1 MONTH OF
FREE
READING

at

www.ForgottenBooks.com

By purchasing this book you are eligible for one month membership to ForgottenBooks.com, giving you unlimited access to our entire collection of over 1,000,000 titles via our web site and mobile apps.

To claim your free month visit:

www.forgottenbooks.com/free877098

ISBN 978-0-266-66339-3
PIBN 10877098

This book is a reproduction of an important historical work. Forgotten Books uses
state-of-the-art technology to digitally reconstruct the work, preserving the original format
whilst repairing imperfections present in the aged copy. In rare cases, an imperfection in
the original, such as a blemish or missing page, may be replicated in our edition. We do,
however, repair the vast majority of imperfections successfully; any imperfections that
remain are intentionally left to preserve the state of such historical works.

PUBLICATIONS

OF THE

AMERICAN

CONOMIC ASSOCIATION

THIRD SERIES, VOLUME III

PUBLISHED FOR THE
AMERICAN ECONOMIC ASSOCIATION
BY THE MACMILLAN COMPANY
NEW YORK
LONDON : SWAN SONNENSCHEIN & CO.
1902

HB
|
A5
ser. 3

CONTENTS OF VOLUME THREE, THIRD SERIES.

PUBLICATIONS

OF THE

AMERICAN ECONOMIC ASSOCIATION

THIRD SERIES.   ISSUED QUARTERLY.
VOL. III, NO. I.   PRICE, $4.00 PER YEAR.

PAPERS AND PROCEEDINGS

OF THE

FOURTEENTH ANNUAL MEETING

WASHINGTON, D. C.

DECEMBER 27–30, 1901

FEBRUARY, 1902

PUBLISHED FOR THE
AMERICAN ECONOMIC ASSOCIATION
BY THE MACMILLAN COMPANY
NEW YORK
LONDON: SWAN SONNENSCHEIN & CO.

PRESS OF
ANDRUS & CHURCH,
ITHACA, N. Y.

CONTENTS.

4 *Contents.*

AMERICAN ECONOMIC ASSOCIATION.

The American Economic Association is an organization composed mainly of persons interested in the study of political economy or the economic phases of political and social questions. As may be seen by examining the list of members and subscribers printed in this volume, not only are all universities and most prominent colleges in the country represented in the Association by their teachers of political economy and related subjects, but even a larger number of members come from those interested as business men, journalists, lawyers or politicians in the theories of political economy or, more often, in their applications to social life. There are further more than one hundred subscribers, nearly all being large libraries.

The first two meetings of the Economic Association in 1885 and 1887, and the meetings of 1897, 1898, 1900, and 1901, were at the same place as those of the American Historical Association. Joint sessions and less formal gatherings of the members of the two Associations were thus held. The annual meetings give opportunity for social intercourse among the teachers and public men composing the Association's membership. They contribute also to create and cement acquaintanceship and friendship between teachers of economics and cognate subjects in different institutions, and so to counteract any tendency to particularism which the geographical separation and the diverse traditions of American colleges might be deemed to foster.

The Publications of the Association, a complete list

of which is printed at the end of this volume, were begun in March, 1886. The first series of eleven volumes was completed by a general index in 1897. The second series, comprising two volumes, was published in 1897–99, and in addition thereto the Association issued, during 1896–99, four volumes of Economic Studies. In 1900, a third series of quarterly Publications was begun with the Papers and Proceedings of the Twelfth Annual Meeting, and has been continued since with ample amount and variety of matter. It is intended to add to these quarterly numbers, from time to time, such monographic supplements as the condition of the treasury and the supply of suitable manuscript may make possible.

The American Economic Association is the organ of no party, sect or institution. It has no creed. Persons of all shades of economic opinion are found among its members, and widely different views are given a hearing in its annual meetings and through its publications.

The officers of the Association and the contributors to its Publications receive no pay for their services. Its entire receipts are expended in printing and circulating the Publications and in the slight expenses attendant upon the annual meetings. Any member, therefore, may regard his annual dues either as a subscription to an economic publication, a payment for membership in a scientific association, or a contribution to a publication fund for aiding the publication of valuable manuscript that might not be accepted by a publishing house governed primarily by motives of profit, and that could not be published by the writer without incurring too heavy a burden of expense.

CONSTITUTION.

ARTICLE I.

NAME.

This Society shall be known as the AMERICAN ECONOMIC ASSOCIATION.

ARTICLE II.

OBJECTS.

1. The encouragement of economic research, especially the historical and statistical study of the actual conditions of industrial life.

2. The publication of economic monographs.

3. The encouragement of perfect freedom of economic discussion. The Association as such, will take no partisan attitude, nor will it commit its members to any position on practical economic questions.

4. The establishment of a bureau of information designed to aid members in their economic studies.

ARTICLE III.

MEMBERSHIP.

Any person may become a member of this Association by paying three dollars, and after the first year may continue a member by paying an annual fee of three dollars. On payment of fifty dollars any person may become a life member, exempt from annual dues.[1]

ARTICLE IV.

HONORARY MEMBERS.

The Council may elect foreign economists of distinction not exceeding twenty-five in number, honorary

[1] NOTE—Each member receives all reports and publications of the Association.

members of the Association.   Each honorary member shall be entitled to receive all reports and publications of the Association.

ARTICLE V.

OFFICERS.

The officers of the society shall consist of a President, three Vice-Presidents, a Secretary, a Treasurer, a Publication Committee, and a Council.

ARTICLE VI.

COUNCIL.

1. The Council shall consist of an indefinite number of members of the society, chosen, with the exception of the original members, for three years.   It shall have power to fill all vacancies in its membership, and may add to its number.

2. It shall elect the President, Vice-Presidents, Secretary, and Treasurer, which officers, with the Chairman of the Publication Committee, shall constitute an Executive Committee with such power as the Council may entrust to it.

3. The Council shall organize itself into a number of standing committees upon the various lines of research undertaken.   These committees shall prepare reports from time to time upon such subjects relating to their respective departments as they may select, or as may be referred to them by the Council.   These reports shall be presented to the Council at its regular or special meetings and be open to discussion.   All papers offered to the society shall be referred to the appropriate committees before being read in Council.

4. The Council shall have charge of the general interests of the society, and shall have power to call meet-

ings and determine what reports, papers, or discussions are to be printed, and may adopt any rules or regulations for the conduct of its business not inconsistent with this constitution.

5. The Council shall elect a Committee on Publications, which shall consist of six members, so classed that after the first election the term of two members shall expire each year. This committee shall have charge of and responsibility for the scientific publications of the Association.

ARTICLE VII.

AMENDMENTS.

Amendments, after having been approved by a majority of the Council, may be adopted by a majority vote of the members present at any regular meeting of the Association.

BY-LAWS.

1. The President of the Association, who shall be *ex-officio* a member of the Council, shall preside at all meetings of the Council and Association, and perform such other duties as may be assigned to him by the Council. In case of inability to perform his duties, they shall devolve upon the Vice-Presidents in the order of their election, upon the Secretary and Treasurer, and upon the Chairmen of the Standing Committees, in the order in which the committees are mentioned in the list.

2. The Secretary shall keep the records of the Association, and perform such other duties as the Council may assign to him.

3. The Treasurer shall receive and have the custody

of the funds of the Association, subject to the rules of the Council.

4. The following Standing Committees shall be organized:

    (1). On Labor.
    (2). On Transportation.
    (3). On Trade.
    (4). On Public Finance.
    (5). On Industrial and Technical Education.
    (6). On Exchange.
    (7). On General Questions of Economic Theory.
    (8). On Statistics.
    (9). On Teaching Political Economy.

The Executive Committee may appoint such special committees as it may deem best.

5. At any meeting called by the general summons of the President five members shall constitute a quorum.

6. Papers offered for the consideration of the Council, shall be referred by the Secretary, each to its appropriate committee.

7. In order to encourage economic research, the Association proposes to render pecuniary assistance in the prosecution of the same, and to offer prizes for the best monographs upon selected topics. It stands ready to accept and administer any fund placed at its disposal for either purpose.

8. The Executive Committee shall have power at any time to add new members to the Council.

9. The Executive Committee shall assign all members of the Council to one of the Standing Committees, and shall appoint the Chairmen of the Committees.

10. It shall be the duty of the Chairman of the respective Committees to organize and direct the work of the same, under the general control of the Council.

OFFICERS

President

EDWIN R. A. SELIGMAN
Columbia University

Ex-Presidents

*FRANCIS A. WALKER, LL.D.
Massachusetts Institute of Technology
*CHARLES F. DUNBAR, LL.D.
Harvard University
JOHN B. CLARK, LL.D.
Columbia University
HENRY C. ADAMS, LL.D.
University of Michigan
ARTHUR T. HADLEY, LL.D.
Yale University
RICHARD T. ELY, LL.D.
University of Wisconsin

Vice-Presidents

THEODORE MARBURG
Baltimore
FRED M. TAYLOR, Ph.D.
University of Michigan
JOHN C. SCHWAB, Ph.D.
Yale University

Secretary and Treasurer

FRANK A. FETTER, Ph D.
Cornell University, Ithaca, N. Y

Publication Committee

JACOB H. HOLLANDER, Ph.D., Chairman
Johns Hopkins University, Baltimore, Md.
THOMAS N. CARVER, Ph.D.
Harvard University
DAVIS R. DEWEY, Ph.D.
Massachusetts Institute of Technology
WILLARD C. FISHER, A.B.
Wesleyan University
WILLIAM A. SCOTT, Ph.D.
University of Wisconsin
FRED M. TAYLOR, Ph.D.
University of Michigan

COUNCIL

VICTOR ROSEWATER, Omaha, Neb.
LEO S. ROWE, University of Pennsylvania.
FREDERICK W. SANDERS, Leipzig, Germany.
EDWIN R. A. SELIGMAN, Columbia University.
MARY ROBERTS SMITH, New York City.
GRAHAM TAYLOR, Chicago, Ill.
W. G. LANGWORTHY TAYLOR, University of Nebraska.
CHARLES W. TOOKE, University of Illinois.
D. COLLIN WELLS, Dartmouth College.
NATHAN A. WESTON, University of Illinois.
ROBERT H. WHITTEN, Albany, N. Y.
STUART WOOD, Philadelphia, Pa.
ARTHUR YAGER, Georgetown, Kentucky.

Term of office expiring in 1904.

HENRY C. ADAMS, University of Michigan.
J. H. ARNOLD, Redfield, South Dakota.
JOHN W. BLACK, Colby University.
ERNEST L. BOGART, Oberlin University.
FREDERICK C. CLARK, Ohio State University.
JOHN B. CLARK, Columbia University.
JOHN R. COMMONS, Washington, D. C.
CHARLES H. COOLEY, University of Michigan.
JOHN CUMMINGS, Cambridge, Mass.
ARTHUR M. DAY, Columbia University.
HENRY CROSBY EMERY, Yale University.
WASHINGTON GLADDEN, Columbus, Ohio.
JOHN H. GRAY, Northwestern University.
FREDERICK B. HAWLEY, New York City.
GEORGE K. HOLMES, U. S. Department of Agriculture.
FREDERICK C. HOWE, Cleveland, O.
CHARLES H. HULL, Cornell University.
JOHN HYDE, Washington, D. C.
ALVIN S. JOHNSON, Bryn Mawr.
DAVID KINLEY, University of Illinois.
MARTIN A. KNAPP, Washington, D. C.
HENRY W. LAMB, Brookline, Mass.
CHARLES W. MACFARLANE, Philadelphia, Pa.
FREDERICK W. MOORE, Vanderbilt University.
HARRY T. NEWCOMB, Wayne, Pa.
J. PEASE NORTON, New Haven, Conn.
SIMON N. PATTEN, University of Pennsylvania.
WILLIAM R. PATTERSON, State University of Iowa.
CARL C. PLEHN, University of California.
JESSE E. POPE, University of Missouri.
HARRY H. POWERS, Cornell University.
WILLIAM A. RAWLES, Indiana University.

GEORGE E. ROBERTS, Washington, D. C.
MAURICE H. ROBINSON, Yale University.
EDWARD A. ROSS, University of Nebraska.
FRANK R. RUTTER, Washington, D. C.
JOHN C. SCHWAB, Yale University.
WILLIAM A. SCOTT, University of Wisconsin.
HENRY R. SEAGER, Washington, D. C.
ERNEST A. SMITH, Allegheny College.
OLIVER M. W. SPRAGUE, Harvard University.
FRED M. TAYLOR, University of Michigan.
THORSTEIN B. VEBLEN, University of Chicago.
G. O. VIRTUE, Winona, Minn.
C. S. WALKER, Massachusetts Agricultural College.
ULYSSES G. WEATHERLY, Indiana University.
MAX WEST, U. S. Department of Agriculture.
WALTER F. WILLCOX, Cornell University.
H. PARKER WILLIS, Washington and Lee University.
WILLIAM F. WILLOUGHBY, U. S. Department of Labor.
CARROLL D. WRIGHT, U. S. Department of Labor.
WALTER A. WYCKOFF, Princeton University.
JAMES T. YOUNG, University of Pennsylvania.

Term of office expiring in 1905.

WILLIAM F. BLACKMAN, Yale University.
JOHN GRAHAM BROOKS, Cambridge, Mass.
WILLIAM M. BURKE, Albion College.
ROBERT C. CHAPIN, Beloit College.
FREDERIC R. CLOW, Oshkosh Normal College.
JAMES W. CROOK, Amherst College.
JOHN F. CROWELL, Treasury Bureau of Statistics.
EDWARD T. DEVINE, New Rochelle, N. Y.
RICHARD T. ELY, University of Wisconsin.
ROLAND P. FALKNER, Library of Congress.
HENRY W. FARNAM, Yale University.
HENRY FERGUSON, Trinity College.
IRVING FISHER, Yale University.
WORTHINGTON C. FORD, Boston Public Library.
HAMLINE H FREER, Cornell College.
HENRY B. GARDNER, Brown University.
GEORGE P. GARRISON, University of Texas.
FRANKLIN H. GIDDINGS, Columbia University.
NICHOLAS P. GILMAN, Meadville, Pa.
FRANK J. GOODNOW, Columbia University.
ELGIN R. L. GOULD, New York City.
FREDERICK C. HICKS, University of Cincinnati.
JACOB H. HOLLANDER, Johns Hopkins University.
EDMUND J. JAMES, University of Chicago.

EMORY R. JOHNSON, University of Pennsylvania.
EDWARD D. JONES, University of Michigan.
LINDLEY M. KEASBEY, Bryn Mawr College.
GUSTAV A. KLEENE, Peoria, Ill.
ISIDOR LOEB, University of Missouri.
FRANK L. McVEY, University of Minnesota.
JESSE MACY, Iowa College.
MILO R. MALTBIE, New York City.
BALTHASAR H. MEYER, University of Wisconsin.
HERBERT E. MILLS, Vassar College.
WILLIAM Z. RIPLEY, Massachusetts Institute of Technology.
BENJAMIN H. RIPTON, Union College.
ALBERT SHAW, New York City.
DELOS DeWOLF SMYTH, Hamilton College.
JOHN L. STEWART, Lehigh University.
ALFRED H. STONE, Greenville, Miss.
FRANK W. TAUSSIG, Harvard University.
CHARLES A. TUTTLE, Wabash College.
THOMAS K. URDAHL, Colorado College.
FRANCIS WALKER, Adelbert University.
LESTER F. WARD, Washington, D. C.
ADNA F. WEBER, Albany, N. Y.
HORACE WHITE, New York City.
GEORGE R. WICKER, Dartmouth College.
ALLYN A. YOUNG, Madison, Wis.

LIST OF MEMBERS.

* Life Members. † Subscribers. ° Honorary Members.

ABBOTT, LYMAN, D.D., *The Outlook*, 287 Fourth Avenue, New York City.
ABBOTT, SAMUEL WARREN, M.D., Secretary State Board of Health, 142 State House, Boston, Mass.
ABRAMS. ALVA E., 78 High Street, Hartford, Conn.
ABREU, J. M., War Department, Washington, D. C.
ADAM, J. N., Buffalo, N. Y.
ADAMS, BROOKS, Quincy, Mass.
ADAMS, CHARLES FRANCIS, South Lincoln, Mass.
ADAMS, HENRY CARTER, Prof., Univ. of Mich., Ann Arbor, Mich.
ADAMS. THOMAS S., Ass't Prof., University Heights, Madison, Wis.
ADAMS, WILLIAM W., 111 June Street, Fall River, Mass.
†ADELBERT COLLEGE LIBRARY, Cleveland, O.
AILES, MILTON E., Treasury Dept., Washington, D. C.

†ALBION COLLEGE LIBRARY, Albion, Mich.

ALDRICH, MORTON ARNOLD, Prof., Tulane Univ., New Orleans, La.

ALLEN, GEORGE HENRY HOWLAND, New Bedford, Mass.

ALLEN, JOHN ROBERT, D.D., Georgetown, Texas.

ALLEN, WALTER S., New Bedford, Mass.

ALLEN, WILLIAM F., South Orange, N. J.

*ALVORD, WILLIAM, 400 California Street, San Francisco, Cal.

AMES, C. H., 110 Boylston Street, Boston, Mass.

†AMHERST COLLEGE LIBRARY, Amherst, Mass.

ANDREW ABRAM PIATT, Jr., 10 Russell Hall, Cambridge, Mass.

ANDREWS, ELISHA BENJAMIN, Chancellor of the University of Ne-
    braska, Lincoln, Neb.

*ARMSTRONG, H. C., Jr., Auburn, Alabama.

ARNOLD, J. H., Prof., Redfield, S. D.

ATKINSON, EDWARD, Brookline, Mass.

AUSTIN, O. P., Bureau of Statistics, Treasury Dept., Washingtin, D. C.

*AVERY, ELROY MCKENDREE, 657 Woodlands Hills Avenue, Cleve-
    land, Ohio.

AYERS, EDWARD E., North Andover Depot, Mass.

BACON, MARSHALL L., Tarrytown, N. Y.

BAILY, WILLIAM B., 22 Linwood Street, New Haven, Conn.

BAKER, CHARLES WHITING, *Engineering News*, 220 Broadway, New
    York City.

BAKER, HENRY D., Exmoor Cottage, Highland Park, Ills.

BAKER, MOSES NELSON, *Engineering News*, 220 Broadway, New
    York City.

BALCH, (Miss) EMILY G., Prince Street, Jamaica Plain, Mass.

BALCH, W. M., Fairbury, Neb.

BALDWIN, CHARLES E., Department of Labor, Washington, D. C.

BALDWIN, FOY SPENCER, Prof., 12 Somerset Street, Boston, Mass.

*BALDWIN, SIMEON EBEN, 69 Church Street, New Haven, Conn.

*BALDWIN, SUMMERFIELD, 1006 Charles Street, Baltimore, Md.

*BALDWIN, WILLIAM HENRY, Jr., President Long Island R. R. Co.,
    128 Broadway, New York City.

BARKLEY, RICHARD W., 220 Broadway, New York City.

BARNES, WILLIAM EDDY, Editor of *Age of Steel*, St. Louis, Mo.

BARNETT, GEORGE E., Johns Hopkins University, Baltimore, Md.

BARRETT, DON CARLOS, Prof., Haverford, Pa.

BARROWS, CHARLES H., Springfield, Mass.

BASHFORD, ROBERT M., Madison, Wis.

BASSETT, JOHN S., Trinity College, Durham, N. C.

BATCHELLER, (Mrs.) ALFRED H., 55 Commonwealth Avenue, Bos-
    ton, Mass.

BATCHELLER, ROBERT, North Brookfield, Mass.

†BATES COLLEGE LIBRARY, Lewiston, Me.

*BATTERSON, JAMES GOODWIN, President Travelers' Insurance Co.,
    Hartford, Conn.

BAXTER, SYLVESTER, 32 Murray Street, Malden, Mass.

BEACH, W. G., Pullman, Wash.

BEARD, J. N., D.D., 129 Haight Street, San Francisco, Cal.

BEARDSLEY, CHARLES, Pullman, Wash.

BECHER, FRANKLIN A., 406 Irving Place, Milwaukee, Wis.

BECKHARD, M., 27 Pine Street, New York City.

BEER, GEORGE LOUIS, 65 Pine Street, New York City.

BEER, WILLIAM, Howard Memorial Library, New Orleans, La.

BELLER, WILLIAM F., 55 East 112th Street, New York City.

BEMIS, EDWARD WEBSTER, 178 Kensington St., Cleveland, O.

BENNETT, J. M., The Wyandotte, Columbus, O.

BERARD, EUGENE M., 7 Nassau Street, New York City.

BERRYHILL, JAMES G., 1101 Pleasant Street, Des Moines, Ia.

†BIBLIOTHECA E ARCHIVA PUBLICA DE ESTADO DE AMAZONAS, Caixa Postal 39a, Manaos, Brazil.

BIGELOW, N. P., 308 Tacoma Bldg., Chicago, Ill.

BIGLER, WARREN, Wabash, Ind.

BILGRAM, HUGO, N. W. Corner 12th and Noble Streets, Philadelphia, Pa.

BILLQUIST, C. EDWARD, 11 Broadway, New York City.

*BIXBY, WILLIAM HERBERT, U. S. Engineer Office, Jones Building, Detroit, Mich.

BLACK, JOHN WILLIAM, Prof., 4 Dalton Street, Waterville, Me.

BLACKMAN, WILLIAM FREEMONT, Prof., Yale University, New Haven, Conn.

BLACKMAR, FRANK W., Prof., Kansas State University, Lawrence, Kansas.

BLAIR, JAMES L., Union Trust Building, St. Louis, Mo.

BLANCHARD, NATHAN W., Santa Paula, Cal.

BLEAZBY, ARTHUR J., 1318 L. St., N. W., Washington, D. C.

BLETHEN, Col. A. J., *The Times*, Seattle, Wash.

BLOOD, JOHN BALCH, C E., Equitable Building, Boston, Mass.

BOCOCK, Rev. KEMPER, Swarthmore, Pa.

BODINE, SAMUEL T., Broad and Arch Streets, Philadelphia, Pa.

BOERNER, ARTHUR R., Cedarburg, Wis.

°BODIO, LUIGI, Prof., Rome, Italy.

BOGART, ERNEST LUDLOW, Prof., Oberlin, O.

°BÖHM-BAWERK, EUGEN, Prof., III Beatrix Gasse, 14B, Vienna, Austria.

BOISSEVAIN, G. M., 4 Tesselchade-stratt, Amsterdam, Holland.

BOLLES, ALBERT S., Prof., Haverford, Pa.

BONN, MAX, 30 Broad St., New York City.

BORG, SIDNEY C., 20 Nassau St., New York City.

†BOSTON ATHENÆUM, Beacon Street, Boston, Mass.

†BOSTON PUBLIC LIBRARY, Boston, Mass.

†BOWDOIN COLLEGE LIBRARY, Brunswick, Me.

*Bowen, Clarence Winthrop, *The Independent*, 251 Broadway, New York City.

Bowen, J. Chester, Dept. of Labor, Washington, D. C.

*Bowker, Richard Rogers, *Publisher's Weekly*, 31 and 32 Park Row, New York City.

Boyd, Jackson, Greencastle, Ind.

Breckenridge, Roeliff Morton, 602 W. 125th Street, New York City.

Breed, W. J., 408 Pike St., Cincinnati, O.

Bridges, Hon. Robert, Orillia, King Co., Wash.

Bright, George W., Pres. Boomer Coal and Coke Co., Columbus, O.

Brohough, G. O., Prof., Red Wing, Minn.

Bronson, Samuel L., New Haven, Conn.

†Brooklyn Library, Montague Street, Brooklyn, N. Y.

Brooks, John Graham, 8 Ash Street, Cambridge, Mass.

Brooks, Robert C., Cascadilla Place, Ithaca, N. Y.

*Brough, William, care Paragon Refining Co., Toledo, O.

Brown, Nelson, P., Dartmouth College, Hanover, N. H.

Brown, R. L., Austin, Texas.

Brown, Thomas Edwin, D.D., 1035 Liberty St., Franklin, Pa.

†Brown University Library, Providence, R. I.

Browne, G. Morgan, 44 Pine St., New York City.

Brummer, Leon, 7 Pine St., New York City.

Bryan, Joseph, Richmond, Va.

Bryan, William J., Lincoln, Neb.

†Bryn Mawr College Library, Bryn Mawr, Pa.

†Bucknell Library, Lewisburg, Pa.

†Buffalo Public Library, Buffalo, N. Y.

Bullock, Charles Jesse, Prof., Williams College, Williamstown, Mass.

Bunnell, J. S., San Francisco, Cal.

†Bureau of Education, Washington, D. C.

Burgess, John William, Prof., Columbia University, 323 W. 57th , Street, New York City.

Burke, William Maxwell, Albion College, Albion, Mich.

Butler, Hermon B., 18 Milwaukee, Ave., Chicago, Ill.

†Butte City Free Public Library, Butte City, Mont.

Cake, H. M., 210 Chamber of Commerce, Portland, Ore.

Caldwell, Howard Walter, Prof., University of Nebraska, 511 N. 16th Street, Lincoln, Nebraska.

†California State Library, Sacramento, Cal.

Callender, Guy Stephens, Prof., Bowdoin College, Brunswick, Me.

Campbell, Norman M., Colorado Springs, Col.

*Carnegie, Andrew, 5 W. 51st Street, New York City.

†Carnegie Free Library, Allegheny, Pa.

†Carnegie Library, Pittsburg, Pa.

CARPENTER, GEORGE O., Russell and Compton Avenues, St. Louis, Mo.

CARVER, THOMAS NIXON, Ass't Prof., Harvard University, 75 Frost Street, N. Cambridge, Mass.

CASSOT, ARTHUR, Manager Manhattan Press Clipping Bureau, 2 W. 14th Street, New York City.

CATHERWOOD, ROBERT K. S., Chicago, Ill.

CATOR, GEORGE, 803 St. Paul Street, Baltimore, Md.

CATT, GEORGE W., Room 2407, Park Row Building, New York City.

†CEDAR RAPIDS FREE PUBLIC LIBRARY, Cedar Rapids, Iowa.

CHANDLER. ALFRED D, Brookline, Mass.

CHAPIN, ROBERT COIT, Prof., Beloit College, Beloit, Wis.

CHASE, HARVEY S., 8 Congress St., Boston, Mass.

CHASE, SIMEON B., King Philip's Mills, Fall River, Mass.

†CHICAGO LAW INSTITUTE, County Building, Chicago, Ill.

†CHICAGO PUBLIC LIBRARY, Chicago, Ill.

†CHIYOZO, OTSUKA, 24 Chiyodacho, Kanda-ku, Tokio, Japan.

CHRISTIAN, GEORGE H., Minneapolis, Minn.

†CINCINNATI PUBLIC LIBRARY, Cincinnati, O.

CLAGHORN, (Miss) K. HOLLADAY, Beech Street and Central Avenue, Richmond Hill, N. Y.

CLARK, FREDERICK CONVERSE, Prof., Ohio State University, 15th and Indianola Avenues, Columbus, O.

CLARK, Miss JEANNETTE A., Winona, Minn.

CLARK. JOHN BATES, Prof., Columbia University, 616 W. 113th Street, New York City.

*CLARK, JOHN SPENCER, Secretary Prang Educational Co., 110 Boylston Street, Boston, Mass.

*CLARK, MARTIN, 91 Erie Co. Bank Bldg., Buffalo, N. Y.

CLARK, W. E., 314 W. 113th St., New York City.

CLARKE, ENOS, Kirkwood, St. Louis Co., Mo.

CLARKE, WILLIAM NEWTON, D.D., Hamilton, N. Y.

†CLEVELAND PUBLIC LIBRARY, Cleveland, O.

CLOW, FREDERICK REDMAN, Prof., State Normal, Oshkosh, Wis.

COHN, MORRIS M., Little Rock, Ark.

°COHN, GUSTAV, Prof., Göttingen, Germany.

COLBY, JAMES FAIRBANKS, Prof., Dartmouth College, Hanover N. H.

COLBY, FRANK MOORE, Prof., University Heights. New York City.

COLER, BIRD S., 280 Broadway, New York City.

COLLIN, CHARLES AVERY, 32 Nassau Street, New York City.

†COLUMBUS PUBLIC LIBRARY, Columbus, O.

COMAN, KATHARINE, Prof., Wellesley College, Wellesley, Mass.

COMINGS, A. G., 37 W. College Street, Oberlin, O.

COMMONS, JOHN ROGERS, Bliss Bldg., Washington, D. C.

CONANT, CHARLES A., 29 Corcoran Building, Washington, D. C.

CONANT, LEONARD H., 30 Broad Street, New York City.

CONNER, J. E., Iowa Falls, Ia.

°CONRAD, JOHANNES, Prof., University of Halle, Halle a/S. Germany.

†CONSUMER'S LEAGUE, 105 E. 22d Street, New York City.

*COOK, CHARLES C., 2222 6th Street, N. W., Washington, D. C.

COOK, HOWARD HAMBLETT, M.D., 71 City Hall, Boston, Mass.

COOLEY, CHARLES HORTON, Prof., University of Michigan, Ann Arbor, Mich,

COOLEY, EDWIN GILBERT, Supt. of Schools, Shiller Building, Chicago, Ill.

COOLIDGE, THOMAS JEFFERSON, 64 Ames Building, Boston, Mass.

COOPER, A R., Galt House, Louisville, Ky.

CORSE, FREDERICK M., Prof., 606 W. 115th Street, New York City.

COWDERY, EDWARD G., Milwaukee, Wis.

CRANE, C. R,, 2559 Michigan Avenue, Chicago, Ill.

CRAPO, PHILIP M., Financial Correspondent, Burlington, Ia.

CROCKER, GEORGE GLOVER, 19 Milk Street, Boston, Mass.

CROCKER, URIEL HASKELL, 247 Commonwealth Avenue, Boston, Mass.

CROOK, JAMES WALTER, Prof., Amherst College, Amherst, Mass.

CROSBY, JOHN, 911 New York Life Building, Minneapolis, Minn.

CROSBY, JOHN SHERWIN, 7 W. 108th St., New York City.

CROSSLEY, JAMES J., Winterset, Ia.

CROUTER, A. L. EDGERTON, Mt. Airy, Philadelphia.

CROWELL, JOHN FRANKLIN, Bureau of Statistics, Treasury Dept., Washington, D. C.

CRUM, FRED STEPHEN, Prudential Insurance Co., Newark, N. J.

CRUNDEN, FREDERICK MORGAN, Public Library, St. Louis, Mo.

CUMMINGS, EDWARD, Prof , Harvard University, 104 Irving Street, Cambridge, Mass.

CUMMINGS, JOHN, 7 Thayer Hall, Cambridge, Mass.

CURRAN, JAMES HARRIS, Tome Inst., Port Deposit, Md.

CURTIS, CHARLES EDWARD, City Bank of New Haven, New Haven, Conn.

CUSHING, JOHN PEARSONS, Prof., New Haven, Conn.

CUTTING, R. FULTON, 32 Nassau Street, New York City.

DA COSTA, JOSÉ S., L.L.D., Ca. Garantia da Amazonia, Pará, north of Brazil.

DAISH, JOHN BROUGHTON, Station B, Washington, D. C.

†DALHOUSIE COLLEGE LIBRARY, Halifax, Nova Scotia.

DANIELS, WINTHROP MORE, Prof., Princeton University, Princeton, N. J.

DANSON, J. T., Grasmere, England.

*DAVIS, ANDREW McFARLAND, 10 Appleton St., Cambridge, Mass.

*DAVIS, HORACE, 1800 Broadway, San Francisco, Cal.

DAVIS, JOHN, President Detroit Chemical Works, 515 Cass Ave., Detroit, Mich.

DAVIS, SAMUEL A., Danbury, Conn.

DAWSON, MILES MENANDER, 11 Broadway, New York City.

DAY, ARTHUR MORGAN, Columbia University, New York City.

DAY, EDWARD, 94 Walnut Street, Springfield, Mass.

DAY, FRANCIS A., Box 15, Bayside, R. I.

*DEAN, CHARLES A., Dean Bldg., 60 India St., Boston, Mass.

DEFOREST, ROBERT W., 7 Washington Sq., New York City.

DEGRAFFENRIED, (Miss) CLARE, U. S. Department of Labor, Washington, D. C.

DELMAS, D. M., 901 Claus Spreckles Bldg., San Francisco, Cal.

DEMPSEY, J. HARRY, Census Office, Washington, D. C.

†DENISON UNIVERSITY LIBRARY, Granville, O.

DENNY, CHARLES L., Dexter Horton Bldg., Seattle, Wash.

DERR, ANDREW F., Wilkes-Barre, Pa.

DETRICK, CHARLES R., Stanford University, Cal.

†DETROIT PUBLIC LIBRARY, Detroit, Mich.

DEVINE, EDWARD THOMAS, Circuit Road, New Rochelle, N. Y.

DEWEY, DAVIS RICH, Prof., Mass. Inst. of Technology, Boston.

DEXTER, SEYMOUR, Elmira, N. Y.

DICKMAN, J. W., Fayette, Iowa.

*DILL, ARTHUR C., 821 Cleveland Ave., Niagara Falls, N. Y.

*DILL, JAMES BROOKS, 27 Pine Street, New York City.

DIXON, FRANK HAIGH, Prof., Dartmouth College, Hanover, N. H.

DOBLIN, BENJAMIN, 796 Lexington Ave., New York City.

*DODD, SAMUEL C. T., 26 Broadway, New York City.

DODGE, (Miss) GRACE HOADLEY, 262 Madison Avenue, New York City.

DODGE, RAYMOND E., Publisher *Money*, New York City.

DODGE, WILLIAM EARL, 11 Cliff Street, New York City.

DORNSEIFE, SAMUEL S., 819 Main Street, Kansas City, Mo.

DOUGHERTY, REV. M. ANGELO, Cambridge, Mass.

DOUTHIRT, W. F., Box 72, Glen Ridge, N. J.

†DREXEL INSTITUTE LIBRARY, Philadelphia, Pa.

DROPPERS, GARRETT, Pres. Univ. of South Dakota, Vermillion, S. D.

DUBOIS, W. E. BURGHART, Prof., Atlanta University, Atlanta, Ga.

DUBRUL, ERNEST F., 507 E. Pearl Street, Cincinnati, O.

DUDLEY, CHARLES BENJAMIN, Drawer 334, Altoona, Pa.

DUGGAN, STEPHEN PIERCE, Prof., College of City of New York, New York City.

DUNBAR, R. E., 3 Odd Fellow's Blk., South Bend, Ind.

DUNWOODY, WM. H., Vice-President Washburn Crosby Co., Minneapolis, Minn.

DURAND, EDWARD DANA, Secretary U. S. Industrial Commission, 37 B Street, N. W., Washington, D. C.

DURHAM, EZRA D., Onarga, Ill.

DUTTERA, WILLIAM B., Salisbury, N. C.

DYNES, JOHN HOWARD, 1305 30th St., Washington, D. C.

EASLEY, RALPH M., Secretary of the Civic Federation, First National Bank Building, Chicago, Ill.

EATON, J. SHIRLEY, Havemeyer Bldg., New York City.

ECCLESTON, J. H., D.D., 910 St. Paul St., Baltimore, Md.

EDDY, ARTHUR J., 800 The Temple, Chicago, Ill.

*EDDY, (Miss) SARAH J., 4 Bell Street, Providence, R. I.

EDGERTON, CHARLES EUGENE, 80 V. St., N. W., Washington, D. C.

EDGEWORTH, FRANCIS YSIDRO, Prof., Baliol College, Oxford, England.

EDMONDS, FRANKLIN SPENCER, Central High School, Philadelphia.

ELKINS, STEPHEN BENTON, Elkins, W. Va.

ELLWOOD, CHARLES A., Prof., University of Missouri, Columbia, Mo.

ELY, RICHARD THEODORE, Prof., University of Wisconsin, Madison, Wis.

EMERY, HENRY CROSBY, Prof., Yale University, New Haven, Conn.

†ENOCH PRATT FREE LIBRARY, Reading Room, Baltimore, Md.

ERICKSON, HALFORD, Commissioner of Labor Statistics, Madison, Wis.

ESHLEMANN, M. D., Fresno, Cal.

EWING, JOHN GILLESPIE, Notre Dame, Ind.

FAIRCHILD, A. B., Crete, Neb.

*FAIRCHILD, CHARLES STEBBINS, 76 Clinton Place, New York City.

FAIRLIE, JOHN ARCHIBALD, 524 So. State St., Ann Arbor, Mich.

FALKNER, ROLAND POST, Chief of Department of Documents, Library of Congress, Washington, D. C.

FARNHAM, Miss ANNA LOIS, Bryn Mawr, Pa.

FARNHAM, HENRY WALCOTT, Prof., Yale University, 43 Hillhouse Avenue, New Haven, Conn.

FARQUHAR, ARTHUR B., York, Pa

FARQUHAR, HENRY, Assistant Statistician, Census Office, Washington, D. C.

FARWELL, JOHN, Jr., 148 Market Street, Chicago, Ill.

FAST, RICHARD ELLSWORTH, Prof., University of West Virginia, Morgantown, W. Va.

FELTER, WM. L., 366 Hancock St., Brooklyn, N. Y.

FERGUSON, HENRY, Prof., 123 Vernon Street, Hartford, Conn.

*FERGUSON, WILLIAM C., Richmond, Ind.

FETTER, FRANK ALBERT, Prof., Cornell University, Ithaca, N. Y.

FIELDER, GEORGE L., 255 W. 95th St., New York City.

FILENE, EDWARD A., 453 Washington Street, Boston, Mass.

FILLEBROWN, C. B., 63 Essex Street, Boston, Mass.

FINLEY, JOHN HUSTON, Prof., Princeton University, Lawrenceville, N. J.

FISHBACK, JOHN HOWARD, Interstate Commerce Commission, Washington, D. C.

FISHER, F. COLQUHOUN, 746 W. North Avenue, Baltimore, Md.

FISHER, GEORGE HARRISON, 308 Walnut Street, Philadelphia, Pa.

FISHER, IRVING, Prof., Yale University, New Haven, Conn.

FISHER, WILLARD CLARK, Prof., Wesleyan University, Middletown, Conn.

FISK, GEORGE M , Prof., Tome Institute, Port Deposit, Md.

FITZGERALD, Mrs. R. Y., Mngr. West Side Branch, 38 King St., New York City.

FLOWER, FRANK A., Census Office, Washington, D. C.

FLUX, A. W., Prof., McGill University, Montreal, Canada.

FOLKS, HOMER, 19 E. 88th Street, New York City.

FOLWELL, WILLIAM WATTS, Prof., University of Minnesota, Minneapolis, Minn.

†FORBES LIBRARY, Northampton, Mass.

*FOOTE, ALLEN RIPLEY, Takoma Park, D. C.

*FORD, PAUL LEICESTER, 97 Clark Street, Brooklyn, N. Y.

FORD, WORTHINGTON CHAUNCEY, Boston Public Library, Boston, Mass.

FORREST, J. DORSEY, Prof., Butler College, Indianapolis, Ind.

FORRESTER, FRANK, 1516 Locust Street, St. Louis, Mo.

FORT, IRWIN A., North Platte, Neb.

*FOSTER, E. H., Prof., Glendale, O.

FOULKE, WILLIAM DUDLEY, Richmond, Ind.

FRADENBURGH, ADELBERT GRANT, Adelphi College, Brooklyn.

FRANKENHEIMER, JOHN, 25 Broad Street, New York City.

FRANKLAND, FRED WILLIAM, 346 Broadway, New York City.

FRANKLIN. FABIAN, Prof., 1507 Park Avenue, Baltimore, Md.

FRASER, ALEXANDER HUGH ROSS, Boardman Hall, Ithaca, N. Y.

FREEHOFF, J C., 521 West 123d Street, New York City.

FREEMAN, HARRISON B., Jr., 50 State Street, Hartford, Conn.

FREER, HAMLINE H., Cornell College, Mt. Vernon, Iowa.

FRENYEAR, THOMAS C., 782 Ellicott Square, Buffalo, N. Y.

FRIEDENWALD, HERBERT, 915 N. 16th Street, Philadelphia, Pa.

†FRIEDLEIN, D. E., Krakau, Austria.

FUKUSHIMA, KATSUTARO, Azoto Mura, Abogori, Suruga, Japan.

FULLER, HULBERT, Hotel Belle Vista, San Francisco, Cal.

*FULLER, PAUL, 68 William Street, New York City

FURBER, HENRY JEWETT. Jr., 659 The Rookery, Chicago, Ill.

GAHAN, WILLIAM J., Whitecastle, Iberville Parish, La.

GAINES, JOHN MARSHALL, 422 West End Ave., New York City.

GARCIA, Gen. CARLOS, 118 San Miguel, Havana, Cuba.

GANNETT, HENRY, U. S. Geological Survey, Washington, D. C.

GARDINER, ROBERT H., Gardiner, Me.

GARDNER, HENRY BRAYTON, Prof., Brown University, 54 Stimson Avenue, Providence, R. I.

GARFIELD, HARRY A., Garfield Building, Cleveland, O.

GARRARD, JEPHTHAH, 44 Johnston Building, Cincinnati, O.

GARRISON, GEORGE PIERCE, Prof., University of Texas, Austin, Tex.

GARTZ, A. F., 5225 Lexington Avenue, Chicago, Ill.

GAULT, FRANKLIN B., 607 N. I Street, Tacoma, Wash.

GAVIN, FRANK E., 902 Majestic St., Indianapolis, Ind.

GEORGE, JOHN EDWARD, Ph.D., Northwestern University, Evanston, Ill.

GERLING, HENRY JOSEPH, 3936 Page Avenue, St. Louis, Mo.

GIDDINGS, FRANKLIN HENRY, Prof., Columbia University, New York City.

°GIDE, CHARLES, Prof., University of Montpellier, Montpellier, France.

GILMAN, NICHOLAS PAINE, Editor *The New World*, Meadville, Pa.

GILMAN, THEODORE, Box 72, New York City.

GILSON, N. S., Madison, Wis.

GLADDEN, WASHINGTON, Columbus, O.

GLENN, JOHN M., 1103 N. Eutaw Street, Baltimore, Md.

GLESSNER, J. J., care Warden, Bushnell and Glessner Company, Chicago, Ill.

GLICKSMAN, NATHAN, 448 Kenilworth Place, Milwaukee, Wis.

GOODELL, EDWIN B., Montclair, N. J.

†GOODELL, HENRY HILL, President, Amherst, Mass.

GOODNOW, FRANK JOHNSON, Prof., Columbia University, New York City.

GOULD, ELGIN RALSTON LOVELL, 281 Fourth Avenue, New York City.

GOVE, WILLIAM HENRY, P. O. Building, Salem, Mass.

GOWDEY, ESQ., CLINTON, 5 Elm St., Springfield, Mass.

GRAETZ, VICTOR, 1808 H. St., N. W., Washington, D. C.

GRANT, FRANCES W., Monmouth, Ill.

GRAVES, EDWIN DWIGHT, 650 Main Street, Hartford, Conn.

GRAY, JOHN CHIPMAN, 50 State Street, Boston, Mass.

GRAY, JOHN HENRY, Prof., Northwestern University, Evanston, Ill.

GREELY, OTTO E., 104 Phoenix Building, Minneapolis, Minn.

*GREEN, DAVID L, Hartford, Conn.

GREEN, JACOB L., Hartford, Conn.

GREENE, FRANK, Care Bradstreets, 61 Elm St., New York City.

GREENE, THOMAS LYMAN, 43 Cedar St., New York City.

*GREY, EARL ALBERT, Howick, Lesbury, Northumberland, England.

GROTON, W. M., 4814 Regent Street, Philadelphia, Pa.

*GULICK, JOHN THOMAS, Oberlin, O

GULICK, M. D., LUTHER, Pratt Institute, Brooklyn, N. Y.

GUNDAKER, H. GUY, 3421 Walnut Street, Philadelphia, Pa.

GUNTON, GEORGE, Pres., College of Social Economics, 41 Union Square, New York City.

†HACKLEY PUBLIC LIBRARY, Muskegon, Mich.

HADLEY, ARTHUR TWINING, President, Yale University, New Haven, Conn.

HAINES, ROBERT M, Grinnell, Ia.

HALSEY, JOHN JULIUS, Prof., Stanford University, Palo Alto, Cal.

HALLE, ERNST VON, Prof., 50 Achenbachstrasse 2, Berlin, W., Germany.

HAMILTON, JAMES HENRY, 304 Waverly Place, Syracuse, N Y.

HAMLIN, CHARLES SUMNER, 2 Raleigh Street, Boston, Mass.

HAMMOND, MATTHEW BROWN, 905 California Avenue, Urbana, Ill.

HANCOCK, JAMES D., Franklin, Pa.

HANGER, G. W. W., Chief Clerk, Department of Labor, Washington, D. C.

*HANKS, (Mrs.) C. STEDMAN, 53 State Street, Boston.

HANKS, LUCIEN S., Pres. State Bank, 216 Langdon Street, Madison, Wis.

HANSHUE, J. J., Box 345, Lansing, Mich.

*HARDING, W. E., Bethany, N Y.

HARKNESS, GEORGE S., Odd Fellows Building, Stockton, Cal.

HARRIS, S. A., President National Bank of Commerce, 1929 Vine Place, Minneapolis, Minn.

HARTMAN, EDWARD T., 14 Beacon Street, Boston, Mass.

HARTWELL, EDWARD M., City Hall, Boston, Mass.

†HARVARD COLLEGE LIBRARY, Cambridge, Mass.

HASKINS, CHARLES W., Dean of School of Commerce, New York University, 30 Broad Street, New York City.

HATCH, LEONARD W., 57 Lancaster St., Albany, N. Y.

HATFIELD, HENRY RAND, University of Chicago, Chicago, Ill.

*HATHAWAY, FRANK RANDEL, 146 W. 92d Street, New York City.

*HATHAWAY, .HARRISON, M.D., Corner Miami and Fort Streets, Toledo, O.

HATTON, WILLIAM H., New London, Wis.

HAWLEY, FREDERICK B., 141 Pearl Street, New York City.

HAZARD, R. S., Peace Dale, R. I.

†HAZEN, LUCIUS B., Middletown, Conn.

HEIM, EPHRAIM M., Bucknell University, Lewisburg, Pa.

†HELENA PUBLIC LIBRARY, Helena, Mont.

HENDERSON, CHARLES RICHMOND, Prof., University of Chicago, Chicago, Ill.

HENDERSON, HARRY B., Cheyenne, Wyoming.

HERRICK, CHEESEMAN A., Central High School, Philadelphia, Pa.

HERRIOTT, FRANK I., State Treasury, Des Moines, Iowa.

*HEWITT, ABRAM STEVENS, 9 Lexington Avenue, New York City.

HICKS, FREDERICK CHARLES, Prof., University of Cincinnati, Cincinnati, O.

HIESTER, A. V., Prof., 26 Race Avenue, Lancaster, Pa.

HILL, JOSEPH ADNA, Census Office, Washington, D. C.

HITCHCOCK, FRANK H., Dept. of Agriculture, Washington, D. C.

HOBSON, JOHN ATKINSON, Elmstead, Limpsfield, Surrey, England.

HOLDEN, L. E., *The Plaindealer*, Cleveland, O.

HOLLANDER, JACOB H., Prof., Johns Hopkins University, Baltimore, Md.

HOLLERITH, HERMAN, 1054 31st Street, Washington, D. C.
HOLMAN, FREDERICK V., P O. Box 504, Portland, Oregon.
HOLMES, GEORGE K., Department of Agriculture, Washington, D. C.
HOLT, HENRY, 29 West 23d Street, New York City.
HOPKINS, William Rowlandson, 820 Society for Savings, Cleveland, O.
HORNE, PERLEY L., S. Byfield, Mass.
HORTON, GUY B , North Clarendon, Vt.
HOURIGAN, JOHN, 45 Maiden Lane, Albany, N. Y.
HOURWICH, ISAAC, Treasury Dept. Mint Bureau, Washington, D. C.
HOUSTON, DAVID F , 2304 San Antonio Street, Austin, Texas.
*HOUSTON, SAMUEL FREDERIC, Chestnut Hill, Philadelphia, Pa.
HOWARD, BURT ESTES, Prof., Stanford University, Cal.
HOWARD, GEORGE ELLIOTT, 7 Bigelow St., Cambridge, Mass.
HOWE, FREDERICK CLEMSON, Garfield Building, Cleveland, Ohio.
HOWE, SAMUEL T., 1925 West Street, Topeka, Kansas.
HOWES, OSBORNE, 55 Kilby Street, Boston, Mass.
HOXIE, ROBERT F., Washington University, St. Louis, Mo.
HUBBARD, CHARLES MEREDITH, 304 Broadway, Cincinnati, Ohio.
HUBBARD, W, P., 1421 Chapline Street, Wheeling, W. Va.
HUBBELL, HENRY LYNES, D.D , 409 Orange St., New Haven, Conn.
HULL, CHARLES HENRY, Prof., Cornell University, Ithaca, N. Y.
HUNT, ROCKWELL DENNIS, Prof., University of the Pacific, College
    Park, San José, Cal.
HUNT, WILLIAM C., Census Office, Washington, D. C.
HURD, RICHARD M., 59 Cedar Street, New York City.
HURRY, CLARENCE B., 1002 Massachusetts Ave., Washington, D. C.
*HUTCHINSON, CHARLES HARE, 1617 Walnut Street, Philadelphia, Pa.
HYDE, JOHN, Department of Agriculture, Washington, D. C.
†IKEDA, HIDEZO, Dr., 104 S. 13th St., Richmond, Va.
*ILES, GEORGE, 5 Brunswick Street, Montreal, Canada.
ILIFF, WILLIAM S., 450 Equitable Bldg., Denver, Col.
†INDIANA STATE LIBRARY, Indianapolis, Ind.
†INDIANA UNIVERSITY LIBRARY, Bloomington, Ind
†INDIANAPOLIS PUBLIC LIBRARY, Indianapolis, Ind.
INGALLS, MELVILLE E., President Big Four Railway, Cincinnati, O.
INGRAM, F. F., 409 Lafayette Avenue, Detroit, Mich.
°INGRAM, JOHN KELLS, Prof., Trinity College, Dublin, Ireland.
INSULL, SAMUEL, 139 Adams Street, Chicago, Ill.
†IOWA STATE COLLEGE LIBRARY, Ames, Ia.
†IOWA STATE LIBRARY, Des Moines, Ia.
†IOWA STATE NORMAL SCHOOL, Cedar Falls, Ia.
†IOWA STATE UNIVERSITY, Iowa City, Ia.
*IRWIN, DUDLEY M., 71 Board of Trade, Buffalo, N. Y.
ISHIZAKA, M., Aoyama College, Tokio, Japan.
JACKSON, CHARLES C., 24 Congress Street, Boston, Mass.
JACOBSON, MAURICE, Bureau of Statistics, Treasury Department,
    Washington, D. C.

*JAMES, EDMUND JANES, Prof., University of Chicago, Chicago, Ill.

JANSCHUL, J., Prof., Moïka 82, St. Petersburg, Russia.

*JAYNE, HENRY LaBARRE, 503 Chestnut Street, Philadelphia, Pa.

JAYNES, ALLEN B., 67 15th Avenue, Columbus, O.

JEFFREY, JOSEPH A., 581 E. Town St., Columbus, O.

JENKS, JEREMIAH WHIPPLE, Prof., Cornell University, Ithaca, N. Y.

†JERSEY CITY FREE LIBRARY, Jersey City, N. J.

JEVONS, THOMAS E., 1301 Produce Exchange, New York City.

†JOHN CRERAR LIBRARY, Chicago, Ill.

†JOHNS HOPKINS UNIVERSITY LIBRARY, Baltimore, Md.

JOHNSON, ALVIN SAUNDERS, Bryn Mawr College, Bryn Mawr, Pa.

JOHNSON, EMORY R., Prof., University of Pennsylvania, Philadelphia, Pa.

JOHNSON, FRANK S., 2521 Prairie Avenue, Chicago, Ill.

JOHNSON, JOSEPH F., Prof., New York University, Washington Square, New York City.

JONES, EDWARD D., Prof., University of Michigan, Ann Arbor, Mich.

JORDAN, CONRAD N., Asst. U. S. Treasurer, New York City.

JUDSON, FREDERICK NEWTON, 500–506 Rialto Bldg., St. Louis, Mo.

JUSTI, HERMAN, 355 Dearborn Street, Chicago, Ill.

†KANSAS CITY PUBLIC LIBRARY, Kansas City, Mo.

†KANSAS STATE NORMAL SCHOOL, Emporia, Kan.

KASAHARA, SHO, care of B. Kasahara, 4 Akasaka, Omotechome, Tokio, Japan.

KEASBEY, LINDLEY MILLER, Prof., Bryn Mawr College, Bryn Mawr, Pa.

KEATOR, CHARLES E., care of R. Dunlap & Co., Nostrand and Park Avenues, Brooklyn, N. Y.

KEITH, JOHN MEIGGS, San José, Costa Rica, C. A.

KELLER. ALBERT D., Prof., Heidelberg University, Tiffin, O.

*KELLER, ALBERT G., Yale University, New Haven, Conn.

KELLY, JOHN F., 284 West Housatonic Street, Pittsfield, Mass.

*KELSEY, FRANCIS WILLEY, Prof., 55 E. University Avenue, Ann Arbor, Mich.

KENNAN, KOSSUTH KENT, 357 Kane Place, Milwaukee, Wis.

KENNEDY, HENRY H., 600 The Temple, Chicago, Ill.

KENNEDY, J. WILMER, 2 Emmett St., Newark, N. J.

KENT, WM., 12 Sherman Street, Chicago, Ill.

KERR, J. A., Mutual Life Building, Seattle, Wash.

*KEYNES, JOHN NEVILLE, 6 Harvey Road, Cambridge, England.

KIDDER, CAMILLUS G., 27 William Street, New York City.

KILLEBREW, J. B., Nashville, Tenn.

KILPATRICK, THOMAS, 410 N. 22d Street, Omaha, Neb.

KINDER, FRANCIS SHANOR, 2659 California St., Denver, Col.

†KING, P. S. & SON, 284 Great Smith Street, Westminster, London, S. W., England.

KINGHORN, HENRY B., P. O. Box 748, New York City.

KINLEY, DAVID, Prof., University of Illinois, Champaign, Ill.

KINSMAN, DELOS O., Whitewater, Wis.

KLEENE, GUSTAV A., 210 4th Avenue, Peoria, Ill.

KLEIN, JACOB, 902 Rialto Building, St. Louis, Mo.

KNAPP, MARTIN A., Chairman Inter-State Commerce Commission, Washington, D. C.

KNIGHT, GEORGE WELLS, Prof., Ohio State University, Columbus, O.

KUCZYNSKI, ROBERT René, 1808 H Street, N. W., Washington, D. C.

KURSHEEDT, MANUEL AUGUSTUS, 35 Warren Street, New York City.

LADD, CHARLES E., care of Ladd and Tilton, Portland, Ore.

LAMB, HENRY W., Brookline, Mass.

LATHAM, CHARLES K., 559 Cass. Avenue, Detroit, Mich.

LAURENCE, (Miss) MARTHA E., Lake Erie College, Painesville, O.

LAUTERBACH, EDWARD, 22 William Street, New York City.

*LEA, HENRY CHARLES, 2000 Walnut St., Philadelphia, Pa.

*LEESON, J. R., P. O. Box 2221, Boston, Mass.

†LELAND STANFORD JR. UNIVERSITY, Stanford University, Cal.

LeROSSIGNOL, JAMES EDUARD, University Park, Col.

LESLIE, GEORGE D., Census Office, Washington, D. C.

°LEROY-BEAULIEU, PAUL, Prof., Collège de France, Paris, France.

°LEVASSEUR, PIERRE-ÉMILE, Prof., 26 Rue Monsieur-le-Prince, Paris. France.

LÉVY, RAPHÄEL-GEORGES, Prof., 80 Boulevard des Courcelles, Paris, France.

†LIBRARY OF PARLIAMENT, Ottawa, Canada.

LINDSAY, SAMUEL McCUNE, Ass't Prof., University of Pennsylvania, 4844 Cedar Avenue, Philadelphia, Pa.

LIPMAN, F. L., care Wells, Fargo & Co.'s Bank, San Francisco, Cal.

LIPPINCOTT, HAROLD E., Surrogate's Court, County Court House, New York City.

LIVERMORE, WILLIAM R., Lieut.-Col., 89 Pinckney Street, Boston, Mass.

LLOYD, HENRY DEMAREST, 95 Mt. Vernon St., Boston, Mass.

LÖBDELL, NELSON L., Clifton Springs, N. Y.

LOEB, ISIDOR, Prof., University of Missouri, Columbia, Mo.

†LOESCHER AND CO., Corso 307, Rome, Italy.

LOEWY, BENNO, 206 Broadway, New York City.

LOGAN, JAMES, General Manager U. S. Envelope Company, Worcester, Mass.

LOGAN, WALTER SETH, 58 William Street, New York City.

LONGYEAR, JOHN MUNRO, Marquette, Mich.

LOONEY, WILLIAM HENRY, Union Mutual Building, Portland, Me.

LOOS, ISAAC ALTHAUS, Prof., State University of Iowa, Iowa City, Ia.

†LOS ANGELES PUBLIC LIBRARY, Los Angeles, Cal.

*LOUCHHEIM, SAMUEL K., West End Trust Bldg., Cor. Broad St. and S. Penn. Sq., Philadelphia., Pa.

*Low, Seth, Mayor, New York City.

Lowden, Frank O., 184 LaSalle Street, Chicago, Ill.

Lowry, John C., 2115 Green Street, Philadelphia, Pa.

Lyman, Arthur Theodore, P.O. Box 1717, Boston, Mass.

Macomber, A. E., 224 Spitzer Building, Toledo, O.

MacRae, Hugh, Wilmington, N. C.

McCormick, Alexander A., 154 Washington St., Chicago, Ill.

McCormick, Harold F., 7 Monroe Street, Chicago, Ill.

McCrea, Roswell Cheney, State Normal School, Charleston, Ill.

McCreery, J. L., 232 11th Street, N. E., Washington, D C.

*McDuffie, John, The McDuffie School, Springfield, Mass.

McFarlane, Charles William, 421 S. 44th Street. Philadelphia, Pa.

McLain, John S., 1710 Dupont Ave. So., Minneapolis, Minn.

McLean, Francis Herbert, 98 Bleury Street, Montreal, Canada.

MacLean, James Alexander, Prof., University of Idaho, Moscow, Idaho.

MacLean, Simon James, Prof., University of Arkansas, Fayetteville, Ark.

McMackin, John M., Commissioner of Labor Statistics, Albany, N. Y.

McNulty, John J., Prof., College of the City of New York, New York City.

McPherson, Logan G., 203 Water St., Pittsburg, Pa.

MacVeagh, Franklin, 29 Wabash Avenue, Chicago, Ill.

*MacVeagh, Wayne, Brookfield Farm, Bryn Mawr, Pa.

McVey, Frank LeRond, Prof., University of Minnesota, Minneapolis, Minn.

Macy, Jesse, Prof., Iowa College, Grinnell, Iowa.

Macy, V. Everit, 68 Broad Street, New York City.

Maitland, Alexander, 14 E. 55th Street, New York City.

†Malden Public Library, Malden, Mass.

Maltbie, Milo Roy, 52 William Street, New York City.

Mann, E. L., Room 97, 175 Dearborn Street, Chicago, Ill.

Mann, Wilbur Edwin, 1428 Wesley Ave., Columbus, Ohio.

Marburg, F. M., 27 Pine St., New York City.

*Marburg, Theodore, 14 W. Mt. Vernon Place, Baltimore, Md.

Marks, Martin A., 204 Garfield Bldg., Cleveland, O.

°Marshall, Alfred, Prof., University of Cambridge, Cambridge, England.

Marvin, Dwight E., 514 Asbury Ave., Asbury Park, N. J.

†Massachusetts Institute of Technology, Boston, Mass.

†Massachusetts State Library, State House, Boston, Mass.

Mather, Robert, 144 Van Buren St., Chicago, Ill.

Matheson, Alexander E., Janesville, Wis.

Mathews, Byron C., City High School, Newark, N. J.

Mayer, Levy, care of Moran, Krans and Mayer, Chicago, Ill.

MAYNARD, ARCHIBALD B., 195 Manning St., Hillsdale, Mich.

MEAD, EDWIN DOAK, 20 Beacon Street, Boston, Mass.

MEAD, ELLWOOD, Cheyenne, Wyo.

†MECHANICS' INSTITUTE, San Francisco, Cal.

MECK, ALEXANDER VON, Board of Directors, Moscow and Kazan Railway, Moscow, Russia.

MEEKER, ROYAL, 235 W. 123d St., New York City.

†MERCANTILE LIBRARY, Baltimore, Md.

†MERCANTILE LIBRARY, Astor Place, New York City.

†MERCANTILE LIBRARY, St. Louis, Mo.

*MERCER, GEORGE GLUVAS, Drexel Building, Philadelphia, Pa.

MERRIAM, A. R , Prof., 314 Collins Street, Hartford, Conn.

MERRIAM, WILLIAM RUSH, Director of the Twelfth Census, Washington, D. C.

MERRIFIELD, WEBSTER, President, University of North Dakota, Grand Forks, N. D.

MERRILL, WILLARD, 95 Prospect Avenue, Milwaukee, Wis.

MERRIMAN, JAMES, D., 237 Broadway, New York City.

METCALF, HENRY CLAYTON. Tufts College, Mass.

MEYER, BALTHASER HENRY, University of Wisconsin, Madison, Wis.

†MICHIGAN AGRICULTURAL COLLEGE LIBRARY, Agricultural P. O. Ingham Co., Mich.

†MICHIGAN STATE LIBRARY, Lansing, Mich.

MIKAMI, YOSHINAGA, University of Michigan, Ann Arbor, Mich.

MIKKELSEN, MICHAEL ANDREW, 32 W. 123d Street, New York City.

MILLER, ADOLPH CASPER, Prof., University of Chicago, Chicago, Ill.

MILLER, B. K., Jr., 559 Marshall Street, Milwaukee, Wis.

MILLER, FREDERICK A., 1175 Neil Avenue, Columbus, O.

MILLER, WALLACE E., 184 Eldridge St , University Settlement, New York City.

MILLION, JOHN W., Hardin College, Mexico, Mo.

MILLIS, H. A., 6532 Ellis Ave., Chicago, Ill.

MILLS, HERBERT ELMER, Prof., Vassar College, Poughkeepsie, N. Y.

†MILWAUKEE PUBLIC LIBRARY, Milwaukee, Wis.

†MINNEAPOLIS PUBLIC LIBRARY, Minneapolis, Minn.

MITCHELL, JAMES E., Alma College, Alma, Mich.

MIXTER, CHARLES WHITNEY, 125 Mt. Auburn St., Cambridge, Mass.

MOFFETT, SAMUEL E., 351 W. 114th St., New York City.

MOMSEN, HART, Census Office, Washington, D. C.

MONAGHAN, JAMES C., University of Wisconsin, Madison, Wis.

MONIN, LOUIS C., Prof., Armour Inst, of Technology, Chicago, Ill.

MOORE, CHARLES, Senate P. O., Washington, D. C.

MOORE, FREDERICK WIGHTMAN, Prof., Vanderbilt University, Nashville, Tenn.

MOORE, HENRY LUDWELL, 83 Third Avenue, Northampton, Mass.

MOORE, ROBERT, Laclede Building, St. Louis, Mo.

MORAN, THOMAS A., 4710 Vincennes Avenue,, Chicago, Ill.

MORRIS, FRANK R., 301 Pleasant St., Bennington, Vt.

MORSE, (Miss) FRANCES R., 12 Marlborough Street, Boston, Mass.

MORTON, I. W., 49 Vandeventer Place, St. Louis, Mo.

MOSELY, EDWARD AUGUSTUS, Secy. Interstate Commerce Commission, Washington, D. C.

MOSLEY, WAYNE T., 1112 6th Street, N. W. Washington, D. C.

MOURASSE, H. O., 24 Harukimatchi Sautchome, Tokio, Japan.

MOXOM, PHILIP S., 83 Dartmouth Terrace, Springfield, Mass.

MUHLEMAN, MAURICE LOUIS, U. S. Sub-Treasury, NewYork City.

MUNROE, JAMES P., 179 Devonshire Street, Boston. Mass.

MURPHY, CHARLES ROBERT, 665 Prairie Avenue, Decatur, Ill.

MURPHY, JAMES F., 271 Main St., Pawtucket, R. I.

MYERS, WM. STARR, Country School, Charles Street Ave, Baltimore, Md.

NAGEL, CHARLES, Security Building, St. Louis, Mo.

†NEBRASKA STATE LIBRARY, Lincoln, Nebraska.

NEEB, CHARLES W., Stockton Avenue., Allegheny, Pa.

†NEW BEDFORD PUBLIC LIBRARY, New Bedford, Mass.

†NEWARK PUBLIC LIBRARY, Newark, N. J.

†NEWBERRY LIBRARY, Chicago, Ill.

NEWCOMB, SIMON, 1620 P Street, Washington, D. C.

NEWCOMB, HARRY TURNER, Wayne, Pa.

†NEW HAMPSHIRE STATE LIBRARY, Concord, N. H.

†NEW JERSEY BUREAU OF STATISTICS of Labor and Industries, Trenton, N. J.

NEWLIN, THOMAS, Prof., Wilmington, Ohio.

†NEW ROCHELLE PUBLIC LIBRARY, New Rochelle, N. Y.

NEWTON, REGINALD HEBER, D.D., 781 Madison Avenue, New York City.

†NEW YORK PUBLIC LIBRARY, 40 Lafayette Place, New York City.

†NEW YORK STATE LIBRARY, Albany, N. Y.

†NEW YORK UNIVERSITY LIBRARY, Univ. Heights, New York City.

NIELL, CHARLES P., Prof., Catholic University, Washington, D.C.

NIMMO, JOSEPH, JR., Huntington, Long Island, N. Y.

NORTH, SIMON NEWTON DEXTER, 683 Atlantic Ave., Boston, Mass.

†NORTHWESTERN UNIVERSITY, Evanston, Ill.

NORTON, FRED L., 434 Tremont Building, Boston, Mass.

NORTON, J. PEASE, 563 Orange St., New Haven, Conn.

NOYES, ALEXANDER DANA, *Evening Post*, New York City.

†OBERLIN COLLEGE LIBRARY, Oberlin, O.

O'BRIEN, ROBERT L., Wyatt Building, Washington, D. C.

†OHIO STATE LIBRARY, Columbus, O.

†OHIO STATE UNIVERSITY LIBRARY, Columbus, O.

OLCOTT, W. HARRY, Census Office Agricultural Division, Washington, D. C.

†OMAHA PUBLIC LIBRARY, Omaha, Neb.

O'MALLEY, THOMAS F., 7 Hill Building, Somerville, Mass.
†ONTARIO LEGISLATIVE LIBRARY, Toronto, Ont.
PAGE, EDWARD D., 238 E. 15th Street, New York City.
PAGE, THOMAS WALKER, University of California, Piedmont Avenue,
    Berkeley, Cal.
PAINE, ROBERT TREAT, 6 Joy Street, Boston, Mass.
*PALGRAVE, ROBERT HARRY INGLIS, Belton, near Great Yarmouth,
    Norfolk, England.
PARKER, ADELLA M., Seattle High School, Seattle, Wash.
PARKER, FRANCIS W., 1410 Marquette Building, Chicago, Ill.
PARSONS, (Mrs.) HERBERT, 112 E. 35th St., New York City.
PATTEN, SIMON NELSON, Prof., Univ. of Pennsylvania, Philadelphia.
PATTERSON, WILLIAM R., Iowa City, Iowa.
PATTON, JOHN, Jr., Grand Rapids, Mich.
†PEABODY INSTITUTE, Baltimore, Md.
PEARMAIN, SUMNER B., 53 State St., Boston, Mass.
PEARSON, E. C., 175 Remsen Street, Brooklyn, N. Y.
PECKHAM, WHEELER HAZARD, 80 Broadway, New York City.
†PENNSYLVANIA STATE LIBRARY, Harrisburg, Pa.
PERKINS, JACOB H., 14 Victoria Sq., Clifton, Bristol, Eng.
PERSON, HARLOW S., 1024 Hill St., Ann Arbor, Mich.
PETERS, EDWARD T., 131 E Street, N. W., Washington, D. C.
PETTIGREW, E. S., Great Southern Hotel, Columbus, O.
†PHILADELPHIA LIBRARY, Juniper and Locust Streets, Philadelphia,
    Pa.
*PHIPPS, LAWRENCE C., Carnegie Bldg., Pittsburg, Pa.
PIERCE, (Miss) CAROLINE F., Wellesley College, Wellesley, Mass.
°PIERSON, N. G., Prof., The Hague, Holland.
PINCHOT, GIFFORD, 1705 Rhode Island Avenue, N. W., Washing-
    ton, D. C.
PITTS, (Miss) GRACE L., 309 E. Gay Street, Columbus, O.
†PLAINFIELD PUBLIC LIBRARY, Plainfield, N. J.
PLATT, WALTER B., M.D., 802 Cathedral Street, Baltimore, Md.
·PLEHN, CARL COPPING, Prof., University of Cal., Berkeley, Cal.
PLIMPTON, GEORGE A., 70 5th Avenue, New York City.
†POLITICAL SCIENCE CLUB OF YALE UNIVERSITY, New Haven, Conn.
†POMONA COLLEGE LIBRARY, Pomona, California.
POPE, JESSE ELIPHALET, Prof., University of Mo., Columbia, Mo.
POPPLETON, WILLIAM S., Room 314, First National Bank, Omaha,
    Nebraska.
PORTER, WILLIAM H., 56 East 67th Street, New York City.
POWERS, FRED PERRY, 19 Beaver St., New York City.
POWERS, HARRY HUNTINGTON, Ass't Prof., Cornell University,
    Ithaca, N. Y.
POWERS, LEGRAND, 3007 15th Street, N. W., Washington, D. C.
†PRATT INSTITUTE FREE LIBRARY, Brooklyn, N. Y.
PRAUSSNITZ, MARTIN, Grossbeerenstrasse 28B, Berlin, Germany.

PRESCOTT, ARTHUR TAYLOR, Prof., 713 North Street, Baton Rouge, La.

PRESTON, HAROLD, Pioneer Bldg., Seattle, Wash.

PRICE, WILLIAM H., Tufts College, Mass.

†PRINCETON UNIVERSITY LIBRARY, Princeton, N. J.

†PROVIDENCE PUBLIC LIBRARY, Providence, R. I.

PURDY, LAWSON, 111 Broadway, New York City.

PUTNAM, HARRINGTON, 45 William Street, New York City.

QUAINTANCE, H. W., Div. of Methods and Results, Washington, D. C.

†RADICAL CLUB, Scottdale, Pa.

RAMAGE, BURR JAMES, Prof., Sewanee, Tenn.

RAND, GEORGE C., Lawrence Station, N. Y.

RANDOLPH, E. F., 1212 Madison Street, Toledo, O.

RAWLES, WILLIAM A., The Indiana University, Bloomington, Ind.

RAY, JOSEPH G., Unionville, Mass.

RAYMOND, JEROME HALL, Morgantown, W. Va.

RAYNER, ALBERT W., 1814 Eutaw Place, Baltimore, Md.

REESE, D. F., St. Paul, Minn.

†REFORM CLUB, 233 Fifth Avenue, New York City.

RENAUD, FRANK N., Census Office, Agr. Div., Washington, D. C.

REW, M., Grinnell, Iowa.

REYNOLDS, ALLEN H., Walla Walla, Wash.

†REYNOLDS LIBRARY, Rochester, N. Y.

RHOADES, JOHN HARSEN, 559 Madison Avenue, New York City.

†RHODE ISLAND STATE LIBRARY, Providence, R. I.

RHODES, JAMES FORD, 392 Beacon Street, Boston, Mass.

RICE, (Miss) MARY W., 804 Summit Street, Columbus, O.

RICHARDSON, VICTOR P., Janesville, Wis.

RICHMOND, THOMAS C., Madison, Wis.

†RIGBY, W. C, 74 King William Street, Adelaide, South Australia.

RIPLEY, WILLIAM Z., Prof., Massachusetts Institute of Technology, Newton Centre, Mass.

RIPPEY, CHARLES MCKAY, 607 21st Street, N. W., Washington, D. C.

RIPTON, BENJAMIN HENRY, Prof., Union College, Schenectady, N. Y.

RIVES, GEORGE L., 32 Nassau Street, New York City.

ROBBINS, FRANCIS L., 232 Fifth Avenue, Pittsburg, Pa.

ROBERTS, GEORGE E., Director of Mint. Washington, D. C.

*ROBINSON, (Mrs.) JANE BANCROFT, 425 Cass Avenue, Detroit, Mich.

ROBINSON, MAURICE HENRY, Yale University, New Haven, Conn.

ROBINSON, PHILIP A., Dept. of Labor, Washington, D. C.

ROBINSON, SAMUEL ADAM, 135 W. 22d Street, Portland, Ore.

ROGERS, CHARLES B., 161 Park Avenue, Utica, N. Y.

ROGERS, (Mrs.) EMMA W., 413 Orange Street, New Haven, Conn.

ROOT, LOUIS CARROLL, 52 William Street, New York City.

ROPES, WILLIAM LADD, Librarian of Andover Theological Seminary, Andover, Mass.

ROSENTHAL, LESSING, Suite 1007, Ft. Dearborn Bldg., Chicago, Ill.

ROSEWATER, VICTOR, Editor *Omaha Bee*, Omaha, Neb.

ROSS, EDWARD ALSWORTH, Prof., University of Nebraska, Lincoln, Neb.

ROWE, LEO S., Ph.D., Asst. Prof., University of Pennsylvania, Philadelphia, Pa.

RUSHBY, GEORGE, 128 Franklin St., New York City.

RUSSELL, JOHN M., Treasurer Crompton & Knowles Loom Works, Worcester, Mass.

RUSSELL, WILLIAM HEPBURN, Postal Telegraph Building, New York City.

RUTTER, FRANK ROY, U. S. Dept. of Agr., Washington, D. C.

RYDEN, OTTO G., 1947 Maple Ave., Evanston, Ill.

RYMAN, J. H. T., Missoula, Mont.

†ST. LOUIS PUBLIC LIBRARY, St. Louis, Mo.

†ST. PAUL PUBLIC LIBRARY, St Paul, Minn.

SAMS, CONWAY W., 206 Courtland Street, Baltimore, Md.

SANBORN. JOHN BELL, Madison, Wis.

SANDERS, Prof. FREDERIC W., care Knauth, Nachod & Kühne, Leipzig, Germany.

†SAN FRANCISCO NEWS CO , 342 Geary Street, San Francisco, Cal.

†SAN FRANCISCO FREE PUBLIC LIBRARY, City Hall, San Francisco, Cal.

*SANGER, WILLIAM CAREY, Sangerfield, N. Y.

SANO, ZENSAKU, Higher Commercial College, Tokio, Japan.

SATO, SHOSUKE, Director Agricultural College, Sapporo, Hokkaido, Japan.

SAUTER, WILLIAM F., 1637 Diamond Street, Philadelphia, Pa.

SCHAPER, WILLIAM A., University of Minnesota, Minneapolis. Minn.

SCHOFF, WILFRED H., 233 S. Fourth St., Philadelphia, Pa.

SCHWAB, GUSTAV HENRY, 5 Broadway, New York City.

SCHWAB, JOHN CHRISTOPHER, Prof., Yale University, New Haven, Conn.

*SCOTT, AUSTIN, New Brunswick, N. J.

SCOTT, WILLIAM AMASA, Prof., University of Wisconsin, Madison, Wis.

SCOVEL, SYLVESTER FITHIAN, President University of Wooster, Wooster, Ohio.

SCOVIL, SAMUEL. 711 Cuyahoga Building, Cleveland, Ohio.

†SCRANTON PUBLIC LIBRARY, Scranton, Pa

*SCUDDER, DOREMUS, M.D., 44 Warren Avenue, Woburn, Mass.

SEAGER, HENRY ROGERS, Prof., 1731 19th St., N. W., Washington, D. C

SEATTLE PUBLIC LIBRARY, Seattle, Wash.

*SELIGMAN, EDWIN ROBERT ANDERSON, Prof., Columbia University, 324 W. 86th Street, New York City.

*SELIGMAN, ISAAC NEWTON, 58 W. 54th Street, New York City.

SEWALL, JOTHAM BRADBURY, Prof., 17 Blagden Street, Boston, Mass.

SHAW, ALBERT, Editor *The American Monthly Review of Reviews*, New York City.

SHAW, G. W., Prof., Kidder Institute, Kidder, Mo.

SHEPHERD, FRED STRONG, Prof., Asbury Park, N. J.

SHEPHERD, R. P., Prof., 39 W. 132d Street, New York City.

SHEVLIN, T. H., 129 Oak Grove, St., Minneapolis, Minn.

SHIBLEY, GEORGE H., 78 V St., N. W., Washington, D. C.

SHIRASU, C., care of Viscount Kuki, Kobe, Japan.

SHORTT, ADAM, Prof., Queen's University, Kingston, Ont.

SIMES, WILLIAM, Petersham, Mass.

SIMKHOVITCH, (Mrs.) MARY KINGSBURY, 248 E. 34th Street, New York City.

SIMKHOVITCH, VLADIMIR G., Columbia University, New York City.

SIMPSON, JAMES HOPE, care of Bank of Liverpool, Liverpool, Eng.

SITES, CLEMENT MOORE LACEY, Nanyang College, Shanghai, China.

SMALLEY, HARRISON S., 6 South Ave., Ithaca, N. Y.

*SMART, WILLIAM. Lecturer on Political Economy, Queen Margaret College, Glasgow, Scotland.

SMILEY, ELMER E., President University of Wyoming, Laramie, Wyo.

SMITH, CHARLES LEE, Prof., William Jewell College, Liberty, Mo.

SMITH, DELEVAN, Lake Forest, Ill.

SMITH, ERNEST A., Meadville, Pa.

SMITH, J. ALLEN, University of Washington, Seattle, Washington.

SMITH, (Mrs.) MARY ROBERTS, 235 W. 102d Street, New York City.

SMITH, MILTON W., P. O. Drawer 51, Portland, Oregon.

SMITH, SAMUEL G., Prof., Univ. of Minn., 125 College Avenue, St. Paul, Minn.

SMITH, THOMAS GUILFORD, 9 German Insurance Building, Buffalo, N. Y.

SMYTH, DELOS DEWOLF, Prof., Hamilton College, Clinton N. Y.

†SNEDDEN, DAVID S., Stanford University, California.

SNOW, MARSHALL S., Washington University, St. Louis, Mo.

†SOUTH DAKOTA AGRICULTURAL COLLEGE LIBRARY, Brookings, S. Dakota.

SOUTHER, CHARLES EDWARD, 128 Broadway, New York City.

†SOUTHERN, H. & Co., 140 Strand, London, W. C., England.

SOUTHWORTH, C. H., Springfield, Mass.

SPENCER, CHARLES WORTHEN, Prof., Hamilton, N. Y.

SPENCER, JAMES OAKLEY, Prof., Hudson River Institute, Claverack, N. Y.

SPIEGELBERG, FREDERICK, 44 Broad Street, New York City.

SPRAGUE, OLIVER MITCHELL WENTWORTH, 21 Stoughton Hall, Cambridge, Mass.

*SPRAGUE, RUFUS F., Greenville, Mich.

†SPRINGFIELD PUBLIC LIBRARY, Springfield, Mass.

STANTON, EDGAR WILLIAM, Prof., State Agricultural College, Ames, Iowa.

†STEIGER, E. & Co., Newspaper Box 298, New York City.

STEIGNER, GEO. E.. New York Block, Seattle, Wash.

STEPHENS, HENRY MORSE, Prof., Cornell University, 176 Cascadilla Place, Ithaca, N. Y.

STERNS, WORTHY PUTNAM, 1534 U. St., Washington, D. C.

STEUART, WILLIAM M., The Kensington, Washington, D. C.

STEVENS, B. J., Madison, Wis.

STEWART, JOHN LAMMEY, Lehigh University, South Bethlehem, Pa.

STOKES, ANSON PHELPS, 47 Cedar Street, New York City.

STOKES, H. K., 8 Hopkins St., Providence, R. I.

STONE, ALFRED HOLT, Greenville, Miss.

STONE, NAHUM I., 2194 Washington Ave., New York City.

STRAUS, ISIDOR. 6th Avenue and 14th Street, New York City.

STRAUS, OSCAR SOLOMON, 42 Warren Street, New York City.

STRAWBRIDGE, JUSTUS C., N. W. corner 8th and Market Streets, Philadelphia, Pa.

STRONG, THOMAS N., Portland, Ore.

STRONG, WILLIAM H., 134 Jefferson Avenue, Detroit, Mich.

†SWARTHMORE COLLEGE LIBRARY, Swarthmore, Pa.

SWAIN, HENRY H., Prof., Dillon, Mont.

*SWAYNE, WAGER, 195 Broadway, New York City.

SYLVESTER, J. WALTER, Albany, N. Y.

TAKASU, TASUKE, Japanese Legation, Peking, China.

TAKEMURA, KINJI, care of Y. Ikeda, 27 Masagocho Hongo, Tokio, Japan.

†TAMAYA, T. & Co., 5 Guiza Sanchome, Kyobashiku, Tokio, Japan.

TANKA, M. I., Librarian Imperial Library, Tokio, Japan.

TATEISH, SAJIRO, 540 Broadway, New York City.

TAUSSIG, FRANK WILLIAM, Prof., Harvard University, Cambridge, Mass.

TAYLOR, FRED MANVILLE, Prof., University of Michigan, Ann Arbor, Mich.

TAYLOR, GRAHAM, Prof., 43 Warren Avenue, Chicago, Ill.

TAYLOR, WILLIAM G. LANGWORTHY, Prof., University of Nebraska, Lincoln, Neb.

TENNEY, D. K., 108 E. Main St., Madison, Wis.

TENNY, M. A. 435 Beatty St., Pittsburg, Pa.

TE PASKE, ANTHONY, Sioux Center, Ia.

*THOM, DeCOURCEY WRIGHT, 119 E. Baltimore Street, Baltimore, Md.

THOMPSON, SANDFORD, ELEAZER, Newton Highlands, Mass.

THURBER, CHARLES HERBERT, 13 Tremont Place, Boston, Mass.

*THURBER, FRANCIS B. 90 W. Broadway, New York City.

THWAITES, REUBEN GOLD, Secretary of State Historical Society, Madison, Wis.

TILLINGHAST, (Miss) ELIZABETH SHELDON, 364 Mansfield Street, New Haven, Conn.

TIMLIN, W. H., 1600 Grand Avenue, Milwaukee, Wis.

TITSWORTH, JUDSON, D.D., 291 Ogden Ave., Milwaukee, Wis.

TOOKE, CHARLES WESLEY, Prof., University of Illinois, Champaign, Ill.

TUCKER, GEORGE FOX, 616 Barristers' Hall, Boston, Mass.

TUCKEY, EDSON NEWTON, 22 Lynwood, St., New Haven, Conn.

TUTTLE, CHARLES AUGUSTUS, Prof., Wabash College, Crawfordsville, Indiana.

†TWIETMEYER, A., Leipzig. Germany.

TWINING, A. C., Asbury Park, N. J.

†UNIVERSITY OF CALIFORNIA LIBRARY, Berkeley, California.

†UNIVERSITY OF CINCINNATI, Cincinnati, O.

†UNIVERSITY OF COLORADO LIBRARY, Boulder, Colo.

†UNIVERSITY OF GEORGIA, Athens, Ga.

†UNIVERSITY OF KANSAS LIBRARY, Lawrence, Kansas.

†UNIVERSITY OF MICHIGAN LIBRARY, Ann Arbor, Mich.

†UNIVERSITY OF MINNESOTA LIBRARY, Minniapolis, Minn.

†UNIVERSITY OF MISSOURI LIBRARY, Columbia, Mo.

†UNIVERSITY OF NEBRASKA LIBRARY, Lincoln, Neb.

†UNIVERSITY OF OKLAHOMA, Norman, Oklahoma.

†UNIVERSITY OF PENNSYLVANIA LIBRARY, Philadelphia, Pa.

†UNIVERSITY OF ROCHESTER LIBRARY, Rochester, N. Y.

†UNIVERSITY OF TEXAS, Austin, Texas.

†UNIVERSITY OF TORONTO LIBRARY, Toronto, Canada,

†UNIVERSITY OF VERMONT, Burlington, Vt.

†UNIVERSITY OF WASHINGTON, Seattle, Wash.

UPHAM, FREDERIC W., Pres. Board of Review, Old Colony Bldg., Chicago, Ill.

URDAHL, THOMAS K., 730 N. Weber Street, Colorado Springs, Col.

VAN VORHIS, FLAVIUS JOSEPHUS, 1129 Stevenson Bldg., Indianapolis, Ind.

VEASEY, JOHN H., Lomagundi Dist., Rhodesia, S. Africa.

VEBLEN, THORSTEIN B., University of Chicago, Chicago, Ill.

VEDITZ, C. W. A., Bates College, Lewiston, Me.

VENABLE, RICHARD M., 205 E. German Street, Baltimore, Md.

VIETH, HENRY A., 234 11th Street, N. E , Washington, D. C.

VINCENT, GEORGE EDGAR, University of Chicago, Chicago, Ill.

VIRTUE, G. O., Prof., 152 W. Wabash Street, Winona, Minn.

†WABASH COLLEGE LIBRARY, Crawfordsville, Ind.

WADLIN, HORACE G., 20 Beacon Street, Boston, Mass.

*WADSWORTH, H. L., Editor *Mining and Scientific Review*, Denver, Col.

°WAGNER, ADOLPH, Prof., University of Berlin, Berlin, Germany.

WAITE, FREDERICK C., 140 D Street, N. W., Washington, D. C.

WALKER, C. S., Amherst, Mass.

WALKER, FRANCIS, Prof., Adelbert College, 46 Nantucket Street, Cleveland, O.

4

WALKER, T. B., 803 Hennepin Ave., Minneapolis, Minn.

WALLING, WILLIAM ENGLISH, 4127 Drexel Boulevard, Chicago, Ill.

°WALRAS, LEON, Prof., University of Lausanne, Lausanne, Switzerland.

*WALSH, CORREA M., Bellport, L. I.

WARD, EDWARD G., Jr., Department of Agriculture, Washington, D. C.

WARD, JOHN H., 34 Kenyon Building, Louisville, Ky.

WARD, LESTER FRANK, 1321 M Street, N. W., Washington, D. C.

WARNER, ADONIRAM JUDSON, Marietta, Ohio.

WARREN, WILLIAM R., 81 Fulton Street, New York City.

WATKINS, GEORGE P., Trinity College, Hartford, Conn.

WEATHERLY, ULYSSES GRANT, Prof., The Indiana University, Bloomington, Ind.

WEAVER, E. E., Harrodsburg, Ky.

WEAVER, JAMES RILEY, Prof., DePauw University, Greencastle, Ind.

WEBER, ADNA FERRIN, Deputy Commissioner of Labor Statistics, Albany, N. Y.

WEBER, GUSTAVUS A., Bureau of Labor, Washington, D. C.

WEEKS, RUFUS W., 346 Broadway, New York City.

WELLES, F. R., 44 Rue St. Didier, Paris, France.

WELLS, DAVID COLLIN, Prof., Dartmouth College, Hanover, N. H.

WELLS, PHILIP P., 72 Mansfield Street, New Haven, Conn.

WEST, EDWIN P., Dayton, Ky.

WEST, MAX, Department of Agriculture, Washington, D. C.

WEST, WILLIAM L., 330 W. 3rd Street, St. Paul, Minn.

†WEST VIRGINIA UNIVERSITY LIBRARY, Morgantown, W. Va.

WESTENHAVER, D. C., Martinsburg, W. Va.

WESTON, NATHAN AUSTEN, University of Illinois, Champaign, Ill.

*WETMORE, GEORGE PEABODY, Newport, R. I.

WEYL, WALTER E., University of Pennsylvania, Philadelphia, Pa.

WHEELER, FRED B., 30 Chenango Street, Binghamton, N. Y.

WHITE, ALBERT B., Charleston, W. Va.

WHITE, ANDREW DICKSON, U. S. Minister to Germany, Berlin.

WHITE, FRANK, Bismarck, N. D.

WHITE, HERBERT H., Hartford, Conn.

WHITE, HORACE, 18 W. 69th Street, New York City.

*WHITE, JULIAN LEROY, 51 *News* Building, Baltimore, Md.

WHITE, PETER, Marquette, Mich.

WHITE, WALTER PORTER, Oshkosh, Wis.

WHITE, Z. L., 819 East Broad Street, Columbus, Ohio.

WHITNEY, EDSON LEONE, Prof., Lamar, Mo.

WHITTLESEY, (Miss) SARAH SCOVILL, 367 Prospect Street, New Haven, Conn.

WHITTEN, ROBERT HARVEY, State Library, Albany, N. Y.

WICKER, GEORGE RAY, Dartmouth College, 30 N. Main Street, Hanover, N. H.

WILCOX, DELOS FRANKLIN, Elk Rapids, Mich.

WILGUS, JAMES ALVA, Platteville, Wis.

WILLARD, MARTIN STEVENSON, Wilmington, N. C.

WILLARD, NORMAN P., 1532 Marquette Building, Chicago, Ill.

WILLARD, TUTHILL, 156 S. Franklin Street, Wilkesbarre, Pa.

WILLCOX, WALTER FRANCIS, Prof., Cornell University, Ithaca, N. Y.

WILLETT, ALLAN H., Brown University, Providence, R. I.

†WILLIAMS COLLEGE LIBRARY, Williamstown, Mass.

WILLIAMS, Dr. G. C. F., Hartford, Conn.

WILLIAMS, HARVEY LADEW, Saranac Lake, N. Y.

WILLIAMS, TALCOTT, 916 Pine Street, Philadelphia, Pa.

*WILLIAMS, TIMOTHY SHALER, 913 Union Street, Brooklyn, N. Y.

WILLIS, HENRY PARKER, Prof., Washington and Lee University, Lexington, W. Va.

WILLOUGHBY, WILLIAM FRANKLIN, U. S. Department of Labor, Washington, D. C.

WILSON, GEORGE GRAFTON, Prof., Brown University, Providence, R. I.

WILSON, THOMAS, The Aberdeen, St. Paul, Minn.

WILSON, WOODROW, Prof., Princeton, University, Princeton, N. J.

*WINSLOW, WILLIAM COPLEY, 525 Beacon Street, Boston, Mass.

WINSTON, AMBROSE PARÉ, 6127 Kimbark Avenue, Chicago, Ill.

WOOD, FREDERICK A., 295 Pawtucket Street, Lowell, Mass.

WOOD, HENRY, 1654 Massachusetts Avenue, Cambridge, Mass.

WOOD, STUART, 400 Chestnut Street, Philadelphia, Pa.

*WOODFORD, ARTHUR BURNHAM, Prof., "Oak Hill," 469 Whalley Avenue, New Haven, Conn.

WOODRUFF, CLINTON ROGERS, 818–819 Girard Building, Philadelphia, Pa.

WOODWARD, P. H., Connecticut General Life Insurance Co., Hartford, Conn.

WOOLWORTH, JAMES MILLS, Omaha, Neb.

†WORCESTER FREE PUBLIC LIBRARY, Worcester, Mass.

*WORTHINGTON, T. K., *The Daily News*, Baltimore, Md.

WRIGHT, CARROLL DAVIDSON, United States Commissioner of Labor, Washington, D. C.

WYCKOFF, WALTER AUGUSTUS, Prof., Princeton University, Princeton, N. J.

WYLIE, Rev. WM. H., Greencastle, Ind.

YAGER, ARTHUR, Prof., Georgetown, Ky.

YARROS, VICTOR S., 290 LaSalle Avenue, Chicago, Ill.

YOUMANS, G. F., Fort Smith, Ark.

YOUNG, ALLYN A., Madison, Wis.

YOUNG, FREDERICK G., Prof., Eugene, Oregon.

YOUNG, JAMES T., University of Pennsylvania, Philadelphia, Pa.

YOUNG, JOHN P., *Chronicle* Office, San Francisco, Cal.

ZACHRY, JAMES G., 70 E. 54th Street, New York City.

SUMMARY OF MEMBERSHIP.

FEBRUARY 1, 1902.

Honorary members	12
Life members	74
Annual members	749
Subscribers	130
Total	965

GEOGRAPHICAL DISTRIBUTION

OF

MEMBERS AND SUBSCRIBERS.

Alabama	1
Arkansas	3
California	27
Colorado	7
Connecticut	38
District of Columbia	68
Georgia	2
Idaho	1
Illinois	59
Indiana	18
Iowa	19
Kansas	4
Kentucky	5
Louisiana	4
Maine	6
Maryland	23
Massachusetts	102
Michigan	29
Minnesota	21
Mississippi	1
Missouri	26
Montana	4
Nebraska	15
New Hampshire	6
New Jersey	19
New York	183

North Carolina	4
North Dakota	2
Ohio	50
Oklahoma	1
Oregon	7
Pennsylvania	65
Rhode Island	10
South Dakota	3
Tennessee	3
Texas	5
Vermont	3
Virginia	2
Washington	14
West Virginia	8
Wisconsin	33
Wyoming	3
Canada	7
Other foreign countries	54
Total	965

The Fourteenth Annual Meeting of the American Economic Association was held at Washington, D. C., on Friday, Saturday, and Monday, December 27, 28, and 30, 1901. The American Historical Association met at the same time and place, the sessions being in the Columbian University, and joint sessions of the two Associations were held Friday and Monday evenings. The first joint meeting was presided over by General A. W. Greeley, who said in welcoming the two Associations:

Ladies and Gentlemen:

The American people are making history as rapidly to-day as in the olden time, and the world is turning to the United States for the settlement of many economic questions. But we are the happier than the men of old in that we now have time to write history, and to draw those lessons from it which may be of value in an economic direction. It is fortunate for this country that there are members of these two societies, the American Economic, and the American Historical Associations, who are willing to give of their time and of their energy, and to sacrifice their Christmas holidays, to come together in the Capitol city of the nation that they may consult as to how the history of the past may best be written and how we may draw therefrom lessons that will be of value to the United States in particular and to the world in general. When these two societies meet here we feel that they deserve a welcome. A gentleman who does not need an introduction to a

Washington audience, the President of the Columbian University, Dr. Greene, will, on the part of the local committees, extend a word of greeting to the distinguished women and men who have honored us on this occasion.

Rev. Samuel H. Greene gave the following words of welcome:

Mr. Chairman, Ladies and Gentlemen:

In behalf of the corporation and the faculty of Columbian University, it is my privilege to bid you a most cordial welcome, both to this city and to this place where you are now assembled. For the fair city in which you are gathered no words I can say are necessary; she speaks for herself, both in the quality of her citizenship and in the character of work here wrought. It is pleasant for me in behalf of my colleagues in this University to say how heartily welcome you are, both because of the objects which underlie the organizations represented, and the distinguished membership gathered here. The one remembers the days that are gone, and holding them in the light of just history, seeks to make the past and the men that are gone minister to the present and the men that are. The other organization grasps the problems which are ever and anon presenting themselves with the onward progress of the people, and seeks to master them. We trust that in this gathering each of your organizations may more than realize your fondest expectations, and that you may find these sessions the most interesting and profitable of any in your history. I bid you God-speed in your work, and again in behalf of this city, in behalf of Columbian University I bid you a most hearty welcome.

The program, as carried out, was as follows:

PROGRAM.

First Session—Friday, December 27, 8 P. M.

Joint meeting with the American Historical Association,
Gen. A. W. GREELEY in the chair.

1. Address of Welcome : Rev. SAMUEL H. GREENE, President *pro tempore* of the Columbian University.
2. Industrial Liberty. Address by RICHARD T. ELY, President of the American Economic Association.
3. An Undeveloped Function. Address by CHARLES FRANCIS ADAMS, President of the American Historical Association.

Second Session—Saturday, December 28, 10 A. M.

INTERNATIONAL TRADE.

1. The Meaning of the Recent Expansion of the Foreign Trade of the United States. BROOKS ADAMS, Quincy, Mass.
2. Discussion : GEORGE E. ROBERTS, Director of the Mint ; CHARLES A. CONANT, Washington Correspondent of the New York *Journal of Commerce.*
3. Commercial Policy of Europe. WORTHINGTON C. FORD, Chief of the Department of Statistics, Boston Public Library.
4. Discussion : HENRY C. EMERY, Professor of Political Economy, Yale University.

Third Session—Saturday, December 28, 2:30 P. M.

ECONOMIC THEORY.

1. Some Theoretical Possibilities of a Protective Tariff. THOMAS N. CARVER, Assistant Professor of Political Economy, Harvard University.
2. Discussion : GUY S. CALLENDER, Professor of Economics and Sociology, Bowdoin College ; MAURICE H. ROBINSON, Instructor in Political Economy, Yale University.
3. The Position of the Workman in the Light of Economic Progress. CHARLES A. TUTTLE, Professor of Political Economy, Wabash College.
4. Discussion : DAVID KINLEY, Professor of Economics, University of Illinois ; SAMUEL M. LINDSAY, Assistant Professor of Sociology, University of Pennsylvania.

Fourth Session—Saturday, December 28, 8 P. M.

LABOR PROBLEMS.

1. The Negro in the Yazoo-Mississippi Delta. ALFRED H. STONE, Greenville, Miss.
2. Discussion : L. G. POWERS, Chief Statistician for Agriculture, U. S. Census.
3. Conciliation and Arbitration among Miners. HERMAN JUSTI, Commissioner, Illinois Coal Operators' Association.
4. Discussion : CARROLL D. WRIGHT, Commissioner, U. S. Department of Labor.

———

MONDAY, Dec. 30, 9:30 A. M., visits to Census Office and the Library of Congress.

Fifth Session—Monday, December 30, 2:30 P. M.

PUBLIC FINANCE.

1. Porto Rican Finance : A Comparative Study of Spanish and American Systems of Colonial Finance. THOMAS S. ADAMS, University of Wisconsin, late of the Office of the Treasurer of Porto Rico.
2. Discussion : JACOB H. HOLLANDER, Associate Professor of Finance, Johns Hopkins University, Treasurer of Porto Rico.
3. Report of the Committee on Uniform Municipal Accounts and Statistics. MOSES N. BAKER, Chairman, Associate Editor, *Engineering News*.
4. Discussion : CHARLES E. CURTIS, Vice-President of the City Bank of New Haven ; ROLAND P. FALKNER, Chief of Division of Documents, Library of Congress.

Sixth Session—Monday, December 30, 8 P. M.

Second joint meeting with the American Historical Association, Judge MARTIN A. KNAPP in the chair.

1. Party Legislation in Parliament, Congress and State Legislatures. A. LAWRENCE LOWELL, Professor of the Science of Government, Harvard University.
2. Discussion : HARRY PRATT JUDSON, Professor of Political Science, University of Chicago.
3. Historical Materialism and the Economic Interpretation of History. EDWIN R. A. SELIGMAN, Professor of Political Economy and Finance, Columbia University.
4. Discussion : ISAAC A. LOOS, Professor of Political Science, University of Iowa ; E. P. CHEYNEY, Professor of European History, University of Pennsylvania.

MEMBERS IN ATTENDANCE.[1]

Henry C. Adams, Thos. S. Adams, C. H. Ames, M. N. Baker, Simeon E. Baldwin, George E. Barnett, Don C. Barrett, John S. Bassett, George L. Beer, John W. Black, Ernest L. Bogart, Chas. J. Bullock, Guy S. Callender, Thos. N. Carver, Miss Kate Claghorn, John B. Clark, W. E. Clark, Frederick R. Clow, John R. Commons, Chas. A. Conant, Frederick M. Corse, John F. Crowell, John Cummings, James H. Curran, Chas. E. Curtis, John P. Cushing, Winthrop M. Daniels, Arthur N. Day, J. Harry Dempsey, Edward T. Devine, Davis R. Dewey, Rev. M. Angelo Dougherty, E. D. Durand, J. N. Dynes, R. T. Ely, H. C. Emery, J. A. Fairlie, Henry W. Farnam, Miss Anna L. Farnham, A. B. Farquhar, Henry Farquhar, Henry Ferguson, Frank A. Fetter, Irving Fisher, William W. Folwell, J. Dorsey Forrest, A. W. Flux, Herbert Friedenwald, Henry B. Gardner, John E. George, Frank J. Goodnow, Victor Graetz, John H. Gray, James D. Hancock, G. W. W. Hanger, Edward T. Hartman, Edward M. Hartwell, Frederick C. Hicks, Jacob H. Hollander, Isaac Hourwich, C. H. Hull, Maurice Jacobson, A. S. Johnson, E. R. Johnson, L. M. Keasbey, David Kinley, Martin Knapp, R. Kuczynski, G. D. Leslie, Samuel Lindsay, Isidor Loeb, Isaac A. Loos, John J. McNulty, Frank L. McVey, Milo R. Maltbie, Theodore Marburg, Byron C. Mathews, Elwood Mead, Royal Meeker, Adolph Miller, Wallace E. Miller, Frederick W. Moore, Harry T. Newcomb, Joseph Nimmo, J. Pease Norton, Simon N. Patten, George A. Plimpton, H. W. Quaintance, Burr J. Ramage, Maurice H. Robinson, Philip A. Robinson, Henry R. Seager, Edwin R. A. Seligman, Harrison S. Smalley, Ernest A. Smith, Delos D. Smyth, Charles W. Spencer, James O. Spencer, Worthy P. Sterns, John L.

[1] Probably some others did not register.

Stewart, Alfred H. Stone, Nahum I. Stone, William G. Taylor, Reuben G. Thwaites, Charles A. Tuttle, Francis Walker, Adna F. Weber, Gustavus A. Weber, Philip P. Wells, Max West, Peter White, Delos F. Wilcox, W. F. Willcox, H. P. Willis, J. G. Zachry. Total, 114.

COUNCIL MEETINGS.

A meeting of the Council was held Dec. 28, 1901, at 9.30 a. m., at the Hotel Shoreham, President Ely in the chair. The minutes of the previous meeting held in Detroit were read and approved. The committee on convention week reported briefly, and was continued for another year. The report of the Treasurer, Charles H. Hull, was read, which was referred to the Auditing Committee. It is printed below. The acting Secretary read his report for the year, and it was accepted and approved. It is as follows:

REPORT OF THE ACTING SECRETARY.

The members of the Executive Committee were so widely scattered that it seemed wise to omit the customary autumn meeting this year. No difficulty was experienced, however, in settling by correspondence the various questions which arose from time to time.

The special committee on the economic condition of the American Negro, authorized by the Council at the 12th annual meeting[1] and partly appointed last year,[2] has been completed by the addition of two new members. As now constituted it consists of Messrs. Walter F. Willcox, chairman, Ithaca, N. Y.; W. E. Burghardt Dubois, Atlanta, Ga.; Harry T. Newcomb, Philadelphia,

[1] Proceedings, p. 43.
[2] Proceedings 13th meeting, p. 48.

Pa.; William Z. Ripley, Boston, Mass., and Alfred H. Stone, Greenville, Miss. This committee is expected to report at the next annual meeting,[1] using, among other sources of information, certain census returns which will become available before that time. Meanwhile, Mr. Stone presents at this 14th meeting, a paper upon one phase of the same subject.

The special committee on Uniform Municipal Accounts and Statistics has also been continued, and will present a further report at this meeting.

At the 13th meeting the Council resolved, 27th Dec., 1900, to call upon its members to suggest each at least five candidates for membership in the Association.[2]

This request meeting with an encouraging response, the Executive Committee authorized the Secretary to call, in his discretion, upon any other members of the Association for similar suggestions. To the persons thus proposed for membership, the President sent an invitation to join, and as a result, the Association secured about 150 new members. This membership campaign has increased the year's administrative expenses by about $100 over last year's; but inasmuch as it has extended greatly the influence of the Association, and as it bids fair to add at least $500 to our annual income, the expenditure may be regarded as money well invested.

During the year 1901, six members died, two of them being life members; twenty-eight resigned, and eight were dropped for non-payment of dues, making a total loss of forty-two between the date of the last report and December 24th of this year. On the other hand, 221 new members were added, leaving a net gain of 179 members.

---

[1] It will not report until the meeting two years hence. See report below, p. 54.

[2] Proceedings, p. 52.

Allowing for a net loss of three on the subscription list, the net gain of members and subscribers this year is 176. This is the largest increase in the recent history of the Association. In 1890 we had 635 members and subscribers, and from that time to 1897 the total members and subscribers varied little, attaining a maximum of 668 in 1897.[1] In 1898 the net gain was 17, in 1899 it was 32, in 1900 it was 57, this year it was 176. Accordingly, our total numerical strength is now 950, much the greatest in the history of the Association. The secretary may perhaps be permitted to record his opinion, that while this result could not have been reached without the cordial coöperation of the members, it would not have been reached save for the energy of President Ely, who has given much time to advancing the Association's interests.

In entering these new members, the former secretary adopted the plan of dating their membership from January 1, thus synchronizing them with the subscribers and with the volume year, instead of beginning their membership with the first of September as was the plan formerly. No trouble has been experienced in consequence and the advantages are obvious.

In July of this year, there appeared the delayed first volume of Mr. A. McF. Davis's History of Currency and Banking in the Province of the Massachusetts Bay, which was due the previous November. The second volume, completing the work, came out early in September. The reason for the delay in issuing these numbers was explained at the last meeting of the Council. It has added greatly to the difficulties of the secretary's duties throughout the year. It is a pleasure to report,

[1] Handbook, New Haven meeting, p. 47.

however, that we are now up to date with the issue of our series, having issued the Proceedings of the Thirteenth Annual Meeting in April, a monograph on The Theory of Value before Adam Smith, by Dr. Hannah R. Sewall, in October, and A Comparative Study of the Administration of City Finances in the United States, by Dr. Frederick R. Clow, early in December.

The total number of pages actually printed between April and December, omitting advertisements, is 1,387, of which 473 were of the delayed number of last year, and 914 were for the current year. This number (914), though smaller than the number in the last volume (1,162). is larger than that of any other year, except in 1899, when the 4th volume of Economic Studies and an extra volume on the Federal Census were printed.

By a departure from our practice heretofore, Mr. Davis's history is illustrated with thirty-five half-tone plates. While this feature adds to the usefulness of the book, it adds also to the expense, and would have been impracticable had not the author offered to advance the cost of illustrations. By an agreement made with him by the Publication Committee and approved by the Executive Committee, the amount involved is to be refunded to him out of the net proceeds of sales of the extra copies of his books, which was printed in an edition of 2,000 instead of the customary 1,300. The Executive Committee also voted that, inasmuch as the first volume of Mr. Davis's book, though issued for November, 1900, did not actually appear until May, 1901, it should be sent to all new members joining this year. Otherwise, they would have but half of the work.

The renewed contract with the Macmillan Co. for the sale of our Publications has worked smoothly. The net receipts from that source are about $50 smaller than last year. Permission has been granted to Messrs. R. T. Ely and T. B. Veblen to reprint papers contributed by them to the Publications and copyrighted in the name of the Association. Also the Bureau of Statistics of the Treasury Department was allowed to reprint freely from the Essays in Colonial Finance issued by the Association in August, 1900.[1]

In spite of paying the largest bills for printing and distributing publications which the Association has ever met in any one year, in all some $2,620, several hundred of which were properly chargeable to last year's account, we have a balance in the treasury of $1,522, or $150 more than a year ago. The liabilities are several hundred dollars less than at this time last year. This fortunate outcome is due in part to the unexpected receipt of $250 from life members, in part also to the unusually small amount expended by the former secretary in the transaction of an increased amount of office business, but chiefly to the fact that annual dues brought in almost $700 more in 1901 than in 1900. With our present membership we can safely count on a cash income of over $3,200. Though with the increased membership a considerable increase of administrative expenses must be counted on, it will still be possible to print and distribute nearly 1,000 pages per annum without embarrassing our treasury.

In April last, the Secretary and Treasurer, Charles H. Hull, tendered his resignation as Secretary to take effect in June, the new duties imposed on him by a change of his university work, making it impossible for him to continue in that position. The Executive Committee accepted the resignation, and appointed as Acting Secretary the

---

[1] See Monthly Summary of Commerce and Finance for October, 1901, pp. 1359–1378.

undersigned, who has since performed the duties of the office. He has been assisted most generously, however, in many ways, by the former Secretary, whose advice has been helpful and indeed indispensable at every stage of the work.

Respectfully submitted,

FRANK A. FETTER,

Acting Secretary.

The Chair appointed the following committees : As a Nominating Committee, John B. Clark, Walter F. Willcox, Henry C. Emery, Thomas N. Carver, Charles J. Bullock, David Kinley, Davis R. Dewey ; as a Committee on Resolutions : Henry W. Farnam, Henry B. Gardner, Emory R. Johnson ; as Auditing Committee : Carroll D. Wright, Winthrop M. Daniels, John R. Commons.

The Council then adjourned to meet after the general meeting of the evening.

The second meeting of the Council convened Dec. 28, 1901, at 10.30 p. m., in Jurisprudence Hall, President Ely in the chair.

A letter was read from Carl C. Plehn inviting the Association to meet in California next winter, and the invitation was seconded by Adolph C. Miller in person. An invitation was read from the Cincinnati League inviting the Association to meet in that city next year, and a letter from the Mayor of that city seconding the invitation. Edwin R. A. Seligman, on behalf of Columbia University, extended an invitation for the Association to meet in New York. After a discussion on the time and place of the next meeting, the subject was referred to the Executive Committee, with power to act.

A letter from Carl C. Plehn, of the University of California, was read, suggesting the appointment of a committee to consider the subject of index numbers. After discussion it was referred to the Executive Committee, with instructions to correspond with Mr. Plehn, and to consider the possibility of selecting a committee to study and report on the subject of index numbers.

A resolution was submitted by Frederick R. Clow, providing for a special committee on Local Finance, as follows : *Resolved*, That a special committee of five be appointed to consider the study of local finance and report at the next meeting. This committee shall consult the persons most likely to be interested, especially professors of finance in the larger universities, and prepare plans, if it sees fit, for the systematic and comprehensive study of local finance in the United States. The finances of the states shall be included in this inquiry, as well as the finances of the more strictly local bodies.

The committee shall give special attention to the following questions : 1. Are there any states which should be studied in a certain succession, so that the influence of one upon another may be may be more readily traced ? 2. Is there any practicable way to avoid needless duplication of work, such as dividing the field or arranging to have notice given of work that has been undertaken ? 3. Is any plan of coöperation practicable by which different investigators may aid one another while their work is in progress ? 4. Would it be desirable to adopt some plan for publishing the results of the study of local finance ? If the committee favors affirmative answers to any of these questions, it will be expected to prepare definite plans as far as possible.

The subject was referred to the Executive Committee, with instructions to consider the advisability of the plan suggested, and with power to act.

A motion of Emory R. Johnson, as amended, referred

to the Executive Committee, with power to act, the question of the advisability of appointing five members as a Committee on Transportation in accordance with the Constitution, with instructions to lay before the Association, at its next meeting, the facts regarding the concentration of railroads and other important developments in the transportation problem.

The proposition contained in Mr. Tuttle's paper, read before the Association, was referred to the Executive Committee, with power to act.

On behalf of the Committee on the Negro, Walter F. Willcox made a brief report, stating that in the present condition of things, it would not be possible for the committee to present its final report earlier than December, 1903.

The following resolutions were unanimously adopted :

WHEREAS, A committee of this Association, appointed in accordance with a resolution adopted December 30, 1895, and acting in cooperation with a similar committee of the American Statistical Association, presented a memorial to Congress, respectfully calling its attention "to the importance of establishing at once a permanent and independent census office," and

WHEREAS, The statute of March 3, 1899, to provide for taking the Twelfth and subsequent censuses, secured the substantial independence of the Census Office, but not its permanence, and

WHEREAS, A bill to make the present Census Office permanent, in the following terms—is now before Congress ; therefore, be it

Resolved, That the American Economic Association renews its previous expressions of "sympathy with all efforts to improve census methods in the United States," and adopts as its own the words already quoted from its committee's memorial.

Resolved, That the secretary of the Association be instructed to transmit copies of this resolution to the Committees on the Census of the Senate and the House of Representatives.

The auditing committee reported that it had audited and approved the accounts of the Treasurer, and had signed his report.

SUMMARY OF THE TREASURER'S REPORT, 1901.

CHARLES H. HULL, Treasurer,

*In account with the American Economic Association
for the year ending December 28, 1901.*

Debits.

Cash on hand from last report_____		$1,372 81
Sales and subscriptions,		
The Macmillan Company_____	$478 38	
Secretary_____	398 19	
		876 57
Reprints_____		33 34
Life members' dues (5)_____		250 00
Annual dues _____		2,280 35

Credits.

Publication expenses _____		$2,620 09
Expenses of President's office_____		133 53
Expenses of Sec'y and Treasurer's office		459 12
Expenses of Thirteenth Annual Meeting		77 91
Cash in bank _____		1,512 99
Cash on hand_____		9 43
	$4,813 07	$4,813 07

Examined and found correct,
December 28, 1901.

Attest :   CARROLL D. WRIGHT,
WINTHROP M. DANIELS,
JOHN R. COMMONS.

The third meeting of the Council convened December 30, 1901, at 5 p. m., President Ely in the chair.

Davis R. Dewey spoke of the advisability of amending the constitution so as to provide for the election of three members of the Executive Committee to take the place of the vice-presidents, as at present provided. The subject was referred to the Executive Committee for consideration and report at the next meeting.

The Council was asked to consider the advisability of establishing a chapter or branch of the Association in New York. It was pointed out that this was possible under the present constitution. The Executive Committee was authorized to recognize any branch if it seems advisable.

The nominating committee, through its chairman, John B. Clark, reported the following list of nominations for officers for the ensuing year: President, Edwin R. A. Seligman; Vice-Presidents, Theodore Marburg, Fred M. Taylor, John C. Schwab; Secretary and Treasurer, Frank A. Fetter; as members of the Publication Committee, Jacob H. Hollander, chairman, and Thomas N. Carver.

The committee submitted also for re-election to the Council, the names of the forty-seven members whose term of office expires in 1902; also the following list of names of new members to be added to the Council, the same to be distributed by the secretary by lot among the three classes: Thomas S. Adams, George Barnet, Charles A. Conant, Charles E. Edgerton, A. W. Flux, John E. George, John Hyde, Alvin S. Johnson, Martin A. Knapp, J. Pease Norton, George E. Roberts, Maurice H. Robinson, Ernest A. Smith, John L. Stewart, Alfred H. Stone, Nathan A. Weston, Allyn A. Young and Frank J. Goodnow.

The secretary was instructed to cast one ballot for the election of the officers and list of Council members as submitted by the nominating committee.

The President-elect, in response to a general call, addressed the Council briefly.

The committee on resolutions, through its chairman, Henry W. Farnam, reported the following resolutions, which were unanimously adopted:

Resolved, That the sincere thanks of the American Economic Association be tendered to the Columbian University, the local Committee of Arrangements, the Washington Economic Society, the Cosmos Club, Mr. and Mrs. John B. Henderson, the Director and Assistant Director of the Census, and the Librarian of Congress, for their numerous courtesies, which have made the meeting of 1901, peculiarly enjoyable and profitable.

HENRY W. FARNAM,
HENRY B. GARDNER,
EMORY R. JOHNSON,
Committee.

The Council then adjourned.

VISITS.

Most of the members in attendance at the meeting met at the Census Office, at 9.30 a. m., Monday. A short address was made by Frederick H. Wines, Assistant Director, outlining the organization of the Bureau and the plans of the work. The officers in charge of the branches of the work were introduced, and the members were then taken in smaller groups to inspect the methods of work in the population department.

Assembling in the rooms connected with the Division of Documents in the Library of Congress, at 11 o'clock, the Association was addressed by Osgood Putnam, the Librarian, and by Roland P. Falkner, Chief of the Division of Documents. They described the resources of the Library in the fields of economic and social history, and as to public documents of the various countries; explained the lines of work that are now being especially developed, and outlined some of the further plans of the Library looking to its increased usefulness to students of these subjects. The members then visited the different stacks and reading rooms, and were shown the methods of work, mechanical appliances. and administration of the Library.

RECEPTIONS.

A luncheon was given by the Washington Economic

Society to the members of the Association, at the Shoreham Hotel, 1 o'clock, Monday.

The courtesies of the Cosmos Club were extended to the members of the Association throughout the meeting, and on Monday evening a reception was tendered to the Association by the Club.

A reception was tendered Saturday afternoon by Mr. and Mrs. John B. Henderson to the members of the American Historical and the American Economic Associations, and was attended by most of the members of the Association.

PAPERS AND DISCUSSIONS.

INDUSTRIAL LIBERTY.

BY RICHARD T. ELY.

The year 1776 is an epoch-making date in the history of liberty. Every American associates 1776 with the Declaration of Independence, which, however we may look upon it—and all modern criticism just and unjust, to the contrary, notwithstanding—ranks among the greatest and grandest documents of the world's history. It is there asserted, as something axiomatic, as something belonging to the realm of natural law, that liberty is an inalienable right of all men. You all recall the precise words: "We hold these truths to be self-evident;—that all men are created equal, that they are endowed by their Creator with certain unalienable Rights, that among these are Life, Liberty and the pursuit of Happiness." It is furthermore asserted that the very purpose of the institution of government is to secure these rights, and that every government derives its just powers from the consent of the governed.

But the year 1776 witnessed the appearance of a book which so admirably presented the eighteenth century philosophy of industrial liberty, that by common consent of the intelligent it ranks among the world's greatest books. I refer to Adam Smith's "Wealth of Nations", which occupies a pivotal position in modern economic thought, earlier works preparing the way for this master-piece, and subsequent works in economics resting upon the "Wealth of Nations" as a foundation. So profound has been its influence that the centennial of its appearance was deemed worthy of a celebration.

Placing it below the Declaration of Independence in its power over human destinies, nevertheless, I dare to place it in the first rank of publications which deal with human liberty.

The spirit of the age in which he wrote breathes through Adam Smith's " Wealth of Nations ". This spirit is a world-spirit, and the age is cosmopolitan. This spirit finds its most logical, its clearest and fullest expression in the French philosophy and the French public life of the latter part of the eighteenth century. Liberty, equality and fraternity are made the watchwords of the republic.

When we examine the treatment of liberty in the great historical works of this age, we must be impressed with the simplicity of the problem of liberty, as then conceived. Liberty is thought of as a unity, and not as a complex conception, or bundle of rights. Moreover, we find that liberty is presented in its negative aspects. Restrictions and restraints are found upon liberty, and it is thought that once we clear these away, liberty will assert itself as a benign force.

As in the motto of the French republic, so in the Declaration of Independence, and in Adam Smith's " Wealth of Nations ", liberty is associated with equality. Natural equality is held to be a fundamental fact, and not by any means a goal to be reached slowly and painfully. Adam Smith looks upon the brick-layer and the statesman as equal in nature, holding that the vast differences between them are due to the varied effects of environment. Had the environment been changed the statesman would have been the brick-layer and the brick-layer the statesman. This theory of equality runs, as a red thread, through the entire social philosophy of that age, and must be borne in mind by one who would understand the theoretical and practical conclusions reached by that philosophy. The problem which presented itself to our forefathers, and to French statesmen, as well as to English thinkers, was essentially negative. Restrictions must be removed. Favoritism must be abolished, and the laws making possible restrictions and favoritism must be repealed. The restrictions upon liberty which were then noticed were restrictions of a political nature. Consequently the problem of liberty was conceived to be essentially a political problem, as well as a negative one.

Closely associated with this doctrine of equality was the doctrine of the beneficence of self-interest. Inasmuch as men were essentially equal, each one could best guard his own interests individually, provided only the hampering fetters of the law should make way for a reign of liberty. Time does not permit me to follow out, as I would like, the development of this negative view of liberty, which I have presented. From it we may trace out a very clearly marked line of evolution of thought, and a somewhat less clearly marked line of evolution of political practice. Through various writers we reach Herbert Spencer's treatment of liberty as a negative and political problem. The great enemy of freedom, he holds, is the state manifesting itself in laws directing human activity, and in his opinion, leading inevitably to slavery, unless the flow of legislation is in some way checked. We find Herbert Spencer preaching his doctrine of liberty in his "Social Statics" in 1851, and asserting in it the right of man to disregard the state, and in more recent times he expounds his doctrine in articles bearing such titles as these: "The Coming Slavery", "The Sins of Legislators", "The Great Political Superstition."

6

It is but one step from Herbert Spencer to philosophical anarchy which, in the interests of liberty, would abolish the state altogether. We thus reach the termination of one line of logical evolution of liberty, conceived negatively, as something which may exist if political restraints and restrictions upon action are once removed. Very early, however, those whose interests led them to approach social and economic questions from a different point of view, as well as those who examined the problem of liberty more broadly and deeply, began to qualify the theory of liberty which we have just examined. John Stuart Mill occupies an interesting position in the development of the philosophy of liberty, as in him we see radically antagonistic views struggling with each other for mastery. He was brought up a firm adherent of the eighteenth century social philosophy, but was obliged to qualify it increasingly, as he grew older and gained larger knowledge as a result of broadening experience and deeper thought. On the one hand, in the interests of liberty he would prohibit life-long marriage contracts. On the other hand, he sees the limitations imposed upon freedom of action in the social and economic order, and looks forward to a time of collective ownership of land and capital, although he does not profess to see how this collective ownership is to be managed so as to avoid new restrictions upon liberty.

Another stage in the development of thought is clearly reached in the writings of the English philosopher, Thomas Hill Green,[1] who breaks away altogether from the conception of liberty as something to be achieved by negative, political action, holding that true

[1] T. H. Green, " Liberal legislation and freedom of contract ". Works, vol. 3. pp. 365-386.

liberty means the expression of positive powers of the individual, and that it can be reached only as a result of a long and arduous constructive process. Green tells us in these words what he means by liberty or freedom : " We do not mean merely freedom from restraint or compulsion. We do not mean merely freedom to do as we like irrespectively of what it is that we like. We do not mean a freedom that can be enjoyed by one man, or one set of men, at the cost of a loss of freedom to others. When we speak of freedom as something to be highly prized, we mean a positive power or capacity of doing or enjoying something worth doing or enjoying, and that, too, something that we do or enjoy in common with others. We mean by it a power which each man exercises through the help or security given him by his fellowmen, and which he in turn helps to secure for them. When we measure the progress of a society by the growth in freedom, we measure it by the increasing development and exercise on the whole of those powers of contributing to social good with which we believe the members of the society to be endowed ; in short, by the greater power on the part of the citizens as a body to make the most and best of themselves."

As anarchy gives us the logical outcome of one line of thought concerning liberty, so we find another line of thought, regarding liberty, going far beyond the necessary implications of Green's position and terminating in the opposite extreme, socialism.

As Adam Smith's philosophy of liberty is an expression of the eighteenth century, Thomas Hill Green's view may be looked upon as an expression of the philosophy of liberty with which the twentieth century opens. There are various reasons for this change of view. One of the most fundamental is, perhaps, found

in the fact that we have discovered human nature
to be a more complex thing than it was thought to be
in the last quarter of the eighteenth century. Instead
of a very simple psychology, we have a very complex
psychology underlying our twentieth century thought.
Inequalities among men we now know are natural, or
. the natural outcome of the kind of a world in which
we live, inhabited by our kind of beings. Men are
what they are as a result of heredity, as well as environment. Moreover, we have a heredity of environment itself, which is felicitously termed social heredity.
The outcome of this is found in the fact now clearly
perceived by those who think deeply on such subjects,
that in contract men who are, in one way and another
unequals, face each other and that their inequality expresses itself in the contracts which determine their
economic condition.

Another cause of the change in view concerning the
achievement of liberty, is found in the growing complexity of society, especially on its economic side. Men
are brought into society in a real and vital sense by the
relations existing among them, and these relations have
multiplied enormously during the past century. The
economic ties uniting men in society were relatively
few and simple in 1776. Their growth, extensively and
intensively, is a matter of familiar knowledge at the
present time. It is a mere truism to say that our well-
being in industrial matters depends on others, as well as
on ourselves. Our economic well-being is an outcome
of satisfactory relations existing between the individual
and society. Now these relations which bind man to
his fellow-men are to only a limited extent of a political
nature. Consequently it follows that restrictions upon
liberty are, for the most part, outside of and beyond

government. Furthermore, the problem of liberty is only to a minor extent a political problem. And as it is only to a minor extent a political problem, it can never, in any true sense, be secured by a mere repeal of political laws, nor indeed by a mere enactment of political laws. Neither removal of politico-economic restrictions upon freedom of trade, nor enactment of universal suffrage, can give us more than a small, fractional part of liberty.

Our own, familiar, everyday experience teaches us that restrictions upon our positive liberty of action are mainly due to the coercion of economic forces. This coercion of economic forces manifests itself in many ways, but largely in and through contract competitively formed. This is seen, first of all, in what may be called the *problem of the twentieth man.* Nineteen men wish to pursue a certain course of economic action, but are coerced competitively by the twentieth into a line of conduct which they dislike. Nineteen barbers in the city of Madison, Wisconsin, wished to close their shops on Sunday; the twentieth would not agree to close his, and consequently, all the twenty were, and still are, kept open. Nineteen men may desire to work ten hours a day, and may be coerced by the twentieth into working fourteen hours a day. Apparently they are all working fourteen hours a day because they choose to do so, but the choice is not a free one, in any true sense of the word. Even the twentieth man prefers to work ten hours a day, but yields to pressure for the sake of a temporary advantage, and so he is likewise coerced. The freedom which thus expresses itself in contract is in certain cases like the freedom of a slave, who chooses to work rather than to suffer under the lash.

The coercion of economic forces is largely due to the

unequal strength of those who make a contract, for back of contract lies inequality in strength of those who form the contract.   Contract does not change existing inequalities and forces, but is simply the medium through which they find expression.   Wealth and poverty, plenty and hunger, nakedness and warm clothing, ignorance and learning face each other in contract, and find expression in and through contract.   According to the theory of Pufendorf, one of the great jurists of his day, slavery is, historically, an outcome of contract.   I do not think, myself, that this is a correct view of slavery, as a whole, but it unquestionably explains slavery in many instances. Even in our own day contracts have been formed which have been denounced from the bench as virtual slavery. I have in mind particularly the well known cases which, in the present year, were brought before Judge W. C. Bennett in Columbia, S. C.   It appears in the statement of the case by the Judge that negroes entered into contracts whereby they surrendered nearly, if not quite all, those rights which we associate with a condition of freedom.   The form of the contract includes the following :

" I agree at all times to be subject to the orders and commands of said _____ or his agents, perform all work required of me._____ or his agents shall have the right to use such force as he or his agents may deem necessary to compel me to remain on his farm and to perform good and satisfactory services.   He shall have the right to lock me up for safekeeping, work me under the rules and regulations of his farm, and if I should leave his farm or run away he shall have the right to offer and pay a reward of not exceeding \$25 for my capture and return, together with the expenses of same, which amount so advanced, together with any other indebtedness I may owe _____ at the expiration of above time, I agree to work out under all rules and regulations of this contract at same wages as above, commencing _____ and ending _____.

The said _____ shall have the right to transfer his interest in this contract to any other party, and I agree to continue work for said assignee same as the original party of the first part."

Judge Bennett, in addressing his grand jury, declared that this nominally free contract " reduced the laborer to a position worse than slavery." In charging the grand jury he said: " No free man in this commonwealth nor any other free country can be permitted, even if he desires to do so, to barter away his liberty and make himself a chattel; and that is what this contract attempts to do." The Judge spoke of it as most pitiful of all that the poor negroes who had formed such a contract should profess " to be satisfied and contented ".

The sale of children by their parents in times of distress is a frequent phenomenon in many Oriental countries; and prostitution and slavery can in those countries even to-day often be traced back to contracts of one sort and another.

We have in these instances a very extreme form of the inequality expressed in and through contract, nominally free. What is seen in these cases in extreme form can be seen in lesser degree on every hand, even in the most civilized nations. We see from all this that contract gives expression to inequalities, and allows existing social forces to flow on, involving in some cases, a perpetuation and deepening of degradation.

Furthermore, we have lying back of free contract the great institutions of society, property, and the inheritance of property, and vested interests. In short, all that passes down from generation to generation lies back of contract and expresses itself in and through contract.

As a result of the nature of man, of the conditions of existence in a world like ours, and of the great historical institutions which have come down to us, men exist in classes. These classes, in modern times, rest upon an economic foundation. Even the political classes of earlier days had, in the beginning, an economic basis, but the older political classes are, in our day a comparatively small matter. The Century Dictionary defines class as follows : " An order of or rank of persons ; a number of persons having certain characteristics in common, as equality in rank, intellectual influence, education, property, occupation, habits of life."

The existence of classes, which is absolutely necessary, resting upon a foundation beyond the power of man to control, gives complexity to our problem of liberty. A modern jurist has used these words, which have a profound significance in our discussion of the problem of liberty : " There is no greater inequality than the equal treatment of unequals."

The problem of liberty includes the problem of suitable control over the relations which exist among men ; for these relations determine the conditions of our social existence. These relations may be considered individually and socially, and the social action may be either of private or public character. The action of a trades union in its endeavor to secure favorable relations, is private social action ; a statute, determining the length of the working day, is public social action ; and both alike aim, successfully or unsuccessfully as the case may be, to promote liberty. All action which endeavors to remove ignorance and superstition and to strengthen the individual, mentally, morally and physically, is action which endeavors to promote liberty. Necessarily, social action which determines or regulates in any way the relations of men among themselves, must restrict freedom of movement at some point, but where it is wise it increases it more than correspondingly at other points. If we have restriction upon liberty called *2a*, we have in the case of wise, social action an increment of liberty which is certainly *2a* plus something else. The employer may not hire the services of little children, and his liberty to do so is restricted, but the liberty of the children is increased. They are freed from toil, and when provision is made for their wise education and up-bringing, their powers are increased, and they have many fold the liberty to employ themselves in the service of their fellows for their own benefit.

We thus have a vast body of legislation in and through which society seeks liberty. This legislation modifies and qualifies nominally free contract, because nominally free contract may mean servitude of various kinds and various degrees. The aim is the increase of liberty in the positive sense.

Education is one of the lines along which modern society works to secure liberty. It cultivates and enlightens the mind, frees it from enslaving superstition; and, where it is industrial, it cultivates economic powers and aids us in adjusting ourselves in the relations of complex economic society.

Modern legislation, even reluctantly and against the force of prejudice, recognizes increasingly the existence of classes, and the inequalities of powers among human beings. We have one great class in the community, children, for whom we have special laws. Women are another great class, with a nature different from that of men, and with special needs of their own. We have the farmers; we have the class of men engaged in transportation; the men who work for wages; all with their special needs and peculiarities, finding expression in laws applicable to the class to which they belong. To use expression of Judge Cooley in his Constitutional Limitations, we have here simply the recognition of " distinctions that exist in the nature of things ".

It would be interesting, if time permitted, to show how many different kinds of legal inequality there may be where we have nominal legal equality. I can refer here only briefly to one or two points. We have inequality in power to secure needed laws. Consequently we have societies and social action in order to secure needed legislation for those who by themselves are not strong enough to gain the ends sought. The street car employees of Baltimore, some years ago, desired to have their hours of labor reduced from seventeen hours and twenty minutes a day to twelve hours, and by social action, in which many of the men of Baltimore, most eminent in church and state and in private fields, participated, a twelve hour day was secured.

There is inequality on account of the knowledge of law on the part of the various classes, and in the power to avail one's self of the law. Consequently, we have societies formed to remedy this evil, and to promote that liberty which comes from balanced powers. We have our bureaus of justice, and our legal aid societies.

And another thing. We have an immense modern development in this country of the police power of the state, as this power is most infelicitously termed. We mean, as everyone versed in the elements of law knows, the general welfare power of the state, restricting and limiting contract in the interests of freedom. This development of the police power, slow as it is, shows the adaptability of law to changing industrial and economic conditions. It has been said, and truly, that development of law lags behind the evolution of industrial society, so that the law represents a correspondence to a preceding stage or period in industrial development. It has been difficult for our courts to adjust themselves to the restrictions upon nominally free contract, demanded by the interests of a larger and truer freedom. Consequently, in many cases decisions have been rendered which must be condemned by economic philosophy. Fortunately, however, our courts are finding the needed element of flexibility in our constitutional system in the police power, and are recognizing the fact that a new economic world demands new interpretations. Under American conditions, with upright judges of superior intelligence, devoted to freedom as they understand it, this proposition may be safely maintained, as has been well stated by one of our professors of law : " It has ever been true that in matters of great social and political import, our legal decisions and theories have conformed themselves to the current political and social thought, and not our social and political thought to our legal theories." [1]

Among our various state courts I think the truths concerning freedom, which I have so imperfectly brought before you, have been most clearly seen and most explicitly stated by the Supreme Court of Massachusetts. Some years ago, legislation restricting the right of women to work in a factory more than ten hours a day and sixty hours a week was upheld. Significant extracts from the decision of the court in this case, are

[1] Professor A. A. Bruce, University of Wisconsin, in the Record Herald, Chicago, July 7, 1901.

the following : " It does not forbid any person, firm or corporation from employing as many persons or as much labor as such person, firm or corporation may desire ; nor does it forbid any person to work as many hours a day or week as he chooses, it merely provides that in any employment which the legislature has evidently deemed to some extent dangerous to health, no person shall be engaged in labor more than ten hours a day and sixty hours a week. There can be no doubt that such legislation may be maintained, either as a health or police regulation, if it were necessary to resort to either of those sources for power. This principle has been so frequently recognized in this commonwealth that reference to the decisions is unnecessary.

" It is also said that the law violates the right of Mary Shirley to labor in accordance with her own judgment as to the number of hours she may work. The obvious and conclusive reply to this is, that the law does not limit her right to labor as many hours per day or per week as she may desire. It merely prohibits her being employed continuously in the same service more than a certain number of hours per day or week." [1]

The present learned chief justice of that state, Mr. Justice Holmes, has also expressed himself in such a manner concerning the right of the state to regulate free contract in the interests of a larger freedom, as to show a clear insight into the underlying principles involved. [2]

It is natural to expect enlightened decisions on economic questions in Massachusetts, and that for several

---

[1] In Commonwealth v. Hamilton Manufacturing Company, 120 Mass. 385.

[2] I am pleased to quote from a letter received from Mr. Justice Holmes, with his permission, the following : " In my opinion, econo-

reasons. One is the progressive character of the state, due to general enlightenment; another is the altruistic spirit of the age, which finds such gratifying expression in the Old Bay state, and a third is the fact of its high industrial development, as a result of which it has had to deal for a longer period than other states with those questions growing out of an intensive industrial life. Recently, however, two states, viz., Tennessee and West Virginia, industrially far less developed, have taken a leading position in the regulation of contract in the interests of liberty truly conceived. I refer to the decisions of the courts of these states, sustaining statutes prohibiting the maintenance of truck shops, and also providing for weighing of coal. The courts clearly recognize inequalities in bargaining power, lying back of contract, and they also take the position,—and it is un-doubtedly a true one,—that wise legislation of this sort is calculated to prevent industrial strife, disorder and bloodshed, and to maintain the public peace.[1]

The august tribunal which holds its session in this city, the Supreme Court of the United States, has also, on broad grounds of public policy, upheld the statute of the state of Utah, which limits the working day for miners in that state to eight hours.[2] The Supreme Court did not go into the wisdom of this particular statute, and I have no desire to do so on this occasion. It is simply the broad principle of regulation of economic relations in the interests of freedom which is in question. We see the most enlightened courts thus en-

mists and sociologists are the people to whom we ought to turn more than we do for instruction in the grounds and foundations of all rational decisions.''

[1] Harrison v. Knoxville Iron Co., 53 S. W. Rep. 955 (Tenn.). Peel Splint Coal Co. v. State, 15 S. E. Rep. (W. Va.) 1000.

[2] Holden v. Hardy, 169, U. S. 397.

deavoring to develop the idea of public policy in such a way as to bring contract into conformity with industrial conditions.

It is in the police power that we find the peculiarly flexible element in our legal system, and with written constitutions such as we have it is not easy to see where otherwise it is to be sought. The possibilities of development along the line of the police power cannot be limited. Consequently, there is the possibility of an evolution of our law which shall adapt it to our present and future industrial life, and thus secure industrial liberty. Let us take, for example, the doctrine that free contract presupposes "the will as voluntarily manifested." It is quite evident that this must take from certain agreements the character of a valid contract. An agreement made by pressure due to threats to a man's house cannot be a binding contract. Similarly if I see a millionaire, who is drowning, and offer to save his life, on condition that he turn over to me all his property, no court would sustain this agreement as a binding contract.

But is it not possible in some cases to take into account the pressure of economic needs, for example, the hunger of wife and children? Unquestionably, agreements with wage-earners have been extorted by the severest pressure of hunger. Agreements for usurious rates of interest have also been extorted under the pressure of economic need. Courts have frequently found a way to declare such agreements of no binding force. I cannot enlarge upon this thought, and indeed, have no desire to do more than merely to suggest an important line of evolution in the interests of liberty.

Let us take again the principle that the right to contract must not nullify itself, and it seems that from the standpoint of liberty, there can be no doubt whatever about this principle. Yet it is easy for contract to abrogate the right of contract. Whenever a man contracts himself into a condition of virtual slavery, this is the case. I have already cited the well-known cases brought before Judge Bennett of South Carolina. Cases have arisen in Germany, under what is called the "competitive clause" of labor contracts. It seems that there it is quite customary to insist upon a contract with an employee, learning a trade or occupation, that he shall not, after he has acquired his knowledge of the business, enter into competition with his employer. Sometimes there is a limitation upon the period or area within which no competition must be attempted, making the clause a fairly reasonable one. Sometimes, however, a lad utterly incompetent to contemplate the remote consequences of his act, and not having five dollars to his name, will agree under a penalty of perhaps several thousand dollars not to enter into competition with his employer during his whole life, or in the entire German empire, and sometimes it is said, not anywhere in the world. When contracts are carefully scrutinized with respect to their impairment, directly or indirectly, of the right to make future contracts, it will be found that many regulations are necessary in the interests of liberty.

Contracting-out as it is now technically called, offers an interesting illustration of the absolute necessity of limitations upon contract in the interests of public policy. It will readily be conceded that private contract must not stand above public policy, and yet through contracting-out of obligations public policy may frequently, and will frequently be subverted. Let us suppose it is determined to be public policy, as it has been determined in Germany and in England, that accidents to employees, unless brought about by wilful act of the employee, shall be regarded as a part of the expenses of manufacturing plants and agencies of transportation, to be paid for as any other costs of doing business, out of the proceeds of the business.   Unless it is rendered impossible for an employee to contract-out of the obligation this wise provision in the interests of a large industrial liberty will be nullified by private contracts.   Consequently, we find in the most advanced industrial countries the doctrine established by the statute, or coming to prevail in one way and another, that contracting-out of obligations, established in the interests of public policy, cannot be tolerated.

Another line of development in the interests of industrial liberty must consist in opening up and increasing opportunities for the acquisition of a livelihood by the mass of men, in order that back of contracts there may lie a nearer approximation to equality of strength on the part of the two contracting parties.   It is certain that there will be a vast development along this line during the twentieth century, and through this development we shall find liberty expressing itself increasingly through contract.

It is manifest, I think, that philosophical anarchy furnishes us with no ideal.   The absence of all social regulations means the unrestricted tyranny of the strong. Plato clearly saw this when he asserted that "the most aggravated forms of tyranny and slavery arise out of the most extreme form of liberty".[1]

Mazzini also saw this clearly enough, when he said of liberty : "If you enthrone it alone as means and end, it will lead society first to anarchy, afterward to the despotism which you fear.[2]

We have not said all, however, that there is to be said concerning the ideal of anarchy when we have pointed

---

[1] Republic, viii, 564, Jowett's translation, p. 272.
[2] Mazzini, "Rights and wrongs", Publications of the Christian Social Union, pp. 9–10.

out that it can only mean tyranny and despotism. Liberty cannot be an absolute ideal, because authority is needed in society, in order to secure the harmonious coöperation of its various elements, and without social authority we could have no production of wealth, and we should be without the material basis of that large and positive liberty which enables us to employ our faculties in the common service. This social authority rests, for the most part, upon the great institutions of society— property, vested interests, contract and personal conditions. To only a limited extent is there a direct political basis for the authority whereby one man brings into harmonious coöperation other men, in the work of production. The basis of social authority is, for the most part, institutional.

On the other hand, socialism furnishes us with no sufficient ideal of industrial liberty. Going to the opposite extreme from anarchy, it would find a political basis for that social authority through which the industrial coöperation of men is effected. It would limit the range of free choice, and restrict liberty, although to a less degree than anarchy. The true ideal lies midway between anarchy and socialism, and may be termed the principle of social solidarity. According to this principle, the great institutions of society must be conserved, but developed in the interests of liberty positively conceived. There must be a carefully elaborated, and wisely executed regulation of economic relations.

We are indulging in no Utopian fancies but are simply describing the forces which are everywhere manifesting themselves in the most enlightened nations, and are resulting in an evident increase of the sphere of industrial liberty for the masses of men. It is absurd to say that we must not pass any law in the interests of a single class of men, inasmuch as men exist in classes, and indus-

trial laws to be effective must deal with them as they
exist in classes.   And, moreover, no class exists for
itself.   As society becomes real and vital, and means
more and more to us all, it becomes apparent that no one
class exists for itself, and that no one class can exist
apart from all other classes.   While there is such a thing
as vicious legislation in behalf of a few favored individuals,
whatever promotes the interests of any one of the great
and numerous classes in society, either in matters physical, mental, moral or spiritual, advances the interests of
every other class.   " We are members one of another," and
" the eye cannot say unto the hand, I have no need of
thee : nor again the head to the feet, I have no need of
you . . . . . and whether one member suffers, all the
members suffer with it : or one member be honored all
the members rejoice with it ".   The apostle Paul gives in
in these words an expression to a deep principle of modern
industrial society, the principle of social solidarity.

I have sketched thus hastily a theory of industria
liberty.   What I have said, I would have looked upon
as thoughts on industrial liberty, more or less closely
connected.   I have not even attempted an exhaustive
treatment, for which my time is too limited, even had I,
as I have not, the wisdom for a complete presentation.
I trust, however, that what I have presented is in
harmony with industrial evolution and truth.   It is
something, at any rate, if I have at least made it clear
that industrial liberty is a conception having a relative
and not an absolute value ; that it is to be conceived in
a positive rather than in a negative sense ; that it is not
something which can be decreed off-hand, by any legislative body, but rather that it is a social product, to be
achieved by individuals working socially together, and
that it comes, not all at once, but slowly as the result of
a long continued and arduous process.   It is not the beginning of social evolution, but rather one of the goals

of social evolution, and one which must be brought into harmony with other goals, such as equality, also relatively conceived, and fraternity, the only one of the three goals, liberty, equality and fraternity, which can, in any way, be conceived absolutely. We have, then, among others, three goals of industrial evolution—liberty, equality and fraternity—but the greatest of these is fraternity.

MEANING OF THE RECENT EXPANSION OF THE FOREIGN TRADE OF THE UNITED STATES.

BY BROOKS ADAMS.

MR. PRESIDENT :—Before entering upon my subject I shall ask permission to explain my conception of the scope of economics, else, perhaps, I might seem to wander. I regard economics as the study of competition among men, or as an investigation of that struggle for survival which is the primal cause of wars and revolutions, of the strife of classes, of financial panics, and finally of that steady change which goes on from age to age in the type of populations,—a change occasioned by the elimination of such organisms as are unable to adapt themselves to the demands of an ever varying environment. Hence, in my judgment, economics embraces a large section of the whole field of human knowledge and experience, and the man who would deal with economics exhaustively should have many attainments. He should be an archæologist, and versed in military, political, and religious history, as well as in the history of jurisprudence and of institutions. He should be acquainted with numismatics, with mechanics, and with metallurgy. He should be profound in geography. He should be a linguist. Above all he should be a man of the world, familiar with the care of property, with the stock-market, and with methods of transportation and of administration. I certainly, can lay claim to no such equipment, and it is precisely because I have felt my own deficiencies that I thus estimate the qualifications of him who would succeed. Limited as I am, I attempt only to suggest, my hope being to interest abler minds in certain phenomena which I deem vital to us all.

I apprehend that an inquiry into the " meaning of the recent expansion of the foreign trade of the United States" opens the gravest of economic problems, for that expansion is, probably, only one amid innumerable effects of a displacement of the focus of human energy. Such displacements have occurred periodically from the dawn of civilization, and of all phases of human development they are, perhaps, those which merit most to rivet our attention, since they have always been preceded by a wave of superb prosperity, and have left decay behind.

Furthermore, as no event is so far reaching as a shifting of the social equilibrium, so none exacts a more practical treatment, for men's weapons in the competition of life range from the mighty army to the pettiest details of the peasant's household. No economy is too small, no waste is too trifling to be neglected, for at each passing moment nature is selecting those organisms which work cheapest, and rejecting those which are costly. Also nature is omnipotent and merciless.

Thus communities rise and fall in proportion to their economy ; but I insist that economy varies according to circumstances. Economy is adaptation to the conditions under which men compete, and these conditions are only learned through experience. Every science is based on experience, and we can draw no inferences regarding the future save such as we deduce from the past. Accordingly I submit that our inquiries into a subject such as this should begin at the beginning, no matter how remote that beginning may be.

I assume that we shall agree that the phase of development which we call civilization opened with the smelting of the metals, for without relatively cheap metals the arts must have remained rudimentary. With metal man makes his sword, his plough, and his money; he also makes the tools with which he builds decked ships, and convenient wheeled vehicles. Evidently tribes adhering to wood or stone brought into contact with those using iron, bronze, or even copper, were destined to be evicted, enslaved or destroyed. They were comparatively wasteful either in war or peace. Hence ages ago the metals became a condition of existence in the more advanced regions of the world, and the position of the mines necessarily exercised a controlling influence over the current of international exchanges.

I propose to illustrate my theory by an examination of the first recorded displacement of energy, a movement which though comparatively simple, may serve as the prototype of all that have followed. I refer to the destruction of Nineveh. Nineveh's bloom lasted from about 1200 B. C. to toward 700 B. C., and Nineveh owed her supremacy not to natural resources, but to her geographical position, as the converging point of the routes leading from northeastern Asia to the Mediterranean. At an epoch when sea-going ships did not exist, and when the Dardanelles were closed, wares from the Punjab, Cashmir, and China, as well as from southern Siberia and Turkestan, could reach the Mediterranean most easily by one of two routes. Having gained Bactra, merchants might follow the highway which yet passes through Teheran, to the head of navigation on the Tigris. This point is now Mossul, and was formerly Nineveh, and from thence several routes led to the different Syrian ports. Secondly, travellers might cross the Caspian and, following the line of the modern railway to Tiflis and Poti, reach Trebizond by boat, whence the road over which Xenophon marched goes by Lake Van to Nineveh. Of course, staunch ships were unknown at this remote period, and the Greek legends leave no doubt that before the siege of Troy the Black Sea was practically inaccessible. Therefore, in the main, the eastern trade went west by land, and accordingly the chief care of the Ninevite emperors was to police the roads along which this commerce flowed. Hence their endless campaigns both toward Syria and Armenia.

The Phoenician cities served as the outlets of the Mesopotamian empire toward the Mediterranean, and accordingly Tyre and Sidon rose with the rise of Babylon and Nineveh, and fell with their decay. Nor did the Phoenicians themselves prove unequal to their opportunity. They not only found a market for the commodities of the East, but they provided acceptable exchanges. Slaves and metals were the only two European products which Asia would receive in payment for her exports, and of the two the metals were the more important. From the outset the Phoenicians grasped the situation. They laid the basis of their future opulence by developing the copper of Cyprus, and afterward crowned their fortune by discovering the silver and gold of Spain, and the tin of Cornwall.

Meanwhile so long as Greece lay beyond the line of traffic, the Greeks were condemned to poverty. This they understood, and such legends as that of the Minotaur, and of the golden fleece, tell plainly enough of their weakness, and of their aspirations. At last they tried war. They sacked Troy, forced the Dardanelles, penetrated into the Black Sea, and entered on the race for supremacy. Starting from Miletus these adventurers slowly spread along the coast of Asia Minor, and, passing the Bosphorus, planted colonies at all the outlets of the Bactra trade, their most important stations being Panticapaeum, Phasis, and Trapesus. Thus they opened direct water communication between the Oxus and Gibraltar, by way of Corinth and Syracuse. In consequence the lines of transportation straightened, Nineveh fell into eccentricity, and the chronology tells the rest. By about 700 B. C. the Greeks are supposed to have firmly established themselves throughout the Euxine, and fifty years later the prophet Nahum foretold the destruction of Nineveh. The catastrophe did not lag. Nineveh fell in 606 B. C. and Babylon soon followed. In 538 B. C. Belshazzar read the writing on the wall, and by 500 B. C. a new military race reigned in Chaldea. Nevertheless revolution brought no cure, for the disease which wasted Mesopotamia was inanition caused by the diversion of her trade. Accordingly Darius had hardly mounted the Babylonian throne before he planned the annihilation of his successful rival. The Persian invasion of Hellas began with the battle of Marathon in 490, and ended with Platea in 479 B. C. From that defeat Persia never rallied. By 400 B. C. she had rotted to the core, and Xenophon on his march to Trebizond found nothing to oppose him. In 330 the end came with the slaughter of Darius and the triumph of Alexander. Toward 450 B. C. Athens, nourished by the mines of Laurium, reached her zenith, while the superb coinage of Syracuse indicates that this wonderful metropolis of international exchanges culminated contemporaneously.

The inference is that during the Persian wars the world's centre of energy moved from Mesopotamia to the Ionian Sea, and that the consolidation which there took place served as the basis of the economic system which subsequently sustained the Roman empire. This example of a change of social equilibrium is valuable because of its simplicity. It can be readily analyzed because ancient exchanges were comparatively rudimentary. The West had little beyond its metals. The East possessed the rest. During the Roman period manufactures never passed the Adriatic; in agriculture Egypt undersold even Sicily, while Arabia, India and China supplied spices, silk and gems. Europeans had, therefore, to maintain the balance of exchanges with gold, silver, copper and the like, and, as the Romans were not inventive and hardly improved on the Phoenician methods of mining, the waste was prodigious. Moreover, the Romans met defeat in their attempt to open up Germany. Hence while the demand for metal increased, the supply diminished; therefore, the empire had hardly been organized before it began to spend its capital. And as it could neither extend its source of supply, nor meet eastern competition, it became bankrupt when the mines of Spain failed.

These facts suggest inferences which may aid us in interpreting the phenomena of the present time. First: the evidence tends to show that at a remote antiquity the need of metal stimulated men to explore toward the West. In the West they found what they sought. Hence civilization has spread westward. Second: as the source of metallic supply has receded the diameter of the economic system has enlarged, and as the diameter of the circle has enlarged, the centre has been displaced. By such movements the stability of the social equilibrium has been shaken. Third: the social equilibrium has been disturbed, because, as the centre of the economic system has moved, the trade routes have changed to correspond, and the ancient capitals have been thrown into eccentricity. This signifies ruin for the city, and annihilation for the population. Lastly: it seems clear that war is as essentially an instrument of commercial competition, as is trade itself; that, indeed, war is only commercial competition in its intensest form. All the facts point to the conclusion that war is regularly kindled by the heat engendered by the impact upon an established economic system of a system which is consolidating. Hence the outbreak of war at certain stages of development must be regarded as a usual, if not an invariable phenomenon.

To trace in detail the rise of England is impossible. It must suffice to say that during the middle ages the financial metropolis lay in northern Italy, as in a remote antiquity it had lain in Mesopotamia. This equilibrium lasted until the inflow of gold and silver from Mexico and Peru projected the centre of exchanges westward, much as the inflow of the Spanish metals had projected it two thousand years before. Also during the 16th century England laid the basis of her future fortune by robbing Spanish treasure, and when Spain retaliated as Persia had done, the Armada met a defeat as decisive as Xerxes met at Salamis. Thenceforward the current flowed north, and when Great Britain emerged from her conflict with her chief rival in 1815, she held an economic supremacy more absolute than that of Rome. The British supremacy surpassed the Roman because resting on broader foundations. England not only served as the world's distributing point like Nineveh, as the world's carrier and explorer like Phoenicia and as the world's banker like Rome, but her supply of useful metals gave her a substantial monopoly of manufacturing during two generations. Instead of being drained by the East, she undersold India. Lastly down to 1845 English agriculture nearly sufficed for the wants of the English people. Roman agriculture failed after the Punic wars.

No such favorable combination of conditions had previously existed, and an equilibrium so stable defied attack until shaken by the series of events which propelled the United States along the path which must presently end in her supremacy or her ruin. The first link in this chain of cause and effect was the discovery of gold in California in 1848, and upon that discovery has, perhaps, hinged the destiny of modern civilization. A few figures may explain this proposition. Prior to 1848 not only had the United States been a poor country, but she had been a country whose advance had not been very rapid. She had indeed contended with overwhelming difficulties. Her mass outweighed her energy and her capital. Confronted with immense distances, and hindered from comprehensive methods of transportation by poverty, she could not compete with a narrow and indented peninsula like Europe. The change wrought in these conditions by the influx of gold was magical.

In the three years 1800–1802 the imports averaged_____ $ 93,000,000
"   "   "   "   1848–1850 "   "   "   _____ 154,000,000
"   "   "   "   1858–1860 "   "   "   _____ 316,000,000

That is to say there was an increase of 66 per cent. in half a century, and of over 100 per cent. in a decade.

Exports during   1800–1802 averaged____ _____ $ 78,000,000
"   "   1848–1850   "   _____ 140,000,000
"   "   1858–1860   "   _____ 299,000,000

A ratio of growth of 80 per cent. in fifty years, as against upwards of 100 per cent. in ten.

Iron was equally remarkable. In 1847 the exports of iron and steel stood at $929,000, in 1858 they had quintupled, reaching $4,884,000; while the authorities hold that the modern era of iron making opened in 1855.

But, perhaps, the most impressive of these phenomena was the accumulation of capital. In 1848 the total deposits in the savings banks amounted to $33,087,488, an average per capita of $1.52. In 1860 they reached $149,277,504, an average per capita of $4.75. This corresponds pretty well with the growth in purchasing power consequent on the yield of the mines. Between 1792 and 1847 the annual production of gold and silver had been less than $500,000; in 1848 it passed $10,-000,000 and in 1850, $50,000,000.

The stimulus proved decisive. As America was organized in 1848, all bulky commodities lying in the interior, away from navigable waterways, were unavailable, but gold and silver could be transported and sold. They were sold, and from their sale came both capital and credit. A comprehensive railroad system was thereafter attainable. The United States realized her opportunity and strained her means to the uttermost, but she did not anticipate the attack which awaited her, and the destiny of two continents has, apparently, hinged upon the catastrophe which accompanied the liquidation of the debt which she contracted to develop her latent resources.

In 1873 Europe refused to receive silver which then represented to the United States a cash asset of upward of $35,000,000 annually. At the same time a fall in prices set in which reduced the value of wheat and cotton alarmingly. Ruin seemed impending, but the result of that convulsion has not met the anticipations of America's rivals. The United States suffered keenly for years, it is true, but she proved herself equal to the emergency. It has not been the debtor, but the creditor who has ultimately collapsed. What happened is nearly a reproduction of the decline of Nineveh.

Under the stress of competition the centre of metallic production has been projected westward, the seat of commercial exchanges has followed, the trade routes are straightening, London is falling into eccentricity, and Europe is being undersold. Approached from this standpoint the process stands out with the logical precision of a natural law.

When, in 1873, America's creditors rejected her silver, she had to sell her other commodities to them at what prices they would fetch, and the chief of these were farm products. It happened, however, that freights fell proportionately to other prices, and this fall in freight made the shrinkage in the worth of wheat more sensible in London than in Chicago, by the difference between the old and the new cost of transportation across the Atlantic. English farmers could not cope with the situation and presently land began to go out of cultivation. Then rents broke, and soon the aristocratic classes stood on the brink of insolvency. To save encumbered real estate, personal property had to be sold, and the best property the British owned was American securities. These accordingly they sacrificed, at first hesitatingly, then more freely, and at last in masses, until they exhausted the supply. Afterward they borrowed.

America, happily, can now afford to lend, but when first called upon to liquidate in haste, American society shook to its base. Deprived at once of her silver, and of much of the value of her other merchandise, the United States had to meet the deficiency with gold. Accordingly gold flowed eastward. In the single year 1893 the United States exported, on balance, $87,000,000, a sum probably larger than any community has been forced to part with under similar conditions. Such a pressure could not continue. The crisis had to end in either insolvency or relief, and relief came through an exertion of energy, perhaps without a parallel.

In three years America reorganized her whole social system by a process of consolidation, the result of which has been the so-called trust. But the trust, in reality, is the highest type of administrative efficiency, and therefore of economy, which has, as yet, been attained. By means of this consolidation the American people were enabled to utilize their mines to the full; the centres of mineral production and of exchanges were forced westward, and the well known symptoms supervened. The first of these symptoms was war. The peculiarity of the present movement is its rapidity and intensity, and this appears to be due to the amount of energy developed in the United States, in proportion to the energy developed elsewhere. The shock of the impact of the new power seems overwhelming.

Only four years ago, in March, 1897, America completed her reorganization, for in that month the great consolidations at Pittsburg first undersold Europe in steel. Immediately Spain and China disintegrated, England entered on a phase of decay corresponding pretty exactly to that which Spain passed through under Philip II, Germany sought relief by attacking China and attempting to absorb her mines, while Russia collapsed. The reason for these catastrophes apparently is that no nation so suddenly ever attained to such a commanding position as the United States now holds, because no nation ever succeeded in so short a time in developing such resources so cheaply. In truth the United States lying between two continents with ports on either ocean connected by the most perfect of railroads, without mountains to make transportation costly, as in Asia, with the great lakes penetrating the interior, with unlimited gold and silver, iron, coal and copper, with a fertile soil and an enterprising population, and with the whole social system, including industry, transportation and farming, administered with a precision elsewhere undreamed of, enjoys not the advantages of Nineveh or Syracuse, of Rome, of Lombardy, or of England separately, but of all of these combined, and her attack is proportionately cogent. Hence the centre of gravity of human society is shifting very rapidly, the seat of mineral production and of commercial exchanges is migrating westward, the lines of transportation are straightening to correspond, and London is ceasing to be the universal mart. A glance at the charts showing the course of ocean steamers during the past twenty years will indicate the direction of trade.

As with Nineveh, so with London. As the volume of American exports has grown, so has the tide of exchanges set more decisively against Great Britain until her people have literally eaten up the accumulations they once possessed in America. Her accumulations depleted, she now lives by borrowing. Well informed authorities in Lombard Street estimate that during the past summer $400,000,000 of French cash have been in constant use to maintain the balance of the Bank of England and to float the public loans. All admit that the London money market is completely dominated by French bankers. Certainly English shipping retains its relative importance, but its actual profits are problematical, if not to owners, at least to the nation at large. British vessels habitually obtain outward cargoes of coal, and homeward cargoes of provisions or ore. The *Economist* has calculated that 40 per cent. of the coal nominally exported goes to coaling stations and is sold to English seamen. Its price, therefore, becomes an item of freight, and is paid by the purchaser of the merchandise transported. If that merchandise happens to be ore or provisions it is paid by Englishmen, and is dead loss. The British iron mines are failing, the copper mines have failed; therefore ores have to be carried to England. The British fields no longer yield food, therefore Great Britain has to pay Americans to feed her, and pay for the transport of what they have to buy. Meanwhile the British spend upon the basis of the lavish profits of old, even when the profits are gone, and hence comes that drain of gold which once prostrated Rome, and afterward desolated Spain, and which has always lead to pillage. When Philip resolved to crush the Netherlands, Alva boasted that he would make treasure flow from Flanders in a stream a yard deep, and the policy of Philip toward the Dutch was nearly parallel to the policy of Lord Salisbury's cabinet toward South Africa. It is superfluous to observe that with Spain and England alike the speculation failed through lack of military energy.

Germany also has been perturbed. Years ago Germany was organized to meet English competition, and while England regulated the pace Germany paid a dividend on her investments. When American trusts entered the field this profit disappeared, and Germans now comprehend that they must adjust their whole system of agriculture, industry and transportation to a new standard. Furthermore, conceding this to be done, success is problematical, for Germany can never match her bulk against the bulk of the United States, or her mines against American mines. She must always buy her raw material. Also Germany must face the destruction of her beet sugar industry through the loss of the American market by Cuban competition.

Russia has, however, suffered most, for her unwieldy shape and ill-situated ports make her transportation costly, and beside her population is hopelessly archaic and therefore wasteful. Administration is the last and highest product of civilization; a primitive community is primitive, precisely because it lacks the administrative faculty. It is the old struggle between the Stone Age, and the metals. Were the Elizabethans resuscitated and made to compete with us they would assuredly starve; and Russians starve. The vice begins at the base. The communal land-tenure still prevails. That tenure indicates an intellectual development more than three centuries behind the American, and accordingly communal land is supplemented by an appropriate civil service. The payment to officials of fixed salaries instead of fees, is an advanced economic conception. The primitive man holds it to be cheaper for each individual to pay for the service he needs, as citizens now pay doctors or lawyers. The fee system even yet lurks in America. All primitive societies, however, prefer fees, hence the official does not work unless he is paid. Fees breed delay, waste and peculation. So it is that all Russian undertakings are excessively wasteful, and this explains why the Siberian Railway, for example, should have cost two or three times the estimates, and when finished need rebuilding. The industries are in a like plight. The Russians have never yet succeeded in working their gold to a profit, much less their manufactures. Not being rich or mechanical the Russians have had to induce strangers to organize their plants, and, as there is no private demand for steel, they have offered as an inducement a protective tariff and state contracts at high prices. But to pay for the steel thus produced, the government has had to borrow, and the price

8

has gone abroad as dividends. Then more money is needed to keep the works employed, and more loans are made, and when loans cannot be negotiated insolvency supervenes. In Paris they estimate that Frenchmen have this year lost upwards of $150,000,000 in a crisis which borrowing may alleviate but cannot cure. Finally the burden falls upon the peasant, who has nothing but his grain. These unhappy beings without money to buy machinery, or intelligence to use it, without railways, or tolerable roads, without even the stimulus which comes from sole ownership of the land they till, ground down by taxes and subject to military service, are made to compete with the capitalistic system of Dakota, the machinery and energy of Nebraska, and the Pennsylvania Railroad. The conclusion is foregone. They perish by thousands from inanition. This year the London papers announce that Russian competition with American grain has substantially ceased.

These symptoms of energy at home and of collapse abroad point to a readjustment of the social equilibrium on an unprecedented scale. Unless all experience is to be reversed the ferocity of the struggle for survival must deepen until one of the two competing economic systems is destroyed. Were all other signs wanting we can see the shadow of the approaching crisis in the failure of the purchasing power of Europe which is reflected in our declining exports, and in the threats of retaliation which we daily hear.

Supposing the United States to push her advantages home, and drive her rivals to extremity, she appears to lie open to two methods of attack. European nations singly or in combination may attempt commercial exclusion somewhat on the principle on which Napoleon acted against England; or they may adopt a policy which will lead to war, such for example as disregarding the Monroe doctrine. In case of war the United States is vulnerable through her communications. Like all centres of international exchanges the United States must preserve her outlets open else she will suffocate, and these outlets now embrace both oceans. On the same principle the kings of Nineveh, for centuries, waged ceaseless war against the Syrians and Egyptians on the west, and the Armenians on the north, to control the roads to the Black Sea and the Mediterranean.

Such is the first method of attack. The second is by opening regions which shall be to America what America has already been to Europe, to force mineral production once more westward. I forbear to enter upon a discussion of northern China. Those who are interested in the provinces of Shansi and Honan may find full details in Richthoven's work. This much, however, is clear. If such a people as the Germans could subdue those provinces, police them, organize them on the American basis, with labor trained and directed by Europeans versed in the American system, there seems to be no reason why America should not be undersold. The region is not unduly large, or distant from the sea, or costly to develop, or unhealthy, while its coal and iron are unparalleled in value. The problem of future civilization, therefore, promises rather to turn upon the capacity of Europeans to partition and reorganize China, and upon the attitude which the United States may assume toward the experiment, than upon natural physical difficulties.

Here then, I apprehend, lies the field of usefulness for modern economics. These complex questions involving peace and war, prosperity and ruin, are the profoundest which can absorb the mind. On them hinges the existence both of individuals and nations. If economics, dealing with such questions in the light of the past, can in some degree illuminate the future, economists will not have toiled in vain.

We are debating no scholastic issue, but the burning topic of all time. Every rising power has been beset by opponents whom fear and greed have incited to destroy her, and the landmarks of history are the battles which have decided this struggle for survival. Think of the siege of Troy, of Marathon, of Arbela, and of Zama. Think of the sacks of Constantinople and of Antwerp; think of the Armada, of Blenheim, of Trafalgar and of Manila. On each day hung the fate of empires and of millions of men and women. From the dawn of time to yesterday, experience has but one lesson to teach us, the lesson that the conflagration kindled by the shock of two rival economic systems has uniformly been quenched in blood.

Economics can have no aim so high as to strive to shield our country from this ancient destiny by marking the path toward danger. Peril exists not for the sagacious and strong, but only for the feeble and the rash. If we would prosper we must be cautious and be armed. We must be willing alike to yield and to strike. If we cannot make ourselves beloved, at least by concessions we can make it profitable to live with us in peace. On the other hand by preparation we can cause all to fear us, and guard against attack. The prudent man will never fight unless in the last extremity, but if he must he will take care that victory shall be sure.

DISCUSSION.

GEORGE E. ROBERTS: The rise of the United States as an industrial power is a new demonstration that the most important factors in the industrial progress of a country are found in the intellectual and moral characteristics of its people. It has been demonstrated here anew that the secret of industrial prowess is in efficient methods. It is not in long hours of labor, or in habits of economy, or in having a docile, disciplined, but inert population. It is not the cost of labor per day, but per unit of product, that determines industrial superiority. The highest productive capacity is found in those who have energy and fertility of mind, who are most alert and enterprising, who, instead of being bound by custom and tradition, have the impulse to inquire, to contrive and initiate. Such capacity requires individuality in a population, the habit of independent and responsible action; it requires the inspiration of hope and opportunity. Probably there has never been a population on the globe that was equal in these qualities to the people who inhabit the United States. They are an amalgamation of the most vigorous nationalities of the world, brought about by the emigration of the most enterprising individuals of each, that movement in itself, with all it involves, being the most stirring to which human nature could be subjected. They come with their minds awakened and receptive, conservatism and tradition broken down by the act of coming, hope and courage stimulating every faculty. The possibilities offered by this country, the prizes within the reach of all and being daily won, have a most stimulating influence. The

restlessness of our people is the restlessness of those who
see their fellows succeed and are impatient to succeed
themselves. Every unit in the fermenting mass is an
independent and potent factor. Our form of government cultivates this individuality. It identifies and dig-
nifies, and gives responsibility to every man. De
Tocqueville declared that he had no doubt that the
democratic institutions of this country contributed to
the prodigious commercial activity of its inhabitants.
A distinguished German writer says that the Americans
have a quality of daring, of unrest, of assertiveness, of
unexpectedness in action. An English trade journal
explains our industrial progress as due to the restless
energy and strong inventive genius of the American
people. The London *Times* says, "the threatened competition [from the United States] in markets hitherto
our own, comes from efficiency in production such as
has never before been seen."

The industrial supremacy of England, so long maintained, has doubtless been due to the same mental
energy, individual independence, and originality. And
so we may trace the industrial rise of Germany since
1870, in some degree at least, to the mental stimulus
given by her tremendous effort against France, her
victory and the consciousness of an enlarged national
life. Such an awakening makes a people fruitful in
every field of effort. No people who are simply patient,
imitative and industrious, but without this intellectual
life and energy, no people who are conservative rather
than enterprising, can equal the people of the United
States in productive capacity. They will fail to do it
even with capable leadership. Japan has had a marvelous awakening, has a government not lacking in enterprise or ability, and her people are alert and receptive ;

but the fear of Japanese competition often expressed a few years ago has passed away. The attempt to use Chinese labor in cotton factories in China has not been successful. They have not inherited the faculty of adaptability. They will learn, but by the time they learn, the methods will be obsolete. A people who depend for advancement upon imported leaders can never keep pace with a people who are themselves fertile of leaders.

The people of the United States occupy a most fortunate and enviable position at this time. No other country has its population so completely equipped with labor-saving tools and machinery, or has such industrial efficiency, man for man. No other people who approach us in industrial efficiency has such a wealth of natural resources at their command. Mr. Carnegie says that the nation which makes the cheapest steel has other nations at its feet in most branches of manufacturing, and our supremacy in this industry seems to be established.

We have scarcely come to a full appreciation of our new situation, and of the modifications in our policies which it evidently requires. We have been intent upon the development of these natural resources which our people have recognized as the basis of future supremacy. We have encouraged the transplanting of industries, and made what temporary sacrifices were necessary to that end. We have diversified the occupations of our people that every aptitude and talent may have employment, and have had the satisfaction of seeing their genius contribute to the advancement of industry the world over. Our policy in this respect has been one instinctive to a vigorous people, conscious of great latent resources. But there is a danger that we may carry this spirit and policy of independence to a point where it will mean isolation, a suppression of intercourse with other peoples at the very time when we can profit most by intercourse. There is a disposition to regard all that we may buy abroad as representing money lost. We are told that we pay so many millions for a given article of commerce, and the conclusion is easily reached that we ought to produce it at home. This may or may not be profitable. It depends upon what else we have to do. It does not pay a man who can earn four dollars per day to divert his energies to work worth one dollar per day. The professional man and the mechanical expert do not dig their own ditches. The people of the United States are high grade workers. The industrial efficiency to which they have attained is such that they cannot afford to do all their own work, or to be shut up to live within and upon themselves, if they can help it. Thus confined, they would lose the advantages which high grade capacity and extraordinary resources secure in the exchanges. What we want is to do the world's best paid work, to enlarge the markets for the industries which yield us the most profit and in which there are the largest possibilities to establish ourselves in the same profitable position in the exchanges of the world that the most skillful, intelligent and resourceful individuals always hold in the exchanges of a local community.

We are all eager to sell, to find foreign customers, but we need to ponder the wise counsel of our lamented President, that we cannot sell everything and buy little or nothing. We cannot do all the work of the world. Other people must have industries, must prosper, or they certainly cannot buy from us. During the three years which ended June 30th last, the excess of our merchandise exports over imports amounted to $1,739,499,252, a sum which exceeds the present stock of gold in all the banks of Europe. It is manifestly impossible to collect such balances in money. To attempt it would be to occasion financial disturbances that would react upon us, and do us vastly more harm than any scheme of reciprocal trade possibly could, with all allowance to the fears of those who oppose such a policy.

The inhabitants of the tropics have their industries, limited in number, upon which their prosperity and progress depend. If these industries be developed, these people will be utilized' in the economy of the world ; they will rise in the scale of civilization and become buyers and consumers of manufactured goods. If the industries upon which they depend for employment be crushed, if their products be refused a market, these countries will be sealed up to barbarism, their populations denied a sphere of usefulness, and we shall have to withdraw labor from more remunerative employment to do their work.

The recent expansion of our exports is based upon elements of superiority that will endure; but that superiority will avail little unless our relations with other peoples are those of comity and reciprocity. Two policies are open for us to pursue. One is the policy of isolation and exclusion, the policy of doing all our own work, and of being confined to our own work and markets. It is a policy that will sacrifice our advantages. It is inconsistent with the genius and ambitions of our people. The other policy is that of fair trade, of amicable arrangements with others, which, while pressing our products into foreign markets, will recognize the fundamental truth that every country must employ its people in some manner, and that, if we are to supply their wants in some line, they must divert their labor into other lines.   It is impossible wholly to suppress the energies of a people, at least to suppress them and have that people remain a factor in the commercial world. If restricted in one direction, they must expand in another.   Hence no plan for the expansion of our foreign trade can be successful that does not allow for the development and prosperity of our foreign customers.

By education and technical training and by the peculiar aptitude of our people, we may hope to secure industrial supremacy in the sense of commanding the most advanced and progressive industries ; we may hope to enjoy the legitimate advantages of superior productive capacity ; but we must concede to everybody some place in the world of industry, either a section of the earth from which we are wholly excluded, or a share in the exchanges,—and we must seek for permanent trade abroad through policies that contemplate the harmonious advancement of all mankind.

CHARLES A. CONANT : The address of Mr. Brooks Adams is so interesting, both in matter and manner— and gives such a dazzling panoramic vision of the movement of world history—that it requires some courage to contest any of his broad conclusions.   With many of these conclusions I am in agreement.   The struggle among the nations for commercial supremacy is a reality which has grown more stern as the struggle has become more intense with the improvement of machinery, the increase in the mass of capital seeking investment, and the contest even for remote islands and pestilential marshes under the equator in the national hunger for land and competitive opportunities.

I think that Mr. Adams, however, gives too great an importance to the part played by money and the precious metals among the forces contributing to national greatness. According to my view of these problems, the ebb and flow of the precious metals is a consequence and not a cause of national prosperity. To inquire where gold has been plentiful, and hence to argue that gold has been the cause of prosperity, is putting the cart before the horse. Undoubtedly a great commercial nation needs the precious metals for carrying on her exchanges, and would be more or less paralyzed without them. But producing power brings gold, while the possession of mines does not imply the power to retain it. The vital element in national greatness is the capacity to produce goods with economy. When a nation solves this problem of economical production, it may snap its fingers in the faces of its competitors. It draws their gold into its exchequer, in spite of every artificial device which they may employ to hold it. Silver and gold may be a valuable asset in themselves, as they were for our country when the mines of California were opened, and as they were for Australia in contributing to her great development. But the mere possession of mines of gold and silver is a minor element in the struggle for national power. This is proved clearly enough by one of Mr. Adams's own illustrations. Spain was the possessor of the riches of Mexico and Peru, but she could not hold them long against the seductive power of English manufacturing and agricultural energy. The goods and commercial policy of England, though scarcely an ounce of gold or silver has in modern times come from her mines, drew away the gold of Spain, as if by a magnet, three centuries ago, and have continued to attract to London the gold of the world through the centuries which have followed.

It has been said that "gold is a coward." This is

true so far as it implies that gold follows the shining
path of commercial success. The true magnet which
draws gold into any country is the possession of capital.
Capital is much more effective in the form of manufacturing machinery, railways and steamship lines, than in
the form of the precious metals. In these efficient forms
capital commands the precious metals and draws them
from the hands of the most persistent misers. The
capacity for economical production is a vastly better
heritage for any people than a mountain of silver or a
river whose bed shines with gold. This capacity for
producing goods at the lowest cost is not the result
merely of a low scale of wages. Rather is it due to a
high scale of efficiency. Yet it is not the result of individual efficiency alone, although that is most important, but of capacity for organization, invention and
the combining of the factors of production.

Fortunately these powers seem to have reached their
culmination to-day in the Anglo-Saxon race and pre-
eminently among the people of the United States.
Through farming on a large scale, through railway combinations which stagger the world by their immensity,
through the consolidation of banks, through the elimination of weak manufacturing concerns, and the
concentration of the highest efficiency in modern machinery, the average producing power of the American
people has become greater than that of any other. As
a consequence they are beginning to undersell all other
peoples in the markets of the world. These things might
be true as the result of the organizing capacity of a few
minds, even if the productive capacity of the ordinary
worker were the same in America as in Germany, and
the same in Germany as in Japan or the Philippines.
When, however, to this great capacity for organization

is added a higher individual intelligence among the workers, with a resulting increase of capacity to accomplish results, and a higher standard of well-being, increasing both physical and intellectual power, it is obvious that under existing conditions America is capable of all with which she has been credited by the previous speaker and of a continuing series of triumphs in time to come.

It is truly the function of modern economics, as Mr. Adams contends, to seek out the causes of national greatness and endeavor to teach them to coming generations. In a broad sense, however, it is doubtful if the recipe for perpetual life will ever be found for nations any more than for individuals. Birth, youth, vigorous manhood, and then decay have marked the history of all the great states of antiquity, and in spite of occasional cccentricities seem in our own day to be pursuing the same round. If the movement of national life from the beginings up to the zenith of achievement and then downward into the abyss of despair are less clearly marked than in antiquity, it is partly because the close communion of all parts of the earth enables a dying nation to absorb a little of the energy of modern life from her vigorous competitors. Within recent times we have witnessed the regeneration of Japan from a civilization long petrified and and dying; we have seen Algeria and Egypt lifted from the coffin of mediaeval barbarism and breathing the breath of modern life, we are witnessing proposals to give a new birth to the moribund empire of China.

We should guard ourselves against the confident belief that our future is secure in the audacious spirit and inventive genius of our captains of industry. National prosperity has often been sapped at the roots by events having but a remote connection with national character. The change in routes of trade has isolated communities which were once the focus of the world's exchanges. The environment which was favorable to economic progress under one set of conditions has failed under a new set of conditions. It was once the countries with an extended and sinuous coast line, offering many inlets and landing places, which were most fortunately placed for the control of trade. With the construction of railways, great interior areas were suddenly thrown open to commerce, changing coast lines and rivers into subordinate factors and making possible the dominance of the Dakotas and of Siberia as producers of the world's food supplies. Steam power on the ocean worked its revolution, and electricity promises to work new revolutions in its turn. Some invention yet beyond our power of comprehension may destroy the value of every dock at Liverpool or New York, or make waste iron of the world's four hundred thousand miles of rail. Against such conditions even national energy may struggle in vain, if out of the logic of events the new inventions do not spring from the brain and hand of the energetic and governing race.

For the present, and probably for several generations to come, the Anglo-Saxon peoples are the masters of energy, the inventive genius, the power of organization and combination of the world. To them is committed the great trust of teaching to the younger races the civilization which has been built up through the seven centuries of English free speaking and unfettered thinking since Magna Charta, through even the twenty-five centuries which link modern civilization with the arts of Greece and Rome. It seems to me a singularly narrow conception of the duties of our race which desires to put aside this leadership, great as are its burdens, and shut ourselves up to a sort of insular vegetation at home. The conditions of the modern world do not permit the realization of such a dream. New markets must be found for our surplus products, new openings must be found for the great capital which we desire rather to convert into permanent sources of wealth than to consume as it is produced.

To one who has had a glimpse of Oriental life, as has been my privilege in the last few months, the absolute necessity of Caucasian leadership, and the vital part which is played in that leadership by Great Britain and America, stand out among the essential lessons of our time. Great opportunities are opening for American enterprise and capital in the Philippines, and are likely to open soon in China. Untold wealth lies there in agricultural products, the raw materials of manufacture, investment opportunities, in mines of copper, coal and gold. If little has yet been accomplished in extending our trade in our own possessions, it is because there has been time only for the work of preparation. When Congress has passed proper laws, permitting capital to be invested under beneficial conditions in the East, the Philippines, so long the victims of the inertia and oppression of one of the dying races, will blossom into one of the garden spots of the world. The common use in the Orient of American money, which is known everywhere as gold, since it is exchangeable for gold, the reign of American law at Manila, the inquiries there of American capitalists planning great enterprises for the employment of the people and the improvement of the country ; the predominant use of the English tongue in all the marts of trade, and the appearance of the American flag on our cruisers and transports in Japanese and Chinese ports, have opened the sleepy eyes of the East to the dominance of a new power. To the more thoughtful of the Eastern peoples, this dominance of our race, with all that it brings of the world's energy and knowledge, although it may wound their pride of blood, is the promise and the fulfilment of all the best that is attainable from modern civilization, conferring blessings alike on those who bring and on those who receive the new gospel of our high political aims and our irresistible economic power.

HENRY P. WILLIS: I suppose that we have all felt a good deal of pride in hearing about the atmosphere of industrial prosperity in which the people of the United States are now living, and that we experience a good deal of satisfaction in our ability to shut out the foreigner, or at all events leave few chances open to him. Yet I suppose there are some who are glad that, as one of the speakers was kind enough to suggest, the foreigner may yet have an opportunity of doing the cheaper work after the United States has selected the best tid-bits, and has received a suitable remuneration. I think the main reliance in this speaker's argument was the notion of the balance of trade, and in that connection he made considerable use of the statement that has been going the rounds in the press in the past few months about the enormous balance now owing to the United States by Europe. The balance, however, seems to be a vanishing quantity. One who has had exceptional opportunities for looking into the conditions in Europe —I refer to Mr. Vanderlip,—publishes in the current number of a well-known magazine an article in which he gives this information. He says there is no such balance, for after inquiring in the financial centers of

Europe he found no bankers who were willing to admit that there were large balances owing to the United States at the present time. In showing how it is that this notion of a trade-balance has arisen, he points out that a great deal of the alleged balance is due to the under-valuation of goods which are brought to this country, and which for obvious reasons are not stated at their true and market value. In various other ways, he finally argues the whole thing out of existence, and thus disproves the statements which depend upon it for support. Perhaps it would be well to bear this matter in mind when estimating the chances that the foreigner has in competing with the victorious people of the United States. It seems to me that, after all, the whole discussion of the beneficial or injurious effect of a balance of trade is one that might well be sent to join the controversy over the relations of creditor and debtor nations in the historical lumber room.

EDWIN R. A. SELIGMAN : I want to add only a word to the discussion. I think the Association is very much indebted to Mr. Adams for the admirable way in which he has called attention to the elementary forces that are instrumental in the shaping of social destinies. I agree, however, with one of the critics in believing that Mr. Adams has exaggerated that particular phase of the subject resulting in the statement that prosperity is due to the abundance or scarcity of the precious metals.

MR. ADAMS : I beg your pardon. What I said was : The metals in general—all metals—no one particular case.

MR. SELIGMAN : I am very glad to be corrected. I fear, however, that even with this explanation Mr.

Adams will not meet with universal approval in his discussion of the period following the gold discoveries of 1848. There is no doubt that the discoveries of the gold mines in California had a most tremendous influence upon our whole prosperity, but we must not forget that at the same time there were other forces which in my opinion exerted even a greater influence. It was just at that time, at the close of the forties, and beginning of the fifties, that in the United States settlers reached the Mississippi valley, and there was thus opened up the immense productive force of a region with the fruitfulness of which nothing in the world's history has been comparable. It was, therefore, not alone the discovery of gold that caused our prosperity, but it was also the immense impetus given to the production of the supply of wheat which enabled us to become an exporter of food products rather than an exporter of gold. Moreover, there is still another point; for at this period there was a fortunate concurrence of events which took place in Europe whereby for the first time a market opened itself to us for our cereals. It was, in fact, not so much the discovery of gold, as the reaching of the Mississippi valley which has completely changed the whole theory of government of the United States. From that time dates the rise of private corporations on a large scale; from that time dates the remarkable change which has come about in the theory and practice of the industrial relations of the individual to the state. It was not gold that was responsible for this.

There is one other thought which I should like to present to the Association, and that is the thought that because in past ages nations have been like individuals —have had their infancy, their maturity and their decay—it does not follow that such is to be the case in the future. It is, indeed, a fact that up to within a very recent time all prosperity was very largely due, as Mr. Adams has so lucidly and admirably shown, to the shifting conditions of trade routes. But the conditions which made all prosperity depend upon commercial advantages are now passing away. What ever may be said of Karl Marx in other respects, it is undoubtedly true that he for the first time laid his finger on the point of real difference between ancient and modern civilization. Marx pointed out that so far as capital existed as a typical category in the nations of classic antiquity, it was primarily commercial capital. Whatever may have been his mistakes in other respects, he was entirely correct in the assertion that capital, in the sense of industrial capital, is essentially of modern birth, and above all the result of the last few centuries. It is only at the present time that we are beginning to see the results of the harnessing of nature to science. It is only now that we are on the very threshold of that immense development in the field of production, due to the utilization by men of the forces of nature to an extent such as never existed before. What does this mean? It means that science is not national. Science cannot be monopolized. The science of the future, and, therefore, the productivity of the future, is not to be the province of any one nation. It is to be the common possession of all those nations which attain civilization, and which acquire those mental and moral qualities that will enable them to make use of these great gifts.

It follows from this that my dream of the future is a very different one from that of Mr. Adams, and even from that of some of the other speakers. I do not believe that a careful reading of the development of the last few decades, or the last few centuries, leads us to the conclusion that the economic supremacy of the future is to be bound up with any one nation. If that were so, we should despair of the future of the human race. The time is soon coming when all productive opportunities, so far as they rest upon the land and natural resources, will be entirely seized. There will be no new lands, no fresh lands, as has hitherto been the case. Rome, Greece and Babylon—all the rest of them—went down before the new comer, who rushed down upon the old country alive with all the vigor of a young and sturdy race. Very soon there will no longer be any possibility of a new comer, because the whole world will be partitioned up among the few huge empires, each of these impressing its own civilization upon the world. The world of the future, with its mastery of science, is large enough for the existence, not of one great nation, but of a half a dozen great world empires.

That outlook I think is bound to change our views, not alone of the economic future, but of the whole ethical and spiritual future of the world. It does not mean that England is necessarily going down because we are going up. That was a historical mistake of one of the speakers.

I should like to call attention to the fact that when Spain decayed, it was not England, but the Netherlands that attained the mastery of the seas. During the seventeenth century the Netherlands were the great industrial nation of Europe, because it was primarily in the Netherlands that the power of industrial capital first made itself felt, for reasons upon which I need not now enlarge. It is true that England gradually won the supremacy from the Netherlands, but as England went up, the Netherlands did not go down. The Netherlands have remained from that time to this an industrial community of great force and prosperity in every respect. The reason that they have not played a greater role in the world's history is simply because of the small territorial basis on which their prosperity was erected; but the Netherlands of to-day are still rich and prosperous. Now, as I take it, the England of the future is to be in a large way what the Netherlands have been during the last two centuries in a small way. England will remain rich, and its capitalists, like those of Holland, to-day, will be receiving their dividends from funds invested in every part of the world. England will, indeed, not retain the supremacy which a chance combination of events secured for her at the beginning of the nineteenth century, but no nation of the future can again have a monopoly such as that enjoyed recently by England. Not alone the British Empire, but the German and the French and the Russian and the American empire will divide up among them the resources of the world. There is room for all of them. It does not necessarily follow that because we are going up, they must go down.

HENRY B. GARDNER: I had it in mind to say a word along the line developed by Professor Seligman, but he has expressed his thought much better than I can express mine. Still there are some facts I wish to bring out in regard particularly to American trade during the decade of 1850 to 1860. If I understand Mr. Adams, he maintains that in that decade the discovery of the precious metals, and their export, was the main factor in our industrial growth. Professor Seligman has already referred to another important event which took place in that decade, namely, at that time we reached the fertile Mississippi valley in our westward expansion. Still another extremely important fact is that the railway during that decade first began to make itself felt in our industrial life.

Mr. ADAMS: I beg pardon. What I said was that one of the difficulties previous to that time which prevented us from having a railway or industrial system was that we had not the capital, and that the gold which we got from California furnished us with the means for developing the country. That was the precise statement which I made.

Mr. GARDNER: I doubt the accuracy of even that statement. The reason we could not have a railway before that time was that the railway was not invented, and that it took some little time to develop it sufficiently to play a really important part in the industry of the country.

Another important fact was the change in England's trade policy, which occurred during the later forties, and which laid the foundation for the tremendous development of manufacturing industry which followed after 1850. If I remember rightly the growth in our foreign trade during the decade of 1850 to 1860 consisted primarily in the growth of cotton exports. Whereas, out of a total export of some hundred and thirty-five million dollars in 1850, our cotton exports amounted to seventy millions. During the next ten years the exports of cotton increased to over two hundred millions out of a total of three hundred and sixteen millions. That certainly would seem to have been the direct outcome of the new market created in England, and of the improvement in our transportation facilities. I believe that the development of the export of our food products as a principal element in our foreign trade did not come until the decade following the civil war. Thus the increased market for American produce abroad would not seem to have been primarily due to the discovery of the precious metals in the United States. As a matter of fact, the precious metals did not play a principal part in the development of our foreign trade.

I would like also to say just a word in development of the thought which Professor Seligman presented so carefully in regard to the difference between ancient and modern conditions. The civilization of to-day is an industrial civilization, based upon the scientific development of natural resources. It follows that each country's economic well-being depends primarily upon the economic resources at its command, and upon the skill and efficiency with which those economic resources can be developed. It seems to me that this view has a very striking confirmation in what I might call the rehabilitation of the ancient civilizations, civilizations that had gone to decay in the struggle between nations, which Mr. Adams has depicted, but which now, with the help of modern scientific methods, are again taking their places among the producing and prosperous nations of the world. Egypt and India, under English influences, are acquiring a new civilization which bids fair to be a permanent civilization, and we may surely expect the same thing in the case of China. Rivalry between nations will determine their relative importance. It will affect the well-being of the nation by affecting the share which it has in the world's markets, as compared with other nations, but, as industrial life is organized at present, certainly the main determining factor is the industrial resources and the efficiency of the people who handle those resources. So long as resources and efficiency remain in the case of any nation, economic decay, in the sense which has been pictured, is an impossibility.

JOHN F. CROWELL : I had hoped to hear something

in this discussion of the effects of trade expansion in the United States upon the United States, inasmuch as we are primarily interested in this phase of the subject. I take the liberty to bring out a few effects which are bound to result from the expansion of our foreign trade. Our foreign trade has expanded geographically eastward, southward, and westward. The influence of the southward expansion has been to increase the accessions of commodities by way of our gulf ports, and change the whole tide of distribution through the Mississippi valley, thus reducing to a great extent the opportunities which the trunk line railway systems have in the command of the traffic in the interior. Some effect is already manifest in the export withdrawals of provisions, flour and grain by way of the Pacific coast. To-day the five great slaughtering centers and live stock markets on the Missouri and at the lower lakes are competing with the far northwestern ports for the command of live stock, and the Rocky Mountain states and territories are feeling the effects of that active competition between the seaboard ports on the Pacific and these markets in the Mississippi valley. One effect of this three-fold competition among the Gulf lines, the trunk lines, and the transcontinental lines, both in sending in and in bringing out, articles of traffic will be to modify the economic position of producers of the surplus products, especially in the central part of the United States, and gradually to change the level not only of prices but of railway rates and cost of distribution between the interior and the seaboard centers of distribution. These several phases it seems to me are entirely pertinent to the question in hand.

Now turning to the general character of this paper, it seems to me that this morning in the author's discussion we have had a splendid illustration of the deification of

the great economic superstition that the end of all existence is economic welfare. Economic progress is a
function of the social aims of the community, and a
means to these ends, not an end in itself.

The three fallacies in the discussion seem to my mind
to be these : First, that a nation is an independent
trading unit—an assumption which does not correspond
to the fact. A nation with other nations forms a com-
plemental commercial unit ; to be an isolated commercial unit is for a nation simply to dig its grave and put
its head in first. Second, that a nation that does not
have all raw materials for making iron and steel, for example, within its boundary can not compete with a nation that has. In securing raw materials international
boundaries are imaginary lines. It does not cost any
more for Germany, for instance, to haul her ores from
the Gallivera mines in northern Sweden, and ship them
some hundred miles down the Baltic and thence up the
Rhine, than it does to haul the ore from the mines a
hundred miles from the head of the lakes to the Lake
Superior docks, thence eight hundred miles down the
lakes, and then two hundred and seventeen miles to
Pittsburg. What we want is common sense and the
study of geographical distances to burst the bubble of
our fallacious reasoning about our living in a fool's paradise of economic superiority. Third, there is in this
paper the fallacy of reasoning by analogy. Analogy
has been running on all fours all over this platform,
and there is no more fallacious way of reasoning. There
is no analogy at all between the primitive conditions
described in the beginning of this paper and the conditions now prevailing in the United States. Moreover,
the metallic thread that runs through history is not the
secret of history. The secret of history is a very different thing, a spiritual, a moral and an intellectual force.

THE COMMERCIAL POLICY OF EUROPE.

BY WORTHINGTON CHAUNCEY FORD.

The commercial policy of Europe may be looked at from so many points of view that I must begin my study by imposing certain limitations. In place of taking any particular country and defining its commercial position in relation to its neighbors; in place of seeking to lay down any general principle of control or regulation common to all the nations of Europe; instead of undertaking to picture trade in statistics, giving masses of figures of quantity or quality; which may be interpreted in more ways than one; I have sought to find some one feature which would in history explain the trend or development of European commercial relations, and in this development explain the largest number of leading features of the existing situation.

The commercial treaty which was negotiated in 1860 between Cobden, on the part of Great Britain, and Chevalier, on the part of France, introduced a new practice in dealing with the foreign trade of France. The leading principles established by that treaty were the prevention of differential treatment of subjects, shipping, or goods of the contracting powers, by means of the most-favored-nation clause, and the fixture of tariffs by means of tables of duties, to remain in force for a term of years. It will be of little avail to go over the old difference of opinion as to the effect of the treaty on the foreign trade of the contracting countries, a difference that can hardly be reconciled or even measured, because of the intervention of that most disturbing of all social factors—war. The Cobden treaty, imposed upon France by the will of an adventurer and of an autocrat, under persuasion of a very able economist and statesman, marks a convenient starting point for this paper. After 1860 a number of commercial treaties were negotiated among the European nations, and, recognizing the principles established by the Cobden treaty, they pointed to a more liberal system of international trade than had hitherto prevailed.[1]

The Franco-Prussian war and the consequent large indemnity demanded from France laid upon that country a heavy financial burden. The patriotism of the people in responding to the appeal of the government accomplished much by freely lending their savings to the government. In 1870 the holders of *rentes* registered in France were 1,254,000; in 1876, six years later they numbered 4,404,763. But the French people were also obliged to submit to additional taxation, and along with new excises, customs duties were the readiest taxes at hand. Thiers denounced the commercial treaty with England, framed a new and much higher tariff, and went so far as to propose duties upon raw materials of foreign origin, even when no similar material was raised or produced in France.

A new power rose on the woes of France. The accomplished Empire of Germany, now first conscious of its strength in war, and possessed of a ready treasure in the French indemnity, turned to arrange its domestic

---

[1] The conclusion of the Cobden treaty with England was followed by a series of treaties on the part of France and other nations. The French treaties were :—

With Belgium, 1 May, 1861 ; Zollverein, 2 August, 1862 ; Italy, 17 January, 1863 ; Switzerland, 30 June, 1864 ; Sweden and Norway, 14 February, 1865 ; Hanseatic cities, 4 March, 1865 ; Spain, 18 June, 1865 ; Portugal, 11 July, 1866 ; and Austria, 11 December, 1866.

concerns so as to adapt them to the novel conditions. This was no light task. The union of states was not complete, and differences as to policy early developed. France was known to be humbled, but not crushed, an enemy in all probability to be fought again, and at no distant day. In its exuberance of new birth the empire saw visions of a future splendid development, and money flowed in quantities into channels where a profit was promised. Speculation supervened, and after speculation the usual collapse. The crisis was not confined to Germany. The United States has cause to remember the crash of 1873, short as our memory has become for past events. Great Britain too gave examples of banking rottenness and misplaced confidence in foreign investments that foretokened a financial panic, and experienced the full force of the storm. But in Germany and in Austria the conditions were aggravated by the greatly inflated operations. The creation of banks, credit companies, discount companies, advance associations, and other institutions of credit had been carried in 1871 and 1872 to a "prodigious extent" all over Germany, Austria and even Italy; and the capitals had become hotbeds of speculative ventures. Vienna was the weakest, and gave the first signs of collapse in 1872, when the Bank act was suspended —a curious proceeding in a country where the currency was already irredeemable, but taken because of the desire on the part of the government to allay excitement by removing the limit to issues. From Vienna the disturbance spread to the German money markets, and even Russia suffered through a too liberal offering of credit by the banks and credit companies established in 1871 and 1872. France alone passed through no credit shock, for economy was forced upon her by the milliards due to Germany, and speculation had found no place in her markets.

Thus we find a condition of exhaustion in the financial world, and from 1873 to 1879 a general depression of great and trying severity prevailed. In increasing her taxes France could at least plead supreme necessity, for only by extraordinary sacrifices, immediate and future (the effect of which are felt to this day), could she regain possession of her territory and government. As these taxes increased the cost of domestic production, Thiers claimed that he could raise duties on imports without violating the terms of the treaties. This increased cost, he urged, was equivalent to an excise duty, and the treaty with England expressly stipulated (Art. 9) that if either of the contracting powers thought necessary to establish an excise duty on any article of native production or manufacture, an equal duty might be levied on the similar foreign manufacture. In practice the attempt would have been difficult, because of the binding force of existing treaties, and especially difficult in face of the treaty with England, about to expire in February, 1873.

"Cotton from India would of course be liable to the duty if imported direct when the treaty with England shall have expired ; but as Switzerland and Italy by their treaties with France obtained the right of introducing cotton into France, nothing could prevent it from taking that route through either of those countries. . . . Silk from China and Japan, with which countries no treaties of commerce exist, is another article on which he anticipates an immediate revenue. But the Swiss treaty again forms an impediment, and one article of that convention dispenses from the certificate of origin a whole series of articles, among which are silk, cotton,

and other yarns, so that the raw material being excluded from France, would find its way in under the
form of thrown silk, and not only escape the duty but
prejudice an important branch of manufacture. . . . .
There is no treaty with the United States, and American cotton might be taxed immediately ; but for the
next eight months English yarns and tissues, on the raw
material of which no duty had been paid, would continue to enter on the same conditions, and in reality
with a premium equal to the amount of the duty. A
tax may be imposed on wool from the countries of South
America ; but manufacturers would continue to be able to
make their purchases, duty free, from Holland and Spain
until 1875, and from Austria–Hungary until 1876. The
same with oleaginous substances : 22,000 tons of ground
nuts are imported from English colonies, and 26,000
tons from Africa ; a duty will be imposed on the latter,
while for the present the former will enter free ; the importations from Africa would consequently cease, and
the duty would produce nothing. Italy and Switzerland import vegetable oils at a nominal duty, and have
special tariffs for candles, soap, and stearine ; the French
manufacturers would have to manufacture the same
with raw material that had paid tribute to the customs.
Timber from Canada and Russia could be taxed, but the
only result would be that merchants would import it
from Sweden and Norway instead of from those countries." [1]

The most-favored-nation clause in treaties of commerce had thus early become an object of suspicion and
dislike in France, but more for the reason that it
hindered the government from obtaining a larger
revenue from customs than for any supposed decrease of

[1] *Economist*, 6 July, 1872.

trade or pressure of foreign competition. It was no time to make new experiments, and treaties with England and Belgium were contracted, upon much the same lines as the older treaties, denounced in 1872 ; and these treaties were to remain in force till 1877. A general enquiry addressed in 1875 to the chambers of commerce by the Minister of Commerce called out a decided opinion in favor of a renewal of the system of treaties, without any material increase in the conventional or treaty tariff rates.

Other states, urged by their financial necessities and steadily decreasing trade incident to the long period of depression (1873–1879) began to revise their tariffs and always in the direction of higher duties. Spain had passed a new law in July, 1877. Italy adopted a general tariff in May, 1878, and Austria-Hungary in June of the same year. Each of these revisals touched the commercial interests of Germany, and the next stage in the course of events was the tariff of Germany, generally known as the law of 15 July, 1879.

Like other countries of Europe the tendency of old Germany—the Zollverein—after 1860 had been towards low duties and a liberal trade policy. The creation of the empire brought a necessity for larger revenues, for the method of making requisitions upon the members of the new empire involved political as well as fiscal dangers, and an opportunity for industrial development such as could hardly have been presented by isolated kingdoms and principalities. In seeking to foster the industries of Germany by a protective tariff Bismarck admitted a change of heart, but in such a combination of strength, subtility and weakness as his character embodied, inconsistencies were only to be expected. Pleading the failure of the so-called free-trade policy of 1865,

Bismarck defended his tariff as a return to a policy avowedly protective, under which he believed the Zollverein had enjoyed a prosperous career of nearly half a century. Urging a political necessity of abolishing all imperial direct taxation, he claimed the expediency as well as right to impose new indirect taxes. Wishing to have a free hand in directing the course of the new empire, he rejected the idea of close connections or alliances, political or commercial, with the neighboring Powers. To Austria alone did he offer to enter into a closer commercial connection, one that could not but lead to closer political union. But Austria refused to consider the proposals, to her lasting injury, as her statesmen admitted some twenty years after.

If revenue was one of the objects of Bismarck's policy, protection to native industries was another. In defending his change of heart, which had among other results driven from the ministry the able Delbrück, so long the economic guide of the chancellor, he was moderate in his claims. His proposed tariff did not seek to obtain revenue by heavy duties on a few articles, but by many light duties on many commodities, thus escaping the danger of imposing unduly heavy taxation on any one region of the Empire; or of giving too large a protection to a few favored industries. The depression of German manufactures, and the avowed policy of other nations gave support to his position. Not only were complaints received from industries, like the iron and steel, of foreign competition, but agricultural interests made themselves heard in like manner, demanding remedial legislation against foreign imports.

In May, 1879, the tariff bill was laid before the Reichstag, accompanied by a voluminous report explaining its provisions. Commercial treaties, it recited, had not accomplished what had been expected of them, and other countries were less willing to recognize that true reciprocity, on which alone such treaties could be defended. The rapid development of transportation, and of the machinery of distribution had given rise to new and unforeseen conditions ; while the protective policy of such countries as the United States was opposed to the commerce and industry of Germany, and could be met successfully only by similar measures. The tendency was everywhere, except in England, towards commercial restriction. Russia, beginning on January 1, 1877, demanded gold in payment of customs duties, a demand that raised all duties by the difference between the price of gold and the price of paper. The action of Austria–Hungary and Italy was cited, and much was made of the fact that France considered the advisability of following their example.

In framing this tariff Bismarck distinguished between revenue and protective duties, and further divided the protective duties into such as were industrial and such as were agrarian. In subsequent years these distinctions became more marked, as political parties arose connected with one or the other, urging their particular claims, often in disregard of the interests of others, or in defiance of claims better founded on economic conditions and policy. Without the grain duties the tariff would scarcely have come into existence. The industrial protectionists knew that a tariff such as they wished would never pass the Reichstag unless the votes of the agricultural representatives were obtained in its favor. The tariff of 1879, by uniting the agrarian and industrial duties, first made possible a parliamentary compromise between the large landed interest and the large employers of labor. It was an alliance that explains so

10

much of Germany's commercial history since 1879, and one that has come well to the front to-day, demanding its full share of attention at the hands of the government.

His objections to commercial treaties were expressed in curt phrase: " The chances of a large export trade are in these days exceedingly precarious. There are now no more great countries to discover. The globe is circumnavigated, and we can no longer find any large purchasing nations. Commercial treaties, it is true, are under certain circumstances favourable to foreign trade ; but whenever a treaty is concluded, it is a question *Qui trompe-t-on ici*—who is taken in ? As a rule one of the parties is, but only after a number of years is it known which one."

Whatever concessions in existing treaties should prove to be inconvenient might be corrected through a manipulation of railway freights, a power recently given by the state purchase of the railway system of Germany ; but no new treaties were to be entered into that should materially modify the tariff rates of duty or interfere with the future development of pro-tection to home interests. Bismarck deliberately isolated Germany commercially. Austria–Hungary could not but feel that the new policy was hostile to her interests, and again framed new duties which widened her separation from Germany.

The reports of the German chambers of commerce for 1880 were filled with complaints of the effects of the new tariff. These complaints were particularly bitter in West Prussia, the province most intimately connected with Russia. Insterburg, on the frontier, asserted that the immediate effect of the tariff was to pauperize the population by destroying the trade across the border. Memel complained that the duties on grain had ruined the transit business on the Baltic, and that Russia founded a new port in her own dominions, Libau, from which she traded in grain with Scandinavia and Holland, without touching at German ports. Tilsit and Königsberg both dwelt on the ruin of the frontier trade by the new duties. As a whole eighty-five chambers reported and a very large majority were for condemning the new tariff as hostile to trade.

Bismarck's reply was an order that the report of no chamber should be published in the future until some months after it had been submitted to the government. One chamber, on violating this order, was promptly dissolved. He did not hesitate to declare that his new conviction was not to be altered. Speaking in 1881 he said : "Without being a passionate protectionist, I am, as a financier, however, a passionate imposer of duties, from a conviction that the taxes, the duties levied at the frontier, are almost exclusively borne by the foreigner, especially for manufactured articles, and that they have always an advantageous retrospective protectionist action. With regard to the development of our tariff, I am firmly resolved to resist every modification in the other direction, and to assist, with all the means in my power, as far as my influence extends, in the direction of a greater support to a higher revenue raised from frontier duties."

The possibilities involved in a tariff for negotiation, one not seriously intended for actual enforcement, but designed for producing an influence on other nations for diplomatic purposes, were early recognized. And when, in 1876, France entered seriously upon the task of tariff revision, the labor of preparing the draught of a bill was imposed upon the Superior Council of Commerce. In explaining its methods for fixing the duties recommended in the draught, the sub-committee asserted its wish that lower rates could have been given, lower even than those in existing treaties. " But we had to remember that a few months hence our negotiators will be wrestling with foreign negotiators, each party striving to obtain for their own country the most favorable terms. Therefore the duties were augmented in order to enable the purchase of concession by concession. Further, the duties were changed from *ad valorem* to specific, a change imitated by other nations on a general scale.

Could not the government by negotiating agreements with other countries undermine the elaborate structure devised by the legislature, and thus neutralize the very purpose of the duties by granting too much of a reduction in rates ? The danger was foreseen, and an amendment was proposed that the new tariff should form a minimum tariff, below which the treaty rates should not go. M. Tirard, then Minister of Commerce, demanded the instant rejection of the amendment, and Gambetta, then President of the Chamber, remarked that it was nothing less than a denial of the right of government to negotiate. To vote high rates for the purpose of negotiating, and then determine those rates as the minimum, was on its face an absurdity, and no convention based upon mutual concessions of duties could have been obtained. The agrarians, defeated on the general question, gained one point of great moment. The more important agricultural duties, those on grain and meats, were not to be reduced by treaty or convention, and thus remained subject to revision by the legislature whenever it should be deemed expedient.

The new tariff, promulgated May 8, 1881, constituted the basis for negotiating new treaties of commerce, and such treaties were formed as follows: with Belgium, October 31, 1881; Italy, November 3, 1881; Portugal, December 19, 1881; Norway and Sweden, December, 30, 1881; Spain, February 6, 1882; Switzerland, February 23, 1882; Servia, January 18, 1883. Unwilling to come into a definite agreement with Great Britain, and unable to impose the rates of the general tariff on imports from Great Britain without inflicting great injury on French industries, a most-favored-nation treaty was framed. With Austria-Hungary and the Netherlands similar contracts were made, with special provisions applying to certain articles of trade or shipping.

Only one country remained—Germany. The treaty of Frankfort, May 10, 1871, contained an article, (Art. 11) stating that the two contracting governments should take as the basis of their commercial relations the most-favored-nation treatment, with this exception: that under this rule were to be included only such favors as were granted to Great Britain, Belgium, the Netherlands, Switzerland, Austria and Russia. Should the treaties with all these powers be abrogated, France would have control over her commercial relations with Germany; but not otherwise, unless some manner of evading the article of the Frankfort treaty was devised.

While thus retaining the practice of commercial treaties, the French tariff law of 1881 contained a strong leaning towards favoring the agricultural interests of France. The years 1875 to 1880 had not been favorable to the farmers of France, any more than they had been to the rest of Europe, and heavy importations of grain and meats had been made. To quiet the fears and clamors of the agricultural population, the largest and strongest politically, duties upon farm products were increased, but not sufficiently to effect the end proposed. Other measures were invoked, and hygienic reasons were found against imports of foreign food. Hence the movement against American pork and other hog products, and an agitation for increased duties upon imported grain, meats and live animals. Again did other countries follow the same policy.

The committee of the German agriculturalists congress addressed a petition to the imperial chancellor asking that the import of dead meat and all preserved meats from the United States be immediately stopped altogether, as dangerous to the public health,[1] and the land owners of south Germany petitioned for higher railroad freights on farm produce in anticipation of the opening of the St. Gothard tunnel.

A trial of moderate protection only whetted the appetite, and good reasons were urged from many sides why the policy should be extended. International feeling had not, as yet, been excited, save in the natural instance of France and Germany, where the jealousy was largely confined to France. Doubtless the conditions under which commercial relations subsisted between the two states were unduly favorable to Germany. That country had a general tariff only slightly modified, and for a very few articles, by treaty. France, on the other hand, had a general tariff extensively modified by a number of treaties, which in return for concessions made by the states with whom they were signed stipulated for lower duties than the general tariff imposed. Yet by the treaty of Frankfort, and under the most-favored-nation clause in that treaty, France was obliged to extend to Germany every concession her negotiations

[1] *Economist*, April 22, 1882.

had obtained from European governments. While giving nothing, Germany obtained much. The absence of a German conventional tariff was a real grievance of France, and the question was raised whether it would not be well to secure a new and more equal commercial understanding with Germany. Official opinion on the subject was out-spoken to the point of indiscretion: "The treaty of Frankfort concluded between France and Germany at the close of a dreadful war weighs in a very heavy and oppressive manner on our commerce and industry. It cannot be denied that this treaty, which put the seal on our military defeat, placed us at the same time in a situation full of difficulties, not to say in one of ruinous inferiority. The consequences of the treaty of Frankfort have been melancholy for France, and the Germans have perhaps done us more harm by their trade laws than they did by the invasion of their armies. But the treaty of Frankfort in itself is neutral. It is worked against our interest by the help of an economical method which we are at liberty to employ in our turn. The Chambers must decide on that question. The treaty of Frankfort compromises the existence of all our commercial contracts, and it seems time for this treaty to cease to be looked upon as perpetual."[1]

The initiative was taken by Germany, and upon a plan of general tariff revision. Attempts made in April, 1882, and in February, 1883, to modify the tariff of 1879 were unsuccessful, but in 1884 the agricultural classes of Germany began to demand the imposition of higher duties upon grain. The existing rate was one mark per 100 kilog. and the imports had not been excessive. But the effects of the trying six years after 1873 were

---

[1] From Spuller's Report on the situation of the working classes in France, 1884, (Chamber of Deputies, No. 2695).

still felt, and the very abundance of the aid received in
the times of need from the United States gave point to
the complaints of the land owners, especially those in
eastern Germany, of their inability to stand up against
such competition. How little ground existed for the
complaints, indeed how much ground there was to prove
the imports were essential, is seen from the returns of
imports and exports of the four leading cereals, 1880–
1890, (tons = 1000 kilog.).

IMPORTS.

	Wheat	Rye	Barley
1880	227,553	689,563	222,271
1881	361,949	575,454	247,828
1882	687,241	658,280	372,648
1883	641,910	777,046	321,567
1884	754,512	961,560	440,080
Average 5 years	534,633	732,380	320,879
1885	*572,423	*769,701	*438,036
1886	273,280	565,265	353,896
1887	*547,255	*638,544	*511,526
1888	339,767	652,811	444,781
1889	516,887	1,059,731	651,422
Average 5 years	449,922	737,210	479,932

* Years of tariff legislation

While imports remained about the same or increased
in quantity, the exports experienced a marked change.

EXPORTS. (Tons = 1000 kilog.)

	Wheat	Rye	Barley
1880	178,170	26,587	154,409
1881	53,388	11,564	119,318
1882	62,502	15,755	79,743
1883	80,758	12,134	82,824
1884	36,193	6,286	37,265
1885	14,080	4,021	24,706
1886	8,294	3,198	58,080
1887	2,840	3,138	20,748
1888	1,112	2,262	23,245
1889	758	608	22,113

Whatever increase of domestic production of grain occurred in this period was required for home consumption, and Germany ceased to be an exporter of grain in any appreciable quantities. In spite of this growing dependence upon foreign supplies the government favored the demand for higher duties, and a bill, submitted in January, 1885, became a law on May 28, raising the duties on wheat and rye from 1 mark to 3 marks; on barley, from ½ mark to 1½ marks; and on oats, from 1 to 1½ marks. The agrarians had won the day.

But it was not without some danger to the state, for the action aroused a spirit of retaliation. Before the bill had become a law the movement began. In March, 1885, France voted to increase her duties on grain and cattle imported from other countries; and Austria voted to authorize the government to raise the import duties on wheat, flour and bread, to the rates proposed by Germany. If Germany, said the Hungarian Minister of Commerce, had not proposed to raise her corn duties, nobody in Austria-Hungary would have thought of raising the corn duties there, Hungary being a corn-exporting country. Austria-Hungary, concluded the Minister, will certainly not cling to her new tariff in the event of Germany's refraining from augmenting her customs duties.

The new German duties also led to agitation in Sweden, chiefly in apprehension of the result of the contemplated charges on foreign timber, which it was feared would be diastrous to an important Swedish and Norwegian trade. Retaliating motions were introduced into both chambers at Stockholm in favor of an import duty on foreign corn. The agricultural duties in Germany, and those to be imposed on timber, also caused dissatisfaction in Russia. This subject of a revision of the tariff came before the Council of the Empire, and retaliation against Germany and Austria were the motives to decide its adoption, with a general tendency in favor of protection.

Russia alone possessed power to produce serious effect upon German exports, and Russia was more directly concerned in the grain duties of Germany than any other power save Austria-Hungary. Germany was the best market for Russian grain, and Russia was the best and most promising market for German manufactures, especially of iron and steel. The threat of reprisal on the part of Russia for the duties of 1885 passed unheeded at the time, but in 1887 when German agrarians demanded further protection it was realized. The government raised the duties on iron and steel manufactures to an almost prohibitive point, and pledged itself to make no reduction before 1898. The gage thus thrown was promptly accepted by Germany, who again in 1887 pushed up the duties on imported grain. Those on wheat and rye were raised from 3 to 5 marks; that on oats from 1.50 to 4 marks, and that on barley from 1.50 to 2.25 marks, (law of December 23, 1887). We naturally look for some counter-action on the part of Russia, and are not surprised to find the situation is becoming strained, and in more directions than that of commerce.

" There is no denying that Russia is intent upon shutting out the whole world commercially, and upon destroying the German element in its western provinces. One ukase follows the other, and scarcely is one additional impost duty enforced when another is proposed, for the most part duties that must offend Germany more than any other state. On the other hand, the German government are not acting very differently. They continually expel Russian subjects, and raise one customs duty after another, especially those connected with agriculture, whereby Russia, above all, suffers. The last measure which Russia has aimed against Germany is the decree of the 25th May, by which landed property is protected by the laws of Russia only if the proprietor be a Russian. Foreigners may neither purchase nor inherit Russian land, and the heirs of proprietors are left the choice of selling their land in three years time, or becoming naturalized Russians. It is this decree, which is unique in modern legislation, that has caused the order to be given in accordance with which the German government press is warning German capitalists against investing in Russian securities. But we may suppose that if this were the only cause the order would have been given a month ago. We may therefore surely believe that the political attitude of Russia during the last two weeks has something to do with it. The Kölnische Zeitung says that just as Russia is now depreciating German landed property in Russia, so may she some day introduce a high tax on coupons, and thus destroy German capital. Some official papers even assert that if there were a war between Germany and Russia the latter might seize the opportunity, and declare herself bankrupt, and thus pocket two milliards of German money, for that is the sum invested by German capitalists in Russian securities. This bankruptcy would even appear in the light of a patriotic action, because it would weaken the enemy. The official papers, moreover, call attention to the fact that England and Holland have got rid of as much of their Russian stocks as possible, whilst France never consented to take them up, because to deal commercially is to make 'friendship suffer'.

The warning of the German government press is certainly well founded, but it must be remembered that the German government was the first to recommend Russian securities to the German public. With a view to showing Russia its friendly feelings and neighborly good will, the Royal Prussian Seehandlung took an active part in introducing the Russian loans to Germany. The irritation of the German government has not failed to produce an impression upon Russia." [1]

While the attitude of Germany and Russia contained promise of future trouble, more immediate difficulties in maintaining commercial peace was experienced elsewhere. The general tendency to denounce the most-favored-nation clause in commercial treaties, and to accentuate the provisions of national tariffs was producing its effect. France and Italy after fruitless negotiations were engaged in conducting a tariff war, illuminative of the effect of increasing tension on trade questions among European nations. The differences began by the rejection by the French Senate of a treaty of navigation. On the plea of revenue, Italy passed a tariff law which increased many duties, and especially those on textiles and metal goods. It was afterwards asserted that these duties were never intended to be permanent, but were designed to serve as means of negotiation rather than of actual execution. The government found itself too deeply pledged to retreat, and so the high duties became operative. While Austria and other powers acquiesced in the new tariff, France refused to accept the situation, and insisted upon a return to the terms of the treaty of 1881, but in a manner which the Italian legislature

---

[1] *Economist,* July 9, 1887. I have treated more fully of this question in "The Economy of Russia," to be published in the *Political Science Quarterly,* for March, 1902.

could not admit. The French government framed a bill which was intended to impose prohibitive duties upon imports from Italy, and both bodies of the legislature increased the rates so as to make them still more oppressive. Silk and cattle the two leading articles in the trade were taxed almost to exclusion.

The treaties of commerce into which France had so freely entered gave rise to a tariff other than the general tariff, a conventional tariff, in which the duties were lower than those of the general tariff. The protectionists of France, and with them must be counted the agrarian party, had become restive under these arrangements which had yielded substantial reductions upon many rates which they regarded as essential to the industrial and agricultural welfare of France.

" The evident interest of France," M. Meline, already the leader of the high tariff party, said, in the campaign of 1889, "is to remain the mistress of her tariffs. . . . . There should be several tariffs, so that the suppression of the treaties may not be considered as a declaration of war by nations with which France had longstanding commercial relations. To them France will accord a tariff of favor as low as possible, reserving the highest tariff—a defensive one—for countries which refuse to France the most-favored-nation treatment."

The design of this plea was to favor the regulation of customs tariff by legislative enactments rather than by treaty ; and to accomplish this, the Assembly must frame two tariffs : one, general, or a maximum tariff, to be applied to such countries as would not make concessions by treaty ; and the other, a conventional, or minimum tariff, the benefits of which could only be obtained by treaty, that is, by similar reductions in duties or concessions of commercial privileges. The usual *question-*

naire on trade policy was sent by the government to the commercial bodies of France, and the replies were overwhelmingly in favor of terminating the existing treaties, and a large majority were opposed to France entering into any fresh engagements, wishing the nation to preserve entire liberty to modify the tariff duties as required. With these replies before it the Superior Council of Commerce could only make its recommendations accordingly. The existing system of treaties was to be set aside, and a maximum (or general) and a minimum (or conventional) tariff were to be framed. Such treaties as should be contracted were to continue for about five years, and were all to terminate on the same date. Thus the minimum tariff would be subject to revision every five years, and the maximum would be open to revision at all times. A minor advantage urged was that such a plan would free France from the obligations of the Treaty of Frankfort, for the rates of the maximum or general tariff could be applied to Germany, should that step be judged prudent or proper in other respects. The perfected recommendations as they came from the government were full of promises. Agriculture, formerly neglected, was to be fully protected; a perfect balance was to be maintained between agriculture and industry; and labor was to be protected in work and wages. If the tariff of 1881 was silvern, the project of 1891 was golden. Accordingly treaties containing tariffs were denounced early in 1891, and the act was not very favorably received by the other powers. The strain of tariff revision and treaty negotiations was becoming too apparent to be lightly invited or silently endured. Every time the matter was opened it meant higher duties, hostile propositions, and increasingly difficult adjustments. The attitude of the powers on the notification of France was extremely suggestive, and even ominous.

"On January 24, 1891, the Department of Foreign Affairs instructed the French Ministers at Brussels, Berne, Lisbon, Madrid, The Hague, and Stockholm, which had treaties of commerce, with a tariff, to notify the termination of those arrangements, and at the same time to propose to maintain the other commercial conventions relative to navigation, copyright, trade marks, etc. These overtures were a complete failure for only one of the six powers interested accepted the offer. Switzerland replied that all the conventions must stand or fall together; Portugal, that her government was not disposed to extend beyond February 1, 1892, the treaties not referring to customs duties; Spain declined to treat the two questions separately, and reserved her reply relative to the commercial conventions until the French Government had communicated the definite new customs tariff; the answer of Holland was a formal notice to terminate the navigation and copyright conventions; Belgium did the same, and Sweden and Norway appeared alone to enter into the views of the French government."[1]

An interesting question on the powers of the government was here created. It was well stated in the *Debats* and may be thus summarized: "The system adopted or endured by the ministers deprives them almost completely, if not in appearance, at least in reality, of one of the most essential attributes of the executive power, namely, that of negotiating and concluding treaties of commerce. They may indeed sign conventions, at least the bill says nothing to the contrary; but under what conditions? Their hands are bound by the

[1] *Economist*, February 6, 1892.

minimum tariff, which is a bar to any serious negotiations. The approval of the Parliament for treaties of commerce is reserved by the Constitution; but, according to the preamble of the bill, which is, however, somewhat obscure on the point, the benefits of the minimum tariff are never to be accorded by decree, and the consent of the Parliament will always be necessary. The government will not require the permission of the Chambers to increase the tariff, even to prohibition, but it is forbidden to make the reduction of a centime. That the determined majority, ultra-protectionists, mistrustful, and hostile to treaties of commerce, could invent such minute precautions against the government might be understood. But what is inexplicable, strange, novel and irregular, is the attitude of a government which voluntarily and spontaneously asks the Chambers to limit its constitutional liberty of action and fetter its hands."

A necessity arose for defining the meaning and purpose of a minimum. The constitutional aspect could be evaded, as indeed it was. The first article of the bill contained no expressed restriction of the powers of the Government, but the preamble or commentary which accompanied the measure explicitly declared that the fundamental principle on which the economy of the minimum tariff was based, was that it formed a limit "below which it will not be permitted in future to descend." M. Ribot, the Minister of Foreign Affairs, could not recognize this doctrine to the full. Had he done so, he must have admitted that the Government was shorn of its prerogatives, and imprisoned by limits thus determined by the legislature. But his opinion was of little moment for he said the Government would not destroy its own work by reducing, in treaties of com-

merce, the minimum tariff it had itself proposed. This
concession, for such it was, received support from
Meline, who further urged that by making any reduction in the minimum the Government would be disregarding its parliamentary duty, and might be charged
with over riding the manifest intention of Parliament.
The veiled threat embodied in this support was easily
felt. It was equivalent to saying that when the Government came before the Chamber to ask for a ratification
of the concessions in the minimum it might make, it
would feel the resentment of that body. It was to curb
an "arbitrary power" of the Government in tariff
matters, that the minimum had been devised, and the
curb was acting with success. For M. de Freycinet, refusing to deny that he might not be obliged to ask the
chamber to modify one or more articles of the minimum,
practically admitted that no change could be made in
the minimum without the consent of Parliament. The
only difference between the executive and the protectionists was whether the assent should be obtained before the negotiations or after the signing of the conventions.

Such being the position of the minimum in its constitutional aspect, it remains to determine its force in
commercial matters. In his report that has been
admired and imitated even in the United States Congress, M. Meline suggests its militant features: "In
order to give its full effect to our minimum tariff and to
persuade other countries to ask for it, two things are
necessary. First of all there must be a distinct difference between the figures of the two tariffs, so that there
may be a decided gain by taking the minimum tariff, and
decided loss by having to submit to the general tariff.
It is necessary again that the two tariffs should be

applied specifically to the greatest number of these products, since the more the number of these products is
diminished the more the benefit is weakened which
results from the distinction between the two tariffs."

Should a nation not accept the duties thus fixed by
the minimum the rates of the maximum would apply.
But another contingency was foreseen. Suppose the
other nation should not only refuse to accept the minimum thus menacingly offered it, but should make reprisals
and legislate against French products, what powers had
the government in the matter. I again quote the
Meline report, as the clearest statement of the purposes
of this tariff legislation and the best exposition and
defense of extreme protection : "Article 4 of the bill,
foreseeing the eventuality of a nation being tempted to
apply to our products differential taxes, or the régime of
prohibition, have given the French government the
power to reply to such proceedings by employing the
same means. Your commission has thought that it
would be unwise and imprudent to attach to the government alone so great a responsibility as that of fixing
tariffs of reprisal towards a particular nation in cases
where this responsibility did not fall to it under the
ordinary tariffs. Such a measure is, moreover, sufficiently serious to make it desirable that Parliament
should be consulted before any steps are taken. Accordingly we have refused in principle to grant to the
government alone the use of so dangerous a power.
"It might, however, happen that Parliament should
not be sitting at the very moment that it was necessary
to act, in order to guard French interests. In such a
case it is important that the government should not remain unarmed, and your commission has been of opinion
that it should be authorized to take these provisional

measures which may seem necessary to it; we have added only this condition, that when the Chambers next meet these measures should be submitted to the ratification of Parliament."

Of course it followed that the agricultural duties could not so much as be entered in the minimum tariff. The solicitude for the farmer, and the expediency of securing his support for the measure imposed this conduct. As cereals and cattle thus had only a single duty, and that in the general tariff, it also followed that they could not be made the subject of any treaty provision or reduction. If the agricultural interest was neglected in 1881, it was amply cared for in 1891. A duty of five francs on wheat had only recently been voted, and even Meline asserted that "no one would think of raising it", an assertion curiously disproved a few years later, when the duty on wheat was raised.

It will be recalled that in 1879 Germany stood aloof from her neighbors, not wishing to enter into any commercial agreements with them. In 1891 this policy of exclusiveness was reversed. While France was slowly framing a tariff which was intended to be highly protective to home industries, prohibitive on foreign imports and sacrificing colonial interests to the mother country, the countries of central Europe quietly entered into a combination of commercial treaties. The Powers concerned were Germany, Austria-Hungary, Italy, Belgium, and Switzerland. The moving spirit was Germany, whose Chancellor, Caprivi, frankly admitted that a desire to strengthen the Triple Alliance was one of the main objects to be attained. That alliance was for the preservation of peace, "but when we conclude such an alliance of peace we cannot carry on a commercial war with our allies." This ended the commercial iso-

lation of the German Empire which had been one of
the cardinal principles of Bismarck's policy. Doubtless
the experience of fourteen years had enforced the necessity of wider markets for German industries, and had
demonstrated the ease with which the protected manufacturers had combined and exacted prices which with
freer outside competition they would never have been
able to obtain. High profits had attracted new capital
until the productive capacity of existing works and mills
was beyond the consuming ability of the home markets ;
and the duties on materials hindered or prevented an
export trade. "Germany was restricted to her own
markets, which became replete with over-production." [1]

It was now that France realized the advantage to be
derived from the much abused treaty of Frankfort. The
very clause of that treaty which the French had denounced and were quite ready to go to war to break, the
clause mutually granting the most-favored-nation treatment to the contracting states, gave to France all the concessions obtained by Germany in her new commercial
treaties save a few exceptions. It was this alone that prevented such a customs union of central Europe as would
isolate France commercially. It was only when agreements were made with other countries like Italy, Spain
or the United States, that French interests would suffer,
for the most-favored-nation clause would not cover advantages secured from them. We may also note a distinct advance in the new German treaties towards a
better commercial understanding with her neighbors.
The freight rates on railroads were regulated by the
treaties, and foreign goods were subject to the same
treatment as domestic, thus doing away with the use
made by Bismarck of the railroad rates for restricting or

[1] Caprivi.

prohibiting the carriage of imported products. For twelve years, the duration of the treaties, commerce would not be subject to sudden changes in duties or railway tariffs, and the merchant would enjoy a reasonable certainty in his forecasts of prices and profits.

From another point of view the German treaties are worthy of study. The reductions in duties were not very large or many. Of three hundred items included. the duties on one hundred and ninety were not altered. But raw materials were freed from duties, and the country gained by the certainty of free coal, minerals, flax, wool, hair, skins, raw silk, and rags; and by reduced duties on chemicals and machinery, so essential to manufacturers. Even pig iron and steel rails were given lower duties, a recognition of a greater ability in the iron industry to meet foreign competition. Finally the articles wheat and rye could be made subjects of treaty reduction; and a conventional rate of 3 marks 50 pf. against a general rate of 5 marks, favored Austria-Hungary until 1894, when Russia obtained the same reduction upon her grain. Other agricultural products such as flour, wine, cattle and wood, the very articles which France refused to treat upon, were also open to concessions. It would appear that the German statesmen had carefully studied the French commercial policy and deliberately rejected its essential features. This makes the German tariff of 1901 all the more remarkable.

With these two policies before them,—France adopting extreme protection and commercial isolation, and Germany entering upon a conciliatory plan,—the other countries were divided in their imitation. In 1891 Switzerland, hitherto always free from strong protectionist leanings, voted by a referendum the protectionist tariff accepted by the Federal Assembly. Spain adopted

a minimum tariff even higher than that of France and
refused to make any concession. Portugal denounced
all her treaties of commerce, and applied her general
tariff to all countries. The offer by France of her
minimum tariff in exchange for the most-favored-nation
treatment, but with a stipulation that the concession
should be revocable by the French government on
twelve months notice, was not acceptable to Europe.
The offers of Germany were more tempting, and from
Russia alone did France receive any encouragement, an
encouragement which was to carry its price.

The tariff of 1891, and the reappearance of Germany
among the Powers having commercial treaties, altered
the economy of Europe so far as it could be modified by
treaty. The Triple Alliance was now something more
than a political combination; it had behind it commercial and financial bonds and possibilities. France
was isolated; involved in tariff wars with Switzerland,
Italy and Spain, in 1893, and bound to Russia by money
as well as by sentimental ties. Russia, in pursuing a
policy which involved radical protection to the industries established on her territory by foreign capital, increased the rate of her tariffs until first the suspicions and
then the hostility of Germany were aroused. A short
tariff war, during which both countries lost heavily,
ended in a better understanding than had existed since
1882, and in a commercial treaty by which Russian
grain was placed upon the same footing in German
markets as the grain of Austria-Hungary. The treaty,
published in February, 1894, to take effect March 20th,
was opposed by the farmers of Germany, who maintained that any concessions to Russia must injure, even
destroy, their interests.

In 1895 the tariff war between France and Switzerland was brought to an end, but the condition elsewhere indicated the unrest which had settled upon Europe in these years of stagnating trade and general depression. Germany sharpened an instrument of retaliation against discriminating duties on the part of other powers. On May 18, 1895, a law was promulgated to the following effect: " Dutiable goods proceeding from states that treat German ships or products less favorably than those of other states may, in so far as existing treaties are not thereby violated, be burdened with a surtax ranging up to 100 per cent. of the tariff duty imposed on such goods. Goods free of duty in virtue of the tariff may, under the same conditions, be burdened with a duty not exceeding 20 per cent. *ad valorem.*"

This instrument was soon put to the test. In 1896 Spain rejected a commercial treaty offered by Germany, and in consequence Germany raised by fifty per cent. the duties on goods imported from Spain. It was a significant act when England denounced her existing treaties with Germany and Belgium, because they obliged her to share with those countries any advantages in preferential tariffs her colonies might grant.

The last step in this essay is the tariff now pending in Germany, which has been forced upon the country by the "agrarians", the large land owners and their following. Industry has been pushed so far that over production in the great lines has become an insuperable difficulty against controlling with profit the domestic market. No combinations, syndicates or cartels, have succeeded in modifying this condition of increasing strain, and neither colonial nor foreign markets have taken the surplus product. The persistent agrarians had anticipated any action on tariff or commercial treaties by securing a report from an official committee

favoring higher duties upon grain. The warnings of
1891 were forgotten, and the ministerial description of
Germany's economy was passed over, though more true
in 1900 than in 1890. "Germany is now a manufacturing country of the first rank, with a rapidly increasing
population, no longer able to produce all the raw
material she requires, and having a large surplus of
manufactures, for which she must find foreign markets."
Having won a victory on a meat inspection bill, which
virtually restricted within very narrow limits, if indeed
it did not prohibit the importation of American corned
beef, canned meats and sausages, the agrarians demanded
a like prohibitive duty on grain. The existing rates
upon wheat, rye and oats are to be largely increased to
serve as minimum rates, or the lowest admissible in
commercial treaties. The maximum rates are prohibitive, and there are no minimum rates on animals and
meats. It is not strange that such a measure, even as a
suggestion, should excite strong opposition at home and
abroad, as it is a menace to industrial power and a
threat to friendly relations with commercial neighbors.
When the measure was informally accepted by Count
von Bülow, the true extent of the feeling became
known. Russia, Austria-Hungary and Italy at once
threatened retaliation, and the matter is now pending.

What is significant for our purpose is the practical
elimination of the most-favored-nation clause in commercial treaties. After 1860 it seemed to be the very
corner stone of trade agreements. In 1901 it exists
only in a few remaining treaties, more as a relic of the
past than as an active agency of the present.

I have thus traced all too briefly the more important
incidents connected with the recent experiences of certain nations of Europe in tariffs and commercial treaties.

Is it possible to illustrate or explain the economy of these and other nations by the results of these experiences? A trial at least may be made.

Customs tariffs may be explained and defended upon fiscal or upon political grounds. They may be framed and imposed for revenue or for protection, or for a mixed reason, as revenue with incidental protection. These phases have been so thoroughly threshed out in our own politics that the distinctive qualities of each description need not detain us here. One fact is emphasized in the European experience, the desire of each of the nations to protect against foreign competition its own producers and manufacturers, and especially its agricultural interests. Whether it is France, whose wheat fields have until recent years yielded sufficient for the consumption of its nearly stationary population; Germany, who became an industrial nation before 1880, and with a population rapidly increasing from year to year began to depend upon other countries for its food supplies; or Russia, distinctly an agricultural country, but forced by frequent recurrence of famine to harbor its own produce— in one and all, the question of food is a serious commercial problem. It has become all the more serious because of the great political power wielded by the "agrarian party", the party of land owners and cultivators who demand not only that the home market shall be reserved to them, but that the price of wheat in that market shall be satisfactory to them, no matter what it would be under perfectly unrestricted competition, and without regard to the hostility aroused in other nations. The rise in the duty on wheat in twenty years in France, Germany, Italy, Austria and Spain, from a merely nominal rate to one that is a serious obstacle to free movement in grain, is eloquent proof of the extent to which this policy has been carried.

The result is a contradiction in terms. Agriculture is limited by the quantity and capability of the land open to cultivation. and the law of diminishing returns applies too rigidly to permit the realization of the intentions of the legislator who seeks to inject an artificial stimulus into the utilization of land. In 1875 the area of France under wheat was 6,946,981 hectares ; in 1898 it was 6,963,711 hectares. The change in area was small, but by better methods of cultivation the yield in a good year was increased about one fifth. This improvement can hardly be assigned to the effect of the duty, because the duty was intended to maintain prices, and prices have steadily fallen. Before the short crops of the last half of the period 1871–1880 had raised the price of wheat, the import price was 25 francs the quintal. In the last half of the period 1891–1900 it was about 23 francs, but the prices were those of years of failure and heavy importations. In the first half of that decade 16 francs was considered a fair quotation. In Germany and Italy the tendency has been no different, but much wheat land has gone out of cultivation.

An historical parallel may be drawn. The farmers of Italy under the Roman Empire were brought to ruin by the free largesses of grain in Rome. Even with slave labor they could not compete with the grain fields of Sicily, Egypt and northern Africa. As a result the inhabitants left the country regions, and flocked to the city, where they became a congested mass of pauperism, a menace to the state and an increasingly heavy burden to support and keep amused. As there were no industries in Rome, this proletariate could not be employed productively, and only by removing them into the provinces, by colonizing them, could the pressure be relieved. The low-priced or free grain from the provinces accounted for the depopulation of the rural parts of Italy.

Is not this much the situation in Europe to day in spite of all the efforts of government to introduce a corrective? Low cost grain and meats from India, America and Australia, have made agriculture in Europe unprofitable in certain of its great lines of production. The farm is no longer a source of profit and the cities offer greater attractions. The encouragement of industries gives employment to a part of this moving population, emigration is quite as important a factor. What Rome accomplished deliberately and by force, economic forces work quietly and peaceably at the present day, and upon a scale never possible among the ancients. The entire movement of the barbarians from the north on to the Empire sinks into insignificance by the side of ten years migration among the nations of Europe.

In seeking to protect productive interests, other than agricultural there are rigid limits, natural limits as a rule, to the extent of development possible. For example, it would be hardly justifiable to conceive any notable expansion of the iron production of France. In 1880, the iron ore mined in that country was 2,874,263 tons; in 1898 it was 4,731,394 tons, an increase of over 60 per cent. The German production of iron increased in the same period 120 per cent. No amount of stimulus seems able to raise Italian industry beyond a moderate degree of activity. The character of the country and the qualities of the people militate against development, and we find true pauperized peoples in the European family. They make a living, but anything beyond that is acquired at tremendous cost. That such peoples should wish to enter into the industrial race, and seek to become industrially independent and even aggressive, is misplaced ambition, certain to react to their lasting injury.

In place of differentiation of product we see each nation seeking to develop the very interests that will antagonize similar interests in their neighbors. And when the rivalry becomes conscious, the government is called upon to interfere and to grant bounties or subsidies to further the competition. Look at the situation of beetroot sugar in Europe to-day, and attempt to explain it upon any reasonable ground, fiscal or commercial. Each nation has sought to supply its own needs, and carrying the production too far, has been obliged to look for foreign markets. Each nation seeks to obtain a revenue from the consumption at home, but cannot tax what is exported, for that would destroy the export interest upon the continuance of which the industry depends for existence. Each nation has become so involved in a mass of fiscal and commercial regulation that no common understanding is possible, and it is hardly possible to comprehend the detail of the regulation and its effect upon exporter and consumer. Many international conferences have been held upon this subject without result, and the almost yearly change in rate of excise or system of drawback prevents a proper understanding of the actual duties charged and bounties, open or concealed, on exports granted.

The same desire to possess a home and export interest in the face of general foreign competition is shown in other lines. The duties on textiles have been framed to favor the domestic manufacture for export to foreign markets; the absence of duties on raw materials has been imposed by this fact of competition. Germany could not tax cotton and wool, if France and Great Britain admitted these articles free, and no system of drawbacks could compensate for such duties. The duties upon so general an article of use as mineral oil, or upon flour, to maintain a local refining or milling industry, are patent protection for a specific purpose. The general tendency to adopt shipping bounties is of the same nature as the beet-root sugar policy, and may lead to the same costly race for supremacy in national shipping and for competition in the international carriage of goods.

This encouragement of home interests does not stop with home conditions, but soon outruns the needs of the domestic markets. Hence the necessity for obtaining national markets in other parts of the world, colonies, or selling in foreign open markets. In the latter case the competition of other countries is encountered; in the former, colonial markets are usually closed markets, open on favorable terms to national ships and goods, but closed to the ships and products of others. What has been the basis of international agreements for the past twenty years, but the desire to obtain markets, exclusive markets? France in Tonquin, Germany in the Pacific islands, the delimitation of Africa, and the threatened partition of China, one and all had for an aim an outlet for the produce of home manufactures. France applies her general tariff to her colonies and monopolizes their import trade. As a compensation she grants certain favors to colonial goods in her home markets, with a result of becoming embroiled in a tariff war with Brazil. Wherever pressure can be exerted, in Turkey, China and until very recently in Japan, the tariffs are framed, not for the benefit of those nations in tutelage, but for Europe and the United States. Markets are the general need, and enormous risks are run to secure them.

For nearly a quarter of a century the three great powers of continental Europe have been busily engaged in erecting tariff walls to protect their trade, and the smaller powers have imitated them. From the standpoint of an outsider it would appear that this policy is based upon a wrong principle, which if carried much further must bring the elaborate structure of protective tariffs, hitherto tempered by commercial treaties to a crash. Entire self-sufficiency can be secured by no one of the powers, and no matter how far the colonial policy is pushed, there will always be a dependence upon foreign products and upon foreign markets. The inwardness of the question was stated by Sir Robert Peel in 1842, when he argued that "it is of the highest importance to the welfare of all classes in this country that the main sources of your supply of corn should be derived from domestic agriculture. You are entitled to place such a price on foreign corn as is equivalent to the burden borne by the agriculturalist. . . . I certainly do consider that it is for the interest of all classes that we should pay a small additional sum upon our own domestic produce, in order that we may thereby establish a security against those calamities that would ensue if we became altogether, or in a great part, dependent on foreign countries for our supply." [1] History has made strange comment upon this utterance, and yet there is a Peel today in every country whispering the hope of self-sufficiency, a hope that has never yet been satisfied, and with the increasing complexity of world relations becomes more and more impossible.

[1] Quoted in *Quarterly Review*, vol. 189:368.

The mercantile system broke down of its own weight, and that system was based upon high tariffs, a net work of prohibitions, a widely applied system of bounties on production, and export, and navigation laws. The stage was reached when diplomatic relations were controlled by commercial rather than political reasons, if, indeed, we may separate the two. That fiction of the balance of power, useful to the strong and grasping, but ruinous to the weak, was a convenient excuse for maintaining an artificial distribution of authority of governments. It could not produce even a working distribution of industrial and commercial power or privilege, any more than did that logical but monstrous conception of a "continental system" which Napoleon raised to the forefront of his military operations. The ingenuity of the mercantilists and the might of Napoleon were swept away by the mightier and more ingenious development of commerce and manufactures which would not endure such attempts to restrict their growth, or to direct their channels. It seems to me that the world is marching into the repetition of the errors of a restrictive policy, and in this course the United States is among the chief sinners. For it no longer has the excuses which were urged when production was on a comparatively small scale, the machinery of commerce imperfectly organized, and the world not parceled out to such a degree as to leave no large territory subject to acquisition and free colonization. It raises food more than sufficient for its population, its sources of raw materials in coal, iron, copper and cotton are greater than those of any manufacturing nation, its command of high qualities of labor is more varied than elsewhere, its machinery for transportation is highly organized, and improved year by year, and its manufactures are favored in every possible

way. It is surely shortsighted policy to continue unnecessary protection and seeking to monopolize all
branches of production by excluding foreign products.
No general tariff law has been framed in our Congress
without a reference to some special country or description of product. It was England, or the pauper labor
of Europe, or Canada, or the cheap products of Asia,
any excuse however flimsy served the purpose. It
will be Cuba and the Philippines. And now the
historian reviews these arguments of the past with
wonder that they could ever seriously have been
urged, much less believed. The gongs of a Chinese
army are not more deafening than these war cries, or
more useless in the end. The blatant boasts of superiority are yet to be measured by the severe tests of depression.

We have heard much of a combination among European nations against the commercial interests of the
United States, and officialdom has shown periodic
tremors over the possibilities involved in such a combination. But if our sketch of tariff legislation and
treaty practice shows clearly any one fact, it is the utter
impossibility of such a customs or commercial union.
It may have been possible in 1860 ; it had become improbable in 1872 ; and with each succeeding decade the
improbability became the greater, until it has now
reached the stage of the impossible. There are too
many oppositions to be overcome, too many competing interests to be harmonized, too many political considerations to be altered, to allow a general
concensus of opinion and action. Is it possible to
picture an agreement upon wheat, sugar or shipping
bounties ? With the growth of tariff and bounties,
interests have grown into a power that would prevent

concessions and mutual sacrifices, even in the face of a "common enemy". The nearest realization of a European Zollverein was after the French tariff of 1891, when the commercial connections of Germany would have isolated France had it not been for the saving clause in the treaty of Frankfort, the most-favored-nation clause.

Where mischief may be done is in the isolated action of each nation of Europe against the trade of the United States. The damage to our interests may be all the greater because of the conscious imitation of regulation by more than one power. To conciliate opposition by wise concession is the part of true statesmanship; to offer a better use of our undeniably great resources is the true economic policy of the United States, and this betterment cannot be obtained by wilfully closing the best markets to our products. The tariff should not be an implement of offence, of commercial war, but one of revenue and commercial peace. It is never more dangerous than when raised to a fetich and held to be the cause of economic advancement.

DISCUSSION.

HENRY C. EMERY: Mr. Ford's paper presents so clear and accurate an account of the recent tendencies in the commercial policy of European countries that there is almost nothing to add to his statement in a brief discussion of this character. It would be uninteresting to add more minute details to his admirable outline, which in itself leaves little room for discussion. For this reason I am tempted to change what I had in mind to say, and to treat the subject of commercial policy partly from the point of view of the discussion which followed Mr. Adams's paper. The two papers read this morning seem indeed to me to illustrate well two radically opposite points of view. It is a common statement that the last few years have witnessed a revival of mercantilist ideas, not only in the policies of nations, but also in the writings of many economists and historians. This class of ideas is represented in the paper of Mr. Adams, which, although to my mind exaggerated in tone, is in line, except for his treatment of the precious metals, with much recent writing abroad, especially in Germany. Mr. Ford, on the other hand, although not dealing with theory, evidently represents the free trade view of international relations, and it is in reference to economic ideas rather than tariff rates that I wish to consider his paper.

In the first place, commercial policy means something more than the question of protective tariffs and reciprocity treaties. It includes the whole question of how far the power of the state can in any way be exercised to secure economic advantage to the individual nation. The essence of the older mercantilism, stripped of its temporary exaggerations, was that the economic welfare of the state can be advanced by the use of political power, and that, conversely, the political power of the state depends upon economic conditions. That is also the idea of many modern writers, and is evidently the idea of Mr. Adams; that is, that the time inevitably comes in the history of a great growing nation when the continuance of its economic progress will call for an exercise of all its political, or even military, resources. It is not necessary to point out the difference between this idea and the free trade idea. It may be worth while, however, to recall the different conditions under which the free trade movement has appeared in different countries. In England the free trade theory was put into force, and became a practical policy, under the pressure of a strong business party. It was an economic necessity at the existing stage of English industry that foreign trade should be relieved of all restrictions, and that the English manufacturer should not be discouraged by the effort to maintain food prices for the protection of the agricultural interests. In the United States the conditions were, of course, just the reverse, and the practical backing of the free trade theory has come from the southern cotton growers (especially prominent before the civil war), and the western grain producers, both of whom have wanted the freest outlet for exports. In France, on the contrary, the so-called free trade period, that is, the period of commercial treaties, was the result of the influence of one man; and, as Mr. Ford points out, the Cobden treaty was forced by Napoleon III upon a people predominantly protectionist in their views. In Germany the free trade movement was closely connected with the agitation of the doctrinaire liberals, a name that may fairly be applied to them, despite their great services, in that they aimed to apply the whole liberal system of English politics to their own country, without appreciating the great importance of historical national tradition. Free trade was an accepted part of English liberalism, and the growth of the idea in Germany was primarily academic. The movement was supported by the landholders at first, but it is fair to say that there was little strong popular feeling for either side of the question. The coincidence of the removal of the iron duties and the trade depression of the seventies started a reaction, and with the protective tariff of 1879 the new era was inaugurated. It came to be the feeling that a system of free trade, though beneficial to England, where it had been adopted on practical grounds, was certain to prove injurious to a weaker country like Germany, where the industries competing with those of England were being worsted in the struggle. It is not necessary to go into a discussion of these views. Suffice it to say that they were quickly utilized by Bismarck to effect the necessary parliamentary combination, and that since the passing of the act of 1879 the strict free trade idea has had no considerable backing. Speaking broadly, it may be said that, whereas from 1848 to 1860 the leading minds in Germany inclined to free trade, since 1880 exactly the reverse has been true. On the general principle of protection in its widest sense there has been a union of political parties, and a unity of feeling among most economists. This union, however, has been sadly shattered by the proposed agrarian duties. The industrial interests, which formerly had supported moderate agrarian protection, are aroused to fight what seems a distinct attack upon them. They do not demand a reduction of existing tariffs, but merely that they be not raised. The agrarians, however, have some supporters among the well-known economists. I happened to be present at the meeting of the Evangelical-Social Congress in Leipsic in 1897, when Dr. Oldenberg read his famous address on *Deutschland als Industriestaat*, which has been the starting point of most of the discussion of commercial policy in Germany since that time. As is well known, Oldenberg drew a dark picture of the trend of German development towards increased industrialization, and held up the ideal of " economic independence." He was in this instance the academic Sir Robert Peel of whom Mr. Ford spoke. Oldenberg has been well supported by Wagner and Sering among others, but the preponderance of opinion has been strongly against him. It has been vigorously maintained in opposition that the time when Germany can be " independent," in the sense of furnishing her own food and raw materials, has irrevocably passed; that to attempt to return to such a condition would be to limit the growth of population ; and that the true policy to adopt is one that will increase commerce, and give the greatest opportunity to population to expand. But this opposition is based as much upon the mercantile theory as the other. It is in no sense a free trade opposition. Their ideal is that of commercial supremacy, and they urge as a means to this end a vigorous trade, colonial, and naval policy. Some of the most vigorous writings on this subject were contributed to the popular propaganda in favor of increased naval appropriations, and the question of war ships is looked upon as an item in a general commercial policy. Political and military power to secure commercial progress,—this is the essence of mercantilism.

I believe, then, that the changing economic conditions, and the conflicting economic theories, to which I

have referred only briefly, must be carefully studied in
any consideration of commercial policy abroad. The
theories may be wrong, but they are likely to prove too
important in the history of the future lightly to be
brushed aside. For illustration, consider the attitude
of a German economist toward Mr. Ford's remarks on
emigration. Roman farmers were ruined by free grain,
there were no industries to employ them, and emigration was necessary. The same, he says, is true of Germany to-day, and the solution is in the inevitable emigration to other countries. But that is just the one solution that the German will not listen to. He cher-
ishes the idea of a Germany great among the nations of the world, and he not unnaturally believes
that if his country sends annually much of her best
blood to increase the vigor of her " rivals," that her position among the great powers will soon be lost. Hence
a policy of high agricultural protection is advocated, or
else a policy of so stimulating commerce that the surplus can be supported at home. The free trade solution, it is urged, takes no account of the ideal of national greatness.

It has been suggested in the discussion that there is
plenty of room for all nations, and that America is the
best friend of Europe, although the latter fails to recognize it. There certainly is room enough unless several
nations insist upon expanding indefinitely, in which case
the statement is doubtful. It is, indeed, to be hoped that
all nations will hereafter live together in harmony ; but
is it not rather a moral ideal that a practical likelihood ?
I earnestly believe that the idea of national rivalry has
been greatly exaggerated, but I also believe that the
idea has been and will continue to be a potent force in
determining international relations. Right or wrong,

the importance of it should be recognized. Personally I am enough of a mercantilist to believe that in past history the economic interests of nations have sometimes really clashed and that these conflicting interests have determined conflicts of a more destructive kind, and I cannot share the optimistic confidence of those who believe that the history of the future will see no repetition of such occurrences. It appears to me quite likely that the continued growth of modern nations may lead somewhere and sometime to similar conflicts.

It has also been suggested that this theory assumes falsely that economic welfare is the highest good. Such an assumption is doubtless false, but the idea of economic welfare, and of the way to secure it, has played a role of the first importance in history. The economist is primarily concerned with problems of material welfare. Again I confess myself enough of a mercantilist to want my own country to be economically great. I would rather see her great and prosperous together with other countries than at the expense of other countries; but I cannot see why we should be afraid to say that, if the unfortunate time should ever come, when other nations shall resort to violence to oppose our peaceful progress, this nation will be ready to protect, by diplomacy or by force, the prosperity she has justly earned.

BROOKS ADAMS: I wish to say a word on the paper of my friend, Mr. Ford, and to express my entire agreement with it. I can see no antagonism whatever between Mr. Ford's views and my own. I believe that Europe has been forced into its policy by necessities of self preservation. All that he has so well described is a necessity. Men do not make tariffs for fun. It is not an academic business we are discussing now. It is a

question of life and death. The man who is undersold
in the end must die. The first thing we have to do is
to live. If another man man competes with us we undersell him if we can, and if we cannot we crush him,
or else he crushes us. Now there is no use blinking this,
and Mr. Ford has put it in a most direct way, He has
shown that these people have been attempting by tariffs
to become self-supporting in order to prevent themselves
from being undersold, and they have failed. He says
that necessity compels them to this course. They have
to go elsewhere for their food and for their raw material,
and it is the only way they can get outside of their own
country and buy, because the country which has the
raw material does not have to buy. It has the advantage, and therefore it can undersell its neighbors, and
the moment you are undersold that moment you can not
pay for your food and you starve. You see it in Russia
to-day. Now it is this very necessity which Mr. Ford
has pointed out which I believe in, which everybody I
think who has practically wandered about the world in
late years sees in operation. It is this necessity of
having the means of life which is causing the tariff
wars everywhere. Mr. Ford says the policy is going to
break down. When it fails in Russia they have got to
go outside for their bread ; and what does that mean ?
It means that the whole economic system of this world
is crumbling ; crumbling under competition. Now I
do not pretend to say that there will be war, but I say
there has never yet been a time when this condition of
things has been reached when there has not been a war,
because men will fight before they die.

CHARLES W. MIXTER : One idea that has been made
prominent this morning, and one constantly seen in

books and newspapers, is the idea that in Europe they have come to their physical limit,—a limit in respect to industrial resources. Now it seems to me that it is the limit of government—a political, not a physical, barrier —which immediately stands in the way of European countries making very rapid progress.

In a few months there will be a book published on German railroads,—something new in that line. It has been my privilege to talk many times with the author, and the chief thing I have obtained from these conversations is the conviction that there are hundreds of millions of wealth which are *not* being created in Germany because of the exorbitant and inflexible charges on the railroads which, in turn, are caused by the thoroughly vicious system with which the railroads are tied up. It sounds like a fairy tale to say that the government can not reduce the charges on the state railways, but such is the fact. It is for that reason that it is actually paralleling the railroads with canals. At present by far the greater part of the bulky, low-value traffic goes by the canals and rivers. The railroads carry little besides high-class freight and passengers.

What all this means to the industrial development of Germany—the non-creation of wealth there—I need not point out in detail ; it is enough to suggest it. If another Bismarck were to arise with the same grasp and power in internal affairs, that the earlier Bismarck had in foreign policy, it would be possible to make reforms which would enable Germany, for a considerable period, to progress as rapidly as we do.

EMORY R. JOHNSON : It is sometimes unwise to let an error pass without attention, even in a running discussion. I wish merely to state that the greater bulk of the heavier traffic in Germany moves by rail and not by water. If we were to study the amount of coal and iron ore in the western part of Germany, that statement would be fully substantiated. Of course there is a large movement by water, and the traffic that moves by water is of this heavier traffic, but that which moves by water is small in comparison with that which moves by rail. I have no doubt that within a few years the technical development of the German railroads, which are somewhat behind those of the United States, will permit large reductions in the cost, and consequently in the charges, for carriage by rail; but it is a decidedly fallacious statement to say that the greater part of the bulk of traffic in Germany moves by water at the present time.

SOME THEORETICAL POSSIBILITIES OF A PROTECTIVE TARIFF.

BY THOMAS NIXON CARVER.

The wisdom of reopening the tariff question to scientific discussion can be denied only on the ground that economic science has said its last word on the subject. In view of the rapid development of the science during the last twenty years, and the light which recent analyses have thrown on other questions, it would be surprising if some new light had not been thrown upon this question. It would savor somewhat of Bourbonism to assume beforehand that further discussion of a question of this kind is superfluous. Certainly the mere fact that the question happens to be a political one can be no sufficient reason why it should be ignored by a student of economics.

In a paper of this length it will be manifestly impossible to discuss every phase of the question. Therefore it will be narrowed down to the three following questions: 1. Who pays the tariff? 2. Can a protective tariff raise wages? 3. Does a protective tariff necessarily attract labor and capital from the more productive industries into the less productive industries? As a partial answer to each of these questions it will be the purpose of this paper to support the three following propositions:

1. A tariff duty is not necessarily paid by the home consumer.

2. A protective tariff may be so framed as to raise wages.

3. A protective tariff may be so framed as to attract

labor and capital from the less productive into the more productive industries—judged from the standpoint of the community rather than from that of the individual business man.

[1] Whether the home consumer pays the tariff duty or not depends upon whether or not the tariff duty raises the price, in the home market, of the article upon which it is collected. Whether it raises the price or not depends upon whether it reduces the supply of the article in the home market or not ;—it being assumed that the duty will not affect the demand. The effect of a duty is ordinarily to reduce the amount of the article imported. The question is then, will the home product then increase, as a result of the duty, sufficiently to counterbalance the diminution in the amount imported? If the conditions are such that a tariff duty will occasion an increase in the domestic product equal to the diminution in the amount imported, the duty will occasion no change in the total supply on the home market, and consequently no change in the price of the article. But if the domestic product does not increase sufficiently to offset entirely the diminution in the amount imported, there will be a decrease in the total supply on the home market and, consequently, a rise in price.

The question then becomes: Under what conditions will a tariff duty occasion an increase in the domestic product sufficient to counterbalance the diminution in the amount imported? If the duty is laid upon an article not producible at home under existing conditions and at existing prices, there can manifestly be no such increase in the domestic product, and the price will rise

[1] This is in part a reproduction of the author's argument on the same subject which forms a part of an article on the shifting of taxes, published in the *Yale Review*, Nov., 1896.

in consequence of the duty. How large a share of the duty will be added to the price of the article will depend upon the comparative elasticity of the demand and the supply. If the demand is highly elastic while the supply is inelastic, only a small proportion of the duty will be added to the price. That is to say, an elastic demand means that if there is a slight rise in the price of the article to the consumer it would cause a great falling off in the amount purchased. In other words the consumer may be said to have considerable power of resistance. On the other hand, if a considerable fall in the price which the producer can get will cause only a slight falling off in the amount produced, as will happen when there are considerable differences in the cost of producing different parts of the supply, the supply is inelastic. When the demand is elastic and the supply relatively inelastic, the burden of a tariff duty will be borne largely by the foreign producer and only to a slight extent by the home consumer. Reversing the argument we will reach the conclusion that when the demand for the article is inelastic and the supply relatively elastic, the burden of the duty will fall largely upon the home consumer. When both the supply and the demand are very elastic a tariff duty will tend to be prohibitive. That is to say, if a slight rise in the price to the consumer would cause a very large falling off in the amount consumed, and a slight fall in the price to the producer would cause a great falling off in the amount sent to the tariff country, manifestly neither the producer nor the consumer can be made to pay the tariff to any great extent, but the article will practically cease to be imported.

If the article is produced at home, but under the law of expanding cost, commonly confused with the law of diminishing returns, the presumption is that as much is already being produced at any given time as can be at existing prices. The one condition for an increase in the home product is that there shall be a rise in price. It is evident that the domestic product could not increase sufficiently to keep the prices down for the reason that if the prices were kept down there could be no increase in the home production. A duty on such an article would raise the price of the article, and be borne, in part at least, by the home consumer.

In case the duty is laid upon an article which is produced at home under the law of diminishing cost—provided its production has not been monopolized—a different result follows. In a case of this kind, the shutting out of a part of the foreign supply increases the opportunities for the marketing of the home product; and since the home product can be increased without any increase in cost, there is nothing to prevent it from increasing sufficiently to offset entirely any diminution in the amount imported. In this case there is no reason to expect that the price will be higher under the tariff than it would be without the tariff.

The shutting out of a part of the foreign supply may be said to be analagous to a normal growth in the consumption of the article,—at least in so far as it affects the home producers. They find an increase in the consumption of their products, and it makes no difference to them whether this is due to a decrease in importation or to a growth in the normal consumption of the article. Few economists would contend that a normal growth in the consumption of an article which could be indefinitely increased at diminishing cost would cause the article to sell at a higher price. It is the position of this paper that there is no better ground for contending that a tariff

duty on an article already producible at home under the
law of diminishing cost would raise the price of the
article ; or that when there is no natural check, such as
increasing cost, to the home production, there is no
reason why the home production may not increase sufficiently entirely to make up for any falling off in the
amount imported.[1]

If, however, the article is one whose home production
is in the hands of a monopoly, the shutting out of a part
of the foreign product would increase the monopoly's
power over the home market and give it an opportunity
to exact a somewhat higher price than would otherwise
be possible. There is a very wide-spread belief that a
monopoly fixes the price of its product according to a
different principle from that which is followed by a
single producer in a competitive industry, but such is
not the case. In either case the price is fixed at the
point which will yield the largest net income to the
producer. The difference is that the individual producer in a competitive industry has to face a different
set of conditions from that which confronts the monopolists. The competitive producer knows that if he
charges too high a price for his products his sales will
fall off rapidly, not only through the unwillingness of
the public to buy the product, but also through the
underselling of his competitors. If he held a monopoly
he would know that a similar rise in the price of the
product would cause his sales to fall off less rapidly,
because only one, namely the former, of those two forces
would operate. While both the monopolist and the
competitive producer try to sell at the point of highest
net return, that point is likely to be somewhat different

---

[1] In fact there are reasons for believing that the price would fall.
Cf. Marshall : Principles of Economics, 4th Ed., p. 525.

in the two cases, because of the differences in the conditions which confront the two producers. The competitive producer has two checks on high prices where the monopolist has one. Hence monopoly price is likely to be higher than competitive price. A tariff duty which shuts out a part of the foreign product, removes one of the checks upon the power of a monopoly to charge high prices, and changes the location of the point of highest net return.

Whether a protective tariff can increase the price of labor or not depends first upon whether or not it is possible, by means of a tariff, to increase the demand for labor relatively to the demand for other factors of production. If this can be done labor will get a larger share of the total product of the industry of the community. This alone would not prove that the individual laborer would in the end be better off. In the first place, the supply of labor might increase correspondingly, either through immigration or natural increase; in which event there would be no increase in individual wages, even though a larger share of the total product did go to the payment of labor. In the second place, the tariff might diminish the total product of industry so that, even though the laborers did get a larger share of the total, the absolute amount going to them as wages might be no greater than, indeed not so great as, before.

As to the first objection, it needs only to be said that if the tariff increases the demand for labor that will tend to raise wages. Whether or not this tendency will be counteracted by immigration or natural increase depends upon other conditions. If the tariff stimulates immigration or increases the birth rate over what it would be without a tariff, the presumption is that it does so because it increases the demand for labor and raises wages, which is all that this paper contends for. Wages may or may not be subsequently reduced to the old level by other forces counteracting the tendency of the tariff. As the second condition, it is hoped that the third part of this paper will show that a protective tariff does not necessarily diminish the total product of industry.

Owing to the limited space available it is necessary to assume two premises as the basis of the argument for the proposition that a protective tariff may be so framed as to raise wages within the country. (1) The three factors of production, land, labor and capital, are combined in different proportions in the production of different commodities. (2) A selected industry may be stimulated and made to grow by means of a protective tariff. Both these propositions could be proved did space allow, but neither is likely to be disputed by any considerable number. Assuming them to be true, it is only necessary to stimulate, by means of a protective tariff, the production of those articles into which labor enters as the principal factor, leaving unprotected those industries into which labor enters as a relatively less important factor. This is a process of artificial selection in which the variation which makes selection possible is found in the different proportions in which the three factors are combined in the different industries. The favorable variations, from the standpoint of the laboring class, are those industries in which labor is the relatively more important factor, and the unfavorable variations are those in which labor is the relatively less important factor. In order to favor the laboring class it is only

13

necessary to select the favorable variations, that is, to build up by artificial means those industries in which labor is the principal factor. Even though this should result in a corresponding injury to other industries, there would still remain a net gain to labor.

Let us suppose, by way of illustration, that in industry A, at a given period, the best results, from the standpoint of the entrepreneur, are ordinarily obtained by combining 1000 acres of land, 10 laborers and $100,000 worth of capital. These yield a product worth $20,000. In industry B, to get a product of the same value the best results would be obtained from combining the factors in the following proportions: 10 acres of land, 20 laborers and $100,000 worth of capital. Wages and interest are assumed to be the same in both industries. For the sake of simplicity, capital is assumed to bear the same ratio to product in both industries, land and labor being the varying factors. By building up industry B, even at the expense of industry A, there will result a net increase in employment of labor, though a corresponding decrease in the employment of land. This increase in the employment of labor means an increase in the demand for labor, while the decrease in the employment of land means a decrease in the demand for land. The result of this situation would be that a larger share of the total product would go in the payment of wages and a smaller share in the payment of rent.[1]

We need here to guard against the possibility that industry B while using fewer acres of land, might require a kind of land that is so very scarce that the rent charge would be higher than in A. But this is not a necessary

[1] This may possibly be made more concrete by means of the following table. I. represents the conditions as described above. II. represents

condition. It is quite conceivable that the two industries would use the same grade of land. It is even conceivable that industry B, in addition to using fewer acres, would also use a more abundant kind of land where rents were less per acre. The whole difficulty could be avoided by starting with the proposition that in different industries rent charges, wages, and interest, enter in varying proportions. Then by selecting for governmental favor those industries in which wages, rather than rent or interest, form the chief item of expense, the total industry of the country would be affected favorably from the standpoint of the wage receivers.

It goes without saying that an entirely different result would be obtained by selecting for governmental favor those industries in which rent or interest formed the chief item of expense :—a result advantageous to the landlord or the capitalist, but disadvantageous to the laborer. It must be confessed, also, that as protectionism has been applied in the past, especially in England before the repeal of the corn laws, this result was quite as frequently obtained as the other. There is some danger also that it will be so in the future, owing

the situation after industry B has been expanded 50% and industry A has been correspondingly contracted.

I.

Industry A 1000 acres :	10 laborers :	$100,000 capital :	$20,000 product
" B 10 "	20 "	100,000 "	20,000 "
Totals 1010	30	$200,000	$40,000

II.

Industry A 500 acres :	5 laborers :	$ 50,000 capital :	$10,000 product
" B 15 "	30 "	150,000 "	30,000 "
Totals 515	35	$200,000	$40,000

This shows a decrease of 495 in the number of acres used and an increase of 5 in the number of men employed.

to the better lobbying facilities of the land-owning and capitalistic classes.   But that is another matter.

The proposition that protection attracts labor and capital from the more productive to the less productive industries has long been one of the basic principles of the free trade school—the rock on which all protectionist theories were supposed to split.   And it must be confessed that unless this position can be successfully assailed the free-trader will always have the advantage in the argument.

The difficulty with the proposition lies in the double meaning which is given to the word " productive ".   In order to make a true proposition of it that word must be given a certain meaning; but in order to make it a conclusive argument it must have quite a different meaning.   From the standpoint of the individual business man a " productive " industry is a " profitable " [1] industry, that is, an industry which offers the opportunity of making a surplus gain over the cost of running the business.   From the standpoint of the community a productive industry is one which increases the sum total of utilities.   It is the " profitableness " of the industry, rather than its " productiveness " in the latter sense, which causes labor and capital to go into it.   It is only by defining " productive " as " profitable " that one can

---

[1] For want of a better term the words profit and profitable are used here in the more popular sense, which agrees with the use of the terms by the older writers on economics.   Profit is made to include the surplus income of an industry over and above the cost of conducting it   In this broad sense it includes rent and every other form of surplus.   A profitable industry would therefore be one which would yield a surplus income of some kind.   This surplus is what attracts the director of industry and it is the surplus-producing power of an industry which determines whether or not labor and capital shall go into it.

support the proposition that labor and capital will seek those industries which are naturally most productive. In that sense, and in that sense alone, it is quite true that protection attracts labor and capital from the more productive to the less productive industries.

But in order to have any weight as an argument this proposition must mean that protection attracts labor and capital from those industries which create more utilities into those which create fewer utilities. That is to say, the word " productive" must mean something more than " profitable." The difficulty could be met only by showing that a " profitable" industry from the standpoint of the individual business man is always a " productive" industry from the standpoint of the community. If this cannot be shown it would mean that labor and capital, if left to themselves, will, in seeking the largest profits, sometimes go into the less " productive" industries. There would then be a possibility that protection or some other form of government interference might be able to attract labor and capital from the less productive industry whither it would naturally go in pursuit of profits, into a more productive industry whence it would naturally have been excluded by the smallness of the profits. This possibility would become a reality if the relative profitableness of the two industries could be reversed by some kind of government discrimination.

The question then becomes: Are the more " profitable" industries always the more " productive ? " Manifestly not. Saying nothing of certain lines of business which are acquisitive in their nature and not productive at all, there are certain highly productive industries which have very little power of attracting individual enterprise.

To begin with an extreme case, there is the work of maintaining light-houses. This illustration is chosen, not because it is supposed to be typical of those industries which are fitted to receive protection, but solely because it serves to make clear that there may be a productive industry which offers no inducements for private enterprise. On the one hand this work has all the ear-marks of a productive industry. It produces a real utility: this utility is of a materialistic sort and not moral or social, as is that produced by educational and other similar institutions; and it is produced by purely mechanical processes. There is nothing in the nature of the utility produced, or its processes of production, to distinguish this from any money making business. On the other hand, this industry offers no incentive to private enterprise, that is, no opportunity for private profits, for the one sufficient reason that the producer cannot control his product. It will shine upon those who do not pay for it as well as upon those who do. He is therefore not in a position to exact a payment for his product corresponding to its utility.

It will doubtless be objected that this is a case calling for government ownership and operation rather than mere protection, and the point would be well taken. This is a business so completely devoid of opportunity for profitable enterprise that no kind of a protective tariff would be able to make it profitable. Nothing but a subsidy could induce private capital to go into it, and the subsidy would have to cover the whole cost. In · that case the government might just as well, it may be maintained, own and carry on the business. But the difference between this industry and one which would lend itself to protective measures is one of degree only.

Industries differ widely in this particular, that,

whereas one, such as the maintenance of lighthouses, produces a utility that cannot be controlled at all in the interest of the owner; another produces a utility of such a nature that the owner can exact full payment from those who use it; while still another produces no utility at all but is purely acquisitive in its nature. An example of the last, not to come too near home, would be the mediæval baron who took possession of a natural ford, or a mountain pass, and set up his castle and went into the business of collecting toll of all who passed that way.[1] These three industries do not belong to sharply differentiated classes but they shade off gradually into one another. That is to say, there is a gradual shading off from the business which creates utilities far in excess of any amount which the owner of the business can collect, to the business which can collect a revenue far in excess of any utility actually created by it. Here again we have a form of variation which makes artificial selection possible, the favorable variations being those industries which come under the former description.

In considering this aspect of economic life too much has been usually assumed as to the harmony of interests among the different members of the community. Nothing is more fundamental in economic science than the

---

[1] This is a business to which the principle of 'charging what the traffic will bear' applies beautifully. What the traffic will bear is, in this case, determined by the superiority of the ford or pass over the poorest ford or pass over which traffic could afford to go. Let us suppose that instead of merely collecting toll the baron spends some trifling sum in the improvement of the passage, still charging what the traffic will bear. His business then becomes slightly productive but its productiveness is still small as compared with its profitableness. Then let us assume him gradually to increase his expenditures for improvement of the passage until the utility created approximates more and more nearly to the charges collected; at each stage of the process his business will represent some type of business actually carried on among us today.

proposition that there is an antagonism of interests among the different members of the community. If there were a complete harmony of interests, labor and capital might be expected to seek those industries which are most productive from the social standpoint. But, aside from the observable fact that labor and capital do nothing of the kind, it is a matter of common observation and experience, confirmed by reflective analysis, that there is no such harmony of human interests. One man's interest is served by having the labor and capital of the community directed in one line, another's by having them directed in quite a different line. More than that, there is great inequality among individuals in the power of giving direction to the industry of the community. The one who owns land or capital in addition to his own labor power is in better position, other things equal, to determine the direction of business activity than is the one who owns only his labor power. We therefore not only have the certainty that each individual will try to direct business activity in the line most conducive to his own interests and that in many cases his interests will not harmonize with the interests of the community, but also the certainty that the power to give this direction differs greatly among different individuals. Did we not know it as a matter of direct observation and experience, we might predict from these premises that the business activity of the community would not, in all cases, be directed in the most productive lines, and that therefore it would be possible, by some form of discrimination, to attract labor and capital from the less productive to the more productive industries.

The following illustration may add something to the concreteness of this conclusion. Let us suppose that a certain tract of land had been devoted to cultivation of a fairly intensive kind and had been producing enough to pay the wages of 20 laborers, with something left over for rent. Through some change of circumstances the price of wool rises and it is found more profitable to use the land for wool growing. By turning the land into a sheep-run, 19 of the laborers may be dispensed with, and the saving in wages would more than measure the difference between the value of the wool crop and that of the present crop, so that a larger surplus would be left over as rent. There is little doubt that the land would then be devoted to the growing of wool. That would be to the interest of the landlord and against the interests of the 19 laborers, but the landlord is in a better position than they for determining the form of cultivation. There is also little doubt that this would be contrary to the interest of the community. Less wealth would be produced either for consumption or for international trade. Fewer people could be supported, or the same number would be more poorly supported, than formerly. If the 19 men thrown out of employment cannot find a place elsewhere, they will probably, since they want to live, offer their labor at lower wages—enough lower to enable the landlord to get as much rent from the more intensive form of cultivation as he might get by the less intensive form. Here we have the somewhat anomalous situation of an increase in the price of one of the products of industry causing a fall in the price of labor. The key to this anomaly is found in the fact that what is cost to one man is frequently gain to another. Now in this supposed case, which is not altogether a supposed case, there is little doubt that some form of discrimination in favor of the present crop and against wool, would

not only increase the relative share of the produce going
to labor, but the absolute amount of the produce of the
land.

And this is a rule which works both ways. In a
community where land is extensively cultivated it is
presumably because extensive cultivation produces the
best results from the standpoint of the land owner. Any
one of several conditions may induce him to change to
intensive cultivation. (1) A fall in the price of labor;
(2) a fall in the price of the products of extensive cultivation; (3) a rise in the price of products of intensive
cultivation. There lies the opportunity for the protectionist. By some discrimination which will tend to increase the profitableness of the intensive product, or decrease, relatively at least, the profitableness of the extensive product, an absolutely larger and more valuable
product might be created. This would support a larger
number of people, or support them better. They would
have a larger number of products either for consumption or for international trade. Labor and capital
would have been attracted from the less productive to
the more productive industry. Since a protective tariff
is one means by which the relative profitableness of different industries may be changed, it follows that a protective tariff may be a means of increasing the total product of the industry of the community.

DISCUSSION.

Guy S. Callender : Professor Carver judges rightly wherein the strength of the free trade position lies: it is in the claim that under the direction of private enterprise labor and capital, if free to move from one industry to another, tend to seek those industries that are most productive. It is, indeed, for the purpose of earning the largest profits that labor and capital are turned to any particular industry. The individual who controls them is seeking only his own advantage. But, as Adam Smith long ago pointed out, "he is led by an invisible hand" to promote also the economic welfare of the community; because those industries that yield the largest profits are also the ones that in general yield the largest utility to the community—utility being used in a strict economic sense. It is natural to expect that a person seeking to provide a theoretical basis for the policy of protection will attack this time honored doctrine; and nearly every protectionist from Hamilton and List to the present time has, in fact, done so. In the third and most important part of his paper Professor Carver admits that, unless it can be overthrown, the free trader must always have the advantage in the argument.

If I understand him, Professor Carver denies that there is any necessary connection between the "profitableness" of an industry and its "productivity"—that is, between its ability to yield profits to the persons carrying it on, and its ability to produce large utility to the community. I do not suppose he would deny that there are many industries in which "profitableness" and "productivity" are connected ; but he holds that there are

other industries in which there is no such connection,
and that, therefore, labor and capital in seeking industries that yield large profits will leave undeveloped other
industries that are more productive to the community.
It is to prevent this neglect of productive industries for
those more profitable but less productive that the protective policy may be legitimately applied. Now it
seems to me that the value of this argument turns
wholly upon the question of fact, whether this distinction of profitableness and productivity between industries be a true one; and, if so, whether industries that
yield small profits but very large utility exist in any
considerable number, and are of such a nature as to be
capable of development by the protective policy. Upon
these questions of fact the paper seems to me to be far
from satisfactory. Professor Carver points out that
there may be an industry which produces great utility
to the community, but which affords no profit at all,
such as the maintenance of light-houses. He admits
that this is not an industry which could be developed
by protection, though he insists that it differs only in
degree from one that might be so developed; he refrains
however, from giving us any example of such an industry. He then goes on to point out that there may
be also an industry which is purely " acquisitive," *i. e.*,
which yields profits but no utility at all. (Is there any
industry outside of gambling and robbery which
furnishes no utility to the community at all?) He
then invites you to believe that there are all gradations of industry between these two extremes. He
argues that close a connection between profit and productivity implies a much greater harmony of interest
among the different members of the community than
actually exists. He affirms, on the contrary, that an-

tagonism of interest among the different members of the community is "fundamental in economic science "; that, " one man's interest is served by having the labor and capital of the community directed in one line, and another's by having them directed in quite a different line "; that each individual will seek to direct industry in the line most conducive to his own interest; and that, in many cases, his interest will not harmonize with the interest of the community. He makes the further statement that industries differ greatly in the extent to which the persons carrying them on are able to appropriate as profits the utilities which they create.

Now all these statements may, or may not, be true. Their entire truth, at any rate, is not altogether obvious, to say the least. And even if we admit their partial truth, the argument for protection based upon them is not at all conclusive. What we need to know before we can judge of the value of this claim for the protective policy is: (1) How may we distinguish a productive from a merely profitable industry? (2) Do industries that are productive but not profitable actually exist in any considerable numbers? and (3) Are such industries of that kind as do exist capable of being developed by a protective tariff? These are points concerning which Professor Carver has left us very much in the dark, and they are points upon which, I repeat, we need a good deal of enlightenment before this particular argument for protection can have much practical or theoretical value for us—unless indeed economic theory is to be made up of a body of pure speculation based upon hypotheses which have little correspondence with the actual conditions of industry.

It is by no means clear to me from the reasoning in the paper that there is any considerable number of in-

dustries that can yield large utility to the community
without offering large profits to those who undertake
them.   I am still more doubtful as to whether such industries, if they do exist, are of such a nature that they
can be developed by a protective tariff.   And this uncertainty is not much dispelled by a consideration of
the one concrete example of such an industry, which
Professor Carver has given.   He thinks it is possible—
and indeed implies that it has actually happened in
some countries—that the owners of land might find it
profitable permanently to devote it to pasturage, when
it would be very much more useful to the community
if devoted to cultivation.   It seems very doubtful to me,
whether this has ever occurred, or ever could occur, in
any country for any considerable length of time.   A
rise in the price of wool relative to the price of other
products of agriculture would of course cause a diversion of land from cultivation to pasture; but this use
of the land could not continue to be profitable if the
community needed the products of cultivation more
than wool.   If this change diminished the supply of
products of cultivation, the price of those products
would rise until it became more profitable to use the
land for cultivation than for pasture, and labor and
capital would be turned back to cultivation.   I cannot
conceive of the land of a country being permanently diverted from cultivation to pasture unless it should become possible for that country to secure the products of
cultivation more cheaply by international trade than
by domestic agriculture.   In that case, the use of the
land for pasture is not diverting it from a more productive to a less productive industry, because considering
the relation of agriculture to other industries, pasture
farming is the more productive of the two.   England is

the only country where such a change has taken place on a large scale in recent times, and the conditions above mentioned have existed in that country and made the change possible. She would certainly not be richer to-day if she had prevented the change from cultivation to pasture by protection or by any other kind of legislation.

This suggests another point in which his example seems to be at fault. He assumes that the change from cultivation to pasture farming will injure the laboring class, because some of the laborers will be thrown out of employment and can secure employment only by offering their labor at lower wages. This seems to overlook the effect of the change on capital. If pasture farming requires less labor than cultivation, so also does it require less capital; and the same change which leaves a certain amount of labor unemployed, sets free at the same time, a certain amount of capital which must seek employment in other industries. The investment of this capital will create a demand for the labor thrown out of employment at as high wages as was paid in the old industry.

Time will permit me to mention only briefly the second argument of the paper. This argument really depends upon the third for its practical value; for I take it no one would hold it good policy to legislate to give the laboring class a larger share of the product of industry, if by so doing the amount of that product is diminished. Professor Carver has not yet shown us how industries which employ more labor and less capital can be substituted for those in existence without diminishing the total product of industry. The argument as it stands seems to me to justify resistance on the part of the laboring class to the introduction of all labor-saving machinery into industry. According to it we should benefit the laboring class by discouraging the production of grain for example, in which we make large use of capital in the shape of animals and machinery, and encouraging the production of sugar beet or flax in which we can make but little use of capital. This looks very much like the fallacy of the trade unionist who seeks to make wages high by "making as much work" as possible.

In conclusion, I will add this further remark. If Professor Carver be seeking in his paper to establish a new basis for the protective policy, he seems to me entirely to have failed to accomplish his purpose. If, however, he wished only to establish a "theoretical possibility" that the protective policy may be wisely applied, then, if we admit his premises to be true, he has perhaps established his case. But this "theoretical possibility" is of very little practical value. He has yet to show that the conditions which make it true prevail to any considerable extent in modern industry.

MAURICE H. ROBINSON: Economic theory when it realizes its largest possible value becomes simply a body of scientific generalizations founded upon a thorough understanding of existing conditions. Any examination of the theoretical possibilities of a protective tariff ought therefore to take cognizance of any and all conditions that may operate to modify its normal workings. Owing to the complexity of economic phenomena, it is usually convenient to assume the competitive system, since it is fundamental and permanent, formulate the general rule and then notice the effect of modifying conditions whether due to inertia, ignorance, or monopolistic control. Some writers in treating of the effects of a protective tariff are inclined to emphasize the influence of the fundamental conditions, while others enlarge upon the effect of the modifying circumstances; the probability of agreement or disagreement depends largely upon the point of view.

Hamilton assumed that internal competition would permanently protect the home consumer. In his report on manufactures he said: "When a domestic manufacture has attained to perfection and has engaged in the production of it a competent number of persons it invariably becomes cheaper—the internal competition which takes place soon does away with everything like monopoly and by degrees reduces the price of the article to a minimum of a reasonable profit upon the capital employed . . . . in a national point of view a temporary enlargement of price must always be well compensated by a permanent reduction of it." Professor Carver has also, in general, assumed the competitive system in effective working order, except in one case, —that of the ejected laborers. He there implies that there is no opportunity for a readjustment to be effected by the flow of some of the laborers into the rank of tenant or independent farmers. Hamilton grants without argument that there would be a temporary enlargement of the price of the protected goods until the home production could be adjusted to meet the enlarged demand. Professor Carver has instanced one case where he intimates that the industrial organization is so sensitive that the production will automatically and instantaneously be adjusted to meet the enlarged demand—a condition which it would be difficult to realize in fact.

This case needs further analysis. It is probably true

14

that the goods could be produced more cheaply either
at home or abroad for a considerable period of time at
least., Suppose the natural condition were more favorable for the production of the article abroad, the production both at home and abroad being under the law
of diminishing costs, the tariff would cause more of the
goods to be produced at home than under a régime of
free trade and therefore the total cost of all the goods
produced both at home and abroad would be greater.
Hence while the price of goods would fall continuously
in the home market, the selling price would necessarily
be maintained at a somewhat higher level than under
the free importation of the goods. If, on the other
hand, the advantage in the cost of production were
with the home producer, he would inevitably take and
hold the home market without the stimulus of the
tariff. The imposition of a duty would hasten the process, since the factors of production are not perfectly
mobile. Whether the home consumer would get the
benefit of the reduced cost would depend upon the efficacy of internal competition. Should the imposition
of a duty in this case encourage the formation and facilitate the workings of industrial combinations, or trusts,
the consumer would hardly get all the benefits of the
lessened cost of production. Such, in fact, appears to
be the case. Trusts are formed, not for philanthropic
purposes, but to protect the interests or increase the
profits of the interested parties. This end may be accomplished either by lessening the costs of production
or increasing prices. Costs may be reduced by lessening the risks of the industry, by eliminating waste, by
inaugurating economies in processes and in organization. Prices may be increased by eliminating competition and establishing a monopoly. A protective tariff

under the given circumstances puts a premium upon the formation of trusts upon both of the following counts: (1) The protective system increases the risks of production; there are continual tariff changes, "tariff tinkering," "tariff reform," etc., or the fear that such changes are imminent. Furthermore the protected industry is deprived of the steadying influence of the world market, under free trade economic disturbances are partially compensated and widely distributed. The formation of a trust here acts as an insurance agency for the weaker producers. And (2) If such consolidation be at all complete, competition is shut out up to the importing point by the tariff wall. These two influences of a protective tariff working in a different way upon the strong and weak producers, while not the chief causes, tend powerfully toward the same end—industrial consolidation. The weak producer looks upon the combination with favor because he hopes for protection from the risks of the business; the strong one because his chances for monopoly profits are increased. The protective system is thus constantly encouraging the formation of consolidations and permitting them to exact a monopoly profit, provided the independent home producer can be kept out.

It might be supposed that if the imposition of a duty is thus a strong factor in building trusts its abolition would cause their destruction. Such is not the case however. The possibilities of a protective tariff do not end here. The wholesale abolition of duties on trust made goods probably would have a far different effect from that usually expected. For (1) It would have a greater tendency to destroy the independent producer than the trust; and (2) By freeing the home field of the troublesome independent producer it would pave the way for the inauguration of international trusts, whose effective regulation would prove a far more difficult task than the regulation of national trusts have yet proved to be.

It appears from the foregoing analysis: (1) That where the goods upon which a duty is laid are produced at parallel costs both at home and abroad the prices in the home market will be raised, temporarily at least, while the necessary readjustment of the productive forces is being effected; (2) That where the cost of production is less in the foreign market, the imposition of a tariff will throw the burden of increased cost chiefly upon the home consumer; and (3) That, when the cost of production is less in the home market, a duty first stimulates the home producers, then puts so large a premium on the formation of a trust among the producers of the protected line of goods that, in this age of industrial consolidation, it cannot be predicted with any certainty that the saving in costs of production will accrue to the ultimate consumers.

FABIAN FRANKLIN: I should like to say a few words on the third head of Professor Carver's paper. Professor Callender attacked Professor Carver's position by citing the actual circumstances of economic life, but I think that taking the article in the abstract it involves an error which is very fundamental. Professor Carver took the position that the economic doctrine on which the free trade theory rests—that a protective tariff interferes with the pursuit of the most productive industries—contains an essential fallacy. I do not know that I can put better what I want to say (for I have not prepared the argument at all, and it is a little difficult to put the criticism in general terms) than by taking up the illustration of the lighthouse. Professor Carver spoke of the lighthouse as a very productive form of investment, which nevertheless would not spontaneously attract capital to its production, and nobody will deny that it takes government interposition to cause a lighthouse to be erected. But that has nothing whatever to do, so far as I can see, with the question of protection. In the case of the tariff, the question is not whether such and such a thing shall be produced or not, either by governmental action or by private enterprise; the question is in what way the thing shall be acquired by private enterprise. The question of the production of the lighthouse is the question whether it shall be produced or not. Take on the other hand, the matter of the protective tariff. We are going to get cloth in this country, and we are going to get wheat. We are going to get both of them by private enterprise. The thing which the economists a hundred years saw absolutely clearly was that we are going to get these things by private means one way or another. We are either going to make a large quantity of wheat and send part of it abroad and get cloth, or make a smaller quantity and make the cloth ourselves. Which of those things is more productive, taken in the aggregate? It is not a question of net profits by any means. We are going to do the one thing or the other, according to which one of the two things will on the whole be the more productive.

There is no doubt that the government could by the exercise of its powers determine the activities of mankind so as to make them take forms far more useful than those they actually take. The question is whether the interposition of the protective tariff is a case of this kind. That seems to have been overlooked. The analogy of the light-house indicates a wrong point of view. It is not a question of whether we are going to have the light-house or not, and it is not a question of whether we are going to have other things or not, but whether we are going to acquire more readily through the agency of the protective tariff things which we should in any case acquire in one way or the other.

HENRY B. GARDNER: Professor Carver's first point, as I understand it, rests on an impossible assumption. He supposes that under conditions of free trade in the case of an industry subject to the law of diminishing costs part of the product is supplied by home producers and part by foreign producers. Under such conditions, however, the competition between home producers and foreign producers would inevitably go on until one or the other had been driven out. The assumption upon which Professor Carver rests his argument implies an impossible adjustment as a permanent adjustment. It seemed to me, also, that Professor Carver's second and third points are really the same point treated in somewhat different ways. For they are both cases in which through the action of the protective tariff labor and capital may be diverted from industries which require a relatively large amount of land, in proportion to the labor employed, to industries in which there is a demand for a relatively small amount of land, in proportion to the labor employed. The two points seem to be variations of the same fact. Further, in relying on this fact as he does in his second point to show that the protective tariff can lead to increased wages he seems to me to overlook the strongest theoretical argument that can be brought forward in support of his position, an argument which, if I remember rightly, Professor Patten developed some ten years ago, namely, that through a protective tariff we can, under certain circumstances, affect the distribution of industry, and consequently relative prices, within a country in such a way as to diminish the prices of those articles which laborers consume (and increase the earning power of laborers measured in these articles) at the same time that we increase the prices of other commodities and diminish the productive power of the country as a whole. Take for example a country which under conditions of free trade is an exporter of agricultural products and an importer of certain classes of manufactured goods not largely consumed by the laboring classes. Through a protective tariff cutting off the importation of those goods, and compelling their production at home, we divert labor and capital from the agricultural industry to this manufacturing industry. The agricultural industry being subject to the law of diminishing returns, the diversion of labor and capital from it tends to raise the margin of production, to lower the margin of cost, and thereby to reduce the price of agricultural products. At the same time the price of commodities previously imported is increased but if the laborer does not consume these commodities and does consume principally agricultural products, the change will be of benefit to the laborer; his wages will go up, not as measured by his power to purchase commodities in general, but by his power to purchase the particular commodities which he consumes. The increased price of the previously imported commodity will be shifted on to the shoulders of those who consume that commodity, and it is perfectly possible they should be other than the laboring classes. It seems to me that this is the essential fact upon which the theoretical argument should rest; that protection may possibly act in such a way as to raise wages, even though it may diminish the total product.

THOMAS N. CARVER : As to Professor Gardner's suggestion I am quite aware that Professor Patten's argument is quite forcible, but I take it for granted that members of this Association are reasonably familiar with it, and so I preferred to devote my attention to other points that did not seem to have been sufficiently emphasized, as yet. And I am also quite willing to admit that my second point and my third point come together, which is precisely what I intended. I have tried to maintain the position that the protective tariff may increase the demand for labor relatively to the other factors. It is a very important question then whether it does that at the expense of the total product. If it comes about that you can increase the share going to laborers and at the same time possibly increase the total product, there is a double gain, which is precisely the point of which I hoped more would be made.

Now as to the alleged oversight which Professor Franklin has called attention to, I think it is not altogether an oversight. I have discussed the question as though it were not a question wholly of international trade. If you are discussing a theory of international trade, I should at once admit the proposition which Professor Franklin has made. As I look at it, however, it is not a question of international trade—and the strong free trade writers have pushed it back of international trade, and make it a question of production. That is the point, or that is the phase of the question, which it seemed to me most important to discuss. To the contrary of what Professor Franklin has said, we are not going to get the commodities any way. If we

get them we must do it either by producing them ourselves, or by importing them. If we are to import them
we must have something to exchange for them ; but if
we produce less under one policy than under another,
we will have less to exchange. The natural resources
in the country will support a larger population, and
produce more wealth which will enable that larger
population to live under one system than under another.
With another system of industries you will have a
smaller amount of wealth produced, and a smaller
population, and a smaller population would not get the
things. It is not a question of international trade but
a question of production, after all. It is a question of
getting the largest wealth out of the natural resources
and not a question merely of international values, as it
seems to me.

Neither did I entirely overlook the possibility of the
ejected laborers finding employment elsewhere when the
land is turned into a sheep run. I asked, however, if
they could be as well employed elsewhere as they were
employed before? If so, they would have been there
anyway, or some of them would have been there anyway. I assumed that if they were employed on the
land it was because they could be better employed there.
To drive them elsewhere would cause loss to them.

Now it is true, as Dr. Callender has said, that I did
not go into the question of pointing out a large number
of industries to which the principle would apply. I
thought it perhaps sufficient to point the extreme cases
and the medium cases. In my opinion any industry
which pays a large rent is profitable in excess of its
productiveness, I will leave it for members of this Association to determine, whether there are industries
which yield more rent than others, and whether there are

industries which yield less rent.   The amount of rent, as
I understand it, is the excess of the profitableness of the
industry over the productiveness of the industry.   There
are industries which yield very little rent, and there are
industries which yield a great deal of rent and I do not
think I need to enumerate the industries here.

THE WORKMAN'S POSITION IN THE LIGHT OF ECONOMIC PROGRESS.

BY CHARLES A. TUTTLE.

Several years ago an honored president of the American Economic Association expressed the conviction, in his annual address, "that much of the confusion in economic theory and much of the discord in industrial life are alike due to inadequate expression by formal law of fundamental industrial rights."[1] He further declared that "every change in the social structure, every modification of the principle of political or industrial association, as well as the acceptance of a new social ideal, must be accompanied by a corresponding change in those rights and duties recognized and enforced by law."[2] Writing in the same strain, another eminent economist has well said that the economist "should surely examine, with not less care than he bestows on the institutions of positive law, these notions of ideal right of which positive law is only a belated and imperfect, though wonderfully elaborated embodiment."[3] Professor Foxwell, recognizing a "dynamical as well as a statical jurisprudence," says that "if positive law is the basis of order, ideal right is the active factor in progress."[4] The distinguished Austrian economist, Professor Menger, speaking of the juridical postulates of the socialists, declares that "the ideal law of property, from

[1] Henry Carter Adams: Economics and jurisprudence, Economic Studies, 2:7-8.

[2] *Ibid.*

[3] Foxwell, introduction to Menger's The right to the whole produce of labour, p. xii.

[4] *Ibid.*, p. 11.

the economic point of view, would be attained in a system which assured to every laborer the whole produce of his labor, and to every want as complete satisfaction as the means at disposal would allow,"[1] while "our actual law of property, which rests almost entirely on traditional political conditions, does not even attempt the attainment of these economic ends."[2]   Further the brilliant analyses of Professor John B. Clark[3] afford little encouragement to the laborer, though they may prove conclusively that in a static society, in which existing property rights prevail, the laborer would receive the entire product of his labor ; for a static society exists only in the imagination, while the laborer lives in the actual world of incessant change.

Though the socialists' juridical postulates may be faulty, though their economic analyses may be fallacious, they have certainly succeeded in directing the attention of thoughtful men to the intimate relation which has always existed between the economic life of a people and its system of jurisprudence—a relation so close that dynamic forces which vitally change the one, must inevitably lead to corresponding changes in the other.   Is it not possible, nay rather is it not probable, that the existing industrial system, which has been such a potent factor in the economic development of the world, may, like the feudal system, have accomplished its task and have become a hindrance rather than an aid to further progress ?

It is not the purpose of this paper to attempt an exhaustive examination of the workman's position in the light of economic progress.   Time forbids that.   The

---

[1] Menger: The right to the whole produce of labour, p. 2.
[2] *Ibid.*
[3] The distribution of wealth.

paper can merely point out, in the hope to contribute something towards rendering the workman's position more definite and dignified and therefore more human, certain economic rights which should receive legal sanction.

The one fact which characterizes our industrial system more clearly, perhaps, than any other, is specialization—a fact heavy with consequences as regards the individual, his relation to society, and society's relation to him. Specialization is the dynamic which has changed society from an aggregation of amœba-like individuals, economically speaking, into a vital organism in which the differentiating process is unceasingly working. Born of the inability of the isolated man to satisfy his diversifying and multiplying wants, and fostered by diversity in man and in the outside world, specialization has opened the way to scientific discovery, mechanical invention and geographical exploration; it has steadily narrowed the individual's function from many things to few things, to one thing and to a more and more minute fraction of a thing, and just as steadily extended the field of his influence with the widening of the circle of exchanges, until one small touch on one commodity lays "the world under tribute," and objective realities have finally awakened in the economist's consciousness the idea of the unity of humanity in the struggle with all nature.

Specialization has not only made society the unit in the productive process; but it has made the collective will sovereign. It has given birth to a force, which is not only the "social guarantor of progress," but the guarantor of social control as well. Broadly speaking it has given all men a common purpose and a common master. More particularly, by assigning a specific func-

tion to large numbers of individuals and to many industrial groups, it has brought them into rivalry—competition—in the common master's service. While the civil law
says the individual may choose his occupation and conduct it where and how he may, so far as he does not in-
fringe upon the rights of others, economic law is more
exacting ; for it circumscribes him more or less minutely and dictates not only what he shall do, but where and
how he shall do it.   In the productive process, independence has been supplanted by interdependence.   In
consumption alone does the individual stand upon his
own feet.

The specializing process has not only made the collective will dominant, but it has rendered society fickle
in her treatment of the individual.   Though animated
by the one supreme economic purpose of wresting from
nature, at the least possible cost, the means of satisfaction for the multiplying and diversifying wants of man,
society is continually changing her mind not only as to
what shall be produced, but as to where and how, as
well.   Not until man's wants shall have ceased to multiply and diversify and man shall have attained complete mastery over his fully developed powers, not until
science shall have exhausted the secrets of nature and
mechanical invention shall have been brought to absolute perfection, can economic stability exist.

We accept then the fact of progress.   We could not
eliminate it if we would ; we would not if we could.
We readily admit that no state could " be so bad that
the fact of progress would not redeem it."   Nothing
short of an economic millennium can be static.

Why, then, we ask has the workingman always been
hostile to economic progress, particularly that form
which may be characterized as mechanical invention ?

Economists and statisticians may demonstrate, as they have long been doing, that mechanical invention is a benefit to the workingman, yet the workman of flesh and blood trembles when he thinks of it. One cannot, it is true, grasp the fundamental import of industrial progress, unless he conceives of labor as a force and of the laborers as a class; but he must not stop there. It is refreshing to read in a recent number of an economic journal that " the right of the present social order to exist depends upon the laws which govern, not functional, but personal distribution. Our only interest in functional distribution is due to the light which it throws on the vastly more important question of personal distribution." [1] Clearness of analysis requires in discussing the effects upon the laborer of industrial progress, in general, and of mechanical invention, in particular, that we distinguish between the standpoint of the laboring class, in the long run, which receives the ultimate uplift and the existing flesh and blood workman, who receives the first shock, and whose life may be hopelessly blighted by it.

Several years ago, the writer had occasion to address to the chiefs of two of the leading labor bureaus of the country the enquiry whether in their judgment insecurity of employment occasioned by inventions or improvements in the methods or processes of production is now a considerable source of hardship to the laboring classes. Substantially the same evasive answer came back in each case to the effect that " in the long run all displacements, whether due to the introduction of new machines or to any other cause, are compensated by a readjustment of industrial forces; labor-saving devices

[1] T. N. Carver: Clark's Distribution of wealth. *Quarterly Journal of Economics*, 15 : 579.

do not contract, on the contrary they enlarge the field for labor." The Hon. Carroll D. Wright, in his work on The Industrial Evolution of the United States, devotes a chapter to the "displacement of labor" by machinery, giving a number of instances of such displacement, drawn from the First Annual Report of the United States Commissioner of Labor and the late David A. Wells's Recent Economic Changes; yet he fails to give the subject the consideration that its importance demands. Apologizing for the term "labor-saving machinery, which should more properly be called," he says, "labor-making or labor-assisting machinery,"[1] he hastens on to "the permanent good effects of the application of machinery to industrial development, which," he justly says, "all men of sound minds admit."[2] He thinks it "impossible to treat of the influence of inventions, so far as the displacement of labor is concerned, on the individual basis," and maintains that "we must take labor abstractly."[3] He then devotes a chapter to the "expansion" of labor by inventions, and reaches the conclusion, which no one—not even the workman—questions, that "machinery is the friend and not the enemy of man."[4]

But let us consider briefly the immediate effect of mechanical invention upon the workman. He has taken his place, at society's call, for the performance of some more or less specialized function, involving, perhaps, considerable special preparation. He has married, has become the owner, perhaps, of a comfortable home and is responsible for the support of a family. An efficient

---

[1] Carroll D. Wright: The industrial evolution of the United States, p. 325.

[2] *Ibid.*

[3] *Ibid.*, p. 335.

[4] *Ibid.*, p. 342.

new machine is introduced involving "some displacement of laborers." A sudden change of process causes him no longer to be wanted at the point where the change occurs, though at a hundred other points he is more wanted than before. The burden of finding and occupying one of these places falls on him and "for a time the burden may not be a light one." "A dynamic society," says Professor Clark, "keeps a certain number of men in transit from one employment to another." [1] He becomes an unwilling member of that mysterious "army of the unemployed." His savings are spent during the search for employment and his family too frequently reduced to positive want and dependence upon outside assistance. When finally an opportunity for work has been found and the scattered family has been brought together by dint of hard work and self-denial, it is only, perhaps, to repeat the experience in an aggravated form. While it is true that the economist need not trouble himself with any new analysis with regard to those whom Professor Dewey calls "the able-bodied poor, sturdy beggars, shiftless ne'er-do-wells, weaklings, intemperates, feeble, discarded units of society," [2] whom society has always carried upon its shoulders ; yet serious consideration is demanded for that "re-enforcement of men and women who are willing to work, and who in past times have found abundant opportunities to work, but who now find their economic condition so uncertain, their industrial tenure so unstable, that they are frequently without employment." [3]

[1] The theory of economic progress, in Economic Studies, vol. I, p. 17.
[2] Davis R. Dewey: Irregularity of employment. Publications of the Am. Econ. Assoc., 9:528.
[3] *Ibid.*

15

Unfortunately, the displacement of labor by mechanical invention has never received systematic statistical investigation, so far as I am able to learn. The data we have is exceedingly fragmentary and widely scattered. It is to be hoped that the subject may, in the immediate future, receive from statisticians the serious attention that its importance deserves. It is certainly significant that " during the past decade, most of the important industrial nations have made efforts to collect statistical data bearing upon the problem of unemployment." [1] Mr. Willoughby's opinion that " the opponents of the present industrial regime have no more effective argument than the fact that there are men willing and able to work, but unable to find opportunity to do so," [2] deserves the earnest consideration of thoughtful men. Economists and all close observers of industrial conditions must concur in the opinion of Mr. Samuel Gompers, President of the American Federation of Labor, that inventions and improvements in the methods and processes of production are the source of much of the restlessness and hardship of the laboring class of our country.

We revert to our question : How are we to account for the traditional hostility of the workingman towards mechanical invention? It is not necessary to enter into any analysis to prove, even to him, that, in the long run, all classes including the wage-earner, are benefitted. The laborer readily admits all this. The fact that mechanical invention imposes present hardship and suffering upon him does not, in itself, account for his position. The workingman is just as patriotic,

---

[1] William F. Willoughby: The measurement of unemployment. *Yale Review*, 10 : 188–202.

[2] Ibid.

is just as ready to suffer and to lay down his life, if need be, in a noble cause, as any other man. If the benefits of mechanical progress could be attained only through the suffering of the workingman, he would not flinch. But he rightly feels that his own misfortune is not a necessary means to economic progress, but rather an unfortunate attendant circumstance, which society should find a way to eliminate. Herein lies the true explanation of his attitude. He sees clearly that the very force which entails present hardship upon himself places extraordinary profits in the pocket of his employer, and he is told that, through the beneficent workings of competition, this same force will ultimately enormously benefit mankind. The questions persistently rise in his mind:—Why should the cost of industrial progress be thrust upon him? Is not this gross injustice? Does not the economic obligation rest upon society to bear the costs of its progress? If, in response to society's demand, the workman has fitted himself for the performance of a more or less specialized function, is he not economically entitled to indemnification, should society in the interest of mankind, and not because of any shortcomings on the laborer's part, effect the withdrawal of that function by mechanical invention? Is not this right of the workman to indemnification for loss of position through economic progress one of the "fundamental industrial rights" which, in a dynamic society, should find expression in formal law? When society shall assume, formally, the obligation to indemnify the workman displaced by mechanical invention, the hostility of the laborer to this form of industrial progress will cease. By making the indemnity sufficiently large to enable the displaced workman, without financial embarrassment, to find one of the opportunities awaiting him in some other quarter of the field, society would effectively, in Professor Gidding's phrase, "take openly the responsibility for replacing the displaced." [1] It is not public or private charity that the modern wage-earner demands, but economic justice. Society should find some practicable method for converting the workman's economic right into a legal title and thereby enable the laborer to receive with self-respect that which otherwise must too often come to him in the form of humiliating charity.

In the actual world of business the benefits of economic progress do not, at once, accrue to the people; they are, for a time, intercepted by the business owner in the form of enhanced profits, which constitute his chief incentive to improvement. The making and applying of mechanical inventions and of improved methods and processes of production is recognized as one of the most prolific sources of business profits under modern conditions. Though not a constant source of profit, it is always present at a thousand different points and gives promise of constantly recurring as long as the industrial system continues. Every entrepreneur is striving to become the possessor of something in machine or process superior to that which his competitors possess. Success is rewarded by extraordinary profit which continues so long as it is possible, through secrecy and the aid of patent laws, to keep a monopoly of the new contrivance. However, in time, patents expire and secrets become known, and a superior device, if it be an important one, will force itself into general use and thus bring to an end the advantage which priority of possession gives its originator.

[1] Democracy and empire, p. 93.

In the end the public gets the whole advantage. Competition lowers the price to the level of the reduced cost of production, eliminates the extraordinary profit and "leaves, as a permanent result, an increase of productive power, an elevation of the level of human life ".[1] A former president of this association, in his annual address on " The theory of economic progress ", said of the employer : " He can keep his place only by being as efficient as his competitors, and that means that his methods must become continually better. He cannot survive by merely directing his industry as well as he did when he assumed control over it ; he must direct it better and better. The condition of being an employer at all is that of using methods that in efficiency are on a plane with those used by others. One must march abreast of the general rank in order to survive ; and he must sometimes step in advance of the rank if he is to make a profit. The rank will then overtake him in his advanced position ; and the result of the whole movement will be a universal forward step. In the front rank of employers, mere survival ; in advance of the front rank, gain ; by the advance of all to the position of foremost, social progress—such is the sequence." [2]

The mode of economic progress reveals the principle in accordance with which the fund for the indemnification of the displaced workman should be raised. The movement which imposes hardship upon the workman creates first a special profit for the entrepreneur and ultimately " an elevation of the level of human life." The costs of the movement should therefore be borne, partly by the business owner, and partly by the people

[1] Clark : Profits under modern conditions, in Clark & Giddings's The modern distributive process, p. 48.

[2] Clark : The theory of economic progress. Economic Studies, 1 : 10.

as a whole. A portion of the indemnity fund should be drawn from the general tax revenue, in recognition of the fact that the people are ultimately the beneficiaries of the movement; another portion should be raised by some sort of special tax upon the entrepreneur, in recognition of the special profit which he reaps.

It is the writer's belief that the displacement of laborers through mechanical invention will increase rather than diminish with time. We are barely entering upon the era of mechanical invention. At the same time, Professor Clark's analysis[1] has revealed that the tendency of economic progress is to lighten the burden of finding a new opportunity for work. The more minute through specialization the labor function becomes, the more quickly it can be learned. A workman displaced by mechanical invention from one such function, can soon master another. Further, the fact also emphasized by Professor Clark,[2] must not be overlooked that it is possible for the laborer himself to seek and get that type of manual training which will make him more widely adaptable. He may have a broader training and a broader capability than was possible for the workman of former times. While at one time he may perform one minute function, he may, and should, have the power, with a minimum of loss in the transition, to do any one of a score of others. He should try to make his command over many functions so complete, that the vanishing of a single function will never leave him utterly helpless. Thus economic progress, in the two-fold way of simplifying the functions for labor and broadening the workman himself, is reducing the burden of displacement by mechanical invention more and more to the mere necessity for leaving one place and finding an-

---

[1] Clark: The theory of economic progress. Economic Studies, 1 : 10.

other. Yet even this burden, though it may involve little waste of acquired skill, will by no means be a light one, and the economic right of the displaced workman to indemnity is none the less clear.

It is not the writer's purpose to plead for a particular form of indemnity, but rather to establish the economic right of the workmen to indemnity for injury suffered through economic progress, and to indicate the sources from which the indemnity would very properly be drawn. It might take the form, partially, of free public employment bureaus, and perhaps of free railroad transportation. Whatever the form, it is essential that it should be recognized as the workman's economic right, and not as a form of public charity.

This economic claim of the workman is, in reality, but a corollary of a larger and more comprehensive economic right. I refer to nothing less than the economic right of the laborer to his place, " during efficiency and good behavior, without regard to religious, political, or economic opinions and associations "—an economic right, which would secure the laborer's tenure by making the business owner liable to a money damage for the summary dismissal of a faithful and efficient workman. If trade-unionism and collective bargaining, profit sharing and industrial arbitration mean anything, they signify that the workman has quasi-property rights in the business in which he is employed. He may not own a dollar of the capital, he may not own a square foot of the land, he may not own even a minute fractional part of a machine; but the business is more than its capital, its land and its machines, and that the workman does have a quasi-property right in the business no one can deny. The productive process is social, and the traditional business owner, so strongly intrenched in our legal system as an industrial despot, is strangely out of harmony with the spirit of the age. In profit-sharing establishments, the workman is already tacitly recognized as a joint owner in the business. The realization of industrial arbitration would be a long step in the direction of industrial democracy and the recognition of the workman's quasi-property right in business. How happily and significantly did Professor Henry Carter Adams declare before this Association, five years ago, that " the existence of the property right which attaches itself to a citizen of the industrial world in much the same way that political right attaches itself to citizens of a democratic society, is rendered probable by its necessity." [1]

[1] Economics and jurisprudence. Economic Studies, 2:29.

DISCUSSION.

DAVID KINLEY: I fear that I am not able, from the brief examination that I have had opportunity to give the paper before us, to do full justice in whatever point of criticism I may have to offer.

I think we are indebted to Professor Tuttle for laying so much emphasis upon the social point of view. The labor question, the position of the laborer, is something to consider from the point of view of society as a whole. We have had the social point of view emphasized in economic discussions in recent years. It is society that has become the producer, society that has become the consumer; it is society that determines values and determines prices; it is society that has done this and that. Although it seems to me that the idea of "society's" acting is sometimes pushed too far, the fact of its application in theories of production and distribution excuses its application here.

I was impressed especially by one of the points made in the paper, and the failure to carry it to its logical conclusion. The consideration of the condition of the workingman, from the point of view of society should be a consideration of the proper status of the working-class as part and parcel of the producing group. That is a very different question from the consideration of evils incidental to the existing status of the working-man; yet it is to the consideration of a single one of that class of evils that Professor Tuttle has devoted the main part of his paper. The discussion of the proper status of the working-class, as one of the factors of the production, is mentioned in the last page or two in connection with the quasi-property right which many think the workingman has in the productive system of which he is a factor. The main purpose of the writer, however, is to provide a remedy for one evil that exists in the present status of workingmen, rather than suggesting possible development for the improvement of the status of the workingmen as a group, and as one of the factors of the producing system. Nevertheless, we must not underrate the importance of what is put before us,—either the importance of the evil mentioned, or the significance of the proposed remedy.

The workingman occupies a certain status as one of the factors of the group of productive elements. There are certain evil things in that status. It is proper to ask what progress has been made in the elimination of the evils incident to the existing status of the workingman in the past ten, twenty-five, fifty years. We are accustomed to answer the question by saying that wages have increased so much, and prices have gone down so much, and therefore the workingman's condition is better off. I take it, however, that Professor Tuttle thinks that such figures do not after all furnish us an adequate answer. The real point at issue is not whether the workingman to-day is in the same status, socially and economically, that he was fifty years ago; but whether the status of the workingman, when compared with the status of other classes, is better than it was in a similar comparison fifty years ago. It is true that the workingman is less certain of employment than he used to be before the introduction of machinery; it is also true that machinery has offset that loss by furnishing a larger quantity of goods for the individual workingman. But this does not necessarily prove, it seems to me, that the status of workingmen as a group, one of the groups engaged in the production of wealth, is any better than it was, when compared for instance with the progress in the condition of the employer, on the one hand, and the capitalist on the other.

We have been accustomed to think of the workman from the employer's point of view, and the employer's point of view is to look upon labor very much as he looks upon machinery,—as one of the factors which he uses in getting his product. The advantage of the social point of view is that it regards the laborer not with reference to the employer, but as a social group, and measures his progress by the relative readjustment from time to time, of his group to others, as groups, and not as individuals. The important question is : Has the laboring class benefited as much as have other classes from the economic progress of the century ? This is a very different question from asking whether we can find a remedy for the irregularities of employment. There are some things to be said in favor of an affirmative answer to the question I have just asked, and to my mind not the least important is the attitude taken in the recent New York labor conference, which, after all, only reflected or crystalized, the public opinion which favors the recognition (as Professor Tuttle put it toward the end of his paper) of quasi-property right on the part of the laborer in the instruments of production he uses, in the business of which he is a part. It seems to me there is no more encouraging mark of progress in the whole range of this labor question than in the acknowledgment that was made by man after man, at that conference, in public discussion, of the laborer's right to a voice in some phases of the policy of the business of which he is a factor. Now I do not mean to admit any right on the part of the employee to manage the business of his employer. I wish simply to emphasize the fact that public opinion no longer recognizes an unlimited right of the employer against the employee to say " this is my property and I will do as I please with it, and you get out." Public opinion says that such a position may not be longer tol-erated, because the securing of fair play in industrial life concerns society as a whole. But this view must not be pushed too far. The employer's rights are equally entitled to protection, and I think there is some danger of forgetting this. A happy solution is to be found somewhere between the two extremes. If the opinion comes to be established that the laboring man, as such, is to have a voice in the settlement of labor affairs and of the productive processes of which he is so large a part, I think we shall have taken a most important step in advance and one that will be of great advantage for the future of society.

Some recent occurrences, however, seem to indicate a loss in the status of the working class. I refer especially to what I have always felt has been the extraordinary extension of the powers of the courts in the use of the injunction, which, it seems to me, has placed a weapon in the hands of the employing class, to the disadvantage of the laboring class, that neither his own welfare nor justice between the parties requires. I am speaking now of this matter in the light of public policy, not as a matter of law. It is sound law, of course, for the highest tribunal of the land has so decided. It is a fact that the extension of the injunction was based upon an interpretation of a statute passed for an en-tirely different purpose, and not upon a logical deduc-tion from the previous use of the injunction, as the in-junction had been used for three hundred years. That, it seems to me, is a step backwards, not perhaps in the mere use of the equity arm of the law for such purposes, but in the extent to which the thing has been pushed. So the position of the laborer to-day, from the social standpoint, has been advanced by the recognition of his quasi-right to a voice in the management of industry, and has been put a step backward by the curtailment of his rights in the labor contract.

To come now to the particular phase of the question that Professor Tuttle discussed. The ethical principle on which he bases his alleged right of the workingman to compensation is not altogether new. It is not the assertion of a new ethical principle, nor, indeed, the assertion of a new legal principle. As a matter of fact it is simply the application to labor of the principle that law and equity have recognized from the time since there have been English law and equity. When the public takes the property of a man to build a railroad, it idemnifies him; it takes his support away and gives him something for it. Professor Tuttle, it seems to me, applies the general principle underlying this action in another direction. He makes society say to the workingman, "we are making progress at your expense; we will try to see to it that the expense is not altogether yours." But whether his particular proposal to indemnify the workman by giving him a sum of money raised by taxation, partly general and partly specific, is a practicable and wise measure, is a different question. If we attempt to put such a scheme into practice, we would run against the old objection that we would cut the nerve of initiative. If we say to the working class, or to any other class, "here is an easy way to get free from difficulties incident to your employment without effort on your part," we are likely to deaden individual enterprise. It seems to me, therefore, that wisdom requires that we should not do this; that whatever share society takes toward improving the life conditions of the laborer, toward giving part of the benefit of industrial progress to those who suffer from this very progress, should be done in a way that will not be doing one kind of mischief while at the same time it is trying to cure another. I am not at all sure that the proper limits of social action would not be reached if whatever funds should be raised should be so applied as to distribute labor in order to meet the requirements made necessary by new inventions, and tide over the superfluous labor until the readjustment has taken place. If we do even that much we encounter another difficulty; if society acts to that extent it is bound also to say to a man, " here is work; now, take this work; you have been thrown out by this improvement or that improvement, but here is an opportunity now for you to go to work and not suffer ". In other words, if society undertakes to provide indemnification it must also have the power to control action to the extent of being able to make a man who has been thrown out of work by economic progress go to work when an opportunity offers, whether it is work he likes, or not. Now that is a technical curtailment of liberty, but it is a fair question, as our distinguished President put it last night, whether increased opportunities for economic activity and better life would not really enlarge the sphere of freedom of action, despite the apparent restriction.

I wish to repeat in conclusion, therefore, that while I sympathize with the general ethical proposition laid down by Professor Tuttle, it seems to me that his practical proposal would be difficult, if not impossible, to put into effect; and that he has missed the main point of his subject, namely, the improvement of the status of the workingman, rather than the elimination of incidental evils in his present status.

SAMUEL M. LINDSAY: To Professor Tuttle's statement of fact in the interesting paper to which we have just listened I have in the main, no objections to offer. As I understand him, the work of the laborer is becoming more highly specialized and more minutely subdivided into effort requiring longer periods for preparation and this movement is likely to be accelerated with further industrial progress. The substitution of machinery for each new labor function is of the essence of progress, but the difficulty of readjustment on the part of the individual workman has become so great and the necessity for more frequent readjustment so marked as to demand social compensation to be derived from the social surplus which is being rapidly increased as a result of this process.

The experience of England in the past twenty years in working out one of the greatest pieces of modern social legislation,—the Workingman's Compensation Act—may be readily applied to the slightly different problem which Professor Tuttle has presented and will serve perhaps as the best concrete illustration of his reasoning. The Workingmen's Compensation Act assumed that the accidents of industry are incidental to the increased productivity of modern industrial organization which makes so large a use of machinery. They hold that the employer out of his enhanced profits due to the use of dangerous machinery or to methods of organization of his labor force involving new risks to life, limb or health, must partially compensate his workmen or in large part carry their risks. Apply this to the risks of displacement or to the dangers of frequent

and prolonged unemployment due to increasing specialization, and ask the state or the employer or both to
compensate the individual workman and partially to
carry or insure his risk and you have a concrete illustration of Professor Tuttle's main thesis.

We are concerned here only with the theoretical justification of such a plan; in no way with the details of
its possible execution. In the first place I would call
attention to certain changes taking place in industry
which makes it necessary for the employer, following
his economic interests, to prevent the rapid displacement
of workmen on the scale assumed in Professor Tuttle's
discussion. Industrial combinations are perhaps the
most significant and far reaching in their effects of all
recent changes in the industrial world. One result has
been the wider separation of the real director of industrial processes from the workman who does the
work. This necessitates the control of labor at long
range and therefore means that the modern trust must
have a more stable labor force and a more intelligent
workman, even in the lower grades, than was necessary under the larger number of smaller employers.
If the trust succeeds at all, it must more evenly distribute its production and run its factories night and
day and every day in the year. It can therefore give
more steady employment and will necessarily seek to
keep men it has trained in its own more efficient
methods. It will and does seek by all sorts of methods
to keep a solid hold on its labor force by offering
bonuses, interests in the business, relief and pension
features to make it difficult for its men to change from
one industry to another, and it seeks also, and this fact
is still more to the point in our present discussion, to anticipate industrial changes and to train in advance its

own men for the readjustments in work which the introduction of labor saving devices will demand. In proportion therefore as this consolidation in industry goes on, and may be taken as typical of modern economic progress, there is in the very process itself some compensation for the industrial workmen and some provision to carry his risk.

In the second place, it is worth one's while to consider whether it be not true that present economic conditions require the individual workman to choose at an early age his occupation for life. In most of the well organized industries new men are not admitted in any capacity after they have attained the age of 35 and in many well defined occupations the age limit of admission is 25 years. So far therefore as such industries do not provide within themselves for all necessary readjustments of individual workmen they may entail great hardship, but the interesting fact is that those industries which have been able to push the age limit for admission down the furthest and have thus reaped the greatest profit from efficient labor have been able to do so only because they recognize the necessity of carrying the risks of both accident and non-employment through compensation relief and pension features. Should the state become an agent for this purpose it might easily check a movement which has already attained some considerable force from the motives of economic interest in private industry.

The state can compensate the individual workman for his losses due to economic progress and may very properly tax the resources to which Professor Tuttle's paper has directed our attention, without danger of interfering with the normal development of the economic

16

compensation to which I have so briefly, and, in the few minutes at my command, I fear but very vaguely, tried to point. The position of the workman in the light of recent economic progress shows nothing more clearly than the growing need of economic foresight, independence, intelligence and inventiveness, and above all the power to work with others collectively even where there is a sacrifice of individual freedom of action. These are qualities which are the result of what President Ely last evening so aptly called our social heredity and they are the products very largely of education. The compensation the state owes is the maintenance of the best industrial and commercial education not only made available for the children of the workers but for adult workers as well. Adult education in every possible effective form and the maintenance of freedom of thought and of activity will alone suffice to enable the modern worker to use existing economic forces and opportunities in the future as he has in the past to protect his share in the social surplus and in the results of economic progress. Under these conditions virile and efficient workmen will make necessary readjustments, and for those who cannot a wiser and more sufficient public charity will provide and at the same time will eliminate them from the ranks of industrial workers in their own interests as well as in that of their employers and their fellow workmen, and for the ultimate good of the body-politic.

GEORGE ROBERTS: Professor Tuttle's essential point as I understand it is that the benefits of progress are enjoyed by society as a whole, while the losses incident to progress are borne by the individual laborer. There are just one or two suggestions that I desire briefly to make in that connection. The first is that the laborer himself is a part of the society which enjoys these benefits, and that, while he may not derive benefit from the particular step of progress which deprives him of employment, he has been all his life a beneficiary of a thousand such steps of progress to which he himself made no contribution. The fact that he is daily the beneficiary of such progress in every department of industry is to him ample compensation for the risk or loss which he may incur. On the other hand, while the profits of a given step of progress may be enjoyed by capitalists, the capitalist himself is constantly bearing the risk of having his entire investment wiped out by just such progress. So it seems to me that the benefits are being constantly distributed to all the members of the community, laborers as well as capitalists, and the losses likewise more equitably than any system that could be devised by legislative acts.

THEODORE MARBURG : This is the largest question of our day. The turn the discussion has taken this afternoon is a fitting supplement to the papers and discussions this morning. The opinion has been advanced that our Association in its consideration of this topic should confine itself to the economic aspects of industry and of the labor question. I cannot reconcile myself to this view ; it seems to me most fitting to introduce the element of the ethical. Few of us doubt that the career of unexampled economic activity upon which our country has entered points to ascendency in the field of industry. What concerns us is to study the forces which are calculated to make our position secure and enduring. There is reason to believe that the cycles of growth and decay that mark the history of nations were born of conditions that are passing away. It is rash to presume that we shall actually escape the fate of other nations but it should be our care to postpone as long as possible the day of decline and to show some lasting gain to humanity as a result of our activities. That object can be promoted by building up the character of the average man in the United States and to effect this we must give attention to the ethical side of industry and of the labor question. It seems to me entirely fitting that the American Economic Association should endeavor to indicate how far it is safe to go in this direction. If we are not to do it, who is?

What I want to do now is to point out, in a limited way, what we can do and what we cannot do to improve the condition of labor and to develop the laborer, submitting the matter to you in the light of experience as an employer of labor combined with some dozen years of attention to the science of economics.

Mr. Tuttle has suggested indemnity for the man who is displaced by improved machinery. In approaching this question we need as perspective a consciousness not only of the contribution of machinery to wealth, but of the part it has played in increasing opportunity for employment and in increasing wages. The great increase in the number of people following gainful pursuits not only in America, where the phenomenon is partly explained by the existence of new land to be cultivated, but in Europe too, has taken place since the advent of power-machines. It has been shown that in America nominal wages have advanced 82 per cent. and real wages 130 per cent. since 1840. There is no question but that machinery means increased opportunity and increased wages. This gain to the labor world as a whole does not excuse us, of course, from compensating the individual who suffers from this development provided such compensation can be given safely, but the question of indemnity for the individual unfortunately connects itself with the question of the unemployed generally. The individual who is thrown out by improved machinery becomes one of that great body. The problem of the unemployed is a serious and most depressing problem for society, one which I fear will never be wholly solved. Experience only emphasizes the truth of the saying of Christ, " ye have the poor with you alway." We may lessen the numbers of the submerged class, but there is little hope of abolishing the class, and for this reason : it is not his actual inferiority but his comparative inferiority which causes the individual to be worsted in the struggle. The most worthless tramp in the street is superior to the savage who gloats over the victim he is torturing to death, or to the brute who practices cannibalism. But whilst he progressed through his antecedents, through his progenitors and through his inheritance of an ever better social environment, the whole of society has progressed, and it is his comparative inferiority to those about him which punishes him.

Now suppose the government attempt to remedy this, as has been suggested, by offering work to the unemployed, what would that mean? It would mean that you offer a refuge to all who chose to abandon their existing employment. It would invite expressions of discontent on the part of those engaged in private industry. The workman would be quick to find fault and to throw up his job if he could fall back upon the government to give him work. Very soon the government would be the major or the sole employer, and that means socialism. Under that régime the only way you can exact work from the man who is disinclined to work is to imprison him, and that is a return to slavery. Private property is the only safeguard against slavery, and private property could not continue to exist on a liberal scale if the government should offer work to the whole body of the unemployed.

As to the workman's right of indemnity and his right to a voice in the management of industry, I think we confuse matters when we talk about rights in that sense. It is much better to appeal directly to social expediency. If it be socially expedient that the worker should be indemnified, and that he should have a voice in the management, let it be done. If it be not socially expedient, he has no right to it.

Now these are some of the things we cannot do; there are some things we can do. We see this marvelous growth in invention; we note new instrumentalities of exchange and production multiplied to such an extent, that what is done to-day would have been considered an idle dream a generation ago. Notwithstanding this, we find labor still subject to the heavy burden to which Mr. Tuttle and others have referred. We find labor in many industries with a task unduly hard, with nothing connected with it that is elevating and developing to the man himself. We see him leaving his home in the morning before his children are up, and returning after they are in bed. We see very few laborers accumulating enough to relieve themselves of this strain in their old age. They get higher wages, and more for their wages as time goes on, but much of their expenditure is dictated by the necessity of conforming to the habits of their neighbors. The money they expend on the education of their children, and on better housing and food and on recreation is well spent, but it is a question whether the gaudier appearance of the household and the fancy dress of the women add much to the household's real happiness.

And here enters a most important consideration. Unless the laborer did expend his wages, and was under the pressure of this necessity of earning a livelihood, I fear we would not get labor for the more unpleasant and harder work of industry. This is a philosophical fact on which the whole question rests. If the labor world were in an independent position, many of our factories would be compelled to close. It is running against this stubborn fact that makes it all the more incumbent upon us to seek ways in which we can improve the laborer's condition in other directions.

The government cannot make the laborer save; it can do but little to increase wages. We come then to the conditions of labor and the first thing that presents itself to us in this connection is the hours of labor. Here, it seems to me, is the opportunity of the government. It can give the laboring man more leisure; it can establish postal savings banks to increase the opportunity and incentive for saving; it can follow the example of Germany and see that the laborer is provided for in his old age. The most important of these steps is that in the direction of shorter hours. The question is too large to go into adequately in this discussion. I must omit arguments; but I should like to give certain conclusions which I have reached after years of attention to the subject.

In 1881 it looked as if shorter hours would be brought about through the efforts of the laborers themselves, but for lack of a concerted action the movement lapsed. The permanent reduction of hours in the building trades was made possible by the fact that in these trades competition is within a limited circumference. In the general field of industry the individual employer cannot reduce the hours of labor because he would be at a disadvantage with his competitor. The same is true of any single state of the Union. I have reached the conclusion that the object can be attained in a reasonable period only through the intervention of the federal government and that the United States is one of the few countries that could afford the experiment. It is a question which we are inclined to leave to its own solution and whose discussion we are disposed to postpone, but there are two considerations which make it incumbent upon us to act soon. One is the fact that shorter hours must be introduced before our exports of manufactures become too large a percentage of our total exports; the other is that the existence of trusts and the perfection of our industries point to a speedy modification of the tariff, and the maintenance of the tariff is essential to the success of the experiment. It would be rash to hope that the tariff would be restored for the sake of giving shorter hours to labor.

The question is indeed a serious one and calls for great deliberation. Personally I think it would be an entirely safe experiment, particularly if the reduction of hours were gradual through a period of years. The group of men who carried it out would be doing something as far reaching as that which Lincoln did for the black man.

ADNA F. WEBER: The practical difficulties of creating any public or governmental machinery for relieving unemployed workingmen are so great that it might be well to consider what means have been devised by private initiative to secure this end. As is generally known, there has lately taken place in the printing industry the introduction on a large scale of new labor-saving machinery,—the type-setting machine. Ordinarily such a movement would have resulted in the retirement of a host of intelligent, well-paid artisans and the substitution in their place of a much cheaper grade of labor. The distress that such a movement would involve has been avoided by the action of the typographical union, which instead of antagonizing the new machine deliberately agreed to its general introduction, but only under the condition that the machines should be operated by union men at the existing rates of wages, and in many cases, that the hours of work should be shortened. Now it seems to me that this is a great forward step in the method of dealing with displacement of labor. By this system the benefits of invention are not entirely absorbed by the employer, in large profits, and the consumer, in lower prices, but are to some extent shared with the workmen in the trade immediately affected. These workmen secure the permanent advantage of shorter hours, but on the other hand are placed under the temporary disadvantage of having to support a fraction of their number who are temporarily thrown out of employment. It is possible that in other industries trade unions may meet employers in the same way, and thus keep in employment the larger portion of skilled labor without any reduction of wages. In some such arrangement I see more promise of practical performance than in other proposals, while it is supported by the ethical considerations advanced by Professor Tuttle and other speakers.

WILLIAM W. FOLWELL: It seems to me that the trouble with this whole discussion is that it is a purely academic discussion, really not worth our while. We might willingly grant the whole contention of Professor Tuttle's able and very interesting paper. It is the practical question, how to put such a scheme into operation, which alone needs consideration. It is proposed now to indemnify laborers by means of taxation, or by contributions from employers, or both. The first question arises in regard to this taxation—what kind is it to be? Is it to be direct or indirect, local or state, or shall the whole United States be called upon? If you leave this to local taxation, there would be great inequalities and great confusion. I can't conceive off hand how you are going to work any such scheme of taxation. If you propose to compel the employers to contribute to such a fund, who is going to do it? What kind of authority— national, state or local? In any case, who can see beforehand what employees are most likely to be displaced by new machinery? Nobody can tell. Nobody knows what business will be completely ruined and upset to-morrow by new processes or new machinery. Do you propose then to raise a fund in advance, to be kept in some treasury ready for use when some industry, at some unknown and unexpected time, shall be destroyed by a new process or a new invention? We don't do things that way in the United States. It seems to me the practical difficulties of working any such scheme are too great, and we have merely been engaged in a purely academic and theoretical discussion, which is extremely pleasant, but which, it seems to me, is wholly impractical.

JOHN R. COMMONS: One of the difficulties of the effort to combine ethics and economics is that it places us in the position of the politician who is in favor of the theory but against the practice. We are all of us in favor of indemnifying working men for loss which he has incurred through no fault of his own. The economic question as I understand it is simply a question of ingenuity. The business of economics is to work out the scheme by which that theory can be put into practice, and we have been listening here to suggestions on that line. It has been mentioned that in the case of accidents the employer, or the business, rather, in European countries, indemnifies the laborer. We might mention also the establishment of employment agencies. There is one example in this country where a state legislature has met this question in a practical way, and I do not know that it has involved any undermining of initiative. The state of Massachusetts some five or six years ago provided for a large construction for supplying water to the metropolitan district. In condemning the real estate in the area of the water shed provision was made for indemnifying property owners. In the same act provision was also made for indemnifying the laborers who were thrown out of employment in those villages. The law was a very simple one. It did not require that the laborers should accept any job which should be offered to them, but it was estimated that on the whole it would take a man six months to find another job, and then provided that any laborer or′ group of laborers might join in an action before a proper court, and upon proving that they had resided in that place and had had employment for a period of one year, they could collect from the state a sum equivalent to six months' wages. It placed them upon their own initiative and responsibility in the matter of finding a new job and moving out of that town, but at the same it placed the burden of caring for them during this loss of employment, through no fault of their own, upon the state which was to be benefited thereby.

Now, I am not claiming that I have a scheme by which a similar provision could be made for those who lose employment through improvements in mechanical processes. The case mentioned was undoubtedly an enterprise undertaken distinctly by the state with the known result that labor would be displaced. There are more difficult problems of course in the case of laborers displaced by improvements in processes. Probably the difficulty in identifying the laborer who lost the job, would be more important than any other, but it does not strike me that a like difficulty arises in inquiry where the burden should lie. The gain to the employer or the gain to the public is found to be the net income of the employer or the capitalist, or the taxpaying class, and it would seem to me that an income tax, perhaps laid upon corporations, or a tax of similar character would assure, as near as we could possibly assure in any scheme, the advantage gained through increased economics from improved processes. If we set about as economists trying to discover practical means for indemnifying the laborer I think we can find lessons from other countries and different states, and draw upon our own economic foundation for plans which would be practical and would combine theory and practice.

EDWARD T. DEVINE: Professor Tuttle appears to me to have taken hold of one corner of a large problem, from which he has vainly attempted to separate the particular part in which he is interested. It is a curious fact, that those who have become profoundly interested in some one aspect of the great problem of relief, almost invariably begin their propaganda for reform by discovering and insisting upon a great gulf between what they wish to remedy on the one hand, and all other remedial movements on the other. The fact is, however, that the problem of relief is one, whatever the varying causes that create it. Its urgency and its magnitude have not been realized ; more adequate measures are required to meet existing needs. Immigration ; the ravages of sickness, and especially of the great scourge, tuberculosis ; industrial displacement, both in ordinary times, and especially in times of depression ; bad housing conditions, and all the other forces creating dependency, must equally be analysed and understood. When the causes of dependency are found to be social rather than individual, as they are in many instances, we must discover by what method the burden can be transferred from the individual and the family, who now suffer vicariously as an incident to industrial and social progress, and placed instead upon the broad shoulders of the community. Professor Tuttle is right in his contention that industrial displacement, to some extent, presents such a case, but wrong in attempting to show that the displaced laborer has a claim different from that of other dependent families, whose claims are equally against society as a whole. No scheme can be devised which will enable us to compensate a laborer for being displaced. Any such scheme, however carefully guarded, would inevitably put a bonus upon inefficiency, since it is the inefficient who in any well managed industrial enterprise are first allowed to go. Society should, as a matter of sound policy meet such a situation, but should meet it with direct reference to the actual experience of the one who is displaced. The nature of the relief supplied,—whether it be cash payment ; transportation to some other place, where work is to be had ; the supply of tools for new work, or whatever else it may be, must have reference to the past history and the capacity of the individual who is thus aided ; in other words, the situation must be dealt with as a problem of relief precisely as we would deal with the needs of a family whose breadwinner has died from consumption, a cause of dependency for which the community is itself chiefly responsible.

THE NEGRO IN THE YAZOO-MISSISSIPPI DELTA.

BY ALFRED HOLT STONE.

Among the many disturbing questions entering into our complex national life, the one above all others that seems to have provoked discussion in every quarter, is the so-called negro problem. Under this general designation have come to be embraced all the various and complicated questions arising from the contact at many points of the black race with the white. Not since the formation of this government has this discussion ceased, and ignorance has never been a bar to free participation in it. In a discussion of these questions in their broader aspects, though I have devoted some years to their consideration, I can claim no peculiar knowledge—no superior wisdom. The problem is so extensive in its ramifications, it presents so many and such varied phases, that to my mind there is but one proper and reasonable method of considering it: that is, through the analysis and study of its component parts—the attempted grasp and comprehension of the minor and elemental conditions and problems which enter into the composition of the whole. The intelligent study of this question must resolve itself at last into a study of local conditions.

A lifetime spent in the "blackest" of the south's "black belts"; a sharer in the association between the two races in the life of the plantation,—the most constant and intimate association that is possible between them; a thorough acquaintance with the conditions surrounding the negro in a section wherein I firmly believe will be discovered the region of his greatest material possibilities; these constitute my only equipment in venturing upon this discussion. It is to a consideration of local conditions only that this paper is addressed.

In the state of Mississippi, between the 32nd and 35th parallels of north latitude, its entire western border washed by the Mississippi river, and most of its eastern by the Yazoo, extending north from the confluence of those streams at a point just above the city of Vicksburg, lies the strip of territory known as the Yazoo–Mississippi delta. The exact origin of the word delta, as applied to this region, is not clear; though it was probably a simple extension of the old and accepted use of the word, descriptive both of the character and of the peculiar formation of the land built up by the diverging mouths of large silt-bearing streams. The character of the soil certainly justifies such a conclusion, for it is entirely of alluvial formation, detritus deposited during thousands of years in which the Mississippi has poured out its muddy flood waters over the adjacent country.

The Yazoo–Mississippi delta is about one hundred and fifty miles in length, and its greatest width is about one-third of that. Its front along the Mississippi is protected against overflows of that river by an unbroken line of levees, three hundred and ten miles in length, averaging fifteen feet in height, with a maximum of about thirty. The delta differs radically from the rest of Mississippi in many important respects, but in none more than in those wherein the negro is immediately concerned; hence only the nine counties lying wholly within it, Bolivar, Coahoma, Issaquena, Leflore, Quitman, Sharkey, Sunflower, Tunica and Washington, are considered here. The alluvial valley of which these counties form a most important part has been called by the most distinguished member of the Mississippi river commission, Judge Robert S. Taylor, of Indiana, " the cream jug of the continent." Of it he has written: " Nature knows not how to compound a richer soil. It can no more lie idle than the sea can keep still. Every square foot of it riots in vegetable life. . . . . Its [the Mississippi's] floods came down loaded with skimmings from the great watershed above. Overtopping its banks, the enriched water spread far and wide over the alluvial area, so obstructed in its flow by the dense growth covering the land that its slackened velocity compelled it to let fall its load of sediment as it went. Thus the floods built up the valley year by year in layers of fatness, to live again in incalculable crops of grain, fruits and fibers." [1]

By what warrant does this region claim attention in a consideration of America's gravest question? Simply because of the part it plays, and is destined to play, in the lives and fortunes of a constantly growing percentage of America's negro population. This has long been recognized by the authority just quoted. He says: " A feature of special interest in this connection [he was discussing the matter of levee protection] is the opportunity which the reclamation of the alluvial valley offers to the negro to better his condition. One-half or more of its entire area is suitable for cultivation of cotton. A bale per acre of ginned cotton, weighing five hundred pounds, is the standard yield—worth from thirty to fifty dollars according to the ups and downs of the market. . . . The negro is not seizing this golden opportunity as the white pioneer of the Northwest would have seized it, but he is not wholly neglecting it.

[1] Tompkins, Riparian lands of the Mississippi river, p. 234.

17

In considerable and increasing numbers they are buying land and becoming independent cultivators. . . . . Nowhere else in the south are as favorable opportunities offered to the black man as in the reclaimed Mississippi lowlands, and nowhere else is he doing as much for his own up-lifting." [1]

The section of this territory with which we are concerned embraces an area of 5,480 square miles, containing about three and one-quarter million acres of land, with a population of 195,346. Of these but 24,137 are white, while the blacks number 171,209, a proportion of 7.1 blacks to 1 white. This proportion has increased steadily from 4.9 to 1 in 1880 and 6.7 to 1 in 1890, while in Mississippi as a whole it is almost stationary, being now 1.4 to 1, as against 1.3 to 1 in 1890 and 1880. I think I am not in error in stating that the largest proportion of blacks to whites exhibited by the last census for any part of the United States is found in one of the counties of this group, Issaquena, in which it is 15.5 to 1. In the same county the proportion was 15.7 to 1 by the eleventh census, and 11.1 to 1 by the tenth. Of the white inhabitants of the state but 3.7 per cent. are found in the delta, while 18.8 per cent. of all Mississippi's negro population make it their home. Comparison with former censuses shows this per cent. for whites to be practically at a standstill, while that for the negro is steadily increasing. In 1890 these percentages were 3.5 for the white and 17.7 for the negro, and in 1880, 3.4 and 12.6 respectively. From 1880 to 1890 the per cent. of increase of the white population of the United States was 26.7, and that of the negro 13.5. For the state of Mississippi these percentages were 13.7 for the one, and 14.2 for the other. During

[1] *Idem*, pp. 236, 237.

that decade the white population of the delta increased by only 17.3 per cent., while the increase of the black was no less than 60.4 per cent. Between the eleventh census and the twelfth, the white population of the country increased 21.4 per cent., and the negro 18.1. The figures for Mississippi exhibit a white increase of 17.6 per cent., with 22.2 for the negro. In the delta section of the state the increase was 23.5 for the white race, and 30.2 for the black. The last census shows that the negro constitutes 11.6 per cent. of the total population of the country, 58.5 per cent. of that of Mississippi, and 87.6 per cent. of that of the Yazoo–Mississippi delta.

Yet here we hear nothing about an ignorant mass of negroes dragging the white man down ; we hear of no black incubus ; we have few midnight assassinations, and fewer lynchings. The violation by a negro of the person of a white woman is with us an unknown crime ; nowhere else is the line marking the social separation of the two races more rigidly drawn, nowhere are the relations between the two more kindly. With us race riots are unknown, and we have but one negro problem —though that constantly confronts us,—how to secure more negroes.

For many years this region was largely a *terra incognita*, and the story of its development and opening explains the figures of negro population. The character of its white population, and the conditions under which its soil is tilled explain the relations between the white man and the black. Until recently the only means of communication between the delta and the outer world were river boats, for not till 1883 was it penetrated by a railroad. We have only to compare the statistics of negro population of the eleventh census with those of the tenth to see the results of railway construction.

The early settlers were from Virginia, Kentucky and Tennessee. They were all slave holders, and the nature of the enterprises upon which they embarked demanded the possession of means. Hence this section early came to be the seat of large planting operations. There was no place for the man who was unable to own slaves ; no demand for his services, other than as an overseer. There were no small farms, no towns, no manufacturing enterprises, no foothold for the poor white, who is here a negligible, if not an absolutely unknown, quantity.

Every step taken in the development of this section has been dependent upon, and marked by, an increased negro population. The railroad rights of way through its forests have been cut out by the negro, and every mile of track laid by his hands. These forest lands have been converted by him into fertile fields, and their subsequent cultivation has called for his constant service. The levees upon which the delta depends for protection from floods have been erected mainly by the negro, and the daily labor in field and town, in planting and building, in operating gins and compresses and oil mills, in moving trains, in handling the great staple of the country,—all, in fact, that makes the life behind these earthen ramparts,—is but the negro's daily toil. The capital, the devising brain, the directing will, constitute the white man's part, the work itself is the negro's. Nowhere else does manual labor find a higher or more certain wage ; nowhere do better relations exist between employer and employed ; nowhere are capital and labor on better terms. There are no strikes, no lockouts, no combinations, no operating on half time, no reductions of force, and the works never shut down.

One of the gravest causes of trouble between the two races is contact on a common industrial plane. A peculiar effect is almost invariably wrought upon the negro's attitude toward the white man by such association, exemplifying the truth of the old maxim that "familiarity breeds contempt." I am not now discussing its cause, but one who knows the negro masses knows that their ingrained admiration for wealth and station, strong as it is, is no more controlling a mental habit than is their lack of respect for the opposite conditions. This is as true in the mines of the north as in the fields of the south.

If I were asked what one factor makes most for the amicable relations between the races in the delta I should say without hesitation the absence of a white laboring class, particularly of field laborers. It cannot be accounted for on the hypothesis that we have a peculiar class of negroes, for this population is a commingling of blacks from every section of the south, brought here without the slightest process of selection. The white population is composed of the professional class, those engaged in mercantile and manufacturing pursuits, and those interested in cotton planting, either as owners or managers. The white artisans are so few in number as not to affect this division, and the relations between them and the negro are identical with those between the two masses of population. Of the field of manual labor the negro holds a practical monopoly.

In saying[1] that each year his feeling grew stronger "that perhaps in the heat of passion, growing out of

[1] Tuskegee Normal Institute, Annual report, 1901.

racial and sectional prejudice, we have not given the southern people due credit for the immense amount of help rendered the negro during the period he was a slave," that he was then " started on the foundation of agriculture, mechanic and household arts", Booker T. Washington has but given expression to a conviction which unprejudiced study would make universal. I am thoroughly satisfied that the conditions existing here to-day are largely a heritage from the slavery régime. By the violence of the civil strife which wrought the destruction of southern social and economic conditions, the delta was probably less affected than any other equal area in the south. For this its isolation and in-accessibility easily account. Out of the ruin which was the legacy of war to the southern states no section emerged with less of violent change as regarded race relations.

In the *Contemporary Review* for July, 1900, Mr. Philip Alexander Bruce has drawn a faithful picture of the old plantation system of the south. He says truly that " the most distinctive feature of the old industrial order", next to slavery, " was the large plantation." He describes the plantation as having been frequently a small principality in extent, the planter the absolute master of his own domain, " his word the supreme law, his wishes the governing influence." Mr. Bruce then sets against this a picture of agricultural conditions in the south of to-day, telling us that " the ruin of the old plantation system is complete." His portrayal of the essential features of the old system fairly describes existing conditions in the delta. Here the era of small farms has not set in, the process of land division has not begun. On the contrary, most of the large planta-tions are growing larger, and such small farms as do exist have not been erected upon the ruins of larger tracts. Change of ownership has not meant disintegration, but has been effected by sales of property entire.

It may be remarked here, parenthetically, that the census rule treating every tract of land on which agricultural industry is conducted as a farm, while doubtless essential to thorough investigation, is misleading to the student who is ignorant of local conditions that materially modify the application of this method of classification. In the language of bulletin 100, Agriculture in Delaware, "The number of farmers, that is, persons operating farms as owners or tenants, is the same at any period as the number of farms." Thus every holding becomes a "farm", and a tract of 1,000 acres, known locally as a plantation, though entirely under one ownership and management, would appear in census reports as so many different farm holdings, the number being dependent upon the number of tenants living on it during the census year, the average acreage governed by the size of these various, arbitrary and temporary subdivisions. That such figures, unless accompanied by an explanatory note, lead to inaccurate conclusions, is well illustrated in an article in the *Boston Transcript*, May 25, 1901, based upon the showings of the ninth census. Taking Mississippi as a "typical state", the writer concluded—and this was for 1870—that the figures showed " a revolutionary increase in the small farms ", " the great plantations of some states being almost entirely eliminated, as in the black counties of Mississippi."

The plantations of this section vary in size from five hundred to several thousand acres, and the proportion of negroes to white men living on them, from 25 to 1

to more than 100 to 1. Yet there is now no more feeling of fear on the white man's part whether for himself or his wife or his children, than in the days
of slavery. As in the olden time, so now, the word
of the planter or his representative is the law of the
place, and on the one hand we have implicit obedience,
on the other, firmness and moderation. Certainly the
relation of master and slave no longer exists here, but
out of it has been evolved that of patron and retainer.
I so designate it because I know of no other to which
it more nearly approaches. It is not at all one purely
of business, the ordinary relation of landlord and
tenant, or of employer and employee. The plantation
owner or manager expects to do more than merely to see
to the physical needs of the negroes under him, to provide for their wants and look over their work. He is
called upon to settle family quarrels, to maintain peace
and order between neighbors, to arbitrate disputes, to
protect wives from the punishment of irate husbands,
frequently to restore broken conjugal relations upon
terms satisfactory to both parties, to procure marriage
licenses and advise as to divorces, to aid in the erection
of churches, to provide for the burial of the dead, to
give counsel in the thousand and one matters peculiar
to the plantation negro's life, whether whimsical or
grave. Every plantation negro expects the discharge
of these functions as a mere matter of course. Yet further, when in more serious trouble, he looks to the white
man as to a friend, and appeals to him as to a protector, when a possible term in jail or the penitentiary
looms up before him, and lawyers and bail are to be
provided. All these things are mere incidents to the
plantation system, the commonplace affairs of its daily
routine. The negro regards them as his due, in return

for the proprietary interest and pride he feels in the plantation at large, his sense of being part and parcel of a large institution, and the certainty, in his own mind, that he himself is necessary to its success. Then too, there is his never failing assurance of ability to pay his account, no matter how large, his labor, when it is not too wet or too cold, his respect, and his implicit, and generally cheerful, obedience.

The one thing which in the south, directly and indirectly, has been the source of the gravest trouble between the races, and which has most disastrously worked their separation, has been the crime of rape. That it should lead to lynching was inevitable; it was equally inevitable that in time the same mode of punishment would be extended to less grave offenses. At the April meeting of the American Academy of Political and Social Science, Dr. George T. Winston, of North Carolina, presented a most sombre picture of existing southern race conditions. He said: "The southern woman with her helpless little children in solitary farm house no longer sleeps secure in the absence of her husband, with doors unlocked but safely guarded by black men whose lives would be freely given in her defense. But now, when a knock is heard at the door, she shudders with nameless horror. The black brute is lurking in the dark, a monstrous beast, crazed with lust. His ferocity is almost demoniacal. A mad bull or a tiger could scarcely be more brutal. A whole community is now frenzied with horror, with blind and furious rage for vengeance. A stake is driven; the wretched brute, covered with oil, bruised and gashed, beaten and hacked and maimed, amid the jeers and shouts and curses, the tears of anger and of joy, the prayers and maledictions of thousands of civilized people, in the sight of school-houses, courthouses and churches is burned to death. . . . . I do not hesitate to say that more horrible crimes have been committed by the generation of negroes that have grown up in the south since slavery than by the six preceding generations in slavery. And also that the worst cruelties of slavery all combined for two centuries, were not equal to the savage barbarities inflicted in retaliation upon the negroes by the whites during the last twenty years."[1]

This forbidding picture is the best support for my contention that the wisest and most helpful study of this combination of intricate problems is from the local point of view,—the exhibition of conditions as presented upon particular horizons. From contrasts and comparisons some good may finally be realized. To be able to say that to one section of the south, at least, this picture presents not one familiar feature, is possibly alone enough to justify my presence here. I do not deny that this is a true statement of conditions in many sections of the south. I know too well that for many it is not overdrawn. I do not even assert that it is not more nearly typical of the south at large than is my own. But I do say that into the minds of the white men and women of my section, where not far from ninety per cent of all our people are black, where in our rural districts they sometimes outnumber us as much as one hundred to one, the thought of the possibility of rape never comes. Nor do I believe that in all this region there is a single plantation on which may not be found negroes who if left by the owner or manager in charge of his home would not fail to take the life of any man, white or black, attempting violence. They would know what was expected of

[1] Amer. Acad. of pol. and soc. sci., Annals, 18:108-9.

them, and that for the uttermost discharge of that duty not one hair of their heads would be harmed.

What is the cause of this difference between geographic divisions of a common country? I answer that our freedom from this curse is merely incidental to the general relations obtaining between the races, and prop. erly ascribable to the general station and character of the white population, to the persistence of the same relative status between the masses of the two races that existed when the one was master and the other slave. Then the negro was bred to absolute obedience, made to respect the white race because it was white, taught that the person, even the name, of the humblest white woman was something not to be profaned by touch or word or thought. That feeling among the negroes, the result of this training, had enough vitality to project itself through the civil war, and through that period rendered safe the white woman who in the absence of her male protector typified in herself the dominance of her race. Through the influence of novel conditions in the process of time it began to disappear, and synchronously rape came to add its horrors and complications to the race problem. The influences and relations and peculiar lines of contact which wrought in the negro that mental habit are potent to-day in the delta, and in consequence rape is a crime we do not fear. I believe that this psychological habit is still latently persistent in the negro masses, and but requires contact with conditions approaching those which produced it to become again a controlling force. Thus I would account for the fact that in a negro population drawn from every quarter of the south there is absence not merely of the crime of rape, but of even the slightest disrespect to white women.

The peculiar attitude of the negro toward those upon

an equality with himself, makes possible such relations
only where between the masses of the two races there
is rigidly maintained the status of superior and inferior.
This is not possible where a white laboring class comes
into contact with the same negro class. To illustrate my
general proposition, as seen from the negro's own standpoint, I may cite the following. In owning and operating a cotton plantation, I have come into relations with
negroes from all sections of the country, and have had
fair opportunities for observation. Before the abolition
of the system, I was for a time a lessee of convicts from
the state penitentiary. Among the prisoners allotted
me was a particularly bright and efficient mulatto of
about twenty-five years of age. He had a common
school education, and was apt and skillful. He was
serving a sentence for an attempted criminal assault
upon a seventeen year old white girl in a county of my
state where conditions obtain radically different from
those existing with us. I was anxious to know how, if
at all, he accounted for his crime, but he was reluctant
to discuss it. Finally he said to me: "You don't
understand,—things over here are so different. I hired
to an old man over there by the year. He had only
about forty acres of land, and he and his folks did all
their own work, cooking, washing and everything. I
was the only outside hand he had. His daughter
worked right along side of me in the field every day,
for three or four months. Finally one day, when nobody else was round, hell got into me and I tried to
rape her. But you folks over here can't understand,—
things are so different. Over here a nigger is a nigger,
and a white man is a white man, and it's the same with
the women". There was not the slightest intimation
of accessory guilt on the girl's part; his only explana-

tion of his act was that " things were different ". There was no fault upon the part of the attempted victim of his lust. Her only crime was a poverty which compelled her to do work which in the estimation of the negro was reserved as the natural portion of his own race, and the doing of which destroyed the relation which otherwise would have constituted a barrier to his brutality. I do not cite this as a typical instance, for many cases of rape occur wherein there is not even the occasion or opportunity of enforced familiarity. I give it for what it is worth, as the expression of a very intelligent negro.

If my theory is at fault, I should like to be told why it is that the delta negro never assaults a white woman, but does commit rape upon the women of his own race. This section while containing 18.8 per cent. of Mississippi negroes now furnishes 21.7 per cent. of the negro population of the state prison. Of the total number of convicts from the delta, 4.9 per cent. are serving sentences for rape. These convictions are upon presentments to grand juries solely by negroes, and from the circumstances are necessarily had solely upon negro testimony. It is a difficult crime to prove, but taking no account of the alleged cases, of those in which there seemed to the grand jury insufficient evidence to warrant an indictment, of those resulting in acquittals on the ground of consent, and of those which never came to the notice of the law at all, the number of convictions of delta negroes for the rape or attempted rape of negro women, during the past four years, is twelve. In 1898, there were three; one in the following year; three in 1900, and in 1901, to September 30th, there were five. The ages of those committing this crime range from sixteen to fifty-four, all but three being between twenty and

thirty-one. Some have been committed under circumstances as revolting as it is possible for the human mind
to conceive.

Returning to the description of the economic condition of the negroes in my neighborhood let me say a
word as to one of the most discussed features of the
negro's life in the south, the house in which he lives.
In the towns, where the negro rents or owns his home,
it is whatever his ability commands, from a bare
shelter, to a well furnished house containing four to six
rooms. On the plantations the one-room cabin, that
bête noire of social scientists, is not in evidence. They
disappeared many years ago. Where one still stands it
is deserted or temporarily occupied by cotton pickers or
day hands. In the competition for laborers a steadily
improving class of plantation houses is not the least of
the inducements offered. If a family lives in a one-room
cabin, it is a matter purely of choice; there are hundreds of a different kind to be had.

In the cultivation of cotton we have in the delta
nearly every system of labor to be found in the south.
They are roughly divisible into two classes, the more
general being the true metayer, or some modification of
it, and the other the fixed cash rental. Where the
negro does not own the soil he cultivates, his relation
to it is either that of a renter or a cropper. The share
system presents no peculiar features. The cropper furnishes his labor in planting, cultivating and gathering
the crop ; the land owner furnishes the land, the team
and the implements ; and the crop is divided equally between them. The planter advances to the cropper such
supplies as are needed during the year, to be paid for
out of the latter's half of the crop. As soon as a
quantity of cotton sufficient to pay this account has been

delivered to the planter, the cropper frequently receives his portion of the cotton, to be disposed of as he sees fit. The extent to which the cropper exercises control over his cotton varies with the locality.

The features of land renting by negroes vary according to the nature of the tenancy, whether the land is part of a plantation under white supervision, or a small tract, or part of a plantation entirely rented by a non-resident landlord. In the first case the land is rented for a fixed sum per acre, varying, with cotton prices and the character of the soil, from five to seven dollars. Where a lint rent is taken it varies from eighty to one hundred pounds. Generally speaking, the supervision over a renter is not as strict as that over a cropper, and as soon as his account is paid his cotton is at his own disposal. More privileges and a larger measure of independence are considered by the negro as incident to this tenure, and as he becomes the owner of a mule it is his ambition to become a renter. It frequently happens that a planter will rent a mule to a negro who has nothing at all, the uniform rent being twenty-five dollars. Under each of these systems certain general features obtain. The planter takes no deed of trust, for the state statutes give him a lien on the crop for rent and supplies. Nor is it usual to have any written contract other than a mere memorandum. There is generally no definite understanding as to the amount of supplies to be advanced, and it is well within the truth to say that usually the planter is engaged in an effort to keep the negro's account within such limits as will make it safe, while the negro is equally anxious to obtain as much as he can on credit.

The negro discriminates between the two systems, yet when results are considered, when one sees him

squander from year to year the proceeds of his labor,
however obtained, when he is seen to move restlessly
and aimlessly from place to place, gathering less moss
than the proverbial rolling stone, it must appear to the
close observer that, as a matter of fact, the system under
which he works makes but little difference in his
material welfare.

Where the negro rents land not under the supervision
of plantation management, he obtains his supplies from
a merchant or cotton factor.   Here we have the crop
lien system, so often, so earnestly, and, in my judgment,
so unjustly inveighed against.   What the negro obtains
from the factor, and the manner of his getting it, depend
largely upon himself.   Usually his advances consist
only of supplies, furnished him monthly or weekly.
The only money advanced is such as the contingencies of cultivating or gathering the crop make necessary.   The negro is dealt with just as his established
reputation and the value of the security he has to offer
may justify.   The factor's method of self-protection is
to take a deed of trust on the live stock and prospective
crop, and is the same whether the applicant be a two-
mule negro renter, or the white owner of a thousand
acres of land, wanting ten thousand dollars of advances.
The latter attaches his signature to a printed trust deed
like that signed by the former covering his mules
and crop to be grown.   The amount advanced is governed by the character of the individual and the security.   There is, however, this difference; the white
man gets his advances in cash, available at stated intervals, while the negro gets the most of his in the shape
of supplies.   If, however, the negro has established
for himself a reputation and credit, and is entitled to it
under the standard applying to the white man, he can

secure advances in the same manner. On the other hand, if the white man is the owner of only two mules, he gets his just as does the negro. Of negroes of reputation and credit, there are in the delta a great many; of white men without property there are, fortunately for all concerned, extremely few. It is a matter of credit, and not of race.

Nor is the business custom which thus discriminates an arbitrary one. Experience has taught no lesson more severely than that the average negro will throw away—and I use the expression advisedly—whatever money comes into his hands. If he would refrain from this practice for a few generations, he could own from top to bottom and from side to side the section in which I live. Even where money is furnished the ordinary negro, it has to be done most carefully; for experience with padded pay-rolls and cotton that failed to make in the bale what the figures promised in the picking is so common as to excite no comment. Aside, however, from any consideration of honesty, the number of negroes who will not squander and utterly misapply funds coming into their hands—whether received under a solemn obligation to use them in making good the security pledged, a growing crop, or as the result of twelve months of toil—is so small that considerations of common business necessity dictate the course pursued. The negroes who are independent renters supplying themselves, or land owners, constitute practically the small thrifty class.

As to the crop lien system, *per se,* I regard it as distinctly the poor man's opportunity. Under it a negro who is honest—honest with himself in his work, and honest with those with whom he deals—who does not

18

waste his money on excursions, picnics, crap games, whiskey, women and pinchbeck jewelry, can out of this soil easily and quickly become an independent man. The proposition appears too simple to argue. Knowing the capabilities of the soil, the cotton factor knows that it alone can be made to repay what he advances in its cultivation. Upon the security of a lien upon what it shall produce he is willing to make possible its cultivation by one who would otherwise be unable to obtain advances. I believe the figures submitted below will demonstrate that the delta negro, by the exercise of common thrift and economy, can become independent as the result of two or three years labor. But so long as he wastes his money and opportunities, as is now his too common habit, the particular system under which he accomplishes these barren results need occasion economists and himself but little concern. Because better results are not more visible in the way of a greater apparent negro prosperity, we sometimes hear it asserted that even here the black man is denied opportunities for his betterment. This is a superficial observation, based upon conditions resulting from a failure of a proper achievement, rather than from the absence of opportunity.

One of the greatest factors in our demand for negroes is the necessity of securing each year a great number of extra cotton pickers. It is an axiomatic proposition with us that no negro family will pick the cotton which it will raise. Not that it cannot be done; on the contrary in an average year, and by the exercise of due diligence, it can; but it will not. In order to save the crop it is necessary to employ additional pickers. The size of the stalk and the great number of bolls make cotton picking on alluvial land very easy work; the utter disregard, by planter and tenant alike, of the true economy of the situation makes it a lucrative employment. Picking is paid for without much regard to the price which cotton commands. Whether it be worth ten cents per pound or six, the price of picking remains very near to fifty cents per hundred pounds of seed cotton. During the fall months a good picker can easily average two hundred pounds, while many can pick as much as three hundred and fifty, per day. One of the most difficult matters of plantation management is to get the tenant to act upon the proposition that every hundred pounds of cotton picked by himself means a saving to him of the cost of picking. The opening of each season finds most of them clamorous for extra pickers.

To supply this autumnal demand for labor the towns empty themselves of great numbers of their negro population. The vagrant leaves for a season his accustomed haunts, the crap shooter and "rounder", in fewer numbers, betake themselves to the country to earn easily a few unfamiliarily honest dollars, and to ply their vocation among their rural friends, the cooks and washwomen desert their regular callings to such an extent as to make the season a time of dread for urban housekeepers. Yet this source of labor is soon exhausted, and the business of securing pickers from towns outside this section and from other states and other parts of Mississippi is regularly pursued by a number of negro "agents". Of the great number of negroes thus brought yearly into the delta, many remain to make crops themselves, attracted by the superior growth of cotton, and the display of money always incident to the season. I have seen more than a thousand dollars in silver paid out of a plantation office on Saturday night for extra picking alone, and in the presence of a curious, eager throng, coming from sections in which such a thing as a handful of negroes handling so much cash as the result of one week's plantation work would seem almost incredible. Such things, taken with the novel surroundings, the large talk of negroes making more cotton and handling more money than many white farmers elsewhere, the scale on which affairs are carried on, such as the measuring and selling of cotton seed by negroes by the ton instead of the bushel, the evidences of plenty and to spare furnished by the spendthrifts around them—for your delta darkey, especially when in the presence of his brother from some less favored section, is as free a spender as the world affords—all this tends to fire the stranger with a desire to come into this land of plenty. It is thus that much of our labor is recruited, and some of it the best we have especially during the first two or three years of residence.

So far as I can judge, the delta negro presents no peculiar social phenomena. His life is the same which the race leads in sections where its material opportunities are not so great. The only difference I can observe is that there may be a greater tendency to the commission of crimes against the person. For purposes of comparison, I have taken the negroes of a group composed of the nine counties of Mississippi where they are most largely outnumbered by the whites. To this group for convenience I shall apply the local designation, "hill" counties. In this group the proportion of whites to blacks is more than four to one, as against a reverse proportion of more than seven to one in the delta group. We have seen that in the latter the negroes constitute 18.8 per cent. of the total negro population of the state; in the hill group they constitute but 2.6 per cent. We have seen that the delta furnishes 21.7 per cent. of the negro state prison population; the hills contribute 3.4 per cent. A comparison of the crimes of the two groups discloses the fact that 50.1 per cent. of those in the hills and only 19.3 per cent. of those in the delta are burglaries, larcenies, forgeries and arsons. Crimes against the person make up 80.7 per cent. of the offenses of delta negroes, and 49.9 per cent. of those in the hills. It may seem somewhat singular that rape constitutes 6.2 per cent. of the graver crimes of the hill negroes, while, as has been shown, 4.9 are the figures for the delta. It is in the crimes of murder, manslaughter and attempts to kill that the delta negro exhibits his criminal propensity most strongly. These compose 75.8 per cent. of all of their felonies, and 43.7 per cent. of those of the hill negro. In the two crimes of larceny and burglary the hills district is far ahead of the other section, the percentage of total felonies being respectively 40.6 and 15.2.

In the lower class of negroes a predilection for petty gambling amounts almost to a passion. Their opportunity of indulging it depends upon their command of ready money. A majority of the murders committed in this section arise out of gambling. Therefore I would attribute the difference in the relative number of homicidal crimes committed by the negro in the two sections to the delta negro's greater command of money. Any one who has witnessed a genuine crap game, played as only the negro can play it, has no difficulty whatever in understanding how easy it is for human life to be taken in a dispute arising over the most trivial sum. It is an entirely conservative statement to say that on or near every delta plantation may be found from one to four regularly patronized crap tables, while in every town and village from one to a half-

dozen negro crap dives are run.   Around these tables,
specially on Saturday nights and Sundays, gather
crowds of men and boys of all ages, scarcely one in five
without a knife or pistol.   It takes but a word to bring
one or both into the game.   Making no attempt to estimate the number of such affrays in which both parties
are killed, and no trial possible, and not reckoning the
number of killings in which the surviving party
escapes, is acquitted by a jury or hanged, there are now
in the penitentiary from this section alone no less than
one hundred and fifty-four negroes serving sentences for
taking, or attempting to take, human life.   In the
courts of this group of counties there were for these
crimes in 1898 thirty-three convictions; in 1899,
twenty-nine; in 1900, thirty-three; in 1901, to September 30, thirty-seven.

It would be idle to discuss such a matter as the sexual
looseness which marks the conditions obtaining among
the masses of these people.   No new light could be
thrown upon it, and no good accomplished thereby.
It may be safely affirmed that the marriage contract
possesses for them little if any sanctity.   This may
seem a hard saying, but no man acquainted with the
facts will deny its truth.

In discussions of the negro we have been repeatedly
told of late years that the race should be judged by its
best element, and not by its worst, and that statistics of
criminality were an unfair index to negro conditions.
That it is unfair to base opinions and conclusions upon
partial investigations is true.   But it is equally true that
we cannot form just estimates by considering only the few
who have risen superior to general environments and are
confessedly exceptional.   The only true index to the
life of a people is furnished by a study of its masses—

its great general class. It is with this mass in my section that I am dealing, and my statements would lose none of their force or truth by being met with the counter claim that there are negroes here who lead decent, respectable lives. No race as a race can rise superior to the condition of its family unit, and it is the disregard of the marriage relation, the brutality of husbands to their wives and of both to their children, which will probably for a long while most impress the student of the negro masses, rather than the fact that here and there may be found families and individuals who have adopted for themselves standards obtaining generally among another people.

One of the traits which militates most against the negro here is his unreliability. Given certain conditions one may reason to fairly certain conclusions regarding a white man. It is not so with the negro. He presents a bundle of hopelessly unintelligible contradictions. Take his migratory habit for instance as one manifestation of his characteristic unreliability. The desire to move from place to place, the absence of local attachment, seems to be a governing trait in the negro character, and a most unfortunate one for the race. It has led to the fixed conviction on the part of many people having constant business relations with him that in this respect the negro cannot be depended upon at all and that the treatment he receives has but little real effect in shaping his course. It is undeniable that there is abundant ground for the most extreme opinion. His mental processes are past finding out, and he cannot be counted on to do or not to do a given thing under given circumstances. There is scarcely a planter in all this territory who would not gladly make substantial concessions for an assured tenantry. I do not mean for negroes who would stay with him always, and never take advantage of an opportunity for genuine betterment, but merely for such as would remain with him only so long as they were willing to work at all under the same conditions, and should receive honest and considerate treatment at his hands. Yet no planter among us can tell how many or which of his tenants of to-day will be his tenants of another year.

Not all negroes can become landed proprietors, any more than all mill operatives can become mill owners, or all wage earners capitalists. It is inevitable that there must always be a large class of negro tillers of other men's soil, corresponding to relative classes among all the races of mankind. It is then manifestly to the interests of these that they should seek for themselves conditions as nearly as possible approaching actual land ownership,—a fixed tenure, and the comforts of a home. This status need not mark the limit of advancement of all those entering it; it would but afford a stepping stone to such as proved themselves capable of turning good conditions into better. In all that I have said, I would not be understood as claiming that motives of self interest do not operate with the negro at all; I simply and emphatically assert that they do not at all intelligently control him.

The negroes in the delta not only make in the aggregate a tremendous amount of money, but they squander more than any similar class of people of whom I have any knowledge. There is no way of computing the amount expended by them in railway travel alone, but it is an enormous sum. This travel is for the most part entirely aimless, and it is a common thing for a negro to take a trip from a plantation to a town fifteen miles distant, with bare train fare in his pocket, and a crop badly in need of his attention at home. On Saturdays field work is practically suspended and the day is usually given up to such aimless moving about, or to assembling around stations and stores to witness the arrivals and departures of others.

The greatest diversions of these people, however, are excursions and the circus. The former come at irregular intervals, from four to six times a year, and mean trips of from eighty to one hundred and fifty miles. The money spent on this form of amusement is nothing in amount to the annual tribute poured into the coffers of the circus. In the months of October and November two of the largest of these concerns now exhibiting gave a total of ten performances in the delta. Making a careful and conservative estimate of the amounts spent on the three items of railroad fare, incidentals and admissions, the sum total could not have been under fifty thousand dollars.

Among our negroes we have few drunkards, and but few who do not drink; nor is the drinking by any means confined to the men. Considering the prevalence of the habit, the only surprising feature is that so few drunkards should be found.

The line of demarcation between rural and urban life is so indistinct and persons pass so constantly from one to the other that there is not much difference between the negroes of the town and those of the country. In each place we find the good, the bad and the indifferent. As in the country we have the moving, shiftless element, so do we also have the shiftless darkey of the town; as in the one place we have the land owner or prosperous tenant, so in the other we have the man who owns his home, and has steady employment at excellent wages; the "rounder," the pistol carrier and the professional crap shooter alike infest each. Throughout the delta there are negroes filling places of responsibility and trust. In the country the gin crews and engineers are practically all negroes, and there are negro foremen, agents and sub-managers. There are many constables, and there is in my county a negro justice of the peace. In my own town every mail carrier is a negro, and we have a negro on the police force. Some are employed by cotton factors and buyers, and earn from six hundred to a thousand dollars per annum. Others are employees of electric light companies, some are telephone linemen, and some are engaged in merchandising. Wages paid in the country range from fifty to seventy-five cents per day for common hands, though going sometimes to one dollar, up to $1.25 and $1.50 for gin crews. In levee work the commonest laborers receive $1.00 per day, and the more skilled $1.50. In towns the wages vary greatly. Hands in oil mills and compresses are paid from $1.00 to $2.00 per day, while the wages and earnings of porters, hackmen, dray drivers, teamsters, etc., range from ten to sixty dollars per month.

Mississippi makes no separate assessment of the property of the two races, and it is therefore impossible to arrive at the value of the property owned by the negro in the delta. The best that can be done is to estimate it. In 1900 the total assessed value of all the property in this group of counties was $29,095,167. Of this amount railroad property constituted $5,396,008, leaving a balance for realty and personality of $23,699,159. Without going into the methods employed in reaching the result, I conclude that a conservative estimate of the value of negro holdings would be, in round figures, not less than one million dollars. This is probably eucumbered to the extent of one half its value. I give this estimate as a minimum figure, and the correct value may be much greater. It is hardly possible to judge the extent of the increase in negro property, but it is considerable, though by no means in keeping with the opportunities of the race. But even now one cannot travel through this section without observing negro land owners everywhere. They are scattered over its entire area, holding tracts varying in size from a town lot to more than a thousand acres.

In considering the negro's condition and opportunities here, the factors assume important proportions. The amicable relations between the races, the peculiarly fertile soil—the absence of the necessity for fertilizers alone meaning a great deal—and the superior quality of the cotton produced. Of race relations enough has been said ; of the soil it is sufficient to say that it needs no fertilization. It has often been the occasion of curiosity to me to know what became of the fertilizer shown by the eleventh census to have been purchased by these counties. The amount expended is stated to have been only $12,472, it is true, with a value of farms and products of $16,771,090, but I have always doubted the accuracy of even these figures. Commercial fertilizer is an article unknown to us, and not handled by our dealers in plantation supplies.

The figures of the last census showing the comparative cotton acreage yield of this section, the state and the south, are not available, but it is not likely that much variation will be shown from those of the eleventh. These exhibit an average yield per acre of lint cotton for the south of 176.67 pounds, and for the state of Mississippi of 191.03 pounds. The yield of this county group was 257.87 pounds. It is only fair to state that the average of the state was increased by that of counties lying partly in the delta, but which, as explained above, have not been included here. While for a given year we have this average, the standard yield is with us five hundred pounds, and large areas will show a yield ranging between this and four hundred.

The cotton grown on this soil is much superior, both in the quality of its fiber and the length of its staple, to upland varieties. Taking its name from the fact of its growth in the bends of the Mississippi river at a time when it found its way to the port of New Orleans by means of boats plying that stream, it is known to the Liverpool, New Orleans and eastern markets as "benders," and commands a premium of about half a cent per pound over "uplands."

[1] In conclusion I shall submit some of the features and results of a personal experiment with negro labor, carried on under conditions differing somewhat from those generally obtaining. Several years' experience in cotton planting led to certain conclusions relative to the usual manner of handling plantation labor. I became convinced for one thing that too much lattitude was allowed the negro in the matter of his account and in the handling of his crop. Observation and experience satisfied me that better results could be obtained, for both the negro and the planter, by requiring the former to conform more strictly to business rules, and by making the relations between the two, in crop and money matters, more nearly of a purely business character. I also entertained the belief, not yet entirely dissipated that a reliable, industrious, and largely self-sustaining, plantation tenantry could be built up by effort along proper

[1] The plan outlined here was a gradual development. In its execution credit is due Mr. Julian H. Fort, my business associate, and Mr. Carl Owens, manager of Dunleith plantation.

lines, coupled with a degree of liberality at the outset not entirely consistent with the general purpose of putting the negro on a strictly business footing.

Even casual observation will show that the greatest opportunity enjoyed by the negro for acquiring property is as a renter. It was determined, therefore, to adopt the rent system. The greatest objection to it is that, as it ordinarily obtains, it allows the negro privileges which he too often abuses. He does not take kindly to suggestion or direction as to what he shall plant, and wants to put practically all his land in cotton because it is a cash crop; he thinks he should be left free to work his crop when and as he pleases, which means frequently neglect, and oftener improper cultivation; having control of mules, he thinks that he should enjoy the privileges of riding them about the country, when both he and they should be at work, and of neglecting and poorly feeding them, if he so elect; in short, that he should enjoy various privileges and immunities which it is impossible to recite, but which are usually accorded by the custom of the country. These things mean that the negro as a renter is generally undesirable, often troublesome, and that his cultivation of land causes deterioration. To rent and yet avoid the difficulties ordinarily incident to the system was a problem solved by the use of a contract specifying in detail what was undertaken by each party, and reserving to the plantation management absolute control over all plantation affairs.

There is generally a great disproportion between the negro's ideas and his ability of execution; he wants to plant on as large a scale as possible, and will usually "overcrop" himself, undertake more land than he can cultivate, leading to the neglect of some, or all, of it.

It was accordingly determined to allot to each family only so much as it could cultivate thoroughly under all ordinary contingencies, believing that not only more money but an actually greater yield could be had by the tenant from twenty acres well handled than from twenty-five half neglected. Mules and implements were sold at reasonable prices and on two years time, one-half the purchase price payable annually. For handling the crop to the best advantage, as regards economy and grade, a thoroughly equipped gin plant was substituted for a less modern one, aud as a means of lessening the cost of living to the tenant, and of encouraging the raising of corn, it was provided with a mill capable of making an excellent quality of meal, far more nutritious than the purchased, kiln dried article. The latter is operated once a week, the grinding being done for toll only, a bushel of meal being exchanged for a bushel of shelled corn. It may be remarked that during the three years of its operation there has been a marked increase in the demand for its services among the negroes of the neighborhood, many coming to it from distances of five and seven miles. Exercising the contract right of requiring the planting of as much corn as was deemed expedient, it was agreed, in return, that all surplus corn raised by the tenant would be taken off his hands at the market price.

In the accomplishment of the general objects in view, it was of as much interest to the plantation as to the tenant that the best possible price be realized for the latter's cotton. For this and other reasons, the privilege of absolutely controlling his crop was denied him. This was clearly stipulated in his contract, but he was not denied all voice in its disposition. He could sell it to the plantation, if a mutually satisfactory price could be agreed upon, or he could let it go forward with the general crop, and have an accounting for its proceeds. One of the essentials to successful cotton growing here is thorough drainage. With this the tenant has nothing to do, it being stipulated that the land is to be kept well drained without cost to him.

Believing that not only is the laborer entitled to proper shelter, but that comfortable homes are a matter of plantation economy, these tenants are furnished excellently constructed houses, well lighted and heated. Each house has its driven well, kept in repair as an item of plantation expense. These houses, with the exception of some of three and four rooms, contain two rooms each, and are constructed with a view to accommodating a family working eighteen acres of land, that being the amount, per average family, from which the best results are found to be obtainable. It has been determined, however, in order to avoid any possibility of crowding, to add a third room to each of these houses. This is now being done, and within a year there will be no two-room houses remaining. Every effort is made to encourage tenants to raise gardens, and to own cattle and hogs, abundant pasturage being provided free. The proper care of live stock is rendered compulsory by close supervision.

To reduce the matter of advancing supplies as nearly as possible to a business system, a furnishing basis of fifty cents per acre, per month, for supplies only, was fixed upon. Incidentals usually require about twenty-five cents per acre additional. Each month the tenant is furnished a coupon book for the amount, in money, of his supplies, a twenty acre family receiving a ten dollar book, thirty acres securing one of fifteen dollars, and so forth. These books are good only for supplies, such as meat, meal, tobacco, snuff and molasses, but it is agreed with the tenant that such coupons as he may have left in his book at the expiration of each month will be honored for whatever he wants. This is done with a view to encouraging economy, and to enable him to secure "extras" without increasing his account. Getting their meal without cost, by grinding corn, and getting flour in its stead out of their books, none of those who were on the plantation last year failed this year to secure with surplus coupons an abundance of sugar, coffee, rice, etc., at the end of each month to carry them through the following. This system possesses several advantages, not the least of which are that it saves the making of numerous small ledger entries, and enables the tenant to tell at any time during the month, from his unused coupons, the exact amount he has left to his credit, so that he may govern himself accordingly. The negroes regard the system with the utmost satisfaction, and would not exchange it for the usual method of "issuing rations".

To make a success of the system outlined here, three things were absolutely necessary: the utmost patience and good sense at the office, wise management, in the field, and discrimination in selecting tenants. Every negro known to be a professional crap shooter or pistol carrier was run off the place, all families known to be quarrelsome and troublesome were got rid of, and everybody whom it was necessary to compel to work was let go. Under no circumstances is a professional "exhorter", or lodge organizing preacher, allowed on the property. The virtue of patience has been exercised to a degree that has more than once threatened its destruction.

It would be manifestly unfair to judge such an experiment by its first year. This was a most troublesome, and, to the management, rather discouraging experience. Little was accomplished beyond getting affairs in easier running order. The third year is not yet closed, but promises results about in keeping with the second, the complete figures of which are available. There were in cultivation in 1900 thirteen hundred acres. The total value of the product was $54,000, an average of a little more than $41.50 per acre. There were on the place sixty-one families, containing eighty men and eighty-one women, including children old enough to work, and sixty-seven younger children, a total of 228 persons in families. These families occupied sixty-one houses, containing 147 rooms, an average of 1.5 persons to the room. There was an average of 3.7 persons to the family, while the average number of hands who assisted at some stage of the crop was 2.6. In addition to the families, there were eighteen wages hands employed, who, though separately housed, must be added to the number of working hands, giving a total of 179. We thus have an average acreage to the working hand of 7.2, with an average product value of $301.67 per hand. Cotton was raised to the value of $41,000, being 818 bales of 500 pounds average, or 4.5 bales, 2250 pounds, to the working hand. The yield was in excess of 450 pounds per acre of cotton land. It should be stated that while these wages hands assisted in various stages of the crop not all their time was thus employed by any means, for some tenants did not need extra hands at all. They were used, when not in crops, in clearing new land, ditching, and other plantation work.

19

The negroes with whom we started, in January, 1899, with possibly three exceptions, had absolutely nothing, barring their clothing, bedding and furniture,—all of the scantiest and poorest kind. It would be a most liberal estimate to put their entire belongings at that date at an average value per family of $30. Yet they were an average lot of plantation negroes; they were of many ages, and came from many sections; of the older ones, most had had something, but had lost it in shifting from pillar to post, and at fifty and sixty years of age were empty handed; some had lived on a dozen different plantations in as many years. They had thus to start with us actually owing for their first week's supplies. After the lapse of three years, the average value of the property owned by the sixty and more families on the place may be conservatively estimated at $200. This, of course, includes no cash on hand or to their credit on our books. After paying their accounts, the tenants on the place in 1900 received $11,000 in cash. Their balances this year will amount to about the same figure. They have good clothing, their houses are now comfortably furnished, and for cooking purposes the open fire place has given way to the kitchen stove.

The following statement is drawn directly from the plantation ledger of 1900. It is the account of two men who worked together as a family. These hands were above the average in point of steadiness and efficiency, but the account is fairly illustrative of the possibilities to the negro of good soil, fair prices, hard work and economy. It will be noted that the value of their product per acre appears to be greater by about eight dollars than the average of the plantation, but this apparent difference will be explained by stating that in computing the latter the entire acreage of the plantation was included. If we exclude from consideration all raw, first year land, such as was not allotted to renters, the difference will be shown to be very much less.

ACCOUNT.

DEBTS.

Land rent, 21 acres, $6	126 00
Mule, paid for entirely in first year,	100 00
Gear and implements	18 50
Planting seed	10 30
Seed corn	1 15
Supply account	98 25
Sundries	18 20
Picking 6 ½ bales cotton	59 45
Ginning and wrapping 19 bales cotton, 500 lbs. av.	57 10
Mule feed	43 50
	$532 95

CREDITS.

Nineteen bales cotton	865 14
Cotton seed—9.4 tons	117 75
Corn—105 bushels—market price at time, 50 cts.	52 50
	$1035 39

Profits $502.44.

Holding their corn, they had, as the result of the year's operations, property worth $171.00. It will be seen that their cash crop overpaid their account by $449.94.

As to the effect of the showing exhibited here upon the negro, if any, it is impossible to judge. Some of those who had least at the outset and have most to-day are preparing to leave—though they may change their minds in a night, after having made their arrangements to depart, while some have already left. To arrive at a just conclusion on this point at least five years would be required, and only such tenants as removed to other places to continue the tenant relation could be considered in enumerating the removals. It would be manifestly unfair, in considering the extent and influence of a migratory, restless habit, to attribute to it such as were actuated by opportunity and desire to purchase land. Of those who have thus far left the place, not one has done so to become a land owner.

All that I have said of general conditions in the delta applies, in greater or less degree, to all the 29,790 square miles of the alluvial valley of the Mississippi. The future of this territory will inevitably be linked with the future of the American negro. The movements of black population, as indicated by the last three censuses, show this clearly enough. In discussing the conditions surrounding the negro in the Yazoo–Mississippi delta, I have not attempted to present such a picture of rural felicity as John Stuart Mill quotes from Chateauvieux of the metayers of Piedmont. But I am well within the limits of conservatism when I assert that in the material potentialities of his environment the situation of the negro here is infinitely superior to that of any European peasant. It is not claimed that there are no instances of injustice to the negro. Not at all. But I do claim that nowhere else is his general treatment fairer,—nowhere is his remedy more certain. This is but corollary to the proposition that nowhere in the same extent of territory will be found a greater or more constant demand for his labor. Nowhere does he find a better market for his service, nowhere is he freer to change his local habitation.

To say how long conditions, particularly as regards the relations between the races, will remain as they are, would be to enter the field of speculation,—a pastime in which I am not engaged. The presentation which I have attempted is believed to be a not unfaithful portrayal of the present; with what the future holds in store, this paper has no concern.

DISCUSSION.

LE GRAND POWERS: In expressing my profound appreciation of the very able paper of Mr. Stone I believe that I voice the sentiment of all who have listened to it. He has placed the members of the society and all stndents of American social and industrial problems under a lasting obligation for his very lucid statement of the social and economic situation in the black belt of Mississippi. He is a resident of the section under discussion. He has lived and labored with and among the people of whom he has spoken so intelligently. I can not speak from his point of view. I have never visited the counties with which his paper deals, so I must approach the problem mainly from a theoretical point of view. All my studies lead me, however, to believe that Mr. Stone has most faithfully portrayed the conditions that prevail in his section. Permit me, however, to compare conditions as he finds them with those in other parts of Mississippi and in the other states of the nation. I do this that we may ascertain, if possible, what industrial organization offers the greatest probability of the black man rising in the moral, intellectual, and economic scale.

In the nine counties contained in the Yazoo–Mississippi delta the negro, as has been stated by Mr. Stone, is almost the only worker on the farms, in the factories, and about the homes. He performs not less than 95 per cent. of the labor on farms. In such a county as Issaquena he performs not less than 90 per cent. of such labor. Practically then, the negro in these counties does not come into competition with white labor on the same plane. Neither is he associated at any point on an industrial equality with the white man. The negro does the work ; the white man is his acknowledged superior. The two races live and work in worlds that have but little in common.

In these nine counties the twelfth census reports 32,291 separate agricultural holdings, including as a holding or farm the land tilled by a given individual or family or for whose cultivation the tiller assumes a formal responsibility, bears the losses and pockets the gains, if any there be. Of these farms and holdings only 2,629 were operated by whites, and the remainder, 29,662 or 92.9 per cent. were operated by negroes. Of these negro farmers 2,091 or 7.1 per cent. owned some interest, great or small, in the land which they tilled. Let these figures be compared with those of the nine counties in the southeastern part of the state, the counties of Clarke, Greene, Harrison, Jackson, Jasper, Jones, Lauderdale, Perry and Wayne. These counties contain 14,629 farms, of which 9,315 or 63.7 per cent are operated by whites. The proportion of whites is relatively nearly eight times as great as in the nine counties of the delta. In these counties where more than one-half of the work on farms is done by white labor, the negro works where he can compare the results of his labor with those of the white man. He sees white men toiling and struggling and saving under the conditions such as those under which he must toil and save and struggle should he attain any competence or rise in the industrial scale. What is the result? In these counties where there are nearly two white farmers to every black one, there are 5,314 negroes in charge of farms or agricultural holdings. Of their number 2,374 or 44.7 per cent. own the whole or some part of the farms which they till. The number of black farm owners is therefore relatively six times as great as in the delta counties where the black man is never in sight of a white man struggling under the same conditions as himself.

The negro starts in the industrial race heavily weighted. He is terribly handicapped by all the vicious and unreliable qualities which Mr. Stone has pictured. The negro can rise industrially only by the practice of the same virtues which advance the white man. He can acquire those virtues only by imitation or by the hard experience of life. The figures for the two sets of Mississippi counties show that in the nine hill counties with two white farmers for every negro this quality of imitation has been a tremendous uplifting power for the economic advancement of the colored man. In those counties the soil is inferior and the other material conditions less favorable than in the delta, and yet relatively the negro makes six times the progress.

The drifting of the negroes to the delta or their clannish separation by themselves, their drawing away from the white men of the south, is therefore to be considered, from an industrial point of view, a great mistake for the race. Their hope is in the white man of the south. This is true in all parts of the south. In the sections where the whites out-number the negroes, the negro must learn of the white man as his leader and teacher, and by imitation. In the delta and similar sections where the black man is segregated by his own acts or by the acts of others, it is otherwise. For such a section when pondering upon the economic progress of the black man I see but little hope save through experiments such as Mr. Stone has been making, where by the stern lesson of experience the negro is forced to learn what in the hill counties of the south and in the counties of the north the negro learns in part by imitation from the whites.

What is true with reference to industrial matters I believe to be equally true with reference to morals and all that can bless, dignify and ennoble humanity. So far as I have had time critically to study Mr. Stone's figures relating to crime given by him to me in conversation, I read from them the same lesson that I have, from an industrial point of view, found in the census data given here.

The negro's contact and intimate relation with the white race has been and is the most potent factor for elevating their morals, as well as further reducing crime among them. Mr. Stone's figures show that murder, man-slaughter and attempts to kill are at least twice as frequent relatively among the delta negroes as in the counties with a preponderance of whites. He tells us about a large number of attempts at killing and also of rape upon colored women which have never been brought sufficiently to the public attention to be noted. These offences are far less frequent in the other counties. If account be taken of this fact it seems clear that the negro's brutal lust is more devilish in its violence in the delta than elsewhere, only the white women are not its victims. In the same way when account is taken of the relative opportunities for committing crimes against property ranked as felony in the delta and in the other counties, the student finds his hope for the black man centered in the counties where the whites out-number the blacks. The negro is an imitative being. Like all people on a low plane of civilization he needs the influence of example. This is the most important single factor in his elevation, and hence from the moral as well as industrial point of view we are to regret his segregation in the delta counties, or in our city slums where he sees and comes in contact but little with the best side of the white man's civilization, with its patient, continous labor, its personal frugality, its practice of the virtues. But when there is such segregation, again the only hope of any great advance for the negro is not in the material resources of the section where he makes his home, but in the self-sacrificing devotion to his real interests which we find exhibited by Mr. Stone and the best white leaders of the south.

Mr. STONE : I have not had access to the data which Mr. Powers has referred to here, but I want to say a few words which will to a certain extent explain it. In order for these figures to illustrate the conditions as they really are, we must take into consideration the difference in the stability of population,—the length of time the negroes have lived in the nine counties of which he speaks, and the age of the negro population of the section which is covered in my discussion. Take the figures and make a comparison,—a just comparison. You must take the same number of people who have lived in the two districts the same length of time to see what has been accomplished. Now another factor which bears materially upon the value of the conclusions reached by Mr. Powers is that the lands in the counties to which he refers are in very many instances practically valueless. I know of a negro who bought five hundred acres of land over there at a price per acre which was one-fourth what he would pay in my section as rent. He bought it at a dollar and a half per acre, and if he had rented land from me or any other delta planter he would have had to pay six dollars or more per annum. Over in my section of the country, according to the showing made by Mr. Powers, the negroes do not own as much land, but when they do acquire a piece of property they have something which is valuable. There are negroes in my section who are individually able to buy about all the land owned by all the negroes in the counties referred to by Mr. Powers.

Mr. POWERS: I would say that all facts in my possession confirm the statement relating to the average value of land in the several counties, as made by Mr. Stone. But here is a general fact concerning white men as a class which Mr. Stone seems to overlook. They get along in a material way better where material conditions are most favorable. They make better progress on good land than on poor land; in good times than in bad times. The same rule should apply to negroes. I think it does, other things being the same; and when it does not apply we can justly affirm that the difference is due to other causes, and not to the variation in land values to which Mr. Stone calls attention. Thus in Mississippi, in the eastern counties, under the hard conditions described by Mr. Stone, the negroes make some headway in acquiring land. They make a fair showing in which every lover of his kind can justly take interest. It is the reverse, so far as his position is concerned, in the delta counties with their rich, alluvial soil and all material conditions favorable. What is the reason for this difference? What factor is present affecting favorably the negro in the eastern counties with their poor soil, and acting unfavorably upon him in the counties with the good land? I find but one: the presence or absence of the white man and of his example on a plane that the negro can comprehend and imitate. Hence I assert that the negro profits by the example of the white man, and suffers when he can not have him as a model to follow and to imitate.

CONCILIATION AND ARBITRATION IN THE COAL MINING INDUSTRY.

BY HERMAN JUSTI.

The title of this paper would give the impression that a uniform system of conciliation and arbitration designed to settle disputes and to prevent strikes is in general use in the coal mining industry throughout the country. Unfortunately this is not the case. I am not prepared to say exactly how these troubles are treated in other states, and shall, therefore, confine myself to the coal mining industry of Illinois.

JOINT MEETING OF MINERS AND OPERATORS.

The plan pursued in Illinois, it is fair to state, has been made possible by reason of the existence of what is known as the interstate-joint-movement. The movement was inaugurated in January, 1898, following the sad and memorable strike of 1897 by the coal miners and coal operators of Pennsylvania, Ohio, Indiana and Illinois, whereby the two interests adopted a system of joint agreements under which the mining scale the scale of wages and the mining conditions are agreed upon for what is known as the basing point in each of the states named, and these, while always agreed upon during the joint-convention in January and February of each year, do not become effective until April 1st following.

After the interstate convention the coal operators and the coal miners of these respective states are accustomed to meet in joint state convention and enter into another agreement determining mining rates based on basic rates theretofore agreed upon in the interstate convention, and to agree upon such wages and mining conditions not common alike to all the four states but peculiar to and necessary for each state.

In Illinois, where the mining conditions vary more than in other coal-producing states, and where the state is divided into nine scale districts, and some of these into sub-districts, and where it is sometimes necessary for individual mine owners or mining companies to act independently of all other mines because of exceptional or unusual conditions, the coal operators and coal miners, after the adjournment of the joint state convention, hold what are known as sub-district, or district, conventions, or local conferences, and agree upon wages and mining conditions suited to the peculiar needs of these respective districts or mines.

To establish a better understanding of the objects of these numerous conventions it may be well to observe that, primarily, the interstate-joint-movement is founded upon the idea of uniformity based upon equitable trade or competitive conditions.

After the several conventions or conferences in which the coal miners and coal operators have had their hand-to-hand fights and their heart-to-heart talks, it is fair to assume that both miners and operators should have reached a pretty clear understanding, not so much as to what each side believed itself entitled, but as to what it was possible for each side to get, and what must satisfy them during the contract year; and yet time, money, and men are employed to prevent strikes and lockouts and to settle differences and disputes.

After an agreement has once been reached in this manner, it still remains to be seen, despite all the safeguards and precautions provided, how well all of its conditions have been carried out, both by the employer and the employee, when the record is complete and a balance struck at the close of the contract year.

PLAN OF ENFORCING JOINT AGREEMENTS.

The officials of the Mine Workers' Union of Illinois, as the representatives of the miners, see to it that the miners' rights under the terms of the several joint agreements are fully protected, while the commissioner of the Illinois Coal Operators' Association, on the other hand, representing the employer class, contends for compliance with these same joint agreements, in behalf of the operators. The representatives of these two organizations are expected to force jointly upon their members faithful compliance with these agreements; to take up and consider all differences and disputes arising during the contract year; and perform all such useful offices as seem necessary for preserving harmony in the coal-producing industry of the state.

Surprise is often expressed that, despite so many safeguards and precautions—despite so fair a scheme of mutual protection—differences, disputes and conflicts nevertheless occur daily, somewhere, in the state. There is, perhaps, something in or about the atmosphere of a mine that breeds conflict—there may be something in the nature of the work of miners calculated unduly to arouse in their breasts the rebellious spirit implanted in our common humanity. But, be this as it may, the mining camp has been a veritable battle ground, here and elsewhere, from time out of mind. Here is presented a fruitful field for the work of a speculative philosopher; but this paper is presumed to treat only of actualities, of stubborn, difficult, irresistible facts, and I shall not venture into the realm of speculation.

Why, then, is there so much trouble in enforcing an agreement so carefully prepared and seemingly so equitable in all its provisions?

PECULIAR COMPLICATIONS IN ILLINOIS.

Speaking of the coal industry of Illinois, it may be safely suggested that the great difficulty of enforcing strict compliance with these carefully prepared agreements is due to the fact that the mining conditions of the state vary more than anywhere else in the country; that there are over 800 coal mines in the state, of which about 600 represent only five per cent. of the shipping mines; that of the 40,000 miners employed fully 40 per cent. are ignorant of our language; that these agreements are made with an organization of laborers as yet not strong enough always rigidly to enforce them; and that employers of labor until recently each fought the fight in his own way, regardless of consequences entailed upon the coal industry as a whole. It is, then, not so strange, after all, that operators still concede demands of the miners which prove dangerous and mischievous precedents, and that it is, therefore, necessary each year that our joint contracts be drawn with increasing care and precision. Otherwise the miners, with the union behind them, and knowing, as they do, a weak employer's anxiety to keep his mines going at almost any sacrifice, would be uncontrollable. Even so, unjustified demands are made, despite pledges and promises, and, therefore, in the hope of preventing, if possible, any unwarranted demands being made during the contract year, a concluding clause has been inserted in the last two state agreements, which provides that "there shall be no demands made locally that are not specifically set forth in this agreement, except as agreed to in joint sub-district meetings held prior to April 1st." In spite of this wise provision demands have been made locally, and much too often foolishly conceded; but considering the vastness and variety of the coal industry, these have been, comparatively speaking, very few in number, and in themselves trifling in importance, but a concession made, however trifling, is a dangerous precedent, for which the discipline of the miner and the interests of the owner always pay dearly sooner or later.

THE ILLINOIS PLAN OF CONCILIATION AND ARBITRATION.

I am expected to describe the system of conciliation and arbitration in use in the coal mining industry of Illinois. There is not really much system about it. It is, after all, nothing more than a simple, effective, humane, common-sense arrangement of getting together on common ground in the hope of reaching a fair understanding. It is nothing more nor less than a sort of balance-wheel of a great industry—albeit a device intended to keep the men at work long enough to enable them and their employers to think calmly and dispassionately over questions in dispute, certain that if this be done a fair adjustment of all differences will surely be made. In fact our joint agreements provide that where differences or disputes have arisen "the miners and mine laborers and parties involved must continue at work pending an investigation and adjustment." At a period not very remote it was the universal custom to stop a mine whenever any dispute arose or when a demand was made, and idle it remained until the operator yielded or the miners were exhausted. This clause of the joint agreement is still violated far too often ; but even so, it is a tremendous advance movement which has resulted in great saving of time and money to master and men alike. In the hope of still further abating this annoying and costly practice, the miners' organization, at its annual convention of 1901, incorporated a clause in its constitution imposing a fine of "ten dollars upon each miner who from any cause threw the mine idle." Where this penalty is rigidly enforced it has had a salutary effect, but for reasons which must be apparent the penalty has not always been imposed.

In another year it is to be hoped that the penalty will not only be more rigidly enforced, but the United Mine Workers will go even further, and for flagrant violation of the agreement make the punishment, if necessary, expulsion from the union. This may seem to be undue severity, but if the penalty be inflicted only a few times we shall see vastly fewer flagrant violations of the agreement. The miners' organization, like a chain cable, cannot be stronger than its weakest link, and if it be weak at any point it is just where it should be strongest, and that is in its ability to enforce compliance with the contracts entered into between the two organizations. The power of the organization is, as I have said on another occasion, not great enough save where its power is unhappily used for mischief. A strong advocate of organizations, both of the labor and the capital classes, this frank criticism of existing conditions seems necessary. Lest I be accused of neglecting to suggest a penalty to be imposed upon employers shutting down their mines contrary to agreement, or otherwise flagrantly violating it, I beg to say that the Illinois Coal Operators' Association in its constitution makes ample provision for the punishment of its members thus guilty of bad faith. But even were it silent on the subject, or if the operators failed to enforce any prescribed penalties, the miners have it in their power to discipline them, which they always do, and sometimes unlawfully, because they too often convict and punish them before trial.

VALUE OF FRIENDLY COUNCIL.

While I shall try plainly to describe the plan of conciliation and arbitration pursued in Illinois, still it seems that what you most desire to know is not so much how differences and disputes are settled, but what it is that occasions these differences and disputes, and how to prevent them; for it is easy enough for fair men of average intelligence to determine upon a plan by which their difficulties may be settled, if only they can be brought to agree upon the real causes leading up to these difficulties. This is our objective point in Illinois.

With scarcely an exception, every strike that has taken place in our time, even where there has been bloodshed and destruction of property, has finally been settled in friendly council. Our plan is to prevent these senseless and costly strikes, and the many differences and disputes arising between master and men which seem to place them in the attitude of enemies to each other, are settled in the same manner in which the most destructive strikes are finally settled by meeting in friendly council where we try self control long enough to enable us to say: "Come, let us reason together." This is, practically, all there is of the plan pursued in the coal mining industry of Illinois, and of this plan to prevent strikes and to promote harmony and good feeling it can be said, at least, that it is the fairest thus far offered. Under it every inducement for doing right and of avoid-

ing conflict is afforded, and its application proves that
such a plan could have been inspired only by high and
honorable motives. This honest tribute is due the coal
operators of Illinois, who inaugurated the plan in their
state, and to the officials of the mine workers who have
cordially supported it. And yet the plan is not perfect.
It is only a beginning, but it is a good and hopeful beginning, as I shall endeavor to show. That it will be
amplified and improved I confidently believe ; and the
sooner all the coal-producing states organize for the
purpose of dealing with labor questions, the sooner this
amplification and improvement will occur. What we
need in the meantime is patience with our present ills
and a steady purpose to keep the faith in holding to
agreements which we are ever trying to make plainer
in their language and fairer in their provisions. In
truth, growing experience has made it possible to draw
these agreements so that they are becoming ever more
and more exact each year, the aim being to make the
language and terms used so plain that the chances of
misunderstanding any of the terms of the compact are
steadily reduced. Disputes arising during the year,
which have not been covered by the provisions of the
current contract, have been taken up at the next annual convention and clauses inserted in the new agreement designed to cover them, so that, seemingly, nothing is left in doubt.

CARE OBSERVED IN DRAFTING ANNUAL CONTRACTS.

To illustrate the care with which every part of the
agreement is drawn, I will quote section 13 of the
current state agreement ; and I have taken this section
as an illustration because the points it seeks to cover are
the ones which have given operators and miners the

greatest amount of trouble and have been the occasion of oft-repeated strikes and lockouts. This section reads as follows :

(*a*) The duties of the pit committee shall be confined to the adjustment of disputes between the pit boss and any of the members of the United Mine Workers of America working in and around the mine, for whom a scale is made, arising out of this agreement or any sub-district agreement made in connection herewith, where the pit boss and said miner or mine laborer have failed to agree.

(*b*) In case of any local trouble arising at any shaft through such failure to agree between the pit boss and any miner or mine laborer, the pit committee and the miners' local president and the pit boss are empowered to adjust it ; and in the case of their disagreement it shall be referred to the superintendent of the company and the president of the miners' local executive board, where such exists, and should they fail to adjust it—and in all other cases—it shall be referred to the superintendent of the company and the miners' president of the sub-district ; and should they fail to adjust it, it shall be referred in writing to the officials of the company concerned and the state officials of the U. M. W. of A. for adjustment ; and in all such cases the miners and mine laborers and parties involved must continue at work pending an investigation and adjustment until a final decision is reached in the manner above set forth.

(*c*) If any day men refuse to continue at work because of a grievance which has or has not been taken up for adjustment in the manner provided herein, and such action shall seem likely to impede the operation of the mine, the pit committee shall immediately furnish a man or men to take such vacant place or places at the scale rate, in order that the mine may continue at work ; and it shall be the duty of any member or members of the United Mine Workers who may be called upon by the pit boss or pit committee to immediately take the place or places assigned to him or them in pursuance hereof.

(*d*) The pit committee in the discharge of its duties shall under no circumstances go around the mine for any cause whatever, unless called upon by the pit boss or by a miner or company man who may have a grievance that he cannot settle with the boss ; and as its duties are confined to the adjustment of any such grievances, it is understood that its members shall not draw any compensation except while actively engaged in the discharge of said duties. The foregoing shall not be construed to prohibit the pit committee from looking after the matter of membership dues and initiations in any proper manner.

(*e*) Members of the pit committee employed as day men shall not leave their places of duty during working hours, except by permission of the operator, or in cases involving the stoppage of the mine.

(*f*) The operator or his superintendent or mine manager shall be respected in the management of the mine and the direction of the working force. The right to hire must include, also, the right to discharge ; and it is not the purpose of this agreement to abridge the rights of the employer in either of these respects. If, however, any employe shall be suspended or discharged by the company and it is claimed that an injustice has been done him, an investigation to be conducted by the parties and in the manner set forth in the paragraphs (*a*) and (*b*) of this section shall be taken up at once, and if it is determined that an injustice has been done, the operator agrees to reinstate said employe and pay him full compensation for the time he has been suspended and out of employment ; provided, if no decision shall be rendered within five days the case shall be considered closed in so far as compensation is concerned.

APPLYING BUSINESS METHODS TO BUSINESS MATTERS.

Thus it will be seen that the effort of the Illinois Coal Operators' Association and of the United Mine Workers of Illinois is not so much directed to establishing a well-defined and elaborate plan of arbitration or conciliation as it is to prevent all manner of differences and disputes and so obviate the necessity for conciliation or arbitration itself. The idea, after all, is that these agreements are nothing more nor less than business contracts, such as business men generally enter into and peform every day of the year—contracts which must either be respected or repudiated. It is not necessary in other departments of business to establish special tribunals designed to adjust differences that grow out of contracts or agreements between business men, and they should not be necessary in a large percentage of disputes growing out of these agreements between employer and employee. That is what the movement in Illinois is aiming at—the application of business methods to business matters. If respected, the business idea is carried out ; if repudiated, it is war. The issue is clearly defined in clause (*b*) of the section I have read, which plainly binds the men to remain at work pending an investigation and adjustment of any and all differences and disputes arising between the employer and his employees. The miners' officials, under this clause, must keep the men at work. If the men strike, the officials must put them back to work, or admit that they are powerless to do so, or plainly declare their intention to repudiate the contract ; and in either of these contingencies the joint trade agreement idea is doomed.

WHERE MUCH FAULT LIES.

During the current year the largest percentage of suspensions or strikes resulted from a violation of clause (*c*) of section 13, and the class of labor most offending under this provision was primarily the drivers, who refused to work at the scale of wages agreed upon, and then by a refusal of the miners to take their places in order that a suspension of work might be avoided. These drivers are an interesting class, in many respects, and not wholly unlike the mules they drive. They are, as a rule, small men, fleet of foot, hardy, stubborn, and great "kickers." In mines where electric haulage has not yet been introduced they are indispensable. Next to the driver question, most trouble has been occasioned by the demand made for the reinstatement of employees who had been discharged. This subject is covered by clause (*f*) of section 13. If this clause could be rigidly enforced the standing of union labor and the discipline of mines in which it is employed would be established in a way to help enormously union labor and those employing it. But unfortunately the miners' officials are often forced to appear as condoning offenses which they know to be indefensible. These officials often live under the lash of jealous and suspicious subordinates or constituents. If the tenure of office of miners' officials could be lengthened and made more certain, and if instead of the beggarly

salaries they receive they were paid salaries com-
mensurate with the value of services performed, if conservative, intelligent, fair-minded laborers belonging to
the miners' organization would attend the meetings of
their local unions and drive from power the radicals and
mischief-makers so often in control, organized labor
would advance by leaps and bounds, and with the approval and consent of the great army of employers who
now regard them with aversion and fear.

MODUS OPERANDI.

As for the plan pursued in settling all questions referred to the Illinois Commission, it is very simple.
When the disputes or differences arise the representatives of the United Mine Workers meet us by agreement
and with them the miners and operators who are directly
interested. Together these representatives of the two
interests, without observing any prescribed form, meet
and proceed to hear testimony, with a view of eliciting
all the facts bearing upon the questions involved. There
is seldom any attempt made to gain any advantage by
confusing witnesses, and every time it is attempted the
difficulties of settlement are at once increased. Our aim
is to encourage witnesses to tell the truth, in order that
disputes, if settled at all, may be settled upon their merits
solely. The main idea of these investigations is to bring
out clearly the exact facts, and when this is done we
have found that nearly all ordinary troubles adjust themselves before we have been a great while in session.
The great advantage of such meetings is that it affords
employer and employee an opportunity to meet upon
common ground, and that long-standing grievances for
which there had been little or no foundation can be
brushed aside, and that the representatives of miners and

operators alike can avail themselves of an excellent opportunity to explain the meaning of the joint agreements; the purposes they are intended to serve and the importance of complying with the spirit as well as the letter of such agreements.

We have found it all-important whenever disputes or differences arise to take them up promptly. In fact, we are endeavoring to get the local officials of the Miners' Union and the mine manager to settle differences and disputes among themselves, where it is at all possible, because it has been found that all differences and disputes are most readily settled as near their source as possible, and as soon as possible after they arise. Failing in this, the miners are urged to notify their district or state officials without delay, and the operators are also expected promptly to notify their commissioner, for the longer the most trifling differences are allowed to remain unadjusted the more serious they become and the more difficult of settlement; but at the same time both operators and miners are urged, even when the amount of money involved is trifling, to settle only in accordance with every provision and of all the terms of our joint agreements.

TACT WILL PREVENT TROUBLE.

It is safe to say that there is really no valid cause for ninety-five per cent. of these differences and disputes being brought to the attention of the miners' officials and the operators' commission, and very often by the time these differences and disputes reach us, we find it necessary to deal with some offense growing out of contentions and bickerings over the most trifling matter. If, by some magic touch, we could burn into the brain of the mine manager, " A soft answer turneth away wrath," and into the brain of the miner, "A polite request will obtain ten-fold more than a rude demand," we would soon be prepared to dispense with much of the tedious work now performed by those entrusted with the difficult task of preserving peace where it is threatened, or restore it where it has been broken. The work before us is, therefore, largely educational—a vast work to be performed by and at the expense of comparatively few men in the coal-producing industry of a single state. It would be idle to endorse the claim that our conditions in Illinois are ideal, but that there is a marked improvement and a hopeful outlook no careful observer can deny.

Of the scores and hundreds of cases that have been brought before the officials of the United Mine Workers of Illinois, and the commissioner of the Illinois Coal Operators' Association, all with two or three exceptions, have been settled without appeal. It should be borne in mind that every time a dispute is settled, if nothing more has been done, friction at least is relieved, but the settlement of very many disputes means the prevention of strikes.

Strikes, even when limited to a single mine and continuing for a short period of time, entail heavy loss on employer and employee. Three hundred dollars loss per day to the average coal mining company and its men is a very low estimate. It is impossible accurately to determine the aggregate saving as the result of the Illinois Coal Operators' experiment, but one-quarter million dollars would be a low estimate of what has been saved in the past year to miners and mine owners, and this experiment, conducted at a trifling cost, has not only brought mine owners and miners to a better understanding of each other, but it has brought the mine owners themselves together in a closer union and to a more just appreciation of each others' rights and to a recognition of the importance of organization among the employer class.

The cases that were appealed, to which reference has been made, are noteworthy and deserve special consideration. A brief statement will serve to show not only how they are settled, but it will show how, oftentimes, costly and harmful conflicts are averted.

THE DANVILLE DISTRICT CASE.

I shall first cite an appeal from the Danville district in Illinois involving an interpretation of a section in the state agreement, known as section 16. Briefly, the miners and operators in the Danville district had met for the purpose of making their annual sub-district agreement for the scale year beginning April 1, 1901, but a controversy arose over the meaning of section 16 of the state agreement, which reads as follows :

(*a*) The scale of prices herein provided shall include, except in extraordinary conditions, the work required to load coal and properly timber the working places in the mine, and the operator shall be required to furnish the necessary props and timber in rooms or working face. And in long wall mines it shall include the proper mining of the coal and the brushing and care of the working places and roadway according to the present method and rules relating thereto, which shall continue unchanged.

(*b*) If any miner shall fail to properly timber and care for his working place, and such failure shall entail falls of slate, rock and the like, or if by reckless or improper shooting of the coal in room and pillar mines, the mine props or other timbers shall be disturbed or unnecessary falls result, the miner whose fault has occasioned such damage shall repair the same without compensation ; and if such miner fails to repair such damage he shall be discharged. In cases where the mine manager directs the placing of cross-bars to permanently secure the roadway, then, and in such cases only, the miner shall be paid at current price for each cross-bar when properly set.

These provisions do not contemplate any change from

the ordinary method of timbering by the miner for his own safety. The dispute arose over what constituted "ordinary" and what "extraordinary" conditions; or, in other words, what "dead" work should be performed by the miner without further compensation than pay for the coal sent out, and when the company should assume this extra work either by allowing the miner compensation therefor or having the work done by company men.

On April 11 the miners and operators of the Danville sub-district held a joint meeting, and, failing to agree upon an interpretation of the clause, the following action was taken :

"That the question now in dispute in the Danville district, namely, the interpretation and application of the sixteenth section of the Springfield agreement and the method of shearing the entry coal, be referred to Mr. Mitchell and Mr. Justi for settlement, and their decision shall be binding. Work at the mines shall resume and continue pending the settlement under the agreement of 1901 and now in force. In case the decision is against the operators, the miners shall be paid for the work done under protest. The parties herein named are to take up the matter and dispose of it at once. The rock down in the places at the resumption of work is to be cleaned up by the operators."

In accordance with this resolution, Mr. Mitchell, president of the United Mine Workers of America, and the commissioner of the Illinois Coal Operators' Association went to the Danville district and inspected four of the ten mines involved in the controversy. Two days were devoted to examining the conditions in controversy at the mines, one day to taking testimony, and two days to a consideration of the evidence. The interpretation of the section of the agreement in dispute was considered favorable to the operators, although it was in fact simply a reaffirmation of the state agreement. The miners in the Danville district, while they were disappointed, and while they murmured their dissatisfaction, remained at work during the investigation and have remained ever since. Thus 4,000 miners were induced to remain at work pending the investigation. Many times $4,000 was saved to both miners and operators; and a great principle of right was established and maintained. All this was done by the prompt application of simple, wise and humane measures,—measures that it was possible thus promptly to apply because the necessary machinery had been provided by means of organization.

ATTEMPT TO FORCE HOISTING ENGINEERS INTO THE U. M. W. ORGANIZATION.

Another case serving to illustrate the manner in which these joint investigations are conducted, as well as their importance to all interests involved, was the strike of the miners at the Glendale Coal and Mining Company's mines in the Belleville district, near St. Louis, Mo. On July 23, a telegram to the commissioner announced that both of the mines of the Glendale Coal and Mining Company had been shut down by the miners because the company refused to reinstate a hoisting engineer who had been discharged at one of the mines for cause. This hoisting engineer belonged to the United Mine Workers of America, and though not discharged because of this fact, he should have been discharged for it, if for no other, for the Illinois Coal Operators' Association had agreed to employ only members of the National Brotherhood of Coal Hoisting Engineers, with whom it had a contract—all of which was known to the said engineer and to the officials of the United Mine Workers of Illinois. The United Mine Workers of Illinois, it is proper to state in this connection, had sought to force all laborers in and about the coal mines of the state into their organization, whether they belonged to other labor organizations or not. From the idea of "trades-unionism," the larger labor organizations of the United States have long since departed, the idea now being to absorb all the smaller unions, whether they desire to be absorbed or not, and to organize them into great industrial families; and this in the very face of the fact that these smaller unions derive their charters from the American Federation of Labor, as does also the organization of United Mine Workers.

Briefly, the Illinois Coal Operators' Association had entered into an agreement with the National Brotherhood of Coal Hoisting Engineers in October, 1899, and it has been working under the agreement, or a renewal of that agreement, ever since. At the interstate and the state conventions of 1901, the United Mine Workers sought to include in the scale of wages which it was seeking to establish with the coal operators a scale of wages for coal hoisting engineers. This the coal operators not only refused to do, but they succeeded in inducing the United Mine Workers to consent to the insertion of a clause in the state agreement definitely excluding from the jurisdiction of the United Mine Workers the coal hoisting engineers, confident that if such a clause were not included in the agreement serious difficulties would occur at short intervals throughout the contract year. In spite of this agreement, and in violation of it, so clearly and so explicitly drawn, the Mine Workers' Union took into its organization certain coal hoisting engineers; or at any rate it allowed certain coal hoisting engineers to remain. When in due course a coal hoisting engineer was discharged who did not belong to the National Brotherhood of Coal Hoisting Engineers, with whom the Coal Operators of Illinois had a contract, the miners not only threw idle the mine where this engineer had been employed, but they threw idle a second mine operated by the same company—and all this was done not only with the consent of the officials of the local and district organization, but with the approval of the officials of the state organization also. Unable to induce the state officials to order the miners back to work, the Illinois Coal Operators' Association, through its commissioner, filed its protest with the national organization of the United Mine Workers, insisting that the miners be ordered to return to work, and that the claim of jurisdiction by the miners over the engineers be discontinued. A decision was rendered, but it was unsatisfactory to coal operators and coal miners alike. Still, the decision provided that the men should return to work and it was heeded. But as the important question of jurisdiction was ignored in the decision, both organizations consented to refer the question for adjustment to Mr. John Mitchell, national president of the United Mine Workers of America, and to the commissioner of the Illinois Coal Operators' Association. The executive boards of the United Mine Workers of Illinois and of the Illinois Coal Operators' Association met in joint session, and after a calm discussion of the points in dispute, the case was taken under advisement by President Mitchell and the commissioner, who, after due deliberation, agreed that under the contract entered into by the coal operators and the coal miners of the State of Illinois the United Mine Workers of Illinois had no jurisdiction over the hoisting engineers. Thus, a question that had been the occasion of constant trouble and friction and which threatened even greater and more serious complications was happily settled.

Needless as this whole contest seems to have been,

still, under the old régime, this strike would have continued indefinitely or until the employer had submitted
to gross injustice, until he had surrendered a right
guaranteed to him under an agreement which all parties
to it had pledged themselves to keep inviolate. Had it
not been so settled, the probabilities are that every other
mine in the state would have been forced to undergo
the same costly experience.

SUSPENSION OF MINERS' LOCAL AT ATHENS,

Another and most important case, and one which was
brought to the attention of the joint convention of
coal miners and coal operators while in session at
Springfield, last March, was that in which the miners
and operators of the Athens Coal Mining Company, at
Athens, Ill., were involved. Here the miners not only
violated the state agreement, but they defied their own
state organization. They not only refused to work under
the mine manager employed by the Athens Mining
Company, but they drove him from his post and out of
the city in which he lived. The case was investigated
by a joint committee of coal miners and coal operators,
and a unanimous report of this committee declaring the
men guilty was submitted to the joint convention, then
in session, which report the joint convention unanimously approved. Thereupon, the executive board of
the United Mine Workers of Illinois suspended the
"local" at Athens for an indefinite period. The miners
were obliged to remain idle because membership cards
were refused to them, and without these membership
cards they were denied employment at all mines employing union labor. Thus mine and miners were both
idle, and they remained idle for eight weeks, at the expiration of which time the offending miners, admitting

the gravity of their offense and the justice of the punishment imposed, sought to be reinstated in their organization. This the United Mine Workers refused to do without first obtaining the consent of the operators. This consent was finally given, the "local" was thereupon reinstated. The miners were re-employed and work was resumed. But think of the cost! Here was a case where the operator was entirely innocent and yet, while the chief burden of loss fell upon him, he was without recourse upon the offenders, or upon the organization to which they belonged.

In all fairness the loss should have been borne by the United Mine Workers. That the Athens Mining Company had no recourse at law against the United Mine Workers does not alter the case. The very fact itself that these two organizations are only voluntary organizations, having no standing before the law, should serve to make such an agreement the more sacred, because they are bound to each other by only moral obligations; and unless labor organizations proceed upon this idea, trade agreements between them and employers cannot be continued. The time will come, I believe, when the United Mine Workers' organization, like the International Longshoremen's Association,[1] will carry out its agreements to the letter, failing in which they will reimburse the employer for resulting damages. Thus it would fully establish its claim to recognition as a business organization doing business according to accepted business rules

[1] At a meeting of the National Civic Federation held at the Chamber of Commerce, New York city, last May, Mr. Daniel J. Keefe, president of the International Longshoremen's Association, in describing the business methods of that labor organization, said that when members of his association refused to carry out its agreements they were expelled, and their places, if necessary, were filled with non-union men, and any loss resulting from failure on its part to carry out its contracts was borne by the International Longshoremen's Association.

and practices, and entitled to respect, since it would then
possess those established elements which merit success,
namely, a proper regard for its promises and obligations.

The course pursued by the miners' organization in the
Athens case was, I am free to say, well intended ; and it
was, perhaps, all it could do under the then existing circumstances.   No doubt great good resulted, but unfortunately the punishment fell too heavily upon the innocent, while the mischief-makers—the men responsible
for all the trouble, and who rather enjoyed the glory of
having wrought so much mischief—are perhaps as well
cared for as ever in the mines to-day, and stand as well
in their organization as the least guilty of their fellows.
These men the United Mine Workers should have punished by summary expulsion from their organization,
and the other men who followed their leadership should
have been made to pay the loss entailed.

Certainly relief from such evils as are herein described
is imperatively demanded, and it must be afforded if
joint agreements between employer and men are to be
continued ; but when will this relief be afforded, and how
shall that relief be obtained ?

STANDING OF LABOR ORGANIZATIONS BEFORE THE LAW.

I am aware that the incorporation of labor organizations, in order to give them a standing before the law,
is suggested by many able men as a cure-all for strikes
and as the only prevention of the petty tyranny to which
employers of labor are so often subjected, as well as a
means of enforcing agreements entered into between
organizations or companies of employers and labor organizations.   In fact, both the representatives of capital
and of labor seem to believe that the remedy for abuses
practiced both by employers and employees is to be

found in legislation. To me this seems impossible, and I might cite many reasons for this belief, if time permitted. Suffice it to say that if the employer should secure the legislation he desires, injury would surely overtake labor ; and if, on the other hand, the employee should secure the legislation he desires, the difficulties of the employer would be enormously increased.

I am mindful of the fact that even so high an authority on all questions he essays to discuss as Mr. Carroll D. Wright advocates the incorporation of labor organizations and believes that thus both employers and employees would be protected.[1] The weak point, it seems to me, in this idea of the incorporation of labor organizations is that in law it is well nigh impossible to impose upon laborers any prescribed labor conditions. That is to say, you cannot make him perform labor in any certain, defined manner, and that is after all the sum and substance of the agreements entered into between labor and capital. If incorporated, the laborer or the organization to which he belongs could be sued for damages, but if so the case would have to be tried in a magistrate's court, or in the circuit court ; and in these courts the complaint of employers now is that a laborer has the better chance of success. Oftentimes such suits would be tried before juries with a too common bias

---

[1] In his address before the Merchants' Club, Chicago, November 9, 1901, Mr. Wright said : "The great advantages of securing charters would be that the unions would have a standing in court ; they would have a better standing in public estimation, and they would be more likely to select the ablest men for leaders. As legal persons they could enforce their contracts against employers, while they would be responsible for breach of contract on their own part. They have been debarred heretofore from appearing in court by representatives, and have thus lost a great advantage which would have been of the utmost importance to them."

21

against capital. The truth is, that if there is any one
thing that a business man does not like—if there is any
one thing a business man will make many sacrifices to
avoid, and that he does religiously avoid—it is a lawsuit.
On the other hand, if there is anything that an unde-
serving or a radical laborer, or an unworthy or incompetent labor official enjoys—and notably where he has
already made a loophole of escape—it is a lawsuit with
the employer or the capital class. It is to be feared if
the employer class once succeeds in introducing the law
suit as a means of enforcing its agreements with labor
organizations, the chief business of the employer will
thereafter be in the courts; and nowhere else is this so
true as in the coal industry.[1] The coal operator who
goes to law with a labor organization or with a laborer,
it will be found, will be engaged in the law business
more than in the coal business. And here let me observe, that the large fund in the treasury of the United
Mine Workers of Illinois would be a constant temptation to the local unions, composing the general organization of miners, to urge litigation. It is true the lot of
the officials of labor organizations would thus be made
harder, their pathway would be strewn with more thorns,
but this would hardly compensate the employer who
must follow in the same rough path.

VALUE OF PUBLIC OPINION.

Better than law courts or restrictive laws—infinitely
better than police surveillance or military power for the
solution of this problem—is the strong, exacting, en-

---

[1] "Discourage litigation. Persuade your neighbors to compromise
whenever you can. Point out to them how the nominal winner is
often a real loser—in fees, expenses, and waste of time "—ABRAHAM
LINCOLN.

lightened public opinion of a free people, founded upon healthy, honest public sentiment. Public opinion in America is certain to be sound, provided the people are well and correctly informed, and the way to make it sound is to ground it on the truth. Let the employers in every industry in the land organize into associations similar to the one I have sought to describe in this paper. Let them stand firm for their just rights, and no more, and treat with labor as it deserves and as it has a right to expect, and then public opinion will be not only unerring in its verdict but inflexible in enforcing its decrees. Thus organized, the employer class in America will, as a natural sequence, inaugurate and conduct a campaign of education in which the enlightened American laborer will gladly join, that cannot fail of establishing such just and correct standards of right in our business relations as to insure fair wages with proper working conditions to the laborer, and profit and safety to the employer, because if employer and employee are alike organized, each with adequate machinery for conducting its business, the public will no longer be misled by one-sided reports of tyranny on the one hand or oppression on the other.

If labor in recent years has too often practiced forms of tyranny and has committed acts of lawlessness, if it has forced conditions upon the employer that are oppressive, and has made contracts,[1] as often charged, simply to violate them, and if all these combined evils have become so great that they would now seem to call for the

---

[1] All the commercial world ought to be converted to the doctrine that a contract is a binding and not a voidable obligation. Every member of the industrial and commercial organizations of this country ought to understand and swear allegiance to the great principle that as a man agrees to do, so, in truth and honor, he must and shall do.—J. STERLING MORTON.

intervention of courts and the protection of the strong arm of government, let us not forget that in times past it was the arrogance and selfishness so often practiced by the rich and the well-to-do that in due course brought on the present conflict between labor and capital.   Now exalted public spirit and wise unselfishness to be practiced by the same class must restore peaceful relations and just conditions at the same time that labor takes heed lest it add crime to folly by seeking revenge for wrongs, both real and fancied, instead of following such a policy of repression, conciliation and wise business sagacity as the higher dictates of their better natures would suggest and as all law-abiding and justice-loving fellow-citizens will approve.

DISCUSSION.

CARROLL D. WRIGHT: I have listened to Mr. Justi's paper with intense satisfaction, and with gratitude also. For many years I have been a very thorough believer in the efficacy of joint meetings of employers and employees and of all efforts to avoid labor conflicts through the instrumentality of voluntary joint committees. The plan which has been so thoroughly and admirably outlined by Mr. Justi, and which has been put in operation in the coal industry in the State of Illinois, must commend itself to all fair-minded men. I cannot offer any criticisms of the paper but wish to commend it fully and cordially. When it is known that during the past twenty years the cost of strikes and lock-outs, including the wage loss of employees the assistance to employees by labor organizations, and the loss of employers, amounts to the enormous sum of $468,968,581, and that the total number of strikes during that period was 22,793, involving 117,509 establishments and throwing out of employment 6,105,694 employees, it would seem that no effort, consistent with high moral standards, to prevent these great losses and hardships should be neglected.

For many years a large proportion of the great industries of Great Britain have adopted plans similar to those presented by Mr. Justi, and with the most gratifying results. In this country the founders, the stove manufacturers, the mason building trades of Boston, the boot and shoe trade, and some others have worked under similar plans, and with no strikes or lockouts. Following these great experiences, the Publishers' Association and the Typographical Union have made contracts looking to the avoidance of all conflicts. The managers of the coal mining industry in Illinois are to be congratulated upon their wisdom in adopting the methods Mr. Justi has explained. I have no doubt that other great associations of manufacturers and wage-earners will follow these experiences, and I am sure that as soon as employers' associations understand the real benefits of dealing with organized labor they will not hesitate to adopt similar plans.

Of the 22,793 strikes occurring during the last twenty years, 14,457 were ordered by organizations, and 52.86 per cent. of the strikes so ordered were successful; but it is not fair to say that a successful strike, so far as its particular conclusions are concerned, was successful, or that an unsuccessful strike, so far as its particular conclusions are concerned, was unsuccessful. There is something in the psychology of strikes which leads us far beyond the mere statement of cost as related to losses, either of employers or employees. The ethical effects of friendly settlement far transcend any financial results which can be considered, either from the favorable or the unfavorable point of view. The harmonious relations of laborers and capitalists are worth more than the success or the estimated losses of any or all strikes.

Dr. William Jacks, president of the West of Scotland Iron and Steel Institute, in his recent address before that body, says that under wise and prudent and far-seeing leaders, unions are good for the masters as well as the man, and he cites one chief benefit—the advantage of having a recognized head and executive with which to deal where such a large body of men is concerned. Then, he says, boards of arbitration can be established. And Mr. Pierpont Morgan, in one of the conferences relating to the recent steel strike, did not hesitate to say that he much preferred dealing with an organized body of men than with a lot of irresponsible individuals. This position is the correct one, and must be recognized if industry is to avoid labor conflicts. This is seen very clearly in the light of some of the remarks made by Mr. Justi. He says that every strike that has taken place in our time, even where there have been bloodshed and destruction of property, has finally been settled in friendly council, and that the plan of the Coal Operators' Association in its contracts with the man is to prevent these senseless and costly strikes and the many differences and disputes arising between masters and men, which tend to place them in the attitude of enemies to each other, and to settle them in the same manner in which the most destructive strikes are finally settled, namely, by meeting in friendly council. This is consummate wisdom. What a commentary it is upon the experience of the past twenty-five years to know that finally most strikes are settled by the very method which should be taken in the initiative to prevent them. Mr. Justi makes it clear that the main idea of such investigations as he recommends is to bring out the exact conditions, and he states that when this is done they have found in Illinois that nearly all ordinary troubles adjust themselves before the joint boards have been in session any great length of time. It is, he states, all important, whenever disputes or differences arise, to take them up promptly.

Mr. John Mitchell, the president of the United Mine Workers, has stated publicly—and I use his exact words—that "nearly all, I may say all the strikes that have occurred in recent years would have been avoided if both sides could have got together and talked the matter over." Talking the matter over, however, involves organization. There is no use of talking it over with individuals; the conference must be between the parties involved, and at the very outset when a greivance is presented. This is all important, and this association of economists will recognize more clearly than any other body of men the economic advantages of such action. The aggregate saving, as pointed out by Mr. Justi as the result of the Illinois coal operators' experiment, is such as to indicate no other sane course to pursue. He says that one quarter of a million dollars would be a low estimate of what has been saved in the past year to miners and mine owners, and that the experiments have been conducted at a trifling cost. The ethical result of the course adopted has been a better understanding of the two parties, for it has brought the mine owners themselves together in a closer union, to a more just appreciation of each other's rights, and to a recognition of the importance of organization among the employer class.

Organization among the employer class has not heretofore been with a view of settling difficulties, but more along the line of defense. The experience of the Founders' Association is in point. They organized for the purpose of defense and accumulated a large defense fund, but the association found that this was not practical, ethical, or economical. They, therefore, turned their organization to the light and undertook the settlement and adjustment of grievances in the initiative as worth more as a matter of defense than all the war methods which they could adopt.

Senator Hanna, who has had long experience in conducting great business enterprises, has made a declaration, not only of sympathy with labor as such, but of sympathetic recognition of their organizations, that will give great stimulus to this broad idea of joint dealing;

and his acceptance of the chairmanship of the executive committee of the National Civic Federation, whose specific purpose is not only the agitation of the benefits to be derived from the plan of labor conferences in general, but the organization of such conferences, is a step greater than any that has yet been taken to secure industrial peace. The objects of the committee are so high that they far transcend all arbitrary methods of adjustment, whether through the machinery of official boards of arbitration or courts of a compulsory nature.

There are one or two suggestions which I should like to add to those already made by Mr. Justi. One is that the constitutions of the associations of employers and employees should respectively incorporate an article comprehending the necessity of joint agreements. This is the practice of the Builders' Association and the labor orgnizations which are co-operating with that association. Each provides in its by-laws or constitution that all members of the association, by virtue of their membership, recognize and assent to the establishment of a joint committee of arbitration by and between the two bodies for the peaceful settlement of all matters of mutual concern to the two bodies and the membership thereof; and they provide, further, the specific machinery by which this agreement shall be carried out and specify the duty of the delegates which shall be elected respectively as members of the joint committee. This makes the whole matter of discussion and effort at adjustment a part of the organic law of the two bodies to the high contract.

The other suggestion is that each party should make provision for some disciplinary efforts when individual members of the respective associations disobey the constitution or by-laws in respect to joint agreements. This is done in a way by the Illinois Coal Operators' Association and the labor organization with which it deals, but more can be done in this direction.

By these methods and their extension to various industries the time will come when a strike will bring either or both parties to it into public disrepute. I look for the time when the managers of a great industry or the leaders of a labor organization will feel ashamed to participate in an open labor war. This is the high moral plane which makes industrial peace. With a high moral plane secured, the economic results will surely follow.

While commending the paper in the strongest terms, I wish also to say that I am in thorough sympathy with Mr. Justi in his moderate strictures relative to my own position concerning the incorporation of labor unions. The weak point to which he refers—that in law it is well nigh impossible to impose upon laborers any prescribed labor conditions—I have long recognized ; but there need not be any such imposition. There are not only great advantages in incorporation, but certain disadvantages. These disadvantages can all be removed by law relating to the incorporation of organized labor, limiting responsibilities under certain circumstances and conditions ; but, on the whole, and recognizing the weak point mentioned, and recognizing also other points which Mr. Justi did not bring out, I still believe that the advantages of incorporation far outweigh the disadvantages.

The whole trend in England now is along the line of the doctrine laid down by the Law Lords recently that any body of persons, whether incorporated or not, a voluntary association or otherwise, that can work an injury should be held responsible in damages for the results of the injury. This looks likes an inimical decision, but I believe that the philosophic, economic, and moral results will be that employers of labor everywhere, recognizing the advantages of the doctrine, will insist upon the organization of laborers, and thus put the two great elements absolutely essential to prosperity on an equal basis and on a dignified footing before the law.

E. Dana Durand : The experiment in Illinois, which Mr. Justi has so well described to us, seems to me extremely interesting, because it is illustrative of a practice which certainly is going to grow rapidly in this country ; which indeed has already gained a foothold in a good many industries other than coal mining ; and which, as Mr. Wright has just told us, has made greater progress in Great Britain than in this country. I think there is one very significant thing to be gathered from the description of the practice in Illinois, and that is, that there are really two distinct classes of questions with which employers and employees have to concern themselves. Questions of the first class are of a general nature ; they involve the terms of the labor contract. Questions of the second class are of a minor character ; they have to do with the enforcement of the labor contract, or with its interpretation as regards details. The experience in England as well as in the United States seems to show that the greatest success is usually obtained where different machinery is provided for the adjustment of these two different classes of questions. Such different machinery is, as Mr. Justi shows us, provided in the coal industry, both as regards the interstate agreement, and more particularly as regards the Illinois system. That is, the general questions relating to the general contract are decided by one body ; and the minor questions are decided by a different form of action and a different body ; both bodies, to be sure, representing the same organizations of employers and employees.

The annual joint agreement or contract is adopted by a large convention of coal miners and operators. The large membership of the convention seems a significant thing. It enables all interests properly to be represented, and all classes of operators and miners to understand the significance of the terms which are reached. The conference acts by unanimous vote. It does not act by a majority vote. The decision is confined wholly to members of the trade, employers and employees themselves, and in no case, in the mining industry, is any one outside of the trade and unfamiliar with the conditions called in to decide such important questions, affecting the welfare of hundreds of employers and tens of thousands of employees.

This then is the system of collective bargaining, as the phrase has been used in this country and Great Britain—the discussion of questions directly between employers and employees or their representatives. The practice in several other trades is in general similar to that in the coal mines. It is not to be considered arbitration in any strict usage of that term. It does not involve a decision by a person outside the trade of questions with which he can not be familiar.

The other class of questions, being of a minor character, need not be brought before a large body. Moreover they cannot be settled at definite periods of time, as from year to year. They arise at irregular intervals, when one or the other workman or employer brings up some question of interpretation, or attempts to violate the agreement. For a settlement of these minor matters there needs to be machinery constantly on hand ; preferably a small-sized joint board which may hear appeals. Of course the most of these minor differences can be settled by immediate conference between those directly interested, if only they are willing to confer ; but if they cannot come to an agreement then appeal to a body of some dignity and permanence, with some independence because not directly concerned in the dispute, is likely to result in peaceful adjustment without the need of rendering a formal decision. Mr. Justi has shown that in most cases disputes, after a little investigation and negotiation, are settled without authoritative decision. It seems to me that this latter practice may properly be called conciliation, or, if you please, even arbitration. Such a joint board may find it necessary to render an authoritative decision, as it occasionally does in Illinois, and in some rare instances it is possible, and perhaps desirable, that failing a decision otherwise, these minor matters should be appealed to some outside authority to be chosen jointly by the parties interested. This is done at times in this country, and quite frequently in Great Britain. But it certainly is undesirable to resort to outside arbitration as regards general questions of the labor contract, unless in the most extreme necessity ; and most employers and employees in this country believe that it is not wise to resort to arbitration by persons outside the trade at all as regards these greater questions.

PORTO RICAN FINANCE UNDER THE SPANISH AND AMERICAN GOVERNMENTS.

BY THOMAS S. ADAMS.

No fair-minded person who read the press despatches from Cuba or heard most of the speeches in Congress in the stirring days which immediately preceded the war with Spain, could have avoided a certain revulsion of feeling in favor of Spain and the Spaniard. Cuba and Porto Rico, we were told with angry vehemence, were ruled from Madrid, administered by a horde of hungry carpet-baggers, taxed and exploited, pillaged and looted for the benefit of the carpet-bagger and the glory of Spain.

But the abuse of Spain was too continual; the damnation too utter. One was forced to conclude that national prejudice was passing current for knowledge; and if it fell to his lot to make a brief study of the Spanish government of Porto Rico he approached his subject, almost inevitably, with a disposition to ascertain the good which it contained, and with the expectation of finding something far less selfish and barbarous than had been painted.

I have not hesitated to begin with a personal statement of this sort because it will be found not without relevancy in the rather invidious comparison which follows, and because the more fully I have been able to investigate Spanish government and administration, the more inevitably have I been forced to conclude that American criticism of this government and administration is on the whole well founded. So far as Porto Rico is concerned there is no evidence of unusual cruelty or unnecessary physical harshness in the history of Spanish administration. On the other hand, the evidence is indisputable that financially and economically Porto Rico was systematically exploited. And for this evidence one is not forced to accept—nor have I in the present paper accepted—the opinion of the Porto Ricans or the evidence found in the utter corruption of public morals in Porto Rico to-day. The evidence is writ large on the statute books of Spain. Porto Rico was governed from Madrid. It was administered in the interests of Spain, and no effort was made to conceal the fact. The utter unconsciousness on the part of Spain that colonies could exist for any other purpose than the enrichment of the mother country is amazing.

SPANISH GOVERNMENT OF PORTO RICO.

We are concerned here with the government of Porto Rico only on its fiscal side, and there is space for only the briefest treatment of this side. We shall go quickest to the heart of the matter by the brief statement that up to the promulgation of the autonomous constitution of November 25, 1897, which was never fully introduced into Porto Rico, there was no semblance of a native legislature. Legislation emanated from Madrid, from the Cortes, in which Porto Rico was represented by sixteen deputies and three senators; but more usually from the colonial minister, Porto Rico being a crown colony. By this is meant, not merely that the Spanish government was the source of legislation, but that it voted the Porto Rican budget, passed her tax laws, increased or pared her appropriations, laid hands upon the minutiae of fiscal administration—for instance, the rates of taxation, the methods of assessment, the penalties for evasion, etc.,—and through

skillful election laws and the powers conferred upon its
representative in Porto Rico, the governor general, controlled absolutely the modicum of representation which
Porto Rico was allowed in the government.

And looking to the administration of the island, it is
no criticism, but a mere exposition of the provincial
law, to say that the administration was the governor
general and the governor general the administration.
In the later history of the island we catch fleeting
glimpses of a board of authorities, a council of administration, and a provincial deputation. But the first two
were explicitly and the latter was in reality " under the
direct and immediate orders of the governor general."
Not only was he commander in chief of the army and
navy, head of the established church, commissioner of
education, and executive head of the administration,
with plenary power to suspend and appoint officials,
issue administrative orders, remove and fine members of
the provincial deputation and municipal councils, but
in point of fact he exercised these powers, " naming
every employee of the municipal governments," said a
prominent Porto Rican to me, " from alcalde down to
porters and janitors."

It should be said that Spain made some effort both to
divorce the financial administration of the island from
the general administration, and to introduce a certain
element of home rule into the financial administration.
Thus the receipt and disbursement of the insular funds,
the initial drafting of the insular budget, the collection
of customs and the financial administration in general,
were under the control of an intendant, who originally
—that is, by the royal decree of September 12, 1870—
was directly responsible to the colonial ministry at
Madrid.   But as both the governor general and the in-

tendant were agents of the colonial office there was no particular reason why their powers should be independent and coördinate, and accordingly, as time passed, the latter came more and more under the control of the governor general. The annual budget, in late years, was presented not to the colonial minister direct, but to the council of administration which was presided over and controlled by the governor general. This council forwarded the budget, with such suggestions of change as they had to make, to the colonial minister. "Though the government may change the budget," continues the law (March 15, 1895), "in order to present it to the Cortes, and in order to provide for the services and general obligations of the state, it shall always attach thereto, as a report, the one drawn up by the council."

As a matter of fact, there were two budgets and two treasuries. The budget drawn up by the intendant contained all the taxes and the more important appropriations: the contributions of Porto Rico to the home government, for instance, the appropriations for the military and naval establishments, for the church and the judiciary. The expenditures for education, roads, charities—in short, for internal affairs—were first voted by the provincial deputation, which sent their budget to the governor general. He in turn revised it and then sent the original and his modifications to the colonial minister. Here it was again revised and certain taxes or parts of taxes assigned for the payment of expenditures allowed. In this form it was submitted to the Cortes. In the fiscal year 1897–98, the insular budget amounted to 3,536,342 pesos: the provincial budget to 1,217,700 pesos. Hereafter I shall treat the two budgets together.

22

The provincial deputation had existed, with intermissions, since 1870—the year in which Porto Rico was declared a Spanish province. Its members were elected by the qualified voters of Porto Rico, and it had in the abstract important administrative powers : the right of suggesting or voting in the first instance the appropriations for schools and roads, of disbursing its own funds, of revising the municipal budgets, etc. But its meaning and usefulness were vitiated by a farcical election law, by the revision of its budgets in Spain, by the superior powers of the governor general, who could annul any resolution and suspend or fine any member, and by that masterpiece of Spanish ingenuity, the provision that the office of provincial deputy should be honorary, compulsory and liable. This, being interpreted, means that a Porto Rican had to accept the office when tendered ; that while he received no salary, he could be fined for absence or disrespect to authority ; and that, if by his action in the deputation he injured the right of any citizen, he was liable for damages. " Should a resolution of the provincial deputation injure the rights of private individuals," says article 50 of the provincial law of Dec. 31, 1896, " those having contributed by their votes to the adoption of the same shall be held liable for indemnity or restitution to the injured parties before the proper courts."

Perhaps, after all, Spain's greatest obstacle was that, like the notorious Mrs. Ebbsmith, she had a past. She tried desperately in the end to rise above her traditions, and in the autonomous constitution of November 25, 1897, made a heroic effort to grant Porto Rico that measure of fiscal autonomy which both justice and expediency demanded. But repentance came too late, and before the autonomous government could be fully instituted Commodore Sampson was shelling San Juan, and the governor general was forced to declare martial law. Under the autonomous constitution Porto Rico was still compelled to pay her contribution to Spain for "the maintenance of sovereignty" (articles 34–36), and this contribution, which was fixed in advance by the Spanish Cortes, had to be accepted by the legislature of Porto Rico before the ordinary budget could be considered. Again, the evidence is plentiful that Spain had not abandoned the old habit of granting power in one paragraph of the law and withdrawing it by a specious generality in the next. Thus after having granted the municipalities and provincial assembly complete power "freely to raise the necessary revenue to cover expenditures," the whole scheme is put to naught by the modifying clause—"with no other limitations than to make the means adopted compatible with the general system of taxation which shall obtain in the island." Whether Porto Rico was ready for fiscal autonomy or not is a doubtful question over which Spain may rightfully have hesitated. But the manner and time in which the concession was made, the specious promises and doubtful ambiguities with which the law is strewn, yield plentiful evidence of a bad conscience. Spain had wronged her colonies, and the Sagasta constitution is an acknowledgement of the fact.

EXPENDITURES UNDER THE SPANISH GOVERNMENT.

An examination of the Porto Rican budget shows that it was not without reason that the Spanish colonial ministry revised budgets so carefully, prepared the laws in detail and prescribed minutely the procedure of assessment and collection. Spain was careful to retain this right of budgetary revision because 46 per cent. of the aggregate budget of the general government and the provincial deputation was in support of functions maintained almost solely for the benefit of the home government. To be specific, the aggregate insular expenditures in the fiscal year 1897–98 amounted to 4,754,-042 pesos. Of this amount, 2,167,157 pesos, or 46 per cent., were devoted to the support of the established church, the colonial ministry at Madrid, and the military and naval establishments in Porto Rico, all of which were of no benefit, but rather a menace, to Porto Rico itself.

It would be interesting, if time permitted, to speak of the expenditures in detail. 193,610 pesos went to the state church in its purely religious capacity, the judicial and educational services of the clergy being otherwise provided for. The military establishment cost 1,252,377 pesos ; including 11,413 pesos for the " disciplinary brigades of Cuba." The naval station cost 222,-668 pesos. These two expenditures together constituted more than 31 per cent. of the aggregate expenditure of the island ; more than twice as much as was spent upon public works and roads, and more than eleven times as much as was spent upon public schools. Finally, the compulsory contribution levied upon Porto Rico as " the expenses of sovereignty " amounted to 498,501 pesos. This consisted of Porto Rico's quota towards the payment of the expenses of the colonial office—sixteen per cent.—and pensions for retired soldiers, marines and civil employees.

The compulsory contribution toward the payment of the expenses of sovereignty is not, I believe, unknown in the colonial administration of other European states. Thus, according to Professor Seligman's paper on the French colonial fiscal system, France collected about

8,500,000 francs from her colonies in 1898. But over against this France spent, in maintaining military establishments and in positive contributions toward the payment of the local expenses of her colonies, 116,000,-000 francs; thirteen times as much as she collected. On her colonies—on Porto Rico at least—Spain spent nothing.

The remaining expenditures of the insular government and provincial deputations amounted to 2,586,884 pesos, or 54 per cent. of the aggregate expenditures. This amount comprehended the expenses of the judiciary, the treasury department, the post-office and telegraph, for roads, education, public health : in short, the ordinary expenses in general. Such remarks as I have to make upon these expenditures will be introduced later in a comparison with the expenditures under the American régime. The interesting point is that only a little more than one-half of the taxes collected was spent for the normal expenses of the island itself.

REVENUES UNDER THE SPANISH GOVERNMENT.

The revenue system, under Spanish control was characterized by a studious avoidance of debt, great complexity in the system of taxation, and by an excessive emphasis upon indirect taxes and upon customs taxes in particular. The estimated receipts in the fiscal year 1897–98 amounted to 5,157,200 pesos, or somewhat more than $3,000,000. Of this amount, 11 per cent. came from non-tax sources, mining royalties, quotas levied on the municipalities, and the public lottery, $87,000 from the lottery ; 13 per cent. from direct taxes, the graduated poll tax, the system of license taxes and the taxes on land ; 9 per cent. from stamp taxes on the transfer of property, passenger and freight traffic, and commercial documents in general; and 67 per cent. from consumption taxes—the unimportant excise on petroleum, the taxes upon the embarkation and disembarkation of passengers and the loading and unloading of freight, the tax upon exports, and most important of all the customs duties.

The Spanish system of taxation is full of interesting features, that will have to be entirely neglected at this time : the virtues and defects of the lottery as a source of income ; the system of *consumos*, by which the municipalities raised a large part of their revenues from *octrois* upon articles of meat, drink and fuel ; the absence of the sumptuary excise tax ; the multiplicity of stamp taxes, touching almost every written document from a will to a sight draft, highly regressive in general, but including a progressive inheritance tax. We shall have time for only a brief description of the two most important group of taxes, the customs duties and the direct taxes, which together yielded 80 per cent. of the total revenue.

The direct taxes consisted of a territorial or land tax ; a system of license taxes called the industrial and commercial tax, and the passport tax—a graduated poll-tax ranging from twelve cents to twelve dollars. The latter, while a source of continual protest in Porto Rico, was fiscally unimportant and need not be considered here. Its estimated yield in 1897–98 was only 31,000 pesos or $18,600.

The territorial tax, which in an agricultural country like Porto Rico should under ordinary circumstances constitute the very back-bone of the revenue system, yielded in 1897–98 only 410,000 pesos or about eight per cent. of the total receipts. The tax was historically a very old one in Porto Rico, having originated in a quit rent which took the form of a percentage tax upon the net product of land as early as 1816. In recent years it has been divided into two classes, the *agricola* and the *urbana*, both of which were taxes upon the income from real estate. In the country the custom was to ascertain the product of the land from sworn returns of the cultivators, deduct a certain percentage as expenses of production, and value the remainder at certain uniform rates. Thus, on cane or sugar land a deduction of 75 per cent. was allowed for expenses, and on coffee and tobacco land 35 per cent. The net product as thus ascertained was then valued at certain fixed rates; for example, $3.00 a quintal (hundred weight) for sugar, $12.00 a quintal for coffee, etc. Cattle, or the increase of livestock, were similarly taxed in the country. In the cities the tax was on rent with a deduction of 25 per cent. for repairs and losses. The rate of the tax was fixed in the annual budget voted by the Spanish Chambers, usually 5 per cent for insular and 7½ per cent for municipal purposes. The tax was apportioned among the various municipalities; assessed by unsalaried commissions of taxpayers appointed by the municipal councils acting together with an assembly of tax-payers themselves, and the collection was farmed out.

The defects of the tax lie on the face of it. But on the whole, as taxes go, it was not unsuited to the actual conditions of the island. "It corresponded," says Dr. Hollander, in a brief mention of the tax in his formal report to the governor of Porto Rico, " in a rough way with schedules A and B of the present English income tax, and although open to many serious defects, and characteristically perverted and injured by defective administration, yet the system, on the whole, embodied certain elements of equitable and scientific taxation."

The so-called industrial and commercial tax was a cumbersome, intricate and illogical system of graded license taxes which yielded between 4 and 5 per cent. of the total revenues or about 240,000 pesos. The interest on the money spent in writing and devising the law must have been about that amount.

For purposes of taxation the various occupations and professions were divided into five main groups or schedules, in each of which there were a very large number of sub-divisions differentiated in accordance with the kind and size of the business, or the amount of the income, and the size of the town. The first schedule comprehended the smaller merchants and shopkeepers in general. The taxes in this schedule varied in accordance with two main principles : the kind of occupation and the size of the town, there being eight classes of occupations and six groups of towns or forty-eight licenses in all. Thus, a warehouseman in San Juan— the largest city—paid 130 pesos a year, while the keeper of a grog shop in the same city paid only 14 pesos. But a similar warehouseman in Toa Baja would pay only 31 pesos a year, and a similar grog shop in Toa Baja only 3 pesos.

The second schedule or tariff included corporations, banks, and the higher classes of salaried officials; the third, manufacturing establishments; the fourth, handicraftsmen; the fifth, miscellaneous trades and occupations. In all, construing the law as charitably as possible, there were at least 350 different species of occupations and 55 distinct exemptions, including among others,—I quote the law,—"hospitals, charitable institutions and other religious establishments, bull fights, masquerades, and other public entertainments organized by said establishments."

It is needless to say that the law was abused. It is almost impossible to avoid the conclusion that it was made to be abused. Not only was the tariff of licenses arbitrary and illogical, but the distinctions between the classes were as impalpable as thin air. A moderately equitable assessment of the tax was absolutely impossible.

A characteristic instance of the way in which this tax could be abused, was reported some time ago in *Harper's Weekly.* An American in charge of an electric lighting plant in Mayaguez got into difficulties with the municipal authorities by refusing to pay a *consumo* tax of 60 cents a ton on a cargo of coal which he had imported, and in the course of the dispute sued the city. He immediately received notice that his assessment for the industrial and commercial tax had been raised; he had been moved from the class of lighting companies, which paid 120 pesos a year for municipal and insular purposes, to the class of importers who paid 750 pesos a year. Later the municipal authorities learned that he had paid for the coal by drawing a draft on New York, and they promptly moved him into the higher class of importers who also do a banking business. The tax upon the latter class was 1,400 pesos a year. I made some inquiries about this incident while in Porto Rico, and was told that it was true. Whether true or not, it was certainly possible and perfectly representative of the way in which this tax was abused. Surely, Professor Seligman must have overlooked the industrial and commercial tax of Porto Rico, when he said of the property tax, that it was beyond peradventure the worst tax in the civilized world. Or else he regarded Porto Rico as uncivilized.

Consumption taxes. By far the most important group of receipts were the consumption taxes which in 1897–98 yielded more than five times as much as the direct taxes. In this group I have included the import duties, the temporary import duties, the export duties, the taxes on the embarkation and disembarkation of passengers and the loading and unloading of freight, and the *consumo* tax on petroleum.

The latter tax which yielded only about 60,000 pesos is interesting in origin if not important from the standpoint of productivity. About 1890 the Standard Oil Company set up a refinery in Porto Rico. Shortly afterward a royal decree was issued imposing a *consumo* of two and a half pesos per 100 kilograms on all refined petroleum imported or manufactured in the island. The decree concluded with this masterly little clause : " The revenue resulting from this tax has been estimated at 60,000 pesos a year. To avoid expenses of collection, the minister of the colonies is authorized to conclude contracts with the manufacturers or refiners of these products in the island, provided that the stipulated amount be not lower than the estimate in the budget." The Spanish financier seems to have been eminently successful in the taxation of monopolies.

The tax on the loading and unloading of freight and the embarkation and disembarkation of passengers, yielded 245,000 pesos in 1897–98. It seems to have been a specific tax on passengers and on exports and imports ; but the exact rates I have been unable to learn. It was first imposed in 1883.

The export taxes yielded 250,000 pesos in 1897–98, and consisted of small specific duties upon coffee, tobacco and lumber : 1 peso per 100 kilograms of coffee ; 22 centavos per 100 kilograms of tobacco ; 15 centavos per 100 kilograms of lumber. As the total value of the exports of these articles in 1897–98 was about 13,500,-000 pesos, the average *ad valorem* tax—computed by dividing total receipts by total value of exports—is thus seen to be considerably less than 2 per cent. This tax fell almost wholly upon coffee, and under the industrial conditions of the Spanish régime was neither oppressive nor excessively burdensome. And as most of these exports went to Spain, it was not an ungenerous tax.

It is of course impossible to go fully into the subject of the tariff. The import duties in 1897–98 yielded 2,631,000 pesos ; 51 per cent. of the total revenues of Porto Rico from every source. Nothing that I might say could be more significant than this simple fact, although its significance will be more readily recognized when it is supplemented by the statement that the greater portion of this amount came from the taxes upon the foodstuffs. Over 70 per cent. of the import duties were collected on foodstuffs, and 60 per cent. of these foodstuffs consisted of pork, rice, and codfish the staple and peculiar food of the lower classes.

The import taxes consisted of the ordinary tariff charges and a so-called temporary surcharge of ten per cent upon the lowest duties levied in the regular schedule—the law contained a maximum and a minimum tariff, the latter applying to the " more favored " nations which had granted similar privileges to Spain. Imports from Spain and Cuba paid only the temporary tax of ten per cent.

It is probably unnecessary to add that in the opinion of the Porto Ricans the tariff was adjusted in the interests of the Spanish manufacturers. On goods which could be manufactured in both Spain and Porto Rico, it was asserted the tariff charges were excessively low; while on the raw materials needed in these industries the rates were excessively high. To take a simple instance from a memorial prepared for the Spanish colonial ministry by the manufacturers of Ponce, just previous to the American war; it was pointed out that while the duty on soap imported from Barcelona was only 15 pesos per hundred boxes of 1 hundred weight each, the total duty on the raw materials required to manufacture this amount of soap was over 32 pesos.

Again, bitter protests were made by the agricultural interests of Porto Rico against the *consumo* taxes levied upon the more important Porto Rican products exported to Spain. Nominally, goods from Porto Rico were admitted into Spain free of import duties. On the other hand, Spain levied a variety of *consumo* or consumption taxes which were collected at the ports of entry and virtually amounted to import duties of great weight. Thus, sugar was taxed 33⅓ pesetas per 100 kilograms, plus a ten per cent. *ad valorem* tax; while coffee paid 60 pesetas per hundred kilograms. More than one-half of the sugar, and nearly one-fourth of the coffee exported from Porto Rico, went to Spain.

Upon the virtues and defects of the Porto Rican tariff as a whole, I feel that I am not competent to express an opinion. One thing is sure. Indirect taxes must be given a relatively much more important place in Porto Rico than in England or the United States, and there undoubtedly is, as Professor Seligman has said, a prodigious amount of cant expressed about the evils of indirect taxes. Giving these truths due weight, however, it nevertheless appears to me that too much stress was placed upon the customs duties; and in the import tariff itself the ordinary foodstuffs of the poor seem to have been relatively over-taxed. Indirect taxes in general—the taxes which we all forget to complain about in our effort to shift them off upon our neighbors—were sadly overworked. Pluck the goose with the minimum amount of squawk; it is a convenient principle and perhaps a defensible one among a self-governing people who vote their own taxes and, from the financial standpoint, make or mar their own destiny. But as a principle of colonial finance, imposed by a superior upon a dependent people, for the purpose of raising revenues nearly one-half of which were expended in the interest of the superior nation, it lacks every element of justice, and even, I may add, of far-sighted expediency.

DEBT UNDER THE SPANISH RULE.

Let us be just to Spain. Whatever the temptation to do otherwise, Porto Rico was never saddled with a public debt. With the exception of a short period following the emancipation of the slaves, Porto Rico has contracted no permanent debt in the last half-century; and municipal borrowing has been confined to a minimum.

As a matter of fact a small annual surplus was usually secured, and this, at intervals, was borrowed by Spain and used in the settlement of the Cuban difficulties. During the ten years' war, for instance, Spain transferred in this way about $3,000,000, called it a Cuban debt, and made Cuba responsible for its repayment. Of more than $4,000,000 taken at various times, $2,253,516 still remain unpaid: Porto Rico's contribution towards the glorious cause of suppressing Cuban insurrection.[1]

---

[1] See testimony of Mr. Nicholas Daubon in the *Report on the Island of Porto Rico* by Henry K. Carroll, special commissioner for the United States to Porto Rico, pp. 250, 251.

Such, in brief, was the Spanish system of colonial finance. Its efficiency was superficial. It aroused no opposition, because the direct taxes were largely evaded through the complexity of the law and the venality of the officials, while the burden of the indirect taxes was shifted from those who owned property and were able to protest effectively to a sodden, inarticulate peon class which was too ignorant either to protest or to realize the economic causes of its own degradation. The direct taxes were collected efficiently, but their collection was farmed out and the delinquent taxpayer brought to book by an administrative process that was mercilessly effective when unimpeded by bribery. The revenue system supplied the needs of the state, because the government lacked almost all the functions which distinguish the modern from the mediæval state. There were government officials by the hundred, but transportation was by pack-horse; there was a state church supported by taxes which, during the last decade of the preceding century, averaged 200,000 pesos a year, but only 15 per cent. of the population could read and write; there were courts of law, policemen, and a civil registry system; but the state conducted a lottery, gambling was unrestricted, petty thieving was, and still is, universal, and one-half of the children were born out of wedlock.

AMERICAN GOVERNMENT OF PORTO RICO.

A detailed description of the present government of Porto Rico, would be, I take it, superfluous; because he who has had more to do with the formation of the present system than any other one man is present, and because the organic law of the island—the Foraker Act—was thoroughly and even passionately discussed by the American people at the time of its adoption.

The governor of Porto Rico is appointed by the president of the United States and because of the failure of the first legislative assembly to pass a new municipal law, he temporarily retains all the municipal powers conferred upon the governor general by the old Spanish law. Otherwise he differs in no important respect from the chief executive of an ordinary American state.

The executive council—the upper legislative chamber—consists of five native Porto Ricans and the six heads of the administrative departments, at present all Americans. The government is thus a modified form of cabinet government. The lower legislative chamber—the house of delegates—consists of thirty-five members elected by the male citizens of Porto Rico who pay taxes or who can read or write. The right to grant franchises and concessions of a public or quasi-public nature is confined to the executive council, but with this exception the powers of the two legislative houses are equal and coördinate. These powers are of the broadest kind ; they shall extend, says the Foraker Act, "to all matters of a legislative character not locally inapplicable." In many respects they are broader and more inclusive than those of the legislature of an American state. For instance, they can pass and enforce their own excise or internal revenue laws. It is scarcely necessary to add that it is this legislative assembly that frames the budget, votes supplies, fixes the appropriations and determines the taxes by which the revenues are to be raised. The present government of Porto Rico is at San Juan, not at the national capital.

Above and superior to the legislative assembly there, of course, remains the power of Congress, which specifically reserves the right to veto any law of the legislature or annul any franchise granted by the executive council. The important questions for us—and for Porto Rico as well—are simply these: in what degree and in what spirit has Congress legislated for Porto Rico?

The first question may be answered in a few words, though it is a question for the future rather than of the past. There has been a minimum of interference on the part of the home country. Congress has retained control of the tariff, brought the currency of the island into conformity with the American system, prohibited the taxation of exports, and forbidden either the insular or any municipal government to contract indebtedness in excess of seven per cent. of the taxable property within their respective jurisdictions. This comprehends practically the whole interference of Congress in the financial affairs of Porto Rico. The government at San Juan has been given free rein. It is true, moreover, that because of the appointive character of the governor and executive council, the American element at San Juan holds a complete check upon fiscal legislation. But it is equally true that the same negative power is held by the native house of delegates.

Concerning the character of American legislation for Porto Rico up to the present date, judging it solely from the standpoint of Porto Rico's needs and not from the standpoint of our own problem of expansion, I have no hesitation in describing it as legislation of the wisest and most generous nature. From the $2,000,000 refund to Porto Rico of the customs duties collected on Porto Rican imports and exports during the military government, to the much abused Foraker act, there is little or nothing which cannot fittingly be described by the words: "legislation of the wisest and most generous nature."

It was generous because it set aside for the use and benefit of Porto Rico two profitable sources of revenue which under ordinary circumstances are reserved for the federal government; the total customs collections in Porto Rico and the customs collected in the United States upon imports from Porto Rico. It was wise because it placed Porto Rico upon an unique basis by making the internal revenue laws inoperative in the island, and by permitting the insular government to levy and collect a system of excise taxes of its own devising. These were the compensations, and in a degree, the results of the fifteen per cent. tariff that so keenly agitated the sympathies of the people of the United States, and which was so sorely needed by the Porto Rican government at the time it was imposed. Moreover, in so far as that tariff placed Porto Rico upon a colonial intead of the customary territorial basis, it was a most fortunate thing for the pocket books of the Porto Ricans. The insular budget amounts to about two million dollars a year. Of this amount it is calculated that about one-fourth will come from the property tax, 37½ per cent. from the excise taxes, and nearly the same proportion from the customs collections in Porto Rico. The last two items, constituting three-fourths of the total receipts, are federal revenues, and so far as I know to the contrary allotted to no other local government under the jurisdicticn of Congress. The Foraker act may have shunted the car of American progress off on a new and dangerous path, but together with the two million refunding act it has placed Porto Rico upon a financial basis of unexcelled security.

The difference between American and Spanish government is the difference between broad, general guid-

23

ance, and officious, minute and perpetual interference. We have started with a Porto Rican legislature; after 400 years of government, Spain had not succeeded in fully introducing one. We have sent them men who have rigidly abstained from interference in local politics; Spain sent them governors who dictated local politics. We have encouraged and fostered the capacity of self-government. They studiously repressed it. We have voted them large grants of money and in times of public distress, sent them assistance. Spain borrowed from them and failed to repay. We have undoubtedly put our best foot foremost. The task will be to presevere as we have begun.

EXPENDITURES UNDER AMERICAN RULE.

Perhaps the most striking contrast between the Spanish and American budgets of Porto Rico is the simple difference in the amount of expenditures. In the last year of the Spanish régime Porto Rico spent, in round figures and American money, $2,852,-425. The appropriation bills passed by the first legislative assembly amounted in all to $1,976,802.21 This amount Dr. Hollander, in a careful estimate, thinks will probably be increased to $2,000,000 by the legislative assembly now sitting. American sovereignty has thus meant for Porto Rico a reduction in expenditures of about $850,000 a year : 30 per cent. of the entire expenditures under the old régime. We levy no compulsory contributions for the maintenance of sovereignty ; we have no established church to support, and we pay for our own military establishments. Section 12 of the Foraker Act specifically provides that all expenses and obligations contracted for defenses, barracks, harbors, light-houses, buoys and other works undertaken by the United States, shall be paid by the latter and not by Porto Rico.

The army, the navy, the church and the home government cost Porto Rico about $1,300,000 a year under Spanish rule. These expenses disappeared with the Spanish government, but in reality Porto Rico is saving $400,000 or $500,000 a year less than this, and in the near future, I believe, the budget will reach the old figure. The reasons for this are brief and significant. In the last year of Spanish control, for instance, $72,117 was appropriated by the insular government for schools; in the present fiscal year more than $500,000 has been appropriated for schools. In the fiscal year 1897–98, $84,543 were spent upon prisons, charities and public health ; in the present fiscal year there have been appropriated for these purposes $230,575. With regard to the expenditures for public works, highways, and insular police, on the other hand, a word of commendation should be said of the Spanish government. While it is not possible to make as exact comparison in these as in the preceding items, the bare figures show that for roads, public works, etc., there were appropriated in 1897–98, $403,523 : in 1901–1902 only $378,942 : that the Spanish civil guard received $256,356 in 1897–98 the American insular police only $204,350. The testimony is universal that under the Spanish government crimes of violence were vigorously suppressed.

Further comparison between specific expenditures would be both impossible and unprofitable; unprofitable, because we know nothing about the relative efficiency of the services of the two governments. In general, however, I think I am safe in predicting that the mere money cost of the American administration is going to be much higher than that of the Spanish.

This will result from the fact that we are paying laborers, clerks and lower grade employees in general, much higher salaries; and from Spain's peculiar method of making almost all elective and many appointive offices in Porto Rico, honorary and compulsory. Not only provincial deputies, but municipal judges, municipal councillors, syndics, tax assessors, ward mayors and a number of other officials were without compensation—though as I pointed out with reference to the provincial deputation, they were "compulsory and liable." The result was corruption and jobbery of the grossest kind, particularly among the municipal judges. But it made government cheap.

REVENUES UNDER AMERICAN RULE.

The existing revenue system should not require more than a few paragraphs. Less than ten days after the American occupation of Porto Rico, the military government abolished the use of documentary stamps and stamped paper; and a month later the real dues on the inheritance and transfer of property were annulled. Following this came a gradual repeal of the *consumos* or *octrois* which the municipalities had been allowed to levy on meat, drink and fuel; and the abolition of the lottery, the passport tax, the export duties and other minor revenues followed in rapid succession. Amid the complex and multitudinous system handed down by the Spanish, our military government slashed and destroyed, repealed and annulled, until the Porto Ricans came to believe that American government meant exemption from direct taxes, and the military government would have gone bankrupt had it not been for that much abused temporary tariff.

There is of course a good deal of exaggeration in this

statement, but it serves to impress the points I wish to make : that the supplies we sent to Porto Rico after the hurricane together with the activity of the military government—properly destructive—came very near pauperizing certain elements of the population and undoubtedly made the reimposition of adequate direct taxation a very difficult task. The moral atmosphere created by the military government gave Dr. Hollander many a bad quarter of an hour. On the other hand, their destructive work made it necessary and possible to replace the old system by an entirely new one.

The break with the past having been effectively made, it was necessary to adopt an American system. And this in fact was done by the revenue act of January 31, 1901. The last vestiges of the Spanish system—the fixed land tax and the *consumo* taxes—were abolished for insular purposes and replaced by a property tax, a system of excises, and a progressive inheritance tax. The last is so unimportant and so like the inheritance tax employed in the United States, that I shall not speak of it further. Less than $5,000 a year are expected from it.

The property tax is not essentially different from the ordinary property tax of the states. The ordinary exemptions of schools, churches, working tools, etc., have been made. Mortgages are treated as an interest in the property, and where a contract does not exist making the taxes payable by the mortgager they are taxed to the mortgagee. An interesting feature of the tax which worked with conspicuous success was a provision for the exemption of debt. Tax payers were allowed to subtract their debts, when the creditors resided in Porto Rico, by entering upon their schedules a specific list of their creditors and the corresponding amount owed to

each. As soon as the list of debts was received by the
assessor he forwarded a copy to the central office, where
a sort of clearing-house was maintained, from which a
memorandum of each debt was forwarded to the assessor
of the district in which the creditor lived, with instructions to see that it was entered upon the creditor's schedule. The scheme not only worked easily and successfully, but it succeeded in bringing to light an immense
amount of intangible property that would otherwise
have escaped.

The really important changes introduced by the property tax were administrative. The old direct taxes had
been levied by the Spanish Cortes, assessed by nearly two
hundred separate commissions appointed by sixty-six
municipal councils of the island, and collected for a percentage by a private company. " In the assessment particularly, there was no central control, no unity of administration and no uniformity of valuation." Under
the American system the tax is levied by the legislative
assembly, assessed by paid assessors appointed by the insular government and directed by a supervisor of assessment, acting under the general direction of the treasurer. Collection by salaried officials has replaced the old
method of letting out the collection to private parties.
The property tax is expected to yield about $500,000 a
year to the insular government.

By far the most important part of the present revenue
system is the group of stamp taxes ; the documentary
taxes ; the license taxes on dealers in alcoholic liquors,
cigars and fire-arms ; and the excise taxes upon the
manufacture and importation of proprietary medicines,
perfumery, cosmetics, toilet articles, playing cards, fire-
arms, ammunition, oleomargarine, matches, alcoholic
liquors and manufactured tobaccos of all kinds. Speak-

generally the rates of these taxes are considerably lower than those imposed on similar articles in the United States. The estimated yield of the stamp taxes in the present fiscal year is $700,000.

Besides the difference in rates, there are other important differences between the excise system of Porto Rico and that of the United States. In the United States, the stamp is placed upon the package of sale at the time of manufacture, or upon removal from bond, while the most thorough surveillance is maintained both of the sale and manufacture. In Porto Rico, the stamp will be placed on the bill of sale or lading which accompanies the shipment of goods from the factory. These changes were necessitated by the fact that it was impossible to supply bonded warehouses in Porto Rico at present, while the manufacture of rum and tobacco, although relatively much more important industries than those of the United States, could not bear the same rates of taxation. It has been repeatedly demonstrated, moreover, that the manufacturers are unable to pay the taxes upon their stocks of finished products until they are sold, the purchaser, at present, almost always forwarding the stamps required on the goods which he purchases. At the same time, the device of placing the stamps on the retail packages is a failure in Porto Rico. The patient peon is too economical to tear the stamp upon his box of cigarettes or matches. He seats himself in the sun and soaks the stamp off, washes it, and sells it to some unscrupulous manufacturer, in return for more cigarettes or matches. And it was found impossible to root out the practice by any reasonable amount of surveillance, because of the mountainous character of the county, the cost of transportation, the lack of police and the universality of the practice.

Under the present system each manufacturer will be furnished with a stub invoice book, on the page and stub of which he will be required to describe each shipment which leaves his factory. The stamps will then be pasted over the perforated line which separates the stub and the bill, in such a way that when the bill is detached part of each stamp will be left upon the stub and part upon the bill. Manufacturers will be required to return the stubs to the treasury, and merchants the bills, at regular intervals, so that in this way a reliable check can be kept upon the goods manufactured and sold in the island; while a perfect check can be kept upon imports and exports by means of the customs officers and the applications for the exemptions allowed upon exports.

In concluding this hasty summary of the existing revenue system of Porto Rico, it should be said that the customs collected upon goods from foreign countries imported into Porto Rico—the proceeds of which go to the insular treasury—are expected to yield $750,000 in the present fiscal year. This yield, however, is not expected to continue indefinitely. In a few years, owing to the growth of the trade between Porto Rico and the United States, now that the tariff barriers have been removed, the yield of the import duties will probably fall to $300,000 a year or less. The preëminence of the customs receipts is a temporary phenomenon.

Of the estimated revenue of $2,000,000, then, two and a half per cent. or $50,000 is expected from the inheritance tax and miscellaneous sources; $500,000 or twenty-five per cent. from the direct tax upon property; $700,-000 or thirty-five per cent. from the stamp taxes, almost all of which fall on the consumption of liquors and tobacco ; and $750,000 or thirty-seven and one-half per cent. from the import duties.

These figures taken in connection with the corresponding proportions in the Spanish budget of receipts convey with striking emphasis the difference between the American and the Spanish systems of revenue. In the one complexity ; in the other simplicity. In the earlier system thirteen per cent. from direct taxes, nothing from sumptuary excise taxes, and sixty-seven per cent. from customs duties falling in the main upon necessaries ; in the latter twenty-five per cent. from direct taxes, thirty-five per cent. from sumptuary excises, and a little more from the Dingley Tariff. In short, the Americanization of Porto Rico has meant, from the fiscal point of view, first, a substantial reduction in the burden of taxation ; second, a simplification of the system of taxation ; next, a relative increase in the taxation of accumulated property as opposed to taxes upon the sale, consumption and transfer of property ; and finally, a shifting of the center of gravity of the consumption taxes from the consumers of codfish and pork to the consumers of rum and tobacco. Whether the two classes of consumers are essentially different or not, is. I must confess, a doubtful question. It is to be hoped, however, that under the present arrangement the peon will get a little more codfish and a little less rum.

DISCUSSION.

JACOB H. HOLLANDER : The one signal omission in the paper just read is any intimation of the service which Dr. Adams himself rendered in the work of fiscal reconstruction he has described. He was invited to join the treasurer's staff just as a revenue system was being propared for submission to the insular legislature. His services in drafting the general property tax law were most important. He had practically exclusive charge of the difficult work of assessing domestic and foreign corporations, and from first to last his presence in Porto Rico was an aid and a comfort to those charged with the financial administration of the island.

Perhaps the most instructive lesson to a body such as this, in the recent financial experience of Porto Rico, is the mutual obligation in successful public financiering of the financial theorist and the financial administrator. This is not only the well established principle that the best laws may be perverted and abused in execution. But, more fundamentally, that just as no degree of technique can redeem an unsound financial measure, so no fiscal device however faultless in theory is good unless it possesses the possibility of administrative efficiency.

In the fiscal reconstruction of Porto Rico, the fullest opportunity was given for the adoption of scientific principles,—first, by reliance upon presumably expert opinion ; second, by the exemption of the island from the internal revenue laws of the United States, and third, by the grant of full financial power to the insular legislature. It is true that the tariff legislation for the island was not, as in the recent Philippine bill, devised specifically with reference to insular conditions, but much of the inconvenience that might have arisen from this fact was reduced first by executive modifications of the original schedules, and thereafter by the anticipation and realization of free trade with the United States. On the whole in Porto Rico, as not often elsewhere, financial theory had free hand and fair field.

On the other hand the financial theorist will emerge from careful study of the actual details of the fiscal revision of the island with meek heart and chastened spirit. On every side he is confronted with evidence of the overwhelming importance of that which he had heretofore lightly brushed aside as financial technique or relegated to the convenient limbo of financial administration. His exclusive concern has theretofore been, for example, as to what commodities and what rates should enter in an excise schedule, or as to whether a general property tax should exempt mortgages or allow deduction for indebtedness. But his actual expericuce is to find that these considerations are absolutely not one whit more important than the questions whether the payment of the excises should be evidenced by the affixture of a stamp to the commodity or otherwise, and whether the assessment schedule should be ruled in this way rather than that, or contain these questions rather than those. Indeed relative to the ultimate success or failure of his desires they are not so important. He finds that it is no greater sin to neglect local conditions and historical development than to ignore a mental reaction and a subjective preparedness for almost radically different financial institutions. He discovers that canons of taxation, laws of incidence and fiscal rules-of-thumb are as relative to time, place and conditions as the dicta of the classical political economy ; that the economic man has a twin brother in the fiscal man, and that unthinking reliance upon the one is as dangerous as upon the other. His return to academic activity will be signalized by a greater insistence upon the principle of financial relativity, by a bolder assertion of the indissoluble connection of technique with theory, and by a less dogmatic state of mind that will probably tend to make his preachment sounder and his influence greater.

The actual operation of the new revenue system since the beginning of the present fiscal year, July 1, 1901,— the period when the new law went into full operation— is full of interest. For the five months ending November 30, 1901, the ordinary receipts of the insular treasury have been $1,000,542.62. The ordinary expenditures for the same period have been $881,976.64, making an excess of receipts over expenditures of $118,565.98.

This result is, however, somewhat misleading, in consequence of the facts that insular expenditures are not spread proportionately over the twelve months, and also that payments on account of the property and delinquent taxes are heavier in the earlier than in the latter part of the year. A safer procedure would be to compare the insular budget and its estimate of receipts with the actual results for the five months.

The necessary expenses for carrying on the government of the island for the fiscal year beginning July 1, 1901, as authorized by the insular legislature in general and special appropriation bills, aggregated $1,976,802.21. The estimated receipts of the treasury were customs duties $784,775; excise taxes $715,343; property and delinquent direct taxes $500,000—aggregating $2,000,-118; or $23,315.79 more than the authorized expenditures with no account taken of minor miscellaneous receipts.

In each of the three essential sources of revenue, the actual receipts for the five months ending November

30, 1901, have justified the budgetary estimates and in two cases by comfortable margins. Thus, customs have yielded $332,987.57, as against an estimate of $326,989.55, or an actual monthly average of $66,597.51, as against an estimate of $65,397.91. Excises have pro-produced $349,429.77, as against an estimate of $350-658.30; or an actual monthly average of $69,885.95, as against an estimate of $70,131.66. Direct taxation has yielded $274,874.34 as against an estimate of $208,333.30, or an actual monthly average of $54,974.86, as against an estimate of $41,666.66. Finally from minor miscellaneous sources—upon which no reliance whatever was put—has come $17,361.73, exclusive of refunds.

In financial matters five months constitute an insufficient period for safe prophesy as to the results of a twelve-month. But considering the facts at hand and the tendencies now evident, there seems full reason for upposing that with no disturbing factor or unexpecteds occurrence the aggregate budgetary estimate for the fiscal year will be safely realized.

Any word as to the future is even more hazardous. As has been said elsewhere: "Without a dollar of funded or floating indebtedness, with a current income estimated as sufficient to meet the ordinary expenses of government, with large reserve funds to provide for unforeseen or extraordinary contingencies, and with a lighter burden of taxation upon the real economic life of the island than at any time in its history, there seems every reason for regarding the financial future of Porto Rico as bright and auspicious."

It would be ridiculous to suppose that all further necessity for financial legislation in Porto Rico has been removed. But it is only time, experience and specific conditions, that will clearly indicate where and when—

without any departure from fundamental principles—omission, amendment, or addition are desirable. In any event it seems no unwarranted optimism to believe that both in subjective appreciation and in objective fact a secure and enduring financial basis has been laid.

HENRY C. ADAMS: I do not rise with the intention of entering upon a discussion of the points presented in Dr. Hollander's excellent paper, but rather with the purpose of thanking him for the very strong and, I think, very just statement he has made of the importance of administrative considerations in the discussion of financial problems. My feeling has always been that for the scientific understanding of a great industrial or financial system, it is essential that the administrative requirements be taken into consideration. Indeed, I would go so far as to assert that theoretic analysis is likely to miss its highest aim unless one's conclusions be subjected to the test of administration. Dr. Hollander has very properly emphasized the close relation which exists between the theoretic and administrative principles in his discussion of the financial situation in Porto Rico. It is a point of view which even the theorist in economics cannot afford to overlook. And it is certainly propitious for the future of political economy in the United States that we find so large a number of men who have trained themselves in economic theory willing to undertake practical work in administration. In this regard the situation is very different from what it was when a few of us met together in Saratoga for the formation of the American Economic Association. A very respectable number of the members of this Association, either in their capacity as directors of public bureaus, or as experts, have already placed their trained intelligence at the service of the federal government, the state governments and the municipal governments of our country. I could not restrain my desire to avail myself of this opportunity to express my appreciation of the strong statements of Dr. Hollander in this regard.

FEDERICO DEGETAU:[1] There have been some statements here and some impressions made which I desire to rectify. I have not heard the first part of Mr. Adams's study, but from what I have heard it seems to me that it is necessary to make clear some points. You have heard, concerning the situation of Porto Rico under Spanish rule, that there were a superior and an inferior people, as if the Porto Rican people were placed in an inferior political relation towards the Spanish people. I must declare that I know nothing about that, and I am a Porto Rican born. On the contrary, I ought to state that Porto Rico was, from the beginning of the nineteenth century, a province of Spain equal to the other provinces. In some matters, Porto Rico had an autonomy not enjoyed by the other provinces of Spain. I refer especially to the economic relations, in which Porto Rico had an autonomy that your states do not enjoy here; and if you wish to see it confirmed by an American authority, you can read the statement of General Davis concerning the latitude and power given to the government of the island, in his report to the war department on the civil affairs of Porto Rico. The fact that the annual budget of the island was approved by the congress at Madrid would seem to give the impression that Porto Rico occupied an inferior status in relation to the Spanish government. If you think that we were in Porto Rico in the same, or similar, condition in which we are now temporarily—deprived of representa-

[1] Mr. Degetau is resident commissioner from Porto Rico.

tion in that congress—then this would seem true, but it was not so. When we were under Spanish rule, Porto Rico elected her people to represent her In the congress of Spain. We elected sixteen members to the House of of Representatives. I, myself, was lately one of those representatives. We also elected four members to the senate. The congress approved the budget, because in it was vested the national sovereignty. But this authority was not an exclusive at tribute of the Spanish peninsula, but was shared by the people of the island, as it has been seen, whose representatives in the house and senate at Madrid had equal rights and privileges to those of the other provinces.

There is another point on which I ought to dwell. I refer to a matter that is awaiting decision. That is the debt of the treasury of Cuba to the people of Porto Rico. It has been said by Mr. Adams, in his paper, that Spain took the money from Porto Rico in order to use it in the war against Cuba. I have studied that question because it was my duty, and I ought to declare that his statement is not scientifically accurate. In order that you may comprehend the question, I will explain briefly how these things worked under the Spanish rule. The Porto Rican treasury, has, since the beginning of the nineteenth century, been recognized as independent of the treasury of Spain and of the treasury of Cuba. The island of Porto Rico made some loans to Cuba, in many cases when it was not in time of war. Some of these loans had no relation whatever to the war. For instance, once, in order to avoid a monetary crisis in Cuba, Porto Rico gave her some thousands—I do not remember how many. I did not come here prepared to speak, so you will excuse me if I do not give you the figures.

I would be glad to give you some explanation of some

of the other matters treated in the study of Mr. Adams, but I will merely explain the reference to the bull fights mixed in the same clause with educational and charitable institutions for the purpose of taxation. That anomaly is due to the fact that in Porto Rico bull fights were not a general amusement. There is not in any city of the island a "plaza de toros," the special place for such sport which is found in almost every Spanish city. It is a pleasure to state that bull fights were not a popular festival in my native country. The bull fights occurred very seldom in Porto Rico, and were fought by the Spanish officers there in the garrisons. These officers generally dedicated the profits of the feasts to charitable institutions. This was the reason for that provision.

Mr. ADAMS: I was rather careful to choose my language when I stated that three million dollars had been taken by Spain and used in the settlement of her Cuban difficulties. In the time limit of thirty minutes one can't go into details. As a matter of fact the money spent by Spain in the attempt to crush the various insurrections of Cuba was made an obligatory debt on Cuba. Three million dollars was borrowed out of the Porto Rican treasury and sent to Cuba during the ten years' war and thus became a Cuban debt. Of this amount, I understand, a large proportion has never been repaid. It is in this sense and in this way that I meant that Porto Rico had contributed some two million two hundred thousand dollars towards the suppression of Cuban insurrection. I do not think it is a stretch of language to use the words in that meaning.

With respect to the representation of Porto Rico, you are aware that I was careful to point out that Porto Rico

was represented in the Spanish Cortes but if Señor Degatau will take occasion to explain the electoral law in
Porto Rico it will become quite apparent, I think, that
the representation in the Spanish Cortes was more apparent than real.   For instance, if I remember rightly,
and I am trusting to my memory here, to vote in Porto
Rico it was necessary to pay at least twenty pesos direct
taxes.

MR. DEGATAU : I was elected by universal suffrage.

MR. ADAMS : When were you elected ?

MR. DEGATAU : 1898.

MR. ADAMS : How long did the universal suffrage
last ?

MR. DEGATAU : Until the war with the United States,
but it was originally introduced in 1869.   They elected
me first in 1878 and the second time in 1898 and I
served until the war.

MR. ADAMS : When did you say was the interval of
universal suffrage ?

MR. DEGATAU : 1869 to 1874.

MR. ADAMS : What I wanted to call your attention to
was the fact that during the interval between 1876 and
1890, or really up to 1898, the suffrage was so confined
that it was possible for the Spanish administration if it
so wished to control absolutely the representation of
Porto Rico.   The electoral law of 1890 provided I
think—I may be wrong in these figures but I think I
am correct—that an individual to vote must pay twenty
pesos,—twelve dollars—in direct taxes, or he must be
an office holder.   The consequence was at that one time,
I am told, the number of voters in San Juan who voted
because of holding office was greater than the number of
persons who voted because of the payment of the
twenty pesos tax.

UNIFORM MUNICIPAL ACCOUNTS AND STATISTICS.

REPORT OF THE COMMITTEE.

At the last meeting of the Association your committee submitted a report in which the work needing to be done to secure a uniform system of municipal accounts and statistics was reviewed, the part in that work which might best be undertaken by this committee was discussed, and certain conclusions were stated.[1]

The report was supplemented by two appendices entitled : (1) "Uniform Accounting a Prerequisite to National Municipal Statistics," and (2) "Progress toward Uniform Municipal Statistics in the United States." In the latter paper the work was reviewed up to the close of 1900. Since there was practically no discussion of the first report, and the main points at issue have changed little, if at all, during the year, it seems advisable again to bring the report of 1900 before the Association.

Attention is called especially to the eight conclusions printed on pages 260–261 of the Proceedings of the Thirteenth Annual Meeting, upon which the following comments are offered :

In the year which has elapsed since the first report was made it has become evident that conclusions 1 to 4 are pretty generally accepted by those interested in the subject under discussion. No. 5, relating to coöperative efforts, has been even more generously received, and several steps have been taken to carry it into effect.

[1] Publications of the American Economic Association, 3d series, 2 : 254–262.

Nos. 6 and 7, relating to state control and the publication of state summaries, respectively, may be left, with advantage, until this movement has attained more definite shape and greater volume and force than could be be expected in so short a time.

As to the first part of no. 8, the United States Department of Labor, through congressional authorization, is continuing its summaries of statistics for cities of 30,000 and upwards, and it is a pleasure to say the work grows better year by year. The last part of no. 8 might, perhaps, be profitably changed into a general inquiry as to what the present Census Office may undertake with greatest advantage in the way of municipal statistics. This inquiry is more pertinent now than it was a year ago, in view of the fact that there is no prospect that the Census Office will reach the municipal investigations before the latter part of 1902.

Since the Detroit meeting of this Association, a committee of the National Municipal League, of which two members of your committee are likewise members, has been formed. This committee is actively engaged in an attempt to formulate a general system of uniform municipal accounting. It is also trying to bring into unity the efforts of various special societies, like water-works associations, to perfect either schemes of accounting or summaries of statistics for annual reports. The work of the National Municipal League committee, up to May, 1901, is outlined in a published report, copies of which are available here or may be secured from the members of either committee. The League hopes that by the date of its next annual meeting it may be able to present both a series of schedules for municipal accounting, and summaries of the statistics of many branches of the municipal service.

Your own committee requests the members of the Association to co-operate in the general movement by aiding in the formulation of schedules, and by trying to induce city officials generally to apply to their respective municipalities and departments the schedules as formulated. Much of the work is necessarily tentative, and its value cannot be judged until the proposed form of schedules has been tested by actual practice.

> MOSES N. BAKER, Chairman.
> HENRY B. GARDNER,
> ED. W. BEMIS,
> E. DANA DURAND,
> FREDERICK R. CLOW.

DISCUSSION.

CHARLES E. CURTIS : One looks over this report with a feeling of gratitude to the framers of it, and a feeling of appreciation of the large amount of effort that has been put into it, and the chairman and the other members of the committee deserve the hearty thanks of all municipal administrators throughout the country. There are one or two features of it of which I should like to speak, not in a critical way, but merely as a matter under discussion, and to suggest a little different standpoint, possibly, from the one which most economists would take. There is no question but that statistics relating to many subjects will be readily obtained, but where the real friction, if any, will come in gaining these statistics is in the items connected with franchises, and particularly in regard to semi-public corporations. While there is no doubt that in some cases these franchises have been abused, there is, I think, a question as to whether the managers of these properties who will be asked, in some cases have been asked, to furnish data may not have a natural and justifiable reluctance in furnishing it. I have the impression from conversation with such managers that in a good many cases they are less interested in the statistics from other cities than they are alarmed at the attitude and teachings of some of the economists themselves. Now if data of this sort are to be obtained, the coöperation of the semi-public companies is desirable, and they should be assured in some way that the data sought for is to be absolutely impartial, and that the questions asked are to be such as will show the facts only, without any attempt or disposition to use the data to support a theory or notion already conceived. In the appendix to the report is mentioned, on page two hundred and seventy-seven, that "at the last meeting of the National Electric Light Association, held in Chicago in May, 1900, Mr. James B. Cahoon, of Syracuse, N. Y., submitted detailed forms for uniform gas and electric lighting accounts. The convention voted to have the committee prepare a system of uniform accounting to be presented at the next annual meeting"; and a foot-note adds: "One of Mr. Cahoon's chief objects in submitting the paper and schedules was to stem the tide in favor of municipal ownership."

Here, then, were schedules made up for the express purpose of supporting certain propositions. This is to be deprecated. The statistics sought for should neither be intended to support nor refute the argument for municipal ownership, but should be such as will reveal the weak points and the strong points of both public and private ownership.

The report says, on page 265: "But unfortunately the council committees that undertake so many of these investigations are rarely trained statisticians or appreciative of the value of such persons; so the figures are put together somehow, and made to fit a preconceived or ill-conceived theory, and money and perhaps human lives are sacrificed as a result."

Now I believe there are many laymen who fear that in the writings of some of the modern economists the data sought for may be used to fit a pre-conceived or ill-conceived theory, and that is one of the things which should be guarded against very carefully. If the statistics are to be serviceable, the questions asked and the schedules used must be absolutely impartial in their tone. Consider the statistics as used by the labor commissioners in certain states, statistics that have been used by some economists in a way that has supported their theories most vigorously. These are partial statistics, and incomplete; but they are used, and are misleading in their results. It has come to be rather a fad among some people, to condemn semi-public companies, and to demand that the municipalities shall engage in industrial enterprises. Not only should we be interested in statistics as a means of correcting the abuses of private companies, but we should also be equally anxious to secure uniform statistics as a means of checking the abuses of municipalities themselves; and the statistics sought should be such as will show both classes of abuses. The council committees referred to here, in some cases at least, look up to and respect the economists of the day. If that respect is to be maintained, the utmost impartiality in such matters as these must be observed. The statistics will be worth the effort of the laymen whose services you will have to use in getting the data, they will be worth the assistance of the officials of companies and of municipalities, upon one condition. If they are to be used to enable Professor A. to demonstrate that Professor B. was mistaken in his last treatise, they are not worth the labor of the rest of us to obtain. If they are to be used, on the other hand, to enable our municipal administrators more correctly to judge of their own duties, so that they may improve the condition of folks, they will be of value. The words of Professor Van Dyke should be often considered: "Keep me from caring more for books than for folks."

Roland P. Falkner: The report calls attention to the chaotic conditions of all official records of what most vitally concerns the people in the administration of local and municipal government. In a field where opinion can be formed and a guiding policy selected only by processes of comparison, the elements of comparison are wholly lacking. If this variety were the result of wholly different local conditions, and the product of a careful adaptation of means to ends we might applaud the result and rejoice that not a dead uniformity but a strong individuality characterizes our local government. But unfortunately the variety is the result of ignorance, indifference and neglect, the bungling makeshift of unskilled artisans.

The problem before us is how to awaken a popular consciousness of this fact and how when awakened to embody this feeling in remedial action. I venture to think that in the first endeavor we must be far more specific than the report before us. It seems to me that we must draw more generously upon illustrations expressed largely in dollars and cents. The comparability of local administration as an abstraction may be a motive sufficiently powerful to stimulate this body or any other body of specialists to the passage of vigorous resolutions, but not one to move public opinion or incite legislation. In certain lines of municipal activity, in certain states, uniformity of records is already a fact. Can we not draw a picture of "before" and "after" which shall carry the same conviction with the public as is supposed to follow the advertisement of hair restorers? A municipal campaign was not long ago conducted in Philadelphia in which the extravagance of the dominant party formed the keynote of the attack. Figures were adduced to show that in twenty years the municipal expenditures had doubled. No one seemed to have thought that the per capita expenditure had not increased in that proportion, and the fact that in the earlier period the gas works were operated by a trust or commission which turned a net balance only into the treasury, while in the later period under city management the entire operating expenses figured as outlay, though the operation still netted a profit was wholly ignored. A system of uniform municipal accounting equally well adapted to bring out real expenditure under either organization would have obviated such an absurd campaign. It is only by such concrete illustrations piled mountain high that a general principle becomes a popular axiom. For not until the voters seize the facts which are so plain to us can our schemes of reform become anything more than pious wishes.

Supposing, however, that happy day arrived when our efforts have not only convinced aenemic reformers and drawing room agitators that good book-keeping is a necessary adjunct of good government, but have brought it down to the workingman that under the cover of vague and uncertain accounting rascality of all kinds flourishes, how shall they obtain a remedy?

Of all the means pointed out none seems to offer better prospects of success than the passage of the state laws of supervision over accounts, to be kept in accordance with forms prescribed by state authority. Individual cities may reform their methods, but cannot impose them upon others. As object lessons their efforts are of the highest value, and it may well be worthy of municipal enterprise to adopt systems of records so complete and so well adapted to the purpose which they serve that they would be selected by state legislatures as types for the state as a whole.

One of the means which, in my judgment, would more than anything else contribute to hastening the day would be the immediate erection of statistical departments in our states and cities. Such officers should be charged with embodying the results of administrative labor instalments in statements easily comprehended. It is the function of statistics to render book-keeping intelligible, and by book-keeping is here included not only accounts in dollars and cents, but all records dealing with classes of facts whose aggregates, compositions or relations to other facts are matters of social significance. That such an effort to systematize the records of local administration would be beset with difficulties is indubitable, but the horrible examples which such an effort would bring to light would be a cumulative force in the direction of uniform regulation which could not be withstood. I have ever believed that the true way to accomplish reform in statistical methods was first to do with those at hand the best which they could accomplish, demonstrate thus the practical value of statistics and thus create a demand for something better.

HARVEY S. CHASE: The city of Chicago with its annual income of twenty-five or thirty millions of dollars is in a very peculiar situation. The application there of the principles of uniform accounting as laid down by the co-ordinating associations, of which this committee represents one, is probably the most notable application that has been made, or perhaps will be made for some time. It may be worth while to give a brief statement in regard to it.

Through the Merchants' Club of Chicago an investigation of the city's affairs was made a year or so ago. The result of this private investigation was such that the city council entered into contracts with well known accountants to investigate the special assessment ac-

counts running back to the year of the fire, 1871 ; and
to report upon a system intended for the entire reorganization of the city's accounts. These matters are now
nearing completion. The system of accounts was reported at the end of November and has been adopted
almost in its entirety by the city council, and it will be
inaugurated during the year 1902. The situation in
Chicago is peculiar from many points of view, but particularly from the fact that the city government has
never, since the fire, at least, had the revenue necessary
to carry on its work. I find when I speak of Chicago
finances with people in the East that it is the almost
universal opinion that Chicago's revenue has disappeared, or large portions of it, into the pockets of her
officials. This is however a mistaken opinion. " Boodle-
ing" in Chicago has not been more marked than in
other cities. Our investigations prove that such revenue
as has been received by the city has on the whole been
well administered. Indeed it is surprising that the city
officials could have done as well as they have, handicapped as they have been by the financial situation in
which the city finds itself due to state legislation.

The complications between the city, the old town-
system, which still continues in part, the county and
and the state, are extraordinary. The tax levy in Chicago is made early in the year, by the city council.
The valuations of property are made by the town assessors also early in the year. Later they go to the board of
review, a county organization, and are rearranged by it,
and then to a state organization, the board of equalization. It is the end of the year before the city really
knows what its income is ; meantime the expenses have
already been incurred and the money spent. In 1900,
for example, the appropriations were made upon a basis

of valuation of the previous year, which was about three hundred and forty-seven millions of dollars. At the end of the year it was found that the new board of assessors had reduced these valuations to two hundred and seventy-six millions. The city had, therefore, been making illegally expenditures all through that period.

The tax levy is voted in March, but the money is not collected until the following year. It then passes into the hands of the county collector, over whom the city officials have no control. As he is paid a commission on his collections and on the money deposited in the banks, it is for his interest to keep the funds in the banks as long as possible. Finally it is paid over to the city treasurer, who also is given a commission, out of which he pays all the expenses of his office. With these astonishing complications, the necessity for uniform accounting is very evident.

The city usually manages to squeeze out revenue enough to pay its wages and salaries, which are essential and immediate. But it has allowed its bills for supplies to run over into the ensuing year, and sometimes it is eighteen months or more before the bills are paid. Bills have passed through the courts and judgments have been taken against the city amounting to something over three million dollars. A tax-payer recently refused to pay his taxes, upon the ground that the total amount of the debt of the city of Chicago was in excess of the statutory limit (which is five per cent of the assessed valuation), and that he could not be compelled to pay the taxes. The case came before the same judge who had granted the judgment making the excess of debt, and he exempted the tax-payer.

Chicago, it thus appears, has no general fund of money against which appropriations are made, no "working capital." Appropriations are made against the future altogether, and do not represent cash at all.

It has been the custom to charge up in the appropriation bill, estimated items of "loss and cost" upon the collection of the tax (four and one-half per cent.). Each appropriation was thus increased by four and one-half per cent., which anticipated the loss and cost of the tax collections. Also during the course of the year, when the actual "loss and cost" of the previous year had been ascertained, it was charged (debit) to this same account. Now as the expenditures increased, there was a difference between this credit and this charge for "loss and cost" yearly. That is to say, there was a deficiency of the estimated deficiency. Under the statutes, all balances of appropriations must be carried at the end of the year into what is called the "general fund account," a surplus account. So at the end of the year these "deficiencies of deficiencies" were carried into this general fund account and were looked upon as surplus, or as cash.

DR. HARTWELL: It has been intimated by several gentlemen in the course of this afternoon's discussion that the economic man and the fiscal man, as bodied forth in the books, are far to seek and that they be few who find them. Judging from statistics as they are made and used generally, the statistics man belongs in the same category with the economic and the fiscal man. In discussing plans and devising measures to secure reasonable uniformity in municipal accounting and statistics, we do well to recognize the standards of idealistic seekers after scientific truth; but we should not lose sight of the fact that in practice we shall have to depend for the most part upon other kinds of men. Professor

Falkner's suggestion that an attempt to cover the whole or even the larger part of the field of municipal statistics would prove futile at the present time seems to me to be apposite and sound.

It is my belief that municipal statistics, like charity, should begin at home; that they should relate to the objects and needs of local administration and be prepared with the primary purpose of enlightening a local public opinion and of serving local authorities as the basis for intelligent action. Know thyself is an injunction which applies as well to cities as to individuals. So long as a city does not know itself it cannot know other cities, or compare itself with them or profit largely by their experience. The sooner our leading cities are led to insist upon having simple and intelligible financial and statistical reports furnished by their own servants for home use, the sooner will the public and official mind become responsive to the demands of such bodies as this for the adoption of more modern and scientific methods of book-keeping and house-keeping by all cities; and the sooner will it become possible for the student of municipal affairs and for state and national officials and bureaus to secure from city officials and publications such information as is usually unattainable now.

I am not at all disposed to underrate the importance of concerted action in this matter on the part of representative associations of scientific and professional men; but I would emphasize the fact that our efforts are likely to prove abortive unless the present undeveloped state of the art of municipal house-keeping and book-keeping, in most cities, is borne in mind. Our recommendations should be comparatively few and simple and capable of being easily carried out, lest we repel busy and preoccupied officials whose cooperation is requisite for the success of the measures we have in mind.

The results of the most notable attempt hitherto made to report annually upon the scope and cost of municipal administrations in the United States bear upon the question before us. I refer to three series of comparative tables entitled "Statistics of Cities," which have been published by the United States Department of Labor for the years 1898–1900 inclusive, in compliance with an act of Congress passed in the year 1898. There is warrant for the assertion that the act was passed in the confident expectation that the statistics desired could be compiled without great dificulty from such reports as are regularly given to the public by city boards and officials. The experience of the commissioner of labor has proved the groundlessness of that expectation. Commissioner Wright has found municipal reports as a class so confused and misleading that he has been obliged to go behind the returns and resort to the expensive expedient of gathering his material at first hand by means of special agents.

Mr. Baker alluded in his report to the committee of the National Municipal League on uniform municipal accounting and statistics. That committee, of which Mr. Baker, Mr. Chase and others present are members, has been at work for nearly a year. On behalf of the committee which has been in session this morning here in Washington, I wish to express our appreciation of the courtesy of your president in inviting us to take part in your deliberations. At a meeting of the league in May last, our committee reported a provisional set of schedules designed to facilitate the rendering of uniform financial reports by the cities of a given state to a central state board,—our problem being to work out the details of a practicable scheme to effectuate certain general recommendations of the league's "Municipal Programme." Mr. Hangar who has charge of the investigation of the Department of Labor in respect to city statistics declares that if cities of 30,000 inhabitants should adopt the schedules just mentioned, the labor of collecting material for the department's yearly bulletin would be reduced 90 per cent.

This is not the time or place for a detailed statement of the views or plans of our committee, but I may say in passing that they agree substantially with those of your own committee. From our point of view financial statistics are of primary importance at this juncture. We recognize the impossibility of securing the speedy or general adoption of reform methods of book-keeping, and shall content ourselves with proposing forms of return with regard to receipts and expenditures, resources and liabilities, debt, loans, sinking-fund, etc., that may readily be filled out by any comptroller or auditor, without disturbance to his customary methods of procedure. If fiscal officers can be induced to make supplementary reports in accordance with a consistent plan it will be far easier than at present to establish a base line to serve in attempts to map out and cultivate other fields of municipal statistics.

The domain of American municipal statistics, using the term in its scientific sense, presents such wide areas of unsettled not to say unexplored territory that, as I have already intimated, it seems a wiser policy to postpone ambitious schemes of expansion until our home fields have been subjected to a more intensive and productive system of cultivation than is yet common. There is need of caution and self-restraint in instituting comparisons between cities even in such familiar fields as population statistics and the movement of population. Owing to loose methods employed in estimating population in intercensal years even the crude death rates of many leading American cities are open to grave suspicion, and per capita estimates of every description are full of pitfalls. For instance in a carefully prepared paper on certain classes of expenditure by twenty-nine principal cities read in 1898 before the American Society of Municipal Improvements, the population of Baltimore according to an "official estimate" was set at the remarkably round number of 500,000. A few months later the Charities Review published a paper whose writer based certain per capita comparisons relating to out-door relief in Baltimore and other cities upon another "official estimate" of 625,270 as the population of Baltimore in the year 1898—while the official death-rates of the city for the same year were based on an estimated population of 541,000. I asked the health officer how he obtained that figure. He replied that he had asked the two leading Baltimore newspapers "independently on the same day" for their estimates of the city's population. "One said 540,000, the other 541,000, and I took 541,000." In June, 1900, the enumerators of the Twelfth Census could find only 508,957 people in Baltimore. In Boston, where I live, it is impossible to show the monthly movement of population because of our antiquated methods of recording births and marriages. Every spring there is a round-up of babies which resembles the method employed by the average town clerk in the rural districts in gathering his birth statistics. To be sure there is a small fee offered in Boston to stimulate promptitude on the part of physicians in registering births. But the allowance of $0.25 for each certificate of birth filed with the city registrar has not proved altogether satisfactory.

It has been known to work even badly. A few years ago it was found that a certain doctor had certified to the birth of upwards of eighty infants that never existed. Yet the names of those ink engendered babes could not be expunged legally from the records, and when we went to the state house and asked to have the law amended the legislators laughed at it.

Such facts may serve to indicate that the immediate prospects for gathering strictly comparable data throughout the wide range of activities common to cities is not brilliant, to say the least.

CLINTON ROGERS WOODRUFF : My experience has been that the " reformer" to whom Dr. Falkner has referred, is anything but aenemic or dilettante or ineffective. As a rule, those I have known are full-blooded, persistent, (which is of the essence of practicality) and, in the long run, effective. Perhaps he is impractical because he does not know when he is beaten or when to "let up." The economic man and the statistical man we have been told this afternoon are figments of imagination. So is the reformer of the type described by Dr. Falkner.

The subject of uniform municipal accounts is one of prime importance as has been pointed out at this session; and obviously so. We hear much of publicity of accounts for municipalities and for quasi-public corporations, and rightly so ; but publicity without uniformity will aid but little in a study and comprehension of vexed municipal problems.

Although apparently a dry topic and one of narrow application, uniform municipal accounting is one of wide application and of extensive influence. Mr. Chase will bear me out when I maintain that following uniform municipal accounts, as a natural sequence, will come inevitably an improved system of municipal taxation and assessment, and an improvement in the relations of city, county and state. In fact there will be substantial betterment all along the line. The experience of Chicago amply verifies this, and we find in Ohio that the movements for uniform accounting and tax reforms have joined hands and both are being jointly urged by the Ohio state board of commerce.

MR. BAKER: I would like to say in addition that the subject is a very broad, complex, and difficult one; and a satisfactory solution, if any solution be reached, can be obtained only by the assistance of all who are interested in the subject and have given it earnest attention. Therefore, in behalf of this Association, and of various committees deeply interested and hard at work upon the problem, I wish to express the hope that suggestions will be freely made to the several committees, and that your coöperation will be given to the work, and particularly that, coming as you do from so many municipalities throughout the country, you will attempt to bring this important matter to the attention of the proper officials of your own cities. I should like to suggest that those who are willing to go into the matter should send suggestions to the director of the census regarding the collection of municipal statistics, and should also give careful consideration to the municipal inquiries already being made by the United States Department of Labor for cities of thirty thousand and upwards, and decide whether it is wise to bring personal influence upon your representatives in Congress for the extension of the latter work to include smaller municipalities.

THE ECONOMIC INTERPRETATION OF HISTORY.

BY EDWIN R. A. SELIGMAN.

The problem with which we have to deal is the reason of those great changes in human thought and human life which form the conditions of progress. The solution that has been suggested is that to economic causes must be traced, in last instance, those transformations in the structure of society which themselves condition the relations of social classes and the various manifestations of social life. This doctrine is often called "historical materialism" or the "materialistic interpretation of history". Such terms are, however, lacking in precision; for, if by "materialism" is meant the tracing of all changes to material causes, the biological view of history is also materialistic. Again, the theory which ascribes all changes in society to the influence of climate or to the character of the fauna and flora is materialistic, and yet has little in common with the doctrine here discussed. The theory now under consideration is not only materialistic but also economic in character; and the better phrase is not the "materialistic interpretation" but the "economic interpretation" is history.

In another place[1] an attempt has been made to expound somewhat more fully the theory as well as to trace its origin and its connection with earlier doctrines. In still another article[2] the developments of the theory and its applications to the particular facts of history have been studied in some detail. What interests us here is

[1] *Political Science Quarterly*, vol. 16, no. 4.
[2] *Ibid.*, vol. 17, no. 1.

a consideration of the theory itself as a philosophical doctrine. We may best approach the problem from an examination of the objections that have been advanced.

Some of these objections are indeed sound ; but others posess only a partial validity. Let us consider the latter class first.

Among these criticisms the following are most frequently encountered :, First, that the theory of economic interpretation is a fatalistic theory ; second, that it rests on the assumption of historical laws, the very existence of which is open to question ; third, that it is socialistic ; fourth, that it neglects the ethical and spiritual forces of history; fifth, that it leads to absurd exaggerations.[1]

Let us consider first the objection that the doctrine is fatalistic, opposed to the theory of free will, and overlooking the importance of great men in history. It is obvious that this is not the place to enter into a general philosophical discussion of determinism. For our purpose it is sufficient to state that if by freedom of the will we simply mean the power to decide as to an action, there is no necessary clash with the doctrine of economic or social interpretation. Every man has will power, and may decide to act or to refrain from acting, thus showing that he is in this sense a free agent. But whether he decides in the one way or the other, there are certain causes operative within the organism which are responsible for the decision. The function of science is to ascertain what these causes are. All we know thus far is that every man is what he is because of the influences of environment, past or present. We need not here discuss the biological disputes between the

[1] These objections are considered more fully in the *Political Science Quarterly*, vol. 17, no. 2.

Weissmannist and the Neo-Lamarkian; for whether we believe with the one that the only factor in progress is the power of natural selection to transmit and strengthen congenital characteristics, or with the other that acquired characteristics are also inherited, we are dealing in each case with the operation of some form of past environment. Neither Weissmannists nor Neo-Lamarkians deny the obvious fact of the influence of present environment on the individual as such.

Since, therefore, man, like everything else, is what he is because of his environment, past and present—that is, the environment of his ancestors as well as of himself—it is clear that if we knew all the facts of his past and present environment we should be in a much better position to foretell with some degree of precision the actions of every human being. Although a man is free to steal or not to steal, we are even now safe in predicting that under ordinary circumstances an honest man will not steal. His congenital and acquired characteristics are such that under certain conditions he will always elect a certain course of action. In the case of physical environment, the matter is very simple. While an Eskimo may be perfectly free to go naked, it is not a violent stretch of the fancy to assume that no sane Eskimo will do so as long as he remains in the Arctic regions. When we leave the physical and come to the social environment, as we necessarily do in discussing the doctrine of economic interpretation, the essence of the matter is not much changed.

The theory of social environment, reduced to its simplest elements, means that even though the individual be morally and intellectually free to choose his own action, the range of his choices will be largely influenced by the circumstances, traditions, manners and customs of the society about him. The negation of the theory of social environment excludes the very conception of law in the moral disciplines. It would render impossible the existence of statistics, jurisprudence, economics, politics, sociology or even ethics. Social law means that amid the myriad decision of the presumable free-agents that compose a given community, there can be discovered a certain general tendency or uniformity of action, deviation from which is so slight as not to impair the essential validity of the general statement. The controlling considerations are always the social considerations. The choices that influence progress are the social choices—*i.e.*, the choices of the majority.

This is the reason why the great man theory of history has well nigh disappeared. No one, indeed, denies the value of great men, or the vital importance of what Matthew Arnold calls the remnant. Without the winged thoughts and the decisive actions of the great leaders, the progress of the world would doubtless have been considerably retarded. But few now overlook the essential dependence of the great man upon the wider social environment amid which he has developed. While his appearance at a particular moment is indeed a matter of chance, the great man influences society only when society is ready for him. If society is not ready for him he is called not a great man, but a visionary or a failure. Just as in animal life the freak or sport works through natural selection as fixed by the environment, so in human life the great man can permanently succeed only if the social environment is ripe. Biologists tell us that variation in the species is the cause of all progress, but that the extreme limit of successful variation from the parent type in any one case does not exceed a small percentage. The great man represents the extreme limit of successful variation in the human race. It is to him that progress seems to be largely due. But we must not forget that even here the great mass of his characteristics are those of the society about him, and that he is great because he expresses more successfully than others the real spirit of the age of which he is the supreme embodiment.

It is then an obviously incorrect statement of the problem to assert that the theory of economic interpretation, or the theory of social environment of which it is a part, is incompatible with the doctrine of free will. If by determinism we erroneously mean moral fatalism, determinism is not involved at all. The theory of social environment in no way implies fatalism. Social arrangements are human arrangements, and human beings are, in the sense indicated, free to form decisions and to make social choices. But they will invariably be guided in their decisions by the sum of ideas and expressions which have been transmitted to them through inheritance and environment. So far as great men influence the march of progress, they can do so only to the extent that they can induce the community to accept these new ideas as something in harmony with its surroundings and its aspirations. Given a certain set of conditions, the great mass of the community will decide to act in a certain way. Social law rests on the observation that men will choose a course of action in harmony with what they conceive to be their welfare, and on the further observation that the very idea of an organized community implies that a majority will be found to entertain common ideas of what is their welfare. If the conditions change the common ideas will change with them. The conditions, so far as they are social in character, are indeed created by men and may be altered by men, so that in last resort, there is nothing fatalistic about progress. But it is after all the conditions, which because of their direct action or reaction on individuals, are at any given moment responsible for the general current of social thought.

To the extent, then, that the theory of economic interpretation is simply a part of the general doctrine of social environment the contention that it necessarily leads to an unreasoning fatalism is baseless. Men are the product of history, but history is made by men.

The second objection to the theory under discussion is closely related to the first. The economic interpretation of history presupposes that there are historical laws. Yet this is objected to by some. Those, however, who deny the existence of historical laws are evidently laboring under a misapprehension. What they mean is, obviously, that the statement of some particular historical law is false, or that the causes of some definite historical occurrence are so complex and so obscure that it is well nigh impossible to frame a general explanation. But they cannot mean that historical laws do not exist. The mere fact that we have not discovered a law does not prove that there is none.

For what is meant by a scientific law? A law is an explanatory statement of the actual relations between facts. The processes of human thought enable us to classify the likenesses and differences in the myriad phenomena of life, and to subsume the unity underlying these differences. This unity makes itself known to us under the guise of a causal relation of one phenomenon to another. When we have succeeded in ascertaining the relation of cause and effect, we are able to frame the law. But our inability to discover the law does not invalidate the fact of its existence. The relations between the stars existed from the beginning of time; the discovery of the law which enables us to explain these relations is a result of scientific progress.

What is true of the exact sciences is equally true of the social sciences, with the difference that social sciences are immeasurably more complex because of the greater difficulty in isolating the phenomena to be investigated, and in repeating the experiments. But to deny the existence of social laws, for instance, simply because some particular alleged laws may be convicted of unreality would be to repeat the errors formerly committed by some of the extremists among the historical economists and not yet so infrequent as they ought to be. Obedience to law does not mean that the law causes the phenomenon to happen—for that is absurd—but simply that the law gives an explanation of the occurrence.

History, however, is the record of the actions of men in society. But if each phase of social activity constitutes the material for a separate science, with its array of scientific laws, the whole of social activity, which in its ceaseless transformation forms the warp and woof of history, must equally be subject to law. To deny the existence of historical laws is virtually to maintain that there is to be found in human life no such thing as cause and effect.

The third objection to the doctrine is its alleged socialistic character. To this it may be replied that if the theory is true, it is utterly immaterial to what conclusion it leads. To refuse to accept a scientific law because some of its corollaries are distasteful to us is to betray a lamentable incapacity to grasp the elementary conditions of scientific progress. If the law is true, we must make our views conform to the law, not attempt to mould the law to our views.

Fortunately, however, we are not reduced to any such alternative. For notwithstanding the ordinary opinion to the contrary, there is nothing in common between the economic interpretation of history and the doctrine of socialism, except the accidental fact that the originator of both theories happened to be the same man. Karl Marx founded " scientific socialism ", if by that curious phrase we mean his theory of surplus value and the conclusions therefrom. Karl Marx also originated the economic interpretation of history, and thought that his own version of this interpretation would prove to be a bulwark of his socialistic theory.

It is plain, however, that the two things have nothing to do with each other. We might agree that economic factors primarily influence progress, we might conclude that social forces rather than individual whim, at bottom, make history, we might even accept the existence of class struggles; but none of these admissions would necessarily lead to any semblance of socialism.

Socialism is a theory of what ought to be ; historical materialism is a theory of what has been. The one is teleological, the other is descriptive. The one is a speculative ideal ; the other is a canon of interpretation. It is impossible to see any necessary connection between such divergent conceptions. We must distinguish between the principle of economic interpretation in general, and some particular application of the principle. We might agree with the general doctrine and yet refuse to accept the one-sided ideals of the non-socialist, Loria ; we might agree with the general doctrine, and yet refuse to accept the equally one-sided ideals of the socialist, Marx. Even if every one of Marx's economic theories was entirely false, this fact alone would not in any degree invalidate the general doctrine of economic interpretation. It is perfectly possible to be the staunchest individualist and at the same time an ardent advocate of the doctrine of economic interpretation. In fact the writers who are to-day making the most successful application of economic interpretation are not socialists at all. Socialism and "historical materialism" are, at bottom, entirely independent conceptions.

The fourth objection is that the theory of economic interpretation neglects the ethical and spiritual forces of history. This seems more formidable, and it must be confessed that the attempts thus far made by the "historical materialists" to meet the objection have not been attended with much success. On closer inspection, however, some parts of this criticism turn out to be less weighty than has often been supposed. For what, after all, is the realm of ethical and spiritual forces? To answer this question it is necessary to distinguish between the existence of the moral law and its genesis. In another place an attempt has been made to show that there is much reason to believe that from the historical point of view all individual ethics may be considered to be the outgrowth of social ethics. Conscience itself, or the ability to distinguish between good and bad, would then be the historical product of social forces. While the origin of the moral sense is thus to be explained, it is nevertheless equally clear that once developed it leads an existence by itself. The categorical imperative is an undoubted fact of human life. The moral conscience exerts so profound an influence on the individual because it is the crystallization of centuries of social influences. So slow, however, has been the accumulating force of these influences, that the individual is utterly oblivious of its social origin and importance. It would, therefore, be absurd to deny that individual men, like masses of men, are moved by ethical considerations.

What is generally forgotten, however, is not only that the content of the conception of morality is a social product, but that amid all the complex social conditions the economic factors are often of chief significance, and that the influence of pure ethical or religious idealism can make itself felt only within the limitations of existing economic conditions. Slavery, for instance, was not considered wrong by the great Greek moralists, whose ethical views on many other topics were at least on a plane with those of modern times. In the same way the English colonists who at home would have scouted the very idea of slavery soon became in the Southern States of America the most ardent and sincere advocates of the system; even the clergymen of the South honestly refused to consider slavery a sin. Had the Northern and Western States been subjected to the same climatic and economic conditions, there is little doubt that, so far at least as they could keep themselves shut off from contact with the more advanced industrial civilization of Europe, they would have completely shared the moral views of their Southern brethren. Men are what conditions make them ; and ethical ideals are not exempt from the same inexorable law of environment.

To the ethical teachers of the middle ages feudal rights did not seem to be wrongs. The hardy pioneer of New England needed a different set of virtues from those which their successors in a softer age have acquired ; the attempt to subdue the Indian by love, charity and non-resistance would have meant not so much the disappearance of evil, as the disappearance of the colonists. The moral ideal of a frontier society is as legitimate from the point of view of their needs as the very different ideal of a later stage of society. The virtue of hospitality is far more important in the pastoral stage than in the industrial. The ethical relation of master to workmen under the factory system is not the same as under the guild system. The idea of honor and of the necessity of duelling as a satisfaction for its violation is peculiar to an aristocratic or military class; with the change of economic conditions which make for democracy and industrialism, the content of the conception changes.

The economic interpretation of history correctly understood thus does not in the least seek to deny or minimize the importance of ethical and spiritual forces in history. It only emphasizes the domain within which the ethical forces can at any particular time act with success. To sound the praises of mercy and love to a band of marauding savages would be futile; but when the old conditions of warfare are no longer really needed for self-defence, the moral teacher can do a great work in introducing more civilized practices, which shall be in harmony with the real needs of the new society. It is always on the border line of the transition from the old social necessity to the new social convenience that the ethical reformer makes his influence felt. With the perpetual change in human conditions, there is always some kind of a border line, and thus always the need of the moral teacher, to point out the higher ideal and the path of progress. Unless the social conditions, however, are ripe for the change, the demand of the ethical reformer will be the voice crying out in the wilderness. Only if the conditions are ripe will the reform be effected.

The moral ideals are thus continually in the forefront of the contest for progress. The ethical teacher is the scout and the vanguard of society; but he will be followed only if he enjoys the confidence of the people, and the real battle will be fought by the main body of social forces, amid which the economic conditions are in last resort so often decisive. There is a moral growth in society, as well as in the individual. The more civilized the society, the more ethical its mode of life. But to become more civilized, to permit the moral ideals to percolate through continually lower strata of the population, we must have an economic basis to render it possible. With every improvement in the material condition of the great mass of the population there will be a great opportunity for the unfolding of a higher moral life, but not until the economic conditions of society become ideal will the ethical development of the individual have a free field for limitless progress. Only then will it be possible to neglect the economic factor, which may henceforward be considered as a constant; only then will the economic interpretation of history become a matter for archaeologists rather than for historians.

Moral forces indeed influence human society no less than the legal and political forces influence it. But just as the legal system like the political system is very considerably influenced by the economic conditions, so the particular ethical system or code of morality has been at any given period very largely an outgrowth of the social and especially of the economic life. If by materialism we mean a negation of the tremendous power of spiritual forces in humanity, the materialistic conception of history is undoubtedly defective. But if by the economic interpretation of history we mean—what alone we should mean—that the ethical forces themselves are essentially social in their origin and content, and largely conditioned in their actual sphere of operation by the economic relations of society, there is no real antagonism between the economic and the ethical life. The economic conception of history, properly interpreted, does not neglect the spiritual forces in history; it seeks only to point out the terms on which the spiritual life has hitherto been able to find its fullest fruition.

The fifth objection to the doctrine is that it involves absurd exaggerations. We shall not stop in this place to consider some of the extreme applications of the theory, for even though they are quite false, they would not necessarily invalidate the doctrine itself. We must distinguish here, as in every other domain of human inquiry, between the use and the abuse of a principle. The difference between the scientist and the fanatic is that one points the limitations of a principle, where the other recognizes none. To make any science or a theory responsible for the vagaries of its over-enthusiastic advocates would soon result in a discrediting of science itself; wise men do not judge a race by its least fortunate members; fair-minded critics do not estimate the value of a doctrine by its excrescences.

What then shall we say of the doctrine of economic interpretation? That its authors originally claimed too much for it or at least framed the doctrine so as to give rise to misconception, is undoubtedly true. That some of its advocates have gone entirely too far is equally certain. It is above all sure that the choice of the term "historical materialism" is unfortunate. The materialistic view of history, like the utilitarian theory

26

of morals, has had to suffer more because of its name than because of its essence. The one is as little sordid as the other.

The economic interpretation of history, correctly understood, does not claim that every phenomenon of human life in general, or of social life in particular, is to be explained on economic grounds. Few writers would trace the different manifestations of language or even of art primarily to economic conditions; still fewer would maintain that the various forms of pure science have more than a remote connection with social conditions in general. Man is what he is because of mental evolution, and even his physical wants are largely transformed and transmuted in the crucible of reasoning. The facts of mentality must be reckoned with.

The extreme advocates of " historical materialism," however, have sometimes seemed to claim that sociology must be based exclusively on economics, and that all social life is nothing but a reflex of the economic life. No such claim can be countenanced, for the obvious reason that economics deal only with one kind of social relations and that there are as many kinds of social relations as there are classes of social wants. The term "utility" which has been appropriated by the economist is not by any means peculiar to him. And the value which is the expression of this utility and which forms the subject matter of economics is only one subdivision of a far greater class. For all the world is continually rating objects and ideas according to their aesthetic or scientific or technical or moral or religious or jural or political or philosophical value without giving any thought to their economic value. So far as utility and value are social in character, that is depend upon the relation of man to man, they form the subject matter of sociology. Economics deal with only one kind of social utilities or values and can therefore not explain all kinds of social utilities or values. The strands of human life are manifold and complex.

In one sense, then, there are as many methods of interpreting history as there are classes of activities or wants. There is not only an economic interpretation of history, but an ethical, an aesthetic, a political, a jural, a linguistic, a religious, a scientific interpretation of history. Every scholar can legitimately regard past events from a different standpoint.

Nevertheless, if we take a broad view of human development, there is still some justification for speaking of *the* economic interpretation of history as the important one, rather than of *an* economic interpretation among other equally valid explanations. Human life has thus far not been exempt from the inexorable law of nature, with its struggle for existence through natural selection. This struggle has assumed three forms. We find first the original struggle of group with group, which in modern times has become the contest of people with people, of nation with nation. Secondly, with the differentiation of population there came the rivalry of class with class, first of the sacerdotal with the military and the industrial class; later of the monied interest with the landed interest; still later of the labor class with one or all of the capitalist classes. Thirdly, we find within each class the competition of the individuals to gain the mastery in the class. These three forms of conflict are in last resort all due to the pressure of life upon the means of subsistence; individual competition, class competition and race competition are all referable to the niggardliness of nature, to the inequality of human gifts, to the difference in social opportunity.

Civilization indeed consists in the attempt to minimize the evils, while conserving the benefits of this hitherto inevitable conflict between material resources and human desires. As long, however, as this conflict subsists, the primary explanation of human life must continue to be the economic explanation—the explanation of the adjustment of material resources to human desires. This adjustment may be modified by aesthetic, religious and moral—in short, by intellectual and spiritual forces; but in last resort it still remains an adjustment of life to the wherewithal of life.

When the ideal economic adjustment is ever reached —that is, when science will give us a complete mastery over means of production, when the growth of population will be held in check by the purposive activity of the social group, when progress in the individual and the race will be possible without any conflict except one for unselfish ends, and when the mass of the people will live as do to-day its noblest members—then, indeed, the economic conditions will fall into the background, and will be completely overshadowed by the other social factors of progress. But until that period is reached, the economic conditions of the social group and of the mass of individuals must continue to retain their ascendancy. From the beginning of social life up to the present the rise, the progress and the decay of nations have been largely due to changes in the economic relations, internal and external, of the social groups, even though the facility with which mankind has availed itself of this economic environment has been the product of intellectual forces. While the study of the economic factors alone will manifestly not suffice to enable us to explain all the myriad forms in which the human spirit has clothed itself since history began, it is none the less true that as long as the body is not everywhere held in complete subjection to the soul, as long as the struggle for wealth does not everywhere give way to the struggle for virtue, the social structure and the fundamental relations between social classes will be largely shaped by these overmastering influences, which, whether we approve or deplore them, form so great a part of the content of life.

From the purely philosophical standpoint, it may be confessed that the theory, especially in its extreme form, is no longer tenable as the universal explanation of all human life. Whether any monistic interpretation of humanity is possible, is by no means yet decided. At all events none will be possible until that most difficult of all studies—sociology—succeeds in finally elaborating the laws of its existence and thus indicating its claim to be a real science. As a philosophical doctrine of universal validity, it must be conceded that the theory of "historical materialism" can no longer be successfully defended. But in the narrower sense of economic interpretation of history—in the sense, namely, that the economic factor has been of the utmost importance in history, and that the historical factor must be reckoned with, in economics, the theory has been and still is of considerable significance.

Human activity is indeed the activity of sentient beings, so that the history of mankind is the history of mental development; but human life depends upon the relation between the individual and his environment. In the struggle that has thus far gone on between individuals and groups in their desire to make the best of their environment, the paramount consideration has necessarily been economic in character. The view of history which lays stress on these paramount considerations is what we call the economic interpretation of history. They are not the exclusive considerations, and in particular instances the action and reaction of social forces may give the decisive influence to non-economic factors. Taking man, however, for what he is and has thus far been, the underlying influence will, not always indeed, but very generally, be of this economic character. The economic interpretation of history, in its proper formulation does not exhaust the possibilities of life and progress; it does not explain all the niceties of human development ; but it emphasizes the forces which have hitherto been chiefly instrumental in the rise and fall, in the prosperity and decadence, in the glory and failure, in the weal and woe of nations and peoples.

DISCUSSION.

ISAAC A. LOOS: The paper just read is an argument for the economic interpretation of history, regarded as an important aspect of the interpretation of history; it is an argument for reckoning with economic conditions in the interpretation of history. To this cautious and moderate defense of the economic interpretation of history there can be but little opposition.

The first objection I have to urge, in addition to those considered in the paper, to the phrase as it stands and understood in the sweeping sense commonly attached to it, is its one-sidedness. This objection corresponds somewhat closely to the fifth objection considered in the paper. The phrase as it stands and is commonly understood announces its exponent as the defender of a school, an "ism," an exaggeration. It implies that the economic interpretation is final, complete, and all sufficient, and that there is no other aspect to the explanation of history. This large claim Professor Seligman regards as unnecessary, or as necessary only in dealing with the genesis of social institutions. He admits in his answer to what he calls the fourth objection (that the theory of economic interpretation neglects the ethical and spiritual forces of history) that we must regard, for example, the moral sense, once developed as leading an existence by itself. If so, we must reckon with it, once it is developed, as an independent and self-existent factor in the interpretation of existing human life. The same thing must be said respecting intellect and will. When these are once developed, they lead an independent existence and constitute a superorganic or psychical factor as distinguished from the purely physical or the biological factors. The words economic and economics can be so used, indeed, they are very often so used, as to include all these elements separately considered, but at the cost of clear thinking, and even more to the detriment of clear expression.

There is a second objection to the phrase "the economic interpretation of history," namely, its ambiguity, its lack of precision. The word "economic" has too much to do for scientific precision ; it must stand now for subjective utility or rational selection, now for objective utility taking on the double aspect of natural selection under the influence of the pressure of environment on food supply and the food quest or the more direct and simple impact of climatic and geographical conditions. It will make immensely for clearness, therefore, if we speak of these factors as psychical, biological, and material or physical respectively. We can then adjourn the question whether the last be the ultimate ground of the others, and move forward in our attention to the evolution of the sociological factors. I should say then that as a cult or as the watchword of a school the economic interpretation of history is open to a third objection, in addition to the two noted above and in addition to those reviewed in the paper. It is likely to take the student of history and of the social sciences from the sphere of his proper inquiry concerning the course and meaning of history into the sphere of metaphysics. It is better to come to the problem of ultimate origins through the study of philosophy.

In the fourth place I desire to ask whether history be not itself interpretation. To this question the several schools of history may give varying answers, and I leave it to the historians who take part in this discussion to furnish their own answers. Even if we define history as a record of events, have we dismissed our difficulty?

What now can we say constructively? In the first place it must be regretted that the social sciences have suffered and still do suffer seriously from an interminable war of words. For the most part those who defend the so-called "economic interpretation of history" investigate some of the same problems, and they investigate these problems by the same method as those students who are now calling themselves sociologists. Professor Keasbey, for example, under the title of "economic geography," has sketched his conception of the development of human society under the influence of economic motives.[1] He has taken the sociologists to task for giving insufficient attention to economic environment and for giving excessive emphasis to will or purpose where will and purpose do not exist. This is equivalent to saying that the sociologists are not doing their work efficiently when dealing with the genesis of society, or that they have not done their work finally.

It may be admitted, secondly, that we can get along without the word "sociology" if its work be done under other names by essentially the same methods and the same instrumentalities. But how the economists themselves can get away from their own terminology and from the large literature which has been wrought out by them in the past several hundred years is itself a serious problem. But it is a problem with which they are struggling successfully by swelling the ranks of the historians and doing some work, indeed much work, hitherto left undone by the historians. And yet we may ask

[1] Keasbey. The institution of society, The International Monthly, April, 1900; and two papers on Economic geography, in the Political Science Quarterly, vol. 16, nos. 1 and 3.

is it possible, and if possible is it advisable after the terms economic and economics have developed such definite connotation (the word "economy" is open to freer construction) to designate an altogether new set of problems and to give an altogether new direction to the problems worked out by the older economists. Apart from the word "utility" there is no point of connection with the regular school; and utility serves only as a verbal bond, for the concepts attached to the word by the regular school of economists, the earlier and later classical, are primarily metaphysical, or psychical as the later classicists would prefer to say, while the historical or sociological school of economists deal with objective utility on a non-animistic or utilitarian basis.

The German historical school has made a place for the broader problems of the origin and relativity of economic forces and principles in their *Allgemeine Volkswirthschaftslehre.* But even in Germany the word "sociology" is making its way. Professor Simmel is giving a course of lectures in Berlin under the title *Sociologie.* By the side of the historical school or as embraced within it I would place the scientific socialists or the socialist school of economists, and the positive philosophy with its chapters on social physics, as forerunners of the larger and more general social science now commonly described as sociology, developed on the lines of the natural sciences. The recognition, in the paper just read, of the work of the scientific socialists, and of Karl Marx in particular, deserves further emphasis. Much can be said to show that the predecessors of Marx, (Godwin, Thompson, Saint Simon) were in search of a broader basis for the theory of society than either the Smithian or the Ricardian economics postulated. Add to the Marxian analysis of history the doctrine of liberty, and you have in socialism a political philosophy. Socialism need not necessarily be viewed and is not always viewed as a body of economic doctrine; it may also be regarded as a theory of society.

The historical economists and the socialists have been preparing the way for the science of sociology, but the problems stated by them must find their final solution in the larger treatment of society accorded to these problems by the sociologists.

The development of the science of sociology with its appropriate method cannot be ascribed exclusively to the evolution of the positive philosophy under the guiding genius of August Comte, as is so often done, except as that is merged with other currents of thought tending toward the same end, above all the naturalistic which took shape in the development of the natural sciences in the eighteenth and nineteeth centuries giving us Lamarck and Darwin, and the revival of historical inquiry on empirical and Aristotelian lines giving us Savigny and Maine in jurisprudence and the study of institutions, and Roscher, Knies and Hildebrand in the historical school of economics, and Saint Simon, Rodbertus, Marx, and Lassalle in the socialist school of economics, and Ruskin in the art movement. The philosopher Hegel may from some points of view be regarded as the connecting link between the old metaphysics and the new sciences; his contemporary Goethe is an expression of it. Hegel's doctrine of development had as profound an influence on the German founders of historical criticism and scientific socialism as Malthus's theory of the pressure of population on food supply had on the Darwinian theory of natural selection which has played such an immense role in speculative biology. The importance of the sociologists, considered as research students and as a school of thinkers, lies in their clear and frank recognition that all things are tied together at common points, that the universe must be reckoned as a cosmos, and that its evolution can be traced in a serial order of the sciences.

Professor Seligman in the closing paragraph of his paper treats the sociologists with great respect, but he puts them away up in the clouds; and he seems to expect something from them by and by. We shall probably have to wait for some time for anything approaching final results from the work of the sociologists; but it is worth while to concede to them the right of way to deal at first hand with the general problems of social origins, functions, organization and methods of amelioration. Giving attention to the last phase of the problems of society does not read them out of the list of the scientists, any more than engineers are read out by building bridges and sewers. The sociologists are the general interpreters of history; the economists, publicists, politicists, jurists, writers on ethics, and the critics of literature and the arts are its special interpreters. But the interpretation of history is not the entire work of the social scientists. They must address themselves even primarily to the current problems of the life now existing. This they must do in the light of history but not with sole reference to history as a source of light. The social sciences look to the present as well as to the past; and in a measure also to the future. All sciences do. Prediction, not prophecy, is the test of applied sciences. The economic interpreters of history are co-workers with the sociologists; they are keeping the attention of the sociologist to a consideration of the influence of environment and of resources, yet the sociologists are not limited to a consideration of one factor in progress. It is their business to reckon with all the factors, the spiritual and moral forces as well as the material or physical. But the cardinal importance of the last must never be forgotten.

EDWARD P. CHEYNEY: The economic interpretation or explanation of history as usually practiced is an effort to find some economic factor in each series of historical events that will explain them,—tell why they occurred. There are two objections to this practice so serious as to call for its condemnation by historians. The first of these objections is one of method, a theoretical objection. The economic interpretation of history arbitrarily and unjustifiably places one group of historical phenomena in a position fundamental to the others, before investigating all the facts to see whether they should really be so placed.

The mere historian, the plain scientific student of the past, when he enters upon the investigation of any period or aspect of history has a two-fold task before him; first to find out all the facts, and secondly to arrange these facts according to their own nature, to put those together which prove to belong together. That is to say he must go where his facts take him, he must follow his facts not lead them. If they group themselves in such a way as to explain the series of occurrences, so much the better; but he must not impose an explanation upon them. If it should prove in any case that the economic phenomena are the ones that explain the others, well and good, but it may also prove that it is the legal phenomena, or the political or the moral, or the facts of language. The historian has no way of telling what the explanation is beforehand. He must wait till he has arranged his facts and then see which are those that interpret the others. That is to say his method is objective, inductive, impersonal, *a posteriori.* He knows of no interpretation of history except that which history gives of itself.

The economic interpretation of history, on the other hand, as usually understood and applied, seeks first of all for some economic phenomenon or condition which may explain or interpret the events under consideration. When found this is accepted, approved and utilized for purposes of explanation, *because* it is economic in character. That is to say the method is subjective, arbitrary, *a priori.* For instance, suppose one is confronted by the historical problem of the growth of two separate nationalities in the Iberian peninsula, Spain and Portugal. The historian would proceed to gather all the facts bearing on the history of those two countries, arrange these, and strive to discover from them what are the reasons for the separateness of the two states. An advocate of the economic interpretation of history was struck by the fact that the amount and character of the rainfall of the two countries is quite different, seized upon this as being an adequate explanation, and has advanced it as the solution of the problem, because it is an economic explanation. He may or may not be right, but the method by which he has reached his result is evidently quite different from that of the historian.

Another instance may be found in Professor Thorold Rogers's effort to explain the causes of the Peasant's Revolt of 1381. He was so convinced that the cause for the outbreak was economic in its nature that he seized upon the only fact of that kind which suggested itself to him as adequate, and attributed the revolt to the reintroduction by the landlords of the old labor services. When the matter was properly and historically investigated it was found that no such process had taken place and Professor Rogers's generalization in this as in so many other points has been entirely discredited. He approached an historical question in the spirit of an economist and failed accordingly.

We need go no further back than Professor Seligman's paper read this evening to find an instance of the difference in the two methods. He declares that the task of the interpretation of history is the discovery of the reason for human progress. But the historian does not feel himself to be especially interested in investigating the condition of progress. He is engaged simply in studying the history of the past. Sometimes it is progress, sometimes it is decadence; more often it is a condition of things in which some phenomena are those of progress, others those of decay; most often of all it is a condition of things where the question whether the tendencies of the time are those of progress or decay, is purely a question of modern, individual opinion.

No, the two methods are irreconcilable. The scientific historian cannot adopt the economic interpretation of history, because it seems to him fallacious and unscientific, and therefore unjustifiable.

Secondly, there is a practical objection to this process. The time is not ripe for the economic or any other interpretation of history. There is too much to be done in finding out what actually has been to spend time in seeking for its explanation. There are great masses of manuscript material lying unprinted and, therefore, unavailable; there are enormous collections of source material for the study of history printed by governments and associations, and readily accessible, but unanalyzed and unutilized; there are vast numbers of monographs and special studies of individual points which have not yet been worked up into the body of systematized historical knowledge. Whole subjects are still obscure to the last degree. Institutions which have lasted through centuries and affected the great majority of the people, we are still ignorant about, not only in their minute points, but in their very fundamentals. Mediæval serfdom is an institution which has been much dealt with by economists, and yet we have scarcely made a beginning of its study. The scholars who have been at work patiently investigating its phenomena have one after another borne testimony to the inadequacy and preliminary character of their labors. What do we know of the ordinary normal working of the greatest of all mediæval institutions, the church? We have studied it from a polemic point of view, either of criticism or defense, almost entirely. The great part it played in ordinary life during those centuries in which it was the strongest and most active and most enlightened institution in all society is still a sealed book to us. There are many aspects of the Reformation, and even of the French revolution, which have never yet been investigated. There are whole periods, as for instance the fifteenth century, which lies too late for the mediævalist and too early for the student of modern history, which are all but unknown. Historians have only just lately turned from an almost exclusive study of individuals to the study of institutions. They are only gradually extending their study so as to include not only political, legal, and ecclesiastical, but social and economic and many other kinds of facts as well.

History is so vast, varied, uncertain and difficult a field that it is no wonder that historians feel that the work lying to their hands is its investigation rather than its interpretation. What they want above all to do is to reduce this chaotic world of the past to some kind of order.

No student of history can do much reading in the works of those who profess to give its economic interpretation without being half amused, half saddened at the kind of history they are trying to interpret. It is so vague, so mistaken, so filled with discredited and fanciful notions that if it were successfully interpreted it would be an interpretation not of the real history of the world but of some quite suppositious history. This, however, is the fault of the historians. They have not yet got their material into a shape in which it can be safely and profitably put into the hands of another group of scientists as raw material upon which to work.

The study of history now is like this continent was when our ancestors first came to it. Its forests needed to be cut off, its rivers bridged, its mines opened, its distances diminished by roads, railroads and canals. The world of history likewise is not yet ready for its highest uses. There must be much done in the way of explanation, of cultivation, of familiarization, before we can reduce it all to law.

Therefore, for this second reason, the historian must oppose the habit of devoting time and effort to the economic interpretation of history. It is not the work which needs now to be done. However pleasant it would be to be the contemporaries of our great-grand-children and join with them in the work of interpreting the history of the past, it is quite evidently our duty to devote our labor to preparing the material for their hands.

27

NOTE.

The paper of Professor A. Lawrence Lowell, on " Party legislation in parliament, congress and state legislatures," which was presented at the joint-meeting (see program above, page 45) will be printed in full in the Annual report of the American Historical Association, 1901.

INDEX TO NAMES AND LEADING SUBJECTS.

PUBLICATIONS

OF THE

AMERICAN ECONOMIC ASSOCIATION

THIRD SERIES.   ISSUED QUARTERLY.
VOL. III, NO. 2.   PRICE, $4.00 PER YEAR.

THE NEGRO
IN AFRICA AND AMERICA

BY

JOSEPH ALEXANDER TILLINGHAST, M.A.

MAY, 1902

PUBLISHED FOR THE
AMERICAN ECONOMIC ASSOCIATION
BY THE MACMILLAN COMPANY
NEW YORK
LONDON: SWAN SONNENSCHEIN & CO.

PRESS OF
ANDRUS & CHURCH,
ITHACA, N. Y.

PREFACE.

The present study does not claim to be an addition to human knowledge. One familiar with the writings of travelers and ethnologists on the negroes of West Africa, is acquainted with most of the books out of which the first few chapters have been woven ; one acquainted with the history and present condition of the race in the United States, has met most of the statements and arguments embodied in the later portions of the work. The merit of the book, in my judgment, is to be found rather in the fact that it brings together two lines of investigation which have hitherto been kept asunder. The rapidity with which an uncivilized people may be lifted, or may lift themselves, to the plane of an advanced civilization is still undetermined. To realize that many characteristics of the American Negro are part of his inheritance from Africa, and were bred into the race there through long generations, may perhaps strengthen the patience and forbearance of those who seek to expedite his progress. To realize that many faults often attributed to the debasing effects of American slavery, are faults which he shares with his African ancestors and contemporaries, may suggest a juster and more impartial view of the merits and demerits of the economic system which crumbled as a result of the Civil War. That a southern white man, the son of a slave holder, should have selected this subject for investigation, have pursued his work at a northern university, utilizing for the purpose a library, the nucleus of which in this field is a large anti-slavery collection, and have reached results, the tendency of which seems to me in the main eirenic rather than controversial, is a noteworthy sign of the times, suggesting how both sections and both races are coming more and more to coöperation of effort and harmony of conclusions regarding our great problem. The work of Mr. Tillinghast has given me much light upon a question in which for years I have been interested, and I believe that many others of his readers will share my judgment.

WALTER F. WILLCOX.

Ithaca, New York.

TABLE OF CONTENTS.

Physiography of Africa, 6—area of West Africa, 7—subdivisions of upper and lower Guinea, 9—climate, 10—its influence upon men, 13—fauna and flora, 15—minerals, 19.

Negro origin undetermined, 21—migrations, 21—Sudanese and Bantus, 22—principal tribal groups, 23—kind and degree of civilization, 24—physical and psychic characteristics, 26.

Conditions adverse to industrial development, 28—natural selection, 30—status of industry, 31—division of labor, 31—paucity of labor-saving apparatus, 33—currency, 37—products of industry, food, shelter, clothing, 38.

Religion of Senegambia, Sierra Leone, and Liberia, 46—basis of West African religion, 48—sacrifices at the burial of the dead, 49—sacrifices to the gods, 51—priesthood, 53—charms, 55—witchcraft, 56—religion not connected with social morality, 58.

Position of women, 60—polygamy prevails, 60—adultery and seduction, 62—why strong sexual instincts have been developed, 64—family relations, 65—attitude toward useless members, 67—thieving, 67—cheating, 68—robbery and murder, 69—destructive wars, 70—cruelty, 71—cannibalism, 72—impulsive kindness, 72—the " Yam Custom ", 73—the " Annual Customs ", 73—love of crowds, 74—ceremonies connected with birth, 75—marriage, 75—funerals, 76.

Low political development, 80—tribal organization, 81—exceptional cases of Ashanti and Dahomey, 82 — military organization, 82 —

Contents.

THE NEGRO IN AFRICA AND AMERICA.

INTRODUCTION.

It will serve to reveal both the author's point of view and the objects aimed at, if the reasons which led to the study herein presented are stated at the outset.

In a self-governing republic like ours, some homogeneity of citizenship is vital. By excluding the Chinese we have avoided one threatening phase of heterogeneity. But unfortunately no African exclusion act was passed in the days when such action might have delivered us from the black peril, consequently, the homogeneity of our national society, especially in one great section, is dangerously broken. Our nine millions of negroes to-day constitute an ethnic group, so distinct from the dominant race, that we are threatened with inability to assimilate them.

The problem before our country, therefore, is how to reduce the divergence in character between its white and black populations. Obviously the first step toward a solution, if one be possible, is to get a thorough understanding of Negro character, otherwise, we are but groping our way, liable at every step to costly blunders. There is only too much reason to fear that misconceptions in this direction have already led to serious errors in our policy toward the nation's "ward".

Now, character is a product of two fundamental factors, *i.e.*, heredity and environment. The endowment of each generation at birth is dictated by heredity, but all that it acquires subsequently is the gift of environment. Matured character, therefore, is a subtle compound of the two elements.

Through choice or control of environment, deliberate human agency may accomplish much toward influencing the ultimate compound. Of two negro infants, let one be brought up in the African jungle and the other amid the best American culture, and very divergent results would certainly follow. But men cannot manipulate heredity. From generation to generation this mysterious force operates in isolated independence, and we cannot touch it.

Yet heredity is not a fixed unchanging force. By slow and infinitesimal degrees it may be modified through selection, which tends to accumulate advantageous variations in offspring and to eliminate unfavorable ones. Inasmuch as the experience or attainments of one generation within its own life-time affect but slightly, if at all, the physiological germs, through which heredity is transmitted, nothing we can do of set purpose for the parent will decidedly improve the birth-endowment of the child. Its later inheritance through example and home training may be improved, and this is of immense significance. But that is another question. The point now being emphasized is, that heredity proper cannot be manipulated by purposive human devices. If it were open to us to exercise deliberate selection among our own kind, as stock-breeders do among brutes, then the case might be different. We might then modify hereditary force with rapidity, but, as it is, we must wait for Nature to do her work in her own infinitely conservative way. No ethnic group, with its inborn nature moulded for ages in an undisturbed environment, can be radically transformed within ten or twenty generations.

All of the considerations just cited have a deep significance in the problem that faces our country. They have, of course, become very familiar to us in some con-

nections, but they have never been properly recognized
and applied in our efforts to comprehend the present
character of American negroes.

United under our flag are two streams of racial heredity ; the one had its origin and development in the north
temperate zone, the other in the torrid zone.   Before
meeting here, the one had evolved an hereditary endowment, delicately adjusted to the highest civilization recorded in history ; the other remained in benighted
savagery.   We have never for a moment dreamed that
the nature of the Caucasian element in our population
could be understood, if its long career in Europe were
ignored.   Infinite pains have been taken, therefore, to
trace and interpret its history from the beginning.   But
what of the African ?   How many of us have definite
ideas regarding the conditions which moulded him
through and through, long before we took him in hand ?
How many of us have in mind accurate data, by which
to distinguish hereditary survival from acquired character ?   Yet, unless we can do this, we have no measure
of his real progress under American tutelage, and therefore, no basis for estimating his probable future.   We are
left to deal with a compound, the proportion of whose
elements we do not know.

To say that the Negro in Africa was a "savage" tells
little, for there are many species of savage, and many
degrees of savagery.   The Indian is a savage, but he
differs widely from the native of Africa.   Each race has
deeply implanted peculiarities of temperament and aptitude.   A dismissal with the generic term "savage"
does not serve the purpose.   We might as well ignore
all Teutonic history, previous to the landing of the May-
flower, and consider it sufficient to say that our European
progenitors were " civilized."

But it may be questioned whether the African life of the Negro has been completely neglected. As a matter of fact, occasional notice has been taken of it, yet in a manner quite useless for modern purposes. In Philadelphia, as early as 1789, a little book was published by Anthony Benezet, entitled, "Some historical account of Guinea". In it one finds a compilation of facts regarding the natives of West Africa, but the author evinced a strong bias in his selection and grouping of these facts, it being his philanthropic desire to show that the negroes were a much higher people than those interested in the slave-trade represented them to be. A contrary bias is revealed by one Josiah Priest, who published at Albany, in 1844, a work with the title, "The origin and character of the Negro race." This sounds promising ; but the fact that an entire chapter is devoted to proving that "the curse of Noah on the race of Ham, as a judicial act, is endorsed by the law of Moses,"[1] reveals its general spirit. Again, "The Negroes in Negro-land, etc," put forth in 1868, by Hinton R. Helper, as a protest against the pending proposition to enfranchise the freedmen, is simply a catalogue of verbatim quotations from works on Africa, regardless of the region our negroes came from, and selected with a view to prove them as low as possible. In his two volume work, "A history of the American Negro," Geo. W. Williams, himself a mulatto, discusses in an introductory part, the West African natives, but the execution is thoroughly unscientific ; for example, his opening chapter relies almost solely upon scripture texts to prove the unity of human origin, no use being made of ethnological data. He hurries over this part superficially, giving attention principally to the race history in

---

[1] See p. 89, *et seq.*

America, and here he seems to have done conscientious work of permanent value.

This list, while not exhaustive, is thoroughly representative. We remain without such a knowledge of West African society as we need, in order to understand correctly our own negro population. We have been content to make occasional vague allusions to a former condition of savagery, straightway proceeding to seek explanations of negro nature and character in terms of American environment, chiefly that of slavery.

The institution of slavery has loomed so large on our horizon that it has completely overshadowed what went before it in African history. At every mention of negro inefficiency, improvidence, or immorality, it sufficed to recall slavery, and the characteristic was deemed explained. But it is time that we seek a truer conception of the forces that have made the American negro what he is.

To make a beginning in this direction has been the object of the investigation whose results are presented in the following chapters. The negro's heredity and environment, each helping to interpret the other, are studied as found in West Africa, then under American slavery, and finally during free citizenship in our Republic.

PART I.

THE NEGRO IN WEST AFRICA.

CHAPTER I.

WEST AFRICA.

The continent of Africa is a vast plateau. It has been compared to an "inverted plate" of irregular shape.[1] On almost every side the high lands approach the coast-line, then slope rapidly to the sea, sometimes by a gently terraced formation, sometimes by a succession of rugged escarpments. Regarding the continent as divided by parallel 4° north latitude, it is found that the continental plateau is thereby roughly marked off into two halves, of which the southern has an average elevation of from 3,000 to 3,500 feet, while the northern averages only about 1,300 feet. Hence it is that Africa, although considerably smaller than Asia in area, has nevertheless a larger volume of earth above sea-level. It is now becoming usual to designate the northern plateau, stretching from Cape Verde to the Red Sea, as the Sudan, which is again divided into West, Central, and East Sudan. These divisions correspond roughly with the Niger, the Chad, and the Nile basins respectively. We shall hereafter confine ourselves to West Sudan. Similarly, of the southern half of the continent only the western regions in more or less proximity to the Atlantic will call for attention. The portions thus defined are commonly given the general title of West Africa.

West Sudan lies within that vast bulge described by the western coast-line in sweeping around from the

[1] See Stanford's Compendium of geography, "Africa", pp. 5, 277.

Strait of Gibraltar to the Niger delta, with Cape Verde
as its extreme westerly point. In this region the great
table-land extends to within a short distance of the
ocean, then breaks down in escarpments so sharp and
rugged that they long were called by mariners, the Kong
Mountains. The drainage to the west is principally by
the Senegal and Gambia rivers, which reaching the sea
by a series of rapids are not navigable to any distance
from the coast. To the south, drainage for the most
part is through numerous short coastal streams. The
Niger, however, rising not far from the head-waters of
the Senegal and Gambia, flows easterly toward the interior for hundreds of miles, gradually sweeps round in
a great curve, and finally opens into the Gulf of Guinea,
through many mouths. Its Delta was a chief market
for negroes in the days of the slave-trade.

In southwestern Africa we find the same general
characteristics of an inner plateau, extending to two
hundred miles of the sea or less, and then sinking rapidly
to the shore. Here, too, the drainage of the coast is
through many small and rapid streams, while far inland
behind these rises the majestic Congo, which at last
bursts through the mountain fringe and reaches the
ocean down a series of rapids. One other river should
be mentioned, the Ogowe, which drains a large area
lying between the Upper Congo and the ocean, and
empties through a delta about four hundred miles north
of the Congo month.

Our present interest in West Africa is confined to the
region whence negroes were taken for the American
slave-trade. There were three principal markets, about
the mouths of the Senegal and Gambia, the Niger, and
the Congo. These places were preferred because of the
advantage they afforded for loading and unloading ships

and for reaching the interior. But the trade was not confined to them ; all along the coast between the Senegal and the Congo wherever cargo could possibly be landed, it went on briskly.[1] It will be convenient to divide this strip of coast some four thousand miles long into Upper Guinea, or all that portion lying between the Senegal and the Niger Delta, and Lower Guinea or that which stretches south from the coast-angle just east of the Niger Delta down to and including the lower Congo region.

The depth from the coast of this slave-yielding belt cannot be determined with any accuracy. The white traders merely touched the periphery of the continent, and neither knew nor cared about the geographical origin of the slaves. That many were brought from far inland cannot be doubted. Wadstrom tells us how the Moors and Mandingans of West Sudan captured many negroes from about the head waters of the Senegal and Gambia, and took them down stream to the coast.[2] Yet the demand for slaves in northern Africa was such as to take off most of the interior supply, so that relatively few are thought to have reached the distant West Coast. DeCardi learned, too, that a good many of the slaves found along the Lower Guinea coast had come from a distance inland.[3] Still, there is every reason to believe that the overwhelming majority of those negroes, destined for the Atlantic trade, were secured from the more densely populated coast countries and fertile river valleys within two or three hundred miles of the sea. The kings of Ashanti and Dahomey,

---

[1] For an outline of the slave-trading region see " An historical account of Guinea ", by Anthony Benezet, Philadelphia, 1771, pp. 6-7. Also " La traité de Negres ", T. Clarkson, Paris, 1789, pp. 15-6.

[2] " Observations on the slave-trade ", London, 1789, pp. 1-3.

[3] Kingsley, "West African studies ", London, 1889, p. 480.

living within one hundred miles of the sea, captured
and sold whole tribes dwelling in contiguous territories,
and their example was followed by numerous other petty
kings all along the coast.   It is known that before the
close of the slave-trading era numerous districts along
the West African coast had been practically depopulated.
Hence the conclusion seems fairly justified that the vast
majority of negroes exported from Africa to America
came from a belt of coastal territory of immense length,
but only a few hundred miles in width.

A brief mention of the countries usually given distinct names, and constituting the divisions of Upper
and Lower Guinea, is necessary.   First on the north is
Senegambia, which includes the Senegal and Gambia
valleys and all the intervening region.   Next to the
southeast lies Sierra Leone, which has long been under
British control ; and then the so-called republic of Liberia.   At the southeast corner of Liberia is Cape Pal-
mas, from which point the coast line takes an almost
due easterly course, stretching over 1,200 miles till past
the Niger Delta, when it turns southward toward the
Cape of Good Hope.   Until the more recent establishment of European spheres of influence, this long
east and west strip was usually divided into the Ivory
Coast, the Gold Coast, and the Slave Coast, names indicating the commercial article once distinctive of each
region.   That the Slave Coast exported more slaves,
and that the trade was maintained there longer than
anywhere else, was due to peculiar facilities it possessed for smuggling and for evading the cruisers sent
to suppress the traffic.[1]

Beyond the vertex of the angle that enclosed the Gulf
of Guinea, Lower Guinea begins.   First is the Cameroon

[1] See Reclus, " Universal geography ", vol. xii, p. 256.

country, which includes Old and New Calabar, now under German administration; then French Congo, which takes in the country drained by the Gaboon and Ogowe rivers, and finally the Congo mouth and to the south of it, Angola.

The dominating climatic facts affecting this long seaboard are two: (1) it lies entirely within the torrid zone, extending from about 18 degrees north latitude to 10 degrees south latitude; and (2) it is subject to pronounced wet and dry seasons, the former so far predominating as to occupy nearly or quite three-quarters of the year. A tropical temperature therefore prevails continuously, and the humidity is excessive for the greater part of the year. Hence the terribly debilitating effect of the climate upon foreigners. All testimony on the subject abundantly supports the following statement of Du Chaillu:

"The climate of the west coast is sickly and exhausting, not because of its extreme heats, but because of its high *average* temperature and moisture, and the universal presence of malaria. Owing to the prevalence of a sea-breeze [during the day] the mercury is rarely higher than 90° in the shade; but then it rarely falls below 80° for nine months in the year, and even in the remaining three (the dry season) it never gets below 64°." [1]

He mentions here, but does not emphasize, the element of humidity, which, combined with the high temperature, absolutely prohibits any considerable or prolonged

[1] "Explorations and adventures in equatorial Africa", by Paul Du Chaillu, New York, 1868, p. 370. By observations taken along the coast of Upper Guinea, Sir James E. Alexander found that at sea-level the barometer ranged between 29.50 and 29.85 for several months at a time when the height of the wet season was well passed. This gives a suggestion in numerical terms of air-pressure conditions, indicating great humidity. See his "Excursions in West Africa", London, 1840, pp. 116, 120, 149, 237. The annual rainfall throughout the West African coast reaches the height of from 100 to 150 inches—an enormous total compared with that of the great majority of countries. See Stanford's "Compendium", "Africa", p. 317.

exertion. This fact and its bearings will be discussed more fully later.

Some idea of the humidity that prevails during the wet season, is conveyed by this description of its effects. MacDonald says: " So great is the humidity particularly along the coast, that all descriptions of wearing apparel rapidly spoil, that which is not destroyed by the ravages of moth and cockroach being very quickly attacked by mildew and rust." [1] Miss Kingsley also repeatedly alludes to the great difficulty of escaping mildew, one of her emphatic expressions being, "that paradise for mould, West Africa ".[2]

During the briefer dry seasons, however, when the Harmattan wind blows out of the far northern interior every night from sunset till after sunrise, the air becomes so extraordinarily dry as to be very trying to man and beast. Says MacDonald :

"This wind blows with a peculiar effect, drying and parching the skin and drying up the vegetation. A fine dust comes with it, and during its continuance its progress is marked by the creaking of Madeira chairs and sofas, the cracking of veneered articles, and the curling up of papers and the covers of books. . . . The air becomes hot and dry, with very cool mornings and evenings, which to the European are very beneficial, though not so to the natives. . . . . Table salt, which at all ordinary times is in a semi-liquid state, owing to the extreme humidity of the air, becomes solid and hard, and glasses have been known to crack and fall to pieces as they stood upon the table." [3]

Similar effects are described in great detail by Robert Norris, who made a journey to the capital of Dahomey, in 1772.[4] A little after sunrise each day the Harmattan ceases to blow, and there is a calm, during which the

---

[1] " The Gold Coast : past and present ", pp. 65–6.

[2] Travels in West Africa ", p. 33.

[3] " The Gold Coast : past and present ", pp. 64–5.

[4] See his " Bossa Ahadee, King of Dahomey ", London, 1789, pp. 114-15.

heat is stifling, but about 11 o'clock a gentle breeze from the sea rises and lasts nearly till sunset, giving a slight relief during mid-day.   This singular alternation of winds within each twenty-four hours, "goes on with the regularity of clock-work." [1]

With regard to the wet and dry seasons, Du Chaillu explains : "Both the time and duration of the seasons depend upon the latitude and longitude of the place." [2] Whenever the sun is approaching the zenith with reference to a given country, the rainy season commences and continues till it is well past the zenith. As the sun is at the zenith only once each year over countries lying near either tropic, there is but one long rainy season, followed by a shorter dry season while the sun is farthest from the zenith.   In the northerly portions of Upper Guinea, which are near to the tropic of Cancer, these conditions prevail.   In strictly equatorial regions, however, the sun passes the zenith twice, so that there are two wet seasons, succeeded by brief dry seasons.   Such is the case in Lower Guinea.   A rainy period is always introduced by a number of terrific tornadoes, which appear suddenly with little warning and tear their way through the jungle, leaving death and destruction behind them.   In a few days all the streams, which fall very low during the dry season, rise many feet, and often become very dangerous for navigation.

One factor influencing climatic conditions has not yet been mentioned, viz., altitude.   This comes into play on the slope of the plateau.   As the average height thus gained, however, in Upper Guinea is not 1,500 feet, the

---

[1] Reclus, "Universal geography", vol. xii, b. 216.

[2] *Op, cit.*, p. 366.   As Du Chaillu will be frequently cited hereafter, it may be well to say that, while his reliability has been denied, recent exploration has shown that he was truthful and accurate.

result is only to secure slightly cooler nights, with greater heat by day, from the sun's direct rays. In Lower Guinea there are greater altitudes, which sometimes have a night temperature as low as 55°, yet these are little inhabited by the scantily clothed natives, to whom such temperatures are disagreeable. They prefer the coast lands and river valleys, under truly tropical conditions. The desire for communication by water also leads them to prefer the lowlands. Thus, altitude does not decidedly modify climate.

West African climate has proved uniformly disastrous to the health and stamina of white men. Numerous are the mournful records that tell of its ravages among Europeans coming under its sway even for brief periods. Sir A. B. Ellis says:

"Although the Government European officials, both civil and military, remain but for a period of twelve months at a time on the Gold Coast, and then proceed to the United Kingdom for six months to recruit their health, the death rate amongst them is abnormally high. . . There are no colonists, for no one could hope to live in such a climate. Unfortunately there are no statistics kept by the local government from which the death-rate might be computed. It came within my own experience, however, that in one year, and that a not unusually unhealthy one, in a town in which I resided, five deaths occurred and six persons had to be invalided to England out of a European population averaging twenty-four in number. And it must be remembered that in this population there were no aged or infirm persons, no women and no children—all were men in the prime of life." [1]

To the same effect are all available accounts of this region. In Lower Guinea where truly equatorial conditions prevail, it is even worse.

Nor do other alien races seem to enjoy any greater exemption than the Caucasian. In July, 1897, sixteen Chinese laborers were imported into the Gold Coast to

[1] "The Tshi-speaking peoples of the Gold Coast", London, 1887, p. 5.

work the mines, situated in the higher country. By December, although none had died, yet "many of them had been at all times very ill," and they were soon removed, the experiment having proved a failure.[1] The importation of Chinamen and of West Indian negroes, themselves the descendants of West African natives, have both been tried by the Congo Free State, but in each case the "mortality has been terrible—more than the white mortality, which competent authorities put down, for the Congo, at 77 per cent., and the experiment has therefore failed."[2] The French, too, tried to work Annamese prisoners in the French Congo, but in spite of most careful treatment they died with appalling rapidity, one gang of a hundred losing seventy within a year.[3]

While it does not follow, as a matter of course, that because aliens are thus debilitated by the climate, the natives should be affected in like manner, yet the facts indicate that they too are injuriously influenced. Ellis is of opinion that the natives, while far less liable to the destructive diseases caused among aliens, are by no means exempt from them, and in any case are subject to the powerful influences against mental or physical energy and progress.[4] It is by no means infrequent for whole villages to be swept away by disease.

The natural resources and productions of West Africa are rich and varied. As the entire region is within the torrid zone, its indigenous fauna and flora are altogether tropical. To these some few additions have been made by Europeans, but most attempts to introduce plants and

[1] Geo. MacDonald, *op. cit.*, p. 8–9.
[2] Kingsley, "Travels in West Africa", p. 657.
[3] Kingsley, "Travels in West Africa", p. 657.
[4] "Tshi-speaking people, etc.", pp. 5-7.

animals from the north temperate zone have proved unsuccessful, owing to the change of climate and other circumstances.

West Africa has a fauna of the greatest possible interest to the zoologist, but our concern is only with what affects human life. The native is affected both favorably and unfavorably by the animal life that surrounds him, *e. g.*, wild beasts furnish him food, yet they often endanger his life. For food he finds elephants, hippopotami, buffaloes, crocodiles, gorillas, and other powerful denizens of jungle and river very serviceable, when he can overcome them. But his weapons being very inefficient at best, he may be himself destroyed. For religious reasons certain venomous snakes, which cause not a few deaths, cannot be touched. Leopards are everywhere much feared, and are difficult for the natives to destroy. There are several species of food-animals, however, which are not so perilous to hunt, such as antelope, small monkeys, and hares. Some of the tribes rely largely upon these for meat. Elephants have been of immense economic importance to the whole country as the source of ivory, but so rapid has been the slaughter of them, that ivory no longer belongs in the first rank as an article of export.

West Africa abounds in smaller animals and insect life. Most of this is harmless, but there are some species that are serious enemies to the welfare of man. The tsetse fly in many localities renders it out of the question to keep horses. The mosquito, now charged with being the medium of disease-contagion in the case of dreaded tropical fevers, swarms along the coast. One other small pest, the driver ant, demands special attention. There are several species of these ants, which are held in

wholesome respect by man and beast.   Du Chaillu tells
us that

"In the forests of this part of Africa are found vast numbers of
ants, some of whose tribes are so terrible to man, and even to the
beasts of the wood, from their venomous bites, their fierce temper
and voracity, that their path is freely abandoned to them, and they
may well be called lords of the forest." [1]

Writing on the same subject Miss Kingsley gives the
following vivid account :

"I will not enter into particulars about the customary white man's
method of receiving a visit of Drivers, those methods being alike ineffective and accompanied by dreadful language. . . . . The native
method with the Driver ant is different; one minute there will be
peace in the simple African home, the heavy-scented hot night air
broken only by the rythmic snores and automatic side slaps of the
family, accompanied outside by a chorus of cicadas and bull frogs.
Enter the Driver—the next moment that night is thick with hurrying
black forms, little and big, for the family, accompanied by rats, cock-
roaches, snakes, scorpions, centipedes, and hugh spiders animated by
the one desire to get out of the visitors' way, fall helter skelter into
the street, where they are joined by the rest of the inhabitants of the
village, for the ants when they once start on a village usually make
a regular house-to-house visitation." [2]

These active swarms of ants frequently devour weak or
sick persons about a village in a few hours, and they
clear out all vermin more efficaciously than human
agency could do it.

The sea and all streams emptying into it throughout
the entire coast afford a great variety and abundance of
fish.   Among these may be mentioned herring, mackerel,
mullets, soles, and eels.[3]   Herring in particular provide
a staple article of food, not merely for the coast tribes,
but also for many inland peoples, who purchase dried
fish from the former.

Very few domestic animals are seen in West Africa.

[1] "Equatorial Africa ", p. 359.
[2] "West African studies ", pp. 27–8.
[3] MacDonald, *op. cit.*, p. 76. See also John Barbot's "Description
of North and South Guinea ", London, 1746, p. 222.

"The only indigenous domestic animals are the ubiquitous dog, the common variety somewhat resembling the European greyhound, but of coarser build, the cat, the ass, and poultry".[1] Of these the ass is found, however, only in northern Upper Guinea, where there has been contact with the Moors. Goats are kept by some tribes, but are a later introduction by Europeans, and little is made of them. In fact, the climatic conditions and the hostile insects of West Africa seem to be as hard upon the domestic animals known to us as upon our race itself.

As to the flora it is both varied and luxuriant. Many portions of Upper Guinea seem less favorable to arboreal than to herbaceous growth, so that while in some parts extensive forests are found, in others the country is open and prairie-like. From Senegambia to and including the Gold Coast most of the land is covered by dense forests, but in the Slave Coast region the woods are mainly confined to the river valleys and low-lying spots. In Lower Guinea the vast equatorial forest of central Africa extends westward to the Atlantic, a dense jungle thoroughly typical of a fertile and well-watered tropical country.[2] Scattered far and wide are the little villages of the natives, connected only by difficult foot-paths or in some cases by streams, navigable with canoes.

The most valuable of all the trees is the "oil palm", which grows wild in all wooded localities. The nuts from this tree yield abundantly a rich oil, used by the natives for food and as an unguent. It has become a prime article of export, since the breaking up of the slave-trade and the threatened exhaustion of the ivory

---

[1] Stanford, "Compendium", *op. cit.*, p. 327.
[2] Paul Du Chaillu, "A Journey to Ashango-land", pp. 406-7.

2

supply. Another palm supplies " palm-wine", a drink
highly prized throughout West Africa. These palms,
also furnish materials for huts, boat-rigging, and other
uses.[1] The plantain bears huge bunches of a coarse
sort of banana ; the cocoa and cola-nut palms both yield
food. Magnificent ebony and mahogany trees are found
at many points, though they were never valued by the
natives till the rise of foreign trade created a demand
for the timber. A species of large vine grows luxuriantly
in the forests, the milky juice of which makes fine
rubber. This was formerly of no use to the natives,
but since they have learned its commercial value an
ever increasing quantity is now produced for the foreign
market.

With regard to cultivated plants the advent of Europeans brought about the introduction at an early date of
Indian corn and rice, while millet seems to have come
in still earlier from Mohammedan sources. But these
excellent cereals are grown chiefly in certain favorable
parts of Upper Guinea, and are little known elsewhere.
Says Barbot :

" It is positively asserted, that before the Portuguese came to this
coast, the natives neither used, nor so much as knew of bread, made of
any sort of corn : but only such as they made of yams and potatoes
[manioc roots], and a few roots of trees." [2]

The West African population therefore, before the
foreign invasion, was confined to a few vegetable roots
for bread material, and had no cereal food. This is still
the case with the immense majority, who rely upon
familiar indigenous plants, either through ignorance of

[1] John Barbot, *op. cit.*, p. 196. He gives a most detailed and satisfactory account of West African plant-life.

[2] *Op. cit.*, p. 197. These cereals were in more or less use as early
as 1695, when the Sieur Froger visited Upper Guinea, for he mentions them in his " Voyage under Gennes ", p. 31.

any other or inability to overcome inertia and repugnance to new things.

The yam is "a root which grows in the earth like carrots, commonly twelve or thirteen inches long, and as much in circumference." It is of a reddish yellow color, when ripe. What Barbot above calls "potatoes" are not at all the vegetable we know by that name, but "manioc roots" as they have now come to be called. The manioc resembles our dahlia more than any plant, perhaps, familiar to us, both in root and foliage, though the former are larger than dahlia-roots. The "tapioca", now widely used in American households, is a preparation derived from manioc roots. As to fruits, the pineapple and pomegranate are indigenous, and are much used by the natives.[1] One or two varieties of beans, cabbages in some parts, and in others a kind of squash, are frequently to be seen. Curiously enough it is the seeds of the squash which are used, rather than the vegetable itself.

What the potential mineral resources of West Africa may be, is unknown as yet. The only metals ever secured from the earth, and actually utilized by the natives have been gold, iron, and copper. Gold has long been supplied by the Gold Coast country, as its name implies, but is not found elsewhere on the West Coast. Superstitious scruples and ignorance of proper methods prevent the natives from mining for any metal, but they have long procured gold by washing out the sands and gravels of the streams. They pick up the ores of iron and copper where rich veins crop out along the broken escarpments of the great table-land.[2] The amount of

[1] MacDonald, p. 69-70.

[2] See Bosman's "Guinea", in Pinkerton's "Voyages and travels", vol. xvi, pp. 369-375. Also Barbot, *op. cit.*, p. 191 and pp. 227-234. Du Chaillu, in his "Equatorial Africa", p. 122, tells how iron ore is found and smelted.

metal secured under such circumstances and worked up by the extremely crude methods in vogue, is insignificant compared with what civilized men might obtain.   There seems to be little doubt that even such metallurgy as is known among the true negroes of West Africa was acquired from northern or northeastern peoples of superior civilization, and not self-developed.[1]

[1] See p. 21.

CHAPTER II.

ETHNOLOGY AND ETHNOGRAPHY.

The primal origin of the Negro still remains undetermined. But definite knowledge on this point is not essential to the present inquiry. We know with certainty, that the Negro race has inhabited Africa for thousands of years, and that its character during countless generations has been moulded by the influences and conditions peculiar to tropical Africa. It is known, also, that for centuries there has been a migration westward and south-westward across the continent. Superior peoples, developed in the drier, cooler climate of the northeast, and improved by mixture of blood with Semitic races invading Africa by way of Suez, have driven inferior tribes before them, across the continental interior. Brinton says :

"The general tendency of migration in central as in southern Africa, so far as it can be traced in historic times, has been westerly and southwesterly. The densest population has been near the Atlantic coast, as if the various tribes had been crowded to the impassible barrier of the ocean." [1]

This is why Keane declares that "the very worst sweepings of the Sudanese plateau"[2] seem to have gathered along the coast lands of West Africa, and Ellis speaks of the West Coast natives as "the dregs and offscourings of Africa."

This movement is going on to-day, and several tribes, themselves driven onward, have arrived on the West Coast within recent times, displacing slowly the existing occupants. For example, the Dahomey people were an

[1] D. G. Brinton, "Races and peoples", pp. 176–7.
[2] A. H. Keane, "Man : Past and present", p. 54.

inland tribe at the time of the earlier visits of Europeans to West Africa, but by the conquest and wiping out of the Whydahs in the first quarter of the eighteenth century, they reached the sea.   So, too, the Fans were in the interior when visited by Du Chaillu in 1856,[1] whereas Miss Kingsley found them, in 1893, wedging themselves rapidly down to the seaports.[2]   She observes : " In this part of the world (Ogowe River), this great tribe is ousting the older inhabitants of the land."   As this process has been going on for centuries, it is obvious that the negroes living along the western verge of the continent at any given period have not been the best specimens of their race.   This is a fact of the first importance to us, because the slaves brought to our country were taken from these peoples.

Fixing our attention, now, upon this West African population, we find that ethnologists are generally agreed in dividing them into two slightly different types, the Bantu, inhabiting Lower Guinea, and the Sudanese of Upper Guinea.   While Keane thinks that,

"The specialised Negro type, as depicted on the Egyptian monuments some thousands of years ago, has everywhere been maintained with striking uniformity . . . Nevertheless considerable differences are perceptible to the practised eye, and the contrasts are sufficiently marked to justify ethnologists in treating the Sudanese and the Bantus as two distinct subdivisions of the family." [3]

The chief reliance for distinguishing the two is the fact that the Bantus all speak slightly differentiated dialects of a common language, whereas a great diversity of language exists among the Sudanese.   Miss Kingsley says that the Bantus keep their villages cleaner than do the Sudanese ; that they prefer to have their slaves

[1] " Equatorial Africa ", *op. cit.*, p. 90.
[2] " West African studies ", *op. cit.*, p. 399.
[3] *Op. cit.*, pp. 38–39.

live apart in separate quarters, whereas the latter do not, and that female gods predominate among the Bantus, while the Sudanese have male gods principally. [1]

But one may read the accounts of West African native life and character, as seen from Senegambia to Angola, without discovering, unless forewarned by ethnological experts, any significant differences. It would seem, therefore, that the distinction above drawn, has little relevancy to the present investigation. That which the negroes throughout West Africa have in common, includes all important race characteristics, and it is a knowledge of these we are seeking.

A short résumé of the principal tribal groups, with their geographical location from north to south, may be of assistance. In Senegambia dwell the Wolofs, with the kindred sub-groups of Jolofs and Serers, all speaking dialects of one tongue. They are reputed to be the blackest and most garrulous of negroes. The name "Wolof," indeed, signifies "talker." They are a tall, well-built people, and in Peschel's opinion, "the finest of negro races," physically speaking.[2]

South of the Gambia are found the Felups, "an utterly savage full-blood negro people", of whom there are many tribes. It was chiefly from these and the Wolofs that superior Moorish warriors once took hundreds of slaves and sold many at the mouths of the Senegal and Gambia rivers. Still farther to the south near Sierra Leone are the Timni, who occupy a considerable territory. The Sierra Leonese and Liberians have been so changed by intermixture with miscellaneous freed slaves, that they must be excluded from consideration. Mention should be made, however, of the

---

[1] *Op. cit.*, p. 422.
[2] See Peschel, "Races of man", pp. 464-5.

Krus, a tribe which has somehow kept itself tolerably pure. It furnishes still the best labor available anywhere on the coast, the " Kru-boys", as they are called, being relied upon at every sea-port for loading and unloading cargoes.[1]

The remainder of Upper Guinea from Liberia eastward is inhabited by three prominent groups of tribes, ethnically related. These are the Tshi-speaking peoples, who occupy the Gold Coast region ; the Ewe-speaking peoples, who occupy the western half of the Slave Coast ; and, finally, the Yoruba-speaking tribes, including those of Benin, who inhabit the rest of the Slave-coast. Between the Tshis and the Ewes a remnant of the Ga-speaking people remain, but they have long been of minor importance. All are pure negro in type, and differ only in language, and in the fact that there has been a slightly greater development of organization among the Ewes and Yorubas. According to their traditions they all once belonged to a single group, and lived in an open grassy country to the northeast—evidently the inner Sudanese plateau.

The population of Lower Guinea is made up of numerous small tribes. Their names being unfamiliar we may here conveniently designate them by their geographical location, *e. g.*, the Bonny natives and the Cameroon natives. Prominent among the peoples of this equatorial region may be named the M'Pongwes, the Bakalai, and the recently arrived Fans. It will, however, seldom be necessary to mention particular tribes, because they are all nearly alike in character and manner of living.

No one general term will correctly describe the kind and degree of civilization found among the West Africans. They are not pastoral peoples, for they have no

[1] Kingsley, " West African studies ", pp. 54-5.

cattle, sheep, or beasts of burden. In fact, they live under conditions which practically prohibit this mode of life. Only a small portion of their subsistence is derived from hunting, and they cannot be accounted good hunters. Those who live near the sea are good fishermen in their way, and even secure a surplus of fish, which they sell to inland peoples. Mainly, however, they depend for food upon agriculture of a very crude type, supplemented by the free gifts of nature. Yet they are not a fully settled people, cultivating the same lands for long periods, for they move their villages freely hither and thither, when impelled by superstition or temporary danger. They have private property in women, slaves, and movables, but not in land. While they trace kinship still through the female line, yet there are unmistakable signs of a change to kinship through the male line. In view of all these considerations, perhaps we can scarcely do better than to say, that they are in a confused state of transition from the stage of purely nomadic savagery to that of settled agriculture.

But though we may call this a transition stage, there is little evidence of any progress within historic times. Keane declares, indeed, that the West African negroes " have made no perceptible progress "[1] for thousands of years. They seem to have suffered an arrest of development, when driven from more favorable conditions in the north and east. At any rate their culture is on a very low level, and very unprogressive. They have no letters, art, or science ; their industries are confined to very elementary agriculture, fishing, a little hunting, and some simple handicrafts. Cannibalism formerly prevailed almost everywhere, but has largely

[1] *Op. cit.*, p. 84.

disappeared, especially in regions under European influence. Human sacrifice, and executions for witchcraft, are still practically universal, except in regions under the immediate control of white officials. Religion is "grossly anthropomorphic," all natural phenomena are explained by reference to spirits, mostly ill-disposed towards man. Language is in the agglutinative state; only suffixes are used among the Sudanese, but prefixes, alliteration, and suffixes are used among the Bantu.

Physical and psychic characteristics are substantially uniform, only trained observers being able to detect a few differences here and there. The West African negro is usually rather above the average human stature, with arms disproportionately long, and slender legs. He is erect and easy in carriage, and has a well-developed physique. The color varies from a dark chocolate to a deep black, the hair is invariably black with elliptical transverse section, causing it to be "woolly." The face has markedly prognathous jaws, thick, everted lips, a flat nose, and large prominent eyes, always black with yellowish cornea.

The psychic nature of the West African exhibits most of those immaturities so common among uncultured savages, and analogous to childish thought and emotion in more developed races. Ellis says:

"The negroes of the Slave Coast have more spontaneity and less application, more intuition and less reasoning power, than the inhabitants of temperate climates. They can imitate, but they cannot invent, or even apply. . . . . They are usually deficient in energy, and their great indolence makes them easily submit to the despotism of kings, chiefs, and priests, while they are as improvident as they are indolent." [1]

In temperament, says Keane, they are "fitful, passionate, and cruel, though often affectionate and faithful"

[1] "Ewe-speaking peoples", p. 10.

They are sensuous, and possess little sense of dignity and little self-consciousness; "hence the easy acceptance of the yoke of slavery."[1]   In one profoundly important particular they seem peculiarly deficient, *i. e.*, in that strength of will which gives stability of purpose, long staying power, and self-control in emotional crises. There is here a striking contrast with our American Indians in several aspects.   Finally, it may be added, that a passionate love of music and rhythmic motion dominates them to a remarkable degree.

[1] *Op. cit.*, p. 83.

CHAPTER III.

INDUSTRIAL ECONOMY.

The natives of West Africa live under conditions adverse to the growth of industrial efficiency; indeed few regions are more hostile to such a development. Their physical environment deprives them of many motives to labor. The weather is never so cold as to necessitate substantial dwellings or clothes. Less food is required than if they lived in a temperate or frigid climate. So abundant is nature's provision for food and other wants, that with little effort they obtain what is needed. The staple artificial drink, palm-wine, is secured merely by tapping a palm of a variety which grows wild everywhere, and fermenting the juice.[1] Palm-oil, a prominent article of diet, is pressed from nuts produced abundantly by another wild palm. Du Chaillu says of Lower Guinea: "The forests abound in wild fruits and nuts, some of which are eaten. For instance, the pineapple grows wild in all parts of this region and is a delicious fruit".[2] The waters teem with edible fish and the forests with game. Such materials as are needed for simple huts and meagre furniture are everywhere in profusion. It is common for a village to be removed and reconstructed in four or five days.

In the case of cultivated produce, the fertility of the soil and the climatic advantages are such that very large returns are yielded to slight labor. Speaking of grain crops along the coast, Bosman

[1] See Bosman's "Guinea", *op. cit.*, p. 453. He gives a good account of this palm and its manifold uses to the native, aside from its wine-producing capacity.
[2] "Equatorial Africa", p. 46.

said: "It were to be wished that corn were to be produced in our country (Holland) with as little trouble as here;" and of rice along parts of the Upper Guinea coast: "It grows in such prodigious plenty that it is easy to load a ship with it, perfectly cleansed, at one penny or less the pound ".[1] The plantain, a large coarse banana, is a prime article of food, and few cultivated plants yield more food for less labor than the banana. Describing a field of plantains, Du Chaillu says, that the small palms are set about five feet apart, and each tree bears a bunch of plantains weighing from forty to one hundred and twenty pounds. "No cereal could in the same space of ground give nearly so large a supply of food ".[2]

Previous to the appearance of Europeans, the extreme west coast of Africa was completely isolated from the outside world; its inhabitants lived in scattered villages buried in the forest, and remained in dense ignorance of any other desirable objects than the necessities of their own savage life. Among the forces which have helped to civilize other peoples has been the stimulus to effort arising from newly conceived wants, quickened into being at the discovery of commodities, first brought by strangers.

The appearance of Europeans with new and attractive commodities, produced a great effect. To get them in exchange for native products, thousands of negroes were moved to unwonted exertions, while foreigners taught them new and better methods of production. All this, however, has been comparatively recent, and for ages the negroes were without such incitements to industry.

The direct influence of the West African climate is

Op. cit., p. 458.
[1] " Journey to Ashango land ", p. 119.

adverse to persistent effort. Where high temperatures, and low humidity prevail, the rapid evaporation from the body cools it, and permits considerable exertion, as is the case in Egypt. Great humidity, combined with a low temperature, as in the British Isles, has no bad effect. But West Africa enjoys neither of these advantages, it swelters under a torrid heat combined with excessive humidity.[1] Such conditions deaden industrial effort. The white man, whose capacity for energetic and prolonged labor in most circumstances is so great, whose wants are numerous and insatiable, finds himself irresistibly overcome. Rich rewards await those who can put forth a little effort, yet as Ellis says, so intense is the disinclination to work, that even the strongest wills can rarely combat it. In fact, the very will itself seems to become inert.[2]

We are now prepared to appreciate the workings of the vitally important factor of natural selection. It is obvious that in West Africa natural selection could not have tended to evolve great industrial capacity and aptitude, simply because these were not necessary to survival. Where a cold climate and poor natural productiveness threaten constant destruction to those who cannot or will not put forth persistent effort, selection operates to eliminate them, and preserve the efficient. In torrid and bountiful West Africa, however, the conditions of existence have for ages been too easy to select the industrially efficient, and reject the inefficient.

In fact, climatic conditions being such as to make severe and prolonged effort actually dangerous to physique, it is plain that the possession of great energy must be dis-

---

[1] See Herbert Spencer's "Principles of sociology", sec. 16, for an illuminating discussion of the influence of climatic factors.

[2] "The Tshi-speaking peoples, etc.", p. 4.

advantageous. It may seem at first sight that, as it is the tendency of selection to adapt a species to the environment it lives in, the negroes should have become exempt from this danger. But Nature is economical. Why should the Guinea natives be carefully adapted to perform heavy labor in spite of climate, when by reason of that very climate such labor was never required? Hence, very little power for energetic and persevering effort was evolved in the race. Just a modicum of such power suffices the main purpose, and during seven or eight hours of maximum temperature each day, all the animal world, man included, seeks an effortless existence in shady places.

The character developed through ages of selection amid these conditions, whatever else it may contain, is not likely to include the elements of high industrial efficiency. Indeed, measured by the standard of northern civilized peoples, the Guinea native's easy-going indolence, heedlessness, and improvidence seem incredible.

The industrial régime which actually obtains among the peoples under investigation shows well the consequences of these conditions. The economic development of a people is marked by a progressive specialization of industry, the gradual creation of labor-saving apparatus, and the accumulation of property. Let us see where the natives of Guinea stand in these respects.

Division of labor has proceeded but a very little way. The most striking instance of it to civilized observers is that which assigns all agricultural and menial labor to the female sex. Of the region explored by him, Du Chaillu says: " The women not only provide all the food, but they are also the beasts of burden in this part of the world ".[1] In allusion to the rubber-gathering industry, he adds: " Even here I noticed the laziness of

---

[1] " Equatorial Africa ", p. 76.

the black men, and the cruel way in which the women are obliged to work ".[1] Describing life near the Congo, Proyart says, " We have spoken elsewhere of agriculture, it is the women who carry it on. . . . The men, besides an universal prejudice, founded no doubt on their indolence, would think they degraded themselves if they tilled the ground."[2] The men are in part occupied with war, hunting, or fishing; for the rest, their great delight is in endless talking and smoking, accompanied incidentally by what Miss Kingsley touches upon as " that great African native industry—scratching themselves ".[3] Their love of tobacco and their noisy garrulous companionship, which cause the hours to pass by unheeded, are brought out again and again by all writers on West African native life.

Still, a few handicrafts are known among them, and in most of the higher tribes are carried on by a small artisan class. Bosman describes some of the Upper Guinea tribes as having " a very few manual arts ", and mentions as examples the making of wooden or earthen cups, troughs, and the like, arm-rings of gold, copper, or ivory, the weaving of small narrow strips of cloth, and crude blacksmithing.[4] Of the lower Congo natives Proyart says, " Almost all of them are hunters and fishers. . . . . There are also smiths among them, as well as potters, weavers, and salt-makers."[5] Du Chaillu, Miss Kingsley, and others tell of tribes, however, who have never developed any handicrafts, depending upon their more well-to-do neighbors for a few articles, obtained by barter.

[1] *Idem.*, p. 78.
[2] " History of Loango ", by the Abbe Proyart, Paris, 1776 ; found in Pinkerton's " Voyages and travels ", vol. xvi. See p. 574.
[3] " West African studies ", p. 97.
[4] *Op. cit.*, p. 390.
[5] *Op. cit.*, p. 574.

The number of handicraftsmen in any given tribe is small, and their special skill is jealously withheld from the common herd. In some instances, indeed, the population at large regard these men, especially the blacksmiths, with half-superstitious awe. These simple folk exist somehow on an incredibly meagre supply of implements and weapons. Even in the manual arts women are compelled to do all the drudgery of collecting raw material, etc. All these facts reveal how the great mass of male population escapes distasteful toil.

The development of labor-saving apparatus and of skill in its use is on a very low level. So little appreciation do the natives have of such things, that Europeans have found it extremely difficult to persuade the natives to utilize even the most obvious means of saving time and labor. To work at something, which merely promotes in some obscure way an ulterior object, seems to the average Guinea native an incomprehensible policy. Even when he has been made to see that a little more care and effort at first, may save much time and trouble, his aversion to exercising care and his innate happy-go-lucky temperament lead him to neglect such a method.

As illustrating this trait it is said that the natives seem utterly oblivious to the fact that the more crooked a path is the more time and labor will be required to traverse it. As MacDonald puts it :

"A road, which need not be more than two miles in length, is frequently more than three on account of its windings. The native seldom troubles to get over an obstacle in his path, he goes round it like the ant, and the time lost is of not the slightest value to him, and in this respect he is quite at a loss to understand the haste of the European." [1]

[1] *Op. cit.*, p. 81. On one occasion a missionary, en route from Sierra Leone to the United States, gave the writer a very impressive description of the infinite trials of patience to which white men are subject in West Africa owing to the negro's utter indifference to the value of time or the importance of economizing labor.

Ellis somewhere remarks that the white man's "at once" is always interpreted by the natives to mean any time from an hour to a week.

All transportation is effected by canoes, if any sort of water-way is available, or else by head-carriage, *i. e.*, by carrying packs on the head. Sometimes the pack is carried on the back, partly supported by a strap passed over the head. Overland transportation is by human pack-trains, each porter bearing from forty to a hundred pounds. Alluding to these native porters, Bosman says that, " with a burthen of one hundred pounds on their heads, they run a sort of continual trot, which is so swift that we Hollanders cannot keep up with them without great difficulty, though not loaded with an ounce weight." [1] Robert Norris, describing a journey from the Whydah coast to the capital of Dahomey, speaks of the porters, who bore him in a hammock, jogging " on at their usual rate of about five miles an hour." [2]

Water carriage, however, is very much depended upon, and to this end many tribes seek to locate their villages near navigable water. The natives along the sea-coast and river-banks seem very expert canoe-men and fine swimmers. Their canoes are made out of large logs by a rude process of hollowing and burning out. Some are of surprising size. Du Chaillu saw a M'Pongwe canoe sixty feet long, over three feet wide, and three feet deep. [3] But this is exceptional, for usually they are hardly thirty feet in length. In these small craft some of the most daring occasionally take considerable coasting voyages at favorable seasons of the year. Neverthe-

---

[1] *Op. cit.*, p. 479.

[2] "Bossa Ahadee, King of Dahomey ", p. 66. Norris was thus carried on one occasion over forty miles in one day.

[3] "Equatorial Africa, p. 167.

less, even at its best, this canoe carriage is extremely unsafe and vexatiously limited in compass. Du Chaillu and Miss Kingsley again and again lost valuable instruments and goods through the capsizing of canoes. Many lives, also, are annually lost in this way.

In agriculture the implements used are exceedingly simple and inefficient. West Africans have no domestic draught animals, and are ignorant of the plow.[1] Du Chaillu says of the Fan tribes :

"Their agricultural operations are very rude, and differ but little from those of the surrounding tribes. Like them, they cut down the trees and brush to make a clearing, burn everything that is cut down, and then plant their crop in the cleared space. The only agricultural instrument they have is a kind of heavy knife or cutlass, which serves in place of an axe to cut down trees, and for many other purposes, such as digging the holes in which they plant their manioc or plantains. After the clearing is made, the women go around among the burned logs and tree-roots, and stick in their roots and shrubs wherever they can find space ; and nature does the rest."[2]

Again, Barbot tells us that the Upper Guinea peoples,

"Till or dig the ground with an iron tool, made in the shape of a shoemaker's knife, fixed at the end of a small staff. . . . During the time the work lasts, they are never without a pipe in their mouth, and continually talking to one another ; so that they do not advance much in a day, being very averse to hard labour."[3]

The Congo natives " have no other instrument of tillage than a little pointed spade, much like the trowels of our masons ", says Proyart.[4]

The tools used in their handicrafts are likewise of a simple character. The outfit for working iron is practically the same everywhere. It comprises an anvil of stone or iron, formed roughly into a block, a pair of tongs,

[1] Waitz says : " Der Pflug ist so wenig im Gebrauch als die Benutzung von Zugvieh zum Ackerbau oder zu anderen Zwecken." See his " Anthropologie ", bk. ii, p. 80.

[2] *Op. cit.*, p. 125.

[3] *Op. cit.*, p. 39-40.

[4] *Op. cit.*, p. 574.

curiously rigged bellows, and a hammer, shaped and used, however, like the pestle for a mortar. The substantial similarity of these tools throughout West Africa, appearing at wide intervals among tribes which have had no intercourse for centuries, though influenced alike by superior peoples of the interior, suggests that iron-working may have been not an indigenous development, but acquired from external sources.

In pottery-making only the bare hands are used, one hand moulding the wet clay, while it is being revolved by the other. For weaving, among such tribes as have learned the art, they have very primitive forms of the loom, which permit strips only a few inches in width and two or three feet in length to be woven. Some of the Upper Guinea tribes are spoken of by Bosman and others as producing considerable quantities of cotton cloth, owing to better appliances and more skill, derived from Mohammedan sources. In Lower Guinea their raw material consists of grass or the thin cuticle stripped off the leaves of a certain palm, "which is then twisted, and becomes a tolerably firm yarn".[1] Many tribes, however, have no looms, but do a little weaving by hand alone. Proyart describes the textile art of the Congo natives as follows :

"The weavers make their cloths of a grass about two feet high, which grows untilled in the desert plains, and needs no preparation to be put to work. The length of the grass is the length of the web ; they make it rather narrower than long. This cloth is woven like ours, but they make it on their knees, without shuttle or loom ; having the patience to pass the woof through the threads with their fingers. . . . The best workmen do not make more than the length of an ell of cloth in the space of eight days." [2]

There are many tribes who know nothing of weaving

[1] "Equatorial Africa", p. 462. They are able to dye this yarn in two or three colors, and the colored cloths are highly prized.

[2] *Op. cit.*, p. 574.

in any manner, and either do without cloth or secure small quantities by trade.

The West Africans love nothing better than trading. The earliest explorers found the coast tribes exchanging surplus fish with their inland neighbors for game or vegetable food, the gold of the Gold Coast region found its way to distant tribes, and iron implements have been seen in use among peoples who knew nothing of metallurgy. Thus inter-tribal trading has always gone on.

This exchanging is carried on mainly by barter. Hence intending travellers or explorers burden themselves with heavy supplies of tobacco, salt, beads, guns, ammunition, cloths and the like, as the only means of paying their way. They often experience infinite vexations, owing to the difficulties of barter.

Rude forms of money, however, have come into use at many points. Cowry-shells seem to have attained the widest currency, and are mentioned as being in common use in Upper Guinea. They have long been employed for this purpose.[1] Much more local in range are such coinage equivalents as " macutes," or " pieces of cloth made a yard long," found among the Loanda natives in 1666,[2] and the " manilla ", a bracelet of alloyed copper for some time in use along the Ivory Coast, but now "sinking into a mere conventional token." Even slaves were passed from hand to hand at roughly fixed valuations. Du Chaillu says on this point:

" No better illustration could be given of the way in which the slave system has ingrafted itself upon the life and policy of these tribes than this, that, from the seashore to the farthest point in the interior

[1] Waitz remarks: " Nach seiner weiten Verbreitung zu schliessen, muss der Gebrauch der Kauris in Africa sehr alt sein." See " Anthropologie ", ii, p. 103.

[2] See " A Voyage to the Congo ", by Angelo and Carli, in Pinkerton's " Voyages and travels ", vol. xvi, p. 157.

which I was able to reach, the commercial unit of value is a slave. . .
If a man is fined for an offense, he is mulcted in so many slaves. If
he is bargaining for a wife, he contracts to give so many slaves for
her." [1]

One needs only to note the character of these several
forms of currency to see at a glance how poorly they
serve as tools of exchange, and why as a matter of fact,
they are little relied upon. Direct barter, still greatly
predominates.

What are the results of the West African's industrial
régime? The conditions are such that with anything
like steady industry and the exercise of a little foresight, his food supply might be ample and varied. But
just these qualities he has never developed. The consequence is that thousands live much of the time on the
verge of famine. Barbot says: "It is very strange that
the blacks should ever know any scarcity and sometimes
famine, but it is occasioned by their sloth, they being generally careless, void of foresight, and never providing
for casualties." [2] The very ease with which they can
collect food at one season tempts them irresistibly to put
off the labor of providing against worse times. The
preservation of meat or even vegetable food is rendered
very difficult by the moist, hot climate. The insecurity
in which many tribes live continually, by reason of war
or natural phenomena, increases the difficulty of producing and maintaining a full food supply.

Certain staple articles of diet are found nearly everywhere, while less valued articles vary from country to
country. The plantain and manioc furnish the most
universal bread equivalents. The plantain is eaten like
bananas, or "cut in longitudinal strips and fried", or
rolled in leaves and baked. Miss Kingsley speaks of

[1] "Equatorial Africa ", p. 380.
[2] *Op. cit.*, p. 196.

two varieties of manioc, one of which is but little cultivated because it yields poorly.   Of the other she
says,

" The poisonous kind is that in general use, its great dahlia-like roots
are soaked in water to remove the poisonous principle, and then dried
and grated up, or more commonly beaten up into a kind of dough in a
wooden trough. . . . The thump, thump, thump of this manioc beating is one of the most familiar sounds in a bush village." [1]   As to its
dietary value, she remarks : "It is a good food when it is properly
prepared, but when a village has soaked its soil-laden manioc tubers
in one and the same pool of water for years, the water in that pool
becomes a trifle strong, and both it and the manioc get a smell which
once smelt is never to be forgotten." [2]

Hence it is that a disease, known in native parlance as
"cut him belly", is very prevalent.   Livingstone considered manioc to be of poor sustaining quality, for "no
matter how much one may eat, two hours afterward he
is as hungry as ever ".[3]

Perhaps the next most important vegetable food, in
point of universality and of quantity used, is the yam.
Palm-oil is very much used to cook vegetables in or
as a sauce for meat.   The universal drink is palm-wine,
of which the natives are excessively fond.

By no means so widely known, but constituting a part
of the food supply in one locality or another, are rice,
maize, millet, squash-seed, and a few vegetables, such as
cabbage and beans.   Rice is known only in the lowlands
of some parts of Upper Guinea.   Maize, recently introduced, is still unknown to interior tribes, away from contact with the whites.   Millet is confined to relatively few
localities.   It is quite evident, at any rate, that the West
Africans need not lack for a good and varied diet.

For flesh the chief dependence of most tribes is fish.

[1] "Travels in West Africa ", p. 208.

[2] *Idem.*, p. 209.

[3] See his " Travels in South Africa ", pp. 326-7.

Even the inland peoples, not living near streams, get supplies of so-called "dried fish" from their better situated neighbors. Wild game is also drawn upon so far as their very crude methods permit. They are quite indiscriminate in their choice of animals, eating snakes, monkeys, and any other creature that falls in their way. They derive, however, only a most uncertain and meagre supply of food from this source, and when a windfall does occur they proceed to devour immoderate quantities, until famine again threatens. As Miss Kingsley puts it : "The gorge they go in for after a successful elephant hunt is a thing to see—once ".[1]

Some tribes, of a more settled and peaceable character, such as were the Whydahs previous to their conquest by Dahomey, keep small stocks of goats and poultry. But these are apt to be so limited in supply, that they are reserved for special occasions. On the whole, it seems that flesh diet is largely a matter of haphazard.

Their method of "drying" fish is to lay them out in the sun, where they dry up a little, and quickly begin to putrefy. Miss Kingsley says that meat is often "just hung up in the smoke of the fires, which hardens it, blackening the outside quickly, but when the lumps are taken out of the smoke, in a short time cracks occur in them, and the interior part proceeds to go bad, and needless to say maggoty ".[2] Nowhere do the natives make any distinction between the flesh of animals properly slaughtered and of those which have died of disease. They eagerly fall upon the carcass of a hippopotamus, which has been dead for days and lying under the torrid sun.

---

[1] " Travels it West Africa ", p. 211.

[2] *Op. cit.*, p. 210. See also MacDonald, *op. cit.*, p. 68.

A summary of this phase of our subject, may be quoted in the words of Miss Kingsley :

> "The food supply consists of plantain, yam, koko, sweet potatoes, maize, pumpkin, pineapple, and ochres, fish both wet and smoked—and flesh of many kinds—including human in certain districts, and snails and snakes, crayfish, and big maggot-like pupae of the rhinoceros beetle and the *Rhyncophorus palmatorum*. For sweetmeats the sugar-cane abounds, but it is only used chewed *au naturel*. . . . . Out of all this varied material the natives of the Congo Français forests produce dirtily, carelessly, and wastefully a dull indigestible diet." [1]

Next we may consider the character of their houses and furniture. During the pouring rains of the wet season there is much need for a roof, while the nights are sometimes cool enough to make shelter comfortable to a scantily clothed people. But these needs can be met by simple construction with coarse materials.

The style of habitation varies with the locality. MacDonald describes the Gold Coast huts as made of bamboo splits or wattle work, tied securely to a double row of sticks planted all around the intended house-space, and having the interstices of several inches between the two rows filled with loose gravelly clay, thus forming thick impervious walls. The roof has gables, and is made of a frame-work of bamboo into which a thatch of leaves is laced.[2] Du Chaillu describes the huts in the equatorial region, as built of upright poles, to which broad strips of bark are lashed, and roofs of the same material added. Many tribes have round, conical shaped huts, thatched with grass or leaves. Waitz remarks that there is little variety in West African habitations. The difference between those of rich and poor, king and subject, is not one of size and elaboration, but merely of number, the rich having many huts for their

---

[1] *Op. cit.,* p. 208.
[2] *Op. cit.,* pp. 80–81.

many wives, and the poor having but one or two.[1] Not
only the warmth of climate, but the great insecurity in
which most of the tribes live, discourages any further
architectural development.

Ordinarily a village consists of two rows of huts,
lining the sides of a street. Here and there a town may
be found, with two streets crossing at right angles, and
a large public square at the intersection. Very rarely is
the aggregation of houses and population large enough
to be dignified with the title of city, as in the case of
Coomassie, the capital of Ashanti. But the structure of
the huts remains uniform throughout, with an exception
in the case of royal "palaces," so called. Even in
such cases, the palace is distinguished merely by slightly
greater size, and by multiplication of rooms in the form
of adjoining huts, the whole being sometimes enclosed
in high walls. Such was the case with the residence of
the King of Dahomey.

There is very little furniture. "In entering a hut,"
says Proyart, "you perceive a mat, which is the master's
bed, his table, and his seat, some earthenware vessels,
which constitute his kitchen tackle, some roots and
fruits, which are his belly-provisions."[2] Sometimes one
finds rude stools and benches. Miss Kingsley when
travelling through the Ogowe River country, was usually
compelled to choose for a bed between a long, low bench
and the floor.[3] A wooden trough in which to beat up
the manioc, an earthenware or iron pot, some calabashes

---

[1] *Op. cit.*, p. 88. He says: "Der Arme und der Reiche unterschei-
den sich in Rücksicht ihrer Wohnung meist nur dadurch, dass der
eine mehrere, der andere wenigere solchen Hütten besitzt, der
Anzahl seiner Weiber entsprechend, und selbst mit den Königen ist
es oftderselbe Fall." This is corroborated by more recent writers on
life in West Africa.

[2] *Op. cit.*, p. 566.

[3] For example, see her "Travels in West Africa", pp. 178-9.

(a species of large gourd), and, among some tribes, baskets, constitute the outfit of the average native home. Thus, their equipment in furniture and utensils is so meagre, that the West African housewife would be dumbfounded if introduced to even the limited equipment of an average Negro cabin in the United States.

The obtuseness and heedlessness of the Sudanese in all sanitary matters, and of the Bantus in many points, have long been the despair of European administrators. Speaking of the various causes of unhealthiness in Upper Guinea, Bosman says :

> "The stench of this unwholsome mist is very much augmented by the Negroes' pernicious custom of laying their fish, for five or six days, to putrefy before they eat it, and their easing their bodies round their houses and all over their towns." [1]

MacDonald and others comment on the fact that they "build their villages without the least regard to situation or pleasantness." Their custom of burying their dead in the earthen floors of their own huts is one which the whites have found it extremely difficult to suppress. Among none of the true negro stocks, from Senegal to the Niger Delta, does there seem to be any appreciation of cleanliness or of the danger of unsanitary conditions.

But the Bantu tribes show some inclination to maintain cleanliness about their villages. The drying of fish, keeping of corpses for days after decomposition has set in, and other proceedings, very offensive to civilized noses, go on as everywhere, but the villages and individual huts are kept cleaner and neater than in Upper Guinea. Miss Kingsley gives "street cleaning" as one

---

[1] *Op. cit.*, p. 382. All travellers in West Africa find it necessary very soon to accustom themselves to most noisome odors of many kinds, and to all sorts of revolting uncleanliness.

of the distinguishing characteristics of the Bantu peoples.[1]

In regard to clothing, two factors enter, not hitherto requiring mention, viz., the love of personal adornment and the sense of modesty. In the torrid zone clothes are worn not primarily to keep the body warm, but to adorn it and to meet the demands of decency. If warmth were the only consideration, most West Africans would never take the trouble to provide clothing at all. As it is, however, even the cannibal Fans and like tribes have some sort of meagre loin-cloth, a fringe of beaded cords suspended from the waist, or a small apron of leaves. How little this is for protection is shown by the fact that children, up to the age of about ten, run about naked. At the age of puberty, however, some covering is assumed, but usually no more than the loin-cloth, fastened around the hips and reaching down nearly or quite to the knees.[2]

Whether their modesty or their inordinate delight in self-decoration counts the more as a motive in this, it would be hard to determine. Waitz, indeed, declares unhesitatingly that modesty for the most part figures far less than vanity (Eitelkeit) among the negroes.[3] For this opinion there is much evidence. Innumerable instances like the following might be given. Du Chaillu says of the M'Pongwe women :

[1] See her " West African studies ", p. 425.

[2] The best way in which to get a notion of the costumes worn in West Africa, is to examine the illustrations in the books of Miss Kingsley, Du Chaillu, and MacDonald.

[3] He says : " Die Schamhaftigkeit ist est freilich meist weit weniger als die Eitelkeit und die Liebe zum Putze, die den Neger hierbei bestimmt. Die Putzsucht und Prachtliebe ist überhaupt eine seiner hervorstechendsten Eigenschaften." See the " Anthropologie ", ii, p, 87.

"On their bare arms and legs they delight to wear great numbers of brass rings, often bearing from twenty-five to thirty pounds of brass on each ankle in this way. This ridiculous vanity greatly obstructs their locomotion, and makes their walk a clumsy waddle." [1]

Bright cotton cloths, beads, looking-glasses, gaudy umbrellas, silk hats and a variety of such incongruous, but to the African very ornamental, articles are the main stock in trade of European traders there.[2] So strong is the motive here exemplified, that it has brought about considerable industry among many tribes, which never could have been persuaded to work otherwise.

[1] "Equatorial Africa", p. 33.

[2] An invoice of goods given by Atkins, in his "Voyage to Guinea", pp. 160-1, includes all such articles as those mentioned in the text. See, also, an extensive and amusing list given by Matthews, in his "Voyage to Sierra Leone", (1788), p. 144.

CHAPTER IV.

WEST AFRICAN RELIGION.

Religious beliefs and practices in West Africa are not altogether uniform, though in essentials there are few variations. Most of the statements of earlier writers are too unsystematic and superficial to convey a correct understanding of the subject. Fortunately, however, the recent careful and thorough studies by Ellis, of the Upper Guinea peoples, and by Miss Kingsley of the Lower Guinea tribes, supply the requisite knowledge. Taking these as a basis, the observations scattered through the older authors may supply illustration and corroboration at many points.

The religion of the tribes of Senegambia, Sierra Leone, and Liberia has been so modified by Mohammedan and Christian influences, that it is hardly worth while to pause long over it. The Wolofs, Felups, and other groups in Senegambia, or in the country south of it, have long been subject to a growing influx and intermixture of peoples from the interior, chiefly the Mandingans. They are in reality border tribes, situated between Negro-land proper on the south, and Moorish countries on the north and northeast. They came earliest under European influence. Thus it has come about, as Keane puts it, that most of them

"profess themselves Muhammadans, the rest Catholics, while all alike are heathen at heart; only the former have charms with texts from the Koran which they cannot read, and the latter medals and scapulars of the 'Seven Dolours' or of the Trinity, which they cannot understand."[1] He adds further that "Many old rites still flourish, the household gods are not forgotten, and for the lizard, most popular of tutelar deities, the customary milk-bowl is daily replenished."

[1] *Op. cit.*, p. 45.

Among the Felups there is some notion of a superhuman being, " vaguely identified with the sky, the rain, the wind, or thunder-storm." Everywhere the medicine man is feared, courted, but inwardly detested. In Sierra Leone and Liberia are found similar hybrid religions of peculiar and confusing character. The original heathen beliefs persistently survive, as shown, for example, by the universal use of " gree-gree bags," or charms. Miss Kingsley states that she never saw a native there " in national costume without some, both around his neck, and around his leg, just under the knee."[1] These charms are supplied for a substantial consideration, by the medicine men or priests.

Such then, very briefly, is the religion of this region. But as the influence of two great religions, alien to that of the natives, has been at work for several centuries, we may infer that at the beginning of slave-trading times the religion was similar to what is found among the Guinea negroes further south.

Ellis is of the opinion that among the Tshi, the Ewe, and the Yoruba-speaking peoples the rate of development has not been uniform, but that it has been somewhat greater in the east among the Ewes and Yorubas than in the west among the Tshis. This he attributes to the open character of the easterly countries, permitting easier intercourse and exchange of ideas. The Tshis of the Gold Coast have always lived in isolated villages, separated by dense forests. But as one goes eastward the forests dwindle, and the obstacles to overland travel are reduced.[2]

This greater freedom of communication seems to have promoted especially unification and higher organization

---

[1] " Travels in West Africa ", p. 19.
[2] See his " Tshi-speaking peoples ", pp. 8-9.

of religious beliefs and practices. While the religions of all rest upon the same foundation, and in outcome are practically the same, yet in passing from west to east an advance is observed in fusing insignificant local gods into greater gods of more extensive reach and power while the priesthood in the west is found to be more organized, until among the Yorubas it is a compact and powerful order, having a large share in government. The root of all West African religion, however, from the Gold Coast to the lower Congo, is the same, and may now be explained once for all.

So admirable is the brief summary given by Ellis that we cannot do better than to take it as a starting point. It is as follows :—

" Partly through dreams, and partly through the condition of man during sleep, trances, and state of syncope, the Tshi-speaking negro has arrived at the conclusions—

1. That he has a second individuality, an in-dwelling spirit residing in his body. He calls this a ' *kra*.'

2. That he himself will, after death, continue his present existence in a ghostly shape. That he will become, in short, the ghost of himself, which he calls a ' *srahman*.'

No. 1 has been very frequently confounded with No. 2, though they are essentially distinct. The kra existed before the birth of the man, probably as the successive kra of a long series of men, and after his death it will equally continue its independent career, either by entering a new-born human body, or by wandering about the world as a ' *sisa* ', *i. e.*, a kra without a tenement. The general idea is that the sisa always seeks to return to a human body, and become again a kra, even taking advantage of the temporary absence of a kra from its tenement to usurp its place. Hence it is that any involuntary convulsion, such as a sneeze, which is believed to indicate that the kra is leaving the body, is always followed by wishes of good health. Usually it only quits it during sleep, and the occurrences in dreams are believed to be the adventures of the kra during its absence. The srahman, or ghost-man, only commences his career when the corporeal man dies, and he simply continues to exist in the ghost-world or land of dead men. There are, therefore, in one sense three individualities to be considered, (1) the man, (2) the in-dwelling spirit, or kra, and (3) the ghost or srahman, though in another sense the last is only a continuation of the first in shadowy form." [1]

[1] " The Ewe-speaking peoples ", pp. 15–16.

Having once conceived these ideas, the natives of West Africa assisted by the medicine men and priests follow them to their logical consequences. All the amazing practices that so dumbfound the foreign visitor, all the apparently silly and inconsequential notions and customs, are in reality the outcome of apparently necessary inferences from their premises. Miss Kingsley says:

"It may seem a paradox to say of people who are always seeing visions that they are not visionaries, but they are not. . . . He is not a dreamer nor a doubter; everything is real, very real, horribly real to him." [1]

If men have their ghosts, then animals must have theirs, and plants, and even inanimate objects, such as weapons and clothes. Therefore, " acting logically upon this belief, he releases these ghosts, or souls, from their material parts, for the ghost-men in Dead-land ".[2] Thus, at the death of the head of the house, more particularly if he be wealthy or of royal family, wives and slaves are killed, that there may be companionship and service for the deceased in Dead-land. In the case of poorer men, these things are done on a scale proportioned to their status. At the death of a king of Ashanti hecatombs of victims die to furnish a suitable retinue for the royal ghost. When King Kwamina died about the year 1800, the funeral ceremonies were repeated weekly for three months, and on each occasion two hundred slaves were slain. At the funeral of the mother of Tutu Kwamina in 1816 three thousand victims died.[3]

The funeral obsequies over a deceased king are called " The Grand Custom," but in addition to these there are the " Annual Customs," when the honors due

[1] " West African studies ", p. 124.
[2] *Op. cit.*, p. 17.
[3] " Tshi-speaking peoples ", p. 164.

4

to the dead are again celebrated in less costly style. During the reign of Bossa Ahadee, King of Dahomey, Robert Norris witnessed one of these periodical celebrations. He says:

"The court was engaged in the celebration of a grand festival, which continues several weeks, and is called the 'annual customs', when the king waters the graves of his ancestors with the blood of many human victims." [1]

He then gives an account of what he saw—a revolting picture of horrible bloodshed. He relates also how, on the death of a king, all is confusion, and how the wives fall to killing each other that their spirits may accompany the king. When Bossa Ahadee died after a long reign, "two hundred and eighty-five of the women in the palace had been murdered, before the announcement of a royal successor to the throne could take place." [2] The same thing on a smaller scale occurs when men of less distinction die. Even where a man is so poor as to have no wives or slaves a goat and some fowls will be killed at his grave. Everything the deceased valued, his weapons, his ornaments, his trophies, together with a stock of provisions, are buried with him. Ellis says in this way no small portion of their wealth disappears continually, the loss at the burial of a single distinguished person running up to many hundred dollars.

Since every object in nature has its kra, the various occurrences, that take place in connection with it, must in the absence of other explanation, be attributed to its miserable spirit.

"Some day a man falls into a river and is drowned. The body is recovered, and is found to present no external injury which in the experience of man would account for death. What then caused the death? asks the negro. Water, alone, is harmless; he drinks it daily,

---

[1] "Bossa Ahadee, etc.", *op. cit.*, p. 86.
[2] *Idem.*, pp. 129–30.

washes in it, uses it for a variety of purposes. He decides, therefore, that water did not cause the death of the man, and having an entity, a spiritual being, ready at hand to whom to attribute the disaster, he concludes that the river's kra, its indwelling spirit, killed the man." [1]

When a bolt of lightning kills someone or sets fire to a house, when a tornado tears through the village, or a pestilence silently destroys it, in short, when anything unusual happens, the native's instant explanation is that some spirit did it.

So literally true is this that the Guinea negroes have no conception of " natural death " or of "accident." All diseases, deaths, or bodily injuries, are supposed to have been caused by man or by some spirit. The distinction between deliberately intended injury to another's person or property and a purely accidental one is not recognized. And so these untaught people go through life dominated at every step by the belief that every success or misfortune is solely due to the mysterious operation of unseen personal agencies.

Inasmuch as men's afflictions make a more lasting impression than their satisfactions, and as the West African's environment is one filled with imposing and dangerous natural phenomena, to him it seems that the malignant ill-disposed spirits are vastly in the majority. Hence, he must propitiate them ; he must flatter them ; appease their avarice ; atone for any insult to them ; and thereby keep them complacent toward himself. Out of this there has arisen much ceremonial, a priesthood, the use of charms, and—most costly delusion of all— witchcraft.

Quite distinct from offerings made to the ghosts of deceased persons are those made to the fetish spirits. The former provide for the comfort and satisfaction of

---

[1] " Ewe-speaking peoples ", pp. 21-2.

the departed ones, but the latter are intended to win the good will of the kras of ocean and river, wind and lightning. A few concrete instances will reveal clearly this deeply ingrained belief and habit of the people.

Du Chaillu gives the following typical example of the way in which disease is dealt with :

"The Camma theory of disease is that Okamboo (the devil) has got into the sick man. Now this devil is only to be driven out with noise, and accordingly they surround the sick man and beat drums and kettles close to his head ; fire off guns close to his ears, sing, shout, and dance all they can. This lasts till the poor fellow either dies or is better." [1]

This is the universal West African method of treating sickness. When it fails (and of course it is well calculated to fail) it is felt that the disease-god has triumphed, and so great is the fear engendered thereby, that it is very common for the entire village to move away. Frequently this is done several times within a year.

Ellis says :

"In time of peace, human victims are sacrificed to the gods whenever their assistance is required in any matter of importance. For ordinary affairs fowls, sheep, or bullocks are sacrificed, there being a regularly ascending scale of sacrifice, according to the urgency of the need of protection or assistance, which culminates in the highest and most costly sacrifice of all, that of a human life." [2]

Not merely, however, are offerings made thus in anticipation, but subsequently in case of success they are repeated as thank-offerings ; in case of failure, still they are repeated to mollify the anger of the gods. Suelgrave witnessed in Dahomey the slaughter of four hundred captives in honor of a victory over a neighboring enemy, by which "above eighteen hundred captives

[1] "Equatorial Africa", p. 282.
[2] "Tshi-speaking peoples ", p. 170.

had been taken and brought to the capital ".[1]   He tells
further how

"The king at the time we were present, ordered the captives of
Tussoe to be brought into the court ; which being accordingly done,
he chose himself a great number out of them to be sacrificed to his
fetiche or guardian angel, the others being kept for slaves for his own
use or to be sold to the Europeans."

Human sacrifices, however, are not equally common
throughout West Africa, for while they are extremely
frequent in Upper Guinea, they are comparatively rare
in Lower Guinea.   In the latter region Miss Kingsley
tells us that the value of the sacrifice is proportioned to
the favor desired :

"Some favors are worth a dish of plantains, some a fowl, some a
goat, and some a human being, though human sacrifice is very rare
in the Congo Français, the killing of people being nine times in ten
a witchcraft palaver." [2]

To deal with the world of spirits a special class of
men exists, variously called medicine men, witch-doctors,
or priests.   They are the professional experts, well
versed in mysterious ways of reaching the spirits, and
mediating directly with them.   Among the Ewes and
Yorubas the original multitude of individual spirits
have become fused into type-gods, *i. e.*, instead of every
stream having its own particular kra, there is one god
of all streams ; instead of every tree having an indwelling spirit, there is a god of the forest, and so on.   Along
with this there has been a parallel development as to
those who negotiate with the gods.   Among the Tshis
all the priests profess to handle all matters indifferently,
be it a case of illness, drowning, or any other misfortune.
But among the Ewes and Yorubas the priesthood is an
organized body, differentiated into those who serve *Wu*,

[1] "A new account of Guinea ", by Capt. Wm. Snelgrave, London,
1734, p. 37.

[2] "Travels in West Africa ", p. 451.

the god of the ocean, those who serve *Mawu*, the god of
the weather, etc. The priests of *Wu* dare not trespass
upon the special sphere of the priests of *Mawu*, and
so a native goes to one or the other according to the
nature of his trouble. There are also priestesses who
serve the phallic deities, and whose chief business is
prostitution. " Properly speaking ", says Ellis, " their
libertinage should be confined to the male worshippers
at the temple of the god, but practically it is indiscriminate. Children born from such unions belong to
the god."

From the humbler medicine men, found in every village, up to the compactly organized and powerful priesthood of Dahomey, the functions of all are essentially
alike, *i. e.*, to cure disease by driving out the evil spirit,
to fend off threatening calamity by appeasing the wrath
of an offended deity, to secure victory in war, good har-
vests, good catches of fish, to detect witches and direct
their proper execution, etc. Priests are present and officiate invariably at every birth, marriage, and death, they
conduct the annual festivals, and set the dates for them ;
in short, nothing in West African affairs can proceed
safely or prosperously without their ceaseless intervention.[1]

Another inference made by the native from his belief
in kras, is that his priest can attract certain good spirits
into little objects, which may then be worn on the person or hung in the hut, and thus afford protection
against the manifold ills that flesh is heir to. Wherever travellers have penetrated Africa, the natives are

[1] For fuller details as to the priesthood, see Ellis, in "The Tshi-
speaking peoples", p. 119, and "The Ewe-speaking peoples", p.
139 ; Kingsley in "West African studies", p. 168, *et seq.* ; and
Waitz in his "Anthropologie", ii, p. 196, *et seq.*

found to believe implicitly in the efficacy of " gree-grees "
or charms.   Anything serves for the purpose, antelope
horns, snail shells, nut shells, so long as some priest has
properly doctored them.   Into these are put " all manner
of nastiness, usually on the seacoast a large percentage
of fowl-dung." [1]   Countless instances might be given of
the eager desire for good charms ; one may be cited from
Du Chaillu :

> " I noticed that they very carefully saved the brain [of the gorilla
> he had shot], and was told that charms were made of this—charms
> of two kinds.   Prepared in one way, the charm gave the wearer a
> strong hand for the hunt, and in another it gave him success with
> women." [2]

On a large scale they have charms to protect a plantation or village, not alone from unseen powers, but from
thieves, human or brute.   As Miss Kingsley says :

> " Charms are not all worn upon the body, some go to the plantations
> and are hung there, ensuring an unhappy and swift end for the thief
> who comes stealing.   Some are hung round the bows of the canoe,
> others over the doorway of the house to prevent evil spirits from
> coming in—a sort of tame watch-dog spirits." [3]

Norris tells that, when the Dahomian invading army
was about to make the passage of a river, which could
easily have been defended, " the infatuated Whydahs
contented themselves with placing the fetiche stake in
the path to oppose the oncoming army." [4]   It was disregarded in this case, and the Whydahs were ruined with
fire and spear.   In smaller affairs, however, so absolute is
the faith of the negroes in the power of these charms,
and such is their dread of them, that any house or plantation known to have a charm of the proper kind in
charge of it, is seldom molested by thieves or petty

---

[1] Kingsley, " Travels, etc.", p. 446.
[2] " Equatorial Africa ", p. 101.
[3] " Travels in West Africa ", p. 450.
[4] " Bossa Ahadee, etc.", p. 69.

marauders.   Thus is their superstition strangely utilized
for the protection of property.

But the feature of their primitive religion that
strikes all civilized observers with the deepest horror
and gloom is witchcraft.   Writing in the early fifties,
Du Chaillu said: "The greatest curse of the whole
country is *aniemba*, sorcery, or witchcraft. . . . At
least seventy-five per cent. of the deaths in all tribes are
executions for supposed witchcraft."[1] He was again
and again horrified and sickened by seeing poor wretches
slain in tortures for this reason, while the utmost per-
suasions known to him were powerless to arrest the
proceedings.   Forty years later Miss Kingsley adds her
testimony in these emphatic words: "The belief in
witchcraft is the cause of more African deaths than anything else.   It has killed and still kills more men and
women than the slave trade."[2] Under its terrible in-
fatuation whole villages have been known actually to
dwindle and disappear through executions of members
in a frenzy of superstitious terror.

To the West African a witch is a man or woman who
has somehow obtained control of evil spirits, and is
using this agency to cause disease, ill-luck, or even
death amongst fellow-tribesmen.   To raise the suspicion of witchcraft is fatally easy, but for the accused to
disprove it, is well-nigh impossible; hence the condition of affairs so well described for us by Miss Kingsley:

"At almost every death a suspicion of witchcraft arises.   The witch-
doctor is called in, and proceeds to find out the guilty person.   Then
woe to the unpopular men, the weak women, and the slaves, for on
some of them will fall the accusation that means ordeal by poison or
fire, followed, if these point to guilt, as from their nature they usually
do, by a terrible death: slow roasting alive—mutilation by degrees be-

[1] "Equatorial Africa ", p. 386.
[2] *Op. cit,*, p. 162.

fore the throat is mercifully cut—tying to stakes at low tide that the
high tide may come and drown—and any other death human ingenuity
and hate can devise." [1]   She adds later : " I have seen mild gentle men
and women turned by it, in a moment, to incarnate fiends, ready to
rend and destroy those who a second before were nearest and dearest
to them.   Terrible is the fear that falls like a spell upon a village when
a big man, or big woman is just known to be dead.   The very men
catch their breaths, and grow gray around the lips, and then every
one, particularly those belonging to the household of the deceased,
goes in for the most demonstrative exhibition of grief.   Long, long
howls creep up out of the first silence—those blood-curdling, infinitely
melancholy, wailing howls—once heard, never to be forgotten."

Then the witch-doctor is hastily summoned, arrives
looking mysterious and very wise, goes through certain
ceremonies, and pronounces guilt.   Instantly a frenzied
mob rushes for the victim, and presently the death-roll
again has been increased.   There may be more than one
victim, for any number may be accused of collusion.

To quote again from Du Chaillu, who saw scores of
executions :

"As usual I heard a harrowing tale of witchcraft in the course of
the day.   Few weeks pass away in these unhappy villages without
something of this kind happening.   A poor fellow was singing a
mournful song, seated on the ground in the village street, and on inquiring the cause of his grief, I was told that the chief of a village
near his having died, and the magic Doctor having declared that five
persons had bewitched him, the mother, sister and brother of the poor
mourner had just been ruthlessly massacred by the excited people,
and his own house and plantation burnt and laid waste." [2]

Such are the religious thought and belief of the West
African natives, and some of the consequences flowing
therefrom.   On every side, and in every detail their
lives are touched and influenced by these delusions.
They attribute every misfortune to evil spirits, and for
success in every move they rely upon friendly spirits.
They sacrifice large portions of ill-spared goods, and even
human blood is poured forth.   Verily, to the Guinea

---

[1] " Travels in West Africa," p. 463.
[2] " Journey to Ashango-land," p. 110.

Negro his religion is no sham or mockery, but the most vividly real and oppressive fact conceivable.

"In every action of his daily life he shows you how he lives with a great, powerful spirit world around him. You will see him before starting out to hunt or fight, rubbing medicine into his weapons to strengthen the spirits within them, talking to them the while; telling them what care he has taken of them, reminding them of the gifts he has given them, though those gifts were hard for him to give, and begging them in the hour of his dire necessity not to fail him."[1]

Yet, in spite of this, his religion has nothing to do with his social morality. It tends to control his conduct toward the gods, but not his conduct toward fellow men. This is a fact of the first importance.

Ellis tells us that in West Africa :

"Religion is not in any way allied with moral ideas," and that the only sins, properly speaking, are "first, insults offered to the gods ; secondly, neglect of the gods.'[2] And as he says further, 'Murder, theft, and all offenses against the person or against property, are matters in which the gods have no immediate concern, and in which they take no interest, except in the case when, bribed by a valuable offering, they take up the quarrel in the interests of some faithful worshipper. . . . . The most atrocious crimes, committed as between man and man, the gods can view with equanimity. These are man's concerns, and must be rectified or punished by man."

Thus the African's code of behavior toward the gods is a matter quite aside from considerations of social morality, and conversely his religion has nothing to do with relations to men.

In reality the West African's religion is simply his science of nature. Civilized peoples have for the most part differentiated their religion from their science. They have certain entities called "forces of nature", which sufficiently explain all natural phenomena. But the conception of an impersonal force, such as gravity or electricity, is utterly foreign to the Negro's mind.

[1] Kingsley, "West African studies," p. 130.
[2] "Tshi-speaking peoples," pp. 10-11. See also the statements of Waitz in his "Anthropologie," ii, pp. 190-1.

Anything that is done must have required the volition
of a being, visible or invisible. Hence his multitude of
spirits, and his methods of dealing with them. Whereas
we have life-saving stations along the sea-coast, a weather
bureau, and boards of health, the African casts human
beings into the sea, offers sacrifices so that the medicine
man may predict or bring good weather, and buys
charms to protect him from disease. His purpose is the
same as ours, but his science is false, and his expenditure futile. With us it is partly the role of religion to
control conduct toward our fellow men ; with the African
it is to guide him safely through the multitudinous
dangers of life arising from the hostile action of countless unseen spirits.

CHAPTER V.

SOCIAL LIFE AND ORGANIZATION.

We shall next consider the institution of marriage and the family, the ceremonials attending various significant events in the life of the individual, and the attitude of individuals toward their fellowmen.

The fundamental fact which determines the social position of women, is that they are property, owned by the men precisely as are slaves or material goods. Upon this fact rests every custom regulating their existence. Women are bought and sold, their virginity is valued solely as a marketable commodity, adultery is simply trespass upon the husband's property rights, seduction or rape is a violence to the parents' property in daughters, and wifehood is but enslavement to the husband's will. Of course, many artful and strong-minded wives manage to get their own way with weaker spirited husbands up to a certain degree. Miss Kingsley remarks on this in her usual vein: "Many a time have I seen a lady stand in the street and let her husband know what she thought of him, in a way that reminded me of some London "slum scenes." [1] But in times of real domestic crisis the husband is apt to reassert his rights in ways more forcible than delicate, and in so doing he is supported by public opinion, including that of other wives in the community.

Polygamy prevails universally, and so deeply rooted is it in the whole social fabric that missionaries have found it scarcely possible to bring over their converts to monogamy. "Polygamy," says Miss Kingsley, "is the

[1] "Travels, etc.", p. 225.

institution, which above all others, governs the daily
life of the native. . ."[1]   The more wives a man has the
more wealthy and distinguished he is, and the greater is
his labor-supply.   A reason everywhere assigned for
plurality of wives is the existence of a custom which
forbids a wife to receive her husband during pregnancy
or while she is suckling a child, this being continued
until the child is two or three years old.[2]   While this
custom could not have given rise to polygamy, being
evidently a concomitant development, yet once established it now operates powerfully against the decline or
abolition of that institution.

Nor must it be supposed that the women dislike polygamy.   They are only too well satisfied with it, the
missionaries find, and resist monagamy with discouraging vehemence.   The more wives, the less work for
each, say they.   Furthermore, there is social distinction
in being the wife of a man who has twenty other wives,
and such a woman looks down with contempt upon her
lower class sisters, who share conjugal rights with only
three or four co-wives.   Little friction seems to arise
among these plural wives.   In explanation of this fact,
however, Ellis says: " No jealousy prevails among the
women, because their affection, if they have any for
their lord and master, is quite passionless, and borders on
indifference."[3]   Waitz thinks that another reason for
the absence of domestic disorders is seen in the fact that
there is always a head-wife, to whom all the rest are
subordinated, and whom in the absence of the husband

---

[1] "Travels, etc.", p. 212.

[2] Ellis, " Ewe-speaking peoples ", p. 206 ; Kingsley, "Travels,
etc.", p. 212.

[3] " Ewe-speaking peoples ", p. 207.

they obey.[1] The custom which requires the husband to live for a time with each wife in succession in her own hut, also furthers the maintenance of peace and conjugal fidelity.

Adultery among these people can only be defined, says Ellis, " as intercourse with a married woman without the consent of her husband, for the men can and do lend their wives, and the latter do not seem to have the right to refuse compliance."[2] Many times was Du Chaillu embarrassed by the earnest proffer of wives by chiefs along the route of his journeys, this being done in strict accordance with their rules of hospitality. He relates how on one occasion his friend, Quengueza, in a fit of generosity, unable to prevail upon his distinguished guest to accept a wife during the time of his visit, actually turned over all his wives to Du Chaillu's men, and they by no means had their white employer's scruples.[3] Nor did the wives on such occasions feel any other sentiment than a kind of chagrin at their rejection by the white guest, his explanation being wholly beyond their understanding.

In fact, these peoples have no conception of chastity as a virtue in itself considered. Ellis says :

"An unmarried girl is expected to be chaste because virginity possesses a marketable value, and if she were to be unchaste her parents would receive little or perhape no head-money for her. . . . A man who seduces a virgin must marry her, or, if her parents will not consent to the marriage, must pay the amount of the head-money. In the latter case, her market value having been received, any excesses she may commit are regarded as of no consequence."[4]

In purchasing wives the substance of the transaction is everywhere the same. On the Gold Coast, for in-

---

[1] *Op. cit.*, p. 110.
[2] " Ewe-speaking peoples ", p. 202.
[3] " Journey to Ashango-land ", p. 76.
[4] " Tshi-speaking peoples ", p. 286.

stance, the fact of purchase is veiled under a form of
present giving. According to MacDonald, when a young
man desires a girl for his wife, he makes known his wish
to her parents. If they agree she is given to him. But
the man must then give a number of " presents," so-
called, to the parents. In Sierra Leone, three cows and
a sheep, or their equivalent, are expected.[1] Further
south, where there are no cattle, the presents consist of
various articles such as decorative ornaments, weapons,
provisions, etc. As a general thing, however, wives are
secured by purchase outright, accompanied, in many
cases, by all the higgling of the market, though custom
usually fixes a rough average price. Thus a man may
have as many wives as he can pay for and look after.
Ordinarily there are from two or three up to ten or fifteen, except in the case of a big chief or king, who is
likely to have scores of them. The king of Ashanti
counted his wives by the hundred, and in the court of
Dahomey there were several thousand.

According to the native code of morality it is only
the wife who can commit adultery, the husband being
at liberty to do as he pleases. The adultery of a wife
is punished with varying severity, from the infliction of
a beating (most common among the masses), up to expulsion and death. The latter is rare, and only occurs
among those of rank and wealth. Frequently the nose
or a hand is cut off.[2] The paramour is punished by
having to pay a fine, or if the wife belongs to a distinguished chief, is liable to death. If unable to pay a
fine, the culprit may be sold as a slave in order to raise

---

[1] Waitz, *op. cit.*, p. 110.

[2] *Idem*, p. 115. He says: "Da die Frau durch die Ehe ganz Eigen-
thum, ein Vermögenstheil des Mannes wird, ist die Ansicht natürlich
dass nur sie, nicht aber der Mann strafbaren Ehebruch begehen
kann."

the amount.   Hence has risen a curious practice, which still further illustrates the laxity of West African notions.   " Many husbands," says Ellis, " encourage frailty on the part of their wives, hoping to profit by the sums they may be able to exact from their paramours." [1] This practice extends throughout all West Africa, and is quite common.   Women of the royal family in Ashanti and Dahomey are permitted to intrigue with men of fine physique, "in order that their kings may be of commanding presence."   Miss Kingsley states that among the Bantus the laws against adultery are severe, but their enforcement is lax.[2]

Clearly, then, sexual purity among the Guinea natives does not rest upon any regard for chastity as such, but merely upon property ownership.   The man must be compensated for any liberties taken with his wives or daughters.   This done, the matter is ended.   The student of West African life finds in the writings on this subject abundant evidence, which need not be repeated here, that very little restraint of the sexual proclivities is exercised.   Indulgence commences at an early age, and continues thereafter with but little impediment.

For this state of things there is probably a good reason. The mortality in West Africa is frightful.   Wars, slave-raids, executions for witchcraft, pestilence, famine, ignorance and neglect in the care of young children, etc., all combine to make the annual drain upon population by untimely death an appalling percentage.   To maintain existence there must be a proportionately high birth rate.   For hundreds of generations therefore, those tribes among whom fertility was greater have tended to sur-

---

[1] " Tshi-speaking peoples ", p. 286.   See also Waitz, *op. cit.* p. 114.

[2] " Travels in West Africa ", p. 497.

vive in the ceaseless rivalry with those less characterized by such traits. It seems likely, therefore, that
selection has developed in the race exceptionally strong
reproductive powers.

Herein seems to lie an explanation of certain problems
of morality, which are to-day the despair of well-wishers
of the negroes. It has surprised some that the negroes
thrive and multiply, wherever transplanted within
warm climates, in spite of close contact with superior
civilization—an experience that seems fatal to most
other races of low culture. If strong sex instincts and
great fecundity were essential under African conditions
to the preservation of race, it is only to be expected that
these traits should prove excessively developed when
civilized conditions of life are substituted. In questions of race preservation the issues are so vital that Nature is not to be turned hither and thither even at the
demand of civilizing reformers.

The family relations are those usually obtaining
among peoples of very backward development. The
father and his children are bound by very weak and uncertain ties, while the mother's affection, though much
stronger, declines as the children reach full maturity
and independence. The description given by Bosman
of the way children are brought up in West Africa, is
possibly a little strong in coloring, but in the main accords with the general idea conveyed by all other writers that touch upon the matter. He says

" Let us see how they educate their children, with whom the men
never trouble themselves in the least, nor the women much, indeed :
the mother gives the infant suck for two or three years, which over,
and they are able to go, then it is—turn out, brats ; if it be hungry
she gives it a piece of dry bread, and sends it abroad wherever it
pleases, either to the market, or to the sea-side to learn to swim, or
anywhere else. Nobody looks after it. nor is it anybody's business to

hinder its progress. These children are as well contented with dry bread as ours with all manner of delicacies ; they neither think of nor know any delicacies, nor are their mothers troubled with them, but do their business undisturbed ; when, on the other hand, if our children can but go alone we are continually perplexed with thousands of fears of some or other accidents befalling them." [1]

The contrast here drawn between the easy-going indifference of African parents and the constant sense of care and solicitude on the part of civilized parents reveals a most significant fact.

There is one singular and striking exception, however, to the general absence of deep affections between family relatives ; that is the mutual love of mother and son. This by comparison with all other ties is, as Miss Kingsley states, a strong and enduring one. Either will support the other as long as able to do so. No explanation of this anomaly is vouchsafed. The Rev. Leighton Wilson says :

"Whatever other estimate we may form of the African we may not doubt his love for his mother. . . . He flies to her in the hour of distress, for he well knows that if all the rest of the world turn against him she will be steadfast in her love, whether he be right or wrong." [2]

Miss Kingsley cites this, too, with approval.[3]

The bearing of children involves little inconvenience or deviation from routine daily life. A few hours after her child has been born, the mother usually goes to the nearest water to bathe. It is a custom widely prevalent in West Africa, that children born with teeth already cut, or twins, are thrown into the bush to die. In some parts the mother of twins is driven out to perish in the jungle. When a mother dies, Miss Kingsley tells us that " very young children they do not attempt to keep, but throw them away in the bush

[1] *Op. cit.*, p. 388. See also MacDonald, p. 39, and Waitz, pp. 122–3.
[2] " Western Africa," p. 116.
[3] " West African studies," p. 373.

alive, as all children are thrown, who have not arrived in this world in the way considered orthodox."[1] Du Chaillu somewhere tells of coming across the emaciated body of a young woman in the forest, who, it was explained, had been driven out from her village for some superstitious reason.

Among the Bantu tribes, the practice prevails of

"helping the old and useless members of the village out of this world by a tap on the head; their bodies are then carefully smoke-dried, afterwards pulverized, then formed into small balls by the addition of water, in which Indian corn has been boiled for hours; this mixture is allowed to dry in the sun or over fires, then put away for future use in the family stew."[2]

Lacking the cannibalistic feature, this practice of getting rid of burdensome individuals, is found everywhere, particularly in times of military stress or threatened famine. This holds true to less degree of rich families, since they are better able to sustain all of their members, yet even they are none too scrupulous under pressure.

Beyond the immediate family relations, the West African recognizes few obligations in control of conduct.

"The individual is supremely important to himself, and he values his friends and relations and so on, but abstract affection for humanity at large or belief in the sanctity of the lives of people with whom he is unrelated and unacquainted, the African barely possesses."[3]

Within his own village, persons and property are protected after a fashion by customs amounting to law, but beyond the village all such protection vanishes. A stranger is fair game, wherever met, unless it may be that his tribe is feared as a powerful and dangerous enemy. And even within the village circle, affliction

---

[1] "Travels, etc.", p. 471. See also appendices to the same, pp. 487, 538, 557.

[2] *Idem*, Appendix I, by M. De Cardi, pp. 565–6.

[3] Kingsley, "West African studies", p. 177.

and suffering rarely elicit any sentiments of pity or sympathetic benevolence.

Descriptions of West African life abound in illustrations of these characteristics. All travelers there find it necessary to guard portable articles very closely, or suffer certain loss. Speaking of the Slave Coast natives, Bosman said : " The Negroes of the Gold Coast are very thievish, but are not to be compared with these. They are acquainted with an hundred several ways of stealing, which would be too long to relate here. I shall only add that no person can provide against them." [1] And of the Lower Guinea natives, Miss Kingsley says that stealing is "a beloved pastime—a kind of game in which you only lose if you are found out." [2] Du Chaillu was frequently well nigh at his wits' end to prevent the steady disappearance of his goods, as they were being carried daily by native porters or canoe-men.

Deception is even more common than theft. Ellis sums up this matter well, when he says that they

"rarely go straight towards the end they wish to attain, but seek to compass it by subterfuges and devious methods. Concealment of design is the first element of safety, and as this axiom has been consistently carried out for generations, the national character is strongly marked by duplicity. The negro lies habitually; and even in matters of little moment, or of absolute indifference, it is rare for him to speak the truth." [3]

Of the Lower Guinea people, Du Chaillu says : " Lying is thought an enviable accomplishment among all the tribes, and a more thorough and unhesitating liar than one of these negroes is not to be found anywhere." [4] Cheating in trade is universal and cannot be prevented. This is one of the most serious drawbacks to doing

[1] *Op. cit.*, p. 482.
[2] " Travels, etc.", p. 312.
[3] " Ewe-speaking peoples ", p. 11.
[4] " Equatorial Africa ", p. 437.

business with the natives. Bosman is moved often to
speak of "the villainous rascality" met with in attempting to trade in Upper Guinea. The rubber
brought down to the coast to sell throughout Lower
Guinea is almost invariably adulterated. In a word,
the natives do not understand any such thing as
commercial morality, and so they instinctively seek
every opportunity to get something for nothing by
lying, stealing, cheating, browbeating, or adulterating.
Yet it has been noted in many instances where the
white man has firmly asserted an ascendency over a few
personal attendants or employees, and followed every
delinquency with swift and unerring discipline, that the
natives, instead of becoming sullen and cunningly vin-
dictive, came to have the greatest respect and attachment for him, and exhibited a fidelity to his interests
never otherwise secured among West Africans. Du
Chaillu found that as long as he was merely kind and
considerate with his porters, they cared less for him and
his fate than when he assumed an attitude of despotic
power, asserted his will with decision, and brooked no
dilly-dallying or deception, on pain of death on the spot.
They then seemed to have a sort of pride in their
master, boasted of the very qualities in him which compelled their obedience, and parted from him with sorrow
at the end of a tour. It is always the strong-minded,
uncompromising, governor or officer along the coast
who becomes the most popular with the natives, and is
most heartily sustained by their public opinion. Otherwise they are only contemptuous, and they cheat, steal
and make trouble.

There is little regard for the life and freedom of those
not members of the same village. We have seen how,
even within the village itself, the lives of the weak are

very little valued. When it comes to outsiders, any excuse is good enough for making away with them. Traders from the interior bringing goods down to the coast are in ceaseless danger of their lives from the intervening tribes; and when robbery occurs no adverse witness is ever left alive.[1] The universality of the custom that the host should taste food and drink before offering it to a visitor, or the wife before giving to her husband, reveals in a startling manner the frequent use of poison. It has been said that "the most prevalent disease in the African bush comes out of the cooking pot," meaning that victuals are poisoned.[2] All this, and more besides, takes place in time of peace, and the horrors of their warfare well nigh surpass description.

To a European witness of native fighting, the destruction of life is appalling. Whole villages are swept out of existence, and their inhabitants either slain on the spot or reserved for sacrificial purposes or slavery. The march homeward of a victorious army or maurading party is, for the captives, an ordeal which words fail to picture. Several missionaries, who saw the return of the Ashanti army with its spoils of war, mostly prisoners, describe the scene as follows:

"The men, who were tied together in gangs of ten or fifteen by ropes round the neck, and presented a pitiable spectacle, were followed by the women, young and old, some with infants on their backs, and others leading little children by the hand, who crouched in terror at their mothers' sides, and were threatened and struck by the cruel spectators. On the day of their arrival fourteen Wassaw men were sacrificed at Bantama to the manes of the former kings of Ashanti."[3]

In another Ashanti war of conquest, as Ellis states,

[1] Kingsley, "Travels, etc.," p. 315.
[2] *Idem*, Appendix I, by De Cardi, p. 560.
[3] Ellis, "A history of the Gold Coast", p. 291.

thousands of men, women and children were slaughtered. The conquest of the Whydahs by the king of Dahomey did not mean their subjection as tributaries, but their utter extinction. The massacre continued for many days, and then large droves of them were driven to Dahomey to survive till such time as they were wanted for the sacrifice.[1] These conquests on a large organized scale are seen only in Upper Guinea, where are found the only strong consolidated kingdoms among West Africans. But among the scattered tribes of Lower Guinea, each including a few villages, an intermittent warfare consisting of forays, marauding expeditions or fights between small groups, goes on constantly.

We are prepared to believe that the African has almost no sensibility to suffering in others, nor compassion for them. Such refinements of the social spirit have never been developed among these peoples. Ellis thinks that their constant familiarity with bloody scenes of torture and death in connection with religious ceremonies or witchcraft executions, has rendered them exceptionally callous and pitiless in the presence of human agony and pain. The exhibition of sentiments of pity by white persons is a standing puzzle to them. After a description of some of the frightful cruelties practised upon war prisoners, Ellis tells that

"the Ashantis were much surprised that the missionaries should exhibit any emotion at such spectacles; and, on one occasion when they went to give food to some starving children, the guards angrily drove them back."[2] He adds further: "Nor is it to prisoners and aliens alone that such barbarity is exhibited by the northern tribes, for an equal indifference is shown to the sufferings of their own people. Servants or slaves, who may fall sick, are driven out

---

[1] Capt. Wm. Snelgrave, *op. cit.*, pp. 1-19.
[2] "Tshi-speaking peoples", p. 173.

into the bush to die or recover as best they may ; and the infirm or helpless are invariably neglected, if not ill-treated. In the village of Abankoro the missionaries saw an orphan boy about five years old, who went about unnoticed and reduced to a skeleton. He was thus neglected because he could not speak, and was regarded as an idiot. He cried for joy when some food was given him, and the kindness of the missionaries to him astonished the people." [1]

Such incidents might be cited almost without end from the various accounts of West Africa.

The lowest level of unsocialized feeling and practice is seen in cannibalism, which once prevailed almost universally, but is now confined within certain tribes. It is noticeable that new arrivals upon the coast from the unknown and isolated interior regions, *e. g.*, the Fans and Dahomians, are cannibals. De Cardi says it was a common thing to see human flesh offered for sale among the natives of Old and New Calabar, before the practice was stamped out under British administration.[2] It survives in disguised forms here and there throughout Lower Guinea, but has practically disappeared in Upper Guinea outside Dahomey, and even there is declining under foreign influences.

It must be added in fairness that an impulsive kindness often lights up somewhat the gloomy picture. Occasionally is met an instance of deep and permanent affection, and sudden fits of benevolent good will are frequently seen, for the race is after all a good humored one when fear or cupidity are not aroused. The pages of Du Chaillu, Miss Kingsley, Livingstone, and others afford not a few examples of unexpected kindness and fidelity, but they also are full of stories of profuse protestations of love and good intention, afterwards wofully

---

[1] "Tshi-speaking peoples", p. 173.

[2] *Op. cit.*, pp. 557-8. Miss Kingsley says that "sacrificial and ceremonial cannibalism is nearly universal."

belied by actions. Fickle and unstable, the moods of the West African are seldom to be trusted long. The attitude taken toward white aliens is hardly a good test, in any case, of the normal state of feeling among themselves.

Passing to the consideration of the more important occasions for social ceremonial, the first in point of importance and universality among the festivals is that of the "Yam Custom", celebrated every year as soon as the priests have pronounced the yams ripe. Yams are a dangerous food until thoroughly matured, hence the custom that none may eat them till the priests have word from the gods that they are ripe. Obviously this is in the nature of a sanitary law. When the restriction is removed, there is great rejoicing and a desire to celebrate the occasion. The ceremonies usually last a week, the priests officiate as principals, and the kings or chief men assist. Human sacrifices are certain to be offered, and this festival, says McDonald, "furnishes the opportunity for the wildest exhibitions of native license and passion. Theft, intrigue, and assault are all forgiven during the continuance of the feast." [1] This description of the Yam Custom, to judge from other accounts, is none too strong, for it seems to be everywhere a time when public opinion winks at anything, and the whole population gives itself up to an orgie of sensual indulgence.

At the "Annual Customs" the kings or chiefs of tribes do honor to the manes of their departed ancestors. [2] Again human sacrifices, proportioned in num-

---

[1] *Op. cit.*, p. 50. See also De Cardi, *op. cit.*, p. 450.
[2] See Ellis, "Ewe-speaking peoples", pp. 129, 168–9; also Kingsley, "West African studies", pp. 146–8.

ber to the wealth and power of the ruler, are in order, and offerings of food and valuables of all kinds are made besides. At this time tributary tribes, if there are any, are expected to send representatives to make fresh acknowledgements of submission, and bring tribute. Any cases for judicature, appealed to the king or head chief from lower officials, are brought forward and settled.

Besides these larger public festivals, there are lesser celebrations on the occasion of the three chief events in every individual life, birth, marriage, and death. Livngstone says that "the chief recreations of the natives of Angola are marriages and funerals."[1] These are times for gathering together in crowds and making an inconceivable hubbub. The African's love of noisy demonstration is alluded to frequently by all travelers in West Africa, sometimes good humoredly, but sometimes resignedly, as if they had been worn out with it. Miss Kingsley is moved to exclaim: " Woe to the man in Africa who cannot stand perpetual uproar! Few things have surprised me more than the rarity of silence and the intensity of it, when you do get it."[2] Du Chaillu was often tormented almost to distraction with the bedlam of noises kept up all night long.[3] Moonlit nights are a time for white people to avoid their villages, for then the whole population remains up till long after midnight, shouting, singing, dancing, and having an uproariously jolly time. MacDonald remarks, philosophically : " It is a

[1] " Travels in South Africa ", p. 446.
[2] " West African studies ", p. 62.
[3] " Equatorial Africa " pp. 134 and 237 ; "Ashango-land ", p. 283.

part of West African nature; nothing can be done without noise." [1]

The ceremonies connected with birth, while showing local variations in details, in substance are everywhere the same. Ellis thus describes them:

"As soon as a woman discovers herself to be pregnant she offers sacrifice to the tutelary deity of the family, and a priestess binds charms about her wrists, ankles and neck, at the same time invoking the god to avert ill-fortune. . . . . During the act of parturition she remains seated on a country stool, surrounded by a number of female visitors, before whom it would be considered exceedingly disgraceful to utter any cry of impatience or pain. . . . The child, after having been washed, has charms bound round it to avert misfortune." [2]

The mother is considered unclean for a week afterwards, but at the expiration of that time she resumes ordinary life. At the end of three months she again makes offerings to the tutelary deity, and then dressed in her choicest ornaments and accompanied by a band of singing women, she visits her neighbors, and there is much rejoicing over her safe delivery.

"Eight days after the birth, the father of the new-born child proceeds with some of his friends to the house where the mother is, and they there seat themselves in a circle in front of the entrance. The child is then brought out and handed to the father, who returns thanks to the tutelary deity." [3]

Often he names the child at this time, but in some parts it is the priest who gives the name. Until very recently it was the custom in some tribes to bury a woman's tenth child alive, while the mother was obliged to isolate herself completely for a year.

A marriage ceremony is a still more elaborate affair. Marriageable age is determined solely by physical development, and is usually between the twelfth and four-

---

[1] *Op. cit.*, p. 227.
[2] "Tshi-speaking peoples", p. 232.
[3] Ellis, "Tshi-speaking peoples", p. 233.

teenth years. At that age the girl is taken to the water-side and washed; offerings are made to the phallic gods, she is attired in the best that her family can afford or borrow, and accompanied by singing girls, is conducted through the village with all possible publicity. Thus her availability as a wife is fully advertised, and it is seldom that suitors are long to be waited for. A suitor having been accepted, he pays over the price agreed upon or sends presents, and the marriage takes place. In preparation for the marriage festival, the groom sends to the bride's home a stock of intoxicants (palm-wine usually), tobacco and pipes, as well as food for a feast. The coming event is heralded abroad with all possible noise and pomp. Finally the feast takes place and is shared in by all the relatives of both parties, "who keep up an orgie," as Ellis terms it, "for many hours." If the husband finds that his wife has been unchaste, and chooses to reject her, he may do so, and demand the return of all that he paid for her.[1]

Still more attractive than marriages in the eyes of the natives are funeral rites. There seems to be about such an occasion a morbid excitement and interest which is fascinating to the negroes. If the deceased person is of any consequence, the entire village takes part in the ceremonies attending the event. Miss Kingsley says:

"To provide a proper burial for the dead relation is the great duty of the negro's life, its only rival in his mind is the desire to have a burial of his own. But, in a good negro, this passion will go under before the other, and he will risk his very life to do it. He may know, surely and well, that killing slaves and women

---

[1] For marriage ceremonies see MacDonald, *op. cit,*, pp. 224-5; Ellis, "Tshi-speaking, etc.", pp. 234-7, "Ewe-speaking, etc.", pp. 155-7.

at a dead brother's grave means hanging for him, when their Big Consul hears of it, but in the Delta he will do it. On the Coast, Leeward and Windward, he will spend every penny he possesses, and on top, if need be, go and pawn himself, his wives, or his children into slavery to give a deceased relation a proper funeral." [1]

This willingness to reduce themselves to beggary, and even to slavery, rather than seem delinquent in furnishing a thoroughly stylish funeral to any member of the family, is a fact attested by all observers in West Africa. [2]

The natives find it very difficult to realize and admit the presence of death or to distinguish death from sleep or some form of temporary insensibility. The consequence is that, in spite of the warm humid climate, they unfailingly retain the corpse unburied until decomposition has proceeded so far as to give no possible escape from the conviction that death has occurred. If a person is dying or insensible from any suspicious cause, endeavors are made, by the most violent methods, to keep the spirit from leaving the body, or else to recall it.

"Pepper is forced up the nose and into the eyes. The mouth is propped open with a stick. The shredded fibres of the outside of the oil-nut are set alight and held under his nose, and the whole crowd of friends and relations, with whom the stifling hut is tightly packed, yell the dying man's name at the top of their voices, in a way that makes them hoarse for days, just as if they were calling to a person lost in the bush or to a person struggling and being torn or lured away from them. 'Hi? hi! don't you hear? Come back—come back? See here. This is your place', etc." [3]

As soon as it is certain that the person is dead, the ceremonies begin. They last from two or three to seven or eight days, according to local habit and the rank of the deceased. The family abstain from food as long as possible, but may drink as much as they like, and usually do drink immoderate quantities of palm

---

[1] "Travels, etc.", p. 491.

[2] See Livingston, *op. cit.*, p. 466, *et seq.*, and Ellis, "Ewe-speaking, etc.", pp. 161-2.

[3] Kingsley, "Travels, etc.", p. 471.

wine. They shave off the hair. Moanings and weird wailings proceed continually from the crowded hut, where the body, after being washed and dressed in full costume, ornaments and all, is propped up in a sitting posture on a stool, and receives the visits of numerous friends and relatives. They address the corpse again and again, reproaching the spirit for having gone away, and giving vent to the loudest lamentations. At intervals the hubbub is hushed, while some female relative offers food to the corpse, beseeching it to take and eat. All watch eagerly, and upon its failure to comply, the lamentations break out afresh. During all this there is a crowd outside as well, sitting about, smoking and talking. Presents to the visitors are always expected, and this renders the occasion very expensive to the family.

At last, when restoration to life is found hopeless, and due honors have been offered, the body is buried. The coffin is large enough to contain various articles valued during life, as well as food and drink. The grave is dug in the earthen floor of the hut itself, and there the coffin is lowered, the earth filled in, and all is smoothed over as before. While widely prevalent, this is not a universal custom, for Du Chaillu found that certain tribes in equatorial Africa had cemeteries at a little distance from the village, where the coffins were merely placed on the surface of the ground, never interred.[1] These native cemeteries present a gruesome spectacle. The custom of burying corpses under the floors of dwelling places is being strenuously put down by European administrators, but only with exceedingly great difficulty.[2]

[1] "Ashango-land, etc.", pp. 132–3. See also Kingsley, "Travels, etc." p. 481.
[2] MacDonald, *op. cit.*, p. 227.

Some of the tribes, as for example, the Fans, have neither coffins nor graves for the reason that their corpses are disposed of as food. Where there are scruples against eating the body of a fellow-villager, it is sold to another village or exchanged for another body from elsewhere. In comparatively minor details there is much variety in funeral rites from one locality to another, and many of the customs are curious and interesting, but not germane to our present subject.

CHAPTER VI.

GOVERNMENT, LAW, AND MILITARY SYSTEM.

Political development in West Africa is on a par with the low stage attained in all other directions. The population, for the most part is in a thoroughly unintegrated condition politically, the largest units of government, with two exceptions, embracing only a few neighboring villages, united by ties of blood. Outside the states of Ashanti and Dahomey, the natives have not risen to the conception of holding conquered enemies as tributaries, thus building up large political units. The vanquished tribes are extinguished by slaughter or held as slaves.

Of the state of affairs in Lower Guinea, where the least governmental development is found, an excellent description in brief form is furnished by M. De Cardi :

"A tribe is composed of a king and a number of chiefs. Each chief has a certain number of petty chiefs under him. Perhaps a better definition of the latter would be, a number of men who own a few slaves and canoes of their own, and do an independent trade with the white men, but who pay to their chiefs from 20 to 25 per cent. as tribute. . . . This collection of petty chiefs with their chief forms what in Coast parlance is denominated a House." [1]

The head of " the house " usually lives in some central village ; branch villages are under the immediate control of petty sub-chiefs. In many respects this organization is patriarchal, the semi-nomadic character of the people heightening the resemblance.[2]

---

[1] *Op. cit.*, 475.

[2] Waitz says : " Bei den meisten Negervölkern zeigen die politischen Einrichtungen in mancher Hinsicht einen patriarchalischen Character." See his " Anthropologie ". II, p. 127. Also Du Chaillu, " Equatorial Africa ", p. 377.

The privilege and authority of the chief depend largely upon personal force or wealth. While the office is to a certain extent hereditary, "the right of succession vesting in the brother of the reigning chief or king," yet the heir must maintain his leadership, for should another of more force arise, the people may desert or grow restive. If a chief is strong-minded and shrewd, he may rule with a high hand, particularly when he secures the support of the priests or medicine men. The latter have much to do with all government in West Africa, and in many regions[1] are feared by both chiefs and subjects. There are scores of tribes where the chief is in close collusion with the priest, and together they have everything their own way, no common man daring for a moment to complain, much less resist.

There have not been wanting, however, instances of governments almost republican in form. Bosman describes one or two such existing in his day (latter half of the seventeenth century) along the Upper Guinea coast. He says :

"The government of Axim consists of two parts, the first whereof is the body of Carboceros, or chief men ; the other the Manceros, or young men. All civil or public affairs which commonly occur are under their administration ; but what concerns the whole land, and are properly national affairs, such as making peace or war, the raising of tributary impositions to be paid to foreign nations, that falls under the cognizance of both parts or members of the government; and on those occasions the Manceros manage with a superior hand, especially if the Carboceros are not very rich in gold and slaves, and consequently able by their wealth to bring over the other to their side."[2]

But the significance of these rare and small examples of

---

[1] For a good illustration, see the story of Ja Ja, King of Opobo, told by De Cardi, *op. cit.*, p. 528, *et seq.*

[2] *Op. cit.*, p. 405.

primitive self-government is very slight.   In population and importance, the single kingdom of Dahomey would far outweigh them all combined.

In the exceptional cases of Ashanti and Dahomey, are seen crudely developed states with tributary peoples. The kingdom of Ashanti consists of Coomassie, the district in which the conquering tribe lived, and a number of tributary provinces, divided in turn into sub-provinces of a few villages each.   These are ruled by chiefs and sub-chiefs respectively, all of whom owe allegiance to the king at the capitol, Coomassie, and pay tribute to him.   Ellis says:

"The power of the king is curbed by a council. . . . It is composed of the king, the queen-mother, the chiefs of Bekwae, Djuabin and Mampon, the general of the army, and a few of the principal chiefs of Coomassie.   This council possesses absolute power, and rules the entire kingdom.   In important matters the provincial chiefs of the second rank are summoned to Coomassie for consultation, but this is really a nominal concession, for the council is so much feared that no individual would venture to vote counter to its known wishes." [1]

The government is in reality an oligarchy, kept very exclusive, and without limits to its power over life and property.   The people of the tributary provinces are often harshly treated.

Land is held under a crude feudal system.   "The land of a tribe as a whole is attached to the stool [throne] of the king, and cannot be alienated from it." [2] By the king it is parcelled out among the chiefs, and by them in turn is allotted to the free men, the latter being obliged in return to answer every call to arms.   Ellis says :

[1] "Tshi-speaking peoples", pp. 276-7.
[2] *Idem*, p. 298.

"The military organization is the same amongst all the Tshi-speaking peoples, the whole of the men capable of bearing arms being divided into town companies. The companies are under the direct command of the captains, whose office is hereditary and the captains owe direct allegiance to the chief of their district." [1]

Each soldier on the mobilization of the army is expected to provide his own commissariat.

Among the peoples next east of the Tshis, *i. e.*, the Ewes, political organization is much like that just described. But Dahomey is, in several respects, worthy of particular notice. It presents a case of unusually developed irresponsible despotism. Snelgrave and Norris tell us that the people there were cowed into abject servility.[2] Under foreign influence matters have improved, but formerly it was the theory that all property belonged absolutely and immediately to the king, who could at any time dispose of it as he chose. The person of the king was so sacred that he was regarded as a demi-god. "The king", says Norris, "never eats in public; it is even criminal to suppose that he ever eats, or that he is so much like other mortals as to want the refreshment of sleep." [3] In approaching him even his chief officers crawl on the ground and kiss the ground repeatedly. Every day in the year must show fresh bleeding heads at the entrance gates to the palace, in order to impress all with the power of the king. His revenue is largely derived from direct taxes and from imposts on trade, from numerous gifts always made by the chiefs and others at the festival of the Annual Custom, "when all the provincial chiefs, the head men

---

[1] "Tshi speaking peoples", p. 299.

[2] "New account of Guinea", ch. i; and "Bossa Ahadee", first section.

[3] "Bossa Ahadee", p. 105.

of villages, the heads of families, and traders, must attend at the capital and bring presents proportionate to their condition."[1] All prisoners of war belong to the king and are disposed of at his command ; also the property of all persons condemned to death or slavery reverts to him. Yet these legitimate revenues do not suffice him, and every device is used to extort more from an unresisting people. For example, it being unlawful for any one to wear cloth of the particular kind worn by the king, he frequently comes out sudddenly in some style of cloth (supplied now by Europeans), which is being innocently worn by many subjects, whereupon they are seized and made to pay fines. In short, the King of Dahomey is a thorough-going despot, ruling without other limitation than the patience of an awed and spiritless people.

The Dahomian military system has interesting peculiarities. A standing army is maintained, consisting of two parts, a male corps, and a female corps, commonly known to Europeans as the "Amazons."[2] In case of need this force is supplemented by all males capable of bearing arms. The Amazons number nearly 3,000 and the male corps about 5,000, but when the entire available military force is called out it reaches 15,000 or 16,000. Dahomey women, accustomed to heavy work and hardship, make nearly as capable soldiers as the men. War is the chief pastime, as well as means of constantly recruiting the supply of victims for sacrifice and slaves. Whenever the king wishes to take the field against some out-lying tribe, he sends for his chief military officer and says, " My house needs thatch ",

---

[1] Ellis, " Ewe-speaking peoples ", p. 170.

[2] Ellis, " Ewe-speaking peoples ", pp. 182-3.

meaning that the skulls which line the inner walls of the palace must be replaced by new ones.[1]

The methods employed in wars, whether large or small, throughout West Africa are substantially the same : to worst the enemy by stealth and treachery. Having decided with all possible secrecy to attack a certain village, the assailants fall upon its sleeping or unsuspecting inhabitants, slaying instantly all who resist or cannot move rapidly, and taking captive the remainder.[2] More courage to fight in the open is displayed by Ashanti and Dahomian warriors, but the treatment of captured populations is everywhere the same. After the ruthless slaughter of every individual, too old, sick, or defective to be of value, the homeward march begins; little or no food is supplied the captives, and all who faint by the wayside are despatched or abandoned to die.

Since the natives possess no form of writing, even of the most primitive sort, no such thing as written laws or records is known. In reality, law is a misleading term to use in connection with these simple folk. What one finds is merely a few customs and usages, having nothing of the precision of written law. So accustomed are we to a highly developed legal system and judical procedure, that it is difficult to refrain from projecting into our notions of primitive law and judicature a definiteness of structure and function not really found there. De Cardi makes the suggestive remark :

"One often hears people who know a little about West Africa talk about native law, but they forget to mention, if they happen to know

[1] Ellis, " Ewe-speaking peoples," p. 188.

[2] Their warfare is well described by Du Chaillu, " Equatorial, etc.", p. 57, *et seq.*

it, that in a powerful chief's house there is only one exponent of the law, and that is the chief himself; for him native law begins to have effect only when it is a matter between himself and some other chief or combination of chiefs, whose power is equal to or superior to his own." [1]

Thus in every case among the common people the chief may interpret the law and the facts almost to suit himself.

The principal customs regulating property and personal relations after a crude fashion may be presented in brief space.[2] There is no private property in land. In Ashanti and Dahomey, to be sure, there is a sort of feudal system, but elsewhere, semi-nomadic habits still prevailing, land is hardly thought of as property. Wherever a village is located for a time, the people use the land in communal fashion. Some tribes, which have become fairly settled and populous, have a few simple regulations with reference to land holding, such as the rule that where a man can get access to his plot of ground only by passing through that of another, the latter must be paid a small consideration for the right of way.

The African's sense of proprietorship in some other things, however, is keen enough. He counts his wealth chiefly in women and slaves, with other things as subsidiary. Yet, curiously enough, wives and slaves may themselves hold property in their own right. If a wife becomes involved in a "palaver," she and her family alone are held responsible, not the husband. By a "palaver" is meant a trial before any native court, *i. e.*,

---

[1] *Op, cit.*, p. 536.

[2] For detailed information see Kingsley, "West African studies", chap. xviii; "Travels, etc.", pp. 485–500; Ellis, "The Tshi, etc.", pp. 280–305, "The Ewe, etc.", pp. 199–228; Bosman, *op. cit.*, p. 404; Waitz, *op. cit.*, p. 141.

before a chief.   In West African annals the word " palaver" occurs with extreme frequency, for the people are
very litigious.

Thieving is punished by a fine, and the stolen goods
or their value must be restored.   Occasionally, when
the theft is large or accompanied by exasperating circumstances, the punishment is death.   As to the collection of debts, Miss Kingsley says:

"The methods employed in enforcing the payment of a debt are appeal to the village head-man or village elders ; or, after giving warning, the seizure of property belonging to the debtor, if possible, or if
not, that of any other person belonging to his village will do.   This
procedure usually leads to palaver, and the elders decide whether the
amount seized is equal to the debt or whether it is excessive." [1]

Interest is always charged and at enormously high rates,
owing to the great insecurity of credit.   From 25 to 50
per cent. is the ordinary rate, calculated on brief periods
of a few months.   Interest is charged also on stolen
goods for the time elapsing till their restoration, a custom which often leads losers by theft to delay prosecution.

The succession of property is through the female, a
survival of the time when paternity was too uncertain to
be relied upon in tracing blood kinship, as it still is for
no small portion of the population.   The children of one
mother belong to her and go with her in case of separation from her husband, a small payment for each being
made to him by the wife or her family.   A man's property is inherited by his uterine brother, or failing a
brother, then by the eldest son of his oldest sister.   If
there is neither brother nor nephew, then, in some tribes,
the property goes to a son, in others, to the principal
native-born slave.   In Dahomey, however, and one or

[1] " West African studies ", p. 435.

two other cases, among the nobility only, primogeniture has become the rule.

Slavery, having existed from time immemorial, is bound up with the whole social and economic organization of West African society. There are, broadly speaking, three kinds of slaves: those captured in war, those purchased from outside the tribe—usually from the interior,—and the native-born slaves. All alike are mere chattels, and by law are absolutely subject to the master's will without redress. But in practice a difference is made, for obvious reasons, between native-born slaves and captives taken from hostile tribes. The latter are numerous, and the severest forms of labor fall to their lot. They are treated with constant neglect and cruelly punished on the slightest provocation. Their lives are at no time secure; they serve as victims for the sacrifice; when sick they are driven into the jungle; in times of scarcity they starve.

Native slaves are those born in slavery, or are tribe members sold into slavery for debt or non-payment of fines, or are children sold by their parents—a frequent practice among the poor. Much more consideration is shown for the native born slaves. They are even accorded the privilege of holding property in their own name, so long as they behave with proper humility toward their masters. Implicit obedience being at all times required of the slave, he can never be held accountable before the law for any action. It is the owner alone who is responsible to others. As the owner, however, has the power of life and death over all slaves, he is apt to deal harshly with any slave who gets him into trouble.

The pawning of persons for debt is exceedingly common. If the debt is never paid in full, the pawn and his descendants become slaves in perpetuity. Meantime the services of the pawn count nothing toward the discharge of the debt. Neither parent may pawn a child without the consent of the other, and in the case of the wife, her relatives also must be consulted. A woman pawned to a man becomes a concubine, and her children belong to him. Not the master of a pawn-slave, but he who put the person in pawn, is responsible for his actions.

Crimes against the person are usually punished by fine. Murder involves the forfeiture of life, unless the criminal or his family can pay the compensation fixed and demanded by the relatives of the murdered person. To be successfully accused of any species of witchcraft, means certain and horrible death. No distinction is made between injury caused unintentionally and that resulting from deliberate purpose. This fact reveals in a striking manner the primitive nature of West African ideas regarding law and judicial procedure.

It may be well to warn the reader against interpreting the above description too rigidly. Europeans, it is said, require years of residence to learn that their precise ideas of law and administration have no existence in the native mind. They find that native justice is a travesty, that witnesses lie with marvelous facility, that the wealthy bribe freely, and that the judges, *i. e.*, ruling chiefs, are actuated in giving judgments by all manner of private considerations. The necessity of conveying notions of primitive human societies through the medium of a vocabulary associated in our minds with things found only amid advanced civilization, is in many ways unfortunate for the accuracy of our conceptions.

CHAPTER VII.

PSYCHIC NATURE.

The discussion of so subtle and complex a theme as the psychic nature of a race, requires the utmost caution. Still, the more significant mental traits, those which are distinctive, may be detected with a fair degree of accuracy. Where many independent observers have received the same impression regarding any point, we may accept that as likely to be correct. So intimately correlated is a people's outer life with its inner constitution, that in describing the former many revelations of the latter are given. From the external life we can infer the psychic nature, just as students of extinct peoples are able to learn much from surviving remains of language, literature, etc. In the foregoing chapters, however, the references to this subject have been too scattered and incidental to give a rounded, complete conception.

On surveying the low culture of West African natives for significant mental products, the first and most striking facts noted are of a negative character. They have no writing, and nothing more than the rudiments of pictorial art, out of which writing is a later development. The nearest approach to a representation of form and color is seen in the idols, kept in fetish huts, and worshipped by some of the Lower Guinea tribes.[1] The goldsmiths of the Gold Coast exhibit considerable ingenuity

[1] Du Chaillu, "Equatorial Africa", pp. 183 and 278–80. These idols are made of wood, rudely shaped into something like human form, and sometimes smeared with color in true impressionist style.

in the fashioning of rude ornaments, and several tribes have produced ivory carvings of curious patterns. Among many tribes one finds not even the traces of a notion of pictorial or plastic art. The musical temperament of the natives has led to greater development in that direction. On the whole, however, it is clear that they have made scarcely a beginning in the arts.

Does this extreme backwardness reflect an inherent deficiency in psychic endowment, or is it due rather to the lack of education and incentive? The latter view is held by many, who believe that civilization may be communicated to such races by the same educational process as is used in training up the rising generation of a civilized people. According to this view, races differ but little in potential capacity, and nothing but wise education is needed to accomplish within a few generations, what the slower process of self-development requires many centuries to achieve. But the widening knowledge of mankind, which anthropology in all its branches is now supplying, the numerous instances of decay and extinction among backward peoples, suddenly called upon to accept civilized life, and a better understanding of the way in which great capacity is brought into being by evolution, are rendering it constantly more difficult to accept this view.

Rather does the evidence from many sources tend to show that psychic nature is developed in close correlation with external conditions, and is unable to respond quickly on the advent of new and highly exacting conditions. Disintegration of the lower culture sets in, but is not replaced *pari passu* by sound development of the new ideas and institutions. The rise of complex industry, of written literature and science, of the fine arts, means the appearance of new criteria or agencies of selection; these, reacting upon a people, fit them by slow healthy progress for still higher things. The entire absence of these agencies in Africa probably means something deeper, therefore, than a mere lack of education for the living generation. It implies that the psychic nature has never been enlarged and refined by selection in response to a progressive environment, and so remains inferior to that of peoples long subjected to the stress and struggle of rapidly advancing standards. Let us proceed to consider the characteristics they present.

Our knowledge of certain of the relations between the mind and its physiological basis in the brain may be taken as fairly established. Although some have set much store on comparison of brain weights, it is felt by conservative anthropologists that the difficulties of using this criterion are too great for it to be of much value.[1] Cranial capacity, however, offers one not so open to objection. It has been found that in this respect the Australian aborigines stand lowest, Africans next, Mongolians next, and highest of all, Caucasians. Reference to tables given by Topinard, shows that while the cranial capacity of the European ranges from 1,550 cubic centimeters upward in the male, and 1,350 in the female, that of the West African ranges from 1,430 and 1,251 respectively.[2] Tylor quotes figures from Professor Flower, giving a mean cranial capacity of 79 cubic inches for the Australian, 85 for the African, and 91 for the Caucasian.[3] Nowhere is it questioned that the

---

[1] See Topinard, "Anthropology" p. 313; Keane, "Ethnology", pp. 42-3.

[2] *Idem*, p. 230. See also "Precis d'Anthropologie", by Hovelacque and Herve, pp. 239-42.

[3] "Anthropology", E. B. Tylor, p. 60.

Negro possesses less cranial capacity than the Mongolian or Caucasian.

But more significant than this, perhaps, is the qualitative comparison of structure and texture in the brain. Topinard says that in the African the secondary convolutions are less complex and rich in minute structure than in the European.[1] Professor A. H. Keane cites with approval the dictum of Waitz : " That the convolutions in the negro brain are less numerous and more massive than in the European appears certain."[2] Keane himself reaches the conclusion that mental energy and capacity depend most intimately upon " the sinuosities or convolutions of the inner white substance, and especially upon the cellular tissue of the thin outer cortex or envelope of grey matter, which follows all the inner convolutions, with which it is also connected by an exceedingly complex nervous system."[3] It is in these structural differences that the greatest significance no doubt lies.

One other factor greatly affecting ultimate mental development, is the length of the period of immaturity, during which the mind remains plastic. Keane says :

"The development of cellular tissue, with a corresponding increase of mental power, apparently goes on till arrested by the closure of the cranial sutures. All the serratures are stated to be more complex in the higher than in the lower races, and their definite closing appears to be delayed until a later period in life amongst the former than amongst the latter. This physiological character . . . . . has recently been noticed by two intelligent observers, Col. Ellis among the Upper Guinea peoples, and Capt. Binger among the West Sudanese generally. ' The black is a child ', says this writer, ' and will remain so ' ; and the sudden arrest of the mental faculties at the age of puberty is attributed to the closing of the sutures."[4]

[1] *Op. cit.*, p. 309.
[2] *Op. cit.*, p. 46.
[3] *Idem*, p. 44.
[4] *Op. cit.*, p. 44.

There seems much probability, too, in the opinion of some, that the marked development of sexual activity among West Africans, with the arrival of puberty, absorbs energy at the expense of mental force. Ellis whose opinion is referred to above, writes as follows :

" In early life they evince a degree of intelligence, which, compared with that of the European child, appears precocious ; and they acquire knowledge with facility until they arrive at the age of puberty, when the physical nature masters the intellect, and frequently completely deadens it. This peculiarity . . . . has been attributed by some physiologists to the early closing of the sutures of the cranium, and it is worthy of note that throughout West Africa it is by no means rare to find skulls without any apparent transverse or longitudinal sutures." [1]

The fact that African children learn easily until the age of puberty, but fail to progress after that time, may be due to another consideration apparently overlooked by the above writers, viz., the difference in the character of knowledge to be acquired in earlier and later stages of education. In the earlier stages it is chiefly the perceptive and imitative faculties, together with memory that are required, but relatively little of the higher faculties of abstract reasoning. These conditions become gradually reversed, however, as the student advances into highly elaborated realms of knowledge. That the African begins to halt on reaching this later stage of acquisition, may be owing to the want of a quality of mind not to be found in brains of coarser texture.

What Captain Binger says, writing contemporaneously with Ellis, but quite independently of him, throws so much light on the point under discussion, that it is well worth quoting in full.

" L'Enfant, par suite des travaux multiples et fatigants auxquels la mère est forcée de se livrer, est bien en retard sur celui des pays civilisés. Porté sur le dos jusquà l'âge de deux à trois ans, époque a

---

[1] " Ewe-speaking peoples ", pp. 9–10.

laquelle il est sevré, le bébé ne peut rien apprendre, le mere ne lui causant jamais, de sorte qu'il ne commence réellement à parler qu'à trois ans et demi ou quatre ans. A partir de cette époque, son intelligence se developpe avec une rapidité surprenante : il a une mémoire extraordinaire et il est capable d'apprendre tout ce qu'on lui enseigne ; il est aussi bien doué que les enfants européens de son âge. Malheureusement, aussitôt qu'il attient l'âge de la puberté, tout developpment intellectual cesse. Cet arrêt complet se produit presque brutalement ; non seulement son intellect reste stationnaire, mais je dirai qu'il diminue ; le memoire s'en va ; d'eveille et d'intelligent qu'il etait, il devient sot, méfient, vaniteux, menteur, dans cette periode, qui quelquefois dure deux ou trois ans, il n'est assimilable qu'à un etre tout a fait inférieur. A cet arrêt intellectual doit correspondre, dans ces regions, la soudure de la boite cervicale, le developpment du crane s'arrête et empêche le cerveau de se dilater davantage.'' [1]

In whatever aspect, therefore, we consider the physiological basis of mental power, whether as to size of brain, or its inner structure, or the length of its plastic period, the natives of Guinea are at a grave disadvantage in comparison with the Caucasian.[2] The low stage of their culture can hardly be deemed the accidental effect of external conditions, for it has its counterpart in the inner constitution of the race. This is what we should expect, knowing that selection operating through many generations brings about a close physical and psychical adaptation of the organism to its environment. We have seen what the West African environment is, and it is obvious that no great industrial system, no science, and no art could be self-developed there in the first instance ; but it is also plain that without the rise of these secondary agencies of selection, the psychic nature could never be adapted to grasp

[1] " Du Niger au Golfe de Guinée ", Paris, 1892, t. 2, p. 246.
[2] Miss Kingsley, it is true, cites the crafty shrewdness of the adult African as somewhat belying this. But crafty cunning is not the same as high intellectual capacity. See her " Travels, etc.", p. 672.

such attainments. The consideration of the general laws of biologic evolution would thus lead us, aside from the evidence above adduced, to believe that the mind of a lower tropical race is unfitted to assimilate the advanced civilization of a strenuous and able northern race.

Yet it would be hasty to conclude that the West Africans are incapable of progress. Though below the modern Caucasian in capacity to master vast knowledge, to handle intricate machinery, and to carry on self-government, they may be able to profit from judicious education and to respond to new stimuli to exertion. With the advent of new standards of efficiency, selection would operate to bring forward those best fitted to the new régime, provided that competition of abler peoples did not enter upon the scene so soon as to overthrow and crush all alike. As for obvious reasons this seems unlikely to happen in torrid West Africa, its inhabitants may have a creditable future before them. Where portions of the race have been removed into other regions, and placed in the midst of able and strenuous competition, the case is altogether different.

The temperamental qualities of the race present some marked and interesting peculiarities. In common with all peoples of low culture, the West Africans are unstable of purpose, dominated by impulse, unable to realize the future and restrain present desire, callously indifferent to suffering in others, and easily aroused to ferocity by the sight of blood or under great fear. More peculiar to themselves are a pronounced aversion to silence and solitude, a passionate love of rhythm in sound and motion, an excessive excitability, and utter lack of reserve.

Nothing so well reveals high development or is so vital to the welfare of a great society as the power to bridle passion, steady the emotions, and keep fixedly to a definite purpose. Infirmity of will means weakness at the root of life. Now, the West Africans give evidence of a marked deficiency in will power throughout every phase of their existence. Their intense emotions, their strong sexual passion, their cupidity, their erratic impulses, are continually breaking control, even at the cost of immediate disaster. The white man from the north, far-seeing, sure-footed, and iron-willed, at first witnesses their infatuated rashness with exasperated amazement, but in the end with resigned patience.

Illustrations of this weakness are strewn thickly through all works on West Africa. A pen-picture of store-keeping in that region is given by Miss Kingsley:

" Whether the native is passing in a bundle of rubber or a tooth of ivory or merely cashing a *bon* (a local check on the store) for a week's bush catering, he is, in Congo Français, incapable of deciding what he will have, when it comes to the point. He comes into the shop with a bon in his hand, and we will say, for example, the idea in his head that he wants fish-hooks—'jupes' he calls them—but, confronted with the visible temptation of pomatum, he hesitates, and scratches his head violently. Surrounding him there are ten or twenty other natives with their minds in a similar wavering state, but yet anxious to be served forthwith. In consequence of the stimulating scratch, he remembers that one of his wives said he was to bring some lucifer matches, another wanted cloth for herself, and another knew of some rubber she could buy very cheap, in tobacco, of a Fan woman, who had stolen it. This rubber he knows he can take to the trader's store and sell for pocket handkerchiefs of a superior pattern, or gunpowder, or rum, which he cannot get at the mission store. He finally gets something and takes it home, and likely enough brings it back in a day or so, somewhat damaged, desirous of changing it for some other article or articles. Remember, also, that these Bantu, like the negroes, think externally in a loud voice ; also, like Mr. Kipling's '*oont*', 'he smells most awful vile ', and . . . accompanies his observations with violent dramatic gestures ; and let the customer's tribe or sex be what it may, the customer is sadly, sadly liable to pick up any portable object within reach, under the shadow of his companions' uproar, and stow it away in his armpits, between his legs, or, if his cloth be large enough, in that." [1]

The difficulties encountered by Du Chaillu every time he started from an African village with his train of porters are thus described :

" When all was arranged—when everybody had taken leave of all his friends, and come back half a dozen times to take leave over again, or say something before forgotten—when all the shouting, and ordering, and quarreling were done, and I had completely lost patience, we at last got away." [2]

Here we have the violently excitable, demonstrative negro, garrulous to the last degree and absolutely heedless of time. Wherever a number of them are together, and they are never seen otherwise, they raise "a perfect word-fog," as Miss Kingsley calls it. Every emotion finds instant and unreserved expression. In joy, in grief, in anger, it is always the same—infinite and unwearied volubility. Tylor notes the perplexing fact that, with no great differences in climatic or physical environment the Indian of Brazil is dull and stoical, while the negro of West Africa overflows constantly with " eagerness and gaiety." [3]

This impulse to a lively, noisy sociability, moulds the racial habits in many ways. Regardless of temperature, there must invariably be blazing fires at night in each village, around which the crowd may gather and make merry. Bright moonlight is always the signal for all-night carousals, accompanied by infinite noise in the shape of tom-tom beating, gun-firing, native music and dancing, etc.

It is but another phase of inconstancy that the West African is never long weighed down by sorrow or mis-

[1] " Travels in West Africa ", p. 204.
[2] " Equatorial Africa ", p. 76.
[3] *Op. cit.*, p. 74.

fortune. His cheerfulness seems irrepressible. He is incapable of nursing long the feelings of anger or revenge, let the provocation be what it may. Barbot remarks that the natives seem "very little concerned at misfortunes, so it is hard to perceive any change in them," and he goes on to say :

"When they have gained a victory over their enemies, they return home dancing and singing, and if they have been beaten and totally routed, still they dance, feast, and make merry. The most they do in the greatest adversity is to shave their heads and make some alteration in their garments : but still they are ready to feast about graves, and should they see their country in a flame, it would not disturb their dancing, singing and drinking ; so that it may well be said, according to some authors, that they are insensible to grief or want." [1]

At the first news of death or disaster there is an outburst of demonstrative grief, but in an amazingly brief time none could tell that anything gloomy had happened. In the moment of discovering a great wrong or injury, there is an outburst of fierce anger, which in a few hours or days, at most, subsides into the habitual easy-going mood.

They are passionately fond of music, and it exerts a very great influence upon their lives. They have several kinds of rude musical instruments. Easily first among them all is the tom-tom, a drum made of a hollow section of log with a skin stretched tightly over one end. The tom-tom accompanies the army to the field, the corpse to its grave, the bridegroom to his wedding, the royal embassy on its journey. Not a festival of any kind can proceed without it. Beaten in rythmical fashion, and with an art that to the native expresses definite ideas, its power over him seems irresistible.[2] Du Chaillu says :

[1] *Op. cit.*, pp. 235-6.
[2] See Ellis, " Tshi-speaking peoples ", pp. 326-7 ; Kingsley, "Travels in West Africa ", p. 181.

"It is curious what a stirring effect the sound of the tam-tam has on the African. It works upon him like martial music does upon excitable Frenchmen; they lose all control over themselves at its sound, and the louder and more energetically the horrid drum is beaten the wilder are the jumps of the male African, and the more disgustingly indecent the contortions of the women." [1]

They have other instruments, horns made of elephant tusks, hollowed out and with holes flute fashion, so that various notes can be blown; also complex instruments, consisting of calabashes of different sizes, with orifices tightly covered with stretched skins; and a few other devices of similar character for producing musical notes.[2]

Music is used, says Ellis, "with three objects, *i. e.*, to stimulate the religious sentiment, the military spirit, and the sexual passion. In the first case the priests have early seen its influence, and have applied it to their own purposes; chiefs and rulers utilize it in the second case, and the youth of the towns and villages in the third, when the drums sound for moonlight dances." [3]   Their numerous dances are invariably accompanied with music and singing. The religious dances, performed by the priests and their special devotees, are wild rythmic leapings and movements of the body, accompanied by facial contortions, expressive, in the eyes of the people, of possession by a spirit. The popular dances chiefly appeal to the sexual nature. Barbot thus describes them:

"The men and women who are to compose the dance divide themselves into equal numbers and couples, opposite to each other, and forming a general dance, they meet and fall back again, leaping, beating their feet hard on the ground, bowing their heads to each other, and snapping their fingers, muttering some words at times, and then speaking loud; then whispering in each other's ears, moving now very slowly and then very fast; men and women running against

[1] "Equatorial Africa", p. 236.

[2] For more detailed accounts of their musical instruments, see Barbot, *op. cit.*, pp. 264-5; Kingsley, "West African studies", pp. 64-6; and Ellis, chapter on "Music" in his "Tshi-speaking peoples."

[3] Ellis, "Tshi-speaking peoples", p. 326.

each other, breast to breast . . . . clapping their hands together, throwing their elephant's tail at one another or clapping it about their shoulders." [1]

Somewhat refined of its grosser features, this dance survives on American soil as the modern negro "cake-walk." In West Africa, however, these dances exhibit all degrees of sex suggestion, and to civilized whites they appear indescribably indecent. Du Chaillu found himself irresistibly moved to depart from the scene of more than one dance especially given in his honor, although he ran serious risk of offending his hosts. No description of the dances could be ventured in his books.[2] These facts are further evidence of the great power in this tropical race of sexual instinct which dominates even the most public festivals.

The racial existence of the Guinea native for ages in the jungles of torrid Africa has given time for the processes of adaptation to do their full work undisturbed. Physical or mental energy have never been exacted or favored by the conditions, nor a genius for searching out labor-saving devices; foresight and self-mastery have not been vital amid prodigal nature and loosely organized society; and so, the Negro in his original habitat has been bred to a happy-go-lucky, improvident existence. For him life is to be taken light-heartedly, never minding the disaster of yesterday or forecasting to-morrow's trouble. He is attracted irresistibly to music and uproarious gaiety, and the more sex suggestion in it the better. When anger or fear arises, the tiger in him is out in a flash and somebody dies a bloody death. At all times and under all circumstances, he carries his emotions on his face and tongue, passionately loves companionship, and forgets each day's sorrow with the sunset.

[1] *Op. cit.*, p. 275.
[2] See " Equatorial Africa ", p. 110 and pp. 176–7.

PART II.

THE NEGRO UNDER AMERICAN SLAVERY.

CHAPTER I.

GENERAL NATURE OF THE CHANGE.

The foregoing study of West African life indicates the nature of the stupenduous task to which our country, during colonial days, was slowly committed. With a continent before them to conquer, our fathers were so in need of labor that they could not be particular in their choice; mere unintelligent muscle, if subject to their direction, would serve the purpose. When the slave trader appeared, offering brute muscle from Africa, economic pressure triumphed over humanitarian scruples, and continued, for over two centuries, to pour into Caucasian society a stream of African barbarism.

" Previous to the year 1740 ", says Bancroft, " there may have been introduced into our country nearly one hundred and forty thousand; before 1776, a few more than three hundred thousand." [1] The census of 1790 revealed the presence of 756,208 blacks, about 17 per cent. of the aggregate population. By 1850, there were 3,638,808, constituting slightly over 16 per cent. It would appear, therefore, that during the period of slavery, about one-sixth of our entire population were West Africans, by birth, or but a generation or two removed.

It must be noted that the importation of negroes from the Guinea coast did not cease until after the Emancipation Proclamation, less than forty years ago.

[1] " History of the United States ", Centenary ed., vol. ii, p. 551.

Prof. W. E. B. Du Bois has shown that the Act of 1807, forbidding the trans-Atlantic slave trade, "came near being a dead letter."[1] In 1836, the consul at Havana reported that "whole cargoes of slaves fresh from Africa were being daily shipped to Texas, . . . that the rate was increasing, and that many of these slaves could hardly fail to find their way into the United States."[2] During the fifties, as Du Bois shows, the trade increased in volume, and thousands of raw Africans were smuggled into the country every year. These facts are confirmed by John R. Spear, who shows, largely from naval records, that the efforts to stop the contraband trade were utterly inadequate, and many streams of black humanity trickled into the country at various points till the fall of the Confederacy.[3] The present writer has heard an eye-witness describe vividly a group of natives, just from Dahomey, seen near an Alabama town shortly before the war. It is a matter of common knowledge in the South that negroes were not infrequently met at that time who could not speak English.

If importation had entirely ceased in 1808, as provided by the Constitution, matters would have been very different. Two generations of negroes would have grown up uncontaminated by fresh infusions of savages, and we should have escaped the burden of assimilating after 1863 no small number of negroes so recently from Africa that they were totally unprepared for their new privileges and responsibilities. They were a bad leaven mingled with the more Americanized negroes.

[1] "The suppression of the slave-trade", New York, 1896, p. 199, *et seq.*

[2] *Ibid.*, p. 165.

[3] "The American slave-trade", by John R. Spear, New York, 1900.

But, in any case, the task of civilizing the population drawn from Africa was a truly gigantic undertaking. Both destructive and constructive work was required. It was necessary to uproot and destroy polygamy, bloody religious rites, and the like, but it was vital that these things should be replaced by monogamy, Christianity, and other civilized institutions. Opposed to the accomplishment of this profound change were two forms of resistance, viz., physical heredity and post-natal or social heredity. By the latter is meant the transmission of ideas and habits from parent to child by example and teaching. The overlapping of generations secures the continuity of this external inheritance, and while it may be modified far more easily than physical heredity, its resistance to change is very great.

Between the inner constitution, transmitted physically, and the outer habits of life, transmitted socially, there arises during a thousand generations of undisturbed existence a delicate adjustment. When, therefore, the attempt is made to replace one stream of social heredity by another infinitely more exacting, the inner nature controlled by physical heredity cannot respond successfully to the new demands. This sudden readjustment, however, the African on our soil has been called upon to make, at first under compulsion, then by pursuasion and assistance. Yet his physical heredity could not possibly be modified on demand to suit the new requirements. While he was a slave the white man could suppress the uprising proclivities, born of other conditions, but could not entirely uproot them. In two ways only could an inner transformation be wrought: (1) by the slow operation of selection, and (2) by race amalgamation.

But the Negro's social heredity was immediately and powerfully affected by the change of environment undergone. When missionaries endeavor to civilize savages the difficulties are greatly heightened by the fact that a change in manner of living is demanded, while the environment remains the same. But the negroes transplanted to this country no longer moved amid the accustomed sights and sounds of their native land. That deeply rooted association of ideas and habits with the background afforded by nature in West Africa, was broken up violently. This rendered much easier the abandonment of traditional customs and the fading from memory of former teachings. This process was greatly accelerated by the complete disappearance on American soil of all tribal differences. The individuals newly arrived from Africa could not understand each other's language or minor habits.

The negroes were promptly subjected in this country to positive and constructive forces of two kinds : (1) the deliberate efforts of the slave owner to enforce new habits by discipline, and (2) the unconscious influences of example and suggestion, calculated to act with peculiar power upon an imitative and susceptible race. It was not alone what the master did with express intention or what the slave did under compulsion, which tended to alter the latter's character ; indeed, it is likely that the healthiest development achieved by him grew out of what passed into his life from above by unconscious processes, which were therefore natural rather than artificial.

CHAPTER II.

SELECTION.

In voluntary migrations, like those of Europeans to America, there is a process of selection, whereby the new region receives a population slightly above the original average in force of character. Only those who have initiative, strength of purpose and courage, will leave the land of their birth for unknown parts. Physically, too, such persons are likely to be sound and full of energy. The push, efficiency, and daring temper of Americans are by many believed to be due in part to this fact. In view of this, it becomes interesting to ascertain how the case stood with those who came from Africa.

The method by which Africa was drawn upon to supply the American labor market led to the most drastic selection that the world has ever seen. Of every thousand natives captured in the jungle only a handful of the hardiest lived to put foot on American shore. This fearful "elimination of the unfit" was due in part to the attitude and methods of the slave-traders, and in part to the African's utter indifference to human suffering and death. In all history there are few passages to equal this in gloomy horror, but it is necessary for us to examine it, for its results abide among us.

With insignificant exceptions the first work of gathering slaves was done not by white men, but by negroes themselves. With no sense of race solidarity, and perfectly callous, the West Africans felt no compunction in selling off their own kind into foreign slavery. They were accustomed to enslaving their enemies, to selling fellow tribesmen for debts or fines, and to pawning or

selling their wives and children. On the appearance of
the white man, offering many tempting commodities in
exchange for these war-captives and slaves, a brisk trade
sprang up. But as the demand for slaves rapidly out-
grew the supply thus provided by the older methods,
there developed far and wide a system of deliberate
slave-hunting. The powerful tribes overwhelmed the
weaker ones, petty kings or chiefs conducted forays
against isolated villages, and bands of slave-catchers lay
in wait at every path and plantation to entrap unwary
stragglers. We have noted above on what a scale the
kings of Ashanti and Dahomey carried on such work.

When a village was captured, all who were judged
non-salable to the white trader, *i. e.*, the aged, the infants, the sick, and the defective, were at once slaughtered. This was in accord with former custom, but the
selection was harsher. On the march to the seaside,
little food was given, and the captives were pushed forward with all possible speed. Every one becoming weak
or ill was promptly killed or abandoned. By the time
the slave-ships were reached, all who fell below a certain rude standard had been eliminated.

Next ensued the expert sifting done by the "factors"
or middlemen, who bought from the native sellers either
as agents, or on their own account in order to sell again
to the ship captains. They were far from accepting all
the human material offered. By long experience they
had become expert in detecting unsoundness or defects,
and they subjected every individual, male and female,
to minute examination and shrewdly devised tests; in
the end there were several classes to accord with a scale
of prices, and all who fell below the minimum standard

were rejected.[1]   These soon found a grievous end.   We are told that "an African factor of fair repute is ever careful to select his human cargo with consummate prudence, so as not only to supply his employers with athletic laborers, but to avoid any taint of disease, . . ."[2] No ship company wanted to load its vessels with "perishable freight," if it was avoidable.

After the thorough sifting before embarkation came the "middle passage," a test of such severity that a cargo rarely reached America without losing a heavy percentage.[3]   Densely crowded together, fed just enough to keep body and soul linked, depressed with vague terrors of the unknown future, only the hardiest could endure till the end.   All weakness or disease that had eluded the vigilance of the buyers in Africa, was sure to be eliminated during this ordeal.

In view of these facts, it is probable that the negro stock landed in America was physically superior to the average of that left behind.   No doubt many were permanently broken in health, but it could not have been so with any large proportion, or the trade could not have flourished as it did.   It is probable that the great majority, being by nature the soundest and strongest, quickly recovered and transmitted to their offspring their congenital qualities.   The conclusion seems justified that the Negro began his American career with an important advantage, secured, however, at frightful cost.

But it would be easy to exaggerate this advantage. Consideration of this process of selection shows that it

[1] See "Capt. Canot: or twenty years in a slaver", by Brantz Mayer, New York, 1854, p. 94, *et seq.*

[2] *Ibid.*, p. 102.

[3] See the "Abstract of evidence taken before a select committee of Parliament on the slave-trade", London, 1791, pp. 38–45.   Also "The American slave-trade", by John R. Spear, New York, 1900, chap. vi, pp. 68–81.

led to physical improvement alone. At every sifting the criteria of selection were those of physique. Mental and moral qualities could not be taken much into account. If in voluntary emigration there is a selection of bold and able characters, in this enforced African emigration it was the bold and able who were most likely to escape capture. In West Africa those who had initiative and energy were likely to become the hunters rather than the hunted.

To appreciate the net result of this extraordinary selection, let us imagine the entire West African population divided into four classes, and consider each in turn. First, those below normal, both physically and mentally; and second, those below par physically, though above it in mental force, would be effectually eliminated. Third, those well above the average, both physically and mentally, were apt to elude capture, and become themselves the captors. Fourth, those above average in physique, but ordinary or even under average in mental force, would, under the peculiar methods of the slave-trade, constitute the major portion of the slaves successfully shipped to this country.

In America the race came under other, though less drastic, selective forces, both artificial and natural. Inasmuch as the slaves were property, absolutely ruled by the will of their owners, the latter could largely control the relations of the sexes with a view, more or less deliberate, to securing rapid improvement of the race. In other words, they could encourage or command marriages or unions of selected partners, and discourage or prohibit unions manifestly contrary to the interests of heredity. Dr. Paul B. Barringer, of the University of Virginia, than whom few could be found better acquainted with the facts of the old regime, has laid much stress upon this significant feature of American slavery. He says:

"In a virgin land of incomparable fertility strong laborers were, of course, extremely useful, and hence much valued. Being valuable they were allowed to multiply, but under a careful selective process of breeding, which outstripped nature itself. Docility, decency, fealty, and vigor were desired, and the slave man having these attributes, with his master's 'pass', scorned the rural 'patroller', and roamed at will to replenish the earth. This selective propagation . . . . not only caused the negroes to increase in numbers, but to improve in kind. . . . . The laws of breeding obtained through centuries of experience with the lower animals had here found a wider and higher field." [1]

This statement is confirmed by a much earlier authority, who wrote on the conditions of slavery as found during the decade immediately preceding the war. Mr. Frederick Law Olmsted,[2] who journeyed through the seaboard slave states about 1854, gives this unmistakable evidence of the fact asserted by Dr. Barringer:[3]

"A slave holder writing to me with regard to my cautious statements on this subject in the *Daily Times*, says: 'In the states of Maryland, Virginia, North Carolina, Kentucky, Tennessee, and Missouri, as much attention is paid to the breeding and growth of negroes as to that of horses and mules."

It would be easy to overstate the extent and deliberateness of this policy, but that it existed in sufficient force to constitute a very important factor in adapting the race to our civilized environment, cannot be doubted.

[1] See his address in the "Proceedings of the Montgomery conference on southern race problems", May, 1900.

[2] Olmsted's books are to-day perhaps the best sources of information to be had on the subject. His sound common sense, sanity of judgment, and remarkable freedom from prejudice, together with keen powers of observation, rendered his studies of peculiar value in view of the all but universal unreliability of other contemporary literature relating to the subject.

[3] See "A journey through the seaboard slave states", New York, 1856, pp. 55-57.

The internal slave trade during the first half of the nineteenth century, led to another form of selection. During the earlier stages of this trade, and continuing with gradually diminishing force to the end, there was a moral repugnance to it sufficient to cause some excuse to be sought for " selling negroes south." This excuse was usually found in the troublesome character of the individuals thus sold. Hence the incorrigibly indolent, unruly, or criminal negroes would be selected. They were shipped to the far south, placed under the gang system of heavy labor on immense plantations, and quickly broken of their unsatisfactory habits, or else— soon eliminated. This process must have tended to improve the average moral quality of the negroes throughout the border states, and to improve the negro population as a whole, in so far as the harder conditions and more unscrupulous discipline of the far south made for the elimination of bad characters.

In West Africa the negroes had been subject to death-dealing agencies of a harsh and wasteful nature : ceaseless warfare, famines, pestilence, religious sacrifices, witchcraft executions, etc. In so far as these were favorably selective, they tended to evolve physical qualities of strength and endurance, along with a psychic nature suited to existence amid scenes of bloodshed and suffering. To meet the enormous mortality, a powerful sexual instinct and great fecundity had been developed. Not living in large compact societies, where delicate social sensibilities and refined virtues have a part in aiding survival, there had been little or no tendency to develop such characteristics.

Transplanted to America, however, the man who had special talents for killing and stealing was likely to be speedily eliminated. Such characters were now subject to master-hands in discipline. On the other hand, he who could best adapt himself to a peaceful, industrious, and self-controlled existence, met with favor. He had decidedly the best chance to survive and propagate his kind. Thus, irrespective of the white man's intentional efforts, this kind of selection must have tended to diminish the savage and increase the civilized elements of the African race nature. But this process is a slow one, and we cannot assume that, independently of artificial agencies, it has accomplished much within the brief career of the race on our soil.

The several processes described in this chapter are such as remould a race. They do what the wisest and most strenuous education can never achieve, since this cannot touch the fundamental endowment, transmitted by germ heredity. The interval to be traversed, however, in passing from West African savagery to American civilization was so immense, that we must beware of losing true perspective in our view of the problem. Allowing the utmost that could reasonably be expected from these selective processes, there still remained at the end of slavery, a wide interval between the Negro and the Caucasian in hereditary racial character.

CHAPTER III.

AMALGAMATION.

We are accustomed to think of but one kind of amalgamation in connection with American negroes, but there have been in reality two kinds. The one was always illegitimate, did not affect the entire mass, and was of doubtful benefit, viz., the crossing of white with black. The other was legitimate, universal, and probably beneficial, viz., that which resulted from the intermingling on our soil of many tribal strains of blood, originally distinct in Africa.[1]

In our Negro population as it came from the western coast of Africa, there were Wolofs and Fulahs, tall, well-built, and very black, hailing from Senegambia and its vicinity; there were hundreds of thousands from the Slave Coast—Tshis, Ewes, and Yorubans, including Dahomians; and mingled with all these Sudanese negroes proper, were occasional contributions of mixed stock, from the north and northeast, having an infusion of Moorish blood. There were other thousands from Lower Guinea, belonging to Bantu stock, not so black in color as the Sudanese, and thought by some to be slightly superior to them.

On our shores, however, all faint ethnic differences were quickly lost. The readiest means of distinguishing one from another—language, customs, and manners—disappeared, and interbreeding proceeded freely. At the close of the period of slavery, this amalgamation had brought about approximate homogeneity. The keenest

[1] Dr. Paul B. Barringer calls attention to this in his address, above cited.

8

and best informed observer would have found it scarcely possible to distinguish with certainty those of Sudanese from those of Bantu descent, or Tshis from Dahomians.

The conditions of slavery were peculiarly favorable to the other kind of amalgamation. So rapidly have conditions changed that it is difficult for the younger generation, even in the old slave states, to realize clearly what they were. Under the anti-bellum régime[1] nearly every household kept a superfluity of " house negroes," the number of these frequently exceeding that of the whites by half or more. Between the two groups existed an intimacy, born of the peculiar relations which bound them together. Slaves could not shift their location and occupation at will, and many lived from cradle to grave in association with the same masters and mistresses. The same house servants, year after year, witnessed with demonstrative emotions every domestic event, whether joyful or sad, and were themselves part of the household life. Their children played with the white children, and all grew up together, thoroughly acquainted with each other, and having many ties of mutual sympathy, in which on the one side there was always a matter-of-fact assumption of superiority, and on the other an equally matter-of-fact recognition of inferiority. Such relations are impossible under the shifting system of free labor.

While this intimacy was favorable to the imparting of the civilization of the white to the black, it also tended in certain ways to react unfavorably upon the white. A writer in *The Southern Cultivator* for June, 1855, says:

[1]It is necessary to anticipate here slightly. The full discussion of the conditions under this regime is taken up in later connections.

" Children are fond of the company of negroes, not only because
the deference shown them makes them feel perfectly at ease, but the
subjects of conversation are on a level with their capacity ; while the
simple tales and the witch and ghost stories, so common among negroes,
excite the young imagination and enlist the feelings.[1] If, in this association the child becomes familiar with indelicate, vulgar, and
lascivious manners and conversation, an impression is made upon the
mind and heart which lasts for years—perhaps for life." [2]

This remark applied particularly to the children of overseers and poor whites, who mingled freely with the
children and youth of the field-negro class.

In connection with this personal intimacy, consider
the facts that the sensual negro mind turned incessantly
to lacivious thoughts and impulses ; that a regard for
chastity had never been developed in the race, and that
the negro female, even had she under the circumstances
been able to refuse compliance with any demands, too
often did not desire to do so. In view of this intimacy,
the sympathetic relations, and the temptations presented
by the presence of a subject race, itself prompted by
strong impulses scarcely controlled by a moral sense, it
is clear why illicit relations came into being under
slavery, became wide-spread, and important in their
results.

It is impossible to measure exactly the extent of this
amalgamation between white and black, for the hybrid
variety thus created, shaded off imperceptibly into
either pure race. So far as Olmsted could observe and
ascertain by inquiry, the proportion of mulattoes to pure
negroes in Mississippi and Louisana just before the war,

[1] In her " Journal of a residence on a Georgia plantation ", Fanny
Kemble says on this point : " All the southern children that I have
seen seem to have a special fondness for these good-natured, childish human beings, whose mental condition is kin in its simplicity
and impulsive emotion to their own, and I can detect in them no
trace of contempt or abhorrence for the dusky skin." See p. 194.

[2] Cited by Olmsted, " Seaboard slave states ", p. 403.

was about one to three.[1] The proportion varying from one locality to another, probably lay somewhere between a fifth and a third of the whole colored population.

It remains to ascertain as far as may be, what were the effects upon the race. Mr. F. L. Hoffman, discussing this subject in his "Race traits and tendencies of the American Negro," says:

"It is an open question whether crossing leads to the improvement or deterioration of races. There is no agreement among high authorities. Gobineau maintains that intermixture of different races leads to final extinction of civilization. Serres and others maintain that crossing of races is the essential lever of all progress. Topinard holds that crossing of races anthropologically remote does not increase fecundity; while M. Quatrefages holds the contrary opinion. Nott, Knox and Perrier hold that intermixture of races would lead to decay, while M. Bodichon declares the era of universal peace and fraternity will be realized by crossing. The latter opinion is shared by Waitz, Deschamps and many others."[2] Mr. Hoffman adds: "I have failed to find in any of the works on Anthropology a statement of facts, which would warrant definite conclusions one way or the other."

Mr. Hoffman has, however, overlooked one eminent authority, who has thrown a flood of light upon the effects of race-crossing. Dr. Paul Broca, in a masterly treatise entitled "The phenomena of hybridity in the genus homo,"[3] does much toward clearing up the confusion, so well stated in the foregoing paragraph, and further makes a special contribution on the subject of Negro-Caucasian crossings.

The trouble has been, as Hoffman points out, that "past inquiries have been directed rather to establishing one theory or another as to the unity or plurality of the human race, than to the more important end of proving in a scientific way whether a race has actually been benefitted intellectually, morally, or physically by cross-

[1] See his "Journey through the back country", p. 90.
[2] See p. 178.
[3] London, 1864.

ing.[1] The anthropologists, says Broca, have been playing fast and loose with the term "race." This term
may be used to denote strictly the primary types of
mankind, *e. g.*, the white, the black, etc., or indiscriminately extended to secondary ethnic types, *e. g.*, Teutons, Slavs, and Semites—all of which are of one "race"
in the wider sense. Seizing upon facts that go to prove
infertility in crossings of the primary types, the poly-
genist argues specific differences and a plural origin for
mankind. The monogenist, on the contrary, finding
that crosses between the so-called Teutonic and Slav
"races," for example, are prolific and sound, concludes
that only varietal differences exist among men, and that
they have a single origin. Until this unscientific looseness in the conception attached to the term "race" is
cured, declares Broca, we need expect nothing but confusion.

Mindful of this cause of error, Dr. Broca reviews the
evidence relating to human hybridity, and reaches the
conclusion that crossings between *some* ethnic groups,
not widely differentiated, are certainly self-perpetuating,
e. g., that of the Celts with the Kimri.[2] He cautiously
points out, however, that it still remains to be proved
that *all* similar crossings are equally sound and fertile.
Now the interbreeding of different tribal stocks from
Africa was an amalgamation of very closely related
ethnic branches. That in this case a perfectly fertile
race resulted, cannot be questioned, and this accords
with Broca's principle, above stated. As it is well
known that continued inbreeding tends to deterioration,
so on the contrary it seems probable that the occasional
remixture of slightly differentiated ethnic branches

[1] *Op. cit.*, p. 179.
[2] *Op. cit,*, pp. 21-4.

tends to improvement.   If this is the case, the American negroes must have benefitted by their intertribal amalgamation on this side of the ocean.

But admitting the soundness and fecundity of such crosses as those between Celt and Saxon, or between Sudanese and Bantu, it does not at all follow that crosses between Negro or Indian and the Caucasian must be the same.   Broca takes up the case presented by the mulattoes in the United States, and offers some very significant facts in relation to it.

Mulattoes born of unions between white women and negroes are so rare that they would merit slight attention here, but for the evidence cited by Broca, showing that they are exceptionally unfruitful.   This conclusion from direct observation of a small range of cases is supported by certain facts revealed by the anatomists.[1]   In unions of white males with black females, however, no anatomical difficulty exists and they are freely fertile.

Broca cites Jacquinot's statement that mulattoes in the European colonies containing negroes, are not self-perpetuating or vigorous in physique.   He then reviews the conclusions of Dr. J. C. Nott, a Southern physician and anthropologist of wide reputation before the war.[2] As the result of many years of observation and record, in the state of South Carolina, Nott maintained the following propositions : (1) that mulattoes are the shortest lived of any class of the human race ; (2) that they are intermediate in intelligence between the blacks and the whites ; (3) that they are less capable of undergoing fatigue and hardship than either pure race ; (4) that

[1] *Op. cit.*, pp. 28–9.

[2] These will be most easily found in a compilation, "The types of mankind", by Nott and Gliddon, Philadelphia, 1871, chap. xii, pp. 372–410.

mulatto women are delicate, distinctly infertile, and have weak children; (5) that when mulattoes intermarry they are less prolific than when crossed with either pure race.[1] Subsequently, having moved to Mobile, and then to New Orleans, Dr. Nott observed that the creole population in those districts were approximately normal in vitality and fecundity. Pondering over this inconsistency in the evidence he recalled that the creoles were a cross between Spaniards, Portuguese, and French on one side, and negroes on the other, whereas mulattoes were a cross of Negro and Teuton. The peoples of Southern Europe with their dark skins, black hair and eyes, and mercurial temperament, might have more affinity with the Negro type than the Teutons, with their fair skin, light hair and eyes, and more phlegmatic temperament. Herein Dr. Nott believed he found the explanation of the greater infertility of mulattoes as compared with creoles.[2]

Examining this opinion critically, Broca inquires whether other considerations might not enter into the problem. Might not the Gulf climate be more favorable than that of South Carolina to a people originally from the torrid zone? But the fact that the pure negro stock multiplied and throve quite normally in South Carolina and even further north, indicated that this could not account for inferior stamina in the mulattoes. As Broca could detect no condition peculiar to the mulattoes, and not affecting the pure blacks equally, Dr. Nott's hypothesis appeared to be the only available explanation. Remarkable confirmation of it is found in the fact that the mulattoes of Jamaica, colonized by Englishmen, are declared by Edward Long, in " History

[1] *Ibid.*, p. 373.
[2] See " Types of mankind ", pp. 374-5.

of Jamaica ",[1] to be under-vitalized and very infertile, whereas those of Cuba, Hayti, and Porto Rica, colonized by Spaniards, are reported healthy and prolific. Jamaica is closely similar to West Africa in climate, and pure negroes thrive there. Such facts, unknown to Nott, and derived from authors unacquainted with his theory, are very significant in its support.

Examining other instances of crossing between the primary types of mankind, and finding much corroboration for the view that such hybrids are of low stamina and fecundity, Broca reaches the following conclusions:

"That mulattoes of the first degree, issued from the union of Germanic (Anglo-Saxon) race with African negroes, appear inferior in fecundity and longevity to individuals of the pure race"; also, "that it is at least doubtful whether these mulattoes, in their alliances between themselves, are capable of indefinitely perpetuating their race; and that they are less prolific in their direct alliances than in their recrossing with parent stocks, as is observed in paragenesic hybridity."[2]

We are now better prepared to appreciate the force of certain facts, different from those utilized by Broca and Nott, and well brought out by Hoffman. He shows that it was the almost unanimous opinion of the army surgeons who examined negro recruits during the war, that the mulattoes were inferior in "vitality and general physical condition."[3] Dr. Gould in his "Statistics of the Sanitary Commission," gives an average chest circumference of 35.8 inches for whites, 35.1 for pure blacks, and 34.96 for mulattoes; a lung capacity of 184.7 cubic inches for whites, 163.5 for pure blacks, and 158.9 for mulattoes; and a respiration rate of 16.4 per minute for whites, 17.7 for pure blacks, and 19.0 for mulattoes.[4]

[1] London, 1774, vol. ii, p. 235. This is alluded to by Broca.
[2] *Op. cit.*, p. 60.
[3] "Race traits, etc.", pp. 182–3.
[4] *Ibid.*, p. 184.

It seems difficult to avoid the conclusion that the Negro-Teutonic hybrid is more or less degenerate in physical vigor and fertility. It is true that in the foregoing discussion no account has been taken of economic and social conditions, and these often affect profoundly a matter of the kind in question. But in our country, mulattoes and pure negroes share equally in any economic and social conditions that are peculiar to the race, or at any rate, if there be differences, they are so slight as to escape detection. Immorality doubtless prevails a little more among the mulattoes, but it is a question whether this is not offset by an economic advantage, for their quicker intelligence enables them by a sort of selection to obtain better paying employments. Thus, it seems fairly safe in this particular case to accept the conclusions based upon biological data.

Amalgamation has not only physical effects but doubtless very important psychic results as well. The mulatto tends to approximate the Caucasian in cerebral structure. Hence, he exhibits more intellectual capacity and nervous energy ; he is more alert and deft in movement, and has more of the Caucasian temperament. Olmsted found that slave-owners preferred pure blacks for heavy, monotonous labor, requiring only brute strength ; but selected mulattoes largely for work involving intelligence and skillful hands.[1] The proportion of them seen among house servants and in positions of some responsibility was much greater than among the field hands. The same thing is to be seen to-day. The writer has observed that the porters, cooks, and waiters on a Pullman train are usually mulattoes, while the laborers in

"Journey through the back country", pp. 90-1.

the gang on the road-bed outside are nearly all black. Similar examples might easily be multiplied. Hence, there is much reason to believe that among the prominent and successful colored people of our day, mulattoes constitute a much larger proportion than they bear to the colored population as a whole. Accurate information on this point, unfortunately, is wanting. The general capacity of the negro race at large for acquiring civilization is certain to be misconceived, if they are credited with the achievements of men who share in Caucasian heredity. Misconceptions of this sort are serious if they lead to mistaken policies.

THE CHANGE IN PHYSICAL CONDITIONS.

In the two preceding chapters we have been investigating the forces that act directly upon germ heredity, determining what the individual shall be at the moment of birth and what he shall transmit in turn to his offspring. But once in the world, he immediately becomes subject to the powerful influences of his physical and organic environment, enveloping him from cradle to grave. The nature and probable effects of the changes undergone by the negroes in passing from West Africa to America we have next to consider.

Let us first get an idea of where West Africa finds its latitudinal parallel in the New World. Senegambia, Sierra Leone, and Liberia are in the same latitude as Central America; the Slave Coast with Venezuela and Guiana. Lower Guinea is opposite to Brazil, both regions lying directly under the equator. The Niger and the Orinoco, the Lower Congo and the Amazon, flow alike through territories luxurious with a tropical flora and fauna. The delta of the Mississippi lies some 1,750 miles further north than that of the Niger; an equal distance north from New Orleans carries one well into Manitoba.

To realize the contrast in climate between West Africa and the eastern portion of the United States, recall the leading facts regarding the former: the uniformly high temperature, the monotony of eternal summer, varied only by excessive humidity during three-fourths of the year and excessive dryness during the remainder. With this compare our own country. The annual mean temperature of South Carolina, Georgia, Alabama, Mississippi, Louisiana, and southern Texas ranges about 65°, with a mean temperature of about 80° for July and from 40° to 50° for January.[1] The isotherm indicating 55° annual mean temperature passes through Washington, Cincinnati and St. Louis; that of 50° passes through or near to New York, Pittsburg, and Omaha. To get roughly the corresponding temperatures for July and January add and subtract respectively from 20° to 25°. The climate does not display well-defined periodic wet and dry seasons, nor extremes of dryness or humidity. Normal barometer readings, anywhere between the Gulf and the Lakes, average about 30.09 inches, as against 29.75 to 29.90 for West Africa.[2] The summers have now and then very close sultry weather, but usually a thunder-storm soon relieves that condition of atmosphere. Mildew and mould cause little trouble.

Only in the Gulf states during the hottest month of the year is a temperature experienced equal to that of West Africa, and even then the much drier atmosphere renders the heat far more tolerable to man and beast. In the more northerly tiers of states during any season the difference is very great. Further comment is unnecessary, so obvious are the many points of contrast. We know that even men from northern Europe have

[1] See charts ix, xiv and xv, in part vi of the report of the United States Weather Bureau for 1897-8.

[2] See the report of the United States Weather Bureau for 1891-2, part vi, pp. 438-443, and compare with Alexander, " Excursions in West Africa ", pp. 116, 120, 145, etc. The barometrical readings cited for this country were "reduced to sea-level" pressures. Those of Alexander, having been taken at sea-level on board ship in West African seaports, are not very satisfactory as data for comparison with the accurate work of our weather bureau, but the writer could not find any other barometrical observations for West Africa.

found our climate peculiarly favorable to vigorous life and energetic activity, and to those from West Africa its stimulating character must have been immense. The northern states of our Union present so great a contrast for people of tropical origin, that it is possible they may never thrive there. But we have no reason to suppose that the transfer to our southern states had, so far as climatic influence is concerned, other than beneficial effects on the health of the negro. Prolonged and energetic activity, whether of body or mind, while an impossibility in West Africa, is here for a large part of the year positively incited by conditions that render a lethargic existence distasteful. It seems reasonable to think also that the variety of season, with its successive changes of natural background and associated activities, industrial and recreative, must have exerted a mild and helpful stimulus, particularly to the psychic life.[1]

Human energy bears a very direct relation to the quantity and quality of nourishment obtained. It is affected by matters of clothing and housing. Finally, much depends upon the maintenance of the body in good working order, its freedom from disease, or effective cure when disease is incurred. In all these points there was a radical change in the condition of the negroes on their transplantation to this country. That this deeply influenced the race we cannot doubt.

The negroes soon became differentiated with the progress of slavery. The "house-servants" and the "field-hands" were two very distinct classes throughout the slave-holding region. The latter again may be divided into those found on the small plantations and farms of the interior and more northerly slave states,

---

[1] The writer does not remember ever to have seen this point brought out anywhere, but it is surely of some significance.

and those of the great plantations of the Atlantic and
Gulf seaboard region.   The circumstances of these
classes were distinct in many respects.

No measurement of their relative numerical importance is possible.   It seems likely that the proportion of slave labor retained for service in or about the
household was considerably larger under the slavery
régime than is now the case under a free labor system.
Under the former all menial work was avoided by the
whites as much as possible, and this tended to increase
the amount of slave labor reserved for that purpose.
The inefficiency of this labor necessitated the employment of more individuals to get a given volume of service performed.   Many expressions of astonishment from
northern and foreign visitors at the number of negroes
used for domestic and personal service throughout the
south might be cited.   "The number of servants
usually found in a southern family of any pretensions",
said Olmsted, "always amazes a northern lady.   In one
that I visited there were exactly three negroes to each
white, and this in a town, where they were employed
solely in the house."[1]   The census of 1890 showed that
under recent conditions 22 per cent. of all our negro
population were then employed in "domestic and personal service."   We should perhaps not err very far in
estimating that something like a fourth of the slaves
were withdrawn from the fields for work of one sort or
another connected with the white household or on the
premises.   How many of the remaining three-fourths
were upon the small plantations, and how many on the
great tobacco, rice, cotton, and sugar plantations, it is
impossible to ascertain.   We know only that either of

[1] "Seaboard slave states", p. 195.

these groups was large enough to constitute a very important portion of the field hand class.

The house-servants generally enjoyed much the same diet as the whites, a distinction being made in the place and manner of serving it. What was left over from the table of the whites went by custom to the kitchen for the servants, and the cooks looked well to it that a surplus was provided, either openly or surreptitiously. Where the servants were put on "rations", they were, nevertheless, pretty sure, with the connivance of the cooks, to get sundry odds and ends from the planter's profusely supplied table. To prevent this would have required an excess of vigilance beyond the patience of most masters and mistresses, and many did not pretend to attempt it. Favorite servants were sure to be indulged in this respect.[1]

The diet of the field negroes was very different. It was based upon certain fixed rations, dealt out once a week or oftener. From a peck to a peck and a half of meal, with from two to five or even six pounds of bacon, according to age, sex, and severity of labor required, was the most widely prevailing ration. But in wheat-raising sections flour would replace meal, or rice in the rice-growing section. Similarly fish, oysters and beef were a prominent element of diet where they could be cheaply furnished. To this ration as a foundation were added other articles of food, varying with the seasons and with different localities. Save on very poorly managed plantations (of which there were of course not a few) there were regular allowances of vegetables in season: sweet-potatoes, Irish potatoes, "roasting ears",

---

[1] With regard to house-servants, see for example "White and black under the old régime", by Mrs V. V. Clayton, pp. 38-9; also Olmsted, "Seaboard slave states", p. 421.

cabbages, beans, and peas. The addition of molasses was widely prevalent and the negroes were especially fond of it; coffee was allowed in some localities, especially during the season of heavy crop-work; and milk was supplied in many places.[1]

It was an almost universal practice to allot to each cabin a small plot of ground, from a quarter to a half acre usually, to the use of which the occupants were exclusively entitled. Thus the opportunity was given to raise vegetables and fruit according to their own choice. Frequently the privilege was given of keeping pigs and sometimes even a cow. It was the exception for plantation negroes to be without poultry. In many cases, however, indolence, thriftlessness, or weariness after hard labor prevented the use of these various opportunities. Still more commonly the negroes sold their produce for money instead of consuming it themselves, a good indication that they got enough to eat free of effort on their own part. On the whole, the carefully formed conclusion of Olmsted on this matter of dietary can scarcely be very far wrong:—"I think the slaves generally —no one denies there are exceptions—have plenty to eat; probably they are better fed than the proletarian class of any part of the world".[2] Certainly the contrast is striking between this diet and that of the race before its removal from West Africa.

Not only did the climate of our country render complete covering of the body necessary, but our civilized

[2] For definite accounts of slave dietaries, see *De Bow's Review of the South and Southwest*, vol. x, pp. 325-6; vol. xiv, p. 177; vol. xxiv, pp. 324-6. Also Olmsted, "Seaboard, etc.", pp. 108-9, 431-2, and 659-60; "Journey through the back country", pp. 15, 50, and 74. The writer should perhaps state that, being a resident in the South, he has secured much information used in this and the next three chapters from persons of whose reliability he is convinced.

[1] "Seaboard slave states", p. 108.

standard of decency demanded it.   Hence the Negro
met here with a new experience.   Great differences,
however, in respect of dress were seen—differences more
striking than any others, perhaps, to the casual observer.   These were partly due to difference of function,
as between house-servants and field-hands, and partly to
differences of climate between the far southern and the
more northerly slave states.   No such marked differences, it may be remarked, existed as regards the amount
of nourishment supplied.

House-servants as a rule were neatly and substantially
dressed.   Being constantly in the presence of the white
household, and expected to perform direct personal services they were required to present a good appearance.
On the smaller or less prosperous plantations the costumes were very plain, but rose to elegance among
wealthy families in town or country.   Servants always
received cast off clothing and favorites received other
gifts in dress.   Love of display led many to spend all
extra earnings or gifts of money upon dress.[1]

A stated outfit of clothing was given out twice each
year to the field negroes.   The kind of clothing supplied depended upon climate and the financial status of
the master.   In the colder states heavy woolen goods
were used, in the far south cotton goods were more suitable.   At a minimum the semi-annual outfit for a man
would be one suit of coat and trousers, two or more shirts,
one pair of shoes, a felt or straw hat according to season,

[1] For detailed accounts of slave outfits, see *De Bow's Review*,
vol. x, p. 326, vol. xiv, p. 177 ; Olmsted, "Seaboard slave states",
pp. 112, 432, 688, and "Journey through the back country", p. 80 ;
Fanny Kemble, "Journal of a residence, etc.", p. 58.   In regard to
this matter the writer has also made many careful inquiries of persons
well acquainted with the domestic economy of ante-bellum days.

several pairs of socks, and not infrequently, underclothes. The women were supplied correspondingly, and usually received one or two gay colored handkerchiefs to tie about their heads, as was customary, particularly on Sundays or festive occasions. From the above minimum the generosity of allowance varied upward, custom requiring in many localities duplicate outfits at each distribution. Blankets were usually supplied to each cabin every second year. Among this class, too, nearly all money earned by extra work or the sale of produce was spent for articles of dress.

It was exceedingly difficult to have the field negroes maintain a satisfactory appearance. They were everywhere very hard on their clothes, partly owing to the character of the work they had to do, and partly to their heedless indifference, save on special occasions when it was desired to make a show. The art of saving wear and tear in clothes was one which this race had never acquired, and it was inevitable that they should proceed most of the time in unconscious thoughtlessness of their clothing. Seeing no clear connection between their own labor and what they received, they could not realize the cost of that which they consumed, and were without motives to avoid wasteful destruction. In consequence of these facts, unless ceaseless oversight was kept up, and supplementary articles of clothing were given out occasionally, the field hands were likely to become dirty and ragged before the next semi-annual distribution came round. This was particularly true where large gangs of them were working under relatively little attention, but not of those on smaller well-managed plantations.[1]

[1] See Olmsted, " Back country ", pp. 79–80; Kemble, " Journal, etc.", p. 52; Harriet Martineau, " Society in America ", vol. i, p. 226, etc.

From the one extreme of neglected, ragged field-hands on the great plantations to the other extreme of refined and elegantly costumed house-servants in the wealthiest families, there were many grades. It is clear, however, that, taken as a whole, the negroes had in the matter of clothing made a long step toward civilized standards. Clothing exercises a subtle influence upon character and it is likely that ninety per cent. of the negroes, at least, would, if called upon, in 1863, to go back to their ancient habit of three-quarter nakedness, have felt as strange as they originally felt in a full costume of hat, suit and shoes.

In the matter of house-shelter we find similar improvement over any former known racial experience. Where brick or stone were to be had cheaply, the houses for slaves would be made of such material, but the typical habitation to be seen almost everywhere was the "log cabin." This was built of hewn logs, with the cracks plastered or boarded up, a clapboard or shingle roof, a chimney with a large fire-place, and frequently a porch at the front or back. Usually the cabins were ranged along one or both sides of the main road leading from the "big house," and distant from it a quarter of a mile or more. These miniature villages, suggestive of the bush villages in the African jungle, were always called "the quarters." On prosperous well-managed plantations the cabins were kept white-washed and clean and the premises were kept neat; where there was slovenly management and poor returns these matters were neglected. It is probable that the proportion of the one to the other was about the same as that of efficient to inefficient farming or business management to be seen in any industrial society. Of the better type of cabin quarters Olmsted said: "They were as neat and well-made as the cottages generally provided by manufacturing companies in New England to be rented to their employees";[1] while Fanny Kemble tells of others which were very dirty and unkept.[2]

Every cabin contained one or two rooms of varying size, and very often a "loft" overhead. By way of furniture there would generally be found in each cabin, on a good plantation, a few "split-bottom" chairs, a bedstead, a plain table, a little tinware with possibly a few pieces of coarse crockery, and the utensils for fireplace cooking, with some exceptions on large plantations where the cooking for the whole quarters was done at a single place. In the far south, where the climate was very mild, the negroes had very little more use for their cabins than for their huts in Africa; they were mere sleeping places and shelters during heavy weather. Fuel was freely allowed, though the negroes went without it often enough, rather than to take the trouble to get it from the woods. Still, here as in Africa, they loved few things better than hot cheerful fires, and generally had them except where they were overdriven with work, which was not common save in a region where artificial heat was little required, *i. e.*, in the Gulf states.

In the matter of medical care and sanitation the contrast with West African conditions reaches its climax. The attempts to prevent and cure disease by futile practices resulting from the belief in malignant spirits were, under the American slave-master, put down with a strong hand. With the greatest vigilance and discipline it was a difficult thing to do, for such beliefs are

---

[1] "Seaboard slave states", p. 659. See also *De Bow's Review*, vol. ix, p. 325.
[2] "Journal, etc.", p. 30.

among the most tenacious of all elements in uncultured human nature. Yet the white man knew that unless something of his own superior knowledge regarding such matters was put in practice among his negroes, it meant temporary, if not total, loss of his laborers. An epidemic of fatal disease at the quarters involving certain and grave losses, every plantation making the least pretense of fair management had rules and regulations relative to cleanliness about the cabins, the prompt reporting of sickness to the overseer or master, and the care of patients. In serious cases a physician was called in to prescribe, and members of the white family helped in the nursing. On large plantations it was usual to select some exceptionally intelligent and trustworthy woman to remain at the quarters permanently to look after the sick, the infirm, and lying-in women. She had to report daily, and the master or overseer went the rounds each day to see that there was no evasion or secret practice of superstitions in place of the right procedure.[1]

Despite the wisest rules, unless ceaselessly watched, the negroes would relapse into the old easy-going way, let filth accumulate, and disease go unattended. Fanny Kemble tells how she strove to get the negroes on her husband's plantation in Georgia to keep their cabins and persons clean and neat, but found it desperate work. They were always good-humored enough about it, and profuse in their protestations of willingness and good intentions, yet if left to themselves there was invariable

[1] See, for example, *De Bow's Review*, vol. xxiv, pp. 321-6. This account of the medical and sanitary care of the slaves is a summary of information gathered from many scattered sources, personal and documentary. Olmsted gives numerous incidental observations on the subject.

backsliding.[1] And so it was everywhere. Any laxity or inefficiency of control led speedily to a happy-go-lucky state of things about the quarters, well enough suited to the tastes and inclinations of the dwellers there, but calculated to create upon civilized eyes and noses something like the impression that is caused in West Africa by shoals of fish "drying" under the tropical sun. When the maintenance of good sanitary conditions and proper care for the sick exacted so much unremitting watchfulness and discipline, there were beyond question many who failed to carry theory into efficient practice; but as compared with the medical practice and hygiene of the Guinea Coast, it is obvious that the negroes experienced an immeasurable gain in these respects through their transfer.

The experience which the American scion of the African race underwent was on the whole one which made for better things in all directions,—better as judged from our civilized point of view, at any rate. That the tremendous readjustment required of the race as managed under slavery was not too much for it, was demonstrated by the one great fact that it multiplied as rapidly as the better conditioned white race. Other peoples in other lands have melted away on contact with civilization. The negroes were brought suddenly into the midst of a strenuous civilization, yet they throve mightily and at the end of two centuries had increased many fold. This is after all the most reliable evidence we have that the race in its American environment met with conditions quite favorable to its survival.

---

[1] "Journal, etc.", pp. 30-1 and 52. A prominent Mississippian, writing in *De Bow's Review*, vol. iii, p. 420, said: "Left to themselves they will over-eat, unseasonably eat, frolic half the night, sleep on the ground, out of doors, anywhere." West Africa still lived in them!

CHAPTER V.

INDUSTRIAL DEVELOPMENT UNDER SLAVERY.

More rapid, at least in its superficial action, than any of the influences hitherto discussed, was the personal influence and discipline of the white man. The social inheritance of ideas and habits, determined by ages of savage existence, dissolved and gave place to, or rather combined with, a profoundly different inheritance derived originally from northern Europe. The resulting compound was a curious and interesting one.

In a society like ours the egoistic and anti-social impulses are controlled by a marvellous mechanism of refined, unobtrusive, and spiritualized agencies, to the influence of which the members of our race are capable of responding. For every overt offender against our written and unwritten law there are thousands who go through life obedient to the subtle suggestions and dictates of public opinion, as expressed through many conscious and unconscious agencies.[1] To this standard of thought, feeling, and action, an exalted one relative to that of undeveloped societies, the individual in American society must accommodate himself or suffer.

But all our ordinary means of exerting social control over the conduct of individuals would have been without effect upon the raw population we received from the Guinea Coast. What to them were our traditions, our industrial standards, our religion, our literature and art, our monogamic family ideals, in a word, our most valued social inheritance? They had a tradition of their own,

[1] See "Social control", by Edward A. Ross, for an illuminating analysis of this general subject.

industrial standards, religion, polygamic family ideals. Appeals to their slightly developed social sensibility could elict no response in action. They could be made to relinquish their own ancient tradition and usages and adopt the new only by force—the unremitting pressure of open, palpable, and resistless force. It might do to wait upon the slow process of missionary effort, unbacked by force, so long as the objects of such effort were far away across the sea. But with thousands of them among us, such a waiting policy involved too serious consequences.

In effect, American slavery was a vast school, in which a superior race drilled an inferior one into useful civilized life. The motive for this astonishing enterprise lay in the fact that all the pecuniary profits were to go to the teachers. Without some such strictly business motive, the teachers, though perhaps willing to help a few missionaries over in Africa, would have left the negroes undisturbed in their native habitat. They were disturbed, they were brought here, they were handed over to the American civilizer to be remodeled, on the understanding that he should receive all surplus material product above net cost—not that there was any conscious bargain to this effect, but in the outcome it amounted to this.

Without the possession of thorough mastery over the physically mature but mentally and morally childish people committed to his charge, he could not have dared to receive them into his community. Hence, these two features, profit and control, were fundamental in the system of slavery, yet they inevitably led to many defects and positive evils. Many of these the thoughtful slave owner realized as keenly as any one, and many he did not. On the other hand, he came to know some things by long experience, which were never rightly comprehended by others not similarly experienced. We are not, however, interested primarily at present either in his point of view or that of his critics, but in that of the negroes themselves. What did it all mean eventually to them?

In his motherland the Negro received a very poor heritage of industrial knowledge and habit from the society that enclosed him. He was acquainted with but few labor-saving tools, and did not comprehend the principle of reaching ultimate ends by indirect means, greatly economizing labor. He never saw people hurry to save time. He was accustomed to make women do all inglorious drudgery. In the day of plenty he gorged himself, and trusted to luck to escape in the day of scarcity. In short, he was the very antithesis of the strenuously energetic, ingenious, and thrifty American.

Yet it was this indolent child of the tropics, of all people in the world, whom an ironical destiny cast into the midst of a great industrial society. It was a critical experience for the race, and probably only the fact that the white man's self-interest led to the protection and training of his Negro property during a transition period of several generations, preserved the latter from fatal consequences. As it was, the negro's industrial deficiencies did not bring upon him the results which most probably would have occurred under free individual competition. What happened was that these evil results came to inhere in the industrial system as a whole, of which his labor was made the basis, and made it weak in competition with that founded on efficient white labor.

The negro's incompetency was by no means the only weakness of American slavery, regarded as an institution for the production of wealth, or as a great industrial school for the negroes. In failing to proportion reward to effort, and offering little incentive to labor except fear, it was unfavorable to the inner development of character. Whether other incentives, powerfully felt by white men, would have proved efficient in urging the negroes to overcome their distaste for steady labor, may be questioned. Still, their absence seems an unfortunate feature of slavery. These incentives were to some extent furnished by the custom of allotting small patches of ground to families for their own use and benefit, and by the fact that a slave might retain all money earned by extra work, after completing the quota required by his master, or that he received for produce, poultry, eggs, etc., raised by himself. Many profited by this fact.

A grave industrial defect in slavery was the absence of any motive in the slave to economize in consumption or to handle tools with care. It seemed of no consequence to the negroes if things were rapidly worn out or recklessly destroyed. This fostered the heedless habits of the race. The only counter-check to this lay in those privileges already mentioned, which provided them a marginal opportunity to earn some money of their own, and so become interested in preserving it carefully.

The industrial evils of the system, above alluded to, were certainly fundamental and militated strongly against the sound improvement of race character. Nevertheless, some remarkable results were attained, so that the negroes were incomparably better prepared for free competition amid our people in 1863, than when they left the slaver's deck.

All those slaves reserved for domestic and personal service about the master's household enjoyed exceptional advantages in being constantly under the direct personal supervision of the whites. The kind of work assigned to them, too, requiring the exercise of intelligence, skill and alertness, tended to develop those qualities.

The female servants employed were cooks, with their assistants or apprentices, house-maids, nurses for the young children, sewing-women engaged in making up the large quantities of clothing required each season, dining-room waitresses, etc. In wealthy households it was common enough for the blacks to exceed the whites in number. It may seem that with so much help at hand the life of a white mistress must have been an easy one. In reality it was far otherwise. The organization and daily direction of all this labor-force usually was a sore burden to the mistress. She had to give out daily provisions to the cook, cut out clothing and supervise the making of it, and instruct the new hands. Dozens of pairs of socks and stockings were to be knitted before the semi-annual distribution; quantities of fruit had to be put up for winter use; the sick and ailing were to be looked after; and throughout all this there were the countless difficulties that arose out of the indolence and thoughtlessness of those under direction. Mrs. V. V. Clayton tells in homely detail of how the mistress of a large household, including a large staff of servants, went through her daily routine at different seasons of the year. There was cutting out and sewing, putting up fruit, "hog killing time," nursing the sick, and ceaseless regulation of numberless other details. Obviously it required no little executive ability to manage such a domestic economy efficiently, and many failed of the best results. Still, the outcome of this training school in domestic work for negro girls was to produce a large class of servants who would perhaps compare favorably with the similar class in any country.[1] Many male servants as well, were employed in various capacities about the house. They enjoyed the same general advantages, and many became as satisfactory in their trained service as any like employees to be found anywhere.

The conditions with field negroes were very different. Except on very small plantations, where the owner looked after his own agricultural operations, and had few hands to direct and train, field negroes had little contact with whites. They were handled in groups, and did not receive careful individual attention. Most of the work assigned to them was simple and monotonous, exacting little intelligence or expert skill. At the height of the crop season, the labor was long and severe, inducing great weariness. The inevitable tendency of these conditions was to deaden intellectual activity, and unfit them for work requiring alert wits and deft hands. This was particularly true on the immense plantations in the rice, cotton and sugar growing sections, and was less and less so as the scale of operations became smaller. A certain amount of this dullness of mind and clumsiness of movement is seen among all agricultural laborers of the lower class, being an inevitable effect of the hard outdoor labor they perform. But the absence of independent will, the subjection to forcible pressure, and

[1] See Mrs. V. V. Clayton's "White and black under the old regime", pp. 38, 39, 50-1, 59, 114-15. See also Olmsted, "Seaboard, etc.", pp. 195-6 and 421 ; Fanny Kemble's "Journal, etc.", pp. 23-4; Miss Martineau's "Society in America", vol. i, p. 224.

the original density of ignorance of plantation negroes,[1] all helped greatly to emphasize such characteristics.

This description, however, applies only to the lowest class during the crop season. With the advent of winter, the plowing, hoeing and harvesting had to give way to occupations that brought in an element of variety and enlivenment. During the slack time there were fresh clearings to be made, fences and out-buildings to be repaired, fuel to be got up, and various left-over jobs to be disposed of.

Not all the negroes outside the house-servant class were mere field laborers. There were two intervening groups of great importance, the mechanics and the sub-overseers. In the ante-bellum days the population of the slave-states was so scattered and the difficulties of transportation so great, that it was impossible to distribute many kinds of manufactured articles, save at prohibitory cost. At the present time when northern and western products can be laid down at almost any point in the south very cheaply, we find it not easy to realize how different it was formerly. The rise of many towns and villages, serving as distributing points, has also facilitated matters greatly for rural districts. Before these great developments, however, the vast majority of plantations had to be nearly self-sufficing. On every large plantation and within every group of small ones there were to be found selected negroes, who had been trained as blacksmiths, carpenters, wheel-wrights, coopers, shoe-cobblers, etc. These men frequently became first-class mechanics, and they were the main dependence for getting all sorts of serviceable home-made manufacturing done. They made and re-

[1] See Olmsted, "Journey through the back country", pp. 81 and 48–9; "Seaboard slave states", pp. 668–9.

paired tools, both wooden and iron, put up buildings, turned out plain furniture, and in many ways rendered the plantation independent of importation from without.[1]

Many thousands of negroes were employed in miscellaneous occupations connected specifically with some local industry. They were relied upon for the labor supply in tobacco factories, sugar mills, cotton gins, saw mills, steamboats, coal and iron mining, extensive coast fisheries, turpentine production, and the like. The workmen in all such industries as these gained an insight into useful forms of production, and had a drill in habits of labor. The class of stupid, densely ignorant field negroes, while large, was far from including all below the relatively aristocratic class of house-servants.

Another class remains to be considered, small numerically, but in some respects more important than any other. It was very common for a master to entrust the management of minor operations to one or more of his negroes who had shown exceptional capacity and trustworthiness. Very frequently, instead of employing a white overseer, a master exercised general supervision himself, and relied upon negro overseers as assistants. Sometimes they were employed in the capacity of stewards, and carried the keys. A typical instance of this is given by Olmsted in his ovservations on a large rice plantation near Charleston :

"We were attended through the mill-house by a respectable looking, orderly, and gentlemanly-mannered mulatto, who was called by his master 'the watchman.' His duties, however, as they were described to me, were those of a steward or intendent. He carried, by a strap at his waist a very large number of keys, and had charge of all the stores of provisions, tools, and materials of the plantations, as well as of all their produce before it was shipped to market. He

---

[1] See Fanny Kemble's "Journal, etc.", p. 27, and Olmsted, "The back country", pp. 76–8 ; "Seaboard slave states", pp. 47, 337–47, 351–4, 564, 668–73.

weighed and measured out all the rations for the slaves and for the cattle; superintended the mechanics, and himself made and repaired, as was necessary, all the machinery." [1]

Here we have, no doubt, the very best type; but in various lesser capacities it was quite common to give able negroes similar opportunities to prove what was in them.

Valuable as they had always been, the members of this small class of selected and trusted negroes, trained to carry responsibility and to manage plantation operations, became indispensable during the civil war. In that struggle the great disparity in white population between the North and the South compelled the latter to call out more and more of its able-bodied white men, until thousands of plantations were stripped of all the whites save women and children. Many a plantation was then conducted for several years by the negro overseer and steward, under no other authority or advice than that of his white mistress. [2] This well known and remarkable fact is a striking indication of the extent to which the "fittest" descendants of that raw population, drawn from Africa, had acquired industrial qualifications under the training of Americans.

In review we may say that the almost homogeneous mass of totally benighted savages unloaded from the slavers and landed on our soil, had gradually differentiated. By 1863 had been evolved at least four classes,—(1) the field-hands proper, (2) the artisans, factory-hands, etc., (3) the house-servants, and (4) the foremen, stew-

[1] "Seaboard slave states," p. 426.

[2] Mrs. V. V. Clayton says that, during the absence of her husband for four years as a general in the Confederate service, she and her four young children were the only white persons on their Alabama plantation. "Old Joe" managed plantation affairs meantime, and was even left in sole charge, when she went to visit her sick husband at the front. "White and black, etc.", p. 116, *et seq.*

ards, etc. Lowest of all were the field-hands, who had acquired the habit of working long and steadily at simple monotonous tasks, under the constant direction of superiors. Otherwise they remained as unenlightened as before; but the habit of labor was something gained for them, since the race never had it before. It is altogether probable also that under the action of selection this class contained many left behind in the evolution of the three higher classes, and innately incapable of much progress. Every race has individuals under, as well as above, average. Among the negroes the former moved slowly in the rear of their race, while the latter progressed more rapidly in varying degrees.

In the second class named, a very marked industrial progress had been attained. Out of a people to whom Du Chaillu's instruments were gods of marvellous power, there had come forth men who worked with or about machinery unburdened with fear, who could handle keen edged tools with good effect, and produce the simpler manufactured articles very successfully. The third class, having enjoyed the greatest advantages of environment and specific teaching, had reached relatively a high level of intelligence of skill in certain phases of industry, and of refinement. But those last mentioned, who, in spite of adverse circumstances, worked their way up to positions of trust and executive responsibility, may be set down as the picked men of their race at the time in question. In them really did the hopes of the negroes lie, for they demonstrated what the race could bring forth at its best. They bore the same relation to all the rest that the entrepreneurs and captains of industry in the dominant race bear to the mass of population.

The industrial progress of the negroes under the tuition and discipline of the American slave-owner, if measured in terms of West African standards, was of enormous importance. There had been positive and constructive achievements, such as placed the American branch far ahead of its contemporaries in the mother land. And yet, so immense had been the distance to be covered before equality with the Caucasian could be reached, and such had been the defects of slavery as an industrial school, that emancipation found the race far behind the whites in competing power.

Olmsted, during his itineraries through the slave states, endeavored particularly to ascertain wherein the negroes were inferior. He found that in amount of work done the average negro did not compare favorably with the white workmen in the free states. The negro never put himself into his work with vim and earnestness. It was his constant study to do as little as possible, consistent with escape from punishment; and so there was formed a deep-seated habit of shamming in every conceivable manner. One prominent Virginia planter said that his negroes "never worked so hard as to tire themselves— always were lively and ready for a frolic at night." Upon this Olmsted remarks: "This is just what I have thought when I have seen slaves at work; they seem to go through the motions of labor without putting strength into them. They keep their powers in reserve for their own use at night, perhaps."[1] Rarely were they too tired for a night frolic, with fiddling and dancing, or a coon and 'possum hunt. Many of them showed that they had plenty of reserved strength for their own projects in spare hours. Olmsted, endeavoring to get at some quantitative comparisons of negro with free white labor, compared the amount of wheat usually harvested by an

[1] "Seaboard slave states", p. 91.

10

equal number of negro and free white cradlers and binders. As a result of this and other calculations, he reached the conclusion that slaves were hardly one-half as efficient as free laborers. Where the "task system" prevailed, as in South Carolina and eastern Georgia, each negro being assigned a definite task to be accomplished each day, they worked "rapidly and well." But, says Olmsted: "These tasks would certainly not be considered excessively hard by a Northern laborer; and, in point of fact, the more industrious and active hands finish theirs often by two o'clock."[1] Evidently such a task would not pass as a good day's work according to our ordinary standards of industry.

Another cause of the inferiority of slave labor was their heedless indifference, clumsiness, and wastefulness. The lightest and best tools could not be given them, owing to excessive breakage or wear and tear. Even with the simplest and stoutest implements, the annual loss in capital was enormous. Further, it was all but impossible to introduce new and improved implements and tools. They were regarded as inconvenient and hateful innovations, and were quickly destroyed, owing partly to shrewd, wilful manipulation to that end, and partly to natural inability to effect readjustment to unfamiliar things. There was no interest to lead to the necessary effort. Nor could fine live stock be introduced, for the same carelessness, and a callous disregard of brute welfare besides, led almost invariably to losses too serious to be borne. Olmsted says:

"When I ask why mules are so universally substituted for horses on the farm, the first reason given, and confessedly the most conclusive one, is, that horses cannot bear the treatment they always must get from negroes; horses are always soon foundered or crippled by them,

[1] "Seaboard slave states", pp. 203-4, 435 and 667.

while mules will bear cudgeling, and lose a meal or two now and then, and not be materially injured, and they do not take cold or get sick if neglected or overworked. But I do not need to go further than to the window of the room in which I am writing, to see, at almost any time, treatment of cattle that would insure the immediate discharge of the driver by almost any farmer owning them at the North." [1]

Finally, there was wide-spread and incessant shamming of sickness among all classes of the negroes in order to avoid work. This evil was one that sorely taxed the patience and resources of every slave-owner. Olmsted states that he rarely failed to find on any plantation, supporting as many as twenty negroes, some that were not at work owing to sickness or injury, real or counterfeited. "It is said to be nearly as difficult to form a satisfactory diagnosis of negroes' disorders as of infants', because their imagination of symptoms is so vivid, and because not the slightest reliance is to be placed on their accounts of what they have felt or done." [2] Everywhere masters and mistresses were constantly between two embarrassing alternatives. If they were lenient and gave the negro the benefit of the doubt, there quickly followed an increase of ailments so great as to be manifestly counterfeit in great part. On the other hand, if they refused to believe in the sickness, they were liable to injure some that were really ill. In the end the masters often made the former mistake and sometimes the latter. Especially common was it for women to get release from labor on grounds of a nature that did not admit of effective investigation. One planter put the matter thus: "They don't come to the field, and you go to the quarters and ask the old nurse what is the matter, and she says, 'Oh, she's not well, master; she's not fit to

[1] *Idem.*, p. 47.
[2] "Seaboard slave states", p. 187.

work, sir,' and what can you do?"[1] Not merely was
there shamming of sickness, but the utmost ingenuity of
the negroes was exercised to invent excuses for procras-
tination, dilatory movements, and all manner of evasions
of real effort. With such a labor-foundation the institution of slavery would inevitably have fallen by the way
sooner or later in the modern struggle of competition.

We must beware, however, of being misled regarding
the actual results of that system. Notwithstanding its
constructive effect on the industrial character of the negroes, they still revealed many serious deficiencies. Was
slavery the cause of these? If so, then with its abolition, we have a right to expect the disappearance of its
effects after the rise of several new generations, subjected to different and opposite forces. If, however, there
lay at the root of these deficiencies another powerful
cause, quite apart from any human institution, then we
are dealing with an altogether different problem. The
true relation of slavery to the industrial inferiority of
the negroes is, therefore, a matter of deep practical concern to us.

The question is : did American slavery develop in the
negro his indolence, carelessness, brutality to animals,
and aptness in deception, or did it merely fail to eradi-
catè them as well as some better devised system might
have done? Every characteristic just named we know
to have been an integral part of the West African's
nature long before any slaver ever touched our shore.
He was indolent, reckless, and improvident, even when
he himself immediately suffered the consequences, instead of an American master. He was inconceivably
cruel to his own fellowmen, not to mention dumb brutes.

[1] *Idem.*, p. 190.

In a word, he was as a native of the Guinea Coast far worse than as an American slave, even in those particulars usually thought of as peculiarly the evil products of slavery.

In the face of this patent fact we must conclude that while our institution of slavery was ill-adapted in some ways to root out these elements of undeveloped character, yet it did not bring them into existence. That they persisted was due to the mighty force of race heredity, obscurely but irresistibly dominating Negro life at every point. Environmental influences, whether for good or evil, may effect much, but what we have just seen is a revelation of man's powerlessness to set aside a fundamental law of nature. With this law must reckon the American Negro, and the nation of which he is a part.

CHAPTER VI.

RELIGIOUS DEVELOPMENT.

In no direction, perhaps, was the readjustment required of the African immigrant more difficult than in that of religion. In every object, animate and inanimate, the Guinea native sees a spirit. To prosper in this life he has to keep on good terms with these spirits. But having attended well to this, his religious duty is done. As to his conduct toward fellowmen, the gods care nothing. His religion has nothing to do with moral conduct. In his thought there is no inconsistency between his piety towards the gods and cruelty or crime against human beings.

Imagine, then, the untutored negro, striving to lay aside these beliefs, rooted in the depths of his soul, and to rise to the comprehension of an exalted monotheistic religion. The conception of a single unlocalized Deity, whose attributes express the loftiest ideals attained by the white race, had never been grasped by the African mind. Instead of attributing every incident, trivial or serious, to concrete personalities, he must explain them in terms of abstract mechanical forces, expressing in indirect manner the will of the one Great Spirit. The negro was told that this Great Spirit is not satisfied with material sacrifices and humble homage, for these, if unaccompanied by obedience to a refined moral code, constitute abominable hypocrisy. He was told that to meet the requirements of the new religion, he must be chaste, truthful, honest and merciful in all human relations. In short, a more profound revolution of thought and conduct than was here involved can scarcely be conceived. Yet nothing less than this was to be achieved, if the negro was to become fit for American society.

Our question is—in what ways and to what extent did the negro's experience under American slavery bring about this readjustment? Human thought and action are moulded by conscious and unconscious agencies. It is questionable whether the deliberate efforts of the dominant race to Christianize the slaves were as effective as various less purposive influences. The transfer from Africa had a strong negative effect. In the utter confusion of tribal distinctions and organization, the former notions and practices tended to disappear. The negroes were thereby released from the domination of their native priesthood, and heard no more of their teachings. The very languages in which all their former religious ideas had been couched were speedily lost. Many of the natural phenomena with which their religious beliefs and rites had been associated, were left in tropical Africa. Human sacrifices, witchcraft executions, licentious orgies at annual festivals, and the like, with all the thoughts and emotions cultivated by them, fell out of use and rapidly faded from memory.

Yet it is easy to overestimate the completeness of this negative experience. If the negroes had been taken in infancy from their native land, before becoming saturated with the native religion, and if they had been so scattered in this country as to give them no opportunity for a separate group life, the new environment would have given almost a *tabula rasa* on which to write new religious ideas. But such was far from the case. The transplanted negroes were adults, already imbued with their native religion. The field-hands living in the "quarters," had much opportunity to pre-

serve by tradition their former ideas.   Hence, much of
the ancient heritage, handed on by social heredity, survives even to this day.

More constructive influences also were acting upon
the race.   As the negroes learned how superior was the
knowledge of their white master, they were profoundly
impressed by the latter's attitude towards accidents, disease, and all occurrences affecting man's welfare.   They
saw the sick cured by nursing and medicine, without a
suggestion of diabolical agencies.   When a person was
accidentally killed, when lightning destroyed property, or
a crop was ruined by adverse weather, they observed
that the far-seeing white man reckoned with no malignant spirits, but explained such incidents on other
grounds.   These facts showed that when their master
reprobated their superstitions as delusions, he was sincere.   Thus, as the negroes acquired confidence in the
white man's ability, this silent influence over their
thoughts grew more effective.   Thus independently of
any effort to instruct them, or force them to act in
harmony with the white man's theory of things, they
underwent a great change of thought and habit.   Affecting first the more capable and alert minds of the race,
these influences of example and suggestion worked
downward throughout the mass.

But the dominant race did not rely solely upon the
agencies just considered to uplift the negroes.   Superstitious practices were strictly prohibited wherever the
results were likely to be injurious or conflict with better
methods known to the white.   Not merely did the
master provide proper methods for the cure of disease,
but he would tolerate no resort to traditional modes of
treatment.   Wherever the latter were detected, they
were suppressed on the spot.   The weird and frantic

ceremonies at a death, the dangerous retention of a corpse till decomposed, the burial of it under the dwelling, and of valuables along with it, were incontinently done away with. Such customs usually are clung to with desperate persistence, and administrators in West Africa to-day find it well nigh impossible to suppress them, even in the districts most fully under their power. But in this country at the close of slavery few vestiges of them remained. The whole sacrificial economy of the former religion was effectively destroyed, and along with it many implied beliefs became lost to memory.

While this destructive work was going on, there was much constructive effort in the shape of religious instruction and exhortation. In hundreds of instances conscientious masters and mistresses made, or encouraged, earnest efforts to enlighten their negroes and impress upon them at least the simpler elements of Christianity. Except in few places, it was customary to have religious services and instruction on Sunday, conducted by the local white clergy, or in remote rural districts, where church facilities were wanting, by negro preachers of more than ordinary intelligence and character.

These humbler ministers of religion performed an important function. Olmsted gives an account of them, based on wide personal observation. He says:

"On almost every large plantation, and in every neighborhood of small ones, there is one man who has come to be considered the head or pastor of the local church. The office among the negroes, as among all other people, confers a certain importance and power. A part of the reverence attaching to the duties is given to the person; vanity and self-confidence are cultivated, and a higher ambition aroused than can usually enter the mind of a slave. The self-respect of the preacher is also often increased by the consideration in which he is held by his master, as well as his fellows; thus, the preachers generally have an air of superiority to other negroes ; they acquire a remarkable memory of words, phrases and forms ; a curious sort of poetic talent is developed, and a habit is obtained of rhapsodizing and exciting furious emotions, to a great degree spurious and temporary, in themselves and others, through the imagination." [1]

Mrs. Clayton describes the negro preacher, Uncle Sam, on her husband's plantation, as one who exercised a a most valuable influence upon all the negroes, commanding their respect as well as that of his master. He held weekly services in a little " chapel " built for the purpose, and also Sunday school for the younger people. [2]

The religion thus transmitted to the masses was unquestionably crude, often sadly distorted, and yet it is probable that the instruction and stimulus thus received were generally as good as the simple hearers were able to assimilate.   Thus the ministry may have been more effective than one purer and more elevated that would have overshot the mark.

Missionary efforts on the part of the churches to provide for Christianizing the heathen population from Africa, were made very early in colonial times.   The favorable opportunities for this work under American slavery had been one of the considerations prominently put forward as an excuse for that institution, and went far· to reconcile the clergy to its adoption.   The " Society for the propagation of the Gospel in foreign parts ", incorporated by William III at London, in 1701, had for one of its objects the Christianizing of the negroes in the American colonies. [3]   Accordingly

[1] " Seaboard slave states ", p. 450.

[2] " White and black, etc.", pp. 23-4.

[3] See " The religious instruction of the negroes ", by the Rev. Charles C. Jones, of Savannah, 1842, p. 8, *et seq.*   In this work will be found an excellent account of the work of this society and of the American churches in the religious instruction of the negroes.

missionaries were sent and the regular colonial clergy
were urged to care for the spiritual welfare of the
slaves.   Masters and mistresses were addressed directly
and urged to promote Christian belief and conduct
among their negroes.   The Bishop of London, for
example, in 1727, addressed a long and earnest letter
" to the masters and mistresses of families in the English
plantations abroad, exhorting them to encourage and
promote the instruction of their negroes in the Christian faith." [1]   The Moravian Brethren were particularly
active in several of the colonies, and accomplished
much.   The Presbyterian, Baptist, and Methodist
churches, named here in the order of their inception
and development in the colonies, also made provision
for the religious teaching of the negroes.   But the
last two denominations succeeded in enrolling the
largest number of converts, and seem to have looked
more than any of the other ecclesiastical organizations
toward the securing of negro converts. [2]   Their great
success was largely due to their methods of evangelization, which strongly appealed to the simple minds and
emotional temperaments of these people.

In these ways an immense force was brought to bear,
tending to transform the negroes' religious life.   That
the light failed to reach all is certain.   Some masters
were indifferent, and a few opposed instruction of any
kind, but the better order and more civilized manners of
negroes controlled by correct religious motives, were too
patent to most slave owners to permit them to make
any objection.   Rather did this consideration lead some

---

[1] *Idem.*, pp. 16–18, the letter being quoted in full.

[2] *Idem.*, p. 53, *et seq.* According to Jones, when the Union was
formed there were some 73,471 Baptists and 12,884 Methodist com-
municants among the negroes, and the number in each case was
growing fast.

who were themselves indifferent to religion, to encourage religious work among their negroes.

It was inevitable that much of the religious teaching should be so little digested as to be without appreciable effect upon the conduct, and it must be admitted that even among the most intelligent and thoroughly instructed of the race, the lofty ideals and exacting moral code of Christianity were but feebly grasped and carried out in life. Nevertheless, when we compare their religious condition in West Africa and at the close of slavery, it is plain that they had made a great step toward something less gloomy, futile, and appallingly wasteful, than their former faith. It is true that their social heredity was not entirely cut off, and the inertia of race habit caused the survival of many superstitions. Belief in the efficacy of charms was still all but universal; a rusty nail wrapped in red flannel was highly valued as a protection against all sorts of ills; belief in witchcraft survived as faith in the power of evil persons to "put a spell" on one. These beliefs were a prolific source of trouble to the owners. "Conjerors", in essence the survivors of the former priests, made a business of selling charms, removing "spells", etc. If a rabbit ran across a path, it was abandoned; a lightning-struck tree was never used for fuel. These things, though harmless compared with what went before, must not be overlooked, for they reveal mental conditions. All in all, however, no small part of that profound readjustment in religious life, defined at the opening of this chapter, had been effected in our negro population by virtue of their experience under slavery.

CHAPTER VII.

SOCIAL DEVELOPMENT.

Let us consider some differences between the petty tribal groups in Africa from which the Negro came, and the great, organic nation for which they must be socialized. Now and then some West African chieftain of unusual ability conquered a number of tribes, but experience has shown that these embryo kingdoms soon fall to pieces. Among the unharmonized village groups perpetual hostility exists. Under such conditions the individual is conscious of membership only in his own small group, and even there his sense of social obligation is little exercised. He has acquired little of that power, fundamental to enlarged social existence, of restraining the desires and passions destructive of orderly coöperation. Killing, torturing, theft and duplicity, are so often virtues to him, that even in his own group they seldom seem disreputable and receive punishment. His sense of family and neighborly obligations—in a word, his psychic nature, has been adapted to social life barely enough to permit of a narrow, turbulent tribal existence.

Our race, which in Europe had developed large national societies, had developed the mental and moral qualities necessary to survival under such conditions: foresight ; ability to harmonize freedom of individual initiative with efficient social organization ; self-restraint combined with self-assertion ; stability combined with adaptability. Respect for life and property, sympathy, integrity, regard for family and fellowman,—these make possible a society progressive and at the same time orderly and conservative.

These subjective adaptations, while to a large extent matters of education, have their limits fixed by innate capacities and instincts. These are determined by heredity, and are not to be reshaped save by the slow processes of selection. A remoulding of the Negro's psychic nature was required to fit him for membership in American society. How far had the Negro character, while subjected to American slavery, been thus socialized? The degree of socialization may be tested in two ways: by the conduct shown in family relations, and by that shown in relation with men in general. In a word, the test of a people's social refinement is found in the moral standards recognized and maintained by it.

We may recall here what was said regarding the loose sex relations and reckless licentiousness of the West Africans. Clearly the task of the slave-owner, coming into possession of such people, and undertaking to regulate them according to white conceptions of chastity and monogamic marriage, was one of superhuman difficulty. Certain exigencies of the institution under which they were held prevented slave marriages from being as inviolable by law and as sacredly respected as was the case among the higher race. The Rev. C. C. Jones said truly enough:

"The married state is not protected by law; whatever of protection it enjoys is to be attributed to custom, to the efforts of conscientious owners, and to the discipline and doctrine of the churches, and also to the correct principle and virtue of the contracting parties" [1]

There was nothing to prevent masters from parting a couple for "incompatibility of temper", or in a division of property, or for any other reason. That only too often they did this, was a serious fault of slavery at a vital point. Yet such parting of slave couples was ex-

[1] "The religious instruction of the negroes", pp. 132–3.

ceptional, few masters resorted to it without strong reasons, and on most plantations many years would pass without any such occurrence. Particularly was it avoided in the case of the house-servants and well-behaved negroes, whose appreciation of the sacredness of monogamic marriage was so much greater. Among the field-hands, much less removed from their original status, strong attachments between husband and wife were, as in Africa, comparatively rare, and separations meant to them neither greatly wounded feelings nor the breach of a sacred contract.

Marriages among the field negroes of the larger plantations were attended with scarcely any ceremony, and thus were not calculated to make much of an impression as really solemn occasions in life. But in the case of negroes on smaller plantations, more intimately known to their owner in person, and especially among house-servants everywhere, marriages were celebrated with considerable ceremony. Says Olmsted :

"When a man and woman wish to live with each other, they are required to ask leave of their master ; and, unless there are some very obvious objections, this is always granted ; a cabin is allotted to them, and presents are made of dresses and house-keeping articles. A marriage ceremony, in the same form as that used by free people, is conducted by the negro preacher, and they are encouraged to make the occasion memorable and gratifying to all by general festivity. The master and mistress, when on the plantation, usually honor the wedding by their attendance, and, if they are favorite servants, it is held in the house, and the ceremony performed by a white minister." [1]

Undoubtedly it is important thus to magnify an occasion, when the individual enters into new responsibilities, so that these will be better realized and remembered.[2]

[1] " Seaboard slave states ", p. 448.
[2] This point is forcibly brought out by Edward A. Ross in his "Social control ", p. 253.

The influences tending toward marital fidelity and chastity among the field negroes failed of securing amongst them a sexual morality even approximating that of civilized peoples. This was due in part to the indifference of masters, and this in turn, in no small degree, to the hopelessness of the task. Reasonable quiet and order in the quarters seemed as much as could be hoped for under the circumstances. In part the failure was owing to strong passions and weak self control, and a lack of any feeling of dishonor in breaking marriage vows or being unchaste. These matters were much better regulated among the house-servants. Not only were they under closer supervision, but they imbibed unconsciously from the whites more of the sentiments and ideals that make against immoral conduct. Probably a distinct majority of the negroes lived out their lives in proper monogamic marriages. In any case it is certain that the negroes on the average had left West African standards far behind by 1863.

It seems probable that there was less advance in parental care for children under slavery than in any other direction. The West African father felt little concern in his children; the mother, while showing impulsive affection for them at times, had no idea whatever of systematically correcting and training them. Thus, at the time the negroes came to this country there had not been developed in the race strong and enduring parental affections nor more than a very slight sense of responsibility for careful bringing up of children.

Now, such were the conditions under slavery that this phase of family life, supremely important in civilized societies, could be very little cultivated. The evil conditions were more aggravated and wide spread than among white working classes of the lower grades, where both father and mother, going out to work, are compelled daily to leave their children. On every plantation the younger children shifted for themselves at the quarters, or were left in charge of one or more older women, entrusted with that duty. These carelessly looked after the little swarm of black children, doing only what was necessary to keep them out of danger and correcting only flagrant disobedience.[1] The parents while about their cabins paid little attention to their own children, save to beat them if exasperated by some unusual misconduct.[2] Parental care was much better in the case of the house-servants, who had the example of the white household constantly before their eyes, and were better able to appreciate the importance of early training.

As might have been expected, the mutual attachments among members of the same family were seldom as deep and lasting as is the case among whites. The capacity for such feeling is a matter of slow growth, and could not possibly be developed suddenly within half a dozen generations. Fanny Kemble was astonished and perplexed by the fact that on the death of a child among her husband's negroes, the parents, nurse, and others "all seemed apathetic and indifferent to the event."[3] Olmsted found that it was so common for negro couples to tire of each other and wish for separation, or else to show no great concern upon separation, that the planters thought nothing of it.[4] Usually, after

[1] Olmsted, "Seaboard slave states ", pp. 423-4.
[2] Jones, "Religious instruction, etc.", p. 113.
[3] "Journal, etc.". p. 95.
[4] "Journey through the back country ", p. 112.

11

the loss of any relative by death or separation,[1] there was an outburst of demonstrative lamentation, very soon followed by returning indifference and cheerfulness. Lack of affectionate concern for the nearest kin was shown often in neglect of them during illness, thus making it necessary for the owner to watch such matters closely.

From our standpoint all this sounds anything but encouraging. But recall how little time had elapsed since the forefathers of these people had lived in complete savagery where selling of relatives or children into slavery, even into foreign slavery, was a commonplace that aroused no protest. At their worst, the American negroes have never witnessed or taken part in scenes of callous cruelty such as were too frequent in West Africa to give occasion for surprise or comment.

In the recognition of wider social obligations considerable progress was made, although the standard attained on the average was still, of course, very low. The Guinea native's propensity to steal, and his remarkable facility in lying, persisted. Just as the officers

---

[1] Olmsted cites, for example, as not inconsistent with his own impressions, the description of a slave auction by a writer in *Chamber's Journal*, Oct., 1853. This writer was much surprised at the absence of emotion among the negroes concerned : "the change of owners was apparently looked forward to with as much indifference as hired servants might anticipate removal from one employer to another. . . . This does not correspond with the ordinary accounts of slave sales, which are represented as tearful and harrowing. My belief is none of the parties felt deeply on the subject, or at least that any distress they experienced was but momentary. . . . One of my reasons for this opinion rests on a trifling incident which occurred. While waiting for the sale, a gentleman present amused himself with a pointer dog, which stood on its hind legs and took pieces of bread from his pocket. These tricks greatly amused the row of negroes . . . . and the poor woman, whose heart three minutes before was almost broken, now laughed as heartily as any one." "Seaboard slave states", p. 37.

and travellers in West Africa were incessantly exasperated by these traits of the negro, so were the American
slave-owners.   Deploring the inveterate habits of the
slaves along the lines in question, Jones said :

"They are proverbially thieves. . . . They steal from each other,
from their masters, from anybody.   Cows, sheep, hogs, poultry,
clothing—yea, nothing goes amiss to which they may take a fancy ;
while corn, rice, cotton, or the staple productions, whatever they may
be, are standing temptations, provided a market be at hand, and they
can sell or barter with impunity." [1]   He adds : "Duplicity is one of
the most prominent traits in their character. . . Their frequent cases
of feigned sickness are vexatious. . . . The number, variety, and ingenuity of the falsehoods, that can be told by one of them in a few
moments, is most astonishing."

The ancient lineage of this trait is familiar to us in the
strikingly similar language of Du Chaillu and Ellis as
to the source of many trials to the white man in
Africa.

To overcome, to any great degree, these weaknesses
of an immature development, was manifestly impossible
within the period of slavery.   Still, many negroes came
to be entirely trusted by their owners in responsible
positions, and there can be no doubt that the class of
honest and reliable characters was steadily growing.
Other elements of social character were being slowly
acquired ; violence to life and property was comparatively rare ; there was a growth of sympathy, and of
a sense of obligation to those in need.   Though much
of this refinement was essentially artificial and of shallow rootage, the American negroes had put off their
more grossly anti-social customs, together with many
associated ideas and sentiments, and had become beings
of a higher social grade.

[1] *Op. cit.*, p. 135.

CHAPTER VIII.

PSYCHIC DEVELOPMENT.

Of all phases of human character, perhaps the most subtle and difficult to understand in their causal relations are temperamental qualities. Why one race is inclined to be phlegmatic, reserved, and stoical, while another is excitable, garrulous, and demonstrative, is a question for which as yet there is no convincing answer. The West African people are emphatically of the latter type. They are exceedingly fond of music and dancing; quickly recover good humor after provocation; are heedless amid misfortune, and love the communal group life rather than that of the family.

These characteristics largely remained with them as slaves in this country. It is true that the very lowest class of field-hands, worked severely in large gangs on the greater plantations and rigidly held in a monotonous routine, tended to become depressed and stolid. In all grades above this, however, the average negro's excitability, love of fiddling, singing and dancing, his readiness for a frolic, his delight in a "crowd" where plenty of talk and gaiety were going on, his unrestrained demonstrations of grief or joy, were proverbial throughout the slave states. Travellers usually were surprised by the exhibition of prevailing cheeriness and good humor where they expected to find sullen despair. Not knowing the natives of Guinea they were not prepared to understand why a negro was not affected by slavery and misfortune in the same way a Caucasian would have been.

Olmsted observed on various occasions that when one

might have expected with good reason to find low-spirited melancholy, such was by no means the case. During a voyage from Mobile to New Orleans, he watched the cargo of slaves, of whom some were going to be sold in the latter city and some were accompanying emigrants to Texas. Disconsolate individuals were the exception, and as a crowd they appeared to have a jolly time, there being "a fiddle or two among them," and plenty of singing, dancing, and continual talk.[1] Similarly he was surprised to find that, on the Louisiana sugar plantations, the negroes looked forward with pleasure to the "grinding season," and preferred it to any other, despite the fact that it involved the hardest labor of the year, requiring at its height eighteen hours a day of both black and white. Inquiring of the negroes why this was so, he found that it was because things were lively, strong coffee was given without stint, and there was abundant noise and "go" about every thing done. Thus, many peculiar propensities of the negroes were gratified.[2]

A typical "ball," as seen on a large cotton plantation of eastern Georgia among the field negroes, is described by Fanny Kemble, as follows:

"At our own settlement I found everything in a fever of preparation for the ball. A huge boat had just arrived from the cotton plantation at St. Simon's, laden with the youth and beauty of that portion of the estate who had been invited to join the party ; and the greetings among the arrivers and welcomers, and the heaven-defying combinations of color in the gala attire of both, surpass all my powers of description. The ball, to which of course we went, took place in one of the rooms of the Infirmary. . . . Oh, my dear E———, I have seen Jim Crow, the veritable James; all the contortions, and springs, and flings, and kicks, and capers you have been beguiled into accepting as indicative of him are spurious, faint, feeble, impotent—in a word, pale Northern reproductions of that ineffable black conception.

[1] "Seaboard slave states", p. 571.
[2] *Idem.*, pp. 681-2.

It is impossible for words to describe the things these people did with their bodies, and, above all, with their faces, the whites of their eyes and the whites of their teeth, and certain outlines, which either naturally or by the grace of heaven, or by the practice of some peculiar artistic dexterity, they bring into prominent and most ludicrous display. The languishing elegance of some, the painstaking laboriousness of others, above all, the feats of a certain enthusiastic banjo player, who seemed to me to thump his instrument with every part of his body at once, at last so utterly overcame any attempt at decorous gravity on my part that I was obliged to secede." [1]

This side-light upon one aspect of plantation life brings into view many characteristics, attesting the persistence of racial heredity.

A high degree of intelligence is incompatable with enslavement as a general thing, and consequently the slave-owners forbade literate education among their negroes. Hence, with negligible exceptions, the mass of them remained totally illiterate until after emancipation. This does not imply that they made no progress in intelligence. It is not likely that lack of schools was as serious a drawback as has been commonly supposed. It is never safe to assume that what is good or bad for a highly developed race is equally good or bad for an undeveloped one.

Literary and scientific culture is the last term in a long series of developments. It is a recent achievement

[1] "Journal, etc,", pp. 96-7. As a companion piece with this scene among the lower class of field negroes, it may be well to give Olmsted's account of how balls were managed among the slave aristocracy: "During the winter the negroes, in Montgomery, have their 'assemblies' or dress balls, which are got up regardless of expense in very grand style. Tickets are advertised 'admitting one gentleman and two ladies, $1 ', and ' Ladies are assured that they may rely on the strictest order and propriety being observed.' Cards of invitation finely engraved with handsome vignettes, are sent, not only to the fashionable slaves, but to the more esteemed white people, who, however, take no part except as lookers on. All the fashionable dances are executed ; no one is admitted except in full dress ; there are regular masters of ceremonies, etc." See "Seaboard slave states", p. 554.

of our own race, and rests upon foundations which it required centuries to build. Before it came to flower and fruitage, civilization had first to strike deep roots into the soil. Without sustentation life cannot grow, which means that without mastery over the processes of production no society can progress. The first lesson for a people to learn is that "labor is the first price, the original purchase money,"[1] that must be paid for all things. No less important is the lesson how to consume with such foresight and self-control as to get the maximum benefit from the products of labor. When these lessons have become part of the character of a people, they are ready to grasp and use a higher culture to advantage. They are then in no danger of losing their equilibrium, for they can then appreciate the true function of literary training.

We are prone to assume that what is good for us must be good for all men. Yet it is not true, for example, that because democratic self-government suits us admirably, it is therefore the best form of government for every people. Because from the high level already attained by us further progress is conditioned upon literary and scientific education, it does not follow that these factors are equally necessary to progress from the level of the Guinea natives. They have yet to learn the elementary lessons of civilization which our race acquired before five per cent. of its members could write their names.

Miss Kingsley's discussion of the attempts in West Africa to civilize the natives through reading and writing is very illuminating. Having shown that, contrary to the supposition of some, polygamy and drink

---

[1] Adam Smith, "Wealth of nations", London, 1893, p. 23.

did not suffice to explain the degeneration revealed by the simi-civilized natives, she says:

"Well! if it is not the polygamy and not the drink that makes the West African so useless as he now is as . . . . a means of developing the country, what is it? In my opinion it is the sort of instruction he has received, not that this instruction is necessarily bad in itself, but bad from being unsuited to the sort of man to whom it has been given. It has the tendency to develop his emotionalism, his sloth, and his vanity, and it has no tendency to develop those parts of his character which are in a rudimentary state and much want it, thereby throwing the whole character of the man out of gear." [1]

By way of explaining the basis of this opinion she says further:

"The great inferiority of the African to the European lies in the matter of mechanical idea. . . The African's own way of doing anything mechanical is the simplest way, not the easiest, certainly not quickest; he has all the chuckle-headedness of that overrated creature, the ant, for his head never saves his heels. Watch a gang of boat-boys getting a surf-boat down a sandy beach. They turn it broadside on to the direction they wish it to go, and then turn it bodily over and over, with structure-straining bumps to the boat, and any amount of advice and recriminatory observations to each other. Unless under white direction they will not make a slip, nor will they put rollers under her. Watch again a gang of natives trying to get a log of timber down into the river from the bank, and you will see the same sort of thing—no idea of a lever, or anything of that sort; and remember that, unless under white direction, the African has never made an even fourteenth-rate piece of cloth or pottery, or a machine, tool, picture, sculpture, and that he has never even risen to the level of picture-writing."

She then points out that most of the education given to the natives has been of the literary kind only. The native

"sees the white man is his ruling man, rich, powerful, and honored, and so he imitates him, and goes to the mission-school classes to read and write, and as soon as an African learns to read and write he turns into a clerk. Now there is no immediate use for clerks in Africa, certainly no room for further development in this line of goods. What Africa wants at present, and will want for the next 200 years at least, are workers, planters, plantation hands, miners, and seaman;

[1] "Travels in West Africa", pp. 668-9.

and there are no schools in Africa to teach these things or the doctrine of the nobility of labour save the technical mission-schools.
Almost every mission on the Coast has now a technical school, just
started, or is having collections made at home to start one." [1]

This very recent movement to lay the main stress in
education upon manual training and discipline in labor
is the result of the experience described by Miss
Kingsley. Her opinions are fully corroborated by other
authorities. M. De Cardi says:

"Thus you will understand me, when I point out to you the weak
spot in nine-tenths of the mission effort. They have been trying to
look after the negro's soul and teaching him Christianity, which in
the native mind is cutting at the root, not only of all their ancient
customs, but actually aims at taking away their living without
attempting to teach them any industrial pursuit which may help them
in the struggle for life, which is daily getting harder for our African
brethren, as it is here in England." [2]

The principle of relativity has been overlooked and it
has been assumed that the needs of the white man and
the savage are the same.

All this does not prove that literary education is in
itself bad for a raw people, but it demonstrates that mere
schooling in matters of intellect will not of itself transform indolent savages into efficient members of a civilized society, and that literary knowledge must be used
only as one of the means to the end sought. Amongst
ourselves each new generation acquires, independently
of schools, invaluable knowledge and habits that the
lower races do not possess at all. We gain them during
youth as unconsciously as we do our mother-tongue.
Precisely for this reason we forget what immense toil
and struggle it costs an uncivilized people to attain the
same ends.

[1] "Travels, etc.", pp. 669–71.
[2] Miss Kingsley, "West African studies", appendix i, p. 561. See
also MacDonald, "The Gold Coast", chap. xii, pp. 316–338.

If the grave mistake made in West Africa had been made here, the disastrous results deplored by administrators in that region probably would have ensued here. We have no reason to assume that our people, in the days of slavery, understood the problem before them any better than the Europeans in West Africa. The facts above cited indicate, therefore, that what the slave-owner did out of pure self-interest, was not so serious a hindrance to progress among the negroes, fresh from Africa, as at first glance it seems.

Notwithstanding his continued illiteracy, the transplanted Guinea native was making progress throughout the period of slavery along the lines most significant to him. He was at school learning the primary lessons of civilization. He was getting rid of ideas and usages incompatible with life in a modern society. He was acquiring a new and superior language; he was being won over little by little to Christianity; he was contracting the habit of labor and becoming familiar with new productive processes; and he was being refined in social feeling and conduct. So far from remaining in a state of arrested progress, he was steadily acquiring those rudiments of character essential to all further development.

PART III.

THE NEGRO AS A FREE CITIZEN.

CHAPTER I.

GENERAL NATURE OF THE SECOND CHANGE.

With the close of the civil war the negroes experienced another alteration of conditions, but one less profound and complete than the first. Many forces that had acted upon the race before emancipation continued in unbroken operation. Let us note them briefly in passing.

It was difficult for the negroes to realize what had befallen them, when their title to freedom was read and explained. There came no sudden change of scene; the same climate with its familiar seasons enveloped them; they moved amid unchanged natural phenomena; they were encircled by the same civilization; they continued in the same occupations; in a word, the environment which enclosed them remained substantially unchanged. It was the nature of their relations to that environment, so far as human law could regulate them, that had been altered. These elements of environment constitute a large proportion of the influences that mould human progress. Favorable to progress before emancipation, they continued favorable after it. Our climate, for instance, has helped steadily to stimulate tropical indolence into northern activity, and the constant influence of a civilized model has tended to substitute American civilization for African barbarism. Unless we bear in mind that these forces persisted, we shall lose perspective, and exaggerate unconsciously the real place of newly introduced forces.

Likewise, heredity continued, changed but slightly with each generation. As under slavery it resisted remoulding influences, so it continued to do under the régime of freedom. The slight tendency to improvement, due to artificial selection of slaves by their owners, came to an end. Since 1863 the hereditary qualities of the race have been subject to natural selection only. There is reason to believe that recent developments are tending to reduce steadily the amount of intermixture between the two races.[1] Thus, it would appear that the racial heredity has undergone improvement (from the standpoint of Americans, of course) with less rapidity since emancipation than before.

So much for the forces that survived with unbroken continuity the abolition of slavery and the cataclysm of war. Others came into operation for the first time with Lincoln's proclamation.

To the negroes emancipation meant objectively the removal of compulsion, and subjectively the rise of new incentives to progress. Very soon came literary education, and, to many, also political power. Gradually has followed a segregation of the negroes, so that they are tending to develop a distinct community within the nation, one having its own public opinion, standards of conduct, and peculiar interests at many points. Both for the negroes and the nation at large, this may prove in the end the most fateful development of all.

We should understand clearly what the removal of compulsion involved. To the freedmen it seemed for a time that all control over them had ceased. In reality,

---

[1] This statement is here made in advance of a fuller discussion, which occurs in the next chapter.

however, there had been merely a transfer of authority from the person of the master to the community at large. It was still as necessary as ever that conduct should be controlled in accordance with civilized order. There was no release from the obligation to earn self-support by labor, to respect life and property, to honor the several relationships of the monogamic family, and, in short, to obey the written and unwritten law of the land. It is not simply that the public authority will enforce such conduct, acting through conscious channels: behind formal law stands a power even more relentless. If the individuals of any class, living in the environment of a strenuously progressive civilization, cannot adjust themselves to its requirements, they must succumb. From this there can be no escape under the law of struggle for existence.

The inertia of habit, once moulded under the discipline of the slave-owner, kept the mature generation of freedmen in the beaten path. It was only among those of the younger generation and its successors that the new conditions could work their full effects for good or evil. It will be for us to investigate these effects throughout the remainder of this study.

The subjective influences of freedom were very powerful for good, yet they were accompanied by grave dangers for the race. On the one hand the negroes now had every motive to put forth real effort in production, to avoid habits of careless wastefulness, and to exercise control over present desires in the interest of future welfare. On the other hand, if they proved wanting in these respects, the consequences were no longer borne by their employers, but by themselves. Personal liberty has, in most cases, been attained by the mass of men in

a community only after a severe struggle. Where it
has been self-developed it is almost secure ; if it has been
a gift from others, the inner qualities needed to maintain
it are far less likely to exist.   Social existence is impossible unless the conduct of the individual be controlled
and ordered according to certain fundamental principles.
If the individual has such command of himself that he
is able to regulate conduct from within, then for him
great personal freedom is safe ; but if not, the regulation
must be from without.   Unregulated action in response
to egoistic desires and passions is in no case to be permitted.   As a native of the Guinea Coast the negro had
very slight self-command ; as a slave in America he had
no opportunity to cultivate this power.   When, therefore, he became a free citizen of the United States, it
was an extremely critical experience and the outcome is
yet to be seen.

Neither education in letters, which became possible to
the freedmen, nor manhood suffrage in self-governing
states, which they suddenly acquired, ever had been
known to the Negro race.   The white man had
slowly and painfully achieved them, and he thus had
learned their functions and limitations.   But such privileges came to the negro all at once, and found him
totally unprepared for their wise use.   Laws of growth
cannot be contemptuously overridden.   Literary culture, not reinforced by industrial training, was productive of mixed results, but the gift of political privileges proved to be almost wholly evil.   Where a gradual,
conservative introduction to political functions might
have been effected with beneficial results, the method
actually tried had deplorable consequences.   Perhaps
the most serious of these was to hasten and aggravate

the alienation of the two races. This, however, was probably inevitable sooner or later. Two groups of men differing in color, temperament, and historical development, as registered in social ideals and sympathies, can not intermingle freely and maintain undifferentiated group life. All theories of abstract rights, all generous hopes to the contrary, must go down before this stubborn law of human affinities and repulsions. Society may find some way to accommodate matters to the law, and thus secure ultimate ends, but the law itself must stand.

CHAPTER II.

INDUSTRIAL PROGRESS.

The progress of any people must depend in the long run upon the efficiency of the individuals as producers and accumulators. The progenitors of our present negro population were indolent and wasteful, lacking mechanical ability, foresight and will in the pursuit of distant objects. But, shielded from individual competition with the whites until four decades ago, the negroes made considerable progress toward American standards of industry. Yet emancipation found them far from equalling white labor in efficiency, and the economic system dependent upon their labor was steadily falling behind in the national development.

Nothing seemed easier to explain than this discrepancy between white and black labor. The black was a slave, with no higher motive to exert himself than fear of punishment; the white was a free man, with abundant incentives to work and accumulate. So clear and dramatic was this contrast that other possible factors in the situation were overlooked. Remove the slave's disabilities, (it was said), give him the incentives of the freeman, and he will presently recover from the ill effects of slavery. The argument seemed sufficient and conclusive. In reality, it was very far from it. The foregoing chapters show that the lack of industrial qualities in the negroes was not due to enslavement alone, but to the effects of an environment enduring for unnumbered generations. So much of their inefficiency as was due to the adverse conditions of slavery might be expected to disappear in the later generations enjoying free citizenship. But so much of it as had its root in hereditary constitution should not be expected to give way before new conditions for centuries. It is in the nature of the case impossible to measure accurately the proportion of inefficiency due to enslavement or to heredity. Some would magnify one, some the other; but certain it is that the importance of the factor of heredity must be more fully recognized than it has been.

Sufficient time has elapsed since slavery passed away for a new generation to come upon the scene. It should be possible for us to ascertain what new traits they are developing as freemen, and what is the significance of these for the future of the race. The industrial capacity our black population is exhibiting to-day, and the progress it is making, are matters of the greatest interest.

A word may be said relative to the scope of the generalizations presently to be made. A large majority of the negroes are still ordinary agricultural or mechanical laborers,[1] constituting practically a single type for the purposes of this investigation. Whenever, therefore, general statements are made it will be this class that is referred to, unless a wider extension is explicitly stated. It will be recognized that there are other classes, small as yet, which must be excepted from many generalizations applicable to the masses of the race. These classes are made up of individuals exceptionally able and forceful. Among their number, too, are many with Caucasian blood in their veins, who thus are not truly representative of African heredity. If the race holds its own, these classes probably will survive and do well, or if it succumbs, they will be the last to go.

[1] See p. 178 for census figures.

12

To ascertain the industrial efficiency of a people, we may observe directly what traits they reveal, or we may note the occupations they tend to engage in, and the use habitually made of what they earn. Let us proceed to apply each of these tests as fully as the available data will permit. On the threshold of the subject of the negro's capacity as a workman, we are met by a puzzling divergence of opinions. "The difficulty", says Hoffman, "in deciding as to the comparative efficiency of white and colored labor is enhanced by the conflict of opinion, even among those most competent to judge of the negro as an agricultural or industrial worker."[1] He quotes the late Gen. Armstrong as saying: "I know of no subject on which you hear such diametrically contrary opinions as you do about the colored people." Some employers of negro labor declare that it is very satisfactory, while many pronounce it thoroughly disappointing and not to be compared with white labor. No one appears to have made an attempt to reconcile and explain this conflict of opinions.

An explanation, almost self-evident as soon as pointed out, is found in the differences in the employers and industries, taken in connection with the industrial traits of the negro himself. Some employers have not the temperament fitting them to rule fellowmen with an iron hand, and they lack the disposition or patience to exercise minute supervision over heedless and unreliable workmen. Again, irrespective of the character of employers, there are industries of such a nature that a large measure of trust and dependence upon the individual laborer is absolutely necessary. In either of these cases it is evident that

[1] Race traits and tendencies, p. 251.

workmen not up to a certain standard of self-reliant skill and steadiness would be declared unsatisfactory. Other employers prefer docile, easily managed laborers, such as can perform hard and comparatively unskilled work, and will submit without friction to thorough subordination. There are industries, though the number is steadily decreasing with the progress of our industrial evolution, in which relatively little independent efficiency is required, or which easily admit of close supervision. Workmen who, under the other conditions above cited, might be counted worthless, might here be considered quite acceptable.

In the light of these distinctions, the apparently inconsistent opinions of negro labor may be harmonized. Those who consider such labor satisfactory, reveal incidentally, by certain adjectives, why they think so. They say, for example, that "the negro is the most docile and tractable of all laborers, and under proper management the most contented and profitable";[1] that he is "eminently successful when directed by intelligent supervision";[2] in other words, that negroes are valuable laborers because they are first-rate muscular machines, submissive and manageable. Those, however, who prefer white to black labor, say either that it is because negroes as a class are unreliable, require too much supervision, and take little pride in doing good work; or that the nature of the industry is such that workmen of independent spirit and trust-worthiness are indispensable. This explanation implies the industrial inferiority of the negroes as compared with whites, save in a narrow range

[1] Mr. Massey, of Friar's Point, Miss., cited by Hoffman in his "Race traits and tendencies of the American Negro", p. 252.

[2] Mr. Killibrew, formerly commissioner of labor in Tennessee, cited by Hoffman, p. 268.

of low-grade employments.   Much evidence upon this point must be furnished, however, before we can accept it as final.

A singularly forcible illustration of the points just brought out may now be considered.   In 1899, at the town of Fayetteville, N. C., a silk mill was established by an able mulatto, Mr. T. W. Thurston, acting as agent for the silk manufacturing interests at Paterson, N. J. Within a short time there were 400 operatives at work with 10,000 spindles.   It was avowedly an experiment with negro labor, and it " has proved a signal success."[1] Let us note carefully the conditions upon which success has depended.   A correspondent of the New York *Journal of Commerce*, writing under date of October 27, 1900, says : " Mr. Thurston, who is evidently a man of ability and strong character and well educated, has a theory of his own in regard to the way in which a negro mill should be managed, and it is of a somewhat startling character."[2]   He then quotes Thurston, who, after stating that his operatives have proved quite satisfactory, adds :

"But no one can make a success of a mill by applying white methods to colored people.   With the latter there is but one rule to follow, that of the strictest discipline.   Call it military despotism, if you will.   There are no indulgences in this mill.   Kindness would be construed as weakness and advantage taken of it to the detriment of our work.   Faults and irregularities are severely punished."

The correspondent then drew out the fact that this discipline takes the form of whipping.

"The punishment is not light; it is severe ; anything else would be a waste of time.   It is upon this system that we have to rely to secure

[1] A very full and interesting account of this mill was given by a correspondent of the *Charlotte Observer*, a leading daily of North Carolina, in its issue of Feb. 11, 1901.   The writer has heard other accounts from eye-witnesses, and these accord fully with the printed sources of information used in the text.

[2] See the *Journal of Commerce*, for Nov. 1, 1900.

a proper performance of duty. All the help engaged here, under twenty-one years of age, are put absolutely under my control, by certificates from their parents or guardians, from six o'clock in the morning to six o'clock at night, and I am free from all responsibilities as to the course I pursue towards them during that time. No one desires more than I do to see the position of my people improved ; but I have no false ideas as to the present condition of the majority of them. They lack the sense of responsibility, and are like children where money is concerned. . . . My methods may be decried by humanitarians, but I am proving their success."

When the mill was first opened this rigid discipline did not exist. The result was that the operatives " were indifferent to their work and behavior, and it was necessary either to correct or discharge them. They preferred the latter, and Thurston, feeling that if he did not have power to discipline the young operatives, he would be compelled to give up," finally resorted to the system already described. This experience illustrates the fact, elsewhere pointed out, that, even under present conditions, the negroes do not feel the same incentives to work, or respond to them as efficiently as the whites. In this case there has been a partial reversion to a former method of securing steady work from an indolent people. Mr. Thurston is clearly of the conviction, founded upon hard experience, that it will not do to rely upon the ordinary incentives in the case of a majority of negroes. Indeed, he says plainly : " Forty years ago they whipped [white] boys in mills, as some of the successful manufacturers of to-day can testify from painful experience, and we are beginning just so many years behind." He attributes the failure of other mills operated by negro workmen to the attempt to treat them like white labor. We have here an instance of an employer, who might well say that his negro operatives are satisfactory and his enterprise a success, but only on condition that he wields a power of discipline over them, such as no body of white workmen would brook for a single day.

Prof. W. E. B. Du Bois, who has made himself an authority upon matters relating to his race, says that "the Negro is, as a rule, willing, honest, and good natured; but he is also, as a rule, careless, unreliable, and unsteady."[1] Mr. Philip A. Bruce, in his careful study of the Virginia plantation negroes, describes them as "steady, docile, and active" only under conditions where they are kept closely under the management of whites. Otherwise, they are restless, continually shifting employment, too heedless to be entrusted with costly agricultural machinery or fine live stock, cheerful and complacent under any conditions of life, and strongly averse to restraint.[2] Reporting from a typical Louisiana sugar plantation, Mr. J. B. Laws states that "the negroes as a rule do not work any harder than is necessary to keep their families alive."[3] He notes the significant fact that Italians are coming in to displace them, because Italians will work steadily as long as wages are paid, whereas the negroes habitually stop work as soon as a little money is paid them, and take a holiday till it is spent. Mr. Alfred H. Stone, after showing that an immense amount of work has been accomplished in the Yazoo-Mississippi delta, tells us that "the capital, the devising brain, the directing will, constitute the white man's part; the work itself is the negro's."[4] The entire paper from which this is quoted witnesses to the fact that negroes can become valuable

[1] "The Philadelphia Negro", Publications of the Univ. of Pennsylvania, No. 14, p. 97.

[2] "The plantation Negro as a freeman", pp. 176–192.

[3] Bulletins of the U. S. department of labor, No. 38, on "The negroes of the Cinclare central factory and Calumet plantation, Louisana."

[4] "The negroes of the Yazoo-Mississippi delta", Proceedings of the Fourteenth Annual Meeting of the American Econ. Ass'n., p. 240.

producers, but only on condition that they are
thoroughly managed by white men.

Let us examine now certain facts relative to the
great staples produced mainly by negro labor. After
pointing out the expert care and close application required by tobacco at various stages of its production,
Bruce states that

"in all those counties of the tobacco region of Virginia, in which
the tobacco crop is cultivated entirely by negroes there has been a
notable decline in the quality of the staple as well as in the character
of its manipulation, now that the majority of the hands, who were
trained for many years under the eye of their master or his overseer,
are fast dying off." [1]

Hoffman shows that, taking five representative counties
of Virginia, whose total negro population much exceeds
the white, there was a decline in the tobacco production
from 30,504,090 pounds in 1859 to 12,123,264 pounds
in 1889.[2] According to statistics furnished by Prof.
Du Bois regarding the production of Prince Edward
County, Virginia, there was a falling off between 1850
and 1890 of over one-half in corn, 23 per cent. in wheat,
one-half in oats, and a third in tobacco.[3] In the greater
staples, therefore, this county shows a heavy decline,
although hay increased from 487 to 2,513 tons; Irish
potatoes from 7,700 to 12,737 bushels; and butter from
47,932 to 133,511 pounds. Yet the white population
was only 4,770 in 1890 as against 9,924 negroes.

Exhaustion of the soil accounts for a part of this decline, and possibly the migration of negroes into towns
for another part. But since 1860 population has
greatly increased, more soil has been brought under
cultivation, and better methods of agriculture have be-

[1] *Op. cit.* p. 183.
[2] "Race traits, etc.", p. 254.
[3] See tables in his study of "The negroes of Farmville, Virginia",
Bulletins of the U. S. department of labor, No. 14, pp. 2-3.

come known. In another Virginia county, Pittsylvania, where the white population exceeded that of the negroes, and had increased more rapidly, the tobacco production rose from 7,800,000 pounds in 1859 to 12,300,000 in 1889.[1] In four counties of Kentucky, which contain less than five per cent. of negro population, the production of tobacco rose from 90,338 pounds in 1859 to 10,044,856 pounds in 1889.[2] Fresh soil in Kentucky might account largely for this, and yet this state has long been settled, and it is questionable whether new land was available for any considerable portion of this enormously increased tobacco-culture. In any case, the great contrasts revealed are of no little significance in the present connection.

Hoffman cites evidence going to show, though it does not prove conclusively, that the production of rice and cotton, once peculiarly dependent upon negro labor, is shifting slowly into white hands. He finds that " with less than one-half as large a colored population as Mississippi, the state of Texas produced in 1894 almost three times the cotton crop of the former state."[3] Even more significant is the fact that " with almost twice the colored population of 1860, Mississippi in 1894 produced less cotton than 34 years ago."[4]

To the same effect is the strong evidence brought out by Prof. Walter F. Willcox, in a careful study of the causes of negro criminality.[5] Speaking of the year 1860, he says: " It would probably be a conservative statement to say that at least four-fifths of the cotton

[1] Hoffman, " Race traits, etc.", p. 254.

[2] *Idem.*, p. 255.

[3] *Idem.*, p. 261.

[4] *Idem.*, p. 261.

[5] See an address delivered before the American Social Science Association, Sept. 6, 1899, on " Negro criminality ", pp. 9–13.

was then grown by negroes; at the present time probably not one-half is thus grown." He finds that tobacco-
culture is "evidently tending to center in Kentucky,
and yet it is the only Southern state in which the number of negroes decreased during the last decade." Similarly the culture of sugar-cane and rice, according to
facts set forth by him, is concentrating into white
hands. Summing up, he says:

> "From all the evidence obtainable it seems clear that southern
> agriculture is become increasingly diversified, and is demanding and
> receiving a constantly increasing amount of industry, energy and in-
> telligence,—characteristics which the whites more generally possess
> or more readily develop."

We may with yet more certainty attribute to the inefficiency of the negroes the fact that they are giving
place to the whites in many occupations. This is particularly true of the skilled trades, requiring long and
patient apprenticeship, followed by steady application.
Bruce says:

> "Indeed, one of the most discouraging features in the character of
> the negroes who have grown up since the war, is their extreme aver-
> sion to the mechanical trades. . . Many who might have been care-
> fully instructed, relinquished the opportunity opened to them as soon
> as they were old enough to support themselves, at which time they
> emigrated to a distance and sought employments more congenial to
> their tastes. The explanation of this antipathy on their part is easily
> found ; such pursuits constrain them to conform more closely than
> they like to a steady routine of work, which is more arduous and try-
> ing on the whole. . . Above all, the laborer is not tied down to one
> spot ; if he grows weary of one locality, he can find occupation else-
> where. But this is not the position of the young mechanic ; his suc-
> cess is largely dependent upon his remaining in one place ; he secures
> patronage by winning a reputation for assiduity and skill in his trade,
> and it is not possible to earn such a reputation as long as he yields to
> his inclination to wander." [1]

In these observations are expressed accurately some of
the most serious weaknesses of the negro. The writer,
in common with others well known to him, has found

---

[1] "The plantation Negro, etc.", pp. 232–3.

nothing more destructive of industrial arrangements than the irrepressible inclination of the younger negroes to shift employers and employments. They are forever in search of some "easier job." The most satisfactory employment, from their standpoint, seems to be one which will afford a bare subsistence and a wide margin for idleness and local migrations.

An able newspaper correspondent in North Carolina recently declared, after carefully looking into the matter, that there is now an unmistakable tendency for "the negro to leave the barber's chair and become a shoe-shine; to lay aside the bricklayer's trowel and carry the hod; to quit the carriage seat and shovel manure; to drop the carpenter's saw and take up the hand-spike."[1] After seeing this statement, the present writer made a number of inquiries and observations along the same line, and the result was a complete corroboration of the correspondent's declaration. In 1894, Prof. Hugh M. Browne, during a speech to a negro audience, said:

"White men are bringing science and art into menial occupations and lifting them beyond our reach. In my boyhood the household servants were colored, but now in the establishments of the four hundred one finds trained white servants. Then the walls and ceilings were whitewashed each spring by colored men; now they are decorated by skilled white artisans. Then the carpets were beaten by colored men; now this is done by a white man, managing a steam carpet-cleaning works. Then the laundry work was done by negroes; now they are with difficulty able to manage the new labor-saving machinery."[2]

Very important and valuable is the testimony upon this point of one who certainly knows whereof he speaks, and whose natural inclination would be against making any grave admission of weakness in his people. With admirable frankness, Booker T. Washington says:

[1] See correspondence of the *Charlotte Observer*, (North Carolina), Jan. 27, 1901, signed H. E. C. Bryant.

[2] From the A. M. E. Zion Church *Quarterly* for April, 1894; cited by W. F. Willcox, in his address on "Negro criminality", p. 12.

"The place made vacant by the old colored man, who was trained as a carpenter during slavery, and who since the war had been the leading contractor and builder in the southern town, had to be filled. No young colored carpenter, capable of filling his place, could be found. The result was that his place was filled by a white mechanic from the North, or from Europe, or from elsewhere. What is true of carpentry and house building in this case is true, in a degree, in every skilled occupation; and it is becoming true of common labor. I do not mean to say that all skilled labor has been taken out of the negroes' hands; but I do mean to say that in no part of the South is he so strong in the matter of skilled labor as he was twenty years ago, except possibly in the country districts and smaller towns. In the more northern of the southern cities, such as Richmond and Baltimore, the change is most apparent; and it is being felt in every southern city. Wherever the negro has lost ground industrially in the South, it is not because there is prejudice against him as a skilled laborer on the part of the native southern white man; the southern white man generally prefers to do business with the negro mechanic rather than with a white one, because he is accustomed to do business with the negro in this respect. There is almost no prejudice against the negro in the South in the matter of business, so far as the native whites are concerned; and here is the entering wedge for the solution of the negro problem. But too often, where the white mechanic or factory operative from the North gets a hold, the trades union soon follows, and the negro is crowded to the wall." [1]

Here are attested the facts not only that there has been an inexorable displacement of the negroes as skilled workmen, but that this has not been due to prejudice against the race in industrial connections. The net result of Prof. DuBois' study of the Philadelphia negroes was to the same effect, save that he is disposed to attribute much to white prejudice against them.[2] It appears that the negroes that were able to hold their own, were trained under slavery. Those that have been free to pursue their own bent, have not followed in the footsteps of their fathers, but have sought less exacting occupations.

The census figures of 1890 showed that 85 per cent. of negro males engaged in gainful occupations were in

---

[1] "The future of the American Negro", pp. 78-9.

[2] See "The Philadelphia Negro", p. 126, *et seq.*

agriculture and domestic service. Of negro females, 52 per cent. were in domestic service and 44 per cent. were in agriculture, leaving 4 per cent. in all other occupations. "Summing up," says Gannett in his paper on this subject, "it is seen that in the matter of occupations the negro is mainly engaged either in agriculture or in domestic service. He has, in a generation, made little progress in manufacture, transportation, or trade." [1] The results of twelfth census on this question are not yet available.

In the qualities so important to economic welfare, those of self-control and wisdom in the expenditure of earnings, the original African was notably weak, and under slavery the instincts of thrift did not develop. We expect to find, therefore, that the mass of the race is marked to this day by the ancestral traits in these regards. Regarding the Louisiana plantation negroes, we are told by Laws that they

"as a rule never save any money, although there are a very few exceptions. They do not know what economy is, and will buy anything that anybody will sell them on credit. . . No thought is given of durability or appropriateness in the purchase of dress or other articles, but only showiness. . . They will not provide in advance for any contingency." [2]

Booker T. Washington tells of finding often a sixty-dollar organ in a scantily furnished cabin, "sewing-machines which had been bought, or were being bought, on instalments, frequently at a cost of as much as sixty dollars, or showy clocks for which the occupants had paid twelve or fourteen dollars." [3] In some cases the owners could not tell the time of day; rarely could any play a tune on the organ, and comparatively few could

[1] "Occupations of the negroes", by Henry Gannett, J. F. Slater Fund, Occasional papers, No. 6.
[2] "The negroes of Cinclare central factory, etc.", p. 117.
[3] "Up from slavery", p. 113.

use the sewing-machine. Of the Virginia plantation negroes Bruce says : " A brief study of the masses of the race reveals that they have many qualities that stand directly in the way of their material improvement, even in the narrowest sense of the term. . . . The most unfortunate of these qualities are carelessness, improvidence, and destructiveness." [1] They will incur debt without other limit than the creditor's caution.[2] Commenting on the fact that the city negroes of Philadelphia had accumulated much less property than might have been expected of them, DuBois says :

" Much of the money that should have gone into homes has gone into costly church edifices, dues to societies, dress and entertainment. If the negroes had bought little houses as persistently as they have worked to develop a church and secret society system, and had invested more of their earnings in savings banks and less in clothes, they would be in far better condition to demand industrial opportunity than they are to-day." [3]

The present writer's personal observations and inquiries in other localities than those above represented,[4] have elicited information fully in accord with the foregoing evidence.

It is scarcely possible to avoid the conclusion, therefore, that the masses of the negroes are still, like their recent ancestors, unable to realize clearly the future and to sacrifice present gratifications in order to provide for it. They spend their earnings upon impulse, injudiciously and wastefully. They exhibit still an inordinate love

[1] " The plantation Negro, etc.", p. 193.
[2] *Idem.*, p. 196. See also " Fourteenth Annual Meeting of the Amer. Econ. Asso.", pp. 251, 253.
[3] " The Philadelphia Negro ", p. 185.
[4] Chiefly in the Carolinas and Washington city. To give a single illustration : During the summer of 1901, an agent for some music house did a thriving business at Morganton, N. C., selling cheap organs to negroes in the surrounding country—negroes who lived in humble cabins and could not play a single tune on the instrument.

for ostentatious display, reckless of consistency and appropriateness.

It would be very misleading, however, to leave the impression that the foregoing facts apply to the entire race. There is a minority, small as yet, which must be excepted from generalizations based upon those facts. They are "the flower of the race," as Bruce puts it, "who alone in the vast swarm of negroes that darken the country like an ominous cloud, give us the least confidence in its capacity."[1] Thousands of negroes have shown themselves possessed of no mean industrial ability. In one vocation or another they have proved their ability to win success, often in spite of great disadvantages. A new class of negroes has made its appearance, a class of small entrepreneurs.[2] Grocery and cigar stores, restaurants, undertaking establishments, brickmaking, upholstering, and enterprises of like character are what negroes are at present attempting. How far this new development will go it is impossible to predict, but there is considerable promise even in its present status. Many negroes, too, have entered, or are trying to enter, professional callings, chiefly those of teaching and the ministry. A few have entered the civil service and clerical positions. The number of doctors and lawyers is slowly increasing.[3]

With regard to the accumulation of property, the census of 1890 showed that of 549,632 farms occupied by negroes, 22 per cent. were owned by them. Of those owned,

[1] *Op. cit.*, p. 216,

[2] See "The Philadelphia Negro", pp. 115-126; also sections headed "Occupations" in "The negroes of Farmville", "The negroes of Sandy Spring, Maryland", Bulletins of the U. S. dep't of labor, Nos. 14 and 32.

[3] "The Philadelphia Negro'", pp. 111-114; "The college-bred Negro", Atlanta University Publications, No. 5, p. 64.

10 per cent. were incumbered with debt. Of the 861,137
homes occupied by negroes, 19 per cent. were owned, of
which 13 per. cent were incumbered.[1] In Philadelphia
DuBois found that between 5 and 6 per cent. of the negroes were home-owners.[2] It is impossible to get at the
aggregate value of property owned by negroes, though
it is known to be very considerable. In three states
only are separate data for whites and blacks available—
Virginia, North Carolina, and Georgia. On the basis
of tax assessments, it appeared that in 1890 negroes
owned 3.1 per cent. of taxable property in Virginia, and
3.5 per cent. in Georgia; in 1891 they owned 3.3 per
cent. in North Carolina.[3] The total taxable property of
the whites in the three states amounted to $978,000,000
as against $32,000,000 owned by blacks. This gives a
per capita of $322 for whites and $16 for blacks. The
close agreement of the percentages for three Southern
states suggests that the figures may be fairly representative. In any case, it is clear that a small minority of
negroes have become owners of property. The aggregate value of this to-day is two or three hundreds of millions of dollars.[4]

This fact appears inconsistent with the various considerations brought out in earlier paragraphs. How are
we to harmonize such contradictory evidence? Certain
further considerations will help us to an explanation.
Increased value does not necessarily imply increased
saving, owing to the "unearned increment," as Hoffman
rightly points out.[5] A further consideration is that, being a propertyless class at the start, the negroes could

[1] Gannett, "Occupations of negroes", p. 16.
[2] "The Philadelphia Negro", p. 184.
[3] Hoffman, "Race traits, etc.", p. 298.
[4] See Hoffman, "Race traits, etc.", p. 287.
[5] *Idem.*, p. 306.

buy only the cheapest real estate in sight—marginal no-rent land. While indefinite appreciation was, therefore, possible, no considerable depreciation could take place. Since the war thousands of whites have lost heavily because of depreciation, while others have become wealthy through appreciation of real estate values. During the same period many negroes have also gained, but scarcely any have lost.

Again, we must make a distinction between the elder generation trained under slavery, and the younger generation. Many of the former were skilled artisans; others had managed plantations as overseers; and all had been accustomed to steady work and plain living. Thus, they had been drilled into habits favoring humble thrift and accumulation. But their children may not be doing as well as their parents did. Bruce has observed that while many of the ex-slaves acquired land, relatively few of them under ten years of age at the close of the war have done so, save through inheritance.[1] The belief that this is true prevails widely in the South, but after careful examination of the insufficient data available, the present writer was unable to reach a definite conclusion.[2] There seemed, however, a strong probability that Bruce's statement contained much truth.

But, irrespective of the above comparatively minor qualifications, it is quite possible to grant that some hundreds of thousands of negroes are altogether successful and prosperous, without in the least contradicting the conclusion toward which we are led by the main body

[1] "The plantation Negro, etc.", p. 224.

[2] There is a great deal of information to be had regarding negro property owners and the amount of their holdings, but extremely little is said by way of indicating the age of these owners. Hence, it is impossible to separate owners old enough to have been slaves, from those grown up since emancipation.

of evidence. As was elsewhere stated, among nearly nine millions of negroes it is perfectly normal for thousands of exceptionally endowed individuals to appear, who are able to far outstrip the racial average. Caucasian blood also has entered as a factor in the case.

The general conclusion we reach, then, is to this effect: that an overwhelming majority of the race in its new struggle for existence under the exacting conditions of American industry, is seriously handicapped by inherited characteristics. Economic freedom has not developed a sense of responsibility and a persistent ambition to rise, as many hoped to see. As a race the negroes are still wanting in energy, purpose, and stability; they are giving way before the able competition of whites in the skilled and better paid occupations; and they fail to husband resources so as to establish economic safety.

13

CHAPTER III.

SOCIAL AND RELIGIOUS PROGRESS.

We shall discuss under one heading the social and religious life of the Negro, although they have heretofore been discussed separately. Since the American negroes became free, there has been a peculiar development tending to combine their social and religious life on a common basis of organization. To discuss either without frequent reference to the other is impossible.

When our colonial forefathers began the importation of Guinea natives, they little dreamed that these people, so manifestly inferior at the time, would ever become free American citizens. This event which took place with abrupt suddenness soon after 1865, illustrated how powerless is legislation to dictate the attitude and action of men in many of the aspects of life. It was impossible to compel the dominant race to receive the negroes as equals, and mingle with them in social and religious activities. In the parlor, at the table, in the pew, whites and blacks will not to-day associate as one people. As for intermarriage and mingling together around the same hearthstone, the very thought is not permitted.

But a social and religious life of some kind the negroes must have; indeed, they are a people whose temperament calls for abundant sociability and religious excitement. There is but one thing for them to do, that is to withdraw to themselves and develop their own organization as a distinct social group. They may vote in common with the whites; they may sue and be sued in the same courts; but they cannot (where numerous) share the same schools, churches, or social recreations. In all these things they are obliged to act separately.

This cleavage between the races does not, as is often supposed, arise from a mere unreasonable prejudice. Individuals cannot find satisfaction in associated life if there be too much diversity in their appearance, tastes, and traditions. But deeper than the contrast between the whites and blacks in physical features is the difference in temper and instincts. The kind of religious services acceptable to most whites does not attract most negroes. The race tradition which is the root of comprehension and sympathy among the whites, means nothing to the negroes. Only yesterday one race was the slave of the other, and the old caste feeling of the master race persists and will persist for generations. In the light of these facts, the lack of affinity between the two races appears natural and inevitable, and it becomes clear how impossible it is for whites and blacks to mingle as a homogeneous people.

Hence it is that a most significant movement has been going on since emancipation. Under slavery the organization of society was such as to keep the negroes widely distributed and in close contact with the whites. For every one of the thousands of small groups of slaves there was a white family, whose example and forcible discipline operated continuously to bring the lower race into line with our mode of life. The significance of this to a very imitative people, striving, in spite of hereditary weakness, to take on highly civilized life, can hardly be estimated. But with the passing of slavery this link between the two races was broken, and each was free to go its own way. Then set in the movement of segregation, so that to-day the negroes are largely isolated from the whites. No longer is there a gathering of dusky faces, beaming with delight, when a wedding occurs among the whites; nor is there any attendance of whites at a negro wedding. When there is a death among the whites, there is now no group of family negroes, hovering about in awe-struck grief; at the negro's grave there are no whites expressing a sympathetic sorrow. In their joys and in their sorrows, in their daily life and conversation, the races live apart, and know but little of each other's inner existence. Thus the negroes are forming a second group within the nation, enveloped by white society, but divided from it, and, in most respects, ever less subject to its influence.

There is a marked tendency also for the negroes to segregate geographically in the " black belt " of the South and in the " negro quarters " of cities and towns.[1] Wherever this begins, the whites move away, thus rendering the isolation of the negroes more complete.

Consider now the consequences of this steadily growing cleavage between two groups, compelled to live together as one nation. On emerging from slavery the negroes had but partially assimilated our civilization. Their adaptation to meet the heavy demands put upon them was hardly adequate. They were making painful progress in learning the primary lessons of our civilization, when, with emancipation, all direct control and discipline vanished. And now they are fast losing the powerful stimulus of immediate contact with the superior civilization they are expected to acquire. To offset all this they have gained the privilege of education in letters. This for the vast majority of them means only a few hours of instruction daily, in a poorly equipped

[1] See Hoffman, "Race traits, etc.", pp. 9-31 ; also Willcox, Proceedings of the Montgomery conference, p. 155.

school-room, during a few months of the early years of childhood. Even if the educational facilities were the best possible, the limitations of class-room training are such that it can never outweigh the other education, which every individual gets from the home and society in which he lives. Obviously the negroes of to-day have before them a desperate struggle, if they are to hold even their present position in American society. The question arises: What are they actually doing?

Monogamic marriage and a sense of parental responsibility for the bringing up of children, are parts of the heritage of the Caucasian. About the home and family have developed an atmosphere of tradition, sentiment, and domestic law. But the negroes have only for a short time been acquainted with monogamic marriage, under slavery they practiced it very imperfectly and mainly under compulsion. Refined, chivalrous sentiments toward the weaker sex, deep abiding affection in the family relations, and a keen sense of responsibility for the distant future of offspring, are late products of a long evolution. At best these higher elements of character had been but crudely developed among the negroes by 1863; yet they must rapidly make good these deficiencies or be undone. The evidence now coming to hand from many sources goes to show, however, that the race is unequal to the tremendous task laid upon it.

In a passage well worth quoting at some length, Bruce describes clearly the change of conditions since emancipation and the results observed to follow:

"Although the institution of slavery did nothing to raise the dignity of marriage or to improve the relations of the sexes, it restricted illicit commerce among the negroes to some extent, because it restrained their general conduct. . . They were especially discouraged from wandering about at night or mingling in large congregations; thus their opportunities of falling into lewd habits were diminished, although the inclination to do so remained unchanged. The personal independence of the present day shows how powerful this inclination was, in spite of the check that was put upon it by the systematic repression of slavery. It is not now reined in by circumstances at all, and the consequence is it is gratified to such a degree that lasciviousness has done more than all other vices of the plantation negroes united, to degrade the character of their social life since they were invested with citizenship. It is in this direction that they seem to be tending most toward a state of nature, and many influences are hastening that event." [1]

That there is little, if any, exaggeration in Bruce's strong statement there is abundant proof. We are told concerning the Calumet plantation negroes that " the families are all broken up by the continual swapping of women going on among the men. The negroes do not want children, and use all manner of means to prevent birth ; " also that "there are numerous children known by all to be illegitimate, and yet this condition of affairs is considered and spoken of as a matter of course."[2] The Rev. D. Clay Lilly, secretary of the Presbyterian Board of colored evangelization, relates :

In one county in Mississippi there were, during twelve months, 300 marriage licenses taken out in the county clerk's office for white people. According to the proportion of the population there should have been in the same time 1,200 or more for the negroes. There were actually taken out by colored people just three." [3]

After an investigation among the " oyster negroes " in the vicinity of Litwalton, Virginia, no less than thirteen per cent. of the children under ten years of age were " reported " as illegitimate.[4] This is believed to be an understatement of the truth, owing to the tendency to conceal illegitimacy. In Farmville, Virginia, it was

[1] *Op. cit.*, p. 178.

[2] "The negroes of the Cinclare central factory, etc.", pp. 102 and 115.

[3] "Proceedings of the Montgomery conference on race conditions and problems in the South ", p. 119.

[4] "The negroes of Litwalton, Virginia " by Dr. W. T. Thom, Bulletin of the U. S. dep't of labor, No. 37, p. 1141.

found by Prof. Du Bois, that fifteen per cent. of all the negro children under ten years were illegitimate,[1] and of a large negro element in Philadelphia, he says: " There is much sexual promiscuity and the absence of real home life." [2]　Regarding the negroes of Sandy Spring, Maryland, where a careful investigation was made, we are told that,

"it is the distinct impression among the older white members of the Sandy Spring community (some of whom have for half a century been doing what they could to help the negroes) that the average moral condition of the negroes is below what it was prior to 1865, and this opinion is shared by a number of the elder conservative negroes." [3]

In the city of Washington, where " the colored race has had exceptional educational and religious opportunities," the percentage of illegitimate births rose steadily from 17.6 in 1879 to 26.5 in 1894.　During the same period the percentage among whites never exceeded 3.6 and in 1894 was only 2.56.[4]　The conditions elsewhere seem to be nearly the same.　In Mobile and Knoxville "the rate of illegitimacy is about 25 per cent. of the total births, against an average of about 2.5 for the whites." [5] Another significant phase of this tendency is revealed in Washington by " the finding of ninety-eight dead infants (negro) in 1888, seventy-one in 1889, sixty-nine in 1890, seventy-five in 1891, and ninety-seven in 1892." A number of living infants were abandoned each year.[6] Much more evidence might be cited, but would only be cumulative in effect.

[1] "The negroes of Farmville, Virginia ", p. 19.

[2] "The Philadelphia Negro ", p. 192.

[3] "The negroes of Sandy Spring, Maryland ", by Dr. W. T. Thom, Bulletin of the U. S. dep't of labor, No. 32, p. 60.

[4] Hoffman, "Race traits, etc.", p. 235.

[5] *Idem.*, p. 237.

[6] The negro in the District of Columbia ", by Edward Ingle, Johns Hopkins Univ. Studies, vol. xi, p. 101.

The crime of rape, directed against white women, has come into existence since the war. The perpetrators of this crime are overcome in many cases by primitive savage passions, which master the criminal's whole being. A great fear is present which impels to murder.

Where sex relations are ill-regulated and unstable, as shown above, there can be but a mockery of monogamic family life. We should hardly expect under such conditions much improvement in the strength and permanence of parental and filial affection. What we might thus infer *a priori* is strongly supported by facts. The swapping of women by the men on Louisiana plantations clearly implies the absence of true conjugal affection and of established parental and filial relations. Dr. Thom found it impossible to get satisfactory statistics of the " economic family " [1] in his investigation of the Sandy Spring negroes, because of a too great fluidity of relationships, too much coming and going under the external form of a family group. One of his difficulties, for example, is thus described : " When small boarding members of a family were traced to their real maternal source, the discovery was sometimes made that the possible family did not have now and had never had visible heads enough." [2] In his report on " The negroes of the black belt," Prof. Du Bois describes a typical rural family as being a numerous, disorderly, quarrelsome, and neglected looking lot, among whom scarcely a spark of real affection was evinced. He then goes on to say, speaking of the district investigated in Georgia :

"In some respects this family is exceptionally bad, but several others are nearly as barbarous. A few are much better, and in the stone-cutter's five-room house one can find clean, decent family life,

[1] The economic family is defined as including " all persons related and unrelated, living in one house under conditions of family life."

[2] " The negroes of Sandy Spring ", p. 86.

with neatly dressed children and many signs of aspiration. The average of the communities, however, is much nearer the condition of the family first described than that of the better one.''[1]

Bruce says in substance of the Virginia plantation negroes that they are quite unable to maintain systematic discipline among their children, because steady watchfulness, temperate correction of small faults, and prompt action in disagreeable matters, are precisely what they are incapable of by nature.[2] Plainly the transition from the polygamic family of West Africa, where women are bought and sold, and family members are pawned into slavery, to the strictly monogamic family life of America, is a journey fraught with enormous difficulty to the transplanted race.

The consequences of the extremely elementary socialization of the West African are revealing themselves among his American descendants. Under the instant and relentless discipline of slavery, anti-social proclivities had small opportunity to manifest themselves. Aside from petty theft and insignificant crimes there was little trouble with the negroes previous to emancipation. But with the liberation of the negroes their obedience to law came to depend upon their voluntary self-restraint, and the weakness of the race at this point has begun to reveal itself to an alarming extent. This phase of the subject has already been so ably and fully treated by Willcox, Hoffman and others, that it does not seem necessary to enter largely into it here. The main facts may be set forth, however, for the present convenience of the reader.

Professor Walter F. Willcox has shown that according to the eleventh census, " in the southern states there

[1] "The negroes of the black belt", Bulletins of the U. S. dep't of labor, No. 22, p. 403.
[2] *Op. cit.*, p. —.

were six white prisoners to every ten thousand whites, and twenty-nine negro prisoners to every ten thousand negroes," while " in the northern states, in 1890, there were twelve white prisoners to every ten thousand whites, and sixty-nine negro prisoners to every ten thousand negroes."[1] Again, in the South the negro prisoners to ten thousand negroes increased 29 per cent. between 1880 and 1890, whereas the white prisoners to ten thousand whites increased only 8 per cent. In the North "the white prisoners increased seven per cent. faster than the white population, while the negro prisoners increased no less than thirty-nine per cent. faster than the negro population." The positive conclusion reached by him is that "a large and increasing amount of negro crime is manifested all over the country."[2]

An important point brought out by this writer is that the attitude of the negroes toward crime by no means coincides with that of the whites. After discussing the lynching of the negro incendiaries at Palmetto, Ga., in 1899, and of Sam Hose shortly after, Professor Willcox says :

"The white Caucasians of the Philippines regard a *juramentado* (a Malay Mohammedan fanatic, who slays Christians as a religious duty) as a peculiarly fiendish individual ; many of the brown Malays regard him as a saint and emulate his deeds. The white Caucasians of Georgia regard Sam Hose as a peculiarly fiendish individual ; many of the black Africans, I fear, regard him as an innocent man and a martyr."[3]

[1] See "Negro criminality", an address delivered before the American Social Science Association at Saratoga, Sept. 6, 1899. Also Hoffman, "Race traits, etc.", pp. 217-234, and a part of Dr. Paul B. Barringer's address before the Montgomery conference on "The sacrifice of a race", "Proceedings", pp. 187-9.

[2] "Negro criminality", pp. 5-6.

[3] *Idem.*, p. 20.

It is of course impossible to determine how far such divergence of opinion between the whites and blacks exists, but as far as it goes nothing could well be more serious and significant.

In the religious life of the American negroes we meet with interesting instances of the survival of racial customs and traits. We have seen that in West Africa the communal life of the village is everything, the private home life, nothing. The African temperament finds no enjoyment in anything unless there are many present and much excitement. Under slavery the propensity of the negroes for the communal group life was almost entirely suppressed. After emancipation the old pastimes were not possible, because too greatly in conflict with the usages of civilized society. But in one direction an opportunity was offered to gratify their instincts without offending the surrounding community, viz., through their church organization. Taking the line of least resistance, they have rapidly developed a church life that resembles in its main outlines the group life of West Africa. In this respect the best class of negroes is not to be distinguished from the average of the race, save in the degree to which refinement and luxury is introduced.

Professor Du Bois, one of the best authorities in this connection, says:

"The Negro church is the peculiar and characteristic product of the transplanted African, and deserves special study. As a social group the Negro church may be said to have ante-dated the Negro family on American soil; as such it has preserved, on the one hand, many functions of tribal organizations, and, on the other hand, many of the family functions. Its tribal functions are shown in its religious activity, its social authority, and general guiding and co-ordinating work; its family functions are shown by the fact that the church is a centre of social life and intercourse; acts as newspaper and intelligence bureau, is the centre of amusements—indeed, is the world in which the negro moves and acts." [1] Later he adds : "Without wholly conscious effort the Negro church has become a centre of social intercourse to a degree unknown in white churches, even in the country. . . . All sorts of entertainments and amusements are furnished by the churches ; concerts, suppers, socials, fairs, literary exercises and debates, cantatas, plays, excursions, picnics, surprise parties, celebrations." [2] To quote another peculiarly significant sentence : "In this way the social life of the negro centres in his church—baptism, wedding and burial, gossip and courtship, friendship and intrigue—all lie within these walls." [3]

In other words, there is a markedly distinct preference for the recreations where many can meet, rather than for the private pleasures of home life. Professor DuBois notes that there are few family festivals ; little notice is taken of birthdays and such occasions for quiet home celebrations. That he misses the underlying reason for this, however, is revealed in the following words of his discussion : " The home was destroyed by slavery, struggled up after emancipation and is not exactly threatened, but neglected in the life of city negroes ".[4] How could slavery destroy a home life that had never existed for the race? It is not the negro "home" that has "struggled up after emancipation", but the ancient racial habit of gregarious communal life, and this is growing to-day at the expense of private home life.

Among the rural negroes these tendencies are not so marked, owing to the greater difficulty of coming together. After stating that the negro churches at Cinclare central factory and Calumet are always well attended, Mr. Laws tells us that " the negroes are naturally a social race and the large attendance at church at both

[1] " The Philadelphia Negro ", p. 201.

[2] *Idem.*, p. 203,

[3] *Idem.*, p. 205.

[4] *Idem.*, p. 196.

places is easily explained aside from religious attraction, as it is the only place where they get together and talk things over ".[1]   Bruce's description of religious activity among the Virginia plantation negroes shows clearly that churches are remarkably well attended simply for the social recreation thus afforded.[2]   The present writer has noted how the town and country negroes of North Carolina seek through their churches the social pleasures, which, among the whites, are provided in private homes. It seems clear, therefore, that this singular movement among the negroes is general.   An impulse from within, working with other forces, is sending the race along lines divergent from those of our national development as a whole.

The inability of the negroes to see the relation between religious profession and moral conduct has perplexed many.   Bruce's statement of the case is admirable :

" The divorce between religion and morality in the life of the negro fills the observer with astonishment, for it seems impossible that he can be both devout and depraved at the same moment ; but if he is suspected in the beginning of hypocrisy, that suspicion is dispelled after a brief association with him. . . . He cannot be charged with religious cant and pretence, however immoral or criminal he may be."[3]

No, it is not necessary to suppose him a hypocrite when he is fervidly religious at church and grossly sinful in his secular life.   It is a case of survival.   Never in the previous history of his race has morality been associated with religion.   For rules of conduct to become interpenetrated with religious associations and sanctions requires a development through an immensely longer period than that of Negro life in America.

---

[1] " The negroes of Cinclare central factory, etc.", p. 118.
[2] " The plantation Negro, etc.", pp. 108–9.
[3] " The plantation Negro, etc,", p. 110.

The manner in which religious services are conducted in the rural churches and open camp-meetings, reveals once more the dominance of heredity. The writer has witnessed many religious meetings of negroes and has heard descriptions of many more. In superficial details they differ here and there, but not in essentials. The account given by Mr. Laws of the average church service on the Calumet plantation, would fit perfectly thousands of others to be seen throughout the South :

"The elder (or preacher) usually prefaces his sermon with the remark that he is not feeling very well, sticks more or less closely to the text, speaking very quietly for a few minutes, but gradually drifts into a vivid description of various thrilling Biblical scenes, as that of Daniel in the lions' den, or of Shadrach, Meschach, and Abednego in the fiery furnace, etc., reaching the climax in seeing ;the New Jerusalem with the four and twenty elders, or something akin. He moves rapidly from one side of the platform to the other, goes through various facial contortions, perspires freely, ' hollers ', and when the whole audience is swaying, moaning, surging, and shouting under intense excitement, the preacher drops his voice for a sentence and sits down exhausted." [1]

Compare with this a West African religious service. The priest dances, gesticulates, " goes through various facial contortions," mumbles and shouts alternately, growing more and more wrought up. Suddenly he sees the spirit or spirits whom he represents. While he fervently calls upon them to support him and his people, all around him the densely packed circle of natives become more and more excited, " swaying, moaning, surging, and shouting under intense excitement," until they are in a half-demented state. Have we not evidence here that the same force is preserving unchanged the color of skin, and the psychic nature ? Or rather, to be more accurate, we should say, not an unchanged nature, but one changing only by infinitesi-

---

[1] " The negroes of Cinclare central factory, etc.", p. 119.

mal degrees, so that ages will be required to accumulate decisive modifications.

Superstition survives to a remarkable degree in negro life. The Guinea native's emotional temperament and imaginative mind, developed for ages amid supernaturalism, easily cause the visionary to appear as the real. Under the influence of music, oratory, and the hypnotism of a crowd, any group of negroes can quickly work themselves into a state of mental exaltation, when the real world dissolves from view. This is but an extreme expression of a cast of mind, which under the stimulus of fear, moves insensibly over the hazy line that divides the natural from the supernatural, and falls under the spell of immaterial images. Hence it is that to-day it may be said:

"plantation negroes, in a convenient distance of churches, schools, and railroads are found to have as firm a belief in witchcraft as the savages of the African bush. . . There are communities of negroes in the tobacco belt of Virginia, to-day, that so far resemble an African tribe as to have a professional trick-doctor, a man whose only employment lies in the practice of the art of witchcraft, but it is probable that he is an unconscious empiric as a rule." [1]

The present writer, although familiar from boyhood with the fact that the belief in "conjurers," witches, spells, the efficacy of charms, etc., prevailed everywhere among the negroes, was surprised to learn from personal inquiries, the extent to which it exists. In the city of Washington there are numerous "doctors," so called, who thrive upon the superstitions of their people, professing to remove "spells," to detect and punish those who have "put spells on" others, to furnish valuable charms, etc. Inquiry in regard to Richmond, Baltimore, and New Orleans, has elicited similar facts. During the summer of 1900 a report got out among the negroes of a community in North Carolina that the ghost of a person

[1] Bruce, "The plantation Negro, etc.", p. 115.

whose death had occurred under unusual circumstances, was "haunting" a certain road. The negroes along the road could not be induced to travel it by night, preferring to go to town by a roundabout path. Such occurrences are common throughout the South. Negroes in rural districts will not use a lightning-struck tree for fuel. A rusty nail or a darning-needle, with red flannel wrapped about it, is worn by thousands of American negroes at this moment as a charm to fend off misfortune. Thus, West Africa survives on American soil.

To avoid misunderstanding it must again be remarked that there are many thousands who have risen far above the average of their race, who constitute an intelligent, civilized aristocracy, in the better sense of that term, and who must be excepted from the generalizations enforced by the foregoing evidence. But they cannot be cited as arguing a capacity in the mass of the negroes to attain American civilization at a pace in harmony with our national progress. Prof. John R. Straton has well said:

"We must not confuse the rapid development of exceptional individuals with the evolution of the race. Picked individuals, strengthened often in mental vigor by infusions of white blood, may grow rapidly; but the evolution of the race comes slowly—a part of each new element of strength being transmitted by the laws of heredity from father to son, and so on to succeeding generations; and so, slowly and painfully, a race advances. It is not a matter of decades, but of centuries. The Negro race as a whole, however, may go forward higher yet in outward forms, but still deep down beneath these things may lie the tendencies which give color to the fear that they are a decaying people." [1]

[1] See the Proceedings of the Montgomery conference, p. 149.

EDUCATIONAL PROGRESS.

Reversion to type takes place where the artificial conditions by which a species has been modified in form and habits, are removed. The system of slavery served as a means of holding the inferior race to at least a semi-civilized mode of life, despite any propensities to the contrary. After the war the negroes, loosed from familiar restraints, were incapable of appreciating the more refined ones in a highly civilized society. It was the belief and dread of many slave-owners that the negroes would revert to savagery; it was the belief and hope of most anti-slavery advocates that the freedmen would attain to the standard of American civilization. The slave-owners failed to realize the inertia of habit, which would prevent in any case, an immediate relapse into savagery. But were they mistaken in their opinion that the Negro was not even potentially a Teuton under a black skin? The abolitionists, moderate and extreme, were right in feeling that slavery was a hideous anachronism, but did they realize adequately the problem to be faced after emancipation? The sword finally determined which body of opinion, and what national policy toward our African population, should prevail. This policy was a natural recoil from the institution held responsible for the freedmen's low status, while less obvious factors in the situation were overlooked in the passion of that period. Those who saw that slavery had failed to give the negroes sufficient incentives to progress, and had denied them education and a voice in government, believed that freedom, education and the ballot, would be effective means of elevating them to the standard of American citizenship.

Formerly the term "education" in ordinary speech meant nothing more than the acquisition of literary knowledge, including, in advanced stages, the classics, higher mathematics, and the natural sciences. If morals and industrial efficiency were thought of at all, it was assumed that young people would acquire them in the home and work-shop. With the advent of kindergartens, manual training, and other additions to the old curricula, we are becoming familiar with a broader conception of education. It includes the training not merely of the intellect, but of the heart and hand as well.

At the time the negroes were freed, the narrower conception prevailed. Hence, in the great effort then inaugurated to educate the negroes, only literary training was supplied, in the belief that this of itself would work wonders for the race. Little thought was given to the fact that the negro child did not have the Caucasian home, and that behind the literary schooling of the white had always existed the nurture of the civilized home; yet without the home no great development of ideals, morality, habits of industry, can be expected. It was forgotten or discredited that the negroes and whites had fundamentally different aptitudes and needs. On this point Dr. J. L. M. Curry has put the truth in few, though emphatic words :

"The curriculum was for a people in the highest degree of civilization ; the aptitude and capabilities and needs of the negro were wholly disregarded. Especial stress was laid on classics and liberal culture to bring the race *per saltum* to the same plane with their former masters, and realize the theory of social and political equality. A race more highly civilized, with the best heredities and environments, could not have been coddled with more disregard of all the teachings of human history and the necessities of the race." [1]

Nor was it realized how immense and difficult a task it would be to provide educational advantages at once for four and a half millions of people.

The census of 1860 showed 4,441,830 negroes in the country, of whom 226,216 were in the north and 4,215,614 were concentrated in the south, where ruin and choas were presently brought on by war. 151,245 free negroes were reported able to read and write, this being three per cent. of the negro population. Among the slaves a few were able to read and write, but probably ninety-five per cent. of the negroes were illiterate.[2] Clearly, with the South exhausted, and millions of whites still in need of education, the providing of satisfactory education for the blacks within two or three decades was absolutely impossible. Illiteracy among the rapidly increasing black population was nevertheless reduced to less than 80 per cent. by 1870, to 70 per cent. by 1880, and to 56.8 per cent. by 1890.[3] In 1900 44.5 per cent. remained illiterate, while a very large proportion of those counted literate had but the smattering of an education.[4] As Dr. H. B. Frissell says:

" Fair provision is made for the city children, but in the great country districts, where 80 per cent. of the southern people live, there are in many localities miserable schoolhouses, school terms that do not average more than three months, and school teachers who are often but poorly equipped for the important work that has been given them to do." [5]

---

[1] Proceedings of the Montgomery conference, etc., p. 109.

[2] In appendices to his " Southern sidelights " Edward Ingle gives much information on this subject in conveniently tabulated form.

[3] Report of the U. S. commissioner of education, 1897–8, vol. ii, p. 2486.

[4] Twelfth Census, vol. 2, p. xcviii.

[5] Proceedings of the Montgomery conference, etc., p. 87.

If education is to be regarded as the great reliance to prevent the negroes from reverting to lower conditions, it would appear (1) that it was poorly devised and inefficient, and (2) that, after a quarter of a century of earnest effort, nearly half the race remained untouched by it. Hence, though we must deplore, we can hardly be surprised at, the situation described in the two preceding chapters. Nor should we blame the generation just past. We have here an instance, not of human fault, but of human limitation.

A wiser policy may guide us in the future. The conception of education as including training of the heart and hand, is being widely recognized. From the foundation of the celebrated Hampton Normal and Agricultural Institute, in 1868, the methods have been based upon this conception.[1] Dr. H. B. Frissell, the present principal, describes the work done there as follows:

"The Hampton school has its workshops as well as its schoolrooms, its farms and saw-mills as well as its church. It is really an industrial village where a thousand young people are being trained in life's industries. Commencing in the kindergarten the children are instructed in the use of the wash-tub and the ironing-table, the hoe and the rake, as well as in music and reading. The work habit—love for the labor of the hand—is created and cultivated throughout the whole course. Every boy is taught agriculture, work in wood, iron, and tin, as well as history, geography, mathematics, and other English studies."[2]

[1] The founder, Gen. S. C. Armstrong, was born in Hawaii, his father being an American missionary and minister of public instruction. Thus young Armstrong became familiar with the methods adopted for the Hawaiians He tells how his early impressions influenced him in developing Hampton Institute : "Illustrating two lines of educational work . . . were two institutions : the Lahaina-luna (government) Seminary for young men, where with manual labor, mathematics and other higher branches were taught ; and the Hilo Boarding and Manual-labor (missionary) School for boys. . . . As a rule the former turned out more brilliant, and the latter less advanced, but more solid men. In making the plan of the Hampton

[2] Proceedings of the Montgomery conference, etc., p. 95.

In Tuskegee institute substantially the same methods are pursued, its organizer and present manager, Booker T. Washington, being a graduate of Hampton. In these institutions the fact is frankly recognized that, however, it may be with whites, the negroes need to be severely drilled into the habit of labor and inspired with a higher standard of morals than exists in their present racial atmosphere. Literary education is not denied; indeed, it is given as freely as practicable, but only as the complement of more vital attainments.

The wisdom of this method of instruction for the negroes has been abundantly proved by results. On this point Dr. Frissell says:

"Scores of letters from southern county and state superintendents bear witness to the industry and thrift of these young people, and their kindly relations with the southern whites. If one will go into the black belt of Virginia he will find scores of Hampton graduates and graduates of other institutions, engaged in the industrial and agricultural leadership of their people, and commanding the respect and confidence of the best men of the white race. He will find a wonderful increase in land holding among the blacks, and a corresponding decrease in crime." [1]

This is not an exaggerated statement of the results achieved at Hampton.[2] Had instruction by this method been given from the beginning to a majority of the race, doubtless the evils never would have gained great headway, and even might have been overcome. If

Institute, that of the Hilo School seemed the best to follow." Graduates of the more pretentious school, where literary culture was attempted rather than manual training, "had frequently been disappointing", while graduates of the mission school turned out more uniformly successful in a practical sense. See "Twenty-two years' work of the Hampton Normal and Agricultural Institute", pp. 1–2.

[1] Proceedings of the Montgomery conference, pp. 95–6.

[2] The writer speaks from information furnished by persons well acquainted with the work being done by Hampton graduates in Virginia.

widely employed now would it suffice to arrest the degeneration of the negroes?

An affirmative answer implies the belief that because a few schools of this type have accomplished excellent results with a few pupils, similar results could be achieved for the race generally by multiplying the institutions. This depends upon whether the material with which Hampton works, fairly typifies the mass of raw material to be improved.

Opening a catalogue of that institution and examining the terms of admission, we discover that it works only with stringently sifted material. Following are extracts from the catalogue, printed as in the original :

"SOUND HEALTH, testimonials of GOOD CHARACTER, and intention to remain through the course, are required of all applicants. Candidates for admission coming from common schools or from other institutions, must present letters of honorable dismissal and of recommendation. . . .

Able-bodied, capable, young men and women of good character are encouraged to apply for admission on the following terms :

1. To work steadily all day for at least an entire year from the time of entering (usually October 1st), and attend night school for two hours five nights a week.

Note.—No one need apply who is not well and strong and capable of doing a man's or woman's work. None under seventeen years need apply. . . .

3. The first three months are probationary . . ..

The utmost economy is expected from the students, in order that they may accumulate money for their expenses in the day school." [1]

Note the severely selective effect of such conditions. Sound health, good character, stringent economy, and great industry make a combination of conditions for

[1] See catalogue for 1896-7, pp. 9-10. One of old date was purposely used here, since we are discussing results gained by past work. The conditions of admission to Tuskegee are similar, but hardly as exacting in detail as those quoted. See any recent catalogue of Tuskegee Institute.

entrance which thousands never can meet. If the youth of the race generally were qualified to enter Hampton on its own terms, the problem would be already half solved. The results attained at Hampton therefore fail to prove that like results could be secured amongst the negroes at large.

Let there be no misunderstanding of the attitude here taken. Under the conditions confronting Hampton and similar institutions, the policy of carefully selecting the students seems thoroughly sound. A maximum of good is thus achieved with the funds available. The method of instruction is probably the best yet devised for up-lifting the negroes. And although Hampton methods could not achieve for the race indiscriminately the same results now gained with picked material, yet a general application of these methods to the negroes, with compulsion if necessary, would improve their condition and at least retard degeneration.

The difficulty of a speedy and general application of these methods is not mainly one of finance. Without easing the rigid discipline maintained at Hampton, (and this certainly never should be permitted), it would become difficult to secure general and steady attendance, as soon as the masses began to be reached. There may be as yet many more individuals than can be provided for, ready and anxious to pass through Hampton or Tuskegee on any terms, but such exceptional material would soon be exhausted upon the inauguration of an extensive system. Hence, nothing short of a vast expenditure of money in multiplying Hamptons and Tuskeegees, coupled sooner or later with compulsory attendance, will avail to arrest the steady reversion to type, now exhibited by the American branch of the race.

That the alphabet and Arabic numerals do not furnish a magic key to civilization has been only too well shown by experience. That efficient, moral, industrial and literary education suffices to civilize picked negroes has been demonstrated. That its general application would be of great benefit to them we cannot doubt. Wisely directed education may largely control character in spite of heredity, but it is well to remember that while efforts toward education often miss their mark, heredity is persistent and unerring.

CHAPTER V.

The assumption was made after the liberation of the negroes, that if they were given constitutional rights they would be ensured against political evils. Fearing that they would be practically re-enslaved under forms of law, unless given an equal share in government with their former masters, the party in power endowed the freedmen with unrestricted suffrage. The experience of the negroes in thus passing almost at once from slavery to full-fledged citizenship, hardly has a parallel in the political annals of mankind.

Neither in West Africa nor under American slavery had the negroes had any opportunity to exercise self-government. Certainly there was nothing in the experience of the natives of the Guinea coast, living in petty despotisms, to develop political capacity or civic virtue. During their enslavement in this country they were never called upon to give a thought to matters of public welfare, and they did not control even their own personal and family affairs. It is true that in so far as they became more civilized, learning to understand and live in harmony with our institutions, they were by so much the better prepared to enter into our political life. But the specific development in political capacity, required for the successful conduct of republican government, the slaves entirely missed. Thus at the close of the war the negroes were still, as when they left Africa, infants in political development. Utterly ignorant of our governmental organization, they were unfitted to acquire rapidly a knowledge of it. They had not even the elemental qualities of character necessary to wise self-government—foresight and self-command.

In this condition they were suddenly given as much political power as the most intelligent citizens of our land. The responsibitities thus laid upon them prematurely, are well expressed by Dr. Curry :

"We are trying . . . to govern upon the theory that every man is a political expert, entitled to have an opinion upon all economic, social, and political questions, and that a majority told by the head, whether that head be covered with hair or wool, is the voice of God. The principle is that one man's opinion upon the most important national and international questions, finance, currency, coinage, tariff, territorial expansion, imperialism, is as good as another's, and that the voter has sufficient knowledge and patriotism to make it safe to trust to him the most important of all human business." [1]

When we consider in the light of this the mental and moral condition of the freedmen, there can be no surprise at the disastrous results that quickly followed their enfranchisement.

Certain conditions, left by the war, affected the negroes particularly. When the negroes received the right of suffrage there was but one issue that they could understand, viz., whether they were to remain free or not, though this was then a dead issue. For them there were but two parties, one of which was identified with the power that had freed them, the other with the power that had sought to keep them in slavery. They ranged themselves in a solid mass on the one side, and have remained there ever since. Not understanding the issues that have arisen in the interval, they have clung to the one issue they could comprehend.

This disregard of real issues, and the rejection of the leadership of white men in their own section, whose interest it was to maintain good government, had an un-

[1] Proceedings of the Montgomery conference, p. 111.

fortunate result. Adventurers from the North, and dem-
agogues at home, who had no interests at stake in the
defeated states, presently acquired the leadership of the
negroes, and received their political support *en masse.*
Partly owing to the fact that negroes were in excess of
whites in many localities, and partly because many
whites were excluded from the ballot by temporary dis-
qualification,[1] a revolution ensued that placed the former
slaves with their new leaders in charge of state and local governments throughout a large portion of the
South. A greater misfortune could hardly have happened to the negroes than to have received their first
political lessons under such leaders.

A foreigner's view of the state of affairs during reconstruction, may perhaps be more impartial than that of
any writer in our own country. Mr. Lecky, the English historian, says :

"The enfranchisement of the negroes added a new and enormous
mass of voters, who were utterly and childishly incompetent. . . For
some time after the war the influence of property and intelligence in
the South was completely broken, and the negro vote was ostensibly
supreme. The consequence was what might have been expected. A
horde of vagrant political adventurers from the North . . . . poured
into the southern provinces and, in conjunction with the refuse of the
mean whites, they undertook the direction of the negro voters.
Then followed, under the protection of northern bayonets, a grotesque
parody of government, a hideous orgie of anarchy, violence, unrestrained corruption, undisguised, ostentatious, insulting robbery, such
as the world had scarcely seen. The state debts were profusely piled
up. Legislation was openly put up for sale. The 'Bosses' were in
all their glory, and they were abundantly rewarded. . . . At length
the northern troops were withdrawn, and the whole scene changed.
The carpet-baggers had had their day, and they returned laden with
southern booty to their own states. Partly by violence, partly by
fraud, but largely through the force of old habits of obedience and
command, the planters in a short time regained their ascendancy.
Sometimes, it is said, they did not even count the negro votes. Gen-

[1] By act of Congress, March 23, 1867. See U. S. Statutes at large,
vol. xv, p. 3.

erally they succeeded in dictating them, and by systematic manipulation or intimidation, they restored the South to quiet and some degree of prosperity. A more curious picture of the effects of democratic equality among a population who were entirely unfitted for it has never been presented." [1]

It was in effect a revolution by force that put the ex-slaves in power. The counter-revolution that restored to power the only residents in the South capable of bringing order out of chaos, was effected by every means that a desperate people could invent. Meantime the impression left upon the minds of the Southern whites was to the last degree unfortunate for the negroes. "Negro domination" became a synonym for all that men of English descent have stubbornly refused to tolerate in government for a thousand years. Unable to protect themselves by legitimate means, because subjected to the federal law, in the making of which, they for the time, had no voice, the whites were compelled to resort to illegal methods. Against an able and politically experienced race, the negroes could not prevail, even in sections where they were much in the majority. Thus, after a brief period of power, the negroes quickly were deprived of it, and have since exercised political rights only on sufferance.

But the danger and dishonor of deliberately ignoring constitutional and legal provisions was keenly felt by the very class that resorted to intimidation and fraud to preserve their civilization. As time went on and the atmosphere became clearer, they began to search for some means by which to effect their object by legal methods. Inasmuch as the states have power to regulate the suffrage so long as they keep within the broad limitations prescribed by the federal constitution, a

---

[1] "Democracy and liberty ", by W. E. H. Lecky, vol. i, pp. 93–4. See also "Union and disunion ", by Woodrow Wilson, pp. 263–4.

movement began about the end of the eighties to secure the main end in view by state constitutional amendments.

In 1890 the state of Mississippi set a precedent by amending her constitution so that after Jan. 1, 1892, no person could vote unless "able to read any section of the Constitution" or "to understand the same when read to him and give a reasonable interpretation thereof."[1] The payment of a poll tax was also required. South Carolina followed in 1895 with an amendment, the effect of which was to require that every voter should be able to read and write any section of the Constitution, or show that he owned and had paid taxes upon property assessed at $300 or more.[2] Louisiana, in 1898, passed an amendment substantially the same in effect as that of South Carolina, but with the addition of a "grandfather clause", which admits illiterate or propertyless whites to the ballot by excusing from the limitations of the amendment all descendants of men who voted previous to the war.[3] North Carolina took similar action in 1900, excepting that no property qualification was required, while the payment of a poll tax was.[4] Alabama and Virginia have very recently passed amendments to the same general end. It is probable that all the states having a large proportion of negro population will ultimately pursue this policy.

It is here no concern of ours to discuss this action as regards its wisdom or justice. It seems to those having to face the problem, to be one of those necessary compromises between ideal principles and actual conditions

[1] See the Annual cyclopedia, vol. xv, pp 559-60.
[2] *Idem.*, vol. xx, p. 705.
[3] *Idem.*, third series, vol. iii, p. 409.
[4] *Idem.*, vol. v. p. 444.

with which our history is full and without which our federal Union never could have existed. But the immediate effect is to disfranchise a large majority of negroes till such time as they can become an intelligent property-owning class, with some appreciation of actual present-day issues and with some interest at stake. Under these circumstances a strong motive is given them to advance themselves in intelligence and material prosperity.

But as the capacity for political self-government is an integral part of general character, the ability to command a proportionate share of governmental power against able competition can hardly exceed the ability to develop industrial importance. In foregoing chapters, however, we have seen that the negroes do not at present give evidence of a general advance in morality or industrial efficiency. It is difficult to avoid the conclusion, therefore, that they are not destined at any early date to regain political power proportionate to their numbers.

Nor can we be surprised at this. Forty years ago the negroes were as little children in political development. To have acquired within forty years what has required the whole range of English and American history for the whites to develop, would have been a marvel without precedent.

Let us glance back over the career of the Negro as we have traced it from his earlier home in Africa. We saw that there the negroes were a semi-nomadic people, living, partly by primitive agriculture, fishing and hunting, and partly upon the free gifts of nature. They had a poor and fluctuating diet, were very scantily clothed, and lived in very simple huts. Their women were made to perform all the drudgery. The value of time and of labor-saving appliances was but dimly appreciated.

They were controlled by present impulses and made no provision for the future.

They dwelt in little village communities and had no regard for life and property outside of these. Even within the village they thought little of destroying the sick or useless, and could not comprehend sentiments of compassion. A large portion of their population was enslaved. Polygamy prevailed, women were bought and sold, and chastity was valued only as a salable commodity. Parental and filial affection, with the exception of that between mother and son, was weak and transient. Social morality was not supported by religion, the gods being supposed to have no interest in the conduct of men toward men.

Their religion was a dark and cruel fetichism. They attributed all events to spirits, to propitiate whom they offered sacrifices, including very often, human victims. They wore charms for protection. Many victims were killed on the charge of witchcraft, and many to supply companionship and service for the departed great in the land of the dead.

With the exception of two or three petty kingdoms, founded upon conquest, the village or group of related villages was the largest political unit known to them. These units were ruled by chiefs in accordance with a few simple customs, interpreted in each special case as the chief might please. Intertribal warfare for slaves and plunder prevailed almost everywhere, and was characterized by horrible cruelties and enormous waste of life.

Such was life along the Guinea coast when Shakespeare was producing his dramas, when Bacon was writing the Novum Organum, when English explorers were sailing every ocean, and English colonists were laying the foundations of our Republic. By a strange destiny the Caucasian and the Negro came to live together under the same flag in North America.

In the course of removal from Africa the negroes were subjected to a drastic selection, which eliminated physically inferior individuals. During slavery a mild form of artificial selection went on. By these experiences the race probably made a gain, which was registered in heredity. The amalgamation in this country of slightly differing tribes was probably beneficial, while that of black with white seems to have resulted in psychic improvement but physical deterioration. The change to a temperate climate, a more steady and substantial diet, and intelligent medical care, was favorable to vigor and energy. Thus the American negroes must have become rapidly superior to their West African contemporaries.

Under white discipline the negroes learned to work more efficiently. The former indolent life of the men was quickly changed into one of useful production, and both sexes acquired skill in many occupations. There gradually appeared at least four classes, viz., the unskilled field-hands, the mechanics, the house-servants, and the sub-overseers and stewards.

The grosser ideas and practices of West African life were soon dropped. Polygamy was forbidden and destroyed as an institution. Monogamy was substituted in form and by thousands was accepted in good faith. Among those more closely associated with the whites, family life became of a much higher type than was ever before known to the Negro race. Christianity was accepted, and though the new religion was debased by many misconceptions and thinly disguised superstitions, it was infinitely superior to the old. The negroes acquired in the English language an improved uniform medium of communication, and along with this their general intelligence was much increased.

At the close of their experience under slavery the negroes had made, therefore, an immense advance in the direction of civilized life. While this was in part founded securely upon a natural basis, it was no doubt due in part to an artificial, forced development. In any case, however, they were still far behind their masters in every element of fitness for highly developed social life. In view of this it was a critical step for them when they ceased to be slaves and became direct competitors of the abler white race in the struggle for life. Since emancipation this competition has relentlessly advanced.

No longer controlled by external force, the negroes have depended for a generation past upon their own self-command. But from time immemorial they have been weak in self-command, they have been dominated by impulse, and inclined to an indolent semi-nomadic existence, and they have possessed an extremely primitive code of morality. Under slavery they were kept widely distributed, in close contact with the whites, so that example and discipline could be very effective against hereditary inclinations. When liberated to follow their own bent, they began to gravitate together until to-day they live isolated, for the most part, from white society. Thus they have lost the stimulus of example, as well as the direct training and discipline, given by the superior race. The strain required to maintain life on the level of the whites is driving the negroes to develop a society of their own, with easier

15

moral standards, better fitted perhaps, to their peculiar temperament. This movement is symptomatic of a dangerous weakness, while at the same time directly contributing to aggravate it.

According to the balance of the evidence now available, it appears that the negroes of the younger generation are restless, unsteady at labor, and impatient of restraint ; that they are yielding place to the whites in many of the better paid employments, and that they are excessively fond of spending for display or other economically unsound purposes. It also appears that in their sexual and family relations there is increasing looseness and instability. Following their strongly gregarious instincts, they are rapidly developing the communal group life afforded through church organization, rather than the private life of the home. Their imperfect socializiation is revealing itself in their criminality, which is increasing at a much greater ratio than the negro population.

Confronted by these facts, we can hardly avoid the conclusion that the heavy task laid upon the American Negro, after liberation from slavery, has proved too much for him, and that this people, considered as a whole, is slowly but surely tending to revert. Seized and transplanted unwillingly, forced sharply into new and severely exacting habits of life, held for a time in this condition of strain, and then suddenly released, the Negro finds it surpassingly difficult to suppress the hereditary instincts that do not harmonize with American social organization. He is finding that two or three centuries are all too brief a period in which to compass almost the entire range of human development.

There is nothing in this conclusion to surprise the

student of evolutionary phenomena. But no right-minded citizen can help deploring it, and hoping that some means may be found of preventing reversion with its inevitable consequence—elimination. Many believe firmly that the magic of education affords the requisite means. Experience has amply demonstrated that mere literary culture will not serve to transform a savage into an efficient member of civilized society. But experience has equally shown that a thorough education of heart and hand, as well as of intellect, will with selected material give valuable results. Applied to all the race, this method could not yield results proportionately great, though a vast amount of good would be done. Meantime, however, only a few thousands are to-day receiving the kind of education critically needed by all the negroes, and almost a half of their number have never received any education at all. In this case a vast educational system is necessary, and under human limitations this cannot be brought into existence and perfected within a brief period. It is not to be forgotten that there are millions of untaught whites also to be provided for. Whatever else happens, hereditary forces, for a time suppressed, will steadily continue to reassert themselves. Obviously, heroic measures are required to reach the millions of negroes.

Surveyed broadly, the outlook for the American negro is not bright. From the native of Guinea to the modern Afro-American is certainly a long step, but from the Guinea natives to the Caucasian builders of our Republic is a yet longer step. It is the hard fate of the transplanted Negro to compete, not with a people of about his own degree of development, but with a race that leads the world in efficiency. This efficiency was reached only through the struggle and sacrifice prescribed by evolutionary law. There are many who believe that a shorter path to greatness exists, since the science of education has been developed. But so long as the powerful conservatism of heredity persists, scarcely admitting of change save through selection of variations, it is to be doubted whether education has the efficiency claimed for it. Time, struggle and sacrifice have always hitherto been required to create a great race. If these are to be exacted of the Negro, he must traverse a long road, not in safe isolation in a country all his own, but in a land filling fast with able, strenuous, and rapidly progressing competitors. Under such circumstances his position can with difficulty be regarded as other than precarious to the last degree.

BIBLIOGRAPHY.

THE NEGRO IN WEST AFRICA.

Adanson, M., "A Voyage to Senegal," 1759 ; see Pinkerton.

Alexander, Sir J. E., "Excursions in West Africa," 2 vols., London, 1840.

Angelo and Carli, "A voyage to Congo," 1667 ; see Pinkerton.

Atkins, John, "A voyage to Guinea," London, 1735.

Barbot, John, "A description of the coast of North and South Guinea," London, 1746 ; see Lintot and Osborne.

Battel, Andrew, "Adventures in Angola" ; see Pinkerton.

Benezet, Anthony, "An historical account of Guinea," Philadelphia, 1771.

Binger, le Captaine, "Du Niger au Golfe de Guinee," 2 vols., Paris, 1892.

Bosman, J., "Description of the coast of Guinea," 1705 ; see Pinkerton.

Brinton, Daniel G., "Races and peoples," N. Y., 1890.

Clarkson, Thomas, "Abolition of the African slave-trade by the British parliament," Wilmington, Del., 1816.

Du Chaillu, Paul, "A Journey to Ashango-land," N. Y., 1867.

Du Chaillu, Paul, "Explorations and adventures in equatorial Africa," N. Y., 1868.

Ellis, A. B., "The Tshi-speaking peoples of the Gold Coast of West Africa," London, 1887.

Ellis, A. B., "The Ewe-speaking peoples of the Slave Coast of West Africa," London, 1890.

Ellis, A. B., "The Yoruba-speaking peoples of the Slave Coast of West Africa," London, 1894.

Ellis, A. B., "A history of the Gold Coast of West Africa," London, 1895.

Froger, the Sieur, "A voyage to Guinea, etc." London, 1696.

Hovelacque and Herve, "Precis d'anthropologie," Paris, 1887.

Keane, A. H., "Ethnology," Cambridge, 1896.

Keane, A. H., "Man : past and present," Cambridge, 1899.

Kingsley, (Miss) Mary, "Travels in West Africa," London, 1897.

Kingsley, (Miss) Mary, "West African Studies," London, 1899.

Lentz, Dr. Oscar, "West Afrika," Berlin, 1878.

Lintot and Osborne, "Collection of voyages, etc.," vol. v, London, 1746.

Livingstone, David, "Missionary travels and researches in South Africa," N. Y., 1858.

MacDonald, George, "The Gold Coast : past and present," N. Y., 1898.

Matthews, John, "A voyage to Sierra Leone," London, 1788.

Merolla, Father Jerom, "A voyage to Congo," 1682 ; see Pinkerton.

Norris, Robert, "Bossa Ahadee : king of Dahomey," London, 1789.

Peschel, Oscar, "The races of man," N. Y., 1876.

Pinkerton, John, "A general collection of the best and most interesting voyages, etc.," vol. xvi, London, 1814.

Proyart, Abbé, "A history of Loango, etc.," 1776 ; see Pinkerton.

Ratzel, Friedrich, "A history of mankind," 3 vols., London, 1896.

Reclus, J. J. E., "Universal geography," vol. xii, London, 1878.

Snelgrave, William, "A new account of Guinea." London, 1734.

Stanford's "Compendium of geography," Africa, 2 vols., London, 1895.

Stanley, H. M., "Through the Dark Continent," 2 vols., N. Y., 1878.

Topinard, Dr. Paul, "Anthropology," London, 1890.

Tylor, E B., "Anthropology," N. Y., 1881.

Waitz, Theodor, "Anthropologie der Naturvölker," band 2, Leipzig, 1860.

Williams, Geo. W., "History of the Negro race in America," N. Y., 1883.

THE NEGRO UNDER AMERICAN SLAVERY.

Abstract of evidence before a select committee of the House of Commons on the slave-trade, London, 1791.

Bandinell, James, "Some account of the trade in slaves from Africa," London, 1842.

Bancroft, George, "History of the United States," Centenary ed., Boston, 1878.

Barringer, Dr. Paul B., "Proceedings of the Montgomery conference," 1900.

Broca, Dr. Paul, "The phenomena of hybridity in the genus homo," London, 1864.

Buxton, T. F., "The African slave-trade," London, 1839.

Clarkson, Thomas, "History of the abolition of slavery," Phila., 1808.

Clayton, Mrs. V. V., "White and black under the old régime," N. Y., 1900.

De Bow, J. D. B., Review of the South and Southwest," New Orleans.

De Bow, J. D. B., "Industrial resources of the South and West," 3 vols., New Orleans, 1853.

Jones, Chas. C., "The religious instruction of the negroes," Savannah, 1842.

Kemble, Fanny, "A journal of a residence on a Georgia plantation," N. Y., 1863.

Long, Edward, "History of Jamaica," 2 vols., London, 1774.

Martineau, Harriet, "Society in America," 2 vols., N. Y., 1837.

Martineau, Harriet, "Retrospect of western travel," 2 vols., N. Y., 1838.

Mayer, Brantz, "Captain Canot ; or twenty years on an African slaver," N. Y., 1854.

Nott, Dr. J. C. and Geo. R. Gliddon, "Types of mankind," Phila., 1871.

Olmsted, Frederick Law, "A journey in the seaboard slave states," N. Y., 1856.

Olmsted, Frederick Law, "A journey through Texas," N. Y., 1859.

Olmsted, Frederick Law, "A journey in the back country," N. Y., 1860.

"Slavery as it is : the testimony of a thousand witnesses," Publications of the Anti-slavery Society, N. Y., 1839.

Smedes, Susan Dabney, "A southern planter," N. Y., 1900.

Spear, John R., "The American slave-trade," N. Y., 1900.

Stirling, James, "Letters from the slave-states," London, 1857.

United States Weather Bureau reports, 1891–2, and 1897–8.

THE NEGRO AS A FREE CITIZEN.

Brackett, J. R., "The progress of the colored people of Maryland since the war," Johns Hopkins Univ. Studies vol. viii, Baltimore, 1890.

Bruce, Philip A., "The plantation Negro as a freeman," N. Y., 1889.

Du Bois, W. E. B., "The Philadelphia Negro," Publications of the Univ. of Pa., no. 14, Phila., 1899.

Du Bois, W. E. B., "The negroes of Farmville, Va.," U. S. Dept. of labor bulletin, no 14, 1898.

Du Bois, W. E. B., "The negroes of the black belt," U. S. Dept. of labor bulletin, no. 22, 1899.

Du Bois, W. E B., "The negro land-holders of Georgia," U. S. Dept. of labor, bulletin no. 35, 1901.

Hoffman, Fred. L., "The race traits and tendencies of the American Negro," Am. Econ. Assoc. publications, vol. xi, N. Y., 1896.

Ingle, Edward, "Southern side-lights," Boston, 1896.

Ingle, Edward, "The negro in the District of Columbia," Johns Hopkins Univ. Studies, vol. xi, Baltimore, 1893.

Laws, J. B., "The negroes of Cinclare central factory and Calumet plantation," U. S. Dept. of labor, bulletin no. 38, 1902.

Montgomery conference on southern race problems," Proceedings, 1900.

Morgan, Dr. T. J., "The Negro in America," Phila., 1898.

"The negroes in cities," (a compilation), U. S. Dept. of labor, bulletin no. 10, 1897

"The college-bred Negro," Atlanta Univ. publications, no. 5.

Thom, Walter T., "The negroes of Sandy Spring, Md.," U. S. Dept. of labor, bulletin no. 32, 1901.

Thom, Walter T., "The negroes of Litwalton, Va.," U. S. Dept. of labor, bulletin no. 37, 1901.

Thomas, Wm. H., "The American Negro," N. Y., 1901.

Thrasher, Max B., "Tuskegee : its story and its work," Boston, 1901.

"Twenty-two years work of the Hampton, etc.," (a compilation), Hampton press, 1893.

Washington, Booker T., "The future of the American Negro," Boston, 1899.

Washington, Booker T., "Up from slavery," N. Y., 1901.

U. S. Commissioner of education, reports, 1897–8, and 1898–9.

NOTE :—This list is not presented as a complete bibliography. It contains only the works actually used in the preparation of the text.

AMERICAN ECONOMIC ASSOCIATION

THIRD SERIES.	ISSUED QUARTERLY.
VOL. III, NO. 3.	PRICE, $4.00 PER YEAR.

A HISTORY

OF

AXATION IN NEW HAMPSHIRE

BY

MAURICE H. ROBINSON, PH.D.

AUGUST, 1902

PUBLISHED FOR THE
AMERICAN ECONOMIC ASSOCIATION
BY THE MACMILLAN COMPANY
NEW YORK
LONDON: SWAN SONNENSCHEIN & CO.

PRESS OF
ANDRUS & CHURCH,
ITHACA, N. Y.

PREFACE.

The field of local financial history, so long unculti-
vated in this country, has during the past two decades
been receiving in some measure the attention its importance demands.   Interest in this subject seems to
have been awakened chiefly through two widely different lines of influence : (1) the extraordinary taxation
necessitated by the financial burdens of the Civil War,
and (2) the introduction of the German methods of historical research into the universities of this country by
American scholars.   The former of the two influences
made its mark earlier, the latter has more effectually
shaped the methods of investigation and has perhaps
exerted the wider sway.   As instances of works on finance
whose inception may be traced with considerable direct-
ness to the influence of war taxation we may mention
the contributions of David A. Wells, Charles F. Dunbar, William G. Sumner, Albert S. Bolles, Henry C.
Adams, and others.   Among investigations due primarily to the influence of German methods of historical
study, Ely's Taxation in American states and cities
(1888) seems to have led the way, and the path thus
blazed has been followed with constantly increasing zeal
until the financial history of the thirteen original colonies has been quite fully explored.

In adding to these financial histories the following
history of taxation in New Hampshire, the writer desires to acknowledge his deep obligation to the authors
who have preceded him, and to call special attention to
three points in the financial history of New Hampshire,
which have seemed to him deserving of more than pass-

ing mention : (1) The healthful influence of the English government in preventing hazardous experiments with currency and the taxes, (2) the early establishment of the legislative authority over the budget, and (3) the very gradual evolution of the system of taxation in the state from provincial times down to the present day. The last may be noticed in tracing the ease with which the state passed over from income theory as a basis for its system of provincial taxes to the property basis of the nineteenth century, a change so gradually effected that the closest student of the subject will find it difficult to decide when the one method was abandoned and the other substituted. This gradual evolution is again noticable in the grafting of the system of corporation taxes so prominent at the present time on to the general property tax system which was the dominant characteristic of the taxation of the first half of the past century. It will be noticed that almost no attention has been given to taxation in the cities. Such omission is due not to lack of interest but to lack of time and space.

In conclusion the author wishes to acknowledge his very great obligation to James Fairbanks Colby, Professor in Dartmouth College, to whose suggestion this study owes its origin. Professor Colby very kindly read the study in the manuscript, and to his helpful criticism it owes much of whatever value it may possess. In preparing the work for the press and in reading the proof the writer has labored under the disadvantage of working far from the sources of authority, and therefore of necessity some errors in citations, and possibly of statement, may have crept in which under more favorable conditions might have been avoided.

Urbana, Ill., January, 1903.

CONTENTS.

CHAPTER I.

AUTHORITY FOR THE IMPOSITION OF TAXES.

SEC. 1. *The Authority of the Towns.* The council of Plymouth had no authority to delegate its power of government over the lands granted to its patentees.[1] The king failed to establish a government over the New Hampshire towns until 1680. Therefore, whatever authority the *de facto* governments possessed over the four New Hampshire towns until the above date must have rested on the voluntary consent of the people. Portsmouth and Dover both received comparatively large additions to their numbers about 1632. From 1633, when the first signs of an elementary political organization appeared, until the date of the respective combinations, authority was exercised by the leading men of the companies owning the patents, with the tacit consent of the people.[2] With the growth of the towns such a government proved unsatisfactory to the law-abiding element,[3] and recourse was had to a political compact, based upon the free consent of the signers, whereby they solemnly pledged themselves to abide by the will of the majority. Unfortunately the Portsmouth compact is lost, and in its absence we may ascribe to the banished church congregation at Exeter the first known agreement in New Hampshire, July 4, 1639, to submit to taxes imposed by the major part of

[1] Decision of Lord Chief Justice, July 20, 1677, given in full in I Belknap's N. H., App., xxviii.

[2] The first governor seems to have been appointed by the patentees. Very soon afterwards the historians speak of the people's electing the officials. I N. H. Prov. papers, 110–119.

[3] Preamble to Dover combination, I N. H. Prov. papers, 126.

the freemen. This agreement is found in the oath [1] of the people, taken probably in connection with the election of the first officials. No especial reference to the power of taxation occurs in the Dover combination, but such power is, of course, implied in the agreement to submit to "all such laws as shall be concluded by a major part of the freemen of our society." [2]

That the Portsmouth combination gave the authorities the power of taxation, either directly or with the approval of a majority vote of the inhabitants, is evidenced by the grant of the glebe on the 25th of May, 1640. [3] Fifty acres of land were granted to the parish to continue in perpetuity for parish uses. As Hampton was thought to be within the boundaries of Massachusetts, it was at once given the powers of a township and entered upon its corporate life in accordance with a system already organized.

SEC. 2. *The Authority of Massachusetts.* By the terms of the union with Massachusetts in 1641, the towns on the Pascataqua, Portsmouth and Dover, were "accepted and reputed under the government of the Massachusetts as the rest of the inhabitants within the said jurisdiction are". [4] A provisional government was provided for until the next meeting of the general court, and until such agreement could be effected the authorities under "the late combination" were empowered "to govern the people there". [4] It was stipulated that the New Hamp-

[1] "We do swear by the great and dreadful name of the high God maker and governor of heaven and earth . . . that . . we will be ready to assist thee [the rulers] with our bodies and our goods and best endeavors." I N. H. Prov. papers, 134.

[2] Dover combination, I N. H. Prov. papers, 126. X N. H. Prov. papers, 700.

[3] Annals of Portsmouth, App., 394-6.

[4] I Mass. Col. rec., 319.

shire towns received into the union should "be subject to pay in church and commonweale as the said inhabitants of the Massachusetts bay do and no others,"[1] with the following qualification: "They shall be exempted from all publique charges other than those that shall arise for, or from among themselves or from any occasion or course that may be taken to procure their own particular good or benefit."[2] Courts were established, the towns were allowed two deputies in the general court, and the next year the freemen in the several towns were formally guaranteed the right of self-government in local affairs. Exeter was assumed to be a part of Massachusetts; Hampton was *de facto* by settlement. Thus the Massachusetts system of taxation was established in the New Hampshire towns almost from the very beginning of the exercise of that sovereign power, and continued for thirty-nine years—a fact that accounts for much that existed in the New Hampshire provincial system of taxation.

SEC. 3. *The Establishment of Legislative Authority.* The commission of 1680,[3] establishing the provincial government in New Hampshire, distinctly recognized the right of the people, through their legal representatives, to impose public taxes. The president and council were authorized, required, and commanded "to issue forth summons for" a general assembly, "within three months after they have bin sworn". In the meantime said president and council were authorized and required "to continue such taxes and impositions as have bin and are now laid and imposed upon the inhabitants

[1] I Mass. Col. rec., 305.
[2] I Mass. Col. rec., 319.
[3] I N. H. Prov. papers, 373-382.

thereof in the best and most equal manner they can, until a general assembly of ye sd province shall be called and other method for yt purpose agreed upon." However, when such assembly should have been legally organized in accordance with the above provision, the assembly was authorized by the royal commission " to consider the fittest ways for rasing of taxes and in such proportion as may be fit for ye support of ye sd government."[1] "All and every such acts, laws and ordinances" made by such general assembly or assemblies " shall first be approved and allowed by the president and council for the time being and thereupon shall stand and be in force until ye pleasure of us, our heirs and successors shall be known whether ye said laws, and ordinances shall receive any change of confirmation or be totally disallowed and discharged." All acts, laws, and ordinances were to be forwarded to the crown by the first ship that should depart thence to England "after their making". Soon after this, February 10, 1680, a special order was issued to constables requiring them to gather in all rates previously levied, giving them the power of distraint, and declaring that the council would cause restitution to be made to any person appearing to them to " be injured by over-rating ".[2] The same day a general assembly was summoned to meet at Portsmouth on the 16th day of March following.[3] The assembly was organized on that date,[4] enacted a body of laws, and exercised the power of taxation granted by the commission in two successive years,[5] without question from any

---

[1] Commission of Governor Cutt, I N. H. Prov. papers, 380.
[2] Coun. rec., XIX, N. H. State papers, 657.
[3] Coun. rec., XIX, N. H. State papers, 658.
[4] Coun. rec., XIX, N. H. State papers, 662.
[5] I N. H. Prov. papers, 424–428.

source. The president and councilors commissioned in 1680 were, without exception, representative men of the province. Many of them had served their towns both in local affairs and as deputies in the larger political life of the general court of Massachusetts.

The appointment of Cranfield as lieutenant governor in 1682 marked the introduction of elements from without the province into the official positions. Although by his commission,[1] May 9, 1682, Cranfield was granted extraordinary powers, he even exceeded his authority.[2] With the consent and advice of the council he was to summon and call general assemblies "as need shall require". The governor was authorized to prorogue and dissolve general assemblies and had a negative upon all legislative acts. He was authorized further to suspend any member from the council and fill the vacancy —the act debarring the member so suspended from sitting in the assembly. The powers of the legislature over the revenue were otherwise unchanged. An assembly was called November 14, 1682,[3] which authorized "a rate of four pence in the pound upon all persons and estates".[4] Out of this tax a present of two hundred pounds was voted to the governor[5] in the hope of securing his favor toward the province.[6] At the second session of the assembly the governor and council proposed a bill for raising revenue, to which the representatives refused their assent. The representatives proposed several revenue bills which the governor declared to be

[1] I N. H. Prov. papers, 433–443.
[2] Report of Lords of Trade, I N. H. Prov. papers, 569–572.
[3] I Belknap's N. H., 192.
[4] Laws, 1682, I N. H. Prov. papers, 448.
[5] Laws, 1682, I N. H. Prov. papers, 448.
[6] I Belknap's N. H., 192.

contrary to law.[1] Cranfield then dissolved the house,
January 20, 1683,[2] and with his council assumed the
whole legislative power. The attempt was made to secure
revenue for the support of the government by means of
excessive fees, fines, and rents[3] from those occupying
lands claimed by the Masonian proprietors, in addition
to the usual excise, tonnage dues, and customs. Failing
in this a third assembly was summoned to meet at
Great Island, January 14, 1684.[4] A bill was presented
to the house "for raising money to defray the expense of
repairing the fort and supplying it with ammunition
and other necessary charges of government." The next
day[5] the house refused to pass the bill and was immediately dissolved. Disappointed in securing a sufficient revenue either by indirect means or through an
assembly, Cranfield, February 14, 1684,[6] secured the reluctant consent of his council to an order continuing "all
such taxes and impositions as have been formerly laid

---

[1] "The governor recommended to them several good bills that had
passed the council, . . they either rejected, or put them into such a
disguise as rendered them altogether useless, and afterwards would
not take notice of any bills which did not arise from themselves ; they
likewise peremptorily insisted to have the nomination of judges and
the appointing of courts of judicature, power solely invested in the
governor by commission from his Majesty ; and lastly, they had prepared bills repugnant to the laws of England, upon which the governor, finding them to act without any regard to his Majesty's service,
or benefit of the province, after he had passed some bills, not knowing where these matters would end, dissolved the assembly." Letter
of Edward Randolph to the Lords of Trade, I N. H. Prov. papers, 491–
496.

[2] I Belknap's N. H., 193 ; Randolph's report, I N. H. Prov. papers,
493.

[3] Weare's Complaint to the crown, I N. H. Prov. papers, 515–519.

[4] I Belknap's N. H., 203.

[5] The members are said to have passed the night in Portsmouth,
probably in consultation with their friends.

[6] I N. H. Prov. papers, 488. The warrants were issued May 10,
1684. *Idem*, 490.

upon the inhabitants."[1] The order was to be kept secret until the need for revenue should appear more pressing. In the mean time the Lords of Trade had sent an order directing Cranfield to make use of an assembly in raising taxes.[2] A fourth assembly was summoned May 27, 1684,[3] but was immediately dissolved on account of their "mutinous and rebellious disposition". The constables were ordered to collect the rate authorized by the council. The people uniformly refused to pay the so-called tax,[4] and the courts to enforce the order. The provost marshal of the province was "impowered and required" to collect the rate and authorized to call upon the constables for assistance "between sun rising and sun setting . . . forceing open dores for the better and more effectual getting in said rates." He was beaten by the men, and threatened with scalding water by the women.[5] The resistance to the tax was intensified by the deep-seated belief that Cranfield was personally interested in the claims of Robert Mason to the lands

[1] "Excepting only the rate of one penny in the pound raised in time of usurpation." I N. H. Prov. papers, 488-9.

[2] I Belknap's N. H., 213.

[3] I Belknap's N. H., 213.

[4] One of the collectors testified "that almost all of them answer that the commissioners directed that the taxes should be raised by the general assembly." I N. H. Prov. papers, 544, 496, 508, 543, 554.

[5] Thurston, the provost marshal, testified : "The wife of Moses Gilman (of Exeter) did say that she had provided a kettle of scalding water for him, if he came to her house, which had been over the fire two days;" also, "certain husbandmen of Hampton did follow the deponent and deputy marshal . . . from the town of Hampton, all on horse-back, into Exeter, being armed with clubs, and there came to the said company John Cotton, minister of Exeter, with a club in his hand, and the said company did push this deponent and his deputy up and down the house, asking them what they did wear at their sides, laughing at this deponent and his deputy for having swords." Deposition of Thomas Thurston, provost marshal, I N. H. Prov. papers, 551-554.

within the bounds of the province.   One of the foremost citizens, Nathaniel Weare, was secretly dispatched to England to secure redress. [1]   The case was referred to the Lords of Trade, a hearing granted, [2] and on March 27, 1685, a decision [3] sustaining the charges of the petitioners was handed down.   As a consequence Cranfield vacated his office.   Thus early in the history of the infant province the old world struggle between the forces of absolutism on the one hand, and the commons on the other, appeared.   The issue was met fairly, fought out, as has been the wont of the English race, in legal channels, and the victory was with the people.

In the next attack the charge was made on a larger field, and the result was more decisive.   In the Andros government, established June 3, 1686, all governmental powers were in the hands of the governor and the major part of his council, nominated by the crown.   The right of the people to impose taxes upon themselves was nowhere recognized.   The revenue from the excise and impost was increased, and on January 13, 1687, Andros and his council attempted to exercise the power of taxation granted them by the crown by authorizing an assessment of " a single country rate of one penny in the pound, according to former usage." [4]   In the absence of records in the Andros period it is impossible to tell whether the New Hampshire towns submitted to the inevitable or made a vain resistance. [5]   With the first rumors of the revolution in England the government of

---

[1] Copy of complaint presented by Weare, I N. H. Prov. papers, 515.

[2] Copy of order of Lords of Trade, I N. H. Prov. papers, 519.

[3] Report of Lords of Trade, I N. H. Prov. papers, 569–570.

[4] Mass. Hist. Coll., vii, 3d series, 171.

[5] The selectmen of Ipswich, Mass., refused to make the levy, and were heavily fined.   I Holmes' Annals, 425.

Andros fell, April 18, 1689.[1] The absolutist reaction
had been met on both sides of the water by the rising
spirit of liberalism. The conflict and the successful
issue further strengthened the New England colonists
to meet succeeding inroads upon their rights in whatever way they might appear.

Left without a government, the New Hampshire
towns—Dover, Portsmouth, Exeter, and Hampton—
made several attempts to form a temporary government.[2]
Through the action of Hampton the plan failed.[3] A
very large element in the four towns naturally desired
to resume their union with Massachusetts, and danger
from the Indians was imminent. A petition drawn up
at Portsmouth, February 20, 1690, addressed to the governor and council of Massachusetts recites that

We, who have been under your government, having been for some
time destitute of power sufficient to put ourselves into a capacity of
defence against the common enemy . . . are necessitate to supplicate
your Honors for government and protection as formerly . . . hereby
obliging ourselves to a due submission thereto, and payment of our
equal proportion (according to our capacity) of the charge that shall
arise for the defence of the country against the common enemy.[4]

The petition, signed by four hundred citizens of the
province of New Hampshire, was granted by the governor and council, approved by the general court, and, on

---

[1] II N. H. Prov. papers, 20.

[2] Town records, given in II N. H. Prov. papers, 30-34.

[3] "But whereas the inhabitants of the town of Hampton meet on
warning for that end [to consider a form of government for the four
towns], the major part by far of the said towne seemed to be ferful
and suspicious of therer neighbor towns [that] they did not intend to
doe as was pretended but to bring them under to theyer disadvantage
which I thought was very ill so to think, yet they would give some
instance of som former acts don." Letter of Nathaniel Weare, Mar.
16, 1690, II N. H. Prov. papers, 43-46.

[4] From the humble address of the inhabitants and trained soldiers
of the province of N. H., Feb. 20, 1689-90, II N. H. Prov. papers, 34-
39.

March 19, 1690, a list of officers for each town was presented and accepted by the above authorities.[1]   During
this second union of two years with Massachusetts, taxes
both local and general were levied and collected "agreeable to former custom ".[2]   With the reëstablishment of
the province, in 1692, the form of government and the respective powers of the governor, council, and assembly
were essentially the same as in the establishment in
1680, with the exceptions that the negative over the
acts of the assembly and the power to prorogue and dissolve said body remained with the governor as in the
Cranfield commission.

The period from 1692 to 1700 was a critical one in
the financial history of the province.[3]   Lieutenant Governor Usher, armed with the powers granted by the
royal commission, attempted at first to become the director and manager of the legislature.   May 12, 1694, he
sent for the lower house and made a speech to them
"about the absolute necessity of raising money " for
military purposes.[4]   On the 17th of the month[5] he sent
down " to the lower house to know whether they had
done anything as to the raising of money for the support of the government in the province as to his proposals layd before them."   Being answered in the negative, he summoned them into his semi-royal presence and
" made a speach to them abt raising money as formerly."
Again, on the 22d of the month, after the house had
asserted their inability to make further appropriations,

---

[1] II N. H. Prov. papers, 40.
[2] II N. H. Prov. papers, 41.
[3] Governor Allen had purchased the Masonian claims and the acting
Governor, Lieut. Gov. Usher, had been an official high in the councils
of the Andros government.
[4] Journal of council and assembly, III N. H. Prov. papers, 18.
[5] Journal of council and assembly, III N. H. Prov. papers, 30.

the lieutenant governor requested the lower house to appoint two members to join with the council to "view the fortifications and report as to what was necessary for their defence." Upon the refusal of the house to make any reply to his message, "the lieutenant-governor sent down and commanded them in their majesties names to sit *de die diem* until they had sent up an answer positive."[1] The house persisted in their refusal to pass the lieutenant governor's revenue bills and two days later were dissolved.[2] For two years—1695 and 1696—the house provided revenue sufficient to meet the ordinary expenses, but refused, on account of their poverty, to make provision for the support of the lieutenant governor or of the fortifications and their garrison. The governor charged them with providing for the "maintenance of the ministry" and "town charges" to the neglect of the support of his royal Majesty's commission,[3] and added that he "shall lay the same before the King . . . and wait for orders and directions from him."[4] He then dissolved the assembly. In the meantime the opponents of Usher, under the leadership of Waldron and Vaughn, had secured the appointment of William Partridge, a popular merchant of Portsmouth who was in political accord with the house of representatives, to succeed Usher as lieutenant governor. The commission was obtained of the Lords Justices in the king's absence, through Partridge's friendship with Sir Henry Ashurst.[5] The popular party were now in control and proceeded to remodel the government in the interests of

---

[1] Journal of council and assembly, III N. H. Prov. papers, 22.
[2] III N. H. Prov. papers, 23.
[3] III N. H. Prov. papers, 46.
[4] III N. H. Prov. papers, 48.
[5] I Belknap's N. H., 207.

the people and to fill the offices with adherents of the popular party. September 15, 1698,[1] Governor Allen appeared, took the oath, and assumed control. A little
later Usher appeared in the province. Governor Allen's
attempted interference with the collection of the tax
previously voted called upon him the just censure of the
house. That body further warned him that unless he
should " see cause to redress their grievances and carry
on with a more moderate conduct,"[2] the house would
make a second application to his Lordship (Lord Bellemont) for relief. The next day, January 7, the assembly voted to continue the " impost, excise and powder
money ", but to keep the income in the treasury until
after the arrival of Lord Bellemont.[3] The governor
attempted to justify his interference with collecting
the last rate upon the ground that " complaint from
several towns of moneys raised and misapplied " had
caused the order " to forbear gathering until the accounts might be examined." He assured the house
that he should " order the moneys to be gathered and
paid to the treasurer," and after advising them " to act
safely " declared the house dissolved January 17, 1699.[4]
Although the officials in sympathy with the house and
the people refused to serve under him,[5] Governor Allen
did not further attempt to control the revenue. With
the accession of Lord Bellemont to the governorship,
July 31, 1699, the first distinct recognition on the part

---

[1] Coun. rec., II N. H. Prov. papers, 276.

[2] Address of the house to Governor Samuel Allen, Jan. 6, 1699, II
N. H. Prov. papers, 289.

[3] Coun. rec., II N. H. Prov. papers, 191.

[4] Governor's address to the house, Coun. rec., II N. H. Prov.
papers, 293.

[5] On the ground that he had violated the king's commission in
allowing Usher a seat in the council.

of a royal governor of the right of the house of representatives to originate and be mainly responsible for public taxes appeared. In his inaugural address before the general assembly, Governor Bellemont, turning to the house, said : " I recommend to you, gentlemen of the house of representatives, the providing for the necessary support of the government, you being the best able to judge what the charge will be and its belonging to you of right to provide the means to defray the charge." [1]

The right of the house of representatives to control the public purse, thus definitely recognized by the royal governor, was enjoyed without question for a third of a century, 1699–1732. During this period the house exercised great freedom, both as to the manner of the levy and as to the amount of the tax. The governor advised the house in regard to taxation, [2] but did not attempt to coerce through repeated vetoes or dissolutions. The governor annually directed the treasurer to lay the accounts [3] before the house of representatives that they might the better estimate the needs of the province. [4] On one occasion the house even entered complaint with the governor that the members of the council were not sufficiently representative of the interests of the province and being chiefly interested in trade had prevented equitable taxation upon the merchant classes. Hence, when Governor Belcher attempted to compel the house to conform the method of taxation to a course marked

---

[1] III N. H. Prov. papers, 67.

[2] See section on Impost, *post.*

[3] See Prov. accounts, 1724–43, V N. H. Prov. papers, 29–32.

[4] Cranfield in 1682 was directed to permit the house to view the accounts from time to time. The same direction was repeated to Governor Allen, 1692. From the latter date the house regularly inspected the accounts without objection before voting the revenue bills.

out by the crown, he was met by an organization strongly intrenched behind custom and supported by a constituency that brooked with impatience any interference from without over local affairs.

In his inaugural address to the legislature Governor Belcher reaffirmed the doctrine laid down by Governor Bellemont. Addressing the gentlemen of the house of representatives he said : "As it is more immediately your province to look into the state of the public revenue, I shall order all the accounts from the last time you had them, to be laid before you, with proper estimates, of what may be the growing charge that you may grant the necessary supplies."[1] In accordance with the king's specific instructions,[2] the house very reluctantly consented (1730) to settle an annual salary of two hundred pounds sterling[3] upon the governor during his continuance in office.[4] Upon the fourth day of the first session Governor Belcher reported that "as the charge of the province will be growing" he had liberty "to emit from time to time what bills of credit may be necessary to defray the expense thereof." During the first session a bill providing for the emission of thirteen hundred pounds in bills of credit to be paid by a tax in 1742 was passed and signed without objection. In the adjourned session, December 3, 1730, an emission of seven hundred pounds was added. In 1731 the house

[1] IV N. H. Prov. papers, 563.

[2] Thirty-second instructions, IV N. H. Prov. papers, 564.

[3] Equal to 600 pounds in bills of credit of the province. IV N. H. Prov. papers, 570

[4] "As to the settlement of a salary, according to his Majesties instructions we have to say that the sum therein mentioned is extraordinary, we being a small and generally poor people, and especially considering the encroachments of our neighbors and the stagnation of our trade from the want of a medium to carry it on." Address of house to Governor Belcher, Aug. 28, 1730, IV N. H. Prov. papers, 565.

and council failed to agree upon a bill for the supply of the treasury and no provision was made for public taxes.

Governor Belcher, addressing the house of representatives in 1732, called attention to the treasury, and said:

By the small account which the commissioners of the treasury will lay before you, you will see there is no money in the treasury and I doubt not you will think it inconsistent with the safety and honor of his majesties government, or the peace and welfare of his subjects for the treasury to remain empty, and that you will therefore in duty to the King and a just regard to the people make the necessary supply to the treasury as early as may be this session.

The house replied that " our circumstances are so that if there should be an additional tax upon the polls and estates of the inhabitants of this province, it would have a greater tendency to fill the publick gaols than supply the treasury," [1] and advised that " some other method must be found out " for supplying the treasury.

The house proposed, May 16th, 1732, an emission of one thousand pounds in bills of credit " to be brought in by a tax on the polls and estates of the inhabitants of this province in the year 1744." [2] The secretary of the council immediately returned the vote with a message from his Excellency that he " cannot make money go beyond the year 1742." [3] Finding that the house was resolved to levy no tax that he could consent to without disregarding the royal instructions, the governor called the house to the council chamber and said:

I am very sorry the great business of the sessions [the supply of the treasury] remains undone, notwithstanding I have so early and so often recommended it to your especial care as a matter more immediately belonging to your house, yet after all I find you are resolved to make no supply of the treasury that can be agreed to by his Majesties council or by me, which is to say you will make none and this you

[1] Address to the governor, IV N. H. Prov. papers, 618.
[2] Journal of house, IV N. H. Prov. papers, 621.
[3] IV N. H. Prov. papers, 622.

persist in under pretence of the difficulty that the supplying the treasury in the usual manner might bring upon the inhabitants : But how specious and vaine is such an *amus'mt*? When a tax of (1000) one thousand pounds for the present yeare would be sufficient, and in time of war it has been common for the province to pay a tax of 2 or 3000 a year without any complaint, altho' the inhabitants were then far less in number and the land not cultivated or improved to any degree as they are now. I find therefore, gentlemen of the assembly, that the assurance that you gave me at the beginnings of the sessions . . . were only words, of course, and on which there was to be no dependence.[1]

The assembly was then dissolved, May 18, 1732.

For the next five years a new house was called annually, the towns returned essentially the same body of men, their bills were non-concurred in the council, the governor berated them for their injustice, incivility, and lack of wisdom, and then dissolved the assembly. In 1733 the house proposed an issue of one thousand pounds in bills of credit to be paid in the next ten years by a tax of one hundred pounds each year, and as a rider a twenty thousand pound loan to run for sixteen years at 5 per cent interest.[2] In 1734 the house voted three thousand pounds in bills of credit to run beyond 1742.[3] In 1735 the house entered a vigorous protest against repeated dissolutions[4] " which seems to compel to a way of acting contrary to the interest of the people we represent." [5] In the same year the house presented a bill for supplying the treasury, specifying minutely the purposes for which the sums should be appropriated and requiring that they should be used for no other ends.

---

[1] IV N. H. Prov. papers, 623.

[2] IV N. H. Prov. papers, 635.

[3] IV N. H. Prov. papers, 655.

[4] IV N. H. Prov. papers, 688 and 692.

[5] " Whatever different sentiments your Excellency may entertain, are very unhappy *presidents*, and that such a matter would be tho't a grievance not only by the representative body of this people, but by assemblys of the neighboring province." Address to the governor, House journal, IV N. H. Prov. papers, 688.

This bill was presented again in 1736, but in slightly modified form. It provided for an emission of four thousand pounds in bills of credit, " to be signed off " in such quantities as the general assembly should order, " to be for such payments and allowances as hereinafter in this act is expressed and for no other uses, intents and purposes whatsoever." A tax for one-half the sum appropriated (£3381 : 14 : 8) was granted " according to such rates and proportions as shall be agreed upon by this court in the spring sessions in the yeare 1742." Payment was to be made in " bills of credit of this province or any of the neighboring governments, or hemp or flax grown in the province at the current price." Each of the above bills was promptly voted down by the council and hence did not reach the governor. The council refused to sanction the bill of 1733 " because the emission of bills on loan was (as the house has been heretofore once and again informed) directly contrary to his $M_a{}^{Jties}$ Royal instructions; " the council further said that the house had united the two parts of the bill so that " if the thousand pounds for the supply of the treasury would not tempt the council to break thro' the King's instructions, their complyance with the King's instructions should defeat the supply of the treasury." [1] The council amended the bill of 1734 by providing that the three thousand pounds " be bro't into the assembly and burnt in thirds, viz: in the year 1740, 1741, 1742." They gave as their reason " that his $M_a{}^{Jtie}$ had prohibited his Excelly to sign any emission of bills to be outstanding beyond that year." [2] The council

---

[1] Message of council to house, Mar. 10, 1733, IV N. H. Prov. papers, 643.

[2] IV N. H. Prov. papers, 655.

objected to the bill as presented in 1735[1] for the following reasons : (1) the governor's salary was not fully provided for ; (2) it provided for a payment of three
hundred pounds to Mr. Tomlinson (the agent of the
house in London); (3) as there was no act giving
bounty on hemp[2] "the council don't think it proper to
grant a bounty ; "[3](4) " there is no fund for the intended
emission as there may be no spring session in 1742, and
if there should be, who knows that the three parts of
the legislature would certainly agree ; " (5) other
than New Hampshire bills were specified in the tax for
calling in the bills. The house immediately signified
their readiness to omit from the list the bills of credit of
other provinces, but otherwise adhered to their bill as
presented. In 1736 the council conceded to the house
all essential points at issue except one : they refused to
sanction the appropriation to Mr. Tomlinson directly,
but would allow it under the guise of a payment " toward
the carrying on the affaire of the lines " under the direction of a committee of both houses.[4] The bill for the
supply of the treasury was accepted by the council and
signed by the governor as it passed the house, March 23,
1737.[5] It authorized the emission of six thousand five
hundred pounds in bills of credit to be paid by a tax of
four thousand pounds in the year 1741, and two thousand five hundred pounds in 1742. Bills of credit of the
province, and hemp, flax, bar iron, and silver were to be
received at prices specified in the act for the tax. The
payment for Mr. Tomlinson was increased to five hundred

---

[1] IV N. H. Prov. papers, 693.
[2] House journal, Jan. 11, 1733, IV N. H. Prov. papers, 655.
[3] They add, " Some, however, are ready to come into a bounty."
[4] IV N. H. Prov. papers, 710.
[5] IV N. H. Prov. papers, 722 and 733.

pounds and the council pacified by appropriating it for the agency in Great Britain. The house secured also an appropriation of five hundred pounds towards defraying the charge of the commissioners and the committee "that are or may be appointed to mark out the boundary lines." The bill was a compromise and its passage marked a truce. The house had prevented a direct tax and had put off the day of payment for the bills of credit to the farthest limit set by the crown. They had secured appropriations for their agent in London, Mr. Tomlinson, and for the commission[1] of the boundary line, two matters in which the house was especially interested and which the governor and his party of the council accepted with ill grace.

The treasury having been supplied, the old differences manifested themselves immediately. Several further appropriations were defeated by the failure of the two houses to agree. In 1738[2] the assembly was dissolved before the treasury bill was reached. The next house was called in 1739,[3] but was prorogued until January 31, 1740.[4] At the opening of the session the governor addressed the "gentlemen of the council and of the house of representatives" as follows: "The last ships from England have brought us his $^{Ma^{jties}}$ declaration of war against the King of Spain and this extraordinary

---

[1] "If some of your *line wretches* had one about their necks, it would be but a piece of justice they richly deserve from the province. I look upon that matter at an end upon the present footing : and pray which of 'em is politician enough to know what to do next? How barbarous would it be for the people of your province to be burdened with taxes to pay the charge of their vile management." Letter [confidential] of Governor Belcher to Secretary Waldron, Aug. 23, 1736, VI N. H. Prov. papers, 879.

[2] V N. H. Prov. papers, 9.

[3] V N. H. Prov. papers, 9.

[4] V N. H. Prov. papers, 10.

event will greatly affect the commerce and safety of the
province, it ought, then, to be your first care in this
sessions to have the publick treasury well supplyed that
the frontiers by sea and land may be put into a state of
defence. You will also take the needful care for paying
the just debts of the province & for the further support of the government." [1] The governor proceeded
to charge the defenceless state of the province to the
failure of the house to provide the necessary means.
With much vigor and ability the house, in turn, defended their action in the past, and charged the negligence
upon the failure of the governor to give his assent to
acts passed by the house. Taking advantage of the
situation, the house expressed their displeasure at the
action of the governor in dissolving the last house before
the appropriations were reached : they affirmed that "if
now we should make that ample supply that your
Excellency recommends & emit such a quantity of bills
as are needful for that purpose unless the period of their
being called in can extend beyond the yeare 1742, we
fear it would be an insupportable burden to the people
and we should bring upon ourselves a greater and more
certain misery than that which we pretend to remedy." [2]
Calling attention to their acknowledged position in
regard to the treasury the house added : "and here we
cannot but take notice that tho' your Excellency
directs your speach to the council conjointly with us as
to the matter of the treasury, we the representatives of
the province look upon ourselves as the persons that are
more immediately concerned and that we are principally
and directly to be appealed to on that head." [3] Three

[1] V N. H. Prov. papers, 11.

[2] Answer to governor's message, House journal, Feb. 15, 1740, V
N. H. Prov. papers, 18-20.

[3] II N. H. Prov. papers, 18.

times within a little more than a year[1] the general assembly was dissolved.   During the August session, 1740,
an appropriation of two thousand pounds in bills of
credit, with a tax of the same amount to be laid in the
year 1742, was made to aid an expedition against the
West Indies.

The stout resistance of the house of representatives to
the arbitrary administration of Governor Belcher[2] bore
its first fruit in the appointment of Benning Wentworth
as governor to supersede Belcher, December 13, 1741.[3]
With Wentworth's administration complete legislative
authority in the imposition of taxes was established.
During his long service,[4] while he did not hesitate to
question the power of the house in regard to other mat-

---

[1] Feb. 26, 1740, Aug. 7, 1740, and Mar. 18, 1741.

[2] The whole controversy over taxation was complicated by the boundary line contest with Massachusetts.   A powerful faction was formed
in New Hampshire under the leadership of Lieutenant Governor Dunbar, Benning Wentworth, Theo. Atkinson, John Rindge, and others.
This faction controlled the house throughout the administration, and
gradually secured an able minority in the council.   The house maintained an agent at the court in London, Mr. Rindge, and afterwards
Mr. Tomlinson, through whose instrumentality the crown was led to
appoint commissioners to settle the boundary and afterwards to dis-
miss Belcher from his position and appoint in his place one of the
leaders of the opposition, Benning Wentworth.   With the new administration came the downfall of Richard Waldron, who had been the
leading figure in provincial politics for many years, and the rise of a
distinct party with marked anti-Massachusetts proclivities.   A feeling
of state patriotism took its rise with the birth of the new party.

[3] It is interesting to notice that Governor Belcher, in one of his last
addresses to the assembly, as in his first, acknowledged the right of
the house to be mainly responsible for the supply of the treasury.   Address to assembly, XVIII N. H. State papers, 117.

[4] Governor Benning Wentworth took the oath of office Dec. 13, 1741.
He was succeeded by his nephew, John Wentworth, June, 1767.   From
June, 1748, to Sept., 1752, the house was dismissed, prorogued, or dissolved thirty-seven times by Governor Benning Wentworth, owing to
a difference of opinion as to their respective prerogatives.   During
this time the house was not legally organized.   Its personnel remained
essentially the same throughout.

ters, he never failed, as the records show, to address the house of representatives when the treasury needed replenishing. The same statement may be made with equal truth[1] of the brief administration of Governor John Wentworth (1767–1775).

The series of contests with the royal governors in regard to the respective rights and privileges, though subjecting the assembly at times to restrictions that savored of absolutism, had very important results beside the more obvious one of developing the idea of independence and the ability to guard their rights. The less obvious results may be stated as follows :—

1. By subjecting the legislature to an authority outside and above itself it prepared the way for a union with the other colonies under a constitutional government when the colonies had freed themselves from the yoke of the mother country.

2. It prevented the untrained frontiersmen from trying experiments in government, by obliging them to conform their laws and institutions to those tried and tested by the experience of centuries in the older civilization of England.

3. The sound financial policy prescribed by the crown and faithfully carried out by the royal governors[2] prevented in New Hampshire that period of wild and extravagant inflation of the currency through which some of the colonies less directly under the royal government passed.

[1] Governor's addresses to the house, VII N. H. Prov. papers, 125, 372, and 385.

[2] Notwithstanding Governor Belcher's arbitrary nature, his quarrelsomeness and duplicity, he was several generations in advance of the province in his thorough knowledge of financial laws. See Belcher papers, Mass. Hist. Soc. Coll.

CHAPTER II.

THE INVENTORY OF POLLS AND OF RATABLE ESTATE, 1680–1775.[1]

SEC. I. *The Basis of Taxation.* The chief source of revenue in New Hampshire during the provincial period was, in common with the other New England colonies, the tax on the general inventory of polls and of ratable estate. The inventory comprised three elements especially enumerated in every important tax law during the period, viz.: polls, specified articles of general property, and "faculty".[2] The principle that the inventory includes only what is enumerated in the act and that all else is exempt, was followed in framing the laws and acts in regard to taxation.[3] This principle as stated above may not have been definitely in the minds of the legislators who framed the earlier laws, but the

[1] The New Hampshire towns were united with the Massachusetts Bay Colony in 1641. During the 39 years of this union Massachusetts developed a complete system of taxation out of which the New Hampshire system grew. In its main outlines the Massachusetts system was as follows: authority for levying taxes was the prerogative of the general court; the objects of taxation were polls, estate, and faculty; the valuation was fixed in some cases by general law, in others by the act of administrative officers; a method of equalization (1) between towns and (2) between counties was gradually evolved which prevented glaring inequalities in valuation; indirect taxes were imposed (1) upon all goods, with certain exceptions, imported into the county in "just proportion with estates rateable in the country," and (2) upon shipping for the support of the harbor fortifications; the assessment and collection were fully provided for, the first by a joint board of assessors and selectmen, and the second by the constables armed with adequate authority. For a full treatment of this subject the reader may be referred to Douglas, Financial history of Massachusetts.

[2] Laws and acts, 1680, 1692, 1728, 1753, and 1770.

[3] Report of N. H. Tax commission, State reports, 1876, 13.

inventories as returned by virtue of those acts disclose that the selectmen and assessors acted upon such an assumption and returned only such forms of property as were especially enumerated. Hence, a comparative study of the inventory as it appeared in the important acts of the provincial period will disclose not only the successive attempts of the legislators to tax all property capable of producing an income, but further the state of the province as regards agriculture, commerce, and the industrial arts.

SEC. 2. *The Act of 1680.* The leading members of the provincial government established over New Hampshire in 1679 had served a more or less extensive apprenticeship in the general court of Massachusetts.[1] One of their number, Richard Waldron, had served almost uninterruptedly since 1654, and had been eight times elected speaker of the Massachusetts house of deputies. Under these circumstances, considering the reluctance with which the people of the province accepted the action of the crown in separating them from Massachusetts, it is not strange that a complete body of laws was imported ready-made from the parent colony during the first session of the legislature, remodelled to suit the simpler conditions, and enacted as the legal code for the new province.

[1] Of the council: John Cutt, president, had served one session ; Richard Waldron, deputy president, twenty-eight sessions ; Richard Martin, one session ; Christopher Hussey, five sessions ; Elias Stileman, secretary, five sessions ; Samuel Dalton, fifteen sessions ; of the deputies : P. Coffin, four sessions ; Anthony Nutter, two sessions ; Thos. Marston, one session : that is, nine out of the twenty-one members of the two houses had served in the Massachusetts legislature a total of sixty-two sessions, through a period of twenty-five years. I N. H. Prov. papers, 369–372.

That portion of the laws of 1680[1] devoted to taxation
required the selectmen to " take a list of all ye male
psons of 16 years old and upwards wth ye valuation of all
their estates according to such rules as are past this
court." The lists were to be returned to a committee
for the whole province consisting of six members, one
each from Dover, Portsmouth, Hampton, and Exeter, together with two of the council, " which committee shall
examine and compare s^d list and bring s^d estates to an equal
valuation," having respect to locality " y^t no towne or
person may be burdened beyond proportion." The
valuation as equalized by the committee was to stand as
a rule or standard of comparison by which other estates
rated by estimation were to be appraised. The forms of
property considered to be susceptible of a uniform rating
without undue injustice were to be appraised as follows
Polls 16 years and upwards, £18; all land within fence,
meadow or marsh, mowable, 5 s. per acre ; (all pasture land
without fence, rate free); all oxen, 4 years old and upwards, £3 ; steers, cows, and heifers 3 years old, 40 s. ;
steers, cows, and heifers 2 years old, 25 s. ; yearlings,
10 s.; horses and mares 3 years old and upwards,
20 s. ; sheep above 1 year old, 5 s. ; swine above 1 year old,
10 s. An omnibus clause followed, " and all other estates
whatsoever in ye hands of whome it is at the time when
it shall be taken, shall be rated by some equal proportion, by ye selectmen of each town wth great care that
pticulars be not wronged." Having thus provided for

---

[1] Province laws, I N. H. Prov. papers, 395-396. The laws of 1680
have generally been considered to have been negatived by the crown.
The evidence is, however, untrustworthy, and the question must at
east be held an open one. The laws certainly registered custom and
seem to have been followed in the case of taxation until the Andros
law, 1686. For a review of the argument pro and con see Shirley,
Early jurisprudence in New Hampshire.

the taxation of the property of the farming classes, the legislators turned their attention to those whose wealth is not so closely connected with the land. "And all ships, ketches, barques, boats and all vessels whatsoever shall be rateable,¹ as also all dwelling houses, warehouses, wharfs, mills, and all handy craftsmen, as carpenters, masons, joiners, shoemakers, taylors, tanners, curriers, butchers, bakers or any other artificers, victuallers, merchants, and inn-keepers shall be rated by estimation." In case of over-rating appeal might be had from the selectmen's decision to the quarter court which was authorized to give relief. But few general exemptions seem to have been intended, and those, in general, included only such property as produced no income. Live stock under one year old, farming implements, farm products, household furniture, books, plate and jewelry, together with articles of personal wear, made up the list. Further it must be noted that in ordering a rate of one and one-half penny in the pound upon the list after it was properly made up, it was enacted that it be laid upon all persons and estates, " yᵉ presdᵗ and council, ministers and elders of churches excepted." ²

In taking the inventory all persons and estates enumerated in the act were included, and such exemptions as are recorded above, viz., president, council, ministers and elders of churches, were made by a special act of the legislature when the tax was voted,—a

¹ By act of assembly which met May 3, 1681, it was ordered that ships, ketches, barques, etc., be rated at " 20s. p tun". I N. H. Prov. laws, p. 40.

² Whether the exemption was held to mean the poll tax, the total tax, or poll tax and property more immediately concerned in securing a livelihood, is uncertain. In the tax list for 1680 the ministers and four of the council were not assessed, the president and five of the council were. See tax lists, 1680-1681.

feature that continued throughout the provincial period, and discloses how closely the representatives kept the purse strings in their own hands.[1] The necessity for stringent oaths in securing the inventory, either on the part of the officers enumerating or the persons rated, had not appeared at this time. Such regulations did not occur until considerably later.

No legislation upon the subject of the inventory is found in the laws enacted during Cranfield's administration. A rate of four pence in the pound upon all persons and estates within the province "according to the valuation thereof last set" was ordered during the session of the legislature that met at Portsmouth, November 14, 1682.[2] The prices at which "specie" was to be received in payment of the taxes were readjusted. From the above facts, in the absence of direct proof, it would appear that the general tax law of 1680 was assumed to be in force at this time and that it was obeyed by the local authorities in assessing the tax upon individuals and their property.

The Andros government, in accordance with the authority granted it by the crown, assumed powers of legislation that had, since the establishment of the New England colonies, remained in the hands of the representatives of the people. In systematizing the revenue laws for the New England colonies, the legislation of Massachusetts as it had developed during the third quarter of the 17th century, formed the basis. Upon

---

[1] In the first tax voted after Cranfield became lieutenant governor no exceptions were made. In the tax of 1692, his Majesty's council, settled ministers, and schoolmasters were excepted. In 1693, two provincial taxes were voted and no exceptions were made save ministers only. From this date the practice generally followed that of the act of 1693.

[2] I N. H. Prov. papers, 488.

the subject of taxation the Andros law of 1687 may properly be considered a codification of the numerous acts which were then in force in the colony of Massachusetts. As the New Hampshire provincial law of 1692 regarding taxation was a reënactment, in many cases verbal, of the Andros law of five years earlier, we may turn directly to the law of 1692.

SEC. 3. *The Act of 1692.* This act was entitled, "An act for y⁰ support of y⁰ government, repairing fortifications, strengthening the frontiers, etc." It was especially provided in the act that it should "stand in force for this particular rate for this year and no longer." The temporary nature of the act[1] was due rather to the fear that the royal governor might attempt to continue taxes without the consent of the legislature than to any dissatisfaction with its provisions.[2] Through the Andros tax law[3] it may be traced directly to the Massachusetts acts of 1647[4] and 1651, whole clauses of the two acts appearing without verbal change. The method of rating houses and lands followed the Massachusetts act of 1657.[5] The method of obtaining the list, the officers and their duties, the list of ratable estate, the tax upon skilled laborers for their "returns and gains", the tax upon the merchants and traders with the provision for abatement in case of over-rating,—all these provisions were identical with those of the above noticed acts of Massachusetts. From this rate her

[1] Province laws, 1692–1702, III N. H. Prov. papers, 164.
[2] By special act of the legislature it was revived annually in assessing taxes into the next century. When it ceased to be observed is uncertain. Its main provisions appeared in the acts of 1770 and 1772.
[3] Douglas, Financial history of Massachusetts, 51.
[4] II Mass. Col. rec., 212.
[5] II Mass. Col. rec., part 1, 288.

Majesty's council, settled ministers, and schoolmasters only were excepted. In succeeding years, when the act was revived for special taxes, ministers only were excepted. The only other exception especially mentioned included "all sorts of cattle under one year old".

Two provisions are especially worthy of note : (1) After providing for an enumeration of "all ye male persons in ye same town, from sixteen years old and upwards, and a trew estimation of all real & p'sonal estates," specifying in general the classes of property to be included, the law required that "all which p'sons & estates are by ye selectmen and commissioners to bee assessed & Rated as hereafter Exprest, viz : Every p'son aforesaid (except before excepted) all others every male at one shilling six pence per head." Then followed a clause specifying that skilled laborers, such as butchers, bakers, etc., "shall be rated for their returns and gains proportionably unto other men for the produce of their estates." (2) To all of which is added, "& all & every p'son aforesaide (except before excepted) shall be assessed & rated at three pence in the pound for every twenty shillings, boath p'sons and estates that shall be found, according to ye rates of cattle hereinafter mentioned." [1] A careful study of the act in comparison with the Massachusetts act of 1647 and of the Andros law of 1687 must convince one that its framers intended that the method of rating polls and estates should follow the method prescribed by the two acts above noted. The act of 1647 provided : "All which p'sons and estates are by ye said commissioners and selectmen to be assessed and rated as here followeth, viz : Every p'son aforesaid (except magtrates) 2 *s.* 6 *d.* by ye head, & all estates boath real and

Laws of the province, 1692, 1702, III N. H. Prov. papers, 105–106.

p'sonal, 1 *d.* for every 20 shillings according to the rates of catall hereinafter mentioned."[1] The corresponding clause in the Andros law is identical with the act of 1647, except that the poll tax is placed at 1 *s.* 8 *d.* per head. The act of 1692 followed the wording of the Andros act, which in turn followed in this particular the act of 1647. Taking the above facts into consideration, the conclusion seems necessary that the act of 1692 intended to assess a poll tax of one shilling six pence per head, and three single country rates of one penny in the pound upon all estates, both real and personal—estates in this case including "faculty" and incomes upon trades as well as the property usually included under that term.

SEC. 4. *Modifications and Additions.* From 1692 until 1770 no general tax law is found among the statutes of the province. During the intervening period various additions and amendments were made either to adapt the existing laws to new conditions or to prevent their evasion as property gradually took on some of the more intangible forms. An act authorizing a tax of £600 in the year 1693[2] exempted only ministers, fixed the proportion among the towns, prescribed that the act of 1692 should be observed by the selectmen and commissioners in the assessment, and in addition empowered the selectmen to favor any persons "aged, decrepid or soe indigent that they are incapable of paying anything."

The same year, 1693, the old conflict between the government and the tax-dodger met the legislator. Evidently the provision in the general tax law of 1692, authorizing the assessors to rate "the estate of merchants, shop-keepers and factors . . . being present to

[1] II Mass. Col. rec., 212.
[2] Laws of the province, II N. H. Prov. papers, 188.

vew or not . . . by the rule of common estymation"—a clause taken from the Massachusetts act of 1657—failed to accomplish its purpose. The preamble of " an act to prevent concealing estates from assessors "[1] recited : " Whereas it is found by experience that several persons doe what in them lye to conceal and secure their estates from time to time and will not give in a true and perfect inventory . . . so that those that make conscience of what they doe, pay more than their proportion." It was accordingly enacted that for every pound of ratable estate so concealed the selectmen and commissioners should have power to rate the persons so concealing, when discovery was made, the sum of five shillings. The above law was reënacted in 1718,[2] but in common with the other provincial tax laws was repealed in 1792.

A significant addition to the tax laws relating to the inventory was made in 1705.[3] The cause of this addition is found in the fact that the "act enjoining every person within this province to give in a true and perfect account of all his ratable estate is found by experience not to attain the end proposed and thereby sundry of Her Majesties good subjects are forced to bear the greater burden." " For prevention thereof " the justices of the court of quarter sessions were required to appoint yearly in December one "freeholder to go through the town he belongs unto, to every inhabitant thereof," to take a just and true account of each person's ratable estate. The freeholder so appointed must be under oath either to the justices of the quarter sessions or to two of her Majesty's justices of the peace, and was authorized to employ assistants to be under like oath. The list must be re-

[1] Laws of province, 1692–1702, III N. H. Prov. papers, 194.

[2] Acts and laws of province, 1696–1725, 99.

[3] Acts and laws of province, 1696–1725, 26.

turned "some time between December and March every
year". The fee for the assessor and assistants was five
pounds, to be assessed and paid by the selectmen and
collected in the usual manner. The centralizing tendency of this act is worthy of notice. Previous to the
above act the inventory had been made up by officers
appointed by the towns. The justices of the quarter
sessions were appointed by the governor and thus the
machinery of provincial taxation was brought more
directly under the control of that part of the government
immediately responsible to the crown.

SEC. 5. *The Acts of 1728 and of 1742.* In the absence
of general tax laws the legislative report of 1727 and
the temporary acts of 1728 and 1742 may serve to indicate the current practice in making up the inventory.
On May 5, 1727, a joint committee of the legislature
was appointed to " project the scheme " for a new proportioning of the province tax. On the tenth of the month
the committee reported that every town should be required to bring into the general assembly at the next
session in May the number of ratable polls, oxen, cows,
horses, swine, houses, and improved lands in each
town, and a valuation of the income of the trade within
each town. The prices at which the specific articles
in the above list must be invoiced were put as follows :
" Polls, 16 years and upwards, 100^d; income upon
trade, 1^d upon ye p^d, the trade to be sworn to if complaint be made ; offices, 1^d upon the product of their income ; ditto on houses and lands improved at six years ;
income deemed to be ye value at 1^d on ye p^{1d}; every ox
4 years old at 4 ; cow at three years old, s2 : 10 ; horse
ditto 4 ; swine one year old s—: 16 ; sheep free for encouragement. Indian and negro slaves ad valorem from

16 to 40 years." [1] The house amended the bill by making the polls ratable at 60 *d.* instead of 100 *d.*, and requiring a new proportion at least once in three years, in both of which amendments the council concurred. This act seems to have failed for want of the governor's signature.

At the May session, 1728, Governor Wentworth in his opening speech urged "that the most material thing that will lye before us is the settling the proportion on the polls, stock and rateable estate of the province so that equal justice may be administered," and recommended a committee for the purpose. [2] A bill was reported, whether from a committee or from a member the records do not specify, which stated in its preamble that there had "arisen many disputes concerning the value of y⁰ polls and the prices that estates should be set at." Therefore, "for the better clearing up of that difference and that justice may be done," it was voted that "all polls be valued at £25 per head; all tillage, meadow and marsh land at six shillings per acre throughout the province, except Kingston and Londonderry [3] which shall be valued at five shillings per acre. All oxen at three pounds each ox, or cows two pounds per cow; horses at three pounds each, swine at ten shillings, negro, Indian and mulatoe slaves at twenty each; the women slaves to be excluded; houses at one pound five shillings each; and the value of y⁰ trades of Portsmouth a thousand pounds, Dover £200, Exeter £200, Hampton Falls 50, Kingston

---

[1] IV N. H. Prov. papers, 295.

[2] IV N. H. Prov. papers, 295.

[3] The number of acres for Londonderry was arbitrarily fixed at four hundred.

20, Derry 5." As first reported this act was for three years, but an amendment was proposed by the council and accepted by the house that the "above scheme be for the present yeare and no longer." The act was approved by the governor and the proportion fixed on the above basis for the year 1728.[1]

From 1728 to 1742 one searches the proceedings of the legislature in vain for acts regulating the making of the inventory. The reason is not difficult to discover. From 1730 to 1741[2] the province was overtasked with two important and exacting controversies: the one relating to the boundary with Massachusetts; the other relating to the respective prerogatives of the governor and council on the one hand and of the representatives of the people on the other. With the advent of Governor Benning Wentworth there came for a time a calmer political atmosphere, and with it increased attention to fiscal matters. Governor Wentworth summoned his first assembly January 13, 1742. On the 23d of June of the same year a bill[3] "for the more equal proportioning the towns" passed the house. June 26 the bill as reported was concurred in by the council and assented to by the governor. The act invoiced "every head £18, all lands 10 s. per acre, a horse £3, an ox £3, a cow 40 s., a three yeare old 30 s., a two yeare old 20 s., a yeare old 10 s., swine 10 s., a double house two stories 40 s., a single house of one room & one story 10 s., & so in proportion for other houses that are otherwise built." An "invoice table" for the town of Chester, dated February 27, 1741,[4] enumerated, in addi-

[1] IV N. H. Prov. papers, 304, 308.
[2] IV and V N. H. Prov. papers.
[3] "The invoices of the several towns and gen'l draught sent up." House journal, V N. H. Prov. papers, 165.
[4] Chase, History of Chester, 259–261.

tion to the articles specified in the act of 1741, mills and colts.[1]   As this was the first inventory returned for the town it is hardly probable that the "invoice men" would have included in this list any classes of property not usually enumerated.   Moreover, from a fragment of an inventory[2] for the same town taken between the above date and 1745, two men in the list were returned for "faculties". The title "mills" does not appear, neither does "houses", single or double. Whether "mills" were included under the head "faculties", as was sometimes the case, is uncertain, owing to the fragmentary nature of the invoice.   A study of inventories in connection with the acts under which they were taken would undoubtedly disclose a considerable divergence between law and actual practice, since the latter was to some extent under the control of local custom.

SEC. 6.   *The Acts of 1753, 1760, 1761, and 1767.* The exit of Governor Belcher was followed by a brief political calm during which the legislature registered the provincial custom regarding taxes in the act of 1742. The calm was of short duration, however.   The province was soon drawn into a struggle with the French and Indians (King George's War, 1744-1748), and later into the distracting political struggle between the house and Governor Benning Wentworth respecting the right to admit new towns to membership in the house, during which controversy, from June, 1748, to September, 1752,[3] the house was not legally organized. Such political controversies are not conducive to the organization of a

[1] The list from Chester returned 152 heads, 50 double houses, 75 single houses, and, in addition to the classes enumerated in the act, 13 mills and 13 colts.

[2] Chase, History of Chester, 262.

[3] V, VI N. H. Prov. papers.

permanent system of taxation, a fact to which the state records bear abundant evidence.

There is no direct evidence that the act of 1753[1] received the signature of the governor.[2]   However, as it met the approval of all the governmental authorities, except possibly of the governor, it may be examined as registering custom if not law.   It provided that the selectmen should take an exact invoice in their town in March, 1753, of all the ratable male polls and ratable estate : namely, of all male polls of 16 years and upwards ; of all Indian, negro, and mulatto slaves and servants (male and female) above 16 years of age ; of the number of dwelling houses ; of all improved lands, namely, arable, orchard, meadow, and pasture land (enough pasture land to keep a cow to be reckoned four acres) ; of the number of acres of each sort and kind ; of all live stock, specifying the number and age except of those under one year ; of all mills and the yearly rent thereof, in the judgment of the selectmen, with repairs deducted.

The acts of 1760,[3] 1761,[4] and 1767[5] were reënactments, largely verbal, of the acts of 1753, with one addition viz., that "the selectmen of the oldest adjoining town shall take the inventory of any town, district, or parish where no selectmen are."   These acts had each the same purpose—to secure the inventory of all polls and

---

[1] Entered the house January 31, 1753 ; reconsidered and amended, at the governor's request, May 9, 1753.   VI N. H. Prov. papers, 175.

[2] The bill passed both houses and was sent to the governor.   It was returned with other bills for a minor correction ; the correction was made and the bill returned.   Then it disappeared from view.   The records indicate that it was followed in bringing in the new invoice. See Journal of house, VI N. H. Prov. papers, 175-209.

[3] VI N. H. Prov. papers, 742.   In the act of 1760 the selectmen were allowed to appoint some one to take the inventory.

[4] VI N. H. Prov. papers, 761.

[5] VII N. H. Prov. papers, 148.

ratable estate in order that a new proportion of the province tax might be made. Hence the valuation of the property was not fixed, as in the case of a general tax law. Nor does there appear to have been any rule or method of assessment fixed by the legislature for the direction of the selectmen or assessors. From the returns of the inventory a proportion [1] was established, and this proportion determined the relative part for each town of the whole of the province tax voted in any year, until a new inventory was ordered and a new proportion made.

SEC. 7. *The Acts of 1770 and 1772.* In 1770 the province was on a specie basis.[2] The debts contracted in the long and disastrous intercolonial wars had been paid partly by the English and partly by the provincial government. The War of Independence, so soon to tax the energies of the colonies to the utmost, however it may have been regarded at this time in the two centers, Massachusetts and Virginia, was not yet considered as a possibility in the province of New Hampshire.[3] Not wars, but roads, industries, trade, commerce, education, and finance furnished the chief subjects of the provincial legislation. Though the tax rate was low,[4] the tax laws

[1] See amount of ratable estate and number of polls and proportion. VII N. H. Prov. papers, 166.

[2] The return to a specie basis was a gradual one and can hardly be attributed to any definite date ; 1767 to 1770 included the period.

[3] See address to the king by the house of representatives, formulated October 29, 1768, and forwarded to England April 14, 1770. VII N. H. Prov. papers, 255.

[4] "It is with the greatest pleasure that I congratulate you that no man can justly say the taxes are heavy, for the whole does not exceed 3 *s.* 8 *d.* proclamation money to each rateable in the province. Perhaps, if exactly known and taken, not 3 *s.* 6 *d.*; an instance, I believe, heretofore unexampled in any province or country whatsoever." From Governor John Wentworth's closing address to the general assembly, April 16, 1770. VII N. H. Prov. papers, 257.

were uncertain and their interpretation subject largely to the individual will of the local officers acting under the influence of local customs and the pressure of local interests.[1] Under such circumstances the legislators turned their attention to framing a temporary tax law, giving as their reasons " there is no rule established by law for making rates and taxes, so that every person may be compelled to pay in proportion to his income, but the same hath been left altogether to the arbitrary determination of the selectmen and of the assessors, which causeth much uneasiness and many complaints." The law of 1770[2] was the result. It provided that " all public rates and taxes shall be made and assessed in proportion to the amount of each person's polls, ratable estate, and faculty." Prices at which the ratable articles were to be inventoried were as follows : male polls 18 years and upward, 18 *s.* each ; male slaves 16–50 years, 16 *s.* ; female slaves 16–50, 8 *s.* ; all live stock was divided into classes according to kind and age, and the value fixed ; all improved lands were to be estimated at 6 *d.* per acre, " provided it does not exceed the sum, which the stock said land does or might keep summer and winter is estimated

[1] A petition, February 21, 1769, to the general assembly, signed by a long list of the citizens of Portsmouth, recited " that the trade and business is signally decayed, that the inhabitants are filled with the most gloomy apprehensions, especially the middling and poorer sort, who look upon themselves to be greatly distressed and aggrieved by the weight of public taxes, which by the present method of assessment fall exceedingly heavy on them, . . . for the remedying of which grievance, and that all the inhabitants may be equally taxed, which at present they are not, the selectmen of the town having no certain rule of law to proceed by as they have in the other provinces on this continent, . . . your petitioners request that you would pass a valuation act obliging every inhabitant of the town to give to the selectmen or assessors a just and true valuation, upon oath, of all his estate, real and personal, under improvement, that each member of the community may bear his equal proportion of public charges of government." XIII N. H. Prov. papers, 273.

[2] Laws, 1824, II, 218.

at;" all houses, mills, warehouses and other buildings,
wharfs, and ferries were to be estimated at one-twelfth
part of their net yearly income; all stock, whether
money at interest or improved in trade, was invoiced at
the rate of one per cent; finally, "any person's faculty
may be estimated by the selectmen of each town or parish at their discretion not exceeding twenty pounds ratable estate." The invoice was to be made in eight
columns: the first for the amount of each person's polls;
the second for the amount of each person's improved
lands; the third for the amount of slaves; the fourth for
the amount of live stock; the fifth for "other real estate";
the sixth for stock at interest or in trade; the seventh
for faculty; and the eighth for the sum total. The invoice was to be "revised, renewed and settled annually"
between the first of April and the first of July. In case
any one should remove from the town or parish where
assessed he was to pay the tax where first rated.
Further, following the Massachusetts law of 1651, it
was provided that "if any person or persons shall come
from any place out of this province to reside or inhabit
in any town or parish in this province for the benefit of
trading, although for less time than a year, such person
or persons shall be rated one year's rate for the polls and
such stock as they bring, either on their own account or
commission, during the residence." In order that there
might be no escape from the provisions of the law, the
selectmen were empowered, in case of refusal to render
under oath an account of all articles of ratable estate as
enumerated in the act when required, to doom equitably
the person according to their judgment, from which
doomage there was no appeal.

In its main features this law, which was continued in
force three years, was reënacted in 1772 for a second

period of three years, with the following changes: (1) Slaves were not rated after forty-five years of age; male polls and male and female slaves were invoiced, respectively, 12 *s.*, 10 *s.*, and 5 *s.* (2) Live stock remained as in the list of 1770, except that it was especially stated that no cattle or horses were to be accounted one year old until they had been wintered two winters. (3) The distinctive provision appears in that clause of the law regarding land, a feature that continued until 1833 as the peculiar mark of the New Hampshire system of taxation.[1] This clause provided that " All improved lands to be estimated as follows, viz.: Orchards, one shilling per acre, accounting so much orchard as will one year with another produce ten barrells of cider one acre; arable land, eight pence per acre, accounting so much land as will produce twenty-five bushels of grain to be one acre; mowing land eight pence per acre, accounting so much land as will produce one ton of hay, one year with another, to be one acre; pasture land three pence per acre, accounting so much land as will summer a cow to be four acres." (4) Mills, wharfs, and ferries were to be rated at one-twelfth part of their net yearly income. (5) Stock, either money at hand or at interest, " more than the person gives interest for," and all money improved in trade was reduced to one-half of one per cent. (6) Right of appeal was granted to any person who considered himself to be overrated in respect to faculty. (7) Another noticeable change consisted in granting liberty to every town and parish "at their annual meeting " to rate all houses, warehouses, and other buildings "so as they are not estimated at more than one-twelfth part of their net yearly income." The provision in regard to the doom-

---

[1] See Wolcott's report, State papers, Finance, Vol. 1, 437.

age of property when the person refused to give in a
list under oath was evidently found to be too iron-clad,
for an exception was made granting right of appeal for
those who were willing to make oath that they were unable to make such inventory. All other features of the
act of 1770 were retained intact, and, with the addition of
a clause empowering the selectmen to make "reasonable and just abatement", the law was complete.

Several features of these two laws deserve especial attention :—

1. They were passed in a time of peace, when no
special stress was laid upon the taxing resources, and
therefore they represented the crystalized experience of
nearly one hundred years' endeavor to lay taxes in proportion to each person's income.

2. The tax upon polls, "faculty", and houses, while
still prominent, showed a tendency toward relatively
less importance, at the expense of stock in trade and
money at hand or at interest, and to some extent of the
common forms of general property.

3. The act of 1772 introduced for the first time in
the colony the method of rating improved land according to its income, the only feature of taxation which is
distinctly the creation of New Hampshire legislation.

4. The principle that no property is taxable unless
especially enumerated had been established. This accounts for the fact that the list of exceptions so prominent in other states was absent here.

5. This act, with sundry additions and modifications,
continued as the basis of the New Hampshire tax system until the adoption of the valuation system in 1833,
thus disclosing that it was temporary only by virtue of
the act of the legislature.

CHAPTER III.

THE PROVINCIAL REVENUE.

SEC. I. *Taxes on the Inventory.* The first instance of a provincial tax made by the legislature of New Hampshire occurred in 1680, soon after the passing of the first tax law. It took the form of "a rate of 1½ *d.* in ye pound upon all persons and estates" with certain exceptions, "according to ye valuation made by this assembly."[1] The method of making the tax on the inventory by rates was soon abandoned, and as early as 1687[2] the tax was placed at a definite sum and apportioned among the towns by the legislature. The amount raised in different years and different periods varied very greatly, according to circumstances. In the first place, the apparent difference was greater than the real owing to the inflation of currency and its consequent depreciation in times of special stress; secondly, the amount voted was always considerably in excess of the wants of the treasury, owing to the expenses, losses, and depreciation of goods taken for taxes and sold in the open market for money; and finally, from the quantity of legislation in regard to the collection and from an inspection of the treasurers' accounts, fragmentary though they be, the conclusion must be reached that whether legally abated or not there was always a considerable proportion of the taxes assessed which the constables were unable to collect.

The uniformity of the province tax from one year to

[1] I N. H. Prov. papers, 399. The rates were usually payable in "specie" or goods at specified values, and an allowance of one-third was made to those who paid in money.

[2] I N. H. Prov. laws, p. 175 *et seq.*

another was impaired by the improvidence of the legislators, who rarely replenished the treasury until obliged
to do so by the accumulation of debts or obligations which
they were unable to postpone. A similar effect was the
result of the spirited and prolonged conflicts between the
house and the governor, who was usually backed by the
council, in which conflicts the house habitually used
their power over the budget to coerce the governor. Up
to 1742 the usual tax was £500 or £1000 annually, the
latter sum not at all unusual ; and under extraordinary
circumstances, £2000 or more. During the French and
Indian Wars, 1754–1763, the annual tax went as high in
1755 as £10,600, a sum equal to about £4240 in Massachusetts money.[1] The tax continued at about £10,000
for several years, but gradually dropped to the normal
amount as the province returned to specie payments,
1770, and the taxes were paid off. The method taken
after 1712 to render the taxes somewhat uniform consisted in issuing bills of credit either to be called in by a
tax laid in succeeding years or to be used as a circulating
medium bearing interest, a subject that will be treated
in a separate section.

The proportion of revenue raised by taxes on the inventory was large. Out of a total revenue of £2045
in 1724, £1028 was raised from the towns in taxes,
£899 from bills of credit, and the remainder was divided
between excise, impost, and interest on bonds. For the
two years 1723-1724 the excise was farmed out for
£300 ; in 1724 the tax to draw in bills of credit, voted
several years before, was £1076. In 1755, when the
highest tax was laid, the revenue from the excise was a

---

[1] The general assembly, March 4, 1756, in payment of salaries voted
to "reckon 15 shillings of our money equal to 6s. of Massachusetts."
I N. H. Prov. papers, 486.

little over £930. From these and similar instances it seems wholly within limits to estimate that from two-thirds to seven-eights of the total provincial revenue during the period under consideration was derived ultimately from taxes upon the polls and upon ratable estate.

SEC. 2. *Taxes on Lands.* The single attempt to levy a general tax upon all lands laid out into townships, improved or unimproved, illustrates the theory of taxation held by the people and their representatives during the provincial period. When this occurred, 1755-6, the province was bearing a load of taxes more than double the usual amount. The resources of the future had been heavily pledged through the issue of bills of credit, and the instructions of the crown to the governor forbade their further emission unless they should be called in during the years already too heavily burdened. Large tracts of land had been granted out into townships, in which grants the governor habitually reserved the two choicest shares for himself, and the members of the council were often among the grantees.

For twenty-five years the towns had been accustomed to an occasional levy upon the lands of the town for special town purposes.[1] The house, as representatives of the people, resolved to try the same method on a larger scale. They first moved January 15, 1755, by a vote "that there be a tax of one penny per acre laid upon all lands laid out into townships improved or unimproved."[2] To which the council immediately "offered objections why they could not concur." Again on the 28th of November, 1755, the house sent up a vote of like

[1] Chase, Hist. of Chester, 75 ; Worcester, Hist. of Hollis, 30.
[2] VI N. H. Prov. papers, 341.

tenor, affirming that a large sum must be raised to defend the frontiers and that it "appears reasonable that the lands protected and benefited thereby should pay a proportion to the charge of protection and defence thereof."[1]   Again the council immediately refused their assent and this time gave their reason, viz. : "They look upon it as unjust for thereby the poorer sort of people would pay the biggest tax" and instanced "Chester, Londonderry, Nottingham, Barrington, etc., etc." Not being able to move the council, the house next attempted the same plan by the use of a "rider", a method now familiar in our legislatures.

The frontiers were in imminent danger, as the French and Indian War was then most threatening. The governor and council were urgent that troops should be dispatched to protect them. The house answered that it was their "unanimous opinion that a suitable number of men be posted on the frontier, provided that all branches of the legislature can agree upon any suitable way to defray the charges thereof."[2]   They proposed an excise and impost act, and innocently attached their "tax of one penny per acre upon all improved and unimproved lands granted or laid out within the province."[3]   The council concurred with amendment that the tax include only the improved land.[4] This was not the land the house wished to reach, and they in turn refused to accept the amendment.   At this point the governor, Benning Wentworth, with much tact urged the granting of means to equip a second expedition against Crown Point in connection with the other colonies, and also to complete the grant for the frontiers.   Notwithstanding

[1] VI N. H. Prov. papers, 448.
[2] VI N. H. Prov. papers, 472.
[3] VI N. H. Prov. papers, 472.
[4] VI N. H. Prov. papers, 473.

the combined influence of the governor and council, the house, in a characteristic reply, signified their desire to aid in the Crown Point expedition and added : "We can think of no way so just and equitable for defraying the charge of the frontiers as that in our vote of ye 23d of January last, and therefore we must in faithfulness to our constituents beg your excellency to excuse us from any charge on that account, unless the lands benefited thereby bear a part therein agreeable to s^d vote and which was the way the house expected to pay the expense when they accepted the report of the committee of both houses."[1]

The council prevented a general land tax, and the house prevented an appropriation for the frontiers. Two theories were presented : the house clearly based their action upon the benefit theory of taxation ; the senate theirs upon the income theory. From these points of view each may have had equally safe ground upon which to stand. Further, the council were undoubtedly more conservative and less ready to inaugurate an entirely new method of taxation for provincial purposes. Finally, it is probable that both parties were selfishly interested : the house, as the representative of the people, in endeavoring to throw the greater burden of taxation upon the wealthy holders of large areas of land ; the council and the governor, as large holders of land, in preventing the plan from taking effect.

Sec. 3. *The Excise.* On the 10th of June, 1680, the council granted licenses "as formerly"[2] to ten persons on payments varying from nothing to eight pounds

---

[1] VI N. H. Prov. papers, 486.

[2] In 1652 Portsmouth laid an excise upon wines, the revenue being paid to the treasurer by those licensed to sell. Adams, Annals of Portsmouth. On April 1, 1680, an officer was appointed by the new government "to receive the powder and customs as formerly, and two

per annum, the total revenue derived being £38 10 s.
1 d. The license system seems to have been continued
until the important act of 1687 through which the Andros government imposed a uniform system of imposts
and excises upon all New England. In 1692 Massachusetts reënacted the Andros law, and a little later
in the same year New Hampshire continued the Andros system by adopting the Massachusetts statute upon
imposts and excises with few verbal changes. The
act provided for an excise on all "wines and brandy,
rum and other distilled liquours, cyder, ale and bear"
sold by retail within the province. All retailers must
obtain a license from one or more justices of the peace,
which license must be renewed quarterly. A retailer
was defined to be one who sold less than two gallons
"strong water" or a "quarter caske" of wine, and a fine
of five pounds was fixed as the penalty[1] for selling without
a license. The rates were fixed at fifty shillings for
every butt of wine, 2 s. 6 d. for every hogshead of
"cyder, ale or bear", current money, and so in proportion. The act was a temporary one, and was renewed
from time to time for short periods until 1732, when a
permanent excise act was passed.

By the act of 1732[2] the excise was laid upon "wines,
rum and other spirits, cyder and perry" retailed and
sold in less quantities than one barrel or quarter cask.
The rates were eight pence per gallon on wines, rum,
or other spirits, and eight pence per barrel for cider or
perry for tavern keepers, inn holders, or other retailers;
for retailers out of doors, six pence per gallon on any

years later, October 13, 1682, the treasurer and collector of customs
were required to submit their accounts to the secretary of the council
to be audited."

[1] III N. H. Prov. papers, 172.
[2] Laws, 1761, p. 134.

wine, rum, or other spirits. The tavern keepers and retailers were allowed twenty per cent for wastage and had to give an account of their sales quarterly under oath. Upon refusal to take the oath a fine of ten pounds was assessed, which would, if paid, stand in full satisfaction of the quarterly excise. Retailers selling less than twenty-five gallons at one time had further to obtain a license from the court of general sessions of the peace, and a penalty of five pounds was provided to be divided into three parts; one-third to the government, one-third to the receiver, and one-third to the informer. One credible " evidence " [witness] was deemed to be sufficient proof. Further, any witness duly summoned had to give evidence under oath or forfeit five pounds to be divided as above. A clause disclosing the difficulties attendant upon enforcing such an act in a seaport town provided that any one selling liquors from a trading vessel in less quantities than at wholesale should be fined five pounds, to be divided as in the preceding cases. The law of 1732 continued in force until 1792.[1]

From the beginning of King George's War, 1744, to the conclusion of the French and Indian War, 1763, the excise was increased by temporary acts.[2] The increased rates, however, do not seem to have more than kept pace with the depreciation of the currency. Finally, by the temporary act of 1767,[3] the rates were fixed in lawful money at one-third those of the act of 1732, and the fines were placed at two pounds in lieu of five pounds. A novel provision of the act defining sales discloses the attempts to avoid the law. The bill provided that all " giving, lending, or commuting of any said liquors, either as

[1] Laws, 1805, 405.

[2] V N. H. Prov. papers, 208, 767, 340 ; VI *Idem.*, 733.

[3] Laws, 1761, temporary acts, 33–34 (the year of return to specie basis).

a reward or for labor or encouragement to labor, that may diminish the price of hire or wages or the charge upon any other commodity or thing whatsoever, whereby the person so giving, or lending, or commuting may directly or indirectly be remunerated or reimbersed therefore shall be esteemed, construed and adjudged to be a sale," [1] and hence under the provisions of the law.

The total annual revenue derived from the excise during the period 1680–1775 varied considerably,[2] but had a growing importance. For the two years 1723–5 it produced £300;[3] for a like period, 1743–5, £929.[4] For the years when taxes were highest, 1755, 1756, 1757, the total revenue was £3515 12 s. 6 d., a sum equal, approximately, to £1400 in Massachusetts money of the same date.[5] With the return to a specie basis, however, the excise revenue was relatively more important. For the year 1772 the receipts were £934 lawful money,[6] or about double the highest revenue from the same source during the period of inflation.

SEC. 4.   *The Impost.*   On April 1, 1680, the general assembly legally continued[7] the Massachusetts sys-

[1] Laws, 1761, temporary acts, 34.

[2] From 1680 to 1720, when the impost was common, the revenue derived from imposts and excises does not appear to have been kept distinct, and hence no accurate statement can be made as to its amount.

[3] IV N. H. Prov. papers, 184.

[4] V N. H. Prov. papers, 208.

[5] Reckoning six shillings Massachusetts money equal to fifteen shillings in New Hampshire bills.

[6] VII N. H. Prov. papers, 302.

[7] Not, however, without a controversy characteristic of the province. On the 24th of the preceding month, Captain Walter Barefoote was summoned before the council " and examyned by w^t pow^r he set up a paper concerning customes to be entered with him, or whether he did set up such a paper there that All persons should enter with him." He answered " that he did set up such a paper and must own it. " He was ordered to appear the next day, when the following " indictment " was read to him : " 1. That you have in a high and presump-

4

tem of customs duties by an act appointing Captain
Elias Stileman "to receive the powder and customs as
formerly."[1] At the same time Richard Martin, the
treasurer of the province, was authorized "to take the
entry of all ships and vessels from foreign ports and to
see to and look after ye act and trade of navigation."[2]
The provincial customs of the first year, according to
Chalmers, arose from taxes on wines and liquors, "and
one penny a pound of the value on the first cost of the
goods imported."[3] Two provisional acts of March 10,
1682, throw light upon the tariff history of the province:
(1) It was ordered that "all ships . . . . or other vessels

tuous manner set up his maj[ties] office of Customs declared it by a
paper in a public place on Grt Island for all Psons concerned to come
to make the entries with you at this Pt, not having leave first from ye
president and council of this province so to doe, w[ch] shews high contempt, being since his Maj[ties] Authority was set up in this place.
2ly. That hereby you have disturbed and obstructed his Maj[ties] subjects both in greater and smaller vessels and such as pass but from
towne to towne harbr to harbr Near adjoining on these occasions, but
must enter and take their passes with and from you, as proved by testimony. 3ly. Yor preemptory Answrs That when any question was
asked you you would Answe[r] My Name is Walter." Barefoote was
sentenced "to pay a fine of ten pounds in money forthwith and
stand committed until it was paid." XIX N. H. State papers, 665-6.

Nearly two years later, March 9, 1682, Barefoote was again brought
before the general assembly for seizing a vessel "without any power
from ye authority under pretence of His Maj[ts] name." Upon examination he answered that he had instructions to seize from Edward
Randolph, Esq., in order to a new trial. The council ordered a fine
of £20 "which they do respit during their pleasure upon his good behavior." "Two accomplices, Wm. Hoskins and Thos. Thurton, were
fined £5 each upon like terms." The three were required "to pay
20 s. in money for fees by equal portions equally or stand committed."
XIX N. H. State papers, 683-684.

[1] XIX N. H. State papers, 611. The revenue from customs for the
year 1680 was £61 3 s. I Chalmers, 511. The total revenue from the
province rate for that year was only £87.

[2] XIX N. H. State papers, 611.

[3] I Chalmers, 511. The same authority says that forty-nine vessels
of from ten to one hundred tons burden entered the port of Portsmouth during six years. See also I Belknap, 187.

belonging to the inhabitants of ye Massachusetts colony, may have free egress and regress into any of the ports or harbors within this province and have free liberty to trade as before our late charge, without being liable to pay powder money or any other duties, but what our own inhabitants are liable to pay for their vessels : Provided ye like order be made by ye general court of ye Massachusetts colony respecting all vessels belonging to the inhabitants of this province." [1] The order was to be understood to apply to vessels coming from foreign ports as well as from the other provinces. (2) It was also enacted " that what goods or merchandise being imported into any of their or our harbors, having paid ye customs at importacion shall not be liable to pay any further or other custom than aforesaid, upon transportation to any of their or our ports ; it appearing by certificate from ye collector from ye place whence such goods came that ye custom is paid. This order not to take place until the like act be made by ye general court of ye Massachusetts colony." In connection with the subsequent history of the two provinces relating to intercolonial trade these acts are significant. [2]

The legislature does not appear to have taken any

[1] I N. H. Prov. laws, p. 46.

[2] From a report to the Lords of Trade made by the council (1682) the following facts regarding the trade of the province are pertinent: "The trade of the province is in masts, planks, boards and staves, and all other lumber, which at present is of little value in other plantations to which they are transported, so that we see no other way for the advantage of the trade, unless his majesty please to make our river a free port. Importation by strangers is of little value, ships commonly selling their cargoes in other governments, and if they come here usually come empty to fill with lumber, but if haply they are at any time loaded with fish, it is brought from other ports, there being none made in our province, nor likely to be until his majesty please to make the south port of the Isles of Shoals part of our government, they not being at present under any." [United to the province 1686.] I Belknap, 184–5.

action regarding the revenue arising from imports or exports during its brief and intermittent sitting while Cranfield was acting governor.   Cranfield, however, by act in council, attempted with one hand to throw Massachusetts into further disfavor[1] with the crown, and, with the other, to fill his pockets with license fees and port dues. An act dated October 22, 1683, to take effect April 1, 1684, charged Massachusetts with evading the navigation acts and " drawing all the ships to Boston " to the injury of the trade of the province and the discouragement of the English merchants and mariners ; affirmed that it was the duty of the governor and council not only to observe said act but also " to use all the care and diligence to prevent the said abuses and discountinance them in others ; " and prohibited, for the above reasons and the advantages that would accrue to the province, the ships and vessels coming " from the colonies to the Massachusetts Bay under the burthen of 100 tons (unless allowed and licensed by the governor by a writing under his hand) from the loading any boards or timber in this province."[2]   A further provision " for the encouragement of shipping and navigation of the merchant and seamen of England " ordered that for a period of three years " all vessels coming from all other of his majesties plantations of what burthen whatsoever shall have free liberty to load and carry

[1] I N. H. Prov. papers, 463-4. " The said colony have, instead of discontenancing all persons that have infringed the said laws and acts, protected and encouraged them in their illegal importations and made these ports places of reception for all foreign prohibited commodities not only as to what hath been consumed within their jurisdiction, but by the sloops under pretence of loading timber (which we find very injurious to the trade of the province) drawing all the ships to Boston, and thereby supplying all the neighboring colonies, totally to the discouragement of English merchants and mariners, and thus we know by experience, having made seijure and condemnation of some prohibited commodities coming from Boston."

[2] I N. H. Prov. laws, 83.

away any boards, timber, or other commodities to any other of his majesty' plantations only paying the usual rate for powder as is and has been usually paid in Barbadoes." [1]   In the brief, 1684,[2] containing the substance of the affidavits, objections, and replies at the hearing before the Lords of Trade in regard to Cranfield's maladministration of his office, he is charged with setting up a license office requiring vessels and sloops from all the other colonies to enter and pay certain fees.[3]

The first systematic act relating to imposts enforced in New Hampshire was the Dudley law of 1686. Its general features, as was the case in the act relating to direct taxes, reappeared through the Massachusetts law of 1692[4] in the first provincial customs act of 1692.[5] This act combined three revenue bills in one; the excise, impost, and tonnage dues. The impost was laid both on goods and wares, and on wines and liquors. Wines were subdivided into three classes and rated as follows : " Fial wines or other wines of the Western Islands, 10 s. money per butt, Maderia wines, 13 s. money, pipe or butt ; sherry, sack, Mallego, Cannary, Mascadalls, tent and Allegant, 20 s. per butt ; brandy, rum and other strong distilled liquors 10 s. hhd.", and so on in proportion. All figures had to be duly entered and the quality and quantity given under oath if required.   Proof of evasion of these regu-

---

[1] I N. H. Prov. papers, 463–4.

[2] I N. H. Prov. papers, 564–9.

[3] " 7th November, 1684, Daniel Gent, master of a sloop of Boston, swears he paid 2 d. for 100,000 feet of boards landed at Broad Island in Governor Cranfield's time and never anything before." "John Usher proves the same paid for the like, though Mr. Cranfield had by letter promised they should go free." Wm. Ardel proved the same for the like. From brief cited above, 568.

[4] The wording is identical for the most part. A careful comparison indicates that the New Hampshire act was copied from the Massachusetts act with few changes.

[5] Prov. law, III N. H. Prov. papers, 168–173.

lations by two credible witnesses caused a forfeiture of
the goods. Further, the goods could be landed only at
certain specified wharfs upon like forfeiture to be divided
as in the case of the excise. In case the same liquors were
exported out of the province, except into the province
of Maine, within three months, two-thirds of the duties
paid were returned, oath having been made as to the
identity of the liquors and that the time limit had been
observed. All goods imported were taxed one penny in
the pound with certain important exceptions, viz : Fish,
sheep, woven cotton, wool, salt, and all sorts of provisions. Goods were to be valued at an advance of ten
per cent above that at the place from whence they
came. Molasses and sugar were rated by the quantity,
four pence for every hogshead of molasses, and eight
pence for the same quantity of sugar. This act was
continued annually by the legislature until 1711, with
some changes.[1] On July 21, 1702, a vote passed the
house, which was concurred in by the council and consented to by the governor, that a tax be raised on all
sorts of goods and merchandise and all manner of lumber[2] that "shall be transported out of or imported into
this province," to continue for one year. In 1703 the
act[3] was renewed for one year with additional duties on

[1] The rates and the list of dutiable goods were changed by an order
of July 30, 1686. This order may not have been approved, however.
I N. H. Prov. laws, p. 111.

[2] In 1695 Lieutenant Governor Usher proposed a duty upon all boards
and staves exported, together with additional duties upon liquors (pro
rata with Massachusetts), to which the house replied that they would
consent to an increase of the impost upon wine and to certain export
duties upon lumber ranging from 2 d. to 1 s. and upon mast yards
and bowsprits transported from beyond the seas from twenty inches
in diameter and upwards 4 d. per inch, provided that the governor
and council would consent to a petition to his Majesty to annex the
province to Massachusetts. III N. H. Prov. papers, 36.

[3] III N. H. Prov. papers, 249.

" rum and other things not mentioned in said last act."
A clause specifying that " masters be upon oath as to
how many thousand they transport," and that the " receiver be upon oath as to lumber transported and goods
imported " indicates the difficulties experienced in gaining a true account of the commerce liable to taxation
under the law. In his message to the house, August 11,
1704, Governor Dudley said: " I know no better article
for the advancement of the revenue than that of lumber,
which was no hard thing these last years . . . and I am
to tell you that laying of that tax is very well taken by
the Right Honorable the Lords Committee of Trade
and Plantations. . . I judge it the most equitable
and easy method, and shall take care it be better collected than heretofore." [1]   August 23 the house replied :
" Also reviving the lumber act we find it not to answer
the proposed end, it also bearing so hard upon those
concerned in lumber, but are willing that all public
charges arising in this province shall be defrayed by
rate on poles and estate." [2]   In 1711, notwithstanding
the advise of Governor Dudley,[3] the impost act was
allowed to expire.

At the spring session of the legislature (May 5,
1712), the governor again called the attention of the
house to the " impost which was abated last year and
is certainly a surprise to the government at home, for
there is everywhere a duty upon shipping and trade
for the support of the public charge in the ease of
the land tax which is always a heavy charge upon the
country." [4]   Considering the almost universal practice
of the time in respect to taxing trade and the weight of

[1] III N. H. Prov. papers, 291.
[2] III N. H. Prov, papers, 294-5.
[3] XIX N. H. State papers, 22.
[4] XIX N. H. State papers, 30.

the royal authority, even though expressed in a wish, the vote of the house, October 14, 1712, "that there be no impost nor duty on exportations in ye province but that it be a free port,"[1] indicates that the representatives of the people possessed a keen sense of their own interests.   The action of the "commons"[2] was so surprising that Governor Dudley again urged the laying of the duties. July 13, 1713, he said: "I must again with all earnestness recommend to you ye Renewal of the Impost . . . there is no government or colony belonging to ye Crown of Great Britain y't Pretends to an open Port or y't doe not bring in ye trade and merchandyse of their province to aid the land tax for ye payment of ye heavy charges of ye war which is as needful in this province as in any other of her Majesties governments ye neglect and inequality whereof will I fear justly offend her Majesties as well as disturb ye other governments on ye shoar of America."[3]   The house persisted in their plan and voted again (1713) that "there be no impost for ye ensuing year."[4]   In 1714, however, upon the presentation of the state of the province by the governor that the regular tax upon polls and estates would be required "to draw in ye bills of credit and thereby discharge the province debt," an act[5] was passed placing a moderate impost

[1] XIX N. H. State papers, 38.

[2] This title is often used in the legislative records in referring to the lower house in New Hampshire in the early part of the eighteenth century.

[3] XIX N. H. State papers, 43.

[4] XIX N. H. State papers, 44.

[5] XIX N. H. State papers, 52. To be in force for one year from June 10, 1714. The imposts were: rum, 8 s. hhd.; ffyall wines, 5 s. pipe ; Maderia, 2 s. pipe ; molasses and sugar, 2 s. hhd.; tobacco, 3 s. hhd., with drawback of ¾ if exported within six months. The duties were : export boards, 1 s.; pine planks, 3 s.; red oak hhd. staves, 6 d.; white oak staves, 9 d.; white oak pipe staves, 1 s.; to which was added an impost of £10 on Indian staves, intended to be prohibitive.

upon rum, wine, molasses, sugar, and tobacco, and an export duty upon lumber manufactured into boards, planks, and staves. By a subsequent act, April 27, 1715, this tax[1] was continued in force until June 10, 1716, so far as it concerned "the duty on rum, wine, sugar, molasses, and tobacco". The drawback limit for exportation of the liquors was reduced to three months.[2] In 1716 the governor again strongly advocated an impost, "what every government in the world hath but we," to which the house, after an experience of two years with the impost, replied that in their opinion "the

[1] XIX N. H. State papers, 62.

[2] As it has been charged that New Hampshire was the offending party in the tariff war between that province and Massachusetts, which culminated in the prohibitive acts of the latter colony in the year 1721, a brief review of some of the facts in the case seems necessary. On the 22nd of July, 1714, the council sent the following message and vote to the house : " Information being given to this board that there is offence taken by yᵉ Assembly of her Majesties Province of yᵉ Massachusetts at the act of impost and duty's of emportation lately made in this province, ordered that Samuel Penhallow and Marke Hunkinge, Esqʳˢ be a committee from this Board to joyne with a committee of ye House of Representatives to meet and confer with such gentlemen as the Govt of Massachusetts shall direct for that purpose to take away any just offence at ye said act for that we would avoy'd any misunderstanding between the two governments of her Majesties Province so happily united for the common safety and preservation of each other. Past in the council *nemine contra dicente.* To which it is answered vizᵗ 1 We are humbly of opinion that it is inconsistent with ye honor of government of this Province to appoynt any committee to be chosen to confer with such of the Massachusetts, about any law of this Prov. If they are agrieved by any act upon their intemation thereof and desire to treat thereon we will then appoynt a committee to confer with theirs. But in yᵉ meintime we pray his Excellency yᵉ Governor to give them all imaginable assurance that we had no intention to affront or injur their government by passing any act and hope they'l have no ill resentment thereof." Six days later, July 28, the house appointed two of their body to be a "committee to joyn with yᵉ committee of yᵉ Massachusetts about their being offended at any law of this Province and make return thereof to the General Assembly."

public charges can most reasonably be borne by an equal tax on all persons and estates." On December 5, 1716, the assembly was dissolved and a new house called, which met January 10, 1717. This house contained eight old members and nine new. Their first act was an impost upon "all liquors imported into this province from beyond the sea"[1] and a duty of "one penny sterling in the pound" upon all European goods. The council at once sent up a vote for a duty on the exportation of lumber. Neither bill became a law.

The house prepared and presented to the governor an able remonstrance against certain conditions that had crept into the council: (1) That originally the council had been chosen proportionally from the towns, but that then "just and good men are laid aside ye whole number residing wthin two miles or thereabouts of one another which hath been the occasion of great difference and animosities and which may further produce inconvenience if not timely prevented, ye council consisting principally of merchants and traders, whereby the revenue due to ye crown by an impost is wholly obstructed." (2) That "tho' we have endeavored an impost several times, it has been opposed by those now in ye council so y^t ye burthen lyes wholly on ye farmers and laborers who have till of late lived in ye hazard of ye lives and many brought to desolation and poverty: whereas ye settlement on our late Govr was on a fund of excise and impost wch impost is now wholly deneyed and the trading part no ways assisting in lighting ye land tax;" (3) "and humbly pray . . . that councilers and courts may be in each town as formerly and that we may not always

---

[1] Rum, 10 *s.* hhd. ; Ffyall wine, 8 *s.* pipe ; Madeira wine, 10 *s.* pipe ; Canary or Posada, 16 *s.* pipe. XIX N. H. State papers, 98.

be outdone by Gent[n] in trade to the great discontent and uneasiness of the farmers and laborers."[1]

The house asked that this remonstrance be laid before the king by the governor, Samuel Shute. The goverernor very shrewdly referred the matter to the council, "men more knowing and acquainted with the affairs of the province" than himself. To the specific charges the council replied : (1) That it had been his Majesty's pleasure to have his council of Portsmouth "in as much as they were gent[n] of the best quality and greatest ability to serve the government in that station ;" (2) "That the newly appointed councillors had for many years served ye public in ye Assémbly to very good acceptance, and did constantly study and endeavor ye benefit and ease of ye people . . . and never opposed any act of impost but when they could not obtain an act of export, wch is ye practice of Great Britian ye Govr assuring us that he himself payed twenty-six pounds sterling for ye export of his own goods, they being ye manufactures of England and now were willing to come into an impost if ye representatives would have concurred with ye vote of ye council for an export."[2] (3) That the judges originally were of Portsmouth and that appointees from Portsmouth took the place of others from the same town.[3]

The house was then dissolved, January 28, 1717.[4] A new house was called, but no further attempts to revive the impost were made during the year. At the opening of the spring sessions, April 29, 1718, Governor Shute

---

[1] III N. H. Prov. papers, 675–6.

[2] The council added "that tho' they are now classed as traders and merchants that they had as good and better estates in lands and land securities than any now in sd house."

[3] III N. H. Prov. papers, 677–8.

[4] III N. H. Prov. papers, 679.

said : "I am glad to find that those coals of contention which were kindled and blowing up amongst us are by your care in your several stations so happily extinguished. All that I have of moment to offer to you at this time is that some speedy method might be thought on, for ye encouragement of raising hemp and other naval stores, W^{ch} will be very acceptable to ye court of Great Britian and highly advantageous to this province as also that there may be an impost and excise W^{ch} I am informed hath been your constant practice before my arrival in this government."[1] In accordance with the usual custom of replying to the governor's message the house answered:[2] "And as to the act of impost, we are of opinion that the charges of the government are more easily defrayed by way of tax upon all persons and estates, and that its most for ye interest of all his Majt^{ies} good subjects of this Prov. to have a free port this year. But we think an act of excise very reasonable and desire one may be p'pared accordingly."[3] The subject of imposts and export duties is not referred to again in the legislative records until May 17, 1721, when Lieutenant Governor Wentworth gave as his opinion that "the keeping our port open is a disadvantage to ye government so hope ye will take it under your consideration."[4] The house prepared a bill and sent it to the council July 11, providing for prohibitive duties upon wines and liquors imported "except from place of growth" and export duties of 2 *s.* per thousand upon lumber except upon that exported to

[1] III N. H. Prov. papers, 732.

[2] The membership of the house was almost identical with that of the preceding house. What influences changed their minds regarding the impost is problematical.

[3] III N. H. Prov. papers, 725 ; XIX *Idem,* 116.

[4] XIX N. H. State papers, 154.

Europe and to the West Indies. The bill proved too
radical for the council and failed to pass that body.
Two days later the house amended the bill[1] by placing
the usual impost duties upon wines and liquors imported from their place of growth and adding an export
duty upon fish of 12 *d.* per quintal, "except what shall
be exported to foreign parts." That the above act was
not intended to represent the policy of the province, but
was considered necessary to secure fair trade with
Massachusetts, is proved by the subsequent action of the
legislature. On October 7 the following bill passed
both houses :—

Forasmuch as the act of impost, etc., lately passed in this province
is resented by the government of the Mass. as injurious to them, upon
which they have enacted the imposing severe, uncommon and un-
neighborly dutys on provisions and other wares and merchandize that
shall be imported and exported to and from y[t] government and being
given to understand that the execution of s[d] act is suspended or does
not commence until the 20th instant, in expectation of a reconsidera-
tion of our act of impost, etc., which they say has occasioned such a
misunderstanding between s[d] governments . . . for the redress-
ing and removing of which voted : That the act of impost and excise
of this Province be repealed so far as relates to impost on liquer and
export on boards provided that the great and general assembly of the
Massachusetts in their next session repeal their said act imposing said
severe duties as also their former act laying double duties on merchandise imported from their province, powder money, double light
money, etc., on the vessels of this province, more than is paid by the
vessels belonging to any other of the neighboring government and
that an order be issued out to the receiver or treasurer that they receive no more until further order from and after this date. But in
case the s[d] great and general assembly of the Mass. do not see meet
to repeal their s[d] Acts so far as affects and relates to this province then
our act to remain in full force notwith-standing.[2]

Nor were the officers of the province wanting in
action. On November 21 the general assembly was
called and Lieutenant Governor Wentworth reported
that

[1] XIX N. H. State papers, 160, 161.
[2] III N. H. Prov. papers, 827-8.

The principal reason of my further proroguing the Genl Assembly to this day was to give the other government time before us to see whether they would repeal an act lately imposed on this government so cruel and oppressive. I am to let you know that since our last sitting Mr. Speaker Pierce and Mr. Treasurer Penhallow accompanyed me to Ipswich when I met Governor Shute according to appointment, and we discussed matters relating to the above act, etc., and came to this resolve, that in case the Mass. will drop all their impositions formerly and lately laid on this government that then and in such case we will do the same, viz., drop all dutys laid by us on them, or in such wise as they do by us. His excellency has promised his best endeavors shall not be wanting for the accommodation thereof. Now in case the Mass. does not redress us, then we have nothing more left us but to state the case fairly and to address his Majesty by our agent Mr. Newman. . . . When our act and that of Massachusetts comes before impartial judges ours will be thought no hardship but w^t one government may lay on another, but theirs will look cruel and oppressive.[1]

On the thirtieth of the same month a committee was appointed from both houses " to form an address to his Excellency to represent to ye government of the Mass^a our desire for the laying all duties aside in each which we suppose will be for the benefit of both provinces." [2] In the spring session, 1722, after several plans had been proposed by the house looking toward the repeal or suspension of the act, it was enacted by the assembly, May 3, 1722, " y^t ye act of this province of the 15th of July, 1721, so far as it relates to the duties of exports and impost be supsended until the province of the Mass^a put their act of export and import in force relating to this province." [3] From this date onward the legislative records upon this subject are silent. From the fact that the matter had occupied an important place in the minds of the legislators for a generation, and that contrary to the advice of the royal governor and notwithstanding the pressing necessity of securing a revenue, the house had

[1] III N. H. Prov. papers, 829-30.
[2] III N. H. Prov. papers, 835.
[3] III N. H. Prov. papers, 311-12.

for a decade generally declared for a free port, the conclusion appears very plausable that the act of 1721 was as effort to secure free trade with the colony of Massachusetts,[1] with which five-sevenths of the foreign commerce of New Hampshire was transacted.[2]

The impost tax was not again renewed during the provincial period. However, several attempts were made to secure revenue from certain persons and commodities imported, which may deserve a brief mention.

In 1732 the crown advised the colonies to lay an impost upon negroes and felons. In answer to the message of Governor Belcher, advising such action, the house said " that there never was any duties laid on either by the gov't and so few br'ot in that it would not be worth

[1] In justice to the province I must protest against both the conclusions reached by Mr. Douglass in his Financial history of Massachusetts, pages 85-87, and the grounds upon which he bases his statements. The preamble of the New Hampshire acts, if relied upon without reference to the action of Massachusetts, would justify the action of New Hampshire as completely as the preamble of the Massachusetts act of September 8, 1721, justifies the latter province. In the interest of historic truth, a careful consideration is asked of the action of both governments and of the facts upon which their actions were based.

[2] From a very interesting paper, made up of replies to queries by the Lords of Trade, January 22, 1730, made either by the secretary or the governor of the province, the following pertinent facts are gleaned: The trade of the province was lumber and fish ; the trade was much the same as it had been for the ten years past ; the province made use of all sorts of British manufactures, amounting to about five thousand pounds sterling per annum in value, which were obtained principally from Boston ; the province sent lumber and fish to the Caribee Islands and received from it rum, sugar, molasses, and cotton ; the province sent the same commodities to Spain and Portugal ; the chief natural product of the province was lumber, generally manufactured and exported to Europe and to West India to the value of one thousand pounds sterling ; the coasting sloops for Boston carried from the province thither in fish and lumber about five thousand pounds (sterling) per annum ; there was no revenue but by poles and estates except £396 by excise and three or four barrels of gunpowder from the shippery. IV N. H. Prov. papers, 532.

the public notice so far as to make an act concerning them." [1] The act of the English government in 1733 forbidding that any duty on British shipping or manufacturers be laid by the provinces [2] would have limited narrowly the field of legislative action had the assembly desired to lay any burdens upon the trade of the other provinces. In 1756, [3] 1760, [4] and 1767 [5] bills were passed by the house providing for an impost on liquors [6] imported into the province. The bills failed to receive the approval of the council and were not pressed by the representatives. They were occasioned by the extraordinary expenses of the French and Indian War of 1756–1763, and at this time represent the unusual rather than the usual methods of securing revenue.

The history of legislation relating to the impost and export duties may be roughly divided into three periods : (1) From 1680 until 1711, when the impost was an established feature of the provincial revenue continuing the system inherited from the parent colony, Massachusetts. (2) From 1711 to 1722, a period which must be regarded as one of unsettled policy, when the large commercial interests demanded and usually secured that freedom of movement so essential to commercial enterprise. (3) From 1722 to the Revolution, when freedom of trade represented the settled policy of the province, and the attempts to secure revenue from imported liquors were temporary in their nature, and may be regarded as

[1] IV N. H. Prov. papers, 617.
[2] IV N. H. Prov. papers, 631.
[3] VI N. H. Prov. papers, 473.
[4] VI N. H. Prov. papers, 733.
[5] VII N. H. Prov. papers, 129.
[6] In 1733 the English government passed an act to prevent the colonies from taxing English manufactured goods imported into America. Hence the field for legislative action after this date was necessarily limited. VII N. H. Prov. papers, 631. VIII *Idem*, 45.

expedients to which the province resorted to relieve some pressing temporary necessity.

SEC. 5. *Tonnage Dues.* By act of the assembly, April 1, 1680, the Massachusetts system of tonnage dues was continued "as formerly". The intention was to provide that all ships of above a certain burden entering the harbor should each trip pay one pound of gunpowder per ton or its equivalent in money.[1] In the Andros law ships above twelve tons were included; by the act of 1692, ships above thirty tons. In 1714[2] the same limit was fixed and seems to have been retained at least until the Revolution. The general law applied to all vessels "all or the major part of the owners whereof are not actually inhabitants" of the province. Exceptions to this law were made at certain periods. In 1693 an act renewing the tonnage dues provided that "sloops or boats that trade along ye shore to be free from paying of powder money that comes into this province for traffic from any port or harbor on this side Connetticutt." This exception in favor of coasters from "this side of Connetticutt" was annually renewed until 1698[3], and probably longer. In 1705, however, Samuel Penhallow, the treasurer, took oath "that since the year 1699 he hath received of all ships or vessels coming into the river the full duty of powder money or species, according to their tonnage and the acts of the province for

[1] The merchants, of course, took advantage of the changing values of money in its relation to powder. The Andros law, 1680, fixed the rate at 12 *d.* per ton, or 1 pound of powder; the law of 1692, 18 *d.*, or 1 pound of powder. On October 17, 1722, Lieutenant Governor Wentworth said in a message that owing to the difference in money, they then received only two-thirds of a pound.

[2] Acts and laws, 1726, p. 64.

[3] III N. H. Prov. papers, 208.

such duty, excepting only the mast ships, who have several times been abated by order of council, or excepting any other in the like nature."[1] From this statement it appears that the general exception in favor of Massachusetts may have been withdrawn as early as 1699, although the language of Treasurer Penhallow is susceptible of a different interpretation. In 1702 the act laying an impost of one pound of powder or its equivalent in money was made permanent. The provincial authorities seem to have regarded the act of 1717, by which the English government prohibited the colonies from laying any impost or powder money dues upon merchant ships of Great Britian trading in the colony, as binding upon them, and to have suspended the provincial act, for in 1720 the house appealed to the London agent to obtain the "royal bounty" that they might continue the act.[2] The Lords of Trade, upon application from said agent, reported,[3] February 13, 1722, that the act (1717) was not retroactive, and advised the province to continue to enforce the provincial act "as it [the act of Parliament, 1717] could have no reference to the act of 1702, and confirmed in 1706." In 1731 the provision of 1693, excepting coasters and Massachusetts vessels provided Massachusetts exempted "coasters and vessels belonging to New Hampshire", was reënacted. In view of the estrangement of the two colonies, due to the boundary line troubles which followed during the next decade, it is improbable that freedom from tonnage dues was long continued; improbable, indeed, that Massachusetts took even temporary advantage of the provision. From the powder money the province seems to have derived sufficient revenue to supply the fort with powder in ordinary times.

[1] III N. H. Prov. papers, 311-12.
[2] XIX N. H. State papers, 144.
[3] IV N. H. Prov. papers, 29.

In case of foreign wars the assembly was obliged to make direct appropriation for its supply.

SEC. 6. *Fines, Fees, and Lotteries.* An elaborate system of fines was a characteristic of the early, and to a less extent, of the later provincial government.[1] Such fines, while not imposed for the sake of revenue, must in the earlier days have added materially to the province's income. Their primary object was to prevent violations of the civil and criminal laws.[2] The marshal was required diligently and faithfully to collect and levy all such fines, "for which he shall have warr't" from the treasurer or other legal authority, to deliver the same to the treasurer or some one legally authorized to receive such fines, and to make return of all fines collected to the next quarter court of sessions in the province.[3] In 1721, on April 19, the house voted that in case the law obliging every town within the province consisting of one hundred families to provide a grammar school was not observed according to law "They [the towns] shall forfeit and pay ye sum of twenty pounds to be applied to defraying ye prov charges."[4] The same year, July 14, the same body voted to fine unlicensed houses five pounds.[5] In the same bill it was provided that "licensed houses should pay 10 shillings every time

[1] A list of fees established in 1682 may be found in I N. H. Province laws, 79. For list of 1686 see I N. H. Province laws, 107.

[2] Some of the characteristic offences for which the persons convicted might be fined, the fine to be handed over to the provincial treasurer, were (1680): drunkenness, 5 s. to £5.; swearing, 10 s. to 20 s.; profaining the Lord's day, 10 s.; contempt of God's or minister's word, 20 s. to 40 s.; lying (above ten years of age), 10 s.; burning fences, 40 s.; breaking down fences, gates, to be amerced according to nature of offence ; defacing land marks, 20 s. to £5 ; unlawful gaming in public houses, by keeper, 40 s.; by each guest, 10 s., etc., etc. Prov. Laws, I N. H. Prov. papers, 382–408.

[3] I N. H. Prov. papers, 400.

[4] XIX N. H. State papers, 150.

[5] XIX N. H. State papers, 162.

they should be found without beer or cyder for the re-freshment of travelers." While the subject of fines does not properly form a constituent part of a history of taxation, the above typical instances may serve to indicate the extent to which they were imposed and the amount of relief that such revenue afforded to the usual forms of taxation.

Fees, or payments for services rendered by the government, were not less prominent than fines, and served to a very marked degree to relieve the ordinary taxation. Fees were regulated by a law as early as April 5, 1698.[1] The act was considerably extended and specific fees revised in 1718,[2] when the table as amended was printed with the session laws of that year. A report[3] furnished to the Lords of Trade, June 22, 1730, by either the governor or the secretary of the province, indicates very clearly the part played in the provincial revenue by the system of fines. This report gives as the ordinary expenses of the government " about fifteen hundred pounds per annum". Out of this sum were paid the governor, the councilors and representatives, the officers and soldiers at the fort, and, as the general assembly " sees meet", the treasurer and secretary. " The judges, justices, sheriffs, clerks, etc. and all other officers' fees are fixed by a law to be paid by the party and persons whom they serve; but they have nothing from the treasury." This system of fees extended to every department of governmental activity. Perhaps in no direction has there been greater advance in economical administration in the present century than in the substitution of fixed salaries for the system of fees and com-

[1] Prov. laws, III N. H. Prov. papers, 211.

[2] Acts and laws of the prov., 1726, pp. 82–87.

[3] IV N. H. Prov. papers, 532-3.

missions that burdened nearly every govermental act
in the eighteenth century.

It is a fact worthy of note that the province of New
Hampshire did not follow in the footsteps of Massachusetts by attempting to secure a part of the province
revenue through the aid of lotteries, although the assembly authorized several lotteries for local purposes,
which will be noticed in connection with the local
revenue. The action of the house in 1760 indicates that
the representatives of the people did not favor such a
plan. A committee in devising a plan to raise eight
hundred men for the Amherst expedition reported in
favor of issuing £1500 sterling bills of credit with interest at 5 per cent to be called in by a tax in the years
1764-6.[1] In connection with the plan they advised a
provincial lottery, the net profits of which should be applied toward paying the interest or a part of the
principal of the sum proposed. This bill was amended in
the house by providing " that there be no provincial lottery", and in its amended form it became a law. In
1769 the governor received instructions from the crown
" not to give his consent to any act for the raising money
by the institution of any public or private lottery without our consent." [2] In this case the province was obedient, and here again the influence of the crown was exerted in favor of a sound and healthy policy.

SEC. 7. *Loans.* From 1709[3] until the formation of
the union in 1787 large use was made of bills of credit

---

[1] VI N. H. Prov. papers, 175.

[2] VII N. H. Prov. papers, 231.

[3] Hildreth, Vol. II, p. 259, states that the first New Hampshire bills
of credit date from 1707, and were issued to aid in the expedition
against Port Royal. Bullock, Monetary Hist. of the U. S., p. 207,
on the other hand, places the first issues at 1709. The writer has
been unable to find any traces of the issue of bills of credit earlier
than 1709.

as a temporary substitute for taxation. In this, as in
other lines of fiscal policy, Massachusetts appears to
have set the example for her younger sister. From
1690 to 1714 Massachusetts had issued about £300,000
in bills of credit, and by allowing a bonus of 5 per cent
when paid into the treasury for current dues she had
succeeded in keeping them at par with coin for twenty
years.[1] Therefore when extraordinary burdens fell
upon the province of New Hampshire the colonial legislature, having the apparently successful outcome of
the policy in Massachusetts as a guide, as naturally
turned to the use of bills of credit as the modern legislature does to the issue of government bonds.

The bills of credit issued by the province were of two
distinct kinds: (1) those issued to pay the running expenses and redeemable by a tax in a subsequent year or
years, and (2) those loaned upon security and bearing a
stipulated rate of interest. The latter form of loan,
issued in considerable quantities, was the expedient
generally resorted to in the case of a great war, and to a
certain extent was the direct predecessor of the modern
war debt. The former from the date of its origin was
used with very great regularity and persistence to pay
the every day expenses of the government.

Without entering upon a detailed description of the
various issues of bills of credit it may prove of interest
here to consider briefly: (1) the causes and conditions leading to the adoption of this policy; (2) the
extent to which bills of credit were used as a substitute
for taxes with the influences determining the same; and
(3) the economic effect of this policy upon the colony
and its citizens.

1. Two causes or conditions which were largely

[1] Felt, Massachusetts currency, p. 52.

responsible stand out with very great prominence : (1) the poverty of the taxpayers and their consequent inability to meet extraordinary burdens in any one year; (2) the extreme scarcity of a common medium of exchange. It was again and again asserted that a higher tax rate would "tend to fill the gaols rather than the treasury." The geographical construction of the province, a triangle with the settlements concentrated at one vertex and the long side opposite to be protected from the attacks of the Indian foes, needs to be considered in this connection. In many cases the bills of credit were issued to equip an expedition against the Indians, or to hold a line of temporary fortifications in time of threatened attack. To this poverty, coupled with the large relative expense of defence, there must be added as a contributing cause the constant dearth of a convenient medium of exchange. The earlier issues of interest bearing bills of credit were largely, if not wholly, due to such scarcity. This same condition prevented the payment and cancellation of such issues until long after the legal date set for their retirement in the original act authorizing the issues.

2. The extent to which bills of credit were employed as a temporary substitute for taxation may be seen from the following table :—

| | —Bills of credit issued.— | | Silver | |
| | Non-interest | Interest | shillings | |
Years.	bearing.	bearing.	per ounce.	Remarks.
1709–1716	£ 9,200 old tenor	£ 1,500 old tnr.	8–9	Indian War
1717	-------------	15,000 old tnr.	10	
1722–1727	12,800 old tenor	-------------	13–16	Indian War
1730–1740	9,800 old tenor	-------------	20–29	
1742–1743	6,000 new tenor	25,000 new tnr.	32	
1745–1746	87,000 new tenor	-------------	35–50	{ Louisburg Expedition
1755–1758	116,250 { second new tenor	-------------	100–120	{ Seven Years' War
1759–1762	68,000 { sterling bills	-------------	120–140	{ Seven Years' War

It will be noticed that the bills of credit were issued chiefly during the time of war. In the case of the earlier issues taxes to redeem the bills were laid within the next five succeeding years. In the later issues the period was longer. The issues of 1745 were payable in taxes laid during the years 1751–1766. The issues of 1755–1757 were payable during the years 1759–1762. The later issues, for 1745–1762, were largely paid out of the funds advanced by the English parliament on account of the Seven Years' War. This fund, being paid in English money, was sufficient to take up a large amount of paper money of the colony. In this case the bills of credit served as a loan to the English government during the war to be repaid after its close. Indeed, in some cases no taxes were provided for the redemption of the bills, it being assumed they were to be paid out of the funds to be paid by England.

3. So far as the expenses for which the bills were issued were not repaid by the English government they served to distribute the burden of taxation, which otherwise must have been intolerable in time of war, over a period of years, thus taking the place of a modern war loan. Here the bills of credit served a wise economic end, and one which could not under the general conditions have been as well met in any other way. The chief evil connected with their use was found in the depreciation which inevitably occurs whenever a government arbitrarily by act of legislation, either directly or indirectly, inflates the amount of currency in actual circulation. The depreciation in this case is best disclosed in the value of silver as shown in the above table.

The use of bills of credit marks a stage in the financial history of the province intermediate between barter and money exchange. The modern system of government loans, both temporary and permanent, was in its infancy. In case of war the demand for immediate revenue was urgent and pressing, the people had little ready money, and consequently were unable to advance a large sum in any single year. The system of loans effected through the use of bills of credit, when not abused, played a justifiable part in the early history of taxation in the colony. When abused it caused great injustice and suffering. In no respect did the English government exert its powers over the finances of the province more wisely than in preventing excessive issues of bills of credit and long delays in their redemption with the consequence depreciation of the provincial paper money. The real temper of the representatives on this subject, a temper often veiled by dangers to which the frontier province was almost constantly exposed, is nowhere better expressed than in an address to the king at the opening of the Seven Years' War, July 26, 1753.

Your Majesties subjects in this province are not desirous of large emissions of paper bills, nor of extending them to farther periods than the situation & condition of the province absolutely require and far from desiring to postpone the payment of any paper bills now out, but willing to sink all at the periods fixed in the several acts emitting the same . . . so that all our paper bills now extant shall be bro't in by the time fixed in the several acts for emitting the same.[1]

[1] Address to the king, VI N. H. Prov. papers, 223-6.

CHAPTER IV.

THE ADMINISTRATION OF THE PROVINCIAL TAXES, 1680–1775.

SEC. 1. *Apportionment.* From the establishment of the provincial government, in 1680, until 1693 the new government followed the Massachusetts system of assessing a rate of one or more pennies in the pound directly upon individuals. In the latter year the legislature, when authorizing the tax, fixed the proportion that each town was to pay—a system that was followed for nearly two centuries. For some years it would seem from the legislative records that the apportionment was made upon the basis of the previous year's levy, taking into account the growth of the towns from year to year.[1] In general a new proportion seems to have been established whenever the growth of the towns demanded it, or when the settlement of new districts made it desirable to include such in the annual levy. The difficulties in the way of a legislature's making an equitable apportionment must have early forced itself upon the legislature, for on May 29, 1724, the house voted "that each town and precinct within the province shall . . . choose some proper person to meet . . . and agree upon rules and measures for the new proportioning the province taxes . . . the best they can and make returns to the assembly."[2] An Indian war delayed further action for some years. In 1729 the selectmen were directed to take an invoice "of the poles and rateable estate[3] in

---

[1] Belknap, Hist. of N. H., 306.
[2] IV N. H. Prov. papers, 381.
[3] IV N. H. Prov. papers, 530.

order that a new proportion may be established." In a similar order in 1732 the legislature required "the person's names with rateable estate carried off ag^t their names." At the beginning of Governor Benning Wentworth's administration, owing to the settlement of the boundary line controversy, a considerable district which had either been subject to Massachusetts or in the disputed territory was added to New Hampshire. A bill for taxing the new district became a law March 18, 1742. The act provided that town governments should be established over the territory added, and that the clerk should "take a true and perfect list and inventory of all rateable polls and estates."[1] Both the clerk and the taxable inhabitants were to be under oath. The returns were to be made to the general assembly. From the inventories thus taken the new towns were apportioned in the province tax for that year. This was substantially the method followed for the apportionment of the province tax to the middle of the nineteenth century. After 1742 a new proportion was made usually as often as once in three years, sometimes annually. After 1772[2] the proportion was regularly published with the sessions laws and legally authorized to be followed "until a new proportion be made."

SEC. 2. *Equalization.* The laws of 1680 provided for a committee of six—one each from the four towns chosen by the assembly together with two of the council—to compare the lists returned by the selectmen and to "bring s^d estates to an equal valuation, having respect to the places where they lye y^t no towne or pson be burthened beyond proportion."[3] After this date no at-

---

[1] IV N. H. Prov. papers, 616.

[2] VII N. H. Prov. papers, 326-329.

[3] Laws, 1680, I N. H. Prov. papers, 397-8.

tempt at equalization was made except through the general laws relating to taxes.[1] Whether this indicates a state of satisfaction regarding the system as administered, or a lack of capacity to grapple with a difficult problem, is an open question. Perhaps the most probable solution is that the legislature in keeping the apportionment so directly in their own hands failed to see that their methods could be improved.

SEC. 3. *Assessment.* Previous to the reëstablishment of the province in 1692 the assessment was made by act of the legislature acting directly upon the local officers, requiring them forthwith to make the rates and to commit them to the constable for collection.[2] In 1692 the provincial treasurer was authorized to issue his warrants to the selectmen, directing them to make the assessment according to the law then established and to commit the same to the constable as before.[3] This method was continued with little change until after the Revolution. Nearly every act relating to assessment during the provincial period recognized a body of men, usually three, called assessors, to act with the selectmen in making the assessment. A study of local institutions indicates that such office was nominal. The records of the town of Concord show that the custom was, from the organization of the town, to elect the selectmen for the time being as assessors ; while there was doubtless a diversity of local custom, the above practice was certainly very prevalent. In 1754 the law relating to assessments was amended by making it the duty of the

[1] The commissioners for the several towns in 1689 were required to meet and "perfect the said lists" for each shire before sending the same to the state treasurer.

[2] Prov. laws, 1680, I N. H. Prov. papers, 399 ; Cranfield's laws, I N. H. Prov. papers, 448.

[3] Prov. laws, 1692, III N. H. Prov. papers, 164-6.

provincial treasurer to send out his warrant annually sometime in the month of May. A second clause of the same law provided that in case the selectmen neglected their duty in making the assessment and in returning the tax within the time prescribed "their persons and estates shall be liable and are hereby subjected to be taken in execution for the sum they were respectively directed to assess and cause to be paid as aforesaid," the warrant to issue from the provincial treasurer and to be executed as in case of delinquent constables. In all cases they were allowed twenty days of grace after the prescribed date before the issuance of the execution.[1] A further safeguard was provided by authorizing the selectmen of a subsequent year to issue executions against delinquent constables when the selectmen of the preceding year had failed for any reason to do so. It thus appears that while the assessment of the province tax was made by the local officers upon the tax payers, they were acting under laws so definite and exacting that any failure to do their duty could not fail to bring the assessment upon their own estates. In order that such remedy might not fail for want of such estate, both law and custom required that only men whose property was sufficient to meet all such demands should be appointed or elected to any responsible office. Whenever any failure to receive the full amount of the provincial tax occurred it was due rather to lax enforcement of the laws, aggravated or made necessary by the economic conditions of the province, than to defects in the law itself.

SEC. 4. *Collection.* The laws relating to the collection of taxes gives a very clear picture of the difficulties experienced in that work. From the establish-

[1] Laws, 1761, 193–4.

ment of the province, 1680, until 1758 the constable was recognized in the laws [1] as the collector of the provincial as well as of the local taxes. Although the custom of employing collectors seems to have been gradually increasing it was not until this latter year, 1758, that this method was legally sanctioned. The preamble gave as the reason that it was "thought by many persons that chosing or agreeing with certain persons to collect the public taxes within the several towns and parishes in this province would be a more expeditious as well as a more convenient method of collecting the same." [2] Accordingly the towns were authorized by act of the legislature (1758) to "chose any number of such persons as they see cause, to collect the public rates, taxes or assessments made annually within the same or may direct and authorize the selectmen of such town or parish, to chose and agree with such persons to be collectors of the . . . taxes . . . aforesaid." This change was the result of experience. It was found that the work could be done more economically when the office of collector was

[1] The office of collector as substitute for a part of the work of the constable is another instance of the English method of making legislation follow rather than precede custom. The origin of the custom of placing the list of taxes in the hands of a collector with a definite agreement to collect the same rather than that of attaching the duties to the office of constable is yet a matter for the investigator to solve. However the office originated, it is clear that collectors were employed before they were authorized by the act of 1758. In 1754, appended to an act to enforce the assessing and collecting of rates and taxes, the following clause appears: "And when any person shall be chosen and appointed to collect rates and taxes by the name of a collector instead of a constable, he shall be thereby invested with the same power and authority in that regard which a constable has, and such collector is hereby subjected to the same kind of process, and to be proceeded against in the same manner in case of neglect of duty therein as constables are."

[2] Laws, 1761, 201. A statement in regard to the revenue for New England under Andros shows that the cost of collection at that time was approximately 17 per cent. I N. H. Prov. laws, p. 176.

divorced from that of constable. The two offices demanded a different form of ability, and in accordance with the principle of the division of labor the method more "expedient as well as convenient" prevailed.

The disagreeable duties of the office caused frequent refusals to serve as constable, and consequently heavy fines for such refusal. It was enacted in 1692 that "if the p'son chosen [constable] shall refuse to serve he shall paye a fine ye sum of five pounds, one half to ye use of ye town, and ye free-holders shall make choice of another."[1] This provision was supplemented in 1698 by a clause authorizing the constable on warrant from a justice of the peace in case the person elected refused to take the. oath of office "to app'hend the body of such person or persons and convey him to his Maj^{ties} prison in the Province there to be secured, untill he pay the s'd fine of five pounds and all necessary charges about the same."[2] By a statute of 1719 it was "provided that no person in commission of any office, civil or military, church office, or member of the house of representatives, for the time being nor any other who hath served as constable within the space of sixty years, shall be chosen to the office of constable."[3] The fine for refusing to serve was continued as in 1692 and 1698, with a provision for a hearing before the session as to whether the person so refusing had just cause for his action. In case he could show no just cause the fine was to be collected by distraint on warrant from the justice to the sheriff or "to any legally constituted constable then in being in such town."

The province held the constable directly responsible,

[1] Laws, 1692, III N. H. Prov. papers, 167.
[2] III N. H. Prov. papers, 207.
[3] Laws, 1726, 135.

in the earlier years of its existence, for the amount committed to him for collection. With this in view one of the first provincial levies provided "y^t if any constable shall faile to clear up his rates within his years, he shall be lyable to have his estate distrained by warrant from ye treas directed to ye marshall or marshalls within this province."[1] Nor did the laws fail to give him whatever aid they were able to, for a subsequent clause added "y^t if any pson or psons w^{th}in this province ratable shall refuse to pay his rate or rates for any estate to the constable, y^t the constable shall have power to seize his person and carry him to the next prison there to remain till he pay his s^d rates, or give good security soe to doe."[2] The above provisions were verbally reënacted in the body of laws made by the first assembly called by Governor Cranfield in 1682.[3] In 1693 the law was amended by providing that in case the constables did not collect and pay in the rates legally committed to them "that their warrant for distraining upon estates according to former act shall alsoe be to apprehend and imprison their person when noe estate appears, until they find estate to answer the law." The clause relating to persons taxed where no estate appeared authorized the constable "by warrant from a justice of the peace to apprehend and imprison such persons until said rates and all necessary charges thereabout be paid." An additional clause indicates that the practice of moving to avoid taxation was then not unknown, for in such cases the sheriff was authorized to levy the rate on the estate "or for want thereof on the person so removing, wherever he is to be found within this province."[4]

---

[1] Laws, 1680, I N. H. Prov. papers, 396.

[2] Laws, 1680, I N. H. Prov. papers, 400.

[3] Laws, 1682, I N. H. Prov. papers, 447.

[4] III N. H. Prov. papers, 187–8.

This order failed in one point, viz., no definite date for settlement was fixed. Hence the assembly corrected this omission during the year by allowing the constable three months to "a' just the accounts" with the proper officers before the warrants for distraint should be issued.

The early laws relating to constables and their duties in collecting rates and assessments were codified by the important act of 1719.[1] This law with but slight modifications continued in force during the provincial period.[2] The act provided that all taxes must be paid in to the officer authorized to receive the same within one month after the expiration of the time allowed for gathering the rate. In case this was not complied with distress was to be made on the constable's real or personal estate "returning the over plus if any." In case no estate was found then such constable was to be imprisoned as usual. In case the constable took goods by distress for taxes he must hold the same at the owner's cost four days and give twenty-four hours' notice in some public place of the sale. In case the person moved out of the town where assessed the constable was given the same power of distraint and imprisonment as he possessed in his own town. A new clause indicates that all property holdings were becoming delocalized, *i.e.*, the citizens of the province often owned land in several townships. In case the owner or tenant of any lands taxable was not a resident of the same town, and no stock, corn, or hay was to be found upon the premises whereon to make distress, any justice of the peace of the province was authorized upon application by the constable to grant a warrant to the constable of the precinct where the occupant resided "to distrain such

[1] Laws, 1726, 15.
[2] Laws, 1759, 36.

occupant by his goods and chattels the full sums at
which such lands are set in such list of assessment, with
the charge of making such distress and to satisfy the
same by sale thereof . . . and in case no goods or
chattles of the party can be found, whereon to distrain
then to commit him to the Common Gaol there to remain without Bail or Main prize until he pay and
satisfy the sums or sum so assessed with the charges."
Whenever new constables were chosen and sworn before
the former constable had completed the collection the
latter were to have full power, notwithstanding, to finish
the collection. A further provision related to the sale
of the real property of a constable when he did not pay
in his rates according to law. Such property first had to
be appraised by two to three freeholders of the town
under oath. Then the sheriff, or his deputy, was authorized to make sale of the lands or houses and to execute
a good and sufficient deed for the same, such deed to be
good and sufficient in the law. A very important saving
clause was appended to this important act : " Provided
that notwithstanding that in no case whatever any distress shall be made or take from any person or persons
of his or their beasts belonging to the plough, nor of
tools or implements necessary for his or their trade and
occupation nor of his or their arms or utensils of household necessary for upholding life, nor of bedding or ap-
parrel necessary for him or themselves or family, any law
usage or custom to the contrary notwithstanding." An
addition of considerable importance was made in 1754
by requiring the selectmen to send to the provincial
treasurer " the name or names of the constable or constables within their respective limits, who shall have
any part of the province tax to collect, the sum each is
to collect, the date of the warrant given him for that

purpose and the time he was ordered to pay the same into the treasury as aforesaid." [1] The law of 1758, authorizing the appointment of collectors, merely clothed the collector with the powers and duties of the constable appertaining to that office as a collector of public taxes. [2]

Notwithstanding the severe penalties prescribed for delinquent constables and collectors, the fact is patent that at all times and in all places in the province there was a most embarrassing and expensive delay in "getting in the rates". The act of 1754, already referred to, asserted that "the neglect or delay of seasonable making and collecting the taxes imposed by law in this province and to be annually paid is very prejudicial to the public affairs." [3] By the treasurer's report, 1760, it appears that on August £4703 was outstanding, representing back taxes for several years. In 1762 a long list of signers petitioned against a play-house at Portsmouth lest it should "carry off the little remaining silver and gold there is now in town and when people make such difficulties in paying the common and ordinary taxes and charges of government that the taxes are seldom collected within the year, through the pretence of poverty, . . . we apprehend it would be destructive to the circumstances of the people as well as their morals." [4] In 1763 the town of New Castle asked the legislature for further time in paying "some back arrearages of taxes, as they were under some difficulties in collecting the same by the constables dying." [5] After investigation the house refused to

[1] Laws, 1761, 194.

[2] Laws, 1761, 201.

[3] Laws, 1761, 193.

[4] VI N. H. Prov. papers, 833–4. Signed by the five selectmen and one hundred and eighty others.

[5] VI N. H. Prov. papers, 877.

allow further delay, " it appearing that some of the s^d taxes had been due nine or ten years."

The chief obstacle to the collection of the taxes was the lack of a stable and convenient currency and the consequent usage of payment in kind, or as the legislature phrased it, in " specie agreeable to the prices fixed and set." A more inconvenient and wasteful method could hardly have been devised, and yet it is difficult to see how it could have been improved with the system of currency then in use. In the first place, the practice of collecting beans of one farmer, beef or pork of another, and tanned shoe leather, codfish, turpentine, or white pine boards of those whose business rendered it convenient for them to pay in such articles was not only expensive, but demanded business qualities not likely to be found in one whose chief duties were those of a police officer. Again, the cost of transportation of such articles as bar iron and lumber, and the loss likely to ensue upon the gathering of such perishable articles as corn, wheat, or pork constituted a direct tax upon the province. Finally, the practice of forcing such a quantity of goods and produce upon the market at times when there was likely to be little demand not only caused an economic loss to the province because the government officials could not accommodate the time of sale to the time of greatest demand, but moreover could have no other effect than needlessly to depress prices throughout the province. This system, which violated every canon of an equitable system of taxation, was aggravated by the constant fluctuations of a most vicious currency.

CHAPTER V

SEC. I. *Introduction.* The chief characteristics of the
period already considered, that from the establishment
of the colony to the Revolution, was the construction of
a complete system of taxation, built upon the theory of
taxing every person in proportion to his income. This
system was inherited from England and was enforced in
the province of New Hampshire both by the Massachusetts government from 1642 to 1679 and by the
royal government inaugurated in 1680 from that date
until its downfall in 1775. The independence secured
through the successful outcome of the Revolutionary
War was economic no less than political. With economic independence came the development of the natural
resources of the province, the establishment of manufactures, the extension of commerce, the more rapid
accumulation of wealth in its varied forms, and with
these economic changes, consequent changes in the
theory and practice of taxation. That these changes
were not effected until long after their crying need had
been painfully demonstrated is undoubtedly true ; such
conservatism in a matter of the first importance to the
permanent welfare of the people is a reason for congratu-
lation rather than the reverse. It testifies not only to
the stability with which the foundations were laid during the provincial period, but what is perhaps of more
consequence, to the conservative character of the people
in the state at the present time.

During the century and a quarter that have elapsed

since the Revolution the important changes inaugurated may be grouped under three heads: (1) From 1775 to 1789 the system inherited from the colonial government was maintained intact. The avowed object was to tax "every person in proportion to his income" and the bases were polls, ratable estate, and faculty.[1] The first significant change occurred in 1789, when the income theory, after having been the ruling idea in New Hampshire taxation from the beginning of the colony, was permanently abandoned, and the taxation of "every person in proportion to his estate" was substituted. As a natural consequence the taxation of a person's "faculty" was no longer attempted. The transition from the income to the property theory had, however, been very gradual. In fact before the outbreak of the Revolution the system had become essentially a general property tax plus a comparatively large poll tax. The act of 1789 registered this fact in the law. (2) The second important change was finally effected in 1833, when the method of fixing the values of large classes of property by the legislature[2] for a term of years was abandoned and all taxable property was thenceforth to be appraised at its true value in money by local officers. (3) A third important change was inaugurated in 1842 by the act making railroad corporations taxable by the state, the tax collected being divided between the towns and the state. This was followed by a series of acts of like nature, culminating in 1879, making the more important corporations directly taxable to the state, the tax in certain cases being partially distributed to the towns, in other cases wholly retained by the state.

[1] Acts, 1776, 1789, 1784, and preceding acts of provincial period.

[2] Vermont took the same step in 1841. See Wood, Hist. of taxation in Vermont.

SEC. 2. *The Inventory of Polls and of Ratable Estate,
1776–1789.* The changes in the inventory introduced
during this period were intended simply to secure an
increased revenue.[1] These changes were of two kinds :
(1) those increasing the valuation of property already
listed, and (2) those increasing the list of ratable
property. An act of 1776[2] increased the valuation of
improved real estate an average of about 50 per cent, the
list otherwise remaining unchanged.[3] A more noteworthy change consisted in a series of acts beginning in
1777[4] making unimproved buildings and lands, whether
owned by residents or non-residents, taxable at a
uniform rate with money, viz., one-half of one per cent
of the real value.

SEC. 3. *The Inventory of Polls and of Ratable Estate,
1789–1833.* The important change in the theory and
practice of taxation adopted into a legal system by the
act of 1789 has already been noted. From this date
onward the avowed object in the framing of the laws of
taxation was " that every person may be compelled to
pay in proportion to his or her estate."[5] Accordingly
no further attempt was made to tax a person's "faculty"
and more attention was given to the valuation of the
property included in the inventory and to the taxation
of new forms of real and personal property. Two results of this change in the revenue system stand out
with some prominence : (1) Less attention was paid to
the poll tax. The rating was again reduced in 1794,
this time to eight shillings, and during the next decade
several classes were legally exempted from its opera-

---

[1] Owing to the financial burdens of the Revolutionary War.
[2] Laws, 1815, appendix, 511.
[3] The valuation of the poll was reduced to 10 *s.* in 1780.
[4] Laws, 1815, appendix, 513.
[5] Laws, 1789, 212.

tion.[1] (2) On the other hand, new forms of property were gradually discovered and added to the list. The forms thus included were public securities in 1792, carriages and bank stock in 1803, jacks, mules, and carding machines in 1809, and fire insurance companies in 1830.

Changes in the valuation of real estate were especially marked. In 1803 the valuation of land was advanced, especially when compared with live stock, one of the chief items in the inventory. Again, in 1830, a general reduction of nearly twenty-five per cent was made in the valuation of all classes of property that were arbitrarily rated by legislative act. In a few cases, however, the valuation was increased. Such a general readjustment of the list indicates clearly that values were undergoing radical changes and that the old method of rating large classes of property by the legislature for a term of years had become, under the influence of a new industrial era, unsuited to these conditions. A fixed list was extremely convenient while values remained relatively stable, and proved equitable, and hence satisfactory, in its workings. When values began to change rapidly and new forms of property were appearing, the market price was nearer the just price than any that could be fixed some months in advance by the state legislature. It is strictly in accordance with the working of natural laws that the rating system was abandoned in 1833 and a less arbitrary method substituted providing that all taxable property should be appraised at its true value in money by the local assessors.

---

[1] In 1798 persons enrolled in the militia, from 18 to 21 years of age ; ministers in active service ; students in colleges ; paupers and idiots; in 1803, the president, professors, and tutors in colleges.

SEC. 4. *The Act of 1833 and its Amendments.* The act of 1833 made comparatively little change in the objects of taxation but a very important one in the method of their valuation. Previous to this date the state legislature established periodically the valuation at which the more important classes of articles should be placed in the list. After this date the work of appraisal was intrusted wholly[1] to local officers.[2] The first section of the act provided that all ratable estate, both real and personal, should be appraised at its full and true value in money; the second section enumerated in full the classes of property that were to be included in the inventory.[3]

This act is therefore worthy of notice, since it was distinctly a decentralizing one, transferring the power of appraising the taxable property from the hands of the state legislature to those of local boards of assessors. It marked, therefore, the flood tide of democracy in the history of taxation in the state. From this date onward the tendency was constantly toward centralization, a movement made necessary by the disintegrating forces set at work in 1833. This tendency to centralization was especially strengthened by two measures: (1) the taxation of railroad corporations in 1842 by the central authorities and the distribution of taxes between the town and the state; (2) the establishment of a board of equalization in 1878, to equalize the valuation placed upon the property by the various local boards of assessors.

SEC. 5. *The Act of 1842 and its Amendments.* The

---

[1] With one exception : stallions kept for service were placed in the list at $10 each until 1837.

[2] The selectmen or boards of assessors in the several towns.

[3] One new class only was added, viz.: locks, canals, and toll bridges. Churches, schoolhouses, and public property, previously exempted by custom, were made so by law.

act of 1842, like that of 1833, introduced a change in the method of taxation of far reaching importance. It excluded railroad stocks from the general inventory of personal estates, and provided for the taxation of railroad corporations as a whole by the central officers of the state. It therefore not only checked the disintegrating tendency of the act of 1833, but also established a method for the taxation of corporations[1] that has since been followed until the corporation taxes form an important part of the state revenue. This early recognition of the fact that local assessors, each working in a limited area, are entirely incapable of reaching the property of corporations and accurately valuing their entire property from the valuation of its separate parts has been of vast importance to the state. Still other provisions regarding the taxation of corporations indicates that the officials were at this early date experiencing difficulty in dealing with these illusive forms of property. Both the corporations and certain of the officers were, under penalties, required to furnish a full and detailed list of the stocks and property subject to taxation.

From the earliest times the deposits of individuals in savings banks were included in the inventory and taxed directly to the depositors. It was not till 1864 that the corporate method similar to that employed in the taxation of railroad property was adopted for savings bank deposits. By an act of that year the taxation of such property was entrusted to state officers, and consequently the deposits of individuals excluded from the invoice.[2]

---

[1] In 1821 an attempt was made to tax banks by placing a tax on their circulation. This method was abandoned after one year's trial.

[2] From 1833 to 1878 no other changes were introduced that affected the general scheme of taxation. Some classes of property were added to the inventory, some exemptions made. The rating of the poll was changed in 1833, 1851, and 1871.

SEC. 6. *The Act of 1878.* As early as 1864 a resolution was adopted by the state legislature calling for a committee to revise the laws relating to taxation and to report to the legislature at its next session.[1] It does not appear, however, that any action was taken, or that the committee was even appointed. The agitation for tax reform was renewed in the early seventies, and as a result a commission[2] was appointed in 1874 "to revise, codify and amend the laws relating to taxation and exemptions therefrom and to recommend such alterations as they find necessary to establish an equal system of taxation."[3] The commission at once prepared and distributed a circular letter " to the assessors and collectors of taxes in every town and to others familiar with the operation of our tax laws and interested in the subject, soliciting information as to the defects of our present system and suggestions as to the proper remedies to be applied." The report stated that as a result "many communications have been received in reply to the circular. Some of them furnish striking information as to the inefficiency of our tax laws, showing that they fail to accomplish the important purposes of a well adjusted system of taxation, inasmuch as they fail to operate upon the taxation with that equality and uniformity without which they must necessarily work mischief to the public and injustice to the individuals and showing also that no amendment to the laws can make the system such in these respects as the highest interests of the state require without an entire change in our policy in some of its distinguishing features." The report further stated that " with a few exceptions (those recom-

---

[1] Laws, 1864, 2856.

[2] Composed of George Y. Sawyer, chairman, Jonas Livingstone, Hiram R. Roberts. The report was the work of Sawyer.

[3] Report of tax commission of 1875.

mending the system proposed by the New York commission of 1871, David A. Wells, chairman), all communications to the commissioners in response to the circular contemplate a continuance of the general policy of the state on the subject of taxation that has prevailed from the earliest period of our provincial history. Most of the amendments of the laws which are suggested are aimed at rendering the system more efficacious in reaching taxable property that now evades taxation, and to bring within the range of assessment other classes of property not now subject to tax; and these objects it is proposed to effect by providing for stringent oaths and severe pains and penalties for tax payers; and for more despotic inquisitional powers over household and private affairs in the hands of government officials."[1]

After a full investigation the commission recognized the undoubted fact that such measures as were found advisable and necessary "to establish an equal system of taxation" would not prove acceptable to public sentiment as voiced by the legislatures of the period; therefore it contented itself with publishing the results of the investigation and in recommending in a general way that taxes be confined to visible, tangible property, that church property be taxed, and that manufacturing establishments be exempted. Notwithstanding repeated failures to secure results, the demand for tax reform was made again and this time with better success. On the 14th of July, 1877, a tax commission was authorized by the legislature to consist of "four commissioners . . . two from each of the political parties . . . together with the state treasurer . . whose duty it shall be to carefully examine into the sources from which the state derives its revenue and ascertain and re-

---

[1] Report of tax commission of 1875, p. 7.

port whether or not all classes of property are equally taxed under the present laws; also to recommend to the next legislature, if possible, some plan of legislation by which the town and city may be relieved to some extent from what is known as the state tax and also to seek new sources of revenue."[1]

The commissioners[2] received their authority on the 14th of November, 1877, and on the 28th organized with Solon A. Carter, the state treasurer, as chairman, and William H. Cummings as secretary. Public hearings of which full notice had been previously given were held, a stenographer employed, and a considerable amount of information collected, both in regard to the sources of the state's revenue under the existing laws, and as to the probable effect of the taxation proposed by the commission. The commission drew up as the fruit of their labors a series of entirely new bills relating to taxation, which the legislature of 1878 adopted in their main features. The laws thus revised were incorporated into the revised laws of that year and have since remained with little alteration the basis of the present system of taxation. The distinguishing feature of the revision of 1878, aside from the special taxes upon the corporations,[3] is the minuteness of provisions relating to the invoice of taxable property, and the severity of the penalties for evasion or fraud.

The secretary of state was required to furnish annually on or before March 1st, to the proper officials, blank inventories requiring "under oath and in answer to interrogatories therein set down, full information to be given therein by the persons or corporations to be taxed,

[1] Laws, 1877, chap. 98.
[2] Solon A. Carter, state treasurer, W. H. Cummings, N. G. Ordway, O. C. Moore, W. H. H. Mason.
[3] See chapter VI.

of the classes in gross and the amount thereof of each
class of his property and estate and the value of such
classes, of his perfonal property and estate liable to taxation and such further information as will enable selectmen or assessors to assess such property and estate at its
true value."[1]   In case the inventory was filled satisfact-
orily and returned to the proper officers before April
15th the tax was to be assessed according to its statements ; in case of wilful omission " to make, deliver and
return such inventory, or to answer any interrogatory
therein," or of false statements or dissatisfaction with
the returns, the selectmen were authorized to " ascertain
otherwise as nearly as may be the amount and value of
the property and estate for which, in their opinion he is
liable to be taxed, and shall set down to such person or
corporation by way of doomage four times as much as
such estate if so inventoried and returned would be
legally taxable."   Corporations were thus placed under
regulations identical with those imposed on individuals.
As an additional safeguard the principal officer of every
bank or corporation was required to furnish to the
proper officer an account of all shares or deposits, the
value thereof, and whether such shares were mortgaged
or pledged.   The penalty for failure to fulfill this duty
was a fine of $400 to be recovered and used for the town.
The iron clad oath[3] required of every taxpayer affirmed
in substance that " according to the best of his knowledge and belief, said inventory contains true statement
of all his or their property liable to taxation and that
he or they have not conveyed or disposed of any property
or estate in any manner for the purpose of evading the

[1] General laws, 1878, 144.
[2] General laws, 1878, 145.
[3] General laws, 1878, 146.

provisions of this chapter." The penalty for false swearing was made a criminal offence by section 9: "if any person shall swear falsely in violation of the provision of this chapter, he shall be deemed guilty of perjury and punished accordingly." [1]

The legislation of 1878 relating to taxation is especially worthy of notice in three points :—

1. It introduced several new taxes upon corporations directly assessable by the state officers.[2]

2. There was very little change made in the general inventory of taxable property.[3] The commissioners of 1878 stated that " the state system of taxation universally in vogue is a property tax. . . This tax is supposed to be equally imposed. . . As a general basis of state, county, and municipal taxation, nearly all are agreed upon this system and it would be difficult to construct a better one. All [improvements

---

[1] General laws, 1878, 146.

[2] See chapter VI, sec. 2.

[3] It made certain specific exemptions, viz. : almshouse on county farms, property of the United States for light-houses and public buildings, reclaimed swamp lands (for agricultural uses) for a period of ten years. The amendments to the act of 1878 were as follows : 1879, explaining certain obscure passages, providing that taxpayers need not estimate the value of property returned, classing for purposes of taxation sea-going vessels as stock in trade, making church property in excess of $10,000 to one society taxable ; 1881, exempting ships and vessels engaged in foreign carrying trade for ten months before the annual assessment, or built during the year, from taxation as stock in trade, but making the net yearly income taxable as personal estate ; 1883, allowing towns to authorize selectmen to distribute blank inventories when they appraised property ; 1885, taxing mica mines as real estate until they declared dividends ; 1889, making fowls kept by one person in excess of $50 worth taxable ; 1895, making " all United States, state, county, city or town stocks and bonds, and all other interest-bearing bonds not exempt from taxation by law " taxable as "stocks in the public funds " ; 1895, exempting live stock, horses, asses, mules, oxen, cows, and other neat stock from taxation under three years, sheep and hogs under one year ; 1897, repealing amendment of 1895 relating to horses, cattle, etc.

suggested] are a departure from the first principle of taxation laid down by the pioneer of English political economists[1] and generally reasserted by his followers." The commissioners believed with M. Say that " the best tax is always the lightest," and adopted as a corollary the proposition that the " lightest tax must be the one that is the most widely and equally diffused." The commissioners of 1876 on the other hand pertinently asked the tax payers to consider this case : " Suppose 30, 40, or 50 per cent. of the property of a certain class, taxable under a system which professes to be an equal and just system because it requires all property to be uniformly taxed, escapes and evades taxation, and that the experience for a long period of time of every state in which such a system has prevailed shows that it will continue to escape ; where is the equality or justice of the system which taxes 50, 60, or 70 per cent. of the property of the class and leaves or is compelled to leave the balance untaxed?"[2] The commission of 1876 further affirmed that in their opinion if the taxation of any classes of property drives such property from the state or necessitates inquisitional or despotic laws, such taxation is at least questionable. The criterion should be, they said, "Sound principles of political economy and not the application of the dogma, that to tax equally is to tax substantially the entire property of the community or to approximate to it as closely as possible."[3] The fact that the state so tenaciously clung to the old system, even after its defects had been made so clear and the remedy had been so plainly disclosed, shows how firmly the theory that is based upon the taxation of all

[1] Adam Smith, Wealth of nations, 1, 654.
[2] Report of tax commission of 1876, 11.
[3] Report of tax commission of 1876, 16.

property was imbedded in the minds of the citizens of the state.

3. The changes introduced in 1878 consisted chiefly in specific provisions for securing more complete returns of the property taxable by law. The investigation of the tax commission of 1876 led to the conclusion that nearly one-half of the personalty legally taxable under the laws of the state failed to bear its just share of the burdens of government. The commission of 1878 reported that the answers received from the selectmen and assessors "are resolvable into the aggregate estimate that three-fourths of the personalty escapes taxation."[1] The commission of 1876

frankly admit that they are unable to frame any law to which a free people would submit or should be asked to submit, that will bring this class of property under actual assessment more effectually than it now is. They believe none can be devised, unless it be by legalizing the methods for raising a revenue adopted by the old English barons of the middle ages in their dealings with contumacious Jews—the application of the thumb-screw and the rack—or at least by clothing the tax officials with despotic and extraordinary powers inconsistent with popular government and degrading to a free people.[2]

The commission of 1878 in discussing the same question reached the same conclusions: "we know of but one alternative; either to make the tax on such property [intangible personalty] so light as to be no inducement to owners to seek evasion; or to compel by the pressure of an oath, the listing of all such property."[3] Unlike the commission of 1876 that of 1878 decided to recommend the inventory under oath, adding the pains and penalty of perjury. Naturally enough the means was justified by the end. "Grant that even the stimulus of an oath will not bring all personal property within the

[1] Report of tax commission, 1878, p. 20.

[2] Report of tax commission, 1876, p. 29.

[3] Report of tax commission, 1878, p. 20.

7

reach of the assessors; even then it cannot be denied that every dollar thus brought forth will swell the aggregate mass of property, lower the rate of taxation and lighten the individual burden."[1] Its efficacy upon this point may be seen from the following table giving money on hand, at interest, or on deposit returned:

1872	$5,200,000	1879	$15,607,999	1893	$6,291,763
1878	4,138,000	1883	8,400,000	1894	5,987,998

Viewed in the light of these facts the words of the commission of 1876 are prophetic:

Threatened pains and penalties and stringent oaths are ineffectual against the temptations and facilities presented for evasions, *and if to any extent they are successful, the success will be but partial.* Cunning and unscrupulous men are never at fault in devising ways and means to defeat revenue or tax laws; and so certain and extensive is the demoralizing effect of a resort to penalties and oaths to make them effectual that a feeling of opposition and resistance to the law is excited that leads multitudes of tax-payers to look upon the threatened penalties as tyrannical and oppressive, and the oaths prescribed as matters of form, and consciences are easily quieted by the thought that the law ought to be violated and the oath disregarded.[2]

SEC. 7. *Exemptions from the Inventory.* It will be remembered that the policy of taxing property only when especially enumerated was established in New Hampshire very early, if not indeed from the origin of the province in 1680. While this statement is strictly true as applied to personal property, it needs qualification when applied to real estate. It will be found upon examination of the statutes that it is usually stated that all real estate is taxable with certain exceptions therein enumerated, consequently it will be noticed that exemptions from taxation refer much oftener to real estate than to personal property. The exemptions from taxation may be divided into two classes: (1) general exemptions, (2) special exemptions.

[1] Report of tax commission, 1878, p. 21.
[2] Report of tax commission, 1876, p. 29.

1. General exemptions apply to all property of the same class or devoted to the same general purpose. The exemption may be either unlimited in time or limited to a term of years. Property which has been granted general exemption from taxation may be best treated by subdividing according to the purposes to which it is devoted.

Public property of the United States is especially exempted by law, as is that of the state or town used for public purposes,[1] and as are almshouses on county farms.[2] It was held also by the supreme court in 1894[3] that "the property belonging to the state and its minor divisions, such as counties and municipalities, which are held by them for public purposes [are] presumptively exempted from the operation of the general tax laws . . . unless the right or duty to tax it was provided for in the most positive or express terms, or by necessary implication." Such exemption grew out of "immemorial usage and universal consent." Chief Justice Smith said :

It is certainly not true that all lands in the town were ever taxed or now are. Lands owned by the town are not taxed, and yet are not exempted by any statute ; the parsonage and school-house lot are of this description. All buildings are to be taxed, but was it ever heard of to tax a meeting-house or school-house? Were the public buildings in Exeter, Concord, Hanover, etc., ever taxed? There are and always have been exemptions where the statute has not expressly made any. They depend upon invariable usage growing out of the reason and nature of the thing. They are not repealed except by express clauses for this purpose, or by provisions necessarily and manifestly repugnant.[4]

For these reasons the supreme court abated a tax on the courthouse and jail of the county of Grafton assessed

[1] Laws, 1857, 1882 ; 1871, 519; Public statutes, 1891, 178.
[2] Laws, 1869, 290 ; Public statutes, 1891, 179.
[3] Grafton Co. *vs.* Town of Haverhill.
[4] Kidder *vs.* French, Smith's N. H. reports, p. 157.

by the town of Haverhill, although the property was not exempted by any statute.

Property devoted to quasi-public uses is also exempted. The church was regarded as a public institution and the minister as a public functionary until the enactment of the toleration act of July 1, 1819.[1] Both had been exempted from taxation by immemorial custom and invariable usage. The first step at variance with the usual practice was taken in 1816, when it was enacted that the real and personal estate of ministers was to be taxable as other estates.[2] Houses of public worship, though previously exempted from the inventory by common consent, were first exempted by specific law in 1842. The report of the tax commission of 1876 urged very strongly a law taxing all church property;[3] the report of 1878 less strongly.[4] The result of the recommendations of the two reports was a temporary abandonment of the historic policy of the state upon this point. An act of 1879[5] made all church property owned by a single corporation or association in excess of $10,000 in value and used exclusively for a place of worship taxable at the same rates as other property for the total valuation of such excess.[6] In 1883 the act of 1879 was repealed by an act providing that " houses of public Worship shall be exempt from taxation."[7] Such is the law to-day.

In the laws of 1872 an act appeared exempting parsonages from taxation. This supposed enactment was re-

---

[1] Laws, 1824, p. 45 ; also Franklin St. Society *vs.* Manchester, LX N. H. Reports, p. 342.

[2] Laws, 1830, p. 39.

[3] Report, 1876, pp. 37–46.

[4] Report of tax commissioners of 1878, p. 10.

[5] Laws, 1879, p. 363.

[6] See Franklin St. Society *vs.* Manchester, LX N. H. Reports, 342.

[7] Laws, 1883, p. 58.

ferred to the supreme court in 1873 for their opinion, and was by them declared invalid on the ground that it did not regularly pass the house of representatives. No further action upon the subject was taken by the legislature until 1889. It was then enacted that " parsonages of religious societies owned by said societies and occupied by the pastors thereof, not to exceed the sum of $2500 to any society[1] " should be exempt from taxation.

With regard to the taxation of the property of seminaries of learning the policy of the state has been more uniform. In 1842 seminaries of learning, exempted by usage before,[2] were first exempted by specific enactment, and since that date there has been no change in the law. The only question has been as to what extent property owned by educational institutions, but not specifically devoted to educational uses, should be exempted from taxation. In 1780 it was enacted that the lands appropriated to the use of Dartmouth College be exempted from taxation.[3] " Under this vote total exemption for all lands owned by the college was for a long time claimed even in favor of tenants for years. But in 1839[4] the supreme court in a case regarding taxes in Lebanon decided that the resolution was temporary in its character, and not a permanent exemption from taxation and that the subsequent adoption of the constitution and passage of general laws for the assessment and collection of taxes terminated the operation of it."[5] The interpretation of the clause enacted in 1842

---

[1] Laws, 1889, p. 52.

[2] See report of commission to investigate exemptions in the state, House journal, 1819, p. 79.

[3] VIII N. H. State papers, p. 879 ; Chase, History of Dartmouth College, I, p. 570.

[4] Brewster *vs.* Hough, X N. H. Reports, 138.

[5] Chase, History of Dartmouth College, I, p. 570.

that " all real estate, except seminaries of learning, is liable
to be taxed" is actually left to the local board of assessors,[1] and accordingly varies from place to place and
from year to year.

It is probable that stock in corporations devoted to
charitable purposes has never been taxed in this state.
The first definite enactment upon this subject occurred
in 1842[2] in the provision that stock in corporations
should be taxed if " a dividend or income is or may be
derived from it." This provision was made more explicit in 1867[3] by the enactment that " stock in corporations shall not be taxed, if the nature and purpose of
the corporation be such that no dividend of its profits is
to be made." The provisions quoted referred to stock of
non-income producing corporations. It was not until
1895[4] that the real estate of public and charitable associations was legally exempted by the enactment that
" all public cemeteries and all property held in trust for
the benefit of public places for burial of the dead and so
much of the real estate and personal property of charitable associations, corporations and societies as is devoted
exclusively to the uses and purposes of public charity
are hereby exempted from taxation."

England's colonial policy prior to the Revolution did
not favor provincial manufactures, and accordingly any
encouragement of local manufactures, either by exemption from taxation or more direct methods, would have
been promptly vetoed by the royal governor. With the
advent of peace in 1783 and the return to normal industrial conditions the young state encouraged several
industries by exempting their property for a term of

---

[1] Subject, of course, to revision on appeal to the courts.
[2] Revised statutes, 1842, p. 102.
[3] General statutes, 1867, p. 116.
[4] Laws, 1895, p. 426.

years. It was affirmed in the preamble of the act that "the manufacturing of oil from flax seed, within this state will furnish employment for poor persons, have a happy influence over the balance of trade, and greatly contribute to the wealth of the good subjects of this state." Therefore it was enacted that "if any person or persons shall, within two years, erect and set up, or if already set up, shall continue, a mill for the manufacturing of oil from flax seed, such mill or building shall not be subject to any tax for ten years."[1] The slitting, rolling, and plating of iron and the making of nails within the state, the preamble stated, "would prevent large sums of money being drawn" out of the state "to foreign countries." This act,[2] accordingly, not only exempted the mills, buildings, forges, and engines for ten years,[3] but also granted an abatement for seven years of the owners' taxes for as many poll taxes of "proper" workmen as were employed in the mill. The same reason was given for the exemption of establishments for the manufacture of sail cloth or duck as was given in the case of the rolling mills, viz.: to keep the money at home. The exemption was for ten years with abatement for poll taxes similar to that granted to the owners of the rolling mills.[4] The manufacture of malt liquors would, it was thought by the legislature, "tend to promote agriculture, diminish the use of ardent spirits, and preserve the health and morals of the people," accordingly the buildings and yards were exempted for ten

[1] Perpetual laws, 1789. p. 196 (passed June 21, 1786).

[2] Perpetual laws, 1789, p. 200 (passed September 2, 1787).

[3] It also offered a premium of £100 and perpetual exemption from taxation for the first mill erected, provided it should be finished within one year from the date of the act.

[4] Perpetual laws, 1789, p. 205. A premium of £50 was given to the first mill, with exemption as in the case of the rolling mills.

years, the owner or owners were exempted from all poll taxes, and the abatement of taxes of workmen allowed as in the two previous cases.[1] The first three of the acts enumerated above were repealed by act of June 18, 1805.[2] The same year, 1805, the buildings, machinery, and stock of cotton mills were exempted from all taxes for five years, provided the mills were operated. By act of December 22, 1808,[3] all establishments for the manufacture of cotton and cotton yarn and of woolen and woolen yarn were exempted upon their capital stock from $4000 to $20,000 for a period of five years. This act was repealed June 22, 1814,[4] but later, in 1816,[5] an act was passed exempting the capital stock of similar industries not exceeding the amount of $10,000 for a period of two years.

In 1819 the policy of exemption was made the subject of a special legislative report.[6] The inquiry was as to the "amount of property exempted from taxation by the several charters" of the corporations in the state. The report stated:

The property freed from taxation is principally that of academies and manufacturing companies, and is exempted either for an unlimited term or for a certain term of years. It is also, in some instances, exempted to a certain extent of capital ; in others according to the net annual income. The amount of corporate property exempted from taxation may be therefore classed under the three following heads :

1. That exempted without limitation of time, $1,112,833.

2. That upon which the term of exemption has not expired, $222,-000.

3. That in which the term has expired or will expire during the present session, $661,000.

---

[1] Laws, 1797, p. 400 (passed December 22, 1792).
[2] Laws, 1805, p. 12 ; Compiled laws, 1805, p. 400.
[3] Laws, 1808, p. 30.
[4] Laws, 1814, p. 503.
[5] Laws, 1816, p. 39.
[6] House journal, 1819. p. 79.

That this investigation occurred during the session of the legislature in which the toleration act became a law was the result of that great movement toward democratization in the United States which reached its height at the middle of the nineteenth century.[1]

From 1816 to 1860 no general acts exempting the capital of industrial enterprises were enacted in this state. The act of July 3, 1860, " to encourage manufactures " required the assent in a legal manner of the towns interested to give it effect.[2] The vote of the town to exempt any such manufacturing industry was to be a contract binding it for the term specified. This act provided that all manufacturing establishments erected by individuals or corporations for the manufacture of cotton and woolen fabrics and all capital and machinery actually used in operating the same should be exempt from taxation for a period of ten years. By act of 1871[3] the exemption upon the same condition was extended to embrace " any establishments . . . for the manufacture of the fabrics of cotton, wool, wood, iron or any other material."[4] As in the act of 1860, the vote of the town making the specific exemption was to be " a contract binding for the term   specified."[5]

---

[1] Bryce, American commonwealth, 3d. ed., vol. 1, p. 451.

[2] The supreme court held in 1890 (LXVI N. H. Reports, p. 274) that the vote must be specific. A vote to exempt any establishment hereafter erected for the manufacture of certain goods would not be sufficient to exempt an establishment afterwards erected.

[3] Laws, 1871, p. 259.

[4] See LXV N. H. Reports, 177. The court held that a vote of the town to exempt a manufacturing establishment in effect exempted the land upon which the building was erected, although such land had been previously taxed.

[5] The justices of the supreme court (Opinion, Laws, 1879, Appendix, pp. 423–425) held that " if the true construction of the state constitution did not authorize the making of these contracts they are binding nevertheless." After referring to well known decisions of

Two amendments to the act of 1871 have been enacted: (1) that of 1885,[1] providing that exemption from taxation should not be granted by one town to any manufacturing industry of another town as a condition of its removal from that town to the bargaining town; (2) that of 1887,[2] providing that "no town shall vote to exempt from taxation any establishment as aforesaid or capital used in operating the same, belonging to any person, form or corporation who shall have been previously exempted by another town in this state." The object of both of these amendments was to prevent manufacturing establishments from moving from town to town at the expiration of each period of exemption in order to escape taxation. The second amendment has accomplished this purpose.

A manufacturing industry of a different character from the above was exempted by act of July 7, 1881.[3] This act, entitled "an act to aid shipbuilding," allowed any town "by vote to authorize its proper officers to make contracts with individuals to exempt from taxation for a period not exceeding ten years all materials of wood, copper, iron and steel used in the construction and building of ships and vessels in such town and the ships and vessels constructed therefrom while in the process of construction." This act appeared unchanged in the public statutes of 1891[4] and is still in force.

the United States supreme court to support their view they continued, "should it now be decided that the true construction of the Constitution does not authorize these ten year exemption contracts, the decision could have no retrospective effects. No such contracts hereafter made would be binding, but those heretofore made under different construction would remain in force. Upon these principles of integrity and fair dealings the government was founded."

[1] Laws, 1885, p. 292.
[2] Laws, 1887, p. 420.
[3] Laws, 1881, p. 442.
[4] Public statutes, 1891, p. 180.

It was not until 1868 that the tide of democratization had receded sufficiently in New Hampshire to allow any public favors to be granted to railroad corporations. By act of July 3, 1868,[1] it was enacted that "the capital of all railroads hereafter constructed in this state shall be and the same is hereby exempted from taxation for the term of ten years from the time of commencement of the construction of such railroads respectively." This enactment appeared unchanged in the general laws of 1878,[2] but was repealed in 1881,[3] and the following provision differing but slightly in its terms was inserted in its place: "But any portion of every railroad which has not been completed and opened for use for the period of ten years from the 15th day of September in each year preceding the time when such tax is assessed shall be exempt from taxation." Since 1881 the law upon this subject has not been changed.[4]

The general policy of the state has been to tax all land, whatever its condition, according to its valuation. From 1796[5] to 1891, however, towns had authority "to exempt unimproved lands of non-residents from any tax or part thereof." This provision was dropped from the laws in the public statutes of 1891. The only exemption now of importance was enacted in 1878,[6] when it was provided "that any person who shall reclaim any swamp or swale lands by underdraining, ditching, or irrigation, either or both, or in any other manner for purposes of agriculture shall be entitled to exemption from taxation on such improvements for a term of ten years from the time when

---

[1] Laws, 1868, p. 151.

[2] General laws, 1878, p. 160.

[3] Laws, 1881, p. 488.

[4] Public statutes, 1891, p. 201.

[5] Compiled laws, 1797, p. 455 ; Revised statutes, 1842, c. 43 ; General laws, 1878, chap. 57, sec. 2.

[6] Laws, 1878, p. 175.

said improvement shall be made to the satisfaction of the selectmen of towns in which said lands are situated." [1]

For the sake of a more complete and symmetrical view of the subject of exemption from taxation, the following enumeration of property never taxed in this state is added: farming implements, farm products, and the young of farm stock; [2] tools of mechanics and artisans; household furniture, books, musical instruments, works of art, plate, jewelry, and personal clothing. [3]

2. Special exemptions are made by special act of the legislature and apply only to the property definitely described in the act. Without entering upon detailed treatment of this topic, the general policy of the state may be outlined.

From the beginning of statehood to 1830 the state favored the establishment of industries not only by general acts but also by special exemptions. Chief Justice Parker, referring to the exemption granted by the act of 1816, said, "and special exemption of different establishments for a much larger amount and for longer term were granted from time to time." [4] The legislative report of 1819, already cited, gives more direct evidence in regard to the nature and amount of such exemptions. The following examples, taken at random, may serve for illustration. At New Ipswich in 1808 [5] a mill was exempted to the amount of $20,000

[1] It was further provided that "the above act shall not apply to lands adjacent to villages or cities which shall be so improved for purposes of building lots or speculation."

[2] Sheep were not taxed until 1830; swine were not taxed until 1874, and since then two to each family have been exempted; carriages are taxed only when exceeding $50 in value.

[3] LX N. H. Reports, 92; Attorney General Tappan estimated that ' fully one-fourth of the sum of the whole valuation, or more than $50,000,000," was exempt from taxation by law.

[4] Smith *vs.* Burley *et al.*, IX N. H. Reports, 423.

[5] Laws, 1808, p. 16.

for twenty years. In 1816[1] a flint glass factory was exempted for five years not exceeding $10,000 in value. In 1820 the above act was continued in force for a second period of five years.[2] In 1827[3] the stock of the New Hampshire Canal and Steamboat Company actually employed in construction and equipment was exempted from taxation until the annual profit equalled 6 per cent on the money actually expended. The next year, 1828,[4] the stock of the Connecticut River Canal Company was similarly exempted, but not to continue over thirty years.

During the period from 1831 to 1860 neither general nor special exemptions were favored. The report of the tax commission of 1876 stated that "for a period of about thirty years preceding 1860, no legislation was had in this state of which we are aware exempting the property of manufacturing or mechanical industries from taxation."[5] The writer's investigation leads him to endorse this view. Nor does there appear to have been any legislation of importance granting special exemptions to other than manufacturing and mechanical industries.

The period from 1860 to the present time has been characterized by the adoption of the policy that was favored in the first, viz., a readiness to grant the aid of the state to establish certain industries that have failed to establish themselves under the stimulus of existing economic conditions. Since under the general laws of the state manufacturing and other industrial establishments are authorized to be exempted by vote of the

[1] Laws, 1816, p. 41.
[2] Laws, 1820, p. 346.
[3] Laws, 1827, chap. 66.
[4] Laws, 1828, chap. 78, p. 334.
[5] Report of 1876, p. 18.

town wherein they were situated the special exemptions granted by the legislature are found to refer to other interests. Thus in 1875[1] Gorham was authorized to exempt the Alpine House[2] and lands for a period of ten years. In 1883 the town of Milford was authorized to exempt Hotel Ponemah for a period of ten years or less. In 1889 Dartmouth College was granted an exemption for ten years on the hotel property known as the Wheelock. In 1874 the Simonds Free High School of Warner was granted exemption on its school fund for the value of $85,000. In 1883 the Orphanage and Home for Old Ladies in Manchester was exempted "so long as used for its present purposes." In 1887 a vote of the town of Hillsborough exempting its town system of waterworks for a period of ten years was legalized. In 1890 the Thompson estate, bequeathed to the state for the benefit of the Agricultural College, was permanently exempted from taxation.[3]

Such, in brief, has been the policy of the state of New Hampshire in regard to exemptions from taxation. While it may be admitted that the state has attempted to tax some classes of property which from their nature are able to elude in most cases the utmost vigilance of assessors and in this way cause inequality of burden while at the same time indirectly promoting dishonesty and disregard of law, it will be readily granted that in respect to household furniture, wearing apparel, tools and implements, and the property of industrial and charitable associations, the state has been singularly liberal in exercising the sovereign power of taxation.

---

[1] Laws, 1875, p. 440.

[2] A hostelry at the foot of Mt. Washington.

[3] For a further list of exemptions see the general index to the laws of 1891 and 1895.

CHAPTER VI.

THE COMMONWEALTH REVENUE, 1776–1900.

SEC. 1. *Taxes on the Inventory.* For convenience we may subdivide the period under consideration into three parts :—

1. From 1776 to 1789. During this period the taxes on the inventory were used largely to liquidate the loans, and were supplemented by important excise and impost taxes. The nominal amount of the tax levied varied with the depreciation of the paper "facilities"[1] in which it was payable. For example, in 1778 the state tax was £80,000 in lawful money ; in 1779, £250,000 for the state and £450,000 for the United States ; in 1780, £2,160,000, one-half for the state, one-half for the national government ; in 1781, £100,000 in bills of the new emission ; in 1784 it reached the normal figure of £25,000 lawful money. During this period an occasional specie tax was imposed : for example, in 1781, £5000 to pay interest ; in 1786, £10,500 for the United States foreign debt ; from 1787 to 1790, from three thousand to five thousand pounds per year for various purposes.

2. From 1790 to 1841. During this period the tax on the general inventory furnished the bulk of the state revenue, and was, in fact, the only permanent and reliable source of income for the state treasury. From 1790 to 1842 the annual tax on the inventory rose from $15,000 to $60,000 : in 1795 it was $26,666.67 ; from 1803 until 1826, $30,000 annually ; from 1829 to 1835, $45,000 ; then, after fluctuating from $35,000 in 1836 to $65,000 in 1835–7, it settled down at $60,000 annually.

[1] That is, bills of credit of the various denominations.

3. From 1842 to the present day. During this period the state tax has been absolutely much larger than in the preceding period, but relatively of decreasing importance. This has been effected by a series of special taxes upon corporations and business interests, beginning with the taxation of railroads by the state in 1843, and expanding into the series of corporation taxes which were particularly characteristic of the tax revision in 1878. From 1843 until 1850 the annual tax on the inventory was continued at $60,000 annually. During the next decade it was placed at $70,000 annually. The tax increased rapidly during the Civil War, and reached a maximum in the years 1865 and 1866 of $750,000 annually. From 1866 it gradually dropped to $400,000 annually, where it remained from 1873 until 1887. Since the latter date the state tax has been fixed at $500,000 per year.

SEC. 2. *Taxes on Railroad Corporations.* Previous to 1842 the stock in all corporations was taxable to the owners as personal property[1] in the towns where they resided. The commissioners appointed in 1842 to revise the statutes reported the law without changes, making its provisions include the stock of railroads as well as of other corporations.[2] After a full discussion of this clause, the legislature adopted an entirely new method—a change of the most far reaching importance in the history of taxation in the state. The act of 1842 provided that " every railroad corporation[3] shall pay to the state treasurer . . . . one per cent on the value of that part of its capital stock ex-

---

[1] Laws, 1833, p. 98.

[2] Commissioners' report, 1842.

[3] At this date there were about one hundred miles of railroad in the state.

pended within this state to be determined by the certificate of the justices of the Superior Court."[1]

The agent of every railroad corporation was required to transmit annually to the state treasurer a certified statement of the shares owned in each town and by whom owned, and any other necessary information. In 1860 an amendatory act made it the duty of the treasurer of a railroad corporation under penalty to keep a book showing the names and residences of the owners of the shares, as well as to make annual returns of the same. This was supplemented by a provision requiring the assessors of the several towns to return the number of shares owned in their respective jurisdictions as a prerequisite to receiving their proportion of the railroad tax. No other change occurred in the law until 1867. The statute is plain in its statement that it was the capital stock that was subject to taxation, and such was the interpretation uniformly put upon it by the justices of the superior court in making the valuation. The general statutes of 1867 made no change in the method of valuation, but altered the rate of taxation by requiring that the " capital "[2] of every railroad corporation expended in the state should be taxed " as near as may be in proportion to the taxation of other property" in the town in which the part of the railroad under consideration was located instead of at the uniform rate of one per cent.[3]

[1] Revised statutes, 1842, p. 103. This tax was to be divided and apportioned as follows : (1) to the several towns in which any railroad might be located one-fourth, each town to receive in proportion to the capital stock expended therein ; (2) to the several towns in which the stock was owned three-fourths of the one per cent paid on the stock owned in such town ; (3) the remainder for the use of the state.

[2] The omission of the word " stock " after the word "capital" was held not to alter the meaning of the phrase.

[3] General statutes, 1867, p. 130.

8

The taxation of railroads was not considered in the report of the tax commission of 1876. The commission of 1878, however, gave the subject ample consideration, both in public hearings in which the railroad corporations were represented, and in their published reports.[1] They stated that

The capital of every railroad expended in this state is required to be taxed as near as may be in proportion to the taxation of other property . . . standing alone this would seem to be a perfectly fair basis, its meaning is unmistakable. The " capital expended " must include the original investment whether of cash or borrowed capital, and the improvements whether made from the avails of new stock or bonds or from the earnings. Does the present method of assessing the railroad tax conform to this law? It does not, because in practice the assessors simply determine the present value of the original capital stock invested. If the original stock, from any cause, has become worthless or has only a nominal value, the assessment is only nominal. This construction of the statute, or rather this invariable practice of the assessors, seems to be based on the doctrine of precedents rather than on the plain intendment of the law.

The commissioners also questioned the equity of the results obtained by the method of distribution in use, on the ground that towns where large blocks of stocks were held temporarily or speculatively or pledged as collateral on the first day of April, or towns where the stations and other buildings were exceptionally valuable, received an undue benefit from the tax apportioned them. On the above ground the tax commissioners recommended an act by which " every railroad corporation in this state (not exempt by law) [should] pay to the state an annual tax upon the actual value of the road, rolling stock and equipments at the average rate of taxation in all the cities and towns of the state,"[2] the valuation and

[1] Report of tax commission, 1878, pp. 15, 43, 173.

[2] Subject to a deduction equal to the amount of tax assessed by local assessors upon buildings and right of way, which tax was to be retained by the towns through which the roads passed.

rate to be determined by a board of equalization. Certain fixed rules were laid down by which the board of equalization was to be governed in determining the valuation; if from mismanagement or any other cause the stock, etc., had only a nominal value, it was recommended that such road be taxed at a fixed sum per mile and for the value of its rolling stock and equipments, such sums to be determined by the state board of equalization.[1] Upon consideration of the above report the legislature adopted the provisions recommended by the commission upon two points: (1) that the tax should be laid upon " the actual value of the road, rolling stock and equipment "; (2) that the actual value and the rate should be determined by the state board of equalization. The legislature clung to the former method of distributing and rating " as near as may be in proportion to the taxation of other property in the several towns and cities in which such railroad is located." It rejected the proposals of the commissioners in regard to the method of fixing the valuation as well as the assessment by the mile when, through mismanagement, the stock had only a nominal value. To facilitate the work of the board of equalization the railroad corporations were required to furnish all necessary information, and upon neglect to do so were made liable to a doomage of two per cent upon capital stock and debt. In other points the act was not essentially changed.

By a subsequent act, August 9, 1881,[2] the law of 1878 was so amended that every railroad corporation was required to pay an annual tax as near as might be in proportion to the taxation of other property in all the towns and cities instead of in proportion to the rate in the

[1] Report of tax commissioners, 1878, pp. 173–5.
[2] Laws, 1881, chap. 53, sec. 1.

several towns in which the railroad was located.[1] Since 1881 the law has not been changed in its essential features.

The revenue received from the taxation of railroad corporations in New Hampshire bears striking testimony to the efficiency of the direct method of taxation of corporate property on the corporation itself. In 1844 the total revenue was $15,635.67, of which $8,405.55 was retained by the state. Ten years later the total income from the same source was $61,590.36, of which $30,420.74 went to the state treasury. In 1864 the tax was not far different. With the industrial expansion following the Civil War a notable increase in revenue from the railroad tax is noticeable. In 1868 it was $203,284.64, of which $111,547.76 was retained by the state. During the twenty years following the annual tax received was from $150,000 to $240,000, the average being not far from $190,000, of which a little less than half went to the state. From 1888 to 1898 the tax regularly increased until it reached a total of over $325,-000, of which about seven-twelfths was distributed to the towns and the remainder used to lessen the state tax upon polls and ratable estate.

SEC. 3. *Taxes on Savings Bank Deposits and on Trust Companies.* Prior to 1864 money deposited in the savings banks of the state was included in the general inventory and taxed as personal property. The expenses of the Civil War necessitated an unprecedented increase in the state tax. Under the old method the accumulations in saving banks were largely escaping taxation. The success of the railroad corporation tax pointed out the way, and the act of 1864 providing for

[1] See decision of the supreme court, B. C. & M. R. R. *vs.* State, LX N. H. Reports, p. 87.

the direct taxation of savings bank deposits by the state was the result. The treasurer of each of the banks was required to make out a detailed list of the depositors and of their deposits,[1] and to pay annually to the state treasurer a tax of three-fourths of one per cent on the accumulated amount, in lieu of all other taxes upon either banks or deposits. In 1889 the provisions of the same act were extended to include the "capital stock and the deposits upon which interest is paid" of all trust companies, loan and trust companies, and other similar corporations in the state. The tax thus assessed and collected by the state treasurer is divided into two parts : (1) that assessed on the deposits of residents of the state, and (2) that assessed on the deposits of non-residents. The former is distributed to the towns and cities in proportion to the share of each in the total deposits; the latter becomes a part of the literary fund and is then by law distributed as state aid to the common schools.[2] The rate of the tax on savings bank deposits was originally three-fourths of one per cent. In 1869 the rate was raised to one per cent, where it remained until 1895, notwithstanding the urgent protests of the banking interests.[3] The taxation of savings bank deposits has been intimately bound up with the taxation of two other classes of property : (1) the real estate held by the banking corporations, and (2) the capital stock of the loan and trust

---

[1] By an amendment of 1865 the bank treasurers were required to make separate lists (1) of the sums deposited by the residents of the state, and (2) of the sums deposited by non-residents. Laws, 1865, p. 3117.

[2] By amendment of 1866. The act of 1864 provided that the tax on deposits of non-residents should remain in the state treasury.

[3] It was stated in a hearing before the tax commissioners of 1878 that the competition of the Massachusetts and of the Vermont savings banks was seriously affecting the deposits in the New Hampshire banks.

companies. In 1872 the real estate held by the banks of the state was excluded from the above tax, being made taxable, as formerly, in the respective towns. In 1891 the treasurers of banks and trust companies were required to separate their general and special deposits from the capital stock, but the rate was to continue at the uniform rate of one per cent on all the classes. In 1895, after considerable discussion, an amendatory act was adopted providing (1) that the rate upon capital stock and upon the special deposits be continued at one per cent, and (2) that the tax upon general deposits upon which interest was paid be reduced to three-fourths of one per cent after deducting, in addition to its real estate, " the value of its loans secured by mortgages upon real estate situated in this state made at the rate not exceeding five per cent per annum."

The tax upon savings bank deposits and other savings institutions is still another impressive example of efficient methods of taxation. The tax is easily and cheaply collected, it is equitable, and it is certain. The following table, comparing the amounts of savings bank deposits with all other personal property returned for taxation for certain years, is worthy of careful study :—

Year.	Savings bank deposits taxed.	All other personal estate taxed.	All real estate taxed.
1860	_____[1]	$28,506,065	$ 77,748,762
1867	$10,297,035	-- ------	------- --
1872	24,654,672	------- --	------- --
1877	30,318,320	---- ----	------- --
1881	31,787,832	36,313,848	123,511,284
1883	38,786,507	37,757,093	128,417,205
1885	43,402,663	36,443,848	130,298,843
1887	56,361,325	37,030,031	131,693,411
1890	63,846,977	35,410,721	140,310,932
1893	77,024,282	35,985,697	150,209,160

[1] Savings bank deposits were included in " All other personal estate".

SEC. 4. *The Revenue from Insurance Companies.*
The revenue from insurance companies has been derived
from two distinct sources : (1) from taxes on the capital
stock or on the business; and (2) from fees of several
kinds. Prior to 1869 shares or stock in insurance companies were taxable to the owner, if the owner was a resident of the state;[1] otherwise they were taxable to the
corporation at the principal office in the state.[2] By an
act of 1869[3] the taxation of foreign insurance companies
doing business in the state was assumed by the central
government. Every such insurance company was required to pay to the treasurer of the state a tax of one
per cent upon the gross amount of premiums received.[4]
All companies wishing to do business in this state had
first to take out a license issued by the insurance commissioner, for which a small fee was exacted.[5] Failure
to furnish the proper information or to pay the assessment after due notice had been given was sufficient cause
for the revocation of the license.

The enactment of the so-called " valued policy law ",
to take effect January 1, 1886, led to the withdrawal,
en masse, of all the foreign fire insurance companies in

[1] In 1852 a retaliatory act was passed providing that insurance companies organized under the laws of any other state should pay the
same taxes, fees, etc., in New Hampshire as such other state imposed
upon any company organized under the laws of New Hampshire and
doing business in such other state. Similar acts were passed in 1891
and in 1895, providing that burdens imposed upon New Hampshire
insurance companies abroad might be offset by retaliatory taxes, fines,
penalties, etc., upon insurance companies from the offending state.

[2] Revised statutes, 1842, p. 104.

[3] Laws, 1869, p. 276.

[4] A sworn statement was required from every insurance company
showing the amount of premiums received in money and in the form
of notes, credits, loans, or any other substitute for money, on persons
or property in the state.

[5] See section on insurance fees, p. 121.

the state.[1] The immediate effect of this withdrawal
was the organization of a considerable number of stock,
mutual, and town insurance companies under state law.
This somewhat unexpected result of legislation intended
to safeguard the interests of the policy holders made a
general law for the taxation of home insurance
companies desirable. At the June session of the legislature in 1869 several stock fire insurance companies
were chartered,[2] of which only the New Hampshire
Fire Insurance Company of Manchester seems to have
been fully organized and to have assumed fire risks. No
provision for its taxation was made in its charter, but
in 1870 the charter was amended so that the company
was directly taxable by the state. The treasurer of the
company was required to make annually a sworn statement to the treasurer of the state of the name and
residence of each of the shareholders in the company
on April first, with the number of shares owned by
such person. Upon such capital stock the company was
required to pay a tax of one per cent, in lieu of all
other taxes against said company or its shareholders.[3]

Subsequently, in 1887,[4] the act for taxing the capital

[1] Fifty-eight companies in all. The law provided, in substance,
that in case of total loss by fire or of other casualty to real estate or
buildings, "the amount of damage shall be the amount expressed in
the contract as the sum insured, and no other evidence shall be admitted on trial as to the value of the property insured." In case of
partial loss the actual damage only was taken.

[2] Laws, 1869, pp. 347–351.

[3] Laws, 1870, p. 483. This tax was to be divided as follows : "One-
fourth of said one per cent shall be retained by the treasurer for the
use of the state and the three-fourths of said one per cent. to be by
him distributed to the several towns in the state in the same proportion that the number of shares owned in each town bears to the whole
number of shares. The tax on all shares owned by persons residing
out of the state shall be retained by the treasurer of the state for the
use of the state."

[4] Laws, 1887, p. 442.

stock of the New Hampshire Fire Insurance Company
was made general, so that all stock fire insurance companies organized under the laws of the state and doing
business in the state were subjected to the same tax, viz.,
one per cent upon the capital stock.[1]

In 1870–1871, the first year in which there was a fair
test of the revenue-producing qualities of the tax, the
amount that was paid into the state treasury by both
foreign and home insurance companies was $11,115.78.
In 1873–1874 it reached its first maximum at $12,179.41.
From this date there was a gradual falling off
until 1879–1880, when the first minimum was reached
at $7,389.79. In 1884–1885 the tax reached $10,-
081.59. The next year, the year of the "exodus",
the tax touched low water mark at $4,831.56. Since
1885 it has regularly increased, and in 1896–1897 the
proceeds of the tax were $26,195.88. The revenue to
the state from the tax on insurance companies has thus
averaged something over $10,000 per year, and in addi-
tion several thousand dollars per year has been distributed to the towns.

In 1867[2] a fee of $5.00 annually was assessed on each
foreign insurance company doing business in the state
for filing a statement of its standing and condition. In
1869[3] an annual fee of $100 was required of every non-

[1] In 1889 the foreign companies began to return, until, on December
1, 1890, thirty-seven of the fifty-eight companies "that made such sudden exit, becoming weary of waiting for the calamity that they had
predicted would fall on New Hampshire, had returned and resumed
business, gracefully conforming to our laws." Message of the governor, I State reports, 1890, p. 6. In 1895 the insurance commissioner
reported that "nearly all the companies that left the state in 1885
have returned and with them many others and they are still coming."
Report of insurance commissioner, 1895, p. xv.

[2] General statutes, 1867, p. 328.

[3] Laws, 1869, p. 276.

resident insurance agent soliciting business in the state. Since that date the fees exacted have been more uniform, as may be seen from the table below :—

	Home insurance companies.		Foreign insurance companies.	
	1870	1889	1870	1889
For filing statement of standing and condition of company annually	$5 00	$5 00	$5 00	$15 00
For license and annual renewal	----	----	5 00	5 00
For filing copy of charter	----	----	----	25 00
For agent's license and annual renewal	----	----	1 00	20 00
For certificate of examination and qualification	----	5 00	----	----
For each service of legal process upon insurance company as attorney	----	2 00	----	----
For each copy of paper on file, ten cents per page ; for certifying the same	----	1 00	----	----

From 1869 to 1887 the commissioner received all fees accruing to the office as his salary and as expenses for clerk hire, etc. By the act of 1887[1] he was allowed an annual salary, and all fees after that date were paid quarterly into the state treasury. The amount of fees thus turned into the state treasury in 1887–1888 was $818. For the first year after the act of 1889, increasing the fees, the amount was $4519. In 1896–1897 the revenue was $9,832.05.

SEC. 5. *Taxes on Telegraph and Telephone Companies.* The direct taxation of telegraph companies dates from 1878. At the session of the legislature held in 1877 a bill was introduced and referred to the board of tax commissioners authorizing a tax of two per cent upon the gross receipts of all telegraph companies doing business in the state. The act recommended by the tax commis-

---

[1] Laws, 1887, p. 428.

sioners, and enacted in 1878,[1] however, provided for a tax of one per cent upon the value of the property of the several companies, including the office furniture and machinery. The appraisal was to be made by the board of equalization at the actual value of the property. The assessment was made annually, in August, by the same authorities, and the tax was payable to the state treasurer on or before the first day of September following. The tax so assessed and paid was to be in lieu of all other taxes. The above act was amended August 9, 1881,[2] by changing the rate of taxation from one per cent to "an annual tax as near as may be in proportion to the taxation of other property throughout the state," and by requiring the state board of equalization to "assess said telegraph property at the average rate of taxation of other property throughout the state."[3] Under the provisions of the act of 1878 the revenue from the taxation of telegraph lines was somewhat less than $1000 annually. Under the act of 1881 the revenue has exceeded $2000 annually, and for the year ending May 31, 1897, was $3,190.40.

Until 1883 the stock and other property of telephone companies was taxed in the same manner as that of other corporations for the taxation of which no special laws existed.[4] The act of September 15, 1883, provided for the assessment of a tax on telephone companies in a manner entirely similar to the taxation of telegraph companies, as described in the preceding paragraph of this section. The revenue from this source has run very nearly par-

[1] Laws. 1878, p. 182.

[2] Laws, 1881, p. 471.

[3] B. C. & M. *vs.* State, LX N. H. Reports, p. 87.

[4] General laws, chaps. 57, sec. 1 ; chap. 53, sec. 5 ; chap. 54, sec. 5.

allel with that from the taxation of telegraph companies. In 1896–97 it was $3,129.60.

Sec. 6. *Fees.* The revenue from fees has been derived from the following sources : (1) license fees from peddlers, hawkers, etc. ; (2) fees for corporation charters ; (3) license fees for the sale of lightning rods ; (4) license fees for the sale of fertilizers ;. and (5) license fees for the practice of dentistry.

1. The fiscal policy of the state in its relation to the business of hawkers, peddlers and itinerant merchants may be grouped by periods as follows :—

(1) From 1821 until 1878. During this period hawkers, peddlers, auctioneers, and itinerant merchants were licensed by a county officer, and the revenue from the license fees was turned into the county treasury.

(2) From 1878 to 1893. The tax commissioners of 1878 recommended that the proceeds of this tax be appropriated to the state treasury, and their advice upon this point was accepted. The applicant for a license, in order to do business under this act,[1] had first to procure of the clerk of the supreme court a state license, for which he paid a small fee ; this license authorized the several county clerks to issue permits to do business within their respective territorial limits.[2] The clerk receipted for the fee on the back of the license,[3] and for-

---

[1] Commercial travellers, venders of fish, fruits, vegetables, provisions, fuel, newspapers, or of the products of their own industry, and those incapable of manual labor, were exempted from the provisions of the act.

[2] The fees for each county were $10 for a hawker or peddler, $20 for an auctioneer merchant, and $50 for an intinerant or temporary merchant. Laws, 1878, p. 104. In 1883 the fee for the last two classes was raised to $100 each.

[3] This receipt on the back of the license was, of course, the licensee's evidence of authority to sell his goods. Selling without license was punishable by appropriate fines of from $100 to $200.

warded the amount to the state treasurer for the use of the state. This act, with the amendment of 1883, was repealed in 1887 and a new act substituted. The act of 1887 [1] was, however, in effect an amendment to the act of 1878. The general license was obtained as before, while the permission to sell in any county was granted directly by the clerk of the supreme court. The list of exemptions was essentially as in 1878, but the schedule of fees was changed to favor those who desired a state license. [2]

(3) From 1893 to the present time. During this period the licenses have been issued by a state officer upon recommendation of a local officer, and the fees have accrued to town, county, or state, according to the territorial limits for which the license has been issued. Under the act of 1893 the applicant for authority to sell goods as a hawker, peddler, etc., must be recommended to the secretary of state [3] by a mayor of a city or by the selectmen of a town. The license is then issued for a town, a county, or the state, as the applicant desires. The fees for a town license are graduated according to the size of the town, varying from $2.00 to $20.00; for a county, $25.00; for the state, $50.00. Temporary or itinerant merchants are licensed directly by the town where they wish to do business. The act of 1893 was, in its nature, a decided reaction against the centralization which had formerly been effected. It bears strik-

[1] Laws, 1887, p. 452.

[2] Hawkers, peddlers, or itinerant venders, $25 for each county, $50 for the state; temporary merchants, $50 for each county.

[3] Soldiers and sailors, disabled either during or since the war, are exempt from the payment of fees, except the $1.00 fee to the secretary of state for drawing up the license. The other classes exempted are not essentially changed, except that those unable to perform manual labor are not exempt.

ing testimony to the spirit of local independence that
still is found in the Granite State.

Under the act of 1878 and its amendments the revenue
from the above source averaged about $1000 annually.
Under the act of 1887 it averaged nearly $2000 per
annum. Under the law of 1893, in 1893–1894 it was
$1550; in 1894–1895, $950; in 1896–1897, $2550.

2. Until 1877 New Hampshire, following the American
custom, paid her legislators for the time expended in
enacting charters, and presented their franchises and
privileges as a free gift[1] to the incorporators. In 1877
this policy was partially reversed. Banking, railroad, insurance, and other corporations were required to pay
certain fees to the state[2] for the privilege of incorporation, and additional fees for subsequent changes. This
act has been twice amended, first in 1889, and second in
1895. The act of 1889 applied only to those corporations which did not carry on all of their business and did
not have their principal office in the state. The tax was
a graduated one, decreasing in rate with the increase in
the authorized capital stock. One per cent on the stock
authorized up to $50,000, it decreased gradually to
three-eighths of one per cent for corporations having
capital stock in excess of $1,000,000. Under this act
corporations within the state, organizing under the so-
called " voluntary laws " relating to corporations, paid
no fees, while the rate for foreign corporations was practically prohibitory. Governor Busiel in 1895[3] called at

[1] See Bryce, American commonwealth, 2d ed., vol. 1, chap. 44, for
an example of European criticism of this policy.

[2] Banks of discount, $1.00 on $1,000 in certified stock ; savings
banks, $100 ; railroads and insurance companies, fifty cents on each
$1,000 authorized capital ; other corporations, $50.00 ; supplementary
acts, $25.00.

[3] Governor's message, State reports, 1895.

tention to these defects in the law, and urged that they be revised to meet the needs of modern conditions. His advice upon the first point fell upon deaf ears; upon the second point the legislature deliberated and as a result the scale of fees was lowered considerably. They now range from $10 for a capital stock of $25,000 to $200 for one of over $1,000,000.

The revenue from charter fees during the first year the act of 1877 was in force amounted to only $740. The maximum revenue received from 1877 to the present time was $15,088.50, in 1877–78, under the act of 1877. In 1890–91, the first year after the amendment was enacted taxing the charters of foreign corporations according to their capital stock, the total revenue was $12,354.50. In 1896–97 the total revenue was $1,360.-00. The aggregate revenue from this source for the twenty years immediately after 1877 was almost exactly $50,000.

3. In 1879[1] the secretary of the board of agriculture was instructed to collect samples of fertilizers sold in the state and to submit them to the College of Agriculture and of the Mechanic Arts for examination. If the results of such examination were found to be satisfactory, the state treasurer was authorized to issue a license, to be countersigned by the secretary of the board of agriculture, to the person or corporation manufacturing or importing such fertilizers. This license legalized the sale of the specified fertilizers, but each bag or barrel offered for sale must display a card giving a list of its constituent parts and the words "State of New Hampshire—Licensed." The fee for the license was $50, to be paid in to the treasury, and the term for which it was valid was one year. During the twenty years in which the

[1] Laws, 1879, p. 353.

sale of fertilizers has been taxed by the state the revenue to the state has approximated $12,500. During the
first decade the revenue averaged about $500 per year;
during the last decade, nearly $1000 per year.

4. The first act[1] on the statute books regulating the
sale of lightning rods was evidently intended to be prohibitory. It dated from 1878 and allowed the state treasurer to grant a license for the sale of lightning rods for a
term of one year to any applicant "if the treasurer shall
be satisfied upon a scientific investigation, that such
lightning rods are sufficient for security against lightning and that the applicant is a person of good moral
character." The sum of $50 had to be paid in advance
to defray the expenses of the investigation. The penalty
for selling without a license was a fine not exceeding
$1000, imprisonment in county jail not exceeding one
year, or both. It is hardly necessary to state that no
licenses were issued under the above law. The next
year, 1879,[2] the law was amended by allowing the state
treasurer upon the payment of $100 to grant a license
for the sale of lightning rods to "any applicant who has
for five years last past been a citizen of the state," provided that the result of the scientific examination were
satisfactory and the applicant filed a bond with the required securities in the penal sum of $1000 to respond
in damages resulting from misrepresentation or fraud.
The constitutionality of the above amendment was
questioned on the ground that it was in conflict with a
provision of the constitution[3] of the United States. A
case involving the validity of the law was brought before the supreme court of the state and the court held

[1] Laws, 1878, p. 179.
[2] Laws, 1879, p. 352.
[3] Art. 4, sec. 2.

the law invalid [1] for the reason given above. The total amount received for license fees under the amendment of 1879 was $500. This sum was refunded [2] by the legislature after the law was declared unconstitutional. The public statutes of 1891 retained all the existing provisions upon the subject of licenses for lightning rod venders except the provision declared invalid. In place of the fees imposed under the amendment of 1879 a uniform fee of $300 each was imposed upon all applicants who were able to file the $1000 bond required under the amendment of 1879. It does not appear that any revenue has as yet (1898) accrued to the state under the above provisions.

5. The practice of medicine and surgery was first regulated by state law in 1875.[3] At the general revision of the laws in 1878 the act was extended to include the practice of dentistry. All persons desiring to practice this profession who were not duly authorized to practice medicine or who had not secured a dental degree from some authorized institution or who had not practiced the profession continuously in the state since January 1, 1875, were required to pass an examination prepared by the New Hampshire Dental Society and to pay certain fees both to the society and to the clerk of the county court. In 1889 a case was brought before the supreme court which involved the validity of the statute on the ground that it discriminated between citizens of the state and those of other states. The court held the statute void and the decision resulted in the act of 1891, establishing a board of denistry, with authority to regulate the practice of the profession. This act provided that

---

[1] State *vs.* Wiggin, LXIV N. H. reports, p. 508.

[2] Laws, 1889, p. 126.

[3] Laws, 1875, p. 449.

9

every person engaged in the practice of dentistry in the state at the specified time, or who was a graduate of some college or institution authorized to give a dental degree, or who had been regularly licensed by the New Hampshire Dental Society should register with the said board. All others desiring to practice the profession were required to pass an examination before the board of dentistry. The fees established by this act were : for a certificate which was to be issued to all practioners, 50 cents ; for a certificate of qualification after the examination, in case such certificate were granted, $5.00. The annual revenue from this source has been small, never having reached $100.

SEC. 7. *Indirect Taxes.* At the outbreak of the Revolution the excise taxes[1] then in force were continued without express enactment until April 9, 1777, when they were legalized by a specific legislative act.[2] By the act of December 26, 1778,[3] the excise tax was discontinued[4] until 1781, when the former policy was revived. The tax was uniform for all kinds of distilled liquors, and the rate was fixed at three pence per gallon for innkeepers and two pence per gallon for ordinary retailers. An account under oath to the proper officers was required at quarterly intervals. In case of refusal to take this oath at the request of the officers a fine of $10 was imposed "in full satisfaction of the quarterly excise". By an amendment of December 28, 1782,[5] the rates were doubled[6] and it was further required that the excise for each county should be sold annually " at pub-

[1] See chap. 3, sec. 3, p. 46.
[2] Perpetual laws, 1789, p. 160.
[3] Perpetual laws, 1789, p. 239.
[4] Perpetual laws, 1789, p. 145.
[5] Perpetual laws, 1789, p. 147.
[6] To counteract the depreciation of the paper currency.

lic vendue to the highest bidder ".[1]   This act was.con-
tined in force until 1787, when it was found that "the
raising a larger revenue to this state by excise than hath
heretofore been practiced and in a more general way appears very necessary."   The act of 1787[2] increased the
rates on distilled liquors[3] and included in the system an
excise tax on clocks[4] and vehicles.[5]   All retailers were
required to take out a license, otherwise they were liable
to a fine of 40 shillings for each offense, one-fourth going
to the prosecutor and three-fourths to the state.   All
persons purchasing by wholesale (twenty-five gallons
and upwards) of those who did not retail or pay excise
were required to pay the regular excise to the farmer or
collector.   This act was continued in force until the
United States government was established in 1789.

2. It was shown in a preceding section[6] that the policy
of maintaining an "open port" was firmly established
in New Hampshire as early as 1725.   While a continuation of the traditional policy of the state was
manifestly impossible after the outbreak of hostilities
in 1775, and impracticable from the close of the war to
the inauguration of the federal government under the
constitution of 1787, the actual policy adopted by the
state was, under the circumstances, singularly liberal.
On the 27th of December, 1776, following the report of
a committee of both houses for regulating trade, etc.,

---

[1] From 1777 to 1782 it seems to have been the custom to "farm
out" the excise tax.

[2] Perpetual laws, 1789, p. 149.

[3] The rates for retailers varied from 4 $d.$ per gallon on New England
rum and other American distilled spirits to 1 $s.$ 3 $d.$ on Medeira wine ;
taverners paid one-fourth more.

[4] 30 $s.$ on every imported clock.

[5] Coach or chariot, £ 6 per year ; fall back chaise, 8 $s.$; other chaise,
6 $s.$, etc., etc.

[6] Chap. 3. sec. 4, pp. 49-64.

the legislature authorized a committee " to repair to the Massachusetts State and there consult with the committee there appointed to bring in a bill for the purpose of regulating trade, etc., and that they make it their business so to conduct matters that a general regulation may take place which may be suitable to the circumstances of the four New England States."[1] It does not appear that this effort to secure uniform trade regulations for New England was successful. Being unable to bring about any rules for the government of trade, New Hampshire for nearly a year, from December 10, 1776,[2] to November 22, 1777,[3] maintained a general embargo.[4] Even after the embargo was abandoued the state legislature exercised large powers over the movements of vessels entering the ports, especially in regard to the exportation of any provisions that might by any chance fall into the hands of the enemy. In general, however, the state maintained the former policy of unrestricted trade until 1784.

By act[5] of the 6th of April, 1781, the state granted to the congress of the United States the right to levy a duty of five per cent upon all goods, wares, and merchandise of foreign growths and manufactures, with certain specified exceptions, imported into the state after March 7, 1781, and a further duty of five per cent upon all prizes condemned in the maritime court of the state, provided that the legislatures of the other states would grant similar duties. The states failed to act, and cousequently matters drifted from bad to worse. Again, on

---

[1] VIII N. H. Prov. papers, 441.

[2] VIII N. H. Prov. papers, 412.

[3] VIII N. H. Prov. papers, 718.

[4] War vessels excepted. Other vessels might be especially excepted by the proper authorities.

[5] XXI N. H. State papers, 869.

four different occasions during the years 1784–86[1] the state of New Hampshire, in accordance with the recommendation of the congress of the United States of April 30, 1784, authorized that body to " enter into treaties of commerce and provide for a due regulation of trade throughout the United States of America," to take effect whenever the other states[2] sanctioned such action on the part of congress. No such general action was secured, however, until the adoption of the Constitution in 1787.

Accordingly the legislature on the 17th of April, 1784,[3] passed an " Act for laying an impost duty on sundry goods imported into this state." The duty was fixed at five per cent upon nails, looking-glasses, China ware, glassware, earthenware and stoneware, and at two and one-half per cent upon all other goods. Hemp, salt, and such articles as were manufactured or grown in the United States of America were exempted. The commercial interests of New Hampshire were at this date too important to submit to a policy of commercial isolation without a struggle. The merchants of Portsmouth were again the leaders in a movement for " free trade". On the 15th of February, 1785, a " petition and memorial of a number of merchants, traders and other inhabitants of the town of Portsmouth "[4] was presented to the legislature with the result that a joint committee was appointed to " confer with the legislature of the commonwealth of Massachusetts, with respect to the trade and commerce carried on between the subjects of the said commonwealth and those of this state," urging

[1] XXI N. H. State papers, 870–3.

[2] See Fiske, Critical period of American history, pp. 142-147, for a brief account.

[3] Laws, 1780, p. 367.

[4] XX N. H. State papers, 197.

the necessity of peace and harmony among the whole, and that, "that commonwealth's laying duties on goods, wares and merchandizes belonging to subjects of this state will have a manifest tendency to disunite them."[1] The instructions for the guidance of the committee stated that "the commercial interests of the commonwealth of Massachusetts and those of this state are so reciprocal and interwoven with each other that it is necessary some laws and regulations should be adopted that may be of mutual benefit and advantage in regulating trade as well by sea as by land, and that such impost acts as have been passed in either or both of said states, to the prejudice of trade or the revenue of either state, or the subjects thereof, be revised and put on a fair and equitable basis for both." In furthering these plans the committee was instructed to "propose and consult on such laws and regulations as shall be judged necessary and convenient for the reciprocal and mutual advantage of each state; and . . . endeavor to obtain a repeal of all such laws and regulations of trade as may be injurious and inequitable to either state or subjects thereof, or in any way embarrass a free and open trade between each other."[2] It was not until October 21, 1785,[3] that the committee was finally appointed and fully prepared to enter on its work. Although it appears that before the New Hampshire committee was ready to proceed on their mission Massachusetts had authorized a similar one, the legislative records of the state are silent regarding the work of the two committees.

From 1786 until 1790, when the revenue laws of the

[1] XX N. H. State papers, 197–8.
[2] XX N. H. State papers, 215.
[3] XX N. H. State papers, 416.

national government took effect, the state, finding her
efforts unavailing to coöperate, either with the nation or
with Massachusetts for a uniform regulation of commerce, pursued a more independent course.   On March
4, 1786, "an act to establish certain impost duties on
various articles imported into this state"[1] stated that
the "laying duties on articles of the produce and manufactures of foreign countries, will not only produce a
considerable revenue to the state, but will encourage
the manufacturing of many of those articles in the
same."   It was thereupon enacted

That from and after the first day of May next, there shall be an
impost duty of 15 per centum *ad valorem* upon all jewels, wrought
gold and silver, brocades or cloth of gold and silver, gold and silver
lace, silk stockings, silk stuffs, silk thread and woolen gloves, shoes
and boots, buckles, pewter spoons, silk, hair and basket buttons,
beaver, felt and castor hats, saddles and bridles, horse harness, ready
made beds and furniture, painted paper, playing cards, chess-men, all
wrought iron excepting artificers tools, all wrought brass excepting
warming pans, all wrought mahogany, nails, bellows, all glass excepting window glass, cheese, loaf sugar and linseed oil ; also upon all
ready made carriages, clocks, clock cases, and watches that may be
imported into this state either by land or water : and an impost duty
of 10 per centum *ad valorem* upon all china, earthen and stonewares,
that may be imported as aforesaid and also an impost duty of 5 per
centum *ad valorem* upon all wines, beer, porter and ale, that may be
imported as aforesaid ; and a duty of three shillings per barrel, on all
pitch, tar, and turpentine imported as aforesaid ; and also a duty of
2½ per centum *ad valorem* upon all goods, wares and merchandize,
that may be imported as aforesaid.

These duties might either be paid in money or secured
by bond, with sufficient securities, to be paid in three
months, after which date interest was charged.   In case
of disagreement as to the value of the goods the impost
officer and importer were authorized jointly to select
two or more reputable citizens to appraise such goods on
oath.   In case the importer and impost officer could not

[1] Perpetual laws, 1789, p. 152.

agree upon the persons, the officer was directed to apply to any justice of the peace for the county, who was then authorized to appoint two or more discreet persons whose appraisal under oath was to be deemed the just value of the goods in question. Both the master of any vessel bringing by sea goods liable to duty and "every waggoner, team driver, carman or other person" importing goods by land exceeding three pounds in value at any one time were required to make certain reports and properly to secure the payment of the duty, or be liable to penalties of £20 and £10 respectively and also to forfeiture of the goods. The impost officers were required " to file a libel" before any justice of the superior court of judicature whenever any goods were seized under this act, and the same court was given full jurisdiction over all cases arising under the law. Perishable goods seized under this law might be sold before the trial occurred. Glass, cast iron, and wrought iron were subject to a duty of two and one-half per cent until January 1, 1787, after which date they paid full rates. A significant clause appeared in a provision " that this act shall not be construed to extend to any rum brought into this state, being the manufacture of any of the United States, or to the article of salt, or the necessary household furniture of any person coming into this state or to any of the articles aforesaid, being the manufacture of any of the United States." This act, by its terms, was " to continue and be in force for the term of two years and to the then next session of the general court."

This important act was modified by two statutes: (1) An act passed June 23, 1786,[1] provided that certain articles used in manufacturing might be imported, by

---

[1] Perpetual laws, 1789, p. 197.

land or by sea, by any person, native or foreigner, duty
free. The articles thus exempted were "spanish and
cotton wool, molasses, raw silk, elephants' teeth, un-
tanned hides, unwrought copper, brass, and steel, pig
iron, goat's hair, camel's hair, fuller's earth, drugs and
wood used in dyeing, tin plates, brass and iron wire, and
all tools and implements used by artificers." (2) A second modifying act, entitled "an act to encourage the
importation of coined gold and silver," was passed June
24, 1786.[1] Although this law failed to relieve the momentary distress owing to the operations of the so-called
tender act,[2] it increased the stock of hoarded gold and
silver and admitted goods free of duty that otherwise
would have either paid a duty or sought other markets.
The act provided that every vessel owned by inhabitants
of the state should be free from all duties except light
money if· it brought gold and silver only, and from
one-half the duties if it brought a sum of money equal
to half its cargo, and so in proportion.[3]

[1] Perpetual laws, 1789, p. 198.

[2] II Belknap, N. H., p. 466. Barstow, N. H., p. 270.

[3] The impost act of March 4, 1786, was again amended on June 27,
1787. Perpetual laws, 1789, p. 149. The object of this amendment
was to "impower the impost officer to enforce the collection of the
revenue" arising under the act. It provided: (1) that the impost
officer or his deputy might enter on board any vessel and remain there
until the time for making the report, and examine and condemn any
part of the cargo (See remonstrance, XXI N. H. State papers, 75) if
it did not compare with the report; (2) that all bonds should be discharged in silver or gold, any tender act to the contrary notwithstanding; (3) that the state treasurer should issue extents if the bonds for
the payment of the impost were not paid when due; (4) that the impost officers should give bond in the sum of £3000 for the payment of
the impost revenue to the state treasurer quarterly, and that in case of
failure extents might be issued against the impost officers; and (5)
that no drawback should be allowed on account of the importation of
gold and silver unless the captain could satisfy the impost officer that
the gold and silver was "on board the vessel when he sailed from
some foreign port."

On June 13, 1788,[1] the general court passed an act continuing the act of March 4, 1786, " so far as the same is consistent with the other impost acts now in force,". for two years, affirming that " the same has been found very beneficial." Upon the assumption of the state debts by the federal government, the latter took formal control of the impost and excise in accordance with the provisions of the federal constitution. It was not till January 16, 1790, however, that the legislature of the state could affirm that " by the operation of the Federal Government the collection of duties and tonnage at the impost and naval office have ceased."[2]

3. In a letter to Colonel M. Weare, president of the council, dated June 10, 1782, Eleazer Russell, collector of the port of Portsmouth, stated,[3] " when the naval office was first ordered by a resolve of the General Court, early in the year 1776[4] no fees were mentioned, and I was advised by the State Committee to make out a list for the several papers to be used that was moderate, which I did, and first shew it to the merchants there in trade who thought it full low—it afterwards had the Saction of the Hon[ble] Committee of the state. When the office was established by law, on November 26, 1778,[5] this list was before the Hon[ble] General Court, and on account of the depreciation they were pleased to order three for one. When paper money ceased to circulate (1780) I knew not what to do. To reduce the law fees by the scale of depreciation[6] brot them very low and produced fractions that I could never make even

---

[1] Perpetual laws, 1789, p. 159.
[2] XXI N. H. State papers, p. 711.
[3] XVIII N. H. State papers, pp. 716-8.
[4] VIII N. H. Prov. papers, p. 194.
[5] N. H. Laws, 1780, p. 132.
[6] Passed September 1, 1781. Perpetual laws, 1789, p. 185.

change. Therefore, I recurd to the original list [1] and it has since been my rule."

4. A resolution of the general court, November 27, 1777,[2] directing the naval officer for the port of Pascataqua (Portsmouth) "to collect and receive for the use of this state all the powder and powder money that shall come due to this state from foreign vessels entering the port . . . . according to the laws of this state and pay the same in to the treasury every three months," indicates that as soon as the embargo act was repealed the laws relating to powder money in force previous to the outbreak of the Revolution were made operative. By "an act to alter and extend the act about powder money," passed April 16, 1784,[3] the former act was amended in two particulars : (1) it was extended "to comprehend all vessels not belonging to any subject or subjects of the United States," and (2) it was provided that in future every ship or vessel liable to pay the powder money duty should pay "two shillings per ton in money and not in powder." The revenue derived from powder money and port fees

[1] XVIII N. H. State papers, p. 684, gives the following list :—

NAVAL OFFICE, New Hampshire, 1776.

For entering every ship and vessel from Massachusetts Coastways	0,,	3,,	0
For clearing to ditto	0,,	3,,	0
For entering from any other of the American States	0,,	6,,	0
For clearing to ditto	0,,	6,,	0
For entering every ship, or vessel from a foreign voyage	0,,	12,,	0
For clearing to ditto	0,,	12,,	0
For every Register	0,,	12,,	0
For recording every Register	0,,	2,,	0
For endorsing every Register	0,,	2,,	0
For every Bond	0,,	2,,	0
For a bill of health	0,,	3,,	0
For a Coket	0,,	2,,	0
For a permit to unload	0,,	1,,	0
For every pass for the Forts	0,,	2,,	0 "

[2] VIII N. H. Prov. papers, p. 721.

[3] Perpetual laws, 1789, p. 159.

seems to have been barely sufficient to provide a harbor light and a small garrison at the port. An act of 1787,. appropriating certain revenues from impost, excise, etc., provided "that the revenue annually received by the naval officer shall be and hereby is appropriated to the support of the garrison and maintenance of the light at ᵗhe castle William and Mary, and the deficiency, should any happen, shall be made up out of the specie taxes due to the state : and the surplus of said revenue, if any there be, shall be and hereby is appropriated to the payment of orders drawn or that may be drawn on the treasury."[1]

SEC. 8.   *The Present Revenue.*   The following statement, taken from the reports of the state treasurer, exhibits the chief sources of the state revenue for the fiscal years 1886–87 and 1896–97 :—

	1886–7	1896–7
State tax	$400,000 00	$500,000 00
Railroad tax [2]	101,191 22	133,045 66
Insurance tax	6,563 32	26,195 66
Interest on deposits	1,416 81	1,994 60
License fees (peddlers)	190 00	2,550 00
License fees (fertilizers)	550 00	1,100 00
Telegraph tax	5,806 73	3,190 40
Telephone tax	195 65	3,129 60
Charter fees		1,360 00
Fees (Insurance Department)		9,832 05

[1] Perpetual laws, 1789, pp. 157–8.

[2] The share of the state in the tax on railroad corporations is somewhat less than one-half. In 1886-7 the total revenue from the railroad tax was $208,182.72.

CHAPTER VII.

THE ADMINISTRATION OF STATE TAXES.

SEC. I. *Assessment.* The act of July 2, 1776,[1] provided that " public rates and taxes shall be made and assessed in proportion to each persons poll, ratable estate and faculty." It did not definitely state that the selectmen should make the assessment, but it assumed such action in a provision requiring that the " Selectmen shall annually take an invoice of each persons poll and estate." However, the act of February 8, 1791, the basis of the succeeding system, enacted

That the selectmen of the several towns in this state be, and they hereby are authorized, empowered and required seasonably in every year to assess the polls and estates within such towns according to the rules and directions of the law, their just and equal proportion of all sums of money granted by the general court for which they shall have warrant under the hand and seal of the treasurer of the state for the time being, and their proportion of all sums of money voted and agreed to be raised by the justices of the court of general sessions of the peace in the same county for which they shall have a warrant under a hand and seal of the treasurer of the same county ; and all such sums of money as shall be voted to be raised at any legal meeting of the inhabitants of their town ; and they shall also assess the polls and estates within such town all such sums of money as they may by any law of this state be authorized and empowered to assess.[2]

They were also authorized to " assess a sum, over and above the sum required to be raised, not exceeding one shilling on every pound," to answer any abatement that might be necessary. In case the selectmen neglected to make the assessment according to the terms of the state treasurer's warrant, the latter officer was directed, as in the case of negligent collectors, to issue his extents against such selectmen. When an execution had been issued and neither the estate nor the persons of the se-

---

[1] Laws, 1815, I App., 511.
[2] Revised laws, 1797, p. 196.

lectmen could be found, the inhabitants of the town were made liable for the amount of the taxes due from the town. By an act of the same date, February 8, 1791,[1] regulating towns and town officers, it was enacted that "any town may choose assessors who shall have the qualifications of selectmen and shall have all the powers of selectmen so far as relates to assessing taxes." It does not appear from the phraseology of the law whether the assessors, when chosen, were to act alone and to assume a part of the usual duties of the selectmen, or to act with the selectmen as a joint board. The act of December 28, 1791,[2] stated that "the selectmen and assessors may assess," but a later act, December 19, 1816,[3] spoke of "the assessors or selectmen acting as assessors." Any uncertainty upon this point was removed on June 26, 1823,[4] by the enactment that "assessors when chosen are to be a joint board with the selectmen for the assessment of taxes."

Since 1823 the law relating to assessments has been slightly modified as occasion has demanded, but in substance it remains to-day as handed down by the Revolutionary government from provincial times. Two important changes in the law have been necessitated by the direct taxation of certain corporations by the state and by the rise and development of the cities. (1) From 1842 until 1878 taxes laid upon railroad corporations were assessed by the justices of the supreme court,[5] from 1878 to the present time by the state board of equalization.[6]

---

[1] Revised laws, 1797, p. 180.

[2] Laws, 1815, I App., p. 541.

[3] Laws, 1816, p. 78.

[4] Laws, 1823, p. 69.

[5] Revised statutes, chap. 39, sec. 4 ; Compiled statutes, chap. 41, sec. 4 ; General statutes, chap. 54, sec. 2.

[6] General laws, chap. 62, sec. 2 ; Public statutes, chap. 64, sec 4.

The state board of equalization has also assessed the taxes upon the telegraph and telephone companies since such taxes were placed under the control of the state authorities in 1878 and in 1883 respectively.[1] Since the state tax upon the deposits in savings banks has been controlled directly by the state (1864)[2] it has been assessed by the state treasurer. The latter officer's duties, however, are merely ministerial, the rate of taxation being fixed by the legislature, and the method of securing the amount of the deposits leaving little to the discretion of the state treasurer. Since 1889[3] the assessment of taxes upon trust companies and similar organizations has been made under the same law as that upon savings bank deposits. (2) The act of 1846, now in force so far as it relates to cities, enacted that " all cities, now or hereafter incorporated shall have, exercise and en-joy all the rights, immunities and privileges and shall be subject to all the duties incumbent upon or appertaining to the town corporations to which they succeed." [4] This act also provided for the election or appointment of as-sessors " who shall perform all the duties relative to the taking of the inventory and the appraisal of property for taxation and in regard to the assessment and abate-ment of taxes . . . . as are now and may be hereafter required by law of selectmen and assessors of towns" and who should be subject to the same liabilities and possess like powers.

[1] In the assessment of the tax upon the railroad corporations the se-lectmen and assessors have since 1860 been required to assist by taking an inventory of the number of shares owned by the several inhabi-tants of each town, and returning the same to the state treasurer an-nually by June first.

[2] Laws, 1864, chap. 4028, sec. 1.

[3] Laws, 1889, chap. 12, sec. 1; chap. 55, sec. 1.

[4] Laws, 1846, chap. 384, sec. 1.

SEC. 2. *Equalization.* Equality of burden in public taxation is required by the provisions of the state constitution. According to the Bill of Rights "every member of the community has a right to be protected by it in the enjoyment of his life, liberty and property; he is therefore bound to contribute his share to the expense of such protection." [1] To carry this provision into effect the legislature is authorized by the constitution "to impose and levy proportional and reasonable assessments, rates and taxes upon all the inhabitants and residents within the said state, and upon all estates within the same." [2] A further provision requires, "in order that such assessments may be made with equality," that "there shall be a valuation of the estates within the state taken anew once in every five years, at least, and as much oftener as the general court shall order." [3] In general, two methods have been employed to give effect to the plain requirements of the constitution: (1) equalization through the apportionment committee of the house of representatives, and (2) equalization through the state board of equalization.

1. From 1775 until the notable revision of the tax laws in 1878, equalization among the towns and counties in the state was the work of the apportionment committee of the house of representatives in establishing a new proportion of the state tax once in four or five years. [4] Whenever a new proportion was ordered, the legislature called upon the selectmen and assessors to make a return of the inventory of the previous April, showing

---

[1] Bill of Rights, art. 12 ; constitution of 1784 ; repeated in constitution of 1792 ; perpetual laws, 1789.

[2] Const. of N. H., part II, art. 5.

[3] Const. of N. H., 1784, 1792, part II, art. 6.

[4] 1775–1808, once in five years ; 1808–1900, once in four years.

the total amount of the taxable property in the several towns. These returns were referred to the apportionment committee of the house of representatives, which did little, if anything, to remedy the glaring inequalities that appeared on their face.[1] The proportional part of each town and of each county in one thousand dollars of the state tax was then calculated, and from this proportion, when a state tax was voted, each town knew at once its share. To a considerable extent before 1833, and almost wholly after that date, when all property instead of being rated was made appraisable by the selectmen and assessors, each town's proportion of the tax depended upon the scale of valuation adopted by the local officers in making the annual inventory. Thus there was a very strong temptation to appraise the property low, so that the town's proportional part of the county and state tax would be lessened.[2] An act of July 10, 1874,[3] attempted to equalize the appraisal of property for the assessment of taxes by providing for a special invoice of the real estate in September of every fourth year. Every invoice was to be returned under oath stating "that we . . . . . appraised all taxable property at its full value and as we would appraise the same in the payment of a just debt due from a solvent debtor."[4] In 1876[5] this act was amended by requiring an annual invoice in April with a new appraisal of "all such real estate as has changed in value in the year next preceding," and a correction

---

[1] See N. H. House and senate journals, 1844, '48, '52, '56, '60, for facts as shown in returns.

[2] General statutes, 1867, chap. 60; Laws, 1868, chaps. 22 and 58.

[3] Laws, 1874, p. 345.

[4] The penalty for the violation of the act was a fine of from $100 to $500, or imprisonment of from three to twelve months, or both.

[5] Laws, 1876, p. 576.

10

of all such errors as were found in the existing appraisal. This system of equalization not only was "loose and inefficient", but also necessitated imposing upon the justices of the supreme court the equalization of the railroad tax, an executive duty which in effect prevented that body from sitting as a court of appeal in cases relating to the valuation of railroad property.

2. The tax commission of 1878 stated that as a result of its inquiry into the tax system of the state it had become thoroughly convinced " that a state board for the equalization of values is a pressing need of the state,"[1] and that " if the new sources of revenue recommended by the commission are adopted, a Board of Equalization will be a necessity."[2] The act of August 17, 1878,[3] providing for a state board of equalization, required that it consist of five members, to be nominated and appointed by the supreme court[4] and commissioned by the governor for a term of two years. The duties imposed upon the board of equalization by the statute were "to assess the taxes upon the several railroads within the state, to perform the duties now devolving upon the apportionment committee of the house of representatives and to perform such other duties as may from time to time be imposed upon them by the State legislature."[5] This act constituted the county commissioners in each

---

[1] Report of the tax commission, 1878, p. 39.

[2] The " new sources of revenue " were adopted in the main, and also the tax commission's recommendation for a state board of equalization.

[3] Laws, 1878, p. 199.

[4] The tax commissioners of 1878, "guided," they said, "somewhat by the almost uniform concurrence in practice in other states," suggested as the personnel of the board the state treasurer, the attorney general, the secretary of state, "and a representative of each of the leading political parties to be appointed by the Governor and council." Report, 1878, p. 39.

[5] Laws, 1878, p. 199.

county local boards of equalization, and the state board of equalization a supreme board of equalization as between counties. The selectmen were required to return inventories to the secretary of state annually, and to the county commissioners once in every four years; the county commissioners were "to visit every town in their county and personally inspect so much of the real and personal estate in said towns" as they deemed necessary to equalize the valuation. After this equalization the chairmen [1] of the several boards of county commissioners were directed to meet with the state board of equalization on a specified date and together with them were made a joint board for "equalizing the apportionment to the different counties so that each county shall pay its just proportion of the state tax." [2] The act definitely stated that "the state board of equalization, together with the county commissioners, as aforesaid, shall have a general supervision of the subject of taxation in the state, as far as it relates to the inventories and the appraisal of the selectmen and assessors in the various cities, towns, and places in the state." [3] The board was required to examine the inventories once in four years, and " if after such examination, such assessments shall be determined relatively unequal, they shall equalize the same by adding or deducting from the aggregate valuation of taxable real and personal estate in such town or towns, such percentage as will produce relative equal and uniform valuation between the several cities and towns in the state." [4] The supreme court of the state was made a

[1] Or any member designated by the board.
[2] Laws, 1878, chap. 73, sec. 4.
[3] Laws, 1878, chap. 73, sec. 6.
[4] Laws, 1878, chap. 73, sec. 7.

final court of appeal from all decisions of the board of equalization.

The act of 1878, constituting a state board of equalization, has been materially modified only by the statutes as revised in 1891.[1]　This revision in effect repealed the clauses making the county commissioners through their representatives a joint board with the state board of equalization for the general oversight of taxation.　The county commissioners[2] are required to visit the towns and personally inspect the property and " decide whether said property is appraised higher or lower than its true value."　But instead of being required to act with the state board of equalization, the representatives of the county commissioners are simply " to give to the board the results of their inspection and all other information upon the subject within their possession."　Such was the relation of the local officers to the board recommended by the tax commissioners of 1878.　Such is their natural relation.

SEC. 3. *Abatement.* Abatement of taxes may be secured in any one of three ways : (1) By action of the selectmen.　The act of February 8, 1791,[3] empowered the selectmen " to abate any taxes assessed either by themselves or by their predecessors upon sufficient reason being shown."　This has since continued to be the law of the state.[4]　(2) By action of the courts of law.　In some cases the supreme court is by law definitely stated to have the power to abate taxes assessed by certain

---

[1] By act of 1885, chap 40, sec. 1, the secretary of the board was voted an annual salary of $600.　By act of 1878, chap. 62, sec. 15, telegraph lines, and by act of 1883, chap. 110, sec. 2, telephone lines as well, were made assessable by the state board of equalization.

[2] Public statutes, p. 107.

[3] Revised laws, 1792, p. 185.

[4] Public statutes, 1891, chap. 59, sec. 10.

authorities.[1] The supreme court may hear all cases in which the question is one relating to the constitutionality of the tax or of the statutes under which the tax was assessed ;[2] and the court may abate the tax if it finds that the tax is "unequal", "unreasonable", or is assessed upon property legally exempted. (3) By action of the legislature. The legislature has always exercised the right of abating taxes whenever it has been shown that good reason existed for such action. Such action more often has been directed toward the relief of towns,[3] but not infrequently toward the relief of railroads[4] and of other corporations.[5]

SEC. 4. *Collection.* The system of taxation established in the eighteenth century by the important act of 1719[6] was continued in force by the Revolutionary government in 1776,[7] and has been maintained in its essential features throughout the nineteenth century. It will be necessary, therefore, to treat here only the more important amendments. These amendments may be grouped for convenience into three classes : (1) those granting to the administrative officers more extensive powers over the collection of taxes, (2) those extending the system of collection to include taxes on corporate property, and (3) those putting a premium upon punctuality in the payment of taxes.

[1] Laws, 1895, p. 448 *et seq.*
[2] 60 N. H. Reports, p. 219 *et seq.*
[3] Laws, 1877, p. 16.
[4] Laws, 1867, p. 17 ; 1863, p. 2723.
[5] Laws, 1878, chaps. 84 and 86.
[6] Chap. IV, pps. 81–82.
[7] The act declared all previous assessments "good and legal", and provided that all officers "take, use and pursue the same method for the collecting and levying of any such taxes or any other taxes that may be legally assessed in the future as the laws of the colony provide and direct for the collecting and levying of the taxes within the same." Laws, 1815, II, p. 16.

1. The amendments of the first class, falling within the years 1781–1821, constituted, in fact, a series of supplementary acts having for their object the better enforcement of the existing laws. An amendment of 1781 [1] stated that " some towns and places in the state liable by law to pay taxes have through meanness or avarice refused and neglected and may hereafter refuse and neglect to choose the proper officers for assessing and levying taxes in the expectation of thereby eluding the payment of their proportion of the public taxes." In such cases the treasurer of the state was directed to issue " executions or warrants of distress" against any two or more inhabitants. These warrants were issued to the sheriff of the county, who was directed to sell the goods or estates in question and to return the proceeds to the state treasurer. The inhabitants whose property had thus been seized were given the right to recover by a suit at law such amounts, with costs, damages, etc., from the other inhabitants of the town. A second amendment of 1789 [2] provided for the sale of real estate [3] whenever personal property was lacking, or whenever the owner " absconded or secreted himself so that his body cannot be arrested." Still a third amendment, dated June 10, 1821, authorized the selectmen to appoint collectors whenever a town refused or neglected to do so. In such cases the selectmen were required to take bonds and make written contracts with such collectors.

2. The second class of amendments, falling within the years 1821–41, were designed to place corporations

[1] Perpetual laws, 1789, p. 219.
[2] Perpetual laws, 1789, p. 183.
[3] The provisions of this amendment were made still more specific by an act of 1827.

as well as individuals under the laws relating to collection. An act of 1827 [1] made all the provisions of the law relating to the duties and powers of collectors apply to corporations as well as to individuals. The act of 1827 was followed by four others, each dealing with some specific point : (1) an act of 1832 provided that a written notice must be given to a proper officer of a corporation, if any such officer lived in the state, before distraining for taxes ; (2) the same act provided that in case of bridge, canal, and similar incorporated companies the franchise and the right to take toll might be sold for taxes due, the usual notice having been given ; (3) an act of 1838 [2] provided that if corporate taxes were not paid within three months from April 1st, and no personal property was pointed out whereon to make distress, then the lands or other real estate might be taken for the taxes ; (4) the act of 1838 was supplemented by one of three years later [3] definitely stating that the personal property of corporations as well as that of individuals was liable to be taken by distress for taxes overdue.

3. The third class of amendments, falling within the years 1834–1867, in general all aimed to secure the prompt payment of taxes, either by allowing a discount for early payment or by charging interest after a certain date. The first act of this nature, passed in 1834, allowed any town by vote to grant a discount [4] to persons paying their taxes before a specified date. No further steps were taken in this direction until 1860, [5] when any

[1] Laws, 1827, chap. 62.

[2] Laws, 1838, p. 350.

[3] Laws, 1841, p. 357.

[4] In 1824 a special act allowed certain towns to grant an abatement for taxes paid in 30, 60, and 120 days, and to distrain for overdue taxes after 120 days. Other towns might adopt such parts of this act as they chose.

[5] Laws, 1860, p. 2271.

town by a vote of a majority of the legal voters in a meeting called for the purpose, or any city by a vote of the city council, was authorized to determine the time after which all taxes assessed upon real and personal property should be charged six per cent interest, to be collected as other taxes. When this clause as modified in the general statutes of 1867 [1] appeared, the statement was definite that " interest at the rate of ten per cent shall be charged upon all taxes not paid on or before the first day of November [2] after their assessment, from that date, which shall be collected with said taxes as incident thereto."

The system is based upon the ultimate responsibility of the property of the individual, which has been effected by the following means: (1) The property and person of the collector is first made responsible by definite provision for seizure and sale of his property through extents issued by the several treasurers, and by further provisions for the imprisonment of the collector, whenever occasion demands such action. (2) In case the above means fail to find property to satisfy the tax, the property of the selectmen is made liable for the amount due; in this case the selectmen have a remedy against the inhabitants for a like sum. (3) In case of the failure of both the above methods, the treasurer may issue extents directly against the property of individuals, who in turn have remedy against all the other inhabitants of the town. Thus the ultimate responsibility is fixed upon the property of the individuals. In cases where either the town fails to appoint the proper officers, or the selectmen fail to appoint the collectors when the town neglects to do so, the extents must first be directed

---

[1] General statutes, 1867, p. 123.

[2] By act of 1872 the date was changed to December 1. Laws, 1872, p. 38.

against the property of the authorities failing to do their
duty.   All the above methods of fixing responsibility
were established during the eighteenth century.

The assessment of a general land tax in 1777[1] on
all lands and buildings not classed as " improved "[2]
made necessary some provision for the collection of the
tax.   It was stated that " great parts of said lands may
be owned by persons unknown or not inhabiting the
towns where the lands lye, and have no personal estate
whereon distress can be made," and therefore some
" equitable " method of collecting the taxes must be devised.   Two methods were provided, the first in 1777,
and the second one year later, 1778.   In the first method
the entire work of collection was entrusted to local collectors.   They were required to advertise the taxes successively for three weeks in the *New Hampshire Ga-
zette.*   In case the taxes remained unpaid at the end of
eight weeks, the collector was required to advertise for
sale and to sell at public auction so much of the lands
as was necessary to pay the taxes and charges, and was
given authority to execute a valid deed to the purchaser.[3]
After six months' trial the above method was found to
cause the non-resident proprietors " vast trouble and expense ",[4] owing to the difficulty they experienced in
finding the collector authorized to receive the taxes, and
to the " exorbitant charges which such constable or
collector has been wont to add thereto."   The act of
1778, therefore, created a state officer to stand between

[1] Revised laws, 1805, p. 422.

[2] It will be remembered that the representatives made several attempts in 1756–7 to secure such a tax, but failed on account of the opposition of the council.

[3] Those in military service or in captivity were granted three months
for redemption after they were at liberty from service or captivity.

[4] Preamble to act of May 23, 1778, amended December 26, 1778.
Laws, 1780, p. 140.

the non-resident proprietors and the collectors. This officer was called the receiver [1] of non-resident taxes, and was authorized to receive all the taxes of non-resident proprietors on lands within the state. The collectors were required to forward without delay the lists of the non-resident taxes for their respective towns to the receiver, who was directed immediately to advertise the list in one of the New Hampshire gazettes for three successive weeks. All taxes unpaid at the end of eight weeks were returned to the collectors, who were then to advertise and sell the lands as under the act of 1777. A subsequent amendment of the same year provided for a more general advertisement both by the receiver and by the tax collector, and required that no more of the lands should be sold than was sufficient to pay the taxes and charges.

By act of 1874 [2] the office of receiver of non-resident taxes was abolished and the entire work of collection entrusted to the local officers. By the terms of the act each collector was required to send a bill of taxes due to all non-resident taxpayers whose addresses were known, and to advertise in specified newspapers before January 1 following all property on which the taxes had not been paid. The cost of collection of non-resident taxes in all cases was borne by the taxpayers. In 1777 the amount was left to the discretion of the collectors, whose charges were described as "exorbitant". The act of 1778 fixed the allowance for collection and charges at the uniform rate of five per cent. The rate was doubled in 1796, and has since remained at ten per cent. A gen-

[1] In 1796 this office was abolished, and its duties transferred to the deputy secretary of state.

[2] Laws, 1874, p. 352.

eral right of redemption [1] for a limited time has been
granted since 1780.   At that time the limit was fixed at
two months.   This limit was extended to six months in
1784, to one year in 1787, and to two years in 1891.

The acts relating to the collection of taxes in unincorporated places fall into two classes: (1) those clothing
the inhabitants of such places with the power to choose
the necessary officers and to grant such officers the authority to collect such taxes, and (2) those granting to
either the county or the state officers the right to make
the collection whenever the places failed to do so themselves.

1. An act for making and establishing a new proportion of the province tax in 1773 stated that "sundry
places which are not incorporated . . . . have no
method to assess the sums to be raised."   Accordingly
certain men were appointed to call meetings of the inhabitants of such unincorporated places "to choose the
necessary officers [2] for assessing and collecting the sums
apportioned and set to their respective names."   This
act and others of temporary nature like it were super-
seded by the permanent act of 1791 "regulating towns"
etc.   The act of 1791 provided that whenever any unincorporated places were proportioned to any public tax,
such places should enjoy the same powers as towns possessed, so far as was necessary to assess and collect such

[1] During the Revolutionary War the right of redemption was granted
to those in service in the war or in captivity until some months after
they were at liberty.   Some other special privileges have been
granted : *e.g.*, in 1851 purchasers of property might pay the taxes,
and such sums must be repaid in order to redeem ; in 1887 those holding a mortgage on property were allowed to pay the tax and then to
hold the property under certain conditions.

[2] The officers were subjected to the same penalties as the like officers
in incorporated places.

tax. In case they refused to do so they were made liable
to the same process as were the inhabitants of incorporated towns refusing or neglecting to collect the tax.

2. After a comparatively short trial it was found that
unincorporated towns " through meanness or avarice "
often refused or neglected to choose the proper officers
"in the expectation of thereby eluding their proportion of
the public taxes." This state of affairs led to the adoption of a second method for the collection of taxes in unincorporated places through state and county officers.
By an act of 1780 [1] the treasurer of the state was authorized to give public notice of the lump sum proportioned
to the lands in unincorporated places, and in case the
taxes were not paid on a specified date to sell so much
of the lands in question as was necessary to pay the taxes
together with the incidental charges. This method was
continued in use until 1831, when the act now in force
was substituted. By the act of 1831 [2] it was enacted
that in case " any taxes are or shall be proportioned
to any place unincorporated having so few inhabitants
as to be incapable of choosing town officers, the treasurer of the state shall assess the proportion of such place
and commit the same to the sheriff of the county where
the said place lies, with a warrant under his hand and
seal empowering said sheriff to collect the same." The
sheriffs were given the same powers and put under the
same limitations as were the collectors in the collection
of the non-resident taxes. If the treasurer failed to receive notice of the appointment of a local collector by
December 31st of any year he was to proceed to assess
and collect the tax by the above method. The tax was

[1] Revised laws, 1805, p. 428.
[2] Laws, 1831, p. 26.

to be assessed in one sum unless the treasurer received notice from the clerk of the proprietors by the above date, certifying the shares belonging to the several proprietors. The law was recast in 1842, and reaffirmed in the general revisions of 1853, 1867, 1878, and 1891 without essential change.

CHAPTER VIII.

SEC. 1. *Relation to the Massachusetts System.* In 1641, when the New Hampshire towns, Dover and Portsmouth, having formally applied by their deputies for admission, were received into the Massachusetts Bay Colony, they pledged themselves to be governed wholly by the said colony, and secured the conditions that they were "to be subject to pay in church and commonwealth as the said inhabitants of the Massachusetts Bay do and no others."[1] In the practical application of the principles worked out in the two provinces while united under a common government we may expect to find certain variations, not only between the two provinces, but also even among the New Hampshire towns. Such differences seem to have been due to the unlike industrial and social conditions of the two colonies.

SEC. 2. *The Parish Taxes.* When the parish coincided with the town there was usually no legal differentiation of the two units ; when, on account of the size of the town, church congregations settled in several localities within the town bounds the organization of their communities into parishes with the legal power of taxation for the support of the ministry was the usual result. As the towns grew in population there came a further differentiation resulting in the formation of church societies of differing creeds within the same territorial limits. Parish taxation illustrates the method of taxation for religious worship in its simplicity. During the early days of the settlement the church was undoubtedly

[1] I N. H. Prov. papers, 156.

supported by voluntary gifts under the pressure of a strong popular opinion.[1] As early as 1633 a pastor was established over the Dover parish, but he was obliged to seek other fields within two years owing to the fact that under the system of voluntary contributions the parish failed to provide for his financial support.[2] This system had proved inadequate in Exeter by the middle of the century, for in 1650 the townsmen were empowered at a meeting of the inhabitants "to make a rate upon such inhabitants of the town as do not voluntarily bring in according to their abilities"[3] to pay their minister's salary. Later, when Rev. Mr. Moody was settled at Portsmouth in 1658, it was stated that he was at first supported by subscriptions, "86 persons having subscribed for the purpose."[4]

With the advent of taxation for ecclesiastical purposes, an effort was made to avoid the more direct forms. Thus in Exeter in 1650 the tax was laid upon the most important industry. It was agreed by the town officers and leading citizens that every inhabitant of the town should pay two shillings for the maintenance of the ministry for every thousand of pipe staves he made. A proportional tax was laid upon other sizes of staves and also upon the prepared "bolts" of which the staves were made. If one sold his products before satisfying the town the penalty was a five fold fine.[5] Perhaps a more common form of taxation for the support of the church was a tax on the sawmills. This tax probably dated from the establishment of sawmills, for in Exeter in 1650, in connection with the tax on staves above

---

[1] Walker, The Congregationalists, p. 231 *et seq.*
[2] I N. H. Prov. papers, 119.
[3] Bell, Hist. of Exeter, 161.
[4] Adams, Annals of Portsmouth, 42.
[5] Bell, Hist. of Exeter, 158. The same tax was raised 50% in 1656.

mentioned, it was provided that "what is due from the saw mills" should also be appropriated to the support of the ministry. The same tax appeared in Dover in 1654.[1] In 1656 the mill taxes in Exeter were especially named and devoted to the ministry, it being further provided that while so taxed the mills should pay no town rates.[2] Later, in 1669, in Dover, forty pounds sterling of the mill rents were "set apart" for the ministry.[3] Such instances tend to show that the tax was adapted to the circumstances of the places, as Dover and Exeter were both largely devoted to the lumbering industry.

In the erection of houses of worship the method followed in Exeter in 1651 seems to have been a typical one. A committee was chosen to call the men to work upon the meetinghouse "as need shall require." As they were to make a rate it is to be presumed that the work was to be equalized according to each man's "abilities". In case of neglect to appear a fine of five shillings per day was to be "seized by the constable."[4] The next year the committee was empowered to require servants "to come forth to work," and owners of teams were to bring their teams when called upon by those in charge.[5] When the more indirect means as stated above failed to produce a sufficient revenue, recourse was had to a tax upon the inventory. The col-

---

[1] I N. H. Prov. papers, 215. Here it is denominated the rent of the sawmills. Whether the use of the word "rent" implies that the mills were owned by the town, or is only intended to specify the returns upon the privileges given the proprietors, is uncertain. As no instance of town proprietorship of sawmills has been discovered, the latter view seems more probable.

[2] Bell, Hist. of Exeter, 165.

[3] I N. H. Prov. papers, 308.

[4] Bell, Hist. of Exeter, 162.

[5] Bell, Hist. of Exeter, 162.

lection was made either by a regular taxgatherer or
sometimes by the pastor himself, probably to save expense of collection.   In the latter case the minister was
authorized, "in case of refusal," to hand the list over to
the constable, who was to collect it by distraint if
necessary.[1]

SEC. 3.   *The School Tax.*   In 1647 Massachusetts
enacted her famous school law requiring every settlement of fifty households to employ a teacher, and one of
one hundred families "to fit for ye University."[2]   In
the first case the selectmen of the town might decide
whether the teacher should be supported by the parents
of the pupils or by the citizens generally.   Bell in his
scholarly history of Exeter says: "The records of the
town contain no imformation in regard to the earliest
schools, as they were probably maintained not at the
public charge, but by the parents of the children who
attended them.   Not for many years after towns were
made by law responsible for the maintainance of schools,
do the records refer to the subject."[3]   The same method
was probably employed in the town of Portsmouth, as it
is not to be presumed that a town whose citizens in 1669
pledged to give £70 annually for seven years[4] to aid in
the erection of a building for Harvard College deprived
its own children of the advantages it thus helped others
to obtain.   On the 2d of April, 1649, the selectmen of
Hampton employed a teacher at a salary of twenty
pounds per annum "in corne and cattle and butter att
price currant . . . to teach and instruct all the children
of our town or belonging to our town, both mayle and

---

[1] Bell, Hist. of Exeter, 166.
[2] II Mass. Rec., 203.
[3] Bell, Hist. of Exeter, 285.
[4] Adams, Annals of Portsmouth, 50.

11

femaile wch are capable of learning."[1] From this date Hampton seems to have supported a free public school the greater part of the time. An appropriation of twenty pounds per annum "for the mayntenance of a school-master in the town of Dover " was voted in 1658.[2]

SEC. 4. *The Highway Tax.* The highway tax in the early period was laid upon polls and teams, those owning teams being required to furnish them during the days set apart for mending the highways. The assessment was a certain number of days' work, or, in case of absence, whether unavoidable or not, a fine of a certain number of shillings per day. Thus in Exeter on June 17, 1644, it was agreed that " 4 days shall be set apart to mend the highways and those that are absent on the specified days shall be fined five shillings for every day." Those having teams had to work them or pay a fine of twenty shillings per day.[3] In Hampton in 1645, upon laying out a certain piece of new road, the total length was divided up into as many shares as there were taxable polls, and a fine of 2 *s.* 6 *d.* was assessed against each person to whom the work was assigned in case he did not have it completed within the specified time.[4] Five years later, 1650, when a vote was taken to repair the same piece of road, each person was required to repair the share that he built. In case of default a fine of 10 *s.* per rod was to be collected by the constable and used to repair that share.[5]

SEC. 5. *Taxes on the Inventory.* It seems probable that taxes on the inventory of polls and of ratable

[1] For a full account of the schools supported in Hampton see Dow, Hampton, I, 473.

[2] Dover Town records, I N. H. Prov. papers, 234.

[3] Bell, Hist. of Exeter, 446, quoting from Exeter Records.

[4] Dow, Hampton, 42.

[5] Dow, Hampton, 42.

estate occupied a much less prominent place in local taxation during the earlier than during the later period.[1] The town officers either served without pay or received their salary in fees and fines. Schools were supported largely by their patrons, the roads were built and repaired by labor, while the ecclesiastical tax was assessed, when possible, on the various forms of industry. Aside from schools, roads, ministers, and officers there were ordinarily few objects toward which the public taxes were appropriated. However, when other means failed the general property tax was laid to supply any deficiency, and in case of an Indian uprising doubtless became very important.

SEC. 6. *Special Taxes and Fines.* The most important source of revenue that may properly be classed under the above heading before 1680 was undoubtedly the taxes assessed on mill privileges. These taxes seem to have been laid on something more than the privilege, for with the original grant there was usually a tract of timber land varying from ten to fifty acres. While the taxes on the mills were often devoted to the support of the ministry, they were also in other cases appropriated to the common town charges.[2] A peculiar instance of a special tax occured in Hampton, January 12' 1668, when the town made it a rule that un-

---

[1] Even in the period of complete independence the towns followed, in general, the provisions of the Massachusetts tax law that was formulated later. For example, in Exeter in 1640 it was voted that the town charges were to be "ratably proportioned among the inhabitants, owners of land and cattle and privileges." Bell, Hist. of Exeter, 48. A month later it was voted that if any one kept town lots vacant they should "pay such charges upon every lot as shall a Rise on the town rates." Bell, Hist. of Exeter, 439.

[2] In Exeter in 1652 one mill was taxed £10, and the total revenue from mills was £35, a sum double the province rate for Exeter in 1680.

married men with no estate upon which taxes could be assessed should be rated on an estate of £20 in the assessment of taxes, town or ministerial, unless the selectmen saw good reason to assess a smaller sum.[1] An application of the idea of taxation by labor, following out the method in vogue in mending highways, occurred in Dover in 1667, when a contract was let by the selectmen for a fortification to be paid for in days' works at 2s. 6d. per day to the amount of £100.[2]

The use of fines in the early times was much more prominent than in the later times. Some of the more common forms were laid (1) on officers for neglect of duty, (2) on citizens for the same offence,[3] (3) as penalties in civil actions, (4) as penalties in minor criminal offences. The primary object was in the interest of good government, not for revenue purposes. Yet the total amount thus exacted must have been considerable.

SEC. 7. *Collection and Exemptions.* The local taxes were collected by the same officers, armed with the same authority, as in the case of the collection of the colonial taxes. Much difficulty was experienced in the collection, owing largely to the lack of provincial currency. The minister was in some cases empowered to collect his own rates, while the collection of the highway tax was superintended by the surveyors. With the growth of the province the duties of the constable as collector be-

---

[1] Dow, Hampton, 59.

[2] The method of paying taxes by labor was rendered almost absolutely necessary by the lack of any suitable medium of exchange. Taxes, when not paid in labor, were usually paid in "specie", *i.e.*, produce, stock, etc.

[3] In Hampton in 1639 a freeman was fined one shilling "for the use of the town" for failure to attend town meeting within half an hour of the time appointed. The constable was to forfeit double the amount if he failed to collect such fines. Dow, Hampton, 15.

came more important, owing to increased town activity and consequently larger taxes.

It seems probable that from the earliest times no property was taxed unless enumerated in the general tax laws. On this account there was no need to enumerate articles that were intended to be exempted, as their omission from the list would accomplish that end. Few special exemptions seem to have been made.

CHAPTER IX.

THE TOWNSHIP REVENUE, 1680–1775.

SEC. 1. *Taxes on Proprietary Rights.* The earliest form of local taxation in townships granted to a company of proprietors consisted in a uniform assessment upon shares. As early as 1673 the proprietors of Hollis entered into a compact agreeing that "if any settler should fail to pay his dues or taxes his lot to be seized by the town and held for payment."[1] A little later, 1689, in Hampton, £75 was raised equally upon shares to pay expenses of contesting the Mason claim. About 1720 this form of taxation became more important, owing to the rapid settlement of the interior, and continued to hold such a place in the early history of each township until the province was organized into full fledged towns. The rate was usually from 10 s. to 50 s. per share, and occasionally several rates were voted in a year. It seems that as an inducement for the proprietors actually to settle a provision such as the following, adopted at a general meeting of the proprietors of Chester, January 11, 1721, was often made : "Voted that each proprietor that does not settle pay ten shillings per year during three years, the whole to be divided yearly among those that settle."[2]

In many cases the charters provided that every proprietor should "pay his proportion of the town charge when and so often as occasion should require the same." To this was added "that upon default of any particular proprietor in complying with the conditions of this charter upon his part such delinquent proprietor shall

[1] Worcester, Hist. of Hollis, 23.
[2] Chase, Hist. of Chester, 15.

forfeit his share to yᵉ other proprietors, which shall be disposed of according to the major vote of the said com-pany at a legal meeting." Acting under such power the proprietors of Rochester in 1727 notified delinquents that they might expect to be voted out. The same year at Concord, at a meeting of the proprietors, it was agreed and voted " that Solomon Martin be admitted and settled in the place of Nathaniel Barker's right, who refusing to pay his proportional charge, the same was paid by the said Solomon Martin to the treasurer, the 8th day of July last."[1] At the same meeting collectors were appointed with power of attorney " to sue for and secure in the law the sum or sums raised on any settler or settlers as afore-said who shall refuse to pay the same."[2] In 1734 an act was passed by the general assembly providing that lands of delinquent proprietors in Rochester might be taken "in execution or extent" and sold to pay taxes. In 1737, upon petition by the inhabitants, the political powers granted by the charter to the proprietors were transferred by act of the legislature to the residents, who were authorized to tax each proprietor's share " 15 shill-ings per acre toward paymᵗ of a ministers salary " so long as they had an orthodox minister there, but to con-tinue no longer than the end of the year 1742.[3]

An instance showing the difficulty experienced by those towns whose charters did not especially authorize the as-sessment and collection of taxes occurred in Gilmanton in 1737. Gilmanton was chartered in 1727, but not settled until 1761. A committee of the proprietors petitioned the legislature for authority to assess and collect taxes, alleging : (1) that the proprietors lived in other towns

¹ Bouton, Hist. of Concord, 86.
² Bouton, Hist. of Concord, 87.
³ McDuffee, Hist. of Rochester, 77-78.

and some of them in Massachusetts, and that the proprietors had no legal authority to levy taxes ; (2) that consequently the growth was retarded and an " unequal burden thrown upon such of the proprietors as are diligent and forward in carrying on the settlement ; " (3) that already considerable expense had been incurred for highways, blockhouses, laying out lots, etc. Accordingly the petitioners prayed that the selectmen would clothe the proprietors with sufficient power to collect the taxes levied. The house agreed to the petition, but the council unanimously rejected it.

The same spirit in the two houses appeared in 1740, when the house passed a bill enabling proprietors to levy and collect taxes, in which the council again non-concurred. It seems probable that the same influence that caused the house in 1756 to favor a provincial land tax and the council to oppose it was active in the cases cited. The student of colonial history, versed in the motives that move legislative action, will doubtless inquire whether there was any relation between the continued refusal of the council to permit a general land tax, in either a direct or an indirect form, and the large holdings of land which that body individually possessed at all periods of our provincial history. It is quite probable that not until the reorganization of the council during the Revolutionary War (1781) did the legislature pass a general law enabling proprietors to tax their rights and collect the sums levied.[1] A combination of proprietary with township taxation constituted an intermediate stage between the early and the later history of taxation in the townships. This happened usually in settling and supporting a minister—a work beneficial both to the proprietors

[1] Laws, 1792, 369.

and to the residents, since it drew settlers and increased the value of the shares. Thus in Nottingham in 1742 a meeting of the proprietors and inhabitants was held at which both the settlement of a minister and the share of each party was agreed upon. Instances of this kind were numerous during the period from 1730 to 1760,[1] but in some cases a failure to agree upon the part each should contribute postponed the settlement of a resident minister for some years.

SEC. 2. *Taxes on Lands of Non-residents.* Previous to 1720 the increase of population in the province was slow, and was confined chiefly to the four original towns. After that date new townships were granted in comparatively large numbers, new settlements were pushed forward, roads laid out, blockhouses built, the land cleared, houses built, churches erected, ministers settled, and all the activities necessitated by subduing the wilderness were witnessed. Land as a measure of ability to bear the public charges became relatively more important. Accordingly we find beginning with the period of active settlement a series of attempts on the part of the actual settlers to secure by special legislation the authority to lay and collect uniform land taxes for local purposes. One of the earlier instances occurred in 1731, when the general assembly authorized the towns of Chester, Nottingham, and Rochester to assess the lands of non-residents for a period of three years with the powers of distraint in case the taxes were not paid. The reason given was that the towns " Labor under inconveniences in carrying on ye public affairs especially supporting the gospel ministry." [2]

---

[1] Chase, Hist. of Chester, 74 ; McDuffee, Hist. of Rochester, 75.

[2] Chase, Hist. of Chester, 75.

There are strong grounds for believing that the tax on lands, especially when it applied only to the lands of non-residents, was introduced into the province through the towns settled under the jurisdiction of Massachusetts. In 1739, when Massachusetts granted a charter to West Dunstable (the last charter granted by that government to a town now within the New Hampshire limits), the citizens of that parish were "empowered to assess and lay a tax of two pence per acre for the space of five years on all the unimproved lands belonging to the non-resident proprietors to be applied to the support of the ministry."[1] This parish was said to contain 70,000 acres, and at that time twenty-five resident families. It is not probable that these twenty-five families owned more than 800 acres each, or a total of 20,000 acres. The tax on the remainder at two pence per acre would have yielded £416 13s.,[2] a tax of no slight importance it will be admitted. The collection of this tax was interrupted by the settlement of the boundary line controversy between Massachusetts and New Hampshire, as a result of which the parish found itself transferred from the jurisdiction of the colony under which it had been organized and settled to that of New Hampshire. The town was incorporated under the name of Hollis, April 3, 1746. As no power was granted the town to tax non-resident lands the town voted that year to lay a tax of 2d. per acre upon all the lands of Hollis "for five years for the support of the gospel ministry and yᵉ arising charges of said town and to petition the Great and General court for Strength to Gather and Get the money of the non-residents."[3] The petition is interesting as indicating

[1] Worcester, Hist. of Hollis, 38.
[2] Worcester, Hist. of Hollis, 41.
[3] Worcester, Hist. of Hollis, 47.

the method of reasoning by which the residents justified
the tax. The petition recited: (1) that the settlers,
"although a considerable progress has been made in
agriculture," found the charges for settling a minister
and building a meetinghouse very burdensome; (2)
"That a considerable part of the best lands in s^d town
belong to non-resident proprietors who make no improvement;" and (3) "That by the arduous begining the
settlement & heavy charges by us already paid has
greatly advanced their lands and they are still rising in
value equal as the resident propri^rs though the charges
hitherto and for the future must lye on ye settler only
unless we obtain the assistance of the Honble Court."[1]
The petition was granted May 14, 1747, but the tax was
limited to four years. During the four years of the tax
the resident landowners increased from forty-eight to
seventy, the non-resident landowners decreased from
thirty-three to twenty-four. Out of a tax of £394 17 s.
8 d. on the land assessed in 1747, the non-resident land
owners paid £256 6 s. 8 d., or more than two-thirds.
The last year of this tax, 1750, the amount of the land
tax paid by the two classes had become much more
nearly equal. The tax seems to have had the salutary
effect of increasing the number of the resident proprietors as well as providing for the support of the
ministry.

This case illustrates the nature of the tax and the
method under which it was authorized and collected.
As the tax was subject first to the will of the town
and second to the legislature no general statement
can be made as to its extent among the towns. The
legislative records show that nearly all the towns along
the Merrimac valley that were settled about the middle

---

[1] Worcester, Hist. of Hollis, 47 ; V N. H. Prov. papers, 886.

of the eighteenth century were empowered to lay such a tax, the tax ranging from one-half to six pence per acre, and extending through periods of from one to six years. In some instances a town at the expiration of its term petitioned for an extension of the period with successful results. In several cases towns failed to receive the power through the reluctance of the council to sanction any general land tax.

During the period of transition in which the wilderness was being transformed into a productive farming country the lands of non-resident owners were growing more valuable through the efforts of the actual settlers, and the tax met all the requirements that the advocates of a sound and equitable system of public taxation could demand. In the cases where the legislature refused to sanction such a tax the evidence indicates that such refusal, whatever may have been the grounds averred, was due to self-interest on the part of large land holders.

SEC. 3. *Revenue from Town Lotteries.* In 1754, in order to suppress private lotteries,[1] "an act for the suppressing of Lotteries" became a law. The preamble to the act stated that "there have been lately set up within this province sundry Lotteries," indicating their recent origin. The act further showed the purposes for which the lotteries already established were designed by placing a penalty of £500 upon any person or persons who should undertake to "set up any lottery or expose for sale or dispose of any estate real or personal by way of lottery." A further clause inflicted a penalty of £200 upon any person or persons who should offer for sale "any lottery tickets for the sale of any estate whatsoever real or personal." The law was not to extend to

[1] Laws, 1761, 197.

any lotteries already begun, nor to those authorized by act of parliament or law of the province.

The first lottery authorized by the legislature was designed for the purpose of opening a harbor at Rye in 1756. The act authorizing this lottery provided that it should be subject to legislative control, and proper safeguards were provided against fraud. Three-fourths of the tickets were blanks, and the profits were to be £6000.[1] After this date lotteries were granted to Portsmouth (1759) for paving streets, to New Castle (1760) for a bridge, to Rye (1764) for building a road, to Stratham (1766) and to West New Market (1768) for building bridges, and to Gosport (1766) for improving the harbor. Some of these appear to have been successful, others failed for various reasons. On the 24th of October, 1768, the manager of the Isles of Shoales lottery appeared in the house and represented that he could not sell the lottery tickets owing to scarcity of money.[2] The managers were authorized by vote of the legislature to give public notice that they would refund all money paid for tickets. This was done and the lottery abandoned. Again, on the 18th of March, 1768, the governor assented to a bill for a lottery to build a bridge over Exeter river.[3] Two years later, March 29, 1770, the petitioners for the Exeter river bridge lottery reported that the two years allowed had expired, and " notwithstanding their utmost diligence used in prosecuting said design they had not been able to complete the same." They were allowed an extension of two years to complete the work.

[1] VI N. H. Prov. papers, 125. See scheme in XIII N. H. Town papers, 361.

[2] VII N. H. Prov. papers, 193.

[3] VII N. H. Prov. papers, 165.

Although private lotteries were effectually suppressed by the act of 1754, [1] the public lottery continued to flourish, and within fifteen years had proved so disastrous to legitimate industry and so prolific of fraud that the institution called out the following instructions from the crown, June 30, 1769 : " Whereas a practice hath of late years prevailed in several of our colonies and plantations in America of passing laws for raising money by instituting public lotteries . . . [and whereas] such practice doth tend to disengage those who become adventurers therein from that spirit of industry and attention to their proper callings and occupations on which the public welfare so greatly depends . . . and also hath been extended to enabling private persons to set up such lotteries by means whereof great frauds and abuses have been committed . . . . it is our will . . . that you [the governor] do not give your assent to any act or acts for raising money by the institution of any public or private lotteries whatsoever until . . . you shall have received our directions thereupon."

SEC. 4. *Revenue from the Public Domain.* The value of the land reserved in the town grants for the purposes of supporting the ministry and public schools depended largely upon the wisdom of the local authorities. By the terms of the charter granted to Chester in 1722 it was provided " That a Proprietor's share be reserved for a parsonage, another for the first minister of the Gospel, another for the benefit of the school." The same provisions were generally made in the charters to other towns granted prior to Governor Benning Wentworth's administration. During his term, 1741-1769, four shares in each township were generally reserved for public purposes, " one whole share for the incorporated

[1] VII N. H. Prov. papers, 231.

[society] for the propagation of the gospel in Foreign parts, one whole share for a Glebe for the Church of England as by law established, one whole share for the first settled Minister of the gospel, and one whole share for the benefit of a school in said town." Dr. Bouton affirms that a careful examination of all the charters granted by the above governor shows that such was the general reservation in the charters of that period. The townships granted by Governor Wentworth during the twenty-five years of his service constituted a very large part of the province. Hence the method that he followed in reserving rights for public purposes may be considered to represent in a broad way the general policy of the provincial government.

The shares granted for the support of the ministry were usually at once occupied by the first settled minister, and became an essential part of his support. The schools, developing slowly, received less benefit, inasmuch as the chief value of land in the period under consideration consisted in its ability to support life under the active care of its occupant. School land was usually rented for a very small sum yearly. In other cases the land was sold for a trifle, and the schools in that case received little benefit.

Sec. 5. *Taxes on the Inventory.* In spite of all the attempts of the town or provincial government to "ease the burden" of taxation upon the polls and ratable estate by means of taxes upon lands or proprietors' rights, the tax upon the general inventory furnished the substantial part of the revenue, local as well as provincial. By the act of 1692 "concerning ye prudential affairs in ye town and Province" the assessments on the inventory were limited to "ye necessary charges arising within these towns."[1]   The more important objects for which taxes were assessed will be considered more in detail in a subsequent section.   It is sufficient here to state that the towns assumed and exercised from the first a large degree of liberty in choosing the objects for which they appropriated the taxes.   By act of 1719 the selectmen were authorized to assess the persons and estates within the town for "such sum and sums of money as hath or shall be ordered, granted and agreed upon from time to time by the inhabitants in any town meeting regularly assembled or the major part of those present at such meeting for the maintenance and support of the ministry, schools, the poor and for the defraying the other necessary charges arising within the said town."[2]

SEC. 6.   *Taxes for the Support of the Ministry.*   The first provincial law " For the support of the ministers of the gospel ", 1682, empowered the selectmen "to make such rates upon all persons and estates in the several towns . . . as may answer the occasions aforesaid."[3]   In 1693 "An act for Maintenance and Supply of the Ministry within this Province"[4] provided that the freeholders might select and make arrangements with a settled minister, "and the selectmen then, for the time being shall make Rates and Assessments upon the Inhabitants of the town for y[e] payment of the Ministers salary as aforesaid, in such manner and form as they do for defraying of other town charges."   Only those who "constantly attend the public worship of God on the Lord's day according to their own persuasion " were excused from paying toward the town minister.   The

---

[1] III N. H. Prov. papers, 167.
[2] Laws, 1761, 31–32.
[3] Provincial laws, I N. H. Prov. papers, 447.
[4] Provincial laws, III N. H. Prov. papers, 189.

law also authorized public taxation "for building and repairing of meeting houses and ministers houses." The act of 1693 was reënacted permanently in 1714, and continued in force till 1792, when it was repealed.   By the act of 1719[1] regulating townships the selectmen were "empowered to assess the inhabitants and others resident within such town and the Precincts thereof and the Lands and Estates within the bounds" such sums as should be granted by a majority in town meeting "for the maintenance and support of the ministry."[2] Only a part of the minister's support was derived from the tax on the general inventory.   His shares from the public domain, one and sometimes two, taxes on proprietary rights, contributions of labor and provisions, and the sale of pews provided a substantial part of his support.   That portion of the minister's salary paid in money ranged usually from about £50 to £100 in lawful money or its equivalent.   Rev. John Pike was settled at Dover in 1686 at £60; Rev. Jeremy Belknap was settled in the same parish in 1766 at £100 per annum.

SEC. 7. *Taxes for the Support of Education.*   The act of 1693[3] providing for the support of the ministry empowered the selectmen in their respective towns to "raise money by an equal Rate and Assessment" upon the inhabitants "as in this present act directed for the maintenance of the ministry" for building and repairing schoolhouses and "allowing a salary to a school master."   Every town failing to provide a schoolmaster was made liable to a fine of ten pounds per annum "to be paid one half to their Majesties, the other half to the poor of the town."   This law was made permanent in

[1] Laws, 1726, 51.
[2] Laws, 1726, 135.
[3] Laws, 1692–1701, III N. H. Prov. papers, 189.

12

1714,[1] but the penalty was omitted. The act of 1719[2] relating to townships authorized the selectmen to make assessments for schools when such tax was voted by the town assembled in a legal meeting.

The same year, 1719, the Massachusetts school law of 1647, requiring every town having fifty householders or upwards to provide a school and of one hundred householders to provide a grammar school, was adopted. The selectmen were empowered to "agree" with a schoolmaster, and to raise money by a rate upon the inhabitants to pay for the same. Any town failing to comply with the terms of the act within six months incurred a penalty of 20 pounds, to be recovered through the court of quarter sessions and appropriated by that court to such school within the province as they deemed to be most in need of aid. An addition to this act passed in 1721[3] stated that "the selectmen of sundry towns . . . neglect to provide grammar schools," and provided that "not only each town but each parish" should support a grammar school as before required by law. In case the town or parish was destitute of such school for one month after the publication of the law, "the selectmen of such town or Parish shall forfeit the sum of Twenty pounds for every such neglect, to be paid out of their own estates and to be applied toward the defraying the charges of the province."

Notwithstanding the excellence of the school law as perfected in 1721, the evidence indicates that public taxation for schools was irregular in time and uncertain in amount. The town of Chester in 1748 voted "that the town defend and secure the selectmen from any

[1] Laws, 1726, 51.
[2] Laws, 1726, 133.
[3] Laws, 1726, 160.

damage they may come at for not providing a Grammar school."[1]   Again in 1756 the same town was warned by an "express from the Court" to provide a grammar school, and thereupon voted "to fulfil and answer the interests of the law if possible."   Amherst, another of the leading towns, shows a similar record.   The town was incorporated in 1762; there were then one hundred and ten tax payers and the largest tax paid by a single individual was £46 18s. 3d.   Yet in the years 1763, 1765, and 1766 no mention was made of any effort to secure an appropriation for schools.   In 1764, 1767, and 1769 the town refused to vote a tax for that purpose. Finally the selectmen were in danger of being "presented" for neglect of duty, and on the 12th of December, 1769, the town voted to "keep a school a part of this year," and granted the sum of £13 6s. 8d. for that purpose.[2]   In the light of such facts it is probable that Gov. Wentworth expressed what was only too true when in 1771 in a message to the assembly he said that "nine-tenths of your towns are wholly without schools or having vagrant teachers . . . . worse than none   . . .   unknown in principle and deplorably illiterate."[3]

SEC. 8.   *Taxes for the Support of Highways.*   The public highways were repaired by labor throughout the provincial period with the exception of the years from 1718 to 1721.   In 1718 the selectmen of their respective towns were empowered and required "to agree with two or more able and sufficient men yearly to mend and keep such ways in Repair, at as moderate a rate as they can and for the payment thereof shall raise money by way

[1] Chase, Hist. of Chester, 278.

[2] Secomb, Hist. of Amherst, 319.

[3] VII N. H. Prov. papers, 287.

of assessment upon the inhabitants of the respective towns as they do for the defraying of their other town charges,[1] Any law, usage or custom to the contrary not-with-standing."

This method was unsuited to the conditions of the province, and was abandoned after a trial of three years. The house inaugurated a movement look-ing toward reëstablishing the former system by a vote on April 21, 1721, "that the highways in y⁰ several towns within this Province may be Repaired by labor under y⁰ direction of surveyors as formerly."[2] The law of April 25, 1721, stated that "it is found by daily ex-perience that the Repairing Highways by Assessments on the several Inhabitants of each town within this province is attended with sundry Inconveniences." The act provided "that hence forwards all Highways...shall be repaired by labor." Every man except the governor, lieutenant governor, ministers, and schoolmasters was required to work or to send a "sufficient man" in his place, or to pay a fine of five shillings per day to be ex-pended under the direction of the surveyors. The sur-veyors were chosen annually by the town, and were authorized "to warn the inhabitants of their several dis-tricts to appear with such necessary tools . . . at such place and time" as they thought best, and to impress such oxen, cart wheels, chains, and yokes as they thought necessary. This law seems to have been gen-erally satisfactory, since it was continued substantially in the above form for nearly a century and a half.

The expense of laying out new highways was borne either by the towns or by the land through which the road passed. The proprietors of Amherst in 1745

[1] Laws, 1726, p. 64.
[2] XIX N. H. State papers, 150.

appointed a committee to lay out highways, and instructed them to lay out no roads except in places
where the owners would give the land for that purpose.[1]
In the case of the public roads undertaken during the
administration of Governor John Wentworth, 1767–1775,
the tax for their support seems to have been laid uniformly upon the lands of the towns through which the
roads passed. The act of 1771 for establishing and
making passable a road from the governor's house in
Wolfeboro to Dartmouth College provided that the proprietors and owners of land within the towns should
make the road " passable to the acceptance of the committee " appointed to lay out and have general charge of
the building of the road, at the charge of the town " by
an equal rate on all the land therein excepting land reserved for public purposes."[2] In case of neglect the land
was to be sold and the proceeds used for building the road.
In 1766 the selectmen of each township were " empowered to raise money . . . & to pay the same out of
the public stock " to make up any deficiency caused by
changing the highways. They were also authorized to
sell the land when the road was abandoned, to buy land
for the new way, and if the money thus received was not
sufficient, to raise the residue by public taxation.

In general throughout the provincial period the
towns voted in public meeting the amount to be expended upon the highways, and the selectmen apportioned this amount among the districts in accordance
with the relative share that each district paid of the
public taxes, the selectmen having also a general oversight of its expenditure. The highway surveyors were

[1] Secomb, Hist. of Amherst, 42.
[2] VII N. H. Prov. papers, 283.

the administrative officers superintending their districts under the direction of the selectmen.

SEC. 9.   *Taxes for Town Charges.*   The act of 1719 "Regulating Townships, Town officers, &c" empowered the selectmen to assess the "Inhabitants and other Residents within such towns . . . and the Lands and Estates lying within the bounds of such towns . . such sum or sums of money as hath or shall be ordered . . . for the maintenance and Support of the ministry, schools, the Poor and for the Defraying the other necessary charges arising within the said town."[1]   These "necessary charges" were small in comparison with later times.   Some of the more important charges were: fortifications, block houses, scouts, watchers, and soldiers in time of Indian warfare; services and expenses of certain officers, such as constable, fence viewers, selectmen, town clerks; the care of certain town property and the fulfilling of certain public functions, such as the maintenance of standard weights and measures, the care of the poor and infirm, with other less common objects for which town action was necessary.   All these "necessary charges" constituted a constant, but not heavy, expense.

SEC. 10. *Administration.*   The first provincial law regulating township affairs was enacted in 1692.[2]   By the terms of this act " ye selectmen of each town within this province or ye major part of them wth a Justice of ye Peace, are Impowered to make assessments on ye visible Estates of ye Inhabitants & of p'sons according to valuation of there incomes, to defraye ye necessary charges arising wthin there towns."   Substantially the same authority was given the selectmen in the act of

[1] Laws, 1726, 135.

[2] Provincial laws, 1692-1702, III N. H. Prov. papers, 167.

1719 [1] " Regulating Townships, Town officers etc." The
duties of these officers and the legal sanctions under
which they were placed by the provincial laws have
already-been noticed in the chapter on the provincial
revenue.

Local taxes were collected by the same officers, acting
under the same general laws, as were the provincial taxes.
The law of 1680 authorized the selectmen, in case the
constable failed to clear up his rates, to direct their
" warrants to ye constables next chosen to distrain upon
the estates of such constables as shall faile of their
duties therein." [2]   The act of 1693 authorizing imprisonment of the constables for neglect of duty " where
no estate appears" applied to local as well as to provincial taxes.   The same is true of succeeding acts, except that the warrant was issued from, and the returns
were made to, the local officers—to selectmen for the
town, to justices of the peace, or to church wardens in
connection with such officials in parish affairs.   The
act of 1758 [3] authorizing towns to employ a collector
instead of constables for the collection of taxes trans-
fered all the rights and duties of the constable to the
collector as regards both local and provincial taxes.

[1] Laws, 1726, 133–8.
[2] Provincial laws, 1680, I N. H. Prov. papers, 396.
[3] Laws, 1761, 201.

CHAPTER X.

SEC. 1. *Taxes on Proprietary Rights.* During the
latter part of the provincial period the proprietary taxes
were of considerable importance ; the proprietors built
roads, at least partially supported public worship and
education, and in many ways paved the way for organic
town life. After the Revolution, however, the state
rapidly filled with settlers, and the township organization
occupied the field partially filled before by the proprietors. The courts of New Hampshire have held that
the act of 4 George I enabling the proprietors of common and undivided lands to sue and be sued virtually
made such proprietors corporations in fact, although not
expressly declared to be such.[1] The original proprietors
and their successors continually exercised such powers.
Moreover, the statutes expressly conferred upon
them the power to assess and collect taxes and to
sell the land of any delinquent. It is not certain
that the act of 1 George III[2] was continued in force
longer than four years. The act of October 28, 1768,[3]
seems to imply that it was then in force. In any
case, an act of June 18, 1771,[4] revived the act in question, and continued it in force for five years, or until
January 1, 1776. The act of April 9, 1777,[5] reëstab-
lished the general system of laws in force at the time

[1] 4 N. H. Reports, p. 101.
[2] Compiled laws, 1815, p. 597.
[3] Compiled laws, 1815, p. 599.
[4] Compiled laws, 1815, p. 601.
[5] Compiled laws, 1815, p. 469.

that the present government was assumed, January 5, 1776. Accordingly the act of 1 George III must have been the law of the state for the greater part of the time from 1760 until 1781, when the first permanent statute on the subject was enacted. [1]

The act of 1781 [2] provided (1) that the proprietors at any legal meeting might vote taxes in proportion to the interests lying in common ; (2) that assessors might be chosen to make the assessment upon the individual interests and commit the list with a warrant to the person chosen to collect the same ; (3) that the interest and property of any delinquent proprietor or owner might be sold for unpaid taxes ; (4) and that liberty of redemption might be granted on the payment of the taxes, interest, and charges within two months [3] from the date of the sale. This act also provided that if the lands were divided before the terms and conditions of the grants or charters were fulfilled, the lots might be assessed their proportion of the taxes voted, as in the case of the common lands. This last provision was amended by act of November 10, 1784,[4] which provided that in cases other than those to fulfill the conditions of the grant, the lots divided or severed might be taxed if the common lands were not sufficient to satisfy the taxes, and at the same time allowed the owners of the severed lots to vote with the proprietors. Both these provisions were repealed by the act of December 22, 1808,[5] which enacted among other things that " no proprietors of common and un-

---

[1] The act of 1781 legalized all acts of proprietors which were passed after the laws of the state on proprietary rights had lapsed as fully as if the said laws had continued in force.

[2] Perpetual laws, 1789, p. 93.

[3] Six months for those engaged in war or in captivity or on public business out of the state.

[4] Revised laws, 1830, p. 114.

[5] Revised laws, 1830, p. 118.

divided lands shall have power to tax any lands holden in severalty; any law to the contrary notwithstanding." The act of June 17, 1796,[1] made the time and mode of redemption the same as in the laws providing for the redemption of land sold for state and county taxes.

Since 1808 there has been no essential change in the laws relating to the taxation of common lands. The meagreness of the legislation, correctly interpreted, indicates, as already stated, that during the nineteenth century the common and undivided lands were of small importance in the fiscal history of the state.

SEC. 2. *Taxes on Lands.* It will be remembered that the land taxes imposed by special acts of the general court of New Hampshire during the ·provincial period were usually for the purpose of supporting the gospel ministry. Such taxes were justified by the "benefit" theory of taxation. During the years 1800 to 1820, when uniform land taxes were somewhat common, they seem to have been justified on the same grounds, but were devoted to other purposes. In all cases the taxes of this nature were to be appropriated to building roads and bridges. The towns making use of these taxes were located in the northern part of the state, in Grafton or Coos County,—regions then thinly settled,— and the roads so built were usually "through roads" designed to form the main line of transportation to more populous parts of this and other states. The tax was usually assessed and expended by a committee appointed by the legislature, though sometimes by the selectmen. In nearly all cases the land owners were privileged to "work out" the taxes so assessed. It does not appear

---

[1] Revised laws, 1830, p. 115. By act of 1798 (Revised laws, 1830, p. 116) the time was stated to be one year.

that uniform land taxes were assessed after 1818 for any purpose.[1]

The accompanying table shows to what extent use was made of such taxes :—

Year.	Rate in cts. per acre.	Town.	Purpose.
1801	3	Danbury,	Roads and bridges
1805	1	Durand,	" "
1805	3	Cockburn,[3]	" "
1805	3	Winslow's Location,	"
1805	3	Whitefield,	
1805	?	Piercy,	
1806	2	Bethlehem,	
1806	2	Franconia,	
1806	2	Lincoln,	
1806	2	Stewartstown,	
1809	2	Elsworth,[3]	
1809	3	Peeling,[3]	
1810	2	Coventry,	
1810	1½	Benton,[3]	
1810	3	Colebrook,	
1810	½	Millsfield,	
1810	2	Errol,	
1812	2	Jefferson,	
1813	3	Alexandria,	
1813	2	Peeling,	
1813	2	Lincoln,	
1813	3	Franconia,	
1814	1½	Eaton,[2]	
1814	3	Barker's Location,	
1816	2	Brettenwoods,	
1816	3	Lincoln,	
1817	4	Dalton,	
1817	4	Durand,	
1818	2	Winslow's Location,	"
1818	2	Paulsborough (Milan),	"
1818	2	Waynesborough,	

SEC. 3. *License Fees.* The state has licensed showmen, ventriloquists, billiard and pool tables, and theatrical and dramatic shows primarily as a police measure,

[1] It was held by the supreme court that the legislature had no right to grant taxes on lands in incorporated and unincorporated places for the purpose of making or repairing roads. 4 N. H. Reports, p. 565.

[2] Unimproved lands. [3] Voted and tax assessed by selectmen.

not for the sake of the revenue that might be obtained from these sources. Still, since the towns and cities have received a small revenue from such licenses, it is necessary to treat the subject very briefly here.

Showmen, ventriloquists, tumblers, rope dancers, persons exhibiting animals, and persons performing feats of agility or slight of hand for pay were first required to take out a license of the selectmen of the town in 1821. The act[1] prescribed fees varying from $3 to $30, the exact amount to be fixed by the town authorities in each case. In 1835[2] the fee was raised to $30—$50; in 1867[3] to $10—$300; in 1876[4] the minimum fee was reduced to $1, making the limits $1 and $300, at which figures it remains at the present time. By act of 1850[5] theatrical and dramatic shows were required to take out a license as provided for showmen, ventriloquists, etc. The discretion of the authorities of the town or city was somewhat limited in 1878[6] by fixing the maximum fee for a license to exhibit in any hall at $5, and again in 1883[7] at $50.

Before 1878 billiard and pool tables and bowling alleys had been taxed to their owners as property, their value being included in the inventory. The tax commission of 1878 recommended a specific tax instead of the former method, and their recommendation was adopted. The license fee was fixed at $10 for each billiard table or bowling alley kept for hire. An annual license was issued on May 1st by the clerk of the town or city, and

[1] Laws, 1821, p. 390.
[2] Laws, 1835, p. 183.
[3] General statutes, 1867, p. 211.
[4] Laws, 1876, p. 568.
[5] Laws, 1850, p. 952.
[6] General laws, 1878, p. 272.
[7] Laws, 1883, p. 25.

the fee was payable to that officer. This act was amended (1) in 1879[1] by allowing the person in charge of a billiard table or bowling alley kept for hire to take out a license for six months at $5, and (2) in 1883 by adding pool tables, and by providing that billiard tables, pool tables, and bowling alleys in connection with any saloon or restaurant should pay a license even if not kept for hire. The amendments of 1879 and 1883 were repealed in 1887, and the original act further amended. The act of 1887[2] provided that licenses of the above description might be granted and revoked by the mayor and aldermen of any city or the selectmen of any town. All other provisions, excepting the privilege of 1879 for a half year license, were essentially unchanged. This act was amended in 1897[3] by making the fee for tables or alleys in connection with summer hotels $4 each in place of the annual license fee of $10.

The revenue from this source, as already stated, though of growing importance, has been insignificant when compared with that derived from direct taxation, as the following table shows :—

Year.	City or town.	From licenses.	Revenue from all sources.
1832	Portsmouth,	$ 6 00	$26,000 00 approx.
1833	Portsmouth,	5 00	28,000 00 "
1841	Chester,	2 00	3,397 48
1845	Manchester,	60 00	30,000 00 approx.
1852	Manchester,	160 00	49,000 00 "
1884	Hanover,	39 50	13,261 31
1885	Hanover,	9 50	11,676 72
1897	Hanover,	120 00	16,390 70
1898	Hanover,	120 00	17,032 20

The policy of licensing taverns and retailers was handed down from provincial days. The act of 1827[4]

[1] Laws, 1879, p. 342.
[2] Laws, 1887, p. 444.
[3] Laws, 1897, p. 32.
[4] Laws, 1827, p. 371.

was the first, however, to impose a fee for the license. The fee imposed by this act was merely nominal—not less than two nor more than five dollars. In the commissioners' report on the revised statutes of 1842[1] the above fees were retained, but the legislature in the final revision[2] struck out the clause imposing a fee, and no fees were thereafter imposed. Since 1849,[3] when town agents were first authorized, and more especially since 1855,[4] when the prohibitory law was enacted, the towns have derived a small revenue from the liquor agencies. In the town of Hanover, which may be considered fairly representative, the revenue in 1876 was $207.70; in 1881, $309.12; in 1884, $413.70; and in 1885, $421.06.

The earlier acts granting licenses to peddlers and hawkers made no direct reference to temporary merchants who rented a store for a part of the year and escaped the assessment on the first of April. An act of June 25, 1858,[5] however, provided for such cases. The fee was fixed at not less than $50 nor more than $100, the proceeds to be for the use of the town. An amendment of 1876[6] reduced the minimum fee to $10, but left the maximum undisturbed. In 1878 the revenue from the above source was made payable to the state treasury. The act of 1893,[7] already referred to, was in one sense a compromise measure—it allowed peddlers or hawkers to choose whether they would have a state, town, or county license. In case the peddler wished a town license, the fees accrued to the town. At the same time the fees

[1] Commissioners' report, 1842, chap. 117, sec. 8.
[2] Rev. statutes, 1842, chap. 117, sec. 7.
[3] Laws, 1849, p. 847.
[4] Laws, 1855, p. 152.
[5] Laws, 1858, p. 1985.
[6] Laws, 1876, p. 568.
[7] Laws, 1893, p. 54.

from the licenses granted to temporary merchants were made payable to the town treasury instead of to the state treasury as had been the case since 1878. The fees for a temporary or auctioneer merchant, trader, etc., were fixed at a specific sum, $50. The fees for peddlers, hawkers, etc., were based upon the population of the town or city in question, viz.: $2 for every town of not more than 2000 inhabitants, and $1 for every 1000 additional inhabitants, but the fee was in no case to exceed twenty dollars. These rates were changed in 1897,[1] as follows :—

For a town with not over 1000 inhabitants, $ 5 00
"   "   "   " from 1000 to 2000   "   8 00
"   "   "   "   " 2000 to 3000   "   10 00
For every additional thousand inhabitants,   1 00

In all the cases referred to the acts were made enforce-able by appropriate fines, the fine usually being divided between the person complaining and the town, city, or county as the case might be.

Since 1842 the towns have derived an increasing revenue from the licensing and taxing of dogs. The introduction of this system, partly for protection, partly for taxation, of regulating the keeping of dogs by licensing them was due to the commissioners of the revised statutes of 1842, who credit the clause to the revised statutes of Maine and of Massachusetts. The act of 1842[2] was permissive, not compulsory: "any town may make by-laws for licensing, regulating or restrain-ing dogs . . . . and may affix penalties not exceeding $5 and the sum to be paid for any license not exceeding two dollars." This act has been amended twice : (1) in 1878,[3] when it was prescribed that whenever any town

[1] Laws, 1897, p. 65.
[2] Revised statutes, 1842, p. 241.
[3] Laws, 1878, p. 149.

neglected to make by-laws as permitted in 1842 the selectmen should make such regulations as they deemed expedient, the sum to be paid for a license to be not less than $2 for a male and $5 for a female dog, and the regulations to be in force until changed either by the town or by the selectmen; (2) in 1891,[1] when every owner or keeper of a dog three months old or over was required on or before the 30th day of April annually "to cause it to be registered, numbered, described, and licensed for one year." The fee was fixed at $2 for a male and $5 for a female, and provision was made for a license for any part of a year after May 1st at proportionate rates. From 1862 to 1893 dogs were also taxed. The first act of this nature, 1862,[2] was passed under the impetus of war expenses, and like many another war tax illustrates the tendency of such taxes to linger long after the necessity for their use has ceased. The rates were $1 and $2 for male and female dogs respectively. The act of 1862 specified dogs "one year old or over". This was amended in 1863[3] by making the tax apply to all dogs no matter how tender the age, and by prescribing that in case any dog appeared to have no owner the person harboring the same should be liable for the tax. This tax continued in force until 1893,[4] when it was repealed. The act of 1891 making license compulsory made the extra tax too burdensome. Outside of the cities small use was made of the provision of 1842. The dog tax of 1862–1893 acted as a substitute to a considerable extent. Under the compulsory act of 1891, however, a considerable revenue has been derived. For instance, in the town of Hanover the revenue in 1897

---

[1] Laws, 1891, p. 371.
[2] Laws, 1862, p. 2607.
[3] Laws, 1863, chap. 2728.
[4] Laws, 1893, p. 9.

was $264.00, and in 1898 was $269.50. The proceeds of the dog tax and license fee has been by law appropriated to two purposes: (1) to pay damages to sheep caused by dogs, and (2) to aid the public schools.

SEC. 4. *Taxes Collected by the State.* In the sections upon the state revenue that part of the insurance tax, the railroad tax, and the savings bank tax distributed to the towns was necessarily described. Aside from the above taxes the town has received a small revenue from what is known as the "Literary fund". But as the proceeds of this tax is appropriated directly to the aid of the common schools, it will be treated under the school taxes.

SEC. 5. *Taxes on the Inventory.* Two questions naturally arise at this point: (1) What limitations, if any, have been placed upon the amount of taxes that may be voted in any town, and what are the purposes for which such taxes may be appropriated? (2) To what extent have the voters exercised the right of taxing themselves? One fact needs to be kept in mind, viz. : it is only in the annual town meetings that the people directly vote the taxes which they themselves are to pay. State, county, and city taxes are authorized by the representatives of the people, not by the people themselves. The New England township is the nearest approach to a perfect democracy that exists in America. But it must be again remembered that the towns derive their powers from the state, and as an organization may be abolished and governed directly through the legislative and executive departments.

As a matter of fact, the purposes for which a town may vote taxes on the inventory have been and are restricted by both statute law and the state constitution. The first act of this nature after the Revolution,

13

February 8, 1791,[1] authorized towns to "grant and vote such sums of money as they should deem necessary for the the settlement, maintenance and support of the ministry, schools, meeting houses, school houses, the maintenance of the poor, for laying out and repairing highways, for building and repairing bridges, and for all the necessary charges arising with the said town, to be assessed on the polls and estates in the same town as the law directs."[2] On comparison it will be seen that the act of 1791 is a substantial copy of the act of 1719.[3] A more important step was taken in 1819, when the church was separated from the state, and the taxation of the towns to support public worship was forbidden[4] except to fulfill existing contracts.[5] Beginning with 1849 the policy of enlarging the sphere of appropriations for the towns is noticeable, and has been followed with increasing vigor until the present; to-day any town may legally raise money for the following purposes: to establish and maintain public libraries and reading-rooms for the free use of all persons of the town;[6] to encourage volunteer enlistment in case of rebellion or invasion;[7] to establish cemeteries and receiving tombs;[8] to purchase parks or commons and improve the same;[9] to set out and care for shade and ornamental trees in highways, cemeteries, commons, and

---

[1] Revised laws, 1792, p. 167.

[2] Revised laws, 1792, p. 173.

[3] See chap. IX, p. 176.

[4] The towns were authorized to raise money to repair meetinghouses belonging to the town in order that they might be made useful for town purposes.

[5] And in that case, when proper notice had been given, persons of other religious persuasion than the minister in charge were not compelled to pay taxes to fulfill existing contracts.

[6] Laws, 1849, chap. 861, sec. 1.

[7] Laws, 1862, chap. 2580, sec. 3.

[8] Laws, 1866, chap. 4221.

[9] Laws, 1866, chap. 4271.

other public places;[1] to publish a town history;[2] to decorate the graves of soldiers in the late Rebellion; the expenditure not to exceed $200 yearly;[3] to provide and maintain suitable coasting and skating places, the expenditure not to exceed $500 yearly;[4] to maintain and record weather observations;[5] to provide and maintain armories for the New Hampshire national guard or reserved militia, the expenditure not to exceed $200 yearly for each organization;[6] to aid or pension disabled, and to bury deceased firemen;[7] to light streets;[8] to procure and erect a monument or memorial building to perpetuate the memory of soldiers belonging to the town that sacrificed their lives in the service of their country.[9]

This list is already a long one, but it is not yet complete. In 1864[10] an enactment provided that any town by a two-thirds vote might raise by tax or by a loan a sum of money not above five per cent of the town valuation to aid the construction of railroads in the state.[11] Under the provision of this law many cities and towns voted considerable sums to aid the railroads then building or soon afterwards commenced. This privilege seems to have been abused,[12] resulting in re-

[1] Laws, 1868, chap. 1 ; Laws, 1875, chap. 39 ; Laws, 1889, chap. 82.
[2] Laws, 1868, chap. 26.
[3] Laws, 1872, chap. 40.
[4] Laws, 1883, chap. 69.
[5] Laws, 1889, chap. 7.
[6] Laws, 1891, chap. 1.
[7] Laws, 1897, chap. 52.
[8] Public statutes, 1891, chap. 40, sec. 4.
[9] General laws, 1878, chap. 37, sec. 4.
[10] Laws, 1864, chap. 2890, sec. 1.
[11] The constitutional convention of 1850 offered an amendment providing that no town or city should either directly or indirectly aid any corporation or take stock therein, but the people at the polls rejected the same by a large vote. Journal of convention, 1850. See 56 N. H. Reports, p. 544.
[12] See 56 N. H. Reports, p. 544 *et seq.* for a list of sums appropriated by various towns under the act of 1864.

action in the sentiment of the voters. Hence the constitutional convention of 1876 proposed the following amendment, which the voters adopted: "the general court shall not authorize any town to loan or give its money or credit, directly or indirectly, for the benefit of any corporation having for its object a dividend of profits, or in any way aid the same by taking its stock or bonds."[1] This amendment to the constitution was followed by a statute passed in 1877[2] providing for the same restriction in statute form.

The towns have depended chiefly upon the direct tax on the inventory for their own use and to pay the county taxes.[3] The revenue from the other sources averages in most cases less than one-fourth of the towns' expenditures. In towns largely devoted to agriculture the natural conservatism of the voters has served to keep the direct taxes low. Indeed, parsimoniousness rather than extravagance in voting public taxes must be considered the fault of the rural communities. It is only in the industrial communities in the larger towns that extravagant taxes are voted. The movement for the constitutional and statutory prohibition of public aid to corporations originated in the cities,[4] where a large number of voters paying only nominal taxes put the citizens owning real estate at their mercy. Yet an examination of the rate of taxation in the various towns in the state will show that the difference in the rate paid by the towns purely agricultural and those largely industrial is less than is generally supposed. The fol-

[1] Laws, 1878, p. 26 ; Constitution of N. H., part 2, sec. 5.
[2] Laws, 1877, p. 51.
[3] The amount distributed to the towns by the state is now usually about equal to the state tax.
[4] Journal of constitutional convention, 1876, pp. 264–269.

lowing list, selected with the view of comparing typical rural with urban communities, shows a difference of only ten per cent on an average for the three years selected in favor of the rural towns, and it will be noticed that only one industrial town shows as high an average for the three years chosen as several of the purely farming towns.

TAX RATE—FARMING TOWNS.

TOWN.	1869–70	1887–8	1895–6	Average
New Hampton	2.35	2.16	1.96	2.16
Fremont	1.50	1.53	1.23	1.42
Northwood	1.95	·1.75	1.83	1.84
Gilmanton	1.90	2.28	2.12	2.10
Hancock	1.46	1.72½	1.52	1.57
Temple	1.86	1.51	1.72	1.70
Westmoreland	1.25	.86	1.35	1.15
Washington	1.80	1.72½	1.30	1.61
Plainfield	1.25	1.57	1.70	1.51
Moultonboro	3.76	3.00	1.60	2.79
Tuftonboro	2.75	2.68	2.34	2.59
Sandwich	3.69	2.70	2.15	2.85
Average	2.13½	2.11½	1.63	1.95

TAX RATE—INDUSTRIAL TOWNS.

TOWN.	1868–70	1887–8	1885–6	Average
Berlin	5.65	1.80	2.50	3.32
Dover	2.20	1.65	2.00	1.95
Rochester	2.37	1.80	2.00	2.06
Tilton	2.20	1.62	1.76	1.86
Franklin	1.80⅔	2.25	1.80	1.95
Manchester	2.48	1.95	1.86	2.06
Nashua	2.80	1.70	2.18	2.23
Hinsdale	2.05	2.15	1.70	1.97
Swanzey	2.63	1.27	1.43	1.78
Newport	1.77	1.71	2.20	1.90
Claremont	1.81½	1.60	2.00	1.81
Conway	2.43	2.01	1.65	2.03
Average	2.53½	1 78	1.81	2.05

The second table, giving the rate by counties for all taxes assessed for state, county, and town purposes during the nine years 1887–1895, shows considerable, difference among the counties. Each county, however,

AVERAGE RATE OF TAXATION BY COUNTIES.

Counties	87–88	88–89	89–90	90–91	91–92	92–93	93–94	94–95	95–96
Rockingham	1.50	1.50	1.62	1.61	1.60	1.64	1.59½	1.68½	1.77
Strafford	1.75½	1.77	1.79	1.88	1.81	1.80	1.77	1.91	1.95
Belknap	1.93	1.88	1.83	1.91	1.83	1.78	1.91	1.92½	1.99
Carroll	2.57	2.18	2.32	2.63	2.12½	2.16	1.90½	1.92	1.84
Merrimack	1.52½	1.55	1.54	1.55	1.57	1.61	1.59	1.67	1.89
Hillsboro	1.71	1.69	1.73	1.63	1.72	1.73	1.70½	1.83	1.85
Cheshire	1.33	1.33	1.39	1.30	1.31½	1.39	1.35½	1.38	1.50
Sullivan	1.63	1.55	1.73	1.64	1.65	1.68	1.66	1.75	1.90½
Grafton	1.66	1.65	1.66	1.64	1.67	1.77	1.73	1.86½	1.84
Coos	1.98	1.78	1.84	1.75	1.72	1.79	1.91	1.91	1.96
Average	1.67½	1.64	1.68	1.667	1.661	1.71	1.677	1.77	1.84

exhibits a strong tendency to raise about the same amount of money in comparison to its valuation year by year, so that there is little change in the rate by counties. A comparison of these rates with those for the year 1869–1870 discloses the fact that the rate is now considerably lower, nominally at least,[1] than it was just after the war, when the towns were paying off the war debt.

The enumeration in the preceding section of the purposes for which the towns may raise money legally is a fairly comprehensive one, but in order to make the picture of local taxation more complete it will be necessary to trace somewhat in detail the historical development of the more important uses to which town taxes are appropriated.

SEC. 6. *Taxes for the Support of Public Worship.* The provincial laws providing for the support of the ministry were continued in force by the act of 1777 until reaffirmed by the act of 1791[2] regulating towns and the choice of town officers.[3] The provincial acts

---

[1] The appreciation of money during the period must, of course, be taken into consideration.

[2] Revised laws, 1792, p. 167.

[3] This statute expressly declared parishes incorporated with town privileges to be towns for all purposes.

continued by the act of 1791 provided for a clergy settled by the towns and supported by public taxation.
While none of the later acts expressly exempted clergymen or their property from taxation, such was the
custom, a custom that was upheld by the courts when
such cases were adjudicated. In 1798[1] it was held by
the highest court in the state "that a minister of the
church and congregation in a town" was not liable to
taxation.[2] This doctrine was reaffirmed in 1815 by the
supreme court.[3] On the other hand, the estate of an
ordained minister, not settled over a corporate society,
was held by the same court in 1807 to be liable to taxation.[4]

The movement for religious toleration began as
early as 1791. William Plummer, a member of the constitutional convention of 1791, proposed as a substitute
for article six of the constitution of 1784 an article
"prohibiting the legislature from compelling any person
either to attend a place of public worship, or to pay
taxes for the purpose of building of churches, or for the
support of religious teachers, except in pursuance of his
own free act and agreement."[5] A second substitute was
also proposed allowing the majority in each parish to
select the pastor and to compel all to contribute taxes to
his support. Neither of the above amendments was accepted by the convention. Instead, an article was submitted to the people providing that in case a minister
was settled in any town, any person might within a

[1] Kelly *vs.* Bean *et al.*

[2] See Shirley, Dartmouth College causes, pp. 70–80.

[3] MS reports cited by Shirley, Dartmouth College causes, p. 71.

[4] Kidder *vs.* French, cited by Shirley, Dartmouth College causes, p.
71. Shirley attributes this decision to the well-known liberal view of
Chief Justice Smith, Wingate dissenting.

[5] Life of William Plummer, p. 116.

certain time dissent against paying any taxes toward his support; also, that when minors became of age or when persons came into the town to live, they might enter such dissent. This dissent was in all the cases to free the person from contributing toward the support of the minister selected by a majority of the town. This amendment was rejected by the people by a vote of 994 for and 3993 against it.[1] This movement, though defeated as a constitutional guarantee, was moving quietly but strongly, and made rapid progress, sometimes by voluntary action, sometimes by judicial decision, sometimes by statute law. The development of parishes within parishes has already been noted. Such, for example, was the formation of the second parish in Exeter in 1755.[2] By 1800 the town of Sanbornton had of its own will granted religious toleration to all societies, and had equitably divided the " parsonage fund ".[3] The first judicial decision favoring religious toleration was given in 1803, Chief Justice Smith holding that although the beliefs of the Congregationalists and Presbyterians were the same, they differed in their church government and discipline to such an extent that they were different sects, and therefor the member of one sect could not be assessed to support the other.[4] About the year 1800 the cases in litigation of this nature were numerous. William Plummer continued to be the leading spirit, and this " branch of business gave him much trouble,"[5] and in some of the cases " he won verdicts of the jury against charges of the court."[6] It is even stated that two of the

---

[1] Journal of convention, X N. H. Prov. and State papers, 113, 141.
[2] Bell, Exeter, 188.
[3] Runnels, Sanbornton, I, 77.
[4] Secomb, Amherst, pp. 275-6.
[5] Life of William Plummer, p. 185.
[6] Life of William Plummer, p. 186.

justices of the superior court in 1799 expressed a decided disapprobation of Plummer's constancy and zeal in supporting those who claimed exemption from taxes for the maintenance of clergymen.[1] To this advice Plummer indirectly replied that so long as he remained at the bar the court would find him a persevering and determined advocate "for the rights of conscience and property both involved in these issues."[2] Two steps were necessary to secure the complete separation of church and state : (1) the taxation of the property of the clergy ; (2) the assumption of the expenses of religious worship by the religious societies.

The first was accomplished in 1816 by an act providing that the "real and personal estate of all ordained ministers of the gospel of every demonination within the state, shall hereafter be assessed and taxed in the same way and manner as other estates."[3] This was the immediate result of a clause in Governor Plummer's message to the legislature stating "the rights of conscience and of private judgment in religious matters are not only secured by the constitution to all men but are in their nature inalienable. Civil and religious liberty have usually flourished and expired together . . . while therefore it becomes every man scrupulously to examine the foundations of his own belief, he cannot guard with too much jealousy against the encroachment of the civil power on his religious liberties."[4]

The passage of the above act was followed on July 1,

---

[1] Life of William Plummer, p. 187.

[2] Life of William Plummer, p. 187.

[3] Laws, 1816, p. 91. This provision was not to effect any preexisting contract.

[4] Governor's message, Senate journal, 1816, p. 24.

1819, by the passage of the so-called "toleration act"[1] whereby the complete separation of the church and state was effected in New Hampshire, and all church organizaations were thereafter obliged to depend upon voluntary contributions to meet their expenses.[2]　Supplementary to the provision releasing the citizen from taxation for the support of religious worship was a clause providing that religious societies might be incorporated and empowered to assess and collect taxes for their own use upon their own members.

SEC. 7.　*Taxes for the Support of Public Education.* Each town was originally a single school district, but owing to the large area of the towns, the lack of means of communication, and the strong spirit of localism

[1] Laws, 1819, p. 246.　The movement for religious toleration in New Hampshire was largely influenced by (1) parallel movements in neighboring states and (2) the varying fortunes of the great political parties.　After about twenty years of partial compulsory taxation for religious worship, Vermont in 1807 adopted complete religious toleration.　Connecticut followed in 1818, at the adoption of her first constitution.　Maine, in formulating her constitution in 1819, provided for complete separation of the church and state.　New Hampshire, by the passage of the act of 1819, preceded Maine in the actual operation of the law, and thus took the third place in the movement that has long since become universal throughout the United States, preceding Massachusetts by fifteen years　The Congregationalists were largely Federalists, the opposing sects Republicans.　The Republicans first came into power in the state in 1805.　From this date until 1816 the parties were evenly matched.　After 1816 the Federalists became permanently the minority party.　The separation of church and state came with the rise of the Republican power in the state.　The Baptists were recognized in law as a distinct sect in 1804, the Universalists in 1805, the Methodists in 1807.　The complete ascendency of the Republican party resulted in 1816 in the passage of the act providing that the estates of all ministers should be taxed; later, in 1819, in the passage of the toleration act.　See Barstow, History of New Hampshire, chap. VII, for a review of the controversy that led to the act of 1819.

[2] With this exception : when there was an existing contract between a town and a minister, the contract was to be fulfilled, but any person, by filing a statement affirming that he was of another persuasion, would be exempted from taxation for that minister's support.

which has at all times characterized the people of New England, the towns began to create temporary districts during the provincial period. This movement increased with the growth of local communities in the towns, and was given legal effect in the act of 1805[1] which provided that towns might sub-divide into districts, determine the limits thereof, and alter them from time to time. Each district was authorized "to raise money for the purpose of erecting, repairing or purchasing a school house in their respective districts, and of necessary utensils for the same." By act of July 6, 1839,[2] such a division was made obligatory upon the selectmen upon application of ten legal voters, a majority being freeholders of the town. These districts were in reality miniature towns whose sole object of existence was to care for the schools included within their territorial area. Their power to raise money by taxes was limited as will be shown later. Of course any town that was not divided was a district.[3]

A centralizing movement began as early as 1845,[4] when two or more contiguous districts were authorized to unite for the purpose of maintaining a high school. This was followed in 1854[5] by a general act empowering any two or more districts in the state by a two-thirds vote of all the legal voters to unite and form one district. The act of 1854 was amended a year later by requiring the assent of only two-thirds of the legal voters present to secure an act of union.[6] For ten years the number of votes required fluctuated be-

---

[1] Laws, 1805, p. 45.
[2] Laws, 1839, p. 398.
[3] Laws, 1840, p. 487. So declared by statute, Dec. 23, 1840.
[4] Laws, 1845, p. 223.
[5] Laws, 1854, p. 1430.
[6] Laws, 1855, chap. 1679.

tween a majority and a two-thirds vote; since 1865[1] the statute has allowed a union by a majority vote of the voters in the districts interested.   Until 1870 the initiative was with the districts only.   By act of July 2, 1870,[2] the initiative was vested also in the towns.   Any town was empowered at any time to abolish the school districts therein, and at once to take possession of the property of the districts and to assess a tax equal to the value of the whole property involved with which to compensate the districts for their school property.   The legislation of 1870 was followed by a slight reaction, in 1874[3] it being enacted that any town having abolished the districts might reëstablish the original districts by a two-thirds vote at any time within two years from the passage of the act.   This reaction was merely temporary. The abolition of the districts and the establishment of the town system was an economic necessity.   For ten years longer the spirit of localism, aided by the well known conservatism of the rural communities, prevented further action.   In 1885 the · legislature enacted that "the division of towns into school districts heretofore existing is hereby abolished, and each town shall hereafter constitute a single district for school purposes."[4] Districts organized under special acts of the legislature were exempted from the provisions of the act.   As a matter of conciliation a provision was added that any town at the end of five years might by a majority vote of all the voters of the district reëstablish the district system in such town.   As a matter of fact, the prejudice

[1] Laws, 1865, p. 3142.
[2] Laws, 1870, p. 409.
[3] Laws, 1874, p. 311.
[4] Laws, 1885, p. 252.

against the law wore away, and at end of the five years the town system was universally maintained.[1]

The amount of the taxes to be raised for the support of the schools, or the rate of taxation for that purpose, was previous to 1789 left wholly to the towns. The act of 1789,[2] which affirmed in its preamble that "the laws respecting schools have been found not to answer the important end for which they were made," was the first state law to fix the amount which each town must raise, by requiring the selectmen of the several towns and parishes "to assess annually the inhabitants of their respective towns according to their polls and ratable estates, in a sum to be computed at the rate of five pounds for every twenty shillings of the proportion for public taxes for the time being and so for a greater or lesser sum." In case the selectmen neglected or refused to make such assessment the property was made liable for the full amount. This rate has at subsequent dates been raised, until in 1898[3] it stood at a sum to be computed at the rate of "five-hundred dollars for every dollar of the public taxes apportioned to such town and so for a greater or lesser sum."[4] In the assessment authorized

[1] During the controversy that preceded the adoption of the law of 1885, the state superintendents of public instruction led the movement, especially the Hon. J. W. Patterson, who unified public sentiment in its favor, and ably explained the system, both on the platform and in his published reports. By this act New Hampshire was the second state in New England to adopt the town system of public schools. See the New Hampshire School reports, 1869-1892.

[2] Laws, 1789, p. 251 ; Revised laws, 1792, pp. 275-6.

[3] Laws, 1895, p. 438.

[4] The rate has varied from £5 for every £1 of the town's proportion of the state tax in 1789 to $500 for every dollar of the proportion in 1895. In 1799 it was $35 ; in 1807, $70 ; in 1852, $135 ; in 1807, $200; in 1870, $350; and in 1893, $400. From 1805 to 1885 the amount raised was distributed among the districts, either by vote of the town in public meeting or in proportion to the valuation of the property in the districts. Since 1885 it has been distributed to various schools by the town board of education.

by the act of 1789 the tax was not to extend to the lands of non-residents. The act of 1799 authorized the taxation of the improved lands and buildings of non-residents, and finally by the act of 1804 the unimproved lands of non-residents were subjected to taxation for school purposes. In addition to the amount required to be raised by law for schools, many of the towns have raised by vote a certain additional sum to be used for the same purposes. No legislation definitely authorizing such action appears earlier than 1842, when such a clause is found in the revised statutes. The act of 1789 and its successors were intended to fix the minimum amount to be raised, and not to prevent the towns from voting additional sums if they chose to do so. A study of the town histories already published shows that in many, if not in the majority of cases, the towns habitually raised more money than was required by law.[1] Since the enactment of the law allowing the towns to subdivide into districts, the districts have possessed considerable power of voting taxes. The act of 1805 permitted the districts to raise taxes for building and furnishing schoolhouses. By the act of December 22, 1808,[2] the districts were authorized to purchase and hold in fee simple so much land as might be necessary for a school lot and yard. But it was not until 1867[3] that the districts were individually permitted to raise additional money for the support of schools.

[1] See also Report of state superintendent of schools, 1876, p. 177. Judge Parker said : "The towns may, if they think proper, vote to raise a larger sum than the selectmen are thus bound to assess, and with a commendable zeal in the cause of education this is often done." Tucker *vs.* Aiken, 7 N. H. Reports, 128.

[2] Laws, 1808, p. 32.

[3] An act of July 8, 1862, permitted schools organized under the Somersworth Act to raise additional sums by a two-thirds vote. This applied chiefly to city schools.

In addition to the revenue raised by direct local taxation, either compulsory under state law or voted voluntarily by the towns and districts, there has been appropriated to the support of the public schools the proceeds of the revenue from three other sources: (1) the literary fund, (2) the dog tax, and (3) miscellaneous sources.

1. The literary fund was established in 1821 [1] by an act requiring all banking corporations established under the authority of the state to have their circulating notes stamped by the treasurer and to pay annually to the state a tax of fifty dollars for every thousand dollars in such notes, or in place of the above tax to pay annually one-half of one per cent on the amount which should at the time constitute the actual capital stock of said bank. This fund was originally intended "for the sole use and purpose of endowing or supporting a college for instruction in the higher branches of science and literature." The fund was allowed to accumulate until 1829, when it amounted to $64,000.[2] By act of December 31, 1828,[3] in accordance with the recommendation of Governor Bell,[4] this fund was directed to be paid over to the towns annually, to be divided severally among them according to the apportionment of the public taxes then existing, and "to be applied by the repective towns to the support of the common free schools, or to other purposes of education, in addition to the sums which may be required by law to be raised." The division of the fund was made annually on the above basis until 1848, when by act of December 13 [5] it was provided that thereafter the fund should be divided ac-

---

[1] Laws, 1821, p. 393.
[2] New Hampshire School report, 1876, p. 290.
[3] Laws, 1828, p. 341.
[4] Governor's message, Journal of house, 1828, p. 16.
[5] Laws, 1848, p. 706.

cording to the number of scholars not less than four years of age [1] who had attended the district schools not less than two weeks of the preceding year. After the introduction of the national banking system, which practically abolished the state banks,[2] the act taxing banks on their capital stock was repealed.[3] By an act of the previous year, 1866,[4] the money received from the tax on the deposits of non-residents in the savings banks was constituted a part of the literary fund to be divided as before. Subsequently, by a joint resolution of June 28, 1867,[5] the governor, with the advice of the council, was directed to sell the public lands of the state, the proceeds to become a part of the literary fund. An act[6] one year later modified the joint resolution of 1867 by providing that the proceeds should be set apart as a school fund to be applied to the purposes of common school education according to the direction of the legislature from time to time. The fund was allowed to accumulate until 1883,[7] when the treasurer was directed to invest it, and it was provided that the proceeds of the funds thus invested should be used for holding teachers' institutes in each county in the state annually under the direction of the state superintendent of public instruction. Since 1866 the non-resident savings bank tax has constituted the greater part of the revenue devoted to the literary fund. However, the fund received a substantial addition by the act of August 14, 1889,[8] providing "for the uniform taxation of the trust com-

[1] Changed to five years in 1878. General laws, p. 226.
[2] Preamble to act of July 5, 1867, Laws, 1867, p. 19.
[3] Laws, 1867, p. 19.
[4] Laws, 1866, p. 3284.
[5] Laws, 1867, p. 28.
[6] Laws, 1868, p. 153.
[7] Laws, 1883, p. 49.
[8] Laws, 1889, p. 76.

panies and other similar corporations." By this act the taxation of such companies was made uniform with the taxation of savings banks, and the taxes on non-resident deposits consequently became a part of the literary fund.

2. The act of June 28, 1867,[1] was the first to provide that the revenue arising from the taxation of dogs, after the payment for damages to domestic animals had been deducted according to law, should be equally divided among the districts in the towns and cities of the state every second year. This act was amended in 1876[2] by providing that each town or city might annually divide the tax as above, or keep it in the treasury as a fund to satisfy any claims for damages to domestic animals. Finally the public statutes of 1891 required that all money arising from this tax not due for damages by dogs should be annually applied to the support of the common schools as other school money.[3]

3. The miscellaneous sources which have contributed to the support of education are four in number: (1) the revenue from local funds, usually the proceeds of the sale of the lots granted to the schools in the original charters; (2) a considerable sum contributed by individuals in money, board, or fuel; (3) a portion of the railroad tax, which is required "to be appropriated as other town money;" and (4) in 1848[4] the balance of the proceeds from the sale of public lands, then in the state treasury, was appropriated to the literary fund to be distributed and used as provided by law.

SEC. 8. *Taxes for the Support of Highways.* The larger part of the expense of constructing and repairing

---

[1] Laws, 1867, p. 2.
[2] Laws, 1876, p. 569.
[3] Public statutes, 1891, p. 25.
[4] Laws, 1848, p. 609.

14

the highways in the state has been borne by the towns, and has been paid by an annual tax upon the polls and estates.[1] In unincorporated places the tax has been laid upon the owners of the land according to their respective interests, generally taking the form of a uniform assessment per acre.[2] However, two exceptions to this general method may be noted : (1) the construction and operation of private roads by chartered turnpike companies, maintained by the toll system ; and (2) the construction of through roads by several towns with an assessment of part or all of the expense upon the county taxes. The private roads were constructed almost wholly within the first two decades of the nineteenth century, and after being in operation for a term of years were surrendered to the towns either gratuitously or for a small compensation. Roads extending through several towns have been constructed and maintained jointly by the towns directly interested, or, as in some cases, partly by the towns and partly by the county.[3] An act of 1831[4] permitted the county officers in case a road was considered " of public and general value " to apportion a part of the expense, not over one-half, to the county. This was followed in 1839[5] by an act providing that the proper officers might require the county to keep in repair any road " of general utility if burdensome to the town." In some cases in addition to those already mentioned the county is required to bear the expense of the highways in unincorporated places. In several cases during the years immediately preceding the Civil War

[1] Revised laws, 1792, p. 280 ; Revised statutes, 1842, p. 126 ; Laws, 1893, p. 24.

[2] Revised laws, 1792, p. 283 ; Laws, 1829, p. 525.

[3] Revised laws, 1792, p. 168.

[4] Laws, 1831, p. 38.

[5] Laws, 1839, p. 383.

the state legislature granted direct state aid to the towns and places in the mountain region for the purpose of building and repairing highways.[1]

The authority for laying out a new highway wholly within one town is vested in the board of selectmen.[2] The same officers are likewise empowered to assess a tax sufficient to cover the expense, such tax to be collected with the regular taxes. Where the road extended through two or more towns, the authority was entrusted under the earlier acts to the selectmen of the towns interested, or in case of disagreement or refusal to act, to the courts;[3] in 1840[4] to the road commissioners, with the approval of the courts; and later, in 1855,[5] to the county commissioners.

The highway tax has in general been " worked out " by the labor of men and teams, although the paying of the tax in money was made permissive in 1823,[6] and obligatory in 1893. The act of 1823 provided that any town by vote might have its highway tax paid in money, the proceeds to be expended under the direction of the selectmen or surveyors. This provision was used chiefly by the larger villages which were not incorporated as precincts or cities and which were therefore under the general laws relating to highways. The act of 1893[7] abolished the district system, and enacted that the highway tax should be assessed, collected, and paid into the treasury as other taxes. The sum thus received was to be expended by elected highway agents under the gen-

---

[1] Laws, 1853, 1854, 1855, 1858, 1859.
[2] Revised laws, 1792, p. 168 ; Revised statutes, 1842, p. 146.
[3] Revised laws, 1792, p. 168.
[4] Laws. 1840, p. 438.
[5] Laws, 1855, p. 1539,
[6] Laws, 1823, p. 90.
[7] Laws, 1893, p. 47.

eral direction of the selectmen. The same act provided
that the highway tax rate should be at least one-fourth
of one per cent of the valuation, but need not exceed
$50.00 per mile. The towns were of course allowed to
raise additional sums to be assessed and expended in the
same way.

CHAPTER XI.

COUNTY TAXATION.

SEC. 1. *Introduction.* An act dividing the province of New Hampshire into counties [1] passed both house and council and received the governor's signature in April, 1769.[2] It was approved by the crown in council, and became effective in March, 1771.[3] This act was the result of persistent efforts on the part of the rural districts, extending over nearly a score of years, to secure the establishment of courts of justice in the various sections of the province. Before 1771 the courts were held at Portsmouth ; after 1771 in one or two centrally located towns in each county. As both province and township preceded the county, the questions raised by the advent of the county obviously related to (1) the purposes to which the revenue was and is applied, (2) the sources of the revenue, (3) the methods of administration.

SEC. 2. *Purposes to Which the Revenue was and is Applied.* The county was created for the purpose

[1] The colony of Massachusetts Bay was divided into "4 sheires" in 1643. Mass. Rec., II, 38. The New Hampshire towns were included within the limits of Norfolk county, with Salisbury as shire town. Dover and Portsmouth were, however, permitted to retain some of their former independence, especially functions of a judicial nature. Although the laws for county purposes were comparatively unimportant, the county was evidently a taxing district during the remainder of the Massachusetts period. In 1658 it was enacted by the general court that the "commissioners of Dover, Portsmouth and York shall annually chose some persons in their several towns to levy the amount of the annual levy, also certain arrears." Mass. Rec., IV, 360. In 1669 the court of election exempted Mr. Edward Hilton from the "county rate" on account of certain official duties undertaken by him for the county. I N. H. Prov. papers, 306. Such acts give evidence that the county system was in use during the period.

[2] VII N. H. Prov. papers, 228-9.

[3] Acts and laws, 1771, p. 207.

of carrying the courts of justice nearer to the people. Its purpose necessarily conditioned to a considerable extent its expenditures, but like all other institutions in New Hampshire the county has been modified by changing conditions during the century and a quarter of its existence.

As a judicial district the county naturally from the first exercised a large authority over the idle, the vagrant, and the disorderly. As early as 1791[1] the court of the general sessions of peace was authorized to provide, at the expense of the county, " a house of correction for the keeping and correcting of rogues, vagabonds, common beggars, lewd, idle or disorderly persons, and in which to employ the poor ; " and it was added that when no such house was provided, " the common prison might be used." All paupers having a " settlement " in any town have been and are now supported by the town. All other paupers were, before 1809, supported by the state. By act of June 27, 1809,[2] however, it was provided that when any person " not an inhabitant of any town or place in this state, nor by the laws thereof the proper charge of any town or place in the same " was in need of relief, he should be relieved by the town, but that the expense should be ultimately paid out of the county treasury. The important act of 1828[3] reaffirmed previous legislature in the main, but in addition authorized " the court of common pleas, if they see fit, to provide, at the expense of any county in the state, all such lands and buildings as may be necessary for the accommodation, support and employment of the poor, who may be chargeable to the

[1] Revised laws, 1792, p. 300.

[2] Laws, 1809, p. 18.

[3] Laws, 1828, p. 296.

county and for a house of correction."[1] Subsequent
legislation has but developed the two lines of work already indicated, so that to-day the county appropriates
its revenue for but two purposes, viz : the administration of justice and the care of the county dependents.[2]

SEC. 3. *Sources of the County Revenue.* The county
revenue arises chiefly from the following sources : (1)
the county tax on the inventory, (2) license fees, (3)
fines, forfeitures, etc., (4) miscellaneous sources.

1. The tax on the county inventory has always been
the chief reliance of the county government. In the
early days it was less important than later because the
county was originally more strictly a judicial district,
and further because the officers were largely paid by
fees. With the extension of the functions of the county
there was a decrease rather than an increase of the
revenue from other sources, and as a consequence the
taxes on the inventory were obliged to bear the greater
burden. To illustrate : in 1832 the town of Portsmouth
paid as its county tax on the inventory $972 ; in
1833, $1,157.67 ; in 1881, $2,407.20 ; in 1891, $1,976.50.
In 1852–3 New Ipswich paid in county taxes $872.70 ;
in 1886–7, $893.98.

2. From 1821 to 1878, and again from 1893 until
1897, the counties received a small income from license
fees imposed upon hawkers and peddlers.[3] The act of
1821 [4] authorized the justices of the court of sessions to

---

[1] By acts of 1841, 1860, 1875, 1883, and 1889 settlements gained prior
to 1796, 1840, 1860, 1870, and 1880 respectively were abolished. By
act of 1897 (Laws, 1897, chap. 31) towns were made liable for care of
only those paupers who had gained settlements within ten years.

[2] A county may in certain cases be required to bear part of the
expenses of constructing and repairing roads.

[3] See chap. VI, sec. 6, pp. 124-126 relating to fees from same source
accruing to the state.

[4] Laws, 1821, p. 389.

grant a license good for one year to any peddler or hawker of good moral character upon the payment of $12 into the county treasury and a fee of one dollar to the clerk for recording the same. The sale of goods grown and manufactured in the United States except feathers, distilled spirits, playing cards, lottery tickets, and jewelry was exempted from the provisions of the act. In 1846[1] the license fee was raised to $25. The act of 1847[2] was the first to discriminate between citizens of the state and those of other states. The fees for a citizen of the state who had been a resident for one year and was reputed to be of good moral character were fixed at from $2 to $20 at the discretion of the court, the license being good for one year as before. A peddler or hawker not a citizen of the state might be granted a similar license upon the payment of $50.[3] The act of 1847 was repealed in 1848 and the rates lowered, but the discrimination continued. The annual rates for a license were to residents $10, to non-residents $20, and a further fee of $20 was exacted if the vendor wished to sell goods which were the property of non-residents.[4] In 1853 a further restriction on eligibility to the business of peddling was introduced by the provision that all licenses must be recorded, for which a fee of 25 cents was imposed, and that the licenses could be granted only to citizens of the United States and residents of New Hampshire for three years. These licenses became void when residence in the state was lost.[5]

[1] Laws, 1846, p. 322. In 1842 the power of granting licenses was transferred to the court of common pleas. Revised statutes, 1842, p. 238.

[2] Laws, 1847, p. 467.

[3] A fee of $50.00 extra was exactad if the applicant wished to sell goods from other states.

[4] Laws, 1848.

[5] Laws, 1853, p. 1341.

The legislation upon this subject in 1858 and in 1859 is exceedingly interesting, not only from the financial but also from the political point of view. The act of 1858[1] provided that the clerk of the court of common pleas might issue a license for peddling to applicants upon evidence of good moral character, of two years citizenship in the United States and in New Hampshire, of a year's residence in the state previous to making the application, and of the payment to the county treasurer of $50 for the license. The license was good for one year, but did not permit the sale of liquor, playing cards, or other articles whose sale was prohibited by law ; nor was it to " prevent any citizen of this state from selling any fish, provisions, farming utensils or other articles lawfully raised or manufactured in this state." An amendment was offered in the house providing that licenses should be issued to citizens of other states upon the payment of a higher license fee, but was rejected by a vote of 195 to 52 upon a call for the previous question.[2] The act of 1858 registered high water mark in the tide of sectionalism and provincialism in the state.

The act of 1859 is one of the first of the indications of that great returning national spirit which was called out by the impending dangers of the period. In the ordinary course of events a statute relating to hawkers and peddlers would hardly be esteemed of sufficient moment to claim the attention of the governor in his annual message. However, Governor Goodwin in his message of 1859 recommended the repeal of the act of 1858, and warned the legislature that while a substitute act seemed desirable it should be framed with great care

[1] Laws, 1858, p. 1991.
[2] House journal, 1858, p. 275.

and discrimination so that it would not interdict the sale of agricultural products of other states.[1] The act of 1859[2] relating to hawkers and peddlers, while discriminating in fees against residents of other states, was much more liberal. The fee for a resident of the state was fixed at $10, and for a non-resident at $10 for each county in which he sold goods; if the goods sold were the property of non-residents, the fee was fixed at $15 for each county where the licensee entered into business. The licenses were granted in all cases by the clerk of the supreme judicial court, and were good for one year. The provisions of the act were not to apply to citizens of the state unable to earn a living by manual labor owing to ill health or decrepitude; nor to those selling fish, fruit, vegetables, provisions, fuel, carriages, farming utensils, live animals, brooms, newspapers, maps, books, pamphlets, and agricultural products of the United States; nor to those selling brittania, brass, and wooden ware, earthen-, tin-, iron-, glass-, or stone-ware, wherever manufactured; nor to any citizen of the state selling any other articles lawfully raised or manufactured in the state, except distilled spirits, playing cards, lottery tickets, and jewelry.

This act was continued in force until the revision of the tax laws in 1878, when the revenue arising from the license fees of hawkers and peddlers was turned into the state treasury. By the act of 1893,[3] in force four years, licenses might be issued by the secretary of state for a town, county, or for the entire state. The fee accrued to the treasury of the district for which the license was issued. The fee for a county

[1] Senate Journal, 1859, p. 32.
[2] Laws, 1859, p. 2092.
[3] Laws, 1893, p. 53.

license payable to the county treasurer was $25., By the act of 1897, now in force, no revenue accrues to the county for the licensing of hawkers and peddlers. The annual revenue from the above source has been small.

3. Fines and forfeitures not specially appropriated to any other body have usually accrued to the county treasury. As early as 1772 it was provided that fines and forfeitures previously accruing to the public treasury should go to the county. An act of February 10, 1791, [1] provided that all fines and forfeitures arising from the escape of prisoners from prisons and goals in the state should go to the county treasury. An act of five years later, June 17, 1796, provided that all fines or forfeitures arising or becoming due upon judgment of any state court should be appropriated for the use of the county. But this was not to affect fines and forfeitures especially appropriated to the town or state. In certain cases where the initiative is taken by private citizens the statutes now provide that one-half of the fine awarded shall go to the county treasury, and one-half to the complainant or the prosecutor.[2] The amount of revenue from this source is sufficient to pay only a part of the expenses caused by its collection, including the cost of suit in the courts necessary to secure judgment. For example, Grafton County in the year 1870–1 [3] received $218.52 in fines out of a total revenue of $42,417.43; in 1896–7,[4] $457.81 out of $59,362.61.

4. The most important of the miscellaneous sources of county revenue are the extensive farms which the several counties in the state acquired about the middle

[1] Revised laws, 1792, p. 137.
[2] Revised statutes, 1842 ; Laws, 1853, p. 98 ; Public statutes, 1891, p. 127.
[3] Report, Grafton County, 1871.
[4] Report, Grafton County, 1897.

of the nineteenth century[1] and have since operated. Upon these farms are supported a part of the county poor, and the revenue from them, when well managed, is considerable.

SEC. 4. *Administration.* The administrative feature of the county taxation is exceedingly simple, owing to the fact that nearly the whole machinery is supplied by either the town or the state. It will be considered under the two following heads: (1) apportionment, and (2) assessment and collection.

1. The apportionment made by the state authorities for the assessment of the state tax is declared by statute to be the basis of the county tax. The work assigned to the county officials is merely advisory. The act of 1878[2] establishing a state board of equalization provided that a representative from each board of county commissioners should meet with the members of the state board of equalization and together form a joint board of equalization for the counties of the state. The act was amended in 1879[3] by striking out the clause providing for a joint board, and by requiring the county commissioners to visit the towns in the county and to equalize the valuation among the towns as far as they were able and to report to the state board. The state board was given absolute authority to modify, as seemed best, the report of the commissioners. As a matter of fact, an able and harmonious board of county commissioners have large influence over the valuations in their own county, and hence in apportioning the state tax among the several counties of the state, and also among the towns within the county.

[1] Under authority of the act of Dec. 16, 1828. Laws, 1828, p. 296.
[2] Laws, 1878, p. 199.
[3] Laws, 1879, chap. 55, sec. 13.

2. By the act of March 19, 1771,[1] the justices of the peace of each county at any court of general sessions of the peace were authorized to make orders for the raising of any sums of money that might be found necessary for the county expenses within each county. This method was continued until 1794, when the present method was introduced. The act of 1794[2] required the county treasurer in September of each year to certify to the judges of the court of common pleas an account of the state of the county treasury, and the said judges were then authorized to determine what taxes were necessary for the ensuing year. The clerk of the court was required to attend the next session of the legislature, where the representatives of the county were authorized to form themselves into a convention for the sole purpose of granting and appropriating taxes for the county. The method prescribed in 1794 has been modified in its administrative details by the acts of 1801 and of 1855. The act of 1801[3] abolished the court of general sessions and divided its powers between the court of common pleas and the county convention, comprised of the representatives in the state legislature from the county. To that convention was given the sole function of granting and appropriating the county taxes. The county revenue was to be paid out by the county treasurer on order from the judges of the court of common pleas. The act of 1855[4] provided for a board of elective county commissioners, which was given general authority over the county government. To this board were granted the powers of the county road commissioners, the powers of the court of common pleas so far as they related

[1] Acts and laws, 1771, p. 207.
[2] Revised laws, 1797, p. 66.
[3] Laws, 1801, p. 581.
[4] Laws, 1855, p. 1539.

to county finances, and the care of county property and of county paupers. The county convention continued all its former powers over the assessment of the county taxes. The taxes thus voted and assessed were required to be collected by the county treasurer as before, *i. e.*, the selectmen of each town assessed the county tax with the town taxes, and the town collector collected the same while collecting the town and state list.[1] All officers assessing or collecting county or town taxes were by an act of 1794[2] placed under requirements and given powers such as the state and town officers possessed in assessing and collecting state and town taxes.

[1] Laws, 1771, p. 207.
[2] Compiled laws, 1815, appendix, p. 545.

BIBLIOGRAPHY.*

*Documents, records, acts, laws, decisions of the courts, etc. essential
in the study of New Hampshire financial history.*

DOCUMENTS AND RECORDS.

Farmer, John, and J. B. Moore, Collections, topographical, historical, and bibliographical, relating principally to New Hampshire.
3 vols. Concord, 1822-24.

Index to the journals of the house of representatives of New Hampshire, 1711-1784. 2 vols. Concord, 1890-1894.

Index to the records of the council of New Hampshire, 1631-1784.
Concord, 1896.

Journals of the senate and house of representatives. Concord, annual
before 1880, biennial since.

Massachusetts Historical Society, Collections.

Massachusetts Bay, Records of. Boston, 1853.

New Hampshire Provincial and state papers. 28 vols. 1867.

New Hampshire Historical Society, Collections. 10 vols. 1824-93.
Proceedings. 3 vols. 1872-1897.

New York, Documents relating to the colonial history of. Albany,
1856.

ACTS, LAWS, AND DECISIONS OF THE COURTS.

Acts and laws passed by the general court or assembly of His Majesty's Province of New Hampshire in New England. Boston, 1699.
Also, Boston, 1726. (With this later edition the session laws for
the years 1718, 1719, 1721, and 1726 were bound, the paging being
continuous, and the whole was reprinted by the state in 1885 as
The acts and laws of 1726.) Also, Portsmouth, 1761. (With this
edition the session acts up to the year 1765 were bound, with
continuous paging, and the whole was reprinted by the state in
1888.) Also, Portsmouth, 1771. Also, Exeter, 1780.

Morrison, C. R., Digest of cases determined in the supreme courts,
1816-1888, reported in the New Hampshire Reports, vols. 1-64,
and including Smith's N. H. Reports. Concord, 1890.

---

*Not including numerous works contained in the author's bibliog-
raphy covering: Reports by state officers, boards, and commissions;
New Hampshire state history; local history; general American history; special works on finance and currency.

New Hampshire laws : Perpetual laws, 1789 ; Revised laws, 1792, 1797, 1805 ; Laws, 1811 ; Compiled laws, vol. I, 1815, vol. II, 1824 ; Revised laws, 1830 ; Revised statutes, 1842, 2d edition, with acts to June, 1850 added, 1851 ; Compiled statutes, 1853, 2d edition, 1854 ; General statutes, 1867 ; General laws, 1878 ; Public statutes, 1891 ; Session laws, annually, 1789–1879 : biennially, 1881 on ; Check list of New Hampshire Laws, 1789–1891, Concord, 1890–91 ; Index to the manuscript laws of New Hampshire, recorded in the office of the Secretary of State, 1679–1883. Concord, 1886.

New Hampshire reports : cases determined in the supreme court. 66 vols. Concord, 1819–1896.

Reports of commissioners to revise statutes, 1842, 1867, 1878, 1890.

LOCAL, GENERAL, AND FINANCIAL HISTORIES CITED IN THE TEXT.

Adams, Nathaniel, Annals of Portsmouth. Portsmouth, 1825.

Belknap, Jeremy, The history of New Hampshire. 3d ed. Dover, 1831.

Bell, Charles H., History of the town of Exeter. Exeter, 1888.

Bouton, Nathaniel, The history of Concord. Concord, 1856.

Chase, Benjamin, History of Old Chester. Auburn, N. H., 1869.

Chase, Frederick, A history of Dartmouth College and the town of Hanover. Vol. I. (J. K. Lord ed.) Cambridge, 1891.

Douglas, C. H. J., Financial history of Massachusetts. New York, 1892.

Dow, Joseph, A history of the town of Hampton. 2 vols.

Felt, J. B., Historical account of Massachusetts currency. Boston, 1839.

Hildreth, R., History of the United States. New York, 1856.

Plummer, William, Jr., Life of William Plummer. Boston, 1857.

Runnels, Rev. M. T., History of Sanbornton. 2 vols. Boston, 1882.

Secomb, Daniel F., History of the town of Amherst. Concord, 1883.

Shirley, John M., The Dartmouth College causes and the Supreme Court of the United States. St. Louis, 1879.

Wood, Frederick, A history of taxation in Vermont. New York, 1894.

Worcester, Samuel T., History of the town of Hollis. Nashua, 1879.

PUBLICATIONS

OF THE

AMERICAN ECONOMIC ASSOCIATION

THIRD SERIES.   ISSUED QUARTERLY.
VOL. III, No. 4.   PRICE, $4.00 PER YEAR.

RENT

IN

MODERN ECONOMIC THEORY:

AN ESSAY IN DISTRIBUTION.

BY

ALVIN SAUNDERS JOHNSON, A.M.

NOVEMBER, 1902.

PUBLISHED FOR THE
AMERICAN ECONOMIC ASSOCIATION
BY THE MACMILLAN COMPANY,
NEW YORK.
LONDON: SWAN SONNENSCHEIN & CO

PRESS OF
ANDRUS & CHURCH,
ITHACA, N. Y.

PREFACE.

It is the belief of the author of the following study that the essential elements of the theory of rent are familiar to all serious students of economics. Present differences in point of view are due, not to ignorance of these elements, but to the fact that authorities disagree as to the proper emphasis which should be laid upon the various aspects of the problem. It is believed that by placing the points at issue in juxtaposition, and by paying due regard both to self-consistency and to relevancy to theoretical needs, it will be possible to approximate a satisfactory view of the problem. No attempt has been made to trace to their original sources the ideas discussed in the following pages. Usually they are the common property of whole schools; and if one author has been cited rather than another, it is because that author seemed to be the best available representative of the idea in question.

That the positive views here advanced are largely based upon the theories of Professor J. B. Clark will, of course, be obvious to every reader. Acknowledgement of indebtedness is further due to Professors E. R. A. Seligman and F. A. Fetter, who have read this study in manuscript and have offered many valuable suggestions both as to form and matter.

ALVIN S. JOHNSON.

Columbia University.

CONTENTS.

CHAPTER V.

CHAPTER VI.

CHAPTER VII.

CHAPTER I.

SEC. 1. Economic science, it has been well said, is not studied because of any inherent interest of its own. Natural curiosity may serve as a sufficient reason for the investigation of physical and vital laws ; interest in the duties and destinies of man may give to ethical and metaphysical studies an intrinsic value ; but divest economics of its bearing upon practical action or ulterior thought, and few would find it worthy of attention. Historically, it was the need for principles of political action that was chiefly responsible for the creation of political economy as a special science ; and in the present day the student usually devotes his attention to economics because he wishes to understand the effects, proximate and remote, of taxation and of governmental control of industry, of trade unions and monopolies ; or, if his interests are those of the scholar rather than those of the practical man, because he wishes to understand the sociological and political effects of economic laws, or because he desires to throw light upon the historical development of society. In any case economic science cannot be considered a sufficient end in itself.

It follows, accordingly, that the results of economic study must not merely be true, but must have a bearing upon practical or intellectual problems that are recognized to be of importance *per se*. The distinctions and classifications of the economist must submit to the two-fold test of truth and relevancy. And as the progress of events and of science brings new problems into the foreground, the old analyses may lose their significance, although they may remain quite true. The work of economic theory, therefore, is never done. Each economic period will demand new analyses, based upon a point of view which is selected by the needs of the time.

It is the purpose of this essay to review the position of the rent of land in modern theory, to consider its nature viewed from the standpoint of economic science of to-day, and to discuss its relations with other economic incomes. It has long been customary with economists to treat rent not as an income *sui generis*, but as one species under a wide genus. Rent has been classed now with one kind of incomes, now with another, as one characteristic or another has seemed to be of vital importance. Economists have not, however, always recognized that it is with reference to qualities which they have themselves selected as relevant that they classify rent with profits or interest or monopoly return. Most frequently they imagine that their classifications are based upon the essential nature of the phenomena under investigation. Reflection will, however, show that if such a classification is possible it is of no importance in economics, since phenomena which are similar in most of their relations may be widely dissimilar in the relations which may properly be called economic. But while economic phenomena are naturally grouped according to characteristics which the economist selects, it is not true that economic analyses may be arbitrary. There are certain problems at the present time which will be recognized to be fundamental in economics. It is with reference to these problems, as the writer conceives them, that the point of view of this essay has been chosen. Criticism of other classifications will accordingly be based not only upon their inherent logic, but also upon their relevancy to the problems of to-day. In adopting such a basis for criticism, injustice is necessarily done to the systems of earlier periods, but not to their survivals in modern economics.

SEC. 2. The rent of land is usually treated as a species of the genus "surplus income." To show that any form of income is a surplus has been regarded as equivalent to demonstrating its kinship with rent. But rent is a category of economic theory, while surplus income may be a category of ethics, politics or sociology, as well as of economics. What is surplus income from the point of view of ethics or sociology may not be a surplus from the point of view of modern economic theory. It is, therefore, not legitimate for the purposes of economic classification to group together all incomes that from one point of view or another may be regarded as surplus. The economic surplus must consist in a part of the social income which exerts upon the central phenomena of economic science an influence differing from that of the incomes classed as non-surplus. It must possess economic potency if it is not to fall outside of the domain of economics ; it must affect phenomena that are recognized as secondary, from the economic point of view, else the term "surplus" is a misnomer.

The classification of the social income into surplus and non-surplus is as old as economic theory, although early writers did not usually treat it as one of fundamental importance, as do many modern writers. But there has been little uniformity in the determination of the concrete forms of income that constitute the surplus. The history of economic science presents a series of surplus funds no two of which cover identically the same elements. This is what one would expect, since those "funds" have been constructed with reference to widely different central problems.

SEC. 3. The first demand upon the resources of a community is the covering of the barest needs of those who procure from nature wealth in its raw form. If nothing is left after this primary need has been met, it is evident that highly elaborative industry, organized government, art, science, and other forms of cultural activity are practically impossible. If, however, an excess of wealth above such primary costs remains, one of the most essential conditions of higher social activities is present.

A surplus of this order was the *produit net* of the Physiocrats. The needs of the agricultural laborer could be met by a portion of the produce of the soil, while such wealth as exceeded the demands of agricultural labor could be employed for the support of trades and arts and government. The extent of the surplus measured a community's potentialities for cultural development.

It is these primary riches, continually renewed, which support all the other states of the realm, which give activity to all the other professions, which cause commerce to flourish, which favor population, which animate industry, which create the prosperity of a nation.[1]

What the Physiocrats were seeking to establish was a material basis for the complex of phenomena that distinguish a civilized and refined community from a barbarous one. The *produit net* had no importance apart from its political and social effects. Again and again we are reminded that it is not really wealth until a population has arisen to demand it.[2] It is of no significance until it has transmuted itself, so to speak, into the activities of the artisan and trading and professional classes. The transformation of surplus revenue into

[1] Quesnay, Grains, printed in Physiocrates, ed. E. Daire, vol. 1, p. 272.
[2] Quesnay, Grains, p. 299.

higher social forms is explained according to the somewhat naïve common sense of the time.

> The assemblage of a number of rich proprietors who reside in a
> single place is sufficient to form what is called a city, where mer-
> chants, manufacturers, artisans, workingmen and domestics come to-
> gether in proportion to the revenues which the proprietors spend
> there. In each case, the magnitude of a city is naturally proportioned
> to the number of proprietors of lands, or rather, the produce of the
> lands which belong to them. The capital city is formed in the same
> way as a city of the provinces, with this difference, that the great pro-
> prietors of the whole state reside in the capital.[1]

Two assumptions are manifestly necessary in order to
give definiteness and meaning to the surplus thus conceived. It is necessary to assume first, that the wages of
labor are fixed at the minimum of subsistence; and
secondly, that population will automatically increase until
the whole product of the soil is consumed by laborers
engaged either in extractive or elaborative industry.
Under these assumptions the *produit net* would be a fair
measure of the labor force at the command of society,
and this, in a society only slightly capitalistic, would be
an approximate measure of its productive powers.

In the later writings of the Économistes we find both
assumptions developing : Turgot states explicitly that
the laborer normally receives his bare living ; and
Malthus, who in his doctrine of rent may be classed with
the Physiocrats, expresses with clearness the assumption
that the surplus tends to create its own consumers, an
artisan class that has to purchase it with their toil.

> Thus the ferti ity of the land gives the power of yielding a surplus,
> a rent, by yielding a surplus quantity of necessaries beyond the wants
> of the cultivators ; and the peculiar quality belonging to the neces- ∨
> saries of life, when properly distributed, tends to strongly and con-
> stantly give a value to this surplus by raising up a population to
> demand it.[2]

[1] Cantillon, Essai sur la nature du commerce, p. 5, 6.
[2] Malthus, Principles of political economy, Boston, 1821, p. 113.

We are not here concerned with the imperfect theory of distribution which assigned to the landlord the entire *produit net*, nor with the fantastic theory of production which imputed it wholly to the soil, or, sometimes, to agricultural labor. What is of interest is the extent of the surplus fund and the significance ascribed to it. The assumptions upon which its definitions are based are sufficiently unreal as applied to modern economic life; but before the development of capitalistic society they were, perhaps, approximately correct. When habits of consumption were fixed and methods of production unchanging, the social development of each community was indeed closely connected with a distinguishable surplus.

SEC. 4. The Physiocrats, then, attempted to establish a physical basis for the growth of that part of society which distinguishes civilization from barbarism. They sought an explanation for the greatness of states con-ceived as units. Assuming at the outset, as they did, that the surplus flowed into the hands of the landowner, they did not enter into a discussion of its distribution among smaller units within the state. Yet they recognized the existence of a capitalist class, and admitted that the laborer could save " by parsimony." Thus a part of the surplus above the bare subsistence of labor remained in the possession of other classes besides the landlords. Unconsciously they had introduced a new class of problems, the further development of which was left to the so-called historical materialists.

An increase in social income, distributed to the different classes of a society in proportion to their original incomes, would increase the happiness of the society as a whole and advance it in civilization and culture. It would also increase its power to cope with other societies

in peace and in war. A surplus thus distributed is
therefore a factor of great importance in international
politics. Increase in social wealth, however, is not likely
to result in a universal augmentation of the original incomes of the members of society. Certain individuals and
classes will almost inevitably receive more than the
average proportion of it. The appearance of a surplus,
therefore, will usually create new class distinctions, or
emphasize those that already exist. The flow of new
income causes one class to gain in power and another to
decline. It is a potent factor in state politics, just as
the surplus which is conceived of as an acquisition of an
entire community is a potent factor in the politics of
the world.

It is, however, only upon the assumption of static
methods of utilization that a surplus of this nature can
at all adequately explain the relative rise and decline of
societies or of social classes. A change in the habits of
consumption, taking place simultaneously with an increase in wealth, may wholly neutralize its social and
political influence. A wealthy state with luxurious
habits is not necessarily more fitted to survive than a
poorer state whose citizens have simpler tastes. If the
development of the personal wants of a class keeps pace
with the increase in its resources, it will not necessarily
gain either in numbers or strength. Now in the ages
preceding the distinctly modern epoch, standards of
consumption were for the most part definite. The surplus of food produced was a rough indication of the
probable magnitude of the non-agricultural population,
and the wealth at the command of a social class was a
not inaccurate index of its probable growth in power.
In modern society, on the other hand, wants are so complex and subject to such great variations that it would

be hazardous to predict the result of any but the most striking changes in income. While, then, a surplus consisting in mere increase in wealth may, even in modern times, occasion changes in the relative political and social position of states and of classes, so many other factors enter into the problem that it is hardly safe to attempt to explain concrete phenomena by the emergence of surplus. The distinction between such surplus and non-surplus parts of income is of great im_ .portance in the discussion of certain historical problems, but it is questionable whether it throws any light upon problems of the present day.

SEC. 5. As a rule the production of goods entails the loss of a certain amount of vital energy, and the consumption of the goods produced restores energy to the human organism. Man has frequently existed in environments which afforded him subsistence only in return for the expenditure of all the energy which he possessed. In such circumstances a change in activities which would require greater exertion would be injurious, and any change in the direction of energy, even though it did not mean an increase in its absolute amount, would be attended with serious risks, and would natually be avoided. Where, on the other hand, the environment has been so favorable that the consumption of the goods created by a day's labor has yielded a quantity of energy more than sufficient to produce an equal amount of goods, variations in the forms of activity have been possible. Where under such circumstances a competition for existence took place among individuals or groups of individuals, a law of survival may have forced the surplus of energy to find a vent in new forms of activity. The presence of surplus energy thus appears as a possible basis for variation in activity, and under the pressure of competition for life may become a real cause of economic and social progress. Such is the part that is assigned to surplus energy in Professor Patten's theory of progress,[1] in which each adaptation to the environment sets free new surplus energy which automatically transmutes itself into progress.

Whether or not one accepts Professor Patten's theory as a satisfactory account of progress, one can hardly deny that it points out a factor which deserves consideration from all who seek for an explanation of the development of a dynamic society out of apparently changeless barbarism. There is accordingly a set of problems which justifies the distinction between the energy which is necessary to conserve human life in its existing conditions and the energy which is free and available for new uses, and which justifies the parallel distinction between the parts of income which may be regarded as the objective forms of such classes of energy.

The three forms of surplus that have been described may indeed be properly denominated surpluses. Those parts of income—or income transmuted into energy—which account for continued, though unchanging, conditions of life represent the non-surplus. Those parts of income that explain change or progress form the surplus fund. If it is indeed the essential function of economics to explain progress or change, political and social, some one of these is rightly termed the economic surplus.

SEC. 6.   Much of the pleasure and pain of life results

---

[1] Theory of prosperity, pp. 186, 187, *et passim*. It is to be observed that in Professor Patten's exposition the first step in progress, from which surplus energy originally results, is mere chance adjustment to the environment. This requires the unnecessary assumption that primitive man actually lived in an environment that barely afforded him subsistence.

from the consumption and production of economic goods. A popular measure of welfare is the net amount of pleasure that results from the entire economic process. It has often been said that the true criterion of economic amelioration is the growth of the surplus of happiness afforded by economic activities. Not increase in power or in wealth or in energy, but increase in the sum of producers' and consumers' rents is the index of progress.[1] One need not accept the growth of surplus satisfaction as an adequate explanation of the meaning of progress, yet it may serve as a working principle in default of a better. The distinction between those satisfactions which are merely sufficient to cover economic discomforts and those which are a net gain to man thus serves to satisfy an intellectual need, and hence requires no further justification.

Psychological science has for a long time protested vehemently against the view which makes economic life a mere balancing of pleasures against pains. The protest has received little attention from economists—probably less than it deserves. Economic conduct consists in a series of options determined by a complex of final causes, of which pleasure and pain may be selected as typical, although they are perhaps not even the most important ones. It would be erroneous, however, to suppose that the adoption of the psychologist's point of view would revolutionize economic theory. Economists are not particularly interested in the analysis of motives. They seek to explain activities, and assume motives merely as a convenient starting point. In every economic act there is a balancing of motives, and what the particular motives may be is to the economist a matter

[1] For a detailed discussion of progress regarded from this point of view see Nicholson, Principles of political economy, iii, book iv.

of small moment. It is convenient to class all motives which make for the performance of an act under a single head, utilities, and all those which dissuade from action under the head of disutilities. Nothing more detailed is needed for the purposes of economic theory.

Whether one chooses to regard economic conduct as the result of a balancing of pleasures and pains, or of utilities and disutilities, defined as above, it is evident that the economic process will usually yield a surplus of pleasure or utility above pain or disutility. Utilities will fall into two classes, those which merely over-balance disutilities, and those which are without any offset. Now it is clear that the former class will account for the totality of economic phenomena. The surplus has no economic potency whatsoever. Whether the motives that lead to an act just outweigh the motives that tend to prevent it, or enormously overbalance them, the act is performed.[1] Whether the pay for the

---

[1] The objection will be raised that the surplus determines the order of economic choices, and therefore possesses economic potency. If the commodity A yields a surplus of ten and B of five, will not A be chosen first? Certainly. But what is the net economic effect of this order of selection if both are chosen anyway? If it is necessary to choose between the two, A yields a surplus of only five, since the choice involves the surrender of B. The question that then arises has to do with the economic potency of the pure surplus of A, represented here by five. Say that the surplus were reduced to one, would not A still be chosen? So long as A affords the least surplus it will be selected in preference to B. It is the part of surplus above the minimum which determines choice that is here affirmed to be of no importance in the explanation of economic conduct.

A kind critic has suggested that if ten units of labor in producing A yield a surplus, while the eleventh just pays, and one unit of labor in producing B just pays, the surplus really determines the apportion-ment of labor. We may say that the first unit in the production of A yields a surplus of 10, the second 9, and so on, down to almost noth-ing. If, however, the surplus on the earlier units of A were reduced to such a mere +, the apportionment would remain the same. It is the extent to which production may be carried on without descending below the minimum ground of choice, and not the amount of the sur-plus, that determines the apportionment.

first hour of a day's labor merely suffices to insure its performance, or is far more than sufficient to do so, the work is accomplished. Whether the former relation of motives holds through the day, or whether each hour up to the last affords an appreciable surplus, the quantity of economic activity remains the same. It cannot be objected that the laborer would refuse to work under the former conditions, or would work less diligently, for in that case the alleged surplus would not be surplus at all, but would form a part of the sum of utilities necessary to determine the choice to work. The same analysis may be applied to the so-called consumers' surplus. If it is indeed a surplus, it is an economic epiphenomenon. Economic theory has no occasion to take cognizance of its existence.

It may be said that if the first hour of labor yields no surplus, the second hour will probably yield a negative surplus, and will therefore be left undone. That is quite true, but it merely signifies that the presence of a surplus serves as a basis for predicting the continuance of labor. It is not therefore a cause of continued labor. The shape of the utility curve gives us important information as to the value of a commodity under varying conditions of supply and demand, but the surplus included by the utility curve plays no part in economics until it ceases to be a surplus.[1]

[1] The price curve of any commodity is theoretically ascertained by establishing the importance of any unit under all possible relations of supply and want. Say that but one unit is in existence, and the importance of it is one hundred. With the same volume of wants, a hundred-fold increase in the number of units of supply may reduce the importance of any unit to ten. It is usually assumed that the theoretically first unit will then yield a surplus of ninety. If we analyze the nature of this alleged surplus, we find that in the first place it contains an element of actual satisfaction, or rather utility. A hungry man does unquestionably receive more pleasure from the

SEC. 7. At any particular time there is a rate of wages that a workman will consider natural and therefore just. A skilled laborer may believe that three dollars a day is a fair wage. Offer him two and a half and he will probably refuse it with indignation. This does not mean that the reduced wage might not cover all the sacrifice that the performance of labor involves, nor does it mean that the money earned in the last hour does not cover the actual disutilities, consisting in weariness and deprivation of liberty, entailed by that hour of labor. When unemployed he may crave the exercise of his accustomed activity, yet he would feel that to work for the low wages would mean the incurring of a net loss. If, on the other hand, he is offered three dollars and a half for a day's labor, he feels that he is receiving a net gain. Manifestly there is no *a priori* reason why three dollars should be the income selected as the preëminently just one. It is a matter of common experi-

first slice of bread which he consumes than from the last. This surplus, however, is insignificant when compared with the total surplus which figures in the diagrams so popular in economic discussions. The second part of the surplus consists in the " pain obviated " by the presence of food. The first part of the surplus is a fact of consciousness, the second part is something which exists neither in consciousness nor outside of it. It is an idea with no foundation in reality.

Hobson, Economics of distribution, p. 41 *et seq.*, has pointed out the true nature of this curious "surplus." Deprivation of food is the destruction of human life ; therefore when the supply of food is threatened the whole worth of life objectifies itself momentarily in the possession of food. The control of the bare means of existence represents the utility of all that one has or ever hopes to have. To assign the utility of all of the goods of life to each one of the necessaries of life is so obviously fallacious that it is astonishing that it has ever been done outside of the popular rhyme that ascribes the loss of horse and rider and battle "all to the want of a horse shoe nail." The subjective surplus, described in the only legitimate way as an actual surplus of satisfaction, does not even give us information with regard to the price curve. That it exists is a ground for optimistic reflections as to human destiny, but it seems to have no further significance in economics.

ence that the standard of just payments varies from age to age and from place to place. The coolie no doubt has his ideas of what is fair in wages, just as the skilled mechanic of America has his. The standards, we can readily see, are based upon experience. What a man has been accustomed to have, and what he sees those whom he regards as of his kind receiving, determines what he will feel should be his in the present.

There are likewise rates of interest that are conceived to be just, and rates that the natural man, at any rate, would pronounce unjust. The same thing is true of prices. These standards, like the standards of just wages, are indisputably the result of experience of what has been or of what is elsewhere the case.

It is possible to divide actual incomes into two parts, one of which corresponds with such standards, while the other measures the variation, positive or negative, from them. The same classification will hold for prices, since prices are merely undistributed incomes. Now it is clear that the first part of income, if isolated, would tend to perpetuate the kinds and volume of the activities which produced it. The second part, whether positive or negative, would lead to a change in such activities. The laborer who feels that he is not treated fairly as compared with others of his kind, who believes that his income is diminished by the existence of negative surplus, will seek to put himself in a position where he may secure greater advantages. He may be personally unable to do so, but his active discontent will serve to urge others who are in a like unfavorable situation, but who are not so specialized that they are unable to change their place in the economic organism, to seek the opportunities that more favored workers possess. If the entire class is degraded, and movement is impossible, there are still likely to be influences at work lessening the efficiency of laborers, and cutting down their numbers. A positive surplus has a similar set of effects, but in the opposite direction.

A surplus of this kind is an evidence of a dynamic change that has taken place. The existence of standards points to the fact that within a certain limited field incomes have been static. A perpetually changing rate could afford no expectation as to the future. Violation of standards shows that a change in the economic situation of the classes who hold standards of income has taken place. But the existence of the surplus has a more important significance for economics than this. It indicates that further dynamic movements must take place. Industry must be rearranged until the surplus annihilates itself in the creation of new standards.[1]

SEC. 8. It is à well recognized fact that the productivity of any economic agent is conditioned both by its own inherent qualities and by its quantitative relations with complementary agents. The productivity of a

[1] The writer is aware of the fact that the term "standard" as employed in this section violates, to a certain extent, established usage. By "standard" incomes we usually mean those which would exist if industry were suddenly to obey the laws of free competition   The term is here used to designate an income which has been established long enough to have become a fixed datum in the social consciousness. If the incomes of all laborers were suddenly to conform to productivity, large numbers of laborers would at first be influenced exactly as though they found themselves in a specially favored environment. Instead of rendering society static, the change would render it intensely dynamic. When, however, the laborers have become accustomed to their new incomes, and look upon them as a matter of course, the dynamic influence of the new order becomes unimportant. Income which is socially regarded as a surplus, even though from the point of view of pure theory it is not a surplus, exerts the dynamic influence of a surplus income. In seeking for a distinction between incomes which account for change and incomes which account for persistence, it appears to be best to define the latter as incomes which are socially regarded as normal.

given agent will increase or decline with the increase or diminution in the quantity of complementary agency combined with it in production. If we assume the worst possible economic position for labor, its economic product will be zero. It will be a "free good," and the entire return which it coöperates in producing will be imputable to the other factors in production. If the quantitative relations are varied, the share of labor emerges and increases, while that of the other factors diminishes. When such changes in the relations of the factors of production actually take place, the resulting increase in income for the favored factor, and decline for the factors which are prejudiced, are at first felt to be surpluses, positive and negative, similar to the surpluses discussed in the last section. They set in motion secondary dynamic forces opposite in direction to the forces which created them. If the secondary force is less powerful than the primary one, it spends itself before it can restore the former quantitative relations, and new standards for the incomes affected are established. When, for example, capital increases relatively to labor, the immediate effect is to create higher wages and lower interest. A positive surplus appears in wages, a negative surplus in interest ; and the effect of the existence of such surpluses is a further dynamic change. Labor will probably increase in volume, while the rate of saving will be somewhat diminished. These effects need not, however, be sufficient to neutralize the effects of the original increase of capital. After the second set of dynamic forces have exhausted their influence, there may be a net gain to labor and a net loss to capital.[1]

[1] As will readily be seen, this is essentially the surplus which appears in Professor Clark's discussion of static incomes. For the sake of simplicity Professor Clark has abstracted from the effects of

If we wish to explain consistently the existence in the present of the standards that are so important in economic life, we can but begin by assuming a time when each concrete income was felt to be a surplus. That surplus, unneutralized by dynamic results, was first crystalized into a standard ; and that standard has received a succession of accretions, as the dynamic forces which create surplus income have exceeded in power the dynamic forces which surplus income itself creates. Standard or static incomes thus resolve themselves into series of surpluses which we may term static, not from their causes but from their freedom from dynamic results.

Sec. 9. It is not claimed that the foregoing classification of surplus funds exhausts the list that economic writings offer. In current theory, however, when an income is classed as surplus, it is usually from one of the points of view which have been enumerated. It is here maintained that for the purposes of economic classification all are not equally significant. Economic science exceeds its domain when it creates classifications that have no immediate bearing upon its own central problems. What those problems will be in the future we have no means of knowing, but in the present economic interest unquestionably centers in the problems of value and distribution in a state of society in which competition rules. Current theory seeks to explain the activities which result in the establishment of standards, and those which cause the standards to change. A present income reacts upon future economic activity. Some in-

the secondary dynamic influences—not overlooked them, as some of the critics of "The distribution of wealth" have supposed. In order to escape a similar misunderstanding, it is here assumed that the standards which may historically be analyzed into surpluses result from the *net* force which remains active after opposing forces have been neutralized.

comes tend to maintain themselves unchanged; others possess a power to induce change, a power which by its own nature must disappear, leaving behind it a permanent income which assimilates itself to the class of standard incomes, tending in like manner to perpetuate itself. The phenomena of standards, of economic persistence, are manifestly primary in a theoretical sense; the phenomena of change, though accounting genetically for the existence of standards, are at any given point of time secondary. Accordingly, to classify as surplus the incomes which at a given time promote change meets the claims of economic logic. The dynamic surplus is the economic surplus *par excellence.*

Normal wages may be taken as a type of standard incomes, and pure profit, or at least certain elements in pure profit, as typical of economic surplus. Where are we to place the rent of land? Does it develop standards which tend to perpetuate themselves, or does it tend to disappear? A satisfactory answer to this question, it is here maintained, would sufficiently determine the position of rent in economic theory. It would decide whether rent is to be classed with wages and interest, or with profits and monopoly return. The conception of rent is, however, far from clear, and its economic relations are the subject of vigorous controversy. It will, therefore, be necessary to define what is here meant by the term rent, and to examine the theoretical validity of the long series of distinctions that have been drawn between rent on the one hand and wages and interest on the other, as well as the significance of the analogies that have led economists to regard rent as a species of profit or of monopoly gain.

CHAPTER II.

SEC. 10. Of the concrete forms of income that have usually been classed as surplus, the rent of land was the earliest to be defined; and so prominent a position has been given to it that the terms " rent" and "surplus" have come to be used interchangeably. If a form of income appears to be a surplus, it is at once treated as a kind of rent; if it presents some of the peculiarities of rent, it is forthwith christened surplus. If rent is regarded as characteristically differential, all incomes that from one point of view or another are differential are called surpluses. If surplus income is defined as residual, all residual incomes are termed rents. It is no wonder, then, that practically every part of the income of society has been classified as rent by one economist or another, and that two of the foremost thinkers of modern economics, Professor Clark and Professor Patten, have—though for widely different reasons—concluded that rent is merely one aspect of an income which from other points of view bears another name.

It is a commonplace of historical economics that land was first given the rank of a factor in production coördinate with labor and capital for the simple reason that in England, the home of classical political economy, the landlords formed a social class distinct from the capitalists and laborers.[1] Land, it is said, is therefore merely an historical category, significant only in a society such as that of England in the early nineteenth century. We may admit that in a country in which all

[1] Held, Zwei Bücher zur socialen Geschichte Englands, 161.

classes share in greater or less degree the benefits of landownership, theorists would not have been so likely to perceive, or at any rate to emphasize, the differences between land and other property which like it produces a permanent income. This does not mean, however, that land, by whatever characteristics it is defined, is to be regarded as a distinct source of income only where landlords are a sharply defined social class. The history of science furnishes numerous examples of truths which remained unknown until the examination of phenomena of a transitory nature drew attention to them. They do not necessarily become untrue or unimportant when the particular need to which they owe their introduction to thought has passed away. When the recipients of the income from land constitute a special class in society, the laws which govern the progress or decline of rent have an additional political and social significance, since such progress or decline must necessarily affect the social constitution.[1] But class problems are beyond the bounds of economics proper, which is at present primarily concerned with the laws governing the production and distribution of wealth, rather than with the more remote sociological effects of such production and distribution.

It will be readily admitted that if land can be distinguished from artificial productive goods by characteristics that are of true economic significance, the rent of land should be treated as a distinct form of income. Any category consists of a group of phenomena which are due to the same general causes, or are affected, in

---

[1] Professor Patten regards the category of ground rent as irrelevant to a study of the economic laws which prevail in a society like that of modern America (Theory of prosperity, p. 5). But the problems which Professor Patten endeavors to solve would at present be called sociological rather than economic.

the main, by the same forces, or which, if they possess causal efficiency, are similar in those effects which are selected as of primary importance.   No one questions the validity of a distinction between labor and capital, and the reason is simply that the two factors naturally con. trast themselves.   Only extremely metaphysical econom. ists are compelled to rely upon class distinctions to mark off the one from the other.   Some writers have indeed classified as interest certain parts of the income of laborers ; as, for example, the reward for acquired skill. Origin in abstinence they assume to be the distinguish. ing characteristic of capital, and acquired skill the result of a sacrifice of present enjoyment for the sake of future gain.   There are, however, other facts besides origin that must be taken into account in the establish- ing of economic categories.   Does an increase in capital diminish the return to acquired skill, or is it rather an increase in population that cuts down the income of skilled laborers ?   Does an increase in skilled labor lower or raise the rate of interest ?   It appears to be reasonable to hold that skilled labor is subject to the same dynamic influences as unskilled labor, not to the influences which affect capital.   It is best, therefore, for the pur- poses of economic theory to restrict rather than to ex- tend the conception "personal capital," and to regard all labor as contrasted with capital.   The characteristics which were at first chosen to distinguish land from capital were unquestionably inadequate for the purpose. There may, however, remain good reason why it is theoretically justifiable to treat land as an independent factor in production.

SEC. 11.   Early political economy found no difficulty in distinguishing between the several factors in produc- tion.   Adam Smith and his immediate followers usually dealt with types that were so chosen as to contrast strongly, not with classifications which were designed to include all phenomena that should logically be included. Labor was represented by the manual worker who gave shape to commodities at the expense of fatigue and pain. Capital was a stock of producers' goods which had been endowed with their usefulness by human agency. "Land" meant a field or meadow which had suffered little transformation beyond the slight changes incident to the growing and gathering of its produce. Toil, goods created by toil, and goods freely given by nature, —these were three perfectly definite categories. Adam Smith, indeed, marred the clearness of this classification by including under land all agricultural improvements. But even where much labor had been spent on improvement, land appeared to be quite distinct from instruments created by labor.

As soon as the work of establishing thoroughgoing classifications was undertaken, it became evident that many other kinds of producers' goods were as truly the free gifts of nature as was land. Hence it came to be the fashion to substitute the term "natural agents" for land. We may take Say and Senior as representatives of this tendency :

Under the term "the Agents offered to us by nature," or, to use a shorter expression, "Natural Agents", we include every productive agent so far as it does not derive its powers from the act of man.[1]

At the same time that the term "land" or "natural agents" was applied to a constantly increasing group of objects, a tendency manifested itself to withdraw from the category of land elements in its productivity which are due to human agency.

[1] Senior, Political economy, p. 58.

A hot house for the raising of exotic plants, a meadow fertilized by
judicious irrigation, owe the greater part of their productive powers to
works and erections, the effect of antecedent production, which form
a part of the capital devoted to the furtherance of actual and present
production. The same may be said of land newly cleared and brought
into cultivation ; of farm-buildings ; of enclosures ; and of all other
permanent ameliorations of a landed estate. These values are items
of capital, though it be no longer possible to sever them from the soil
they are attached to.[1]

A hothouse or an irrigation plant may, in thought at
least, be separated from the land to which it lends
productivity. But when a field is cleared of stones,
there is no material thing, apart from the land itself,
which can be called the product of labor. Such land
is a material object to which utilities have been added
by human exertion. Nothing more, however, can be
said of any of the so-called products of labor. Why
should one say that labor produces a brick, but merely
adds intangible utilities to land? From an economic
point of view as radical a change has taken place in
the land which has been reclaimed from bog or jungle
as in the iron which has been won from the ore. The
terrace gardens of Europe owe their usefulness to
toil; they are the product of labor, if any commodity
can be so designated. But if we admit that land in its
economic aspect may sometimes be the product of labor,
logic demands that we classify as the product of labor all
soil the utility of which has been enhanced by labor.
As applied not to values but to physical objects, " made
by labor " is a quality which does not admit of degrees.
It does not distinguish between an ordinary brick and
the most exquisite products of industry. With such a
quality as the distinguishing characteristic of capital,
coal in the depths of the earth becomes capital the
moment when the first earth is removed from the mouth

---

[1] Say, Treatise on political economy, Biddle, Boston, 1824, p. 16.

of the shaft. The soil of the earth becomes capital when the first furrow is run—indeed much earlier, for as soon as the pioneer sets out for his new home, he has, in effect, expended labor for the reduction to usefulness of virgin soil, and value begins to flow into that soil. In this view the transforming of natural agents into capital is little more than a rite.

SEC. 12. It was inevitable that the more logical economists should discard a distinction which was as colorless as this. Some have decided to designate as capital whatever may be changed at all by human agency, thus leaving to the category of land nothing but the qualities of extension and position. This is practically the view of Professor Commons.

What land furnishes to all industries is simply *room* and *situation*. This is the fundamental idea of land in production and distribution, it is nothing more than the bare surface of the earth. Not land, but capital, embodies the forces, energies and material of nature. . . . . . Soil is capital as soon as labor is employed in clearing the land, draining, fencing, plowing, fitting, fertilizing and planting.[1]

Almost the same position is maintained by Professor Marshall:

When we have inquired what it is that marks off land from those material things which we regard as products of the land, we shall find that the fundamental attribute of land is its extension.[2]

What this is, however, that is bought and sold and "economized" generally under the name of land is not mere "room and situation" or "extension": it is a physical object with numerous qualities of which fertility and capacity for support may be taken as typical. Surface extension is the quality selected for quantitative measurement, just as weight is selected to measure other physical objects of economic importance. Economically,

[1] Commons, The distribution of wealth, p. 29.
[2] Marshall, Principles of economics, p. 192.

extension and weight are not "fundamental," although the objects which possess them could not be conceived without them.   The importance of land varies from zero to a positive quantity of a high degree according to its situation relatively to population.   Situation is not therefore the fundamental quality that endows land with utility.   Beef may be a free good in parts of South America; we should not for that reason say that it is situation alone that gives it value in New York.   Land possesses, indeed, "place utility"; it possesses also elementary and form utilities; and it would be hazardous to declare that for all land one kind of utilities rather than the others is fundamental, and distinguishes land from all other economic goods.

It is not difficult to see what it is that has led to the adoption of such an ethereal conception of land.   It is desired to find a clear distinction between land on the one hand and the products of labor on the other.   Extension and situation are indeed something that labor cannot literally create, while many of the other qualities of land may be artificially produced.   While, however, the value of clear distinctions cannot be denied, this distinction, it is obvious, does not really mark off one class of economic phenomena from another, and is therefore valueless.[1]

SEC. 13. Another view, frequently associated with the foregoing, distinguishes between land and capital on the ground that they do not bear the same relation to cost. The early economists held that capital derived its value from cost, while the value of land was dependent solely upon limitation.   This view appears in Adam Smith,

[1] For a further discussion of the futility of this distinction between capital and land see Fetter, Recent discussion of the capital concept, *Quarterly Journal of Economics*, Vol. XV.

and is still common wherever the cost theory of value survives. But even among those who recognize that the value of capital and land alike is determined by productivity, and that limitation, not cost, is the true determinant of productivity, there are some who are inclined to draw a distinction between the two agents on the ground that the value of capital tends to equal cost, while that of land shows no such tendency. The form of cost that figures here is obviously entrepreneurs' cost— the expenditure in money or its equivalent necessary for the production of a good. It is the contention that the value of a capital good tends exactly to cover this expenditure, while the value of land, in a progressive society, nearly always exceeds the cost of appropriating it and preparing it for use. A conservative expression of this view is that of Sidgwick:

At the same time I think it reasonable to assume that the rent of much agricultural land in England is materially in excess of interest (at the present rate) on the expenditure that would now be required to bring it from its original condition to its present degree of efficiency for supplying its markets with agricultural produce.[1]

The value of land, then, exceeds the cost that was incurred in the appropriation and improvement of the land, while the value of any capital good equals its cost. If we examine the assumptions upon which this view is based, we find that in the case of the capital good the assumption of perfect competition in production and sale is essential to the truth of the proposition. Such competition implies that both buyer and seller possess adequate knowledge of the current production and of probable future changes in its volume, and that there is perfect freedom from all forms of combination and from favoritism on the part of government or quasi-governmental

[1] Sidgwick, Principles of political economy, 3d ed., p. 287.

functionaries. Moreover, it implies that all changes which can not be foreseen will be met by a perfect system of insurance which eliminates risks for the individual producer. Under these conditions all will agree that a capital good as it leaves the producer will have a value exactly equal to its cost. At any later date its value will be less than cost; but we may look upon a worn implement as merely a fragment of a former whole, as a certain number of the utilities that were formerly embodied in the new implement, and may conceive of it as still worth what it specifically cost, the other utilities, destroyed in use, having been replaced out of the sinking fund that a properly calculated capital good would create, or having been paid for in consumers' goods of equal cost and value.

It is obvious that these assumptions are unreal, but they are useful for certain theoretical purposes. If, however, we wish to distinguish between land and capital on the basis of such assumed conditions, we must be careful to apply the same assumptions in discussing the relation of land value to the cost of appropriating and improving it that we apply to capital in the discussion of the relation of capital value to capital cost.

If, in the traditional manner, we postulate a settled community with unoccupied land upon its borders, and trace in imagination the gradual growth of population and the progress of the appropriation of land, assuming force and fraud and favoritism out of existence, as we do in the case of capital, and assuming full knowledge on the part of numerous persons of the current and future demand for the products of the soil, it is obvious that each zone of new land would be appropriated just when the cost of occupation would be covered by the value which the newly occupied land would possess. At that particular time, then, the relation of the value of land to its cost would be identical with the relation of capital value to capital cost. If we use the term "income" in a sufficiently broad sense, this would mean an identical relation of permanent income from property, whether capital or land, to the cost of acquiring that property. If by "income" we mean the goods actually produced, there would, indeed, always be a disparity in the earnings of forms of property of equal value and equal cost. This would result from the fact that each form of property would change in value for reasons partly independent of its current productivity; hence there might be a rise in value which would be estimated as a net addition to the income in goods produced, or a decline which would have to be deducted from such income.

In the circumstances which we have assumed, the value of the land would rise; accordingly a part of the income from the land would take the concrete form of an "unearned increment" in land value. Artificial goods, on the other hand, would deteriorate, but the gross value which they would produce would be so great that the net value which would annually accrue to their owner would be exactly equal to the net annual addition to the wealth of the landowner. Through exchange either property owner could turn his net income into consumers' goods adapted to his use, leaving the sources of his income unimpaired. Social habits, indeed, might discourage a man from alienating that part of his income which consisted in the increased value of land, since such alienation would require either the selling of a part of the land or the creation of a mortgage debt—acts which carry with them the stigma of impoverishment. It is conceivable that a social habit might arise com-

pelling the ordinary capitalist to set aside as permanent
capital a fraction of his annual interest, just as it is
coming to be the approved custom for a corporation to
accumulate a surplus fund. But such a habit would
not alter the economic nature of the increase in wealth.
It would still remain a portion of the net income.

Any one who purchased the land from its original
occupant would, as Sidgwick asserts, pay more for it
than the cost in labor and capital that would then be
required to bring it from its original condition to its
state of productiveness at the time of purchase. But the
cost in labor and capital that the first occupant incurred
in improving the land was only a part of its total cost
to him. Another part consisted in the consumers' goods
which he had to forego in order to hold the land and
secure the increase in value. If to-day I purchase a
piece of land which yields no income, but which I expect to rise in value, it would be obviously absurd to say
that when I sell it ten years from now the total cost to
me will be the price I paid for it. The interest on that
outlay for ten years which I shall forego will be just
as much a part of the cost as the principal. From the
point of view of the individual landowner, the increase
in value of land is the reward for a form of abstinence
which is as true a cost as any which the capitalist undergoes. Assuming perfect competition,—competition enlightened by foreknowledge of future conditions,—the
relation of land value to cost does not differ from the
relation of capital value to cost so far as the individual
buyer or seller is concerned.

Land has not, however, been appropriated under conditions of perfect competition. Favoritism and fraud
have tainted much of the original occupation of land
even in our own relatively just age. Mere chance has

played an enormous part in the distribution to individuals of the value of land, enriching some and des-
poiling others. It is impossible to say whether or not
the total value of the land in this country exceeds its
cost to individuals, including in cost both of the elements discussed above. Moreover, any investor in land
is uncertain whether he will gain through abnormal increase in value, or lose through less than normal increase or positive decline; and uncertainty, it must be
remembered, is itself a form of cost, and must be taken
into account when we estimate total cost.

Yet, when all is said, the great mass of the land value
of to-day is the result of a reasonably calculable rise
which has taken place since the era of wild speculation
and land robbery. That rise is capitalized in the purchase price long before the circumstances of current
production warrant a change in the value of the land, and
to the present landholders it represents the reward for saving. There are still, and probably always will be, spasmodic movements of population which transfer values in
an unforeseen manner from one to another. Chance incomes will always attach themselves to landownership.
But in this respect land can not be placed in a class by
itself. All of the elements that vitiate a competitive
valuation of land influence the market value of capital
goods. No one is unfamiliar with the enormous speculative gains that result from dealing in stocks that represent
nothing but aggregates of capital goods of reproducible
kinds. The increase in the value of wheat which takes
place between October and May is the result of a normal,
inevitable, calculable change in the relation of supply to
demand. The normal increase in land value is the
same, in essence, differing only in the fact that it extends through a period which, measured by the length

of human life, is indefinite. Along with the regular and normal increase in value there are always spasmodic variations which result in great speculative gains and losses. And what is true of land and wheat is true of practically every commodity on the market. Absence of chance income is the exception, not the rule.

Thus if we assume rigidly static conditions, we do not find a difference between land and capital, so far as cost to the individual landowner is concerned. If, on the other hand, we take into account all dynamic factors, we must admit that the value of neither capital nor land corresponds very closely with cost, and that, moreover, it is impossible to prove which factor shows the greatest average variation from cost.

SEC. 14. The question will naturally arise whether this discussion does not overlook distinctions that are of fundamental importance. We may grant that the holding of land involves subjective costs similar to those which are borne by the capitalist, yet we may deny that it is of real social utility that anyone should assume such costs. If one decides that instead of consuming his entire income he will use part of it for the production of a new machine, society is clearly the richer by an additional source of income. But if he uses the same part of his income in the purchase of a right to secure an increase in the value of land, an increase that takes place quite without regard to the act of purchase, wherein is society benefited? Is our stock of land increased, or its productivity enhanced? Again, when new capital is created, productive energy is diverted from the making of goods for consumption to the creation of producers' goods. The abstinence which figures in the creation of artificial capital goods thus means a diminution in the sum of immediate social satisfactions. Is there an analogous cost in the case of land?

As Professor Clark has clearly shown,[1] the capitalization of the expected rise in land value is in modern times one of the the chief immediate inducements to the development of new countries. The earnings of a settler on the Western prairie, apart from the increase in the value of his homestead, were for decades ridiculously low. No one not under the pressure of extreme want would have cared to pass years of his life in a log-house or dug-out if he had had nothing to expect beyond the scarcely marketable products which the soil afforded. Had there been no prospect of increased land value, the progress of settlement would have been far slower than it has actually been. It would have required a material rise in the price of food to extend the area of cultivation. Instead of a condition in which food is far in excess of the bare needs of society, we should have a condition in which the pressure of population upon subsistence would be an indisputable fact. Willingness to assume the abstinence involved in land-ownership has increased the effective land at the disposal of society, and therefore has been of social utility, like any other form of rational economic sacrifice.

But now that practically all the free land of the country has been appropriated, it may seem that this form of abstinence has ceased to be of social importance. It must, however, be borne in mind that the work of developing land, of raising it from a low grade of social utility to a higher one, may continue indefinitely. In this developmental activity the expectation of an increase in value plays an important role. Highways are constructed and streets are graded and paved far beyond

[1] In lectures given at Columbia University, 1899.

immediate needs. These are to a considerable extent paid for out of taxes on wealth which consists in nothing but expectations. Thus the demands of a future society render themselves effective in present time. Of course it is easy to point out cases in which what is here termed abstinence does no one any good. The mere speculator who invests his wealth in land and waits passively for it to increase in value is not thereby increasing the sum of social utility. But the capitalist who merely buys a share in an existing industrial corporation does no more. The wealth existed before he "abstained." The seller of the share, however, secures free wealth which he may employ in producing new capital goods. Thus the buyer of stock indirectly creates capital. In the same way the speculator sets wealth free when he buys land, and may indirectly create either new land or capital.

Much as in the case of capital, a true social cost is connected with this form of individual cost. The labor and capital which are induced to engage in the development of a new country are diverted from the production of immediately available goods. Present satisfactions are sacrificed for the sake of the future.

SEC. 15. Perhaps the most common distinction between land and capital is based upon the alleged fact that the stock of capital is capable of indefinite increase, while the amount of land at the disposal of a community is absolutely fixed. As expressed by Professor Marshall,[1]

The stock of land in an old country at any time is the stock for all time, and when a manufacturer or cultivator decides to take in a little more land to his business, he decides in effect to take it away from some one else's business.

This view has been so ably criticised by recent writers that its deficiencies need only to be outlined here. It is

[1] Principles of economics, p. 603. *Cf.* also Say, Treatise on political economy, p. 2, chap. ix.

3

quite true that if "in an old country" industry has become static so far as the development of land is concerned, one man can add land to his business only by taking it away from another man's business. If capitalization has outlived the dynamic period, the same thing is true of capital. Even while capital is growing, one business ordinarily increases its capital by taking capital from another. The distinction evidently holds only in a society which has so far advanced that the quantity of effective land can not increase, while the quantity of capital may still become greater.[1] Professor Marshall admits that in a new country the stock of land may be materially increased. The extension of roads and canals has had this effect, since they have permitted waste lands to be utilized. The recent vast development of the means of transportation has virtually annexed enormous areas of land to the more settled portions of the world. All this everyone admits. But it is held that as soon as all the land in a country has been occupied and put to economic use, further increase in land is for that country impossible. If, however, it is to be accounted an increase in economic land when a tract of virgin territory is transformed into a cattle range, why should it not be considered a further increase when in consequence of the building of a railroad the same land is converted into fields? To reply that there is no more land because the number of acres has remained the same would be much like declaring that there is no more capital in a steel rail than in an ingot because the number of pounds is unchanged. If we are to think of capital and labor in units of efficiency, we ought to treat land in the same way. The acre of land which supports a highly intensive form of cultivation can not in any economic sense

[1] Clark, The distribution of wealth, p. 338 *et seq.*

be considered as quantitatively equal to one which barely repays the most scanty outlay. Economically it counts for more land. From this point of view it is possible even in an old country to increase the quantity[1] of economic land; and the quantity does actually increase, although the laws which govern that increase are quite unlike those that govern increase in capital.[2]

SEC. 16. The great majority of those who treat land as a separate factor in production define it with reference to one or another of the characteristics discussed above. None of these, as we have seen, possesses any great logical validity. Are we then to drop the terms "land" and "rent," or dissociate the name and the income, designating by the term "rent" one aspect of any concrete income,[3] or total income regarded from the point of view of monopoly advantages,[4] while placing the income itself under profit[5] or interest[6] or even wages?[7] It is merely a question of convenience. If there are im-

---

[1] Of course this does not mean that when land of the third quality, to use the familiar illustration, becomes necessary to meet the demand for food, and rent consequently rises on that of the first quality, we should consider that the good land now represents more units of economic land. If, however, an improvement in agriculture makes fields of the second quality as fertile as those that were formerly classed as of the first quality, or if improvements in transportation give free access to market to a tract classed with poor land on account of unfavorable situation, it may properly be said that the quantity of economic land at the disposal of society has been increased. And just as an increase in labor lowers the wages of each unit of labor, so what I have termed an increase in land would obviously lower the rent of each unit of land.

[2] For a more complete discussion of this and some other aspects of the same problem see Fetter, The passing of the old rent concept, *Quarterly Journal of Economics*, vol. xv.

[3] Clark, The distribution of wealth, p. 350.

[4] Patten, Theory of prosperity, p. 8.

[5] Patten, Theory of prosperity, p. 114.

[6] Clark, The distribution of wealth, p. 336.

[7] Patten, Theory of prosperity, p 121.

portant economic laws which affect in a peculiar way a group of productive goods which practically coincides with what is ordinarily meant by land, there would seem to be good reason for retaining the old terminology, even if by so doing we run the risk of being classed with those who divide economic goods into the products of man and the gifts of nature, or with those who derive value from cost, or with the champions of other outlived notions.

The most fundamental proposition in the theory of production and distribution is that with an increase in the number of units of any productive agent, if other things remain the same, there will be a decline in the productivity of each unit of that agent, measured in terms of goods created, and a still greater decline in value productivity (defining value as the power to purchase a given complex of goods). So far as the decline in productivity measured in goods is concerned, the cause of this is evidently the greater competition of the increased number of units for opportunity to combine with the complementary agents essential to production, and the consequent necessity of utilizing the inferior powers in such complementary agents. A similar cause lies at the bottom of the additional decline in value productivity; for in an economy based upon exchange, each producing group is merely an element in the great complementary group which creates the social commodity, and the individual groups compete with each other for the most favorable combining positions. Any increase in that competition naturally results in a decline in income.

This proposition may be merely formal, as when it is said that an increase in manufacturing capital without a corresponding increase in mercantile capital would mean a relative decline in the earnings of the former kind of capital. The statement is of course true, but the assumption is not real, because normally an increase would take place simultaneously in both branches. In order to account for an actual fall in the earnings of manufacturing capital, we should not care to investigate its relation with commercial capital, because we should know that the latter was suffering in the same way and from the same causes. If labor and capital were so related that any increase in the one implied a parallel increase in the other, we could not explain any change in the rate of wages by reference to changes in the volume of capital. To make our assumptions real, it is necessary to treat as units all productive goods which are so related that their incomes increase or decline in consequence of the same causes.

It has been amply demonstrated that there is no close connection between increase in capital and increase in labor, hence an examination of the effect of an increase in capital upon wages is something more than an exercise in logic. It is not a merely hypothetical truth that an increase in capital will raise wages. If wages rise, one would naturally infer an increase in the amount of capital available. This applies, however, only to general wages. An increase in unskilled labor might result in higher wages for skilled labor, provided that the movement from one class to the other is sluggish. New capital may increase one form of capital goods while leaving other forms unchanged in quantity. It may, therefore, be necessary to divide capital and labor into several distinct groups if we are to have approximately satisfactory explanations of such rates of income as prevail in actual society. It does not, however, seem to be a straining of the truth to say

that in a reasonably long period the influences that tend
to degrade one form of labor will also injure all other
forms, and that a fall in the interest from one class of investments in capital goods will eventually cause a decline in interest from all others.

Economically available land is, as we have seen, quite
capable of increase ; but an increase in capital does not
usually imply a corresponding increase in land.   An increase in land, on the other hand, may take place without any increase in capital which could be regarded as its
cause. There have been many attempts to account for the
fact that in spite of the enormous increase in the total
capital of the western nations the rate of interest has
rather increased during the past century than declined.[1]
Certainly the virtual annexation to civilized society of
continents of land, due to improvements in transportation,
is largely responsible for this apparently anomalous condition.   At times the annexation of new land has unquestionably outrun the creation of new capital, and the
rate of interest has risen ; at other times it has lagged
behind.   The important point is that increase has not
uniformly affected both factors simultaneously. And the
reason is not hard to find.   The causes that have led to
the development of new territory have been very different
from those which have resulted in the steady growth of
capital.   Transportation agencies have been created for
political as well as for economic reasons ; thus land has
been annexed whether capital was overflowing or not.
Another thing that has entered into the development of
new countries is the spasmodic movement of population,
and with this movement increase in capital has had
little or nothing to do.   We may therefore conclude that
the laws governing an increase in capital are very dif-

---

[1] Nicholson, Principles of political economy, III, p. 139.

ferent from those which govern an increase in land. It is accordingly justifiable to assume an increase in capital without an increase in land in order to explain a particular rate of interest; and except in a society in which neither land nor capital is increasing, or in which they happen to increase at the same rate, we must separate the two factors, and investigate their reciprocal relations, as well as their joint relations with labor.

If we attempt to classify the productive goods that from this point of view are to be called "land," we should in the first place include all agricultural land, whether "made land" or not, provided that by the creation of irrigation works or of drainage ditches or similar improvements such land could not be very considerably increased without the expenditure of a proportionately greater quantity of energy and capital. We should also include building sites, so far as they could not be increased at practically "constant cost" in capital and labor. We should exclude all elements of fertility which are normally destroyed and renewed; for whether natural or artificial, a fall in interest would cause a corresponding decline in their earning power. We should include permanent improvements which can not be extended indefinitely without diminution in productiveness; as, for example, ditches that drain limited bogs, embankments that prevent overflow, and the like. For even if these improvements could be reproduced at a lower cost, there is no occasion to increase their number; and therefore to diminish their productivity. We should also include so-called natural monopolies—mines, roadways possessing exclusive advantages—in short, every productive good except labor which normally increases in productivity simultaneously with a general fall of interest. And just as in considering the rate of interest on any particular form of capital it may be necessary to analyze capital into several classes of investments which are affected unequally by dynamic influences, so it may be necessary in the study of particular classes of rents to distinguish several rent-bearing categories. The influences which result in an increase in the agricultural lands at the disposal of society may be very different from those which bring new mines within reach. But in treating of the relation of land as a whole to capital and labor we may disregard such distinctions.

SEC. 17. There is a further reason why it would seem to be expedient to keep land and capital distinct in economic theory. A great part of the significance of economic theory depends on the possibility of establishing units of productive agency independently of their actual product. We speak of the tendency of capital and labor to seek conditions of equalized productivity, of the decline or rise in interest or wages, of normal and abnormal earnings. If we define our unit of productive agency as that quantity of productive goods which actually creates a unit of value, all of these and similar propositions are either truisms or absurdities.

It is customary to define as a unit of productive agency a quantity which will under assumed conditions produce a given value.[1] This implies that such a unit is physically determinable and recognizable under diverse conditions. Two laborers, engaged in unlike occupations, may be said to represent equal numbers of units of labor if they could change places without loss of productivity. This is of course a case of exaggerated simplicity. Yet there are in actual industry large numbers of laborers who may be employed indifferently in

---

[1] *Cf.* Clark, The distribution of wealth, chap. xxiv—The ultimate standard.

several occupations. When, however, two laborers are so specialized that it would be impossible for them to change places, a notion of their comparative efficiency may still be obtained if there are unspecialized laborers normally working with them who may serve as "common denominators." Without the presence of such unspecialized laborers, it would be obviously impossible to reduce the various kinds of labor to units of efficiency which would be determined independently of their immediate value product.

Artificial instruments of production are in the highest degree immobile.[1] They are designed for a single use, and rarely could one be found which would serve as a common measure for two others of unlike kinds. The unit of capital must therefore be determined in some other way than by direct comparison of finished instruments. It is generally true that capital goods which are employed in the creation of ultimate utilities are the product of other goods that are less specialized. The material and labor that enter into the production of guns do not differ widely from those which are used in the manufacture of sewing machines. The amount of capital in the two forms of goods cannot be compared directly, but it is possible to compare the quantities of the practically homogenous productive agency that has entered into them, and thus we may obtain an indirect measure, correct only under perfect competition, of the capital in unlike instruments.

If land is to be reduced to units of efficiency, it will have to be treated in the way in which we have treated labor. Land is highly mobile,[2] it successively enters into different employments; and, moreover, land in

---

[1] Clark, The distribution of wealth, p. 118.

[2] Clark, The distribution of wealth, p. 298.

different occupations may frequently be compared by simple physical tests. Some forms of land are, indeed, of no value except for a single use. But there is almost always some economically mobile land which is employed in the same industry and which may serve as a measure of the efficiency of the immobile forms.

If the several factors of production were each divided into non-competing groups,—if, for example, a hard and fast line could be drawn between skilled and unskilled labor, between city lots and farming land, between monopoly and competitive capital,—it would be meaningless to speak of units of labor as a whole, or of capital or land. If skilled labor produced the same amount of wealth as unskilled labor, it would yet be without significance to affirm that there were the same number of units of each kind, since no other common measure than their actual value product would exist. We might, indeed, so define our unit as to make the products of units of both kinds the same, but any dynamic change that could occur would in all probability affect units of different kinds in different degrees. The only way to restore the former equality would be to reapportion the units of one kind or the other, a procedure suspiciously like forcing scientific results. It would probably be better under such circumstances to make six factors of production instead of three. There is nothing sacred about the traditional threefold division of the science. But the facts of competition through margins are perhaps numerous enough to justify the retention of the simpler classification.

There is, however, reason why land should be treated as distinct from capital Capital does, indeed, compete with land, but only as labor competes with land. The primary relation of capital to land is coöperative, not competitive. As we have seen, an increase in capital normally increases the productivity of land. If we are to call land capital, and divide it into units which shall be equal in productivity to other units of capital, we should need after each dynamic change a new apportionment of units, a species of theoretical stock-watering the utility of which is not apparent.

It may be said that in classifying with land mines and monopoly situation I have committed myself to a position not differing in nature from that of those who classify land with capital. To this charge I hasten to plead guilty. There is no way of equating mines to agricultural land except in terms of value productivity. There are no margins between the two forms of agency. My defense is that the dynamic influences which increase our control over minerals are more similar to those which govern increase in land than to those which are responsible for an increase in capital, and that an increase in capital or of labor affects both alike. For the sake of economy in thought, it is best to make only as many distinctions as are necessary for the solution of the problems at hand. In a study of the static laws of income, there is no reason for a distinction between land and capital. In a study of the most general dynamic influences, it is useful, I believe, to distinguish three factors in production. In a more detailed dynamic study, it would probably be necessary to divide each factor into as many classes as can for any length of time stand in a complementary, rather than a competitive relation with each other.

Sec. 18. Land, then, we shall treat as a separate factor in production. We can not distinguish land from capital on the ground that it is not made by labor, for labor adds utilities to land, and does no more in the case

of any other commodity. We shall not abstract from
land all qualities that can possibly be due to labor,
because by so doing we should have to apply the term
land to something which is not economic at all. Nor is
it possible to distinguish between land and capital on a
basis of their relations to cost. Land has a cost which
under free competition would equal its value, just as the
value of capital under free competition equals the cost of
production. When industry is dynamic, the unqualified
law of cost governs the value of neither capital nor land.

What appears to be, on the whole, the clearest distinction between land and capital, that the quantity of land
is fixed for all time, while the quantity of capital may
increase, proves on examination to involve a confusion
of economic with geographic land. The surface of the
world is indeed permanently fixed, but the part which is
accessible to man changes in magnitude. It is the latter
alone which has significance in economics. Economic
land is subject to increase, and so does not differ from
labor and capital in this respect.

But the laws which govern the increase of land are
not identical with those which cause capital to increase:
consequently, when interest is rising, rent may fall; indeed, it would probably do so. Rents may rise in a period of falling interest. Accordingly, if it is desired to
account for a change in the rate of interest, it is necessary
to contrast land with capital, and to examine their reciprocal quantitative relations. We distinguish between
capital and land, then, on the ground that such a distinction throws light upon changes in income and in
prices, the fundamental phenomena with which economic
theory has to deal.

By the term rent we shall designate the income which
the owner of land actually receives. That income would,

under perfect competition, equal the part of the product of industry which the land specifically produces. It may, perhaps, be convenient to designate as the " rent fund " what the land actually produces, whether the present laws of distribution give it to the landowner or not. That rent, so defined, is an independent form of income follows from the fact that land is an independent factor in production. It is necessary now to consider whether rent as a whole is to be classed with interest and wages on the one hand, or with profits and monopoly gain on the other. It is hardly necessary to define wages and interest. The actual incomes of the laborer and capitalist are generally here called wages and interest. There is a wages fund and an interest fund, consisting in the theoretical product of labor and of capital respectively. Profits and monopoly return may be left for later definition.

SEC. 19. Economic science deals with the ordinary phenomena of business life, and receives its conceptions. originally from popular thought. At first it accepted uncritically the categories of common sense. Where the business man saw a distinction between phenomena, the economist was inclined to discover one. Eventually it became necessary to supplement the grounds upon which the distinction had originally been based by new ones of a purely theoretical nature. Accordingly we find in current conceptions elements derived from popular thought and elements due to theoretical analysis. Thus it is customary to characterize the rent of land as an unearned or exploitative income, as did those who *l* wrote before the development of economic theory, or who have remained uninfluenced by it, and as differential or residual, as only an economist would do. This is not necessarily illegitimate. It is possible that both common sense and theory may have contributed elements essential to a satisfactory conception. It will, however, be convenient to keep the two sets of characteristics distinct and to study each separately.

In the popular view, the distinguishing quality of ground rent is that it is unearned, that it is *par excellence* the income which is secured not by virtue of any useful activity, but through social, political, or legal privileges. The facts of land appropriation lend color to such a view. Everywhere history or tradition recalls a time when "the whole product of labor was the laborer's." Nothing could be more natural than that a condition in which land yields a rent should be accounted for as a result of the gradual subjection of the masses to favored classes who were shrewd enough to secure a part of the social income without producing anything. And this view has frequently been reflected in economic writings, from the slur which Adam Smith cast upon the landlords, who " love to reap where they never sowed," to the vociferous declamations of Henry George and his disciples.

In order to establish a distinction between earned and unearned incomes, it is essential that the meaning of the word " to earn " should be perfectly definite. An income is earned when a certain relation exists between the merit of the recipient and his reward. But what is the test of merit in economic conduct, and what is the proper relation it should bear to reward ? To undergo fatigue and pain for the sake of producing economic goods is recognized to be economically meritorious. It is safe to affirm that the majority of those who write on economics still consider disutility to be the common characteristic of all forms of labor, and hold that it constitutes an ideally just basis for the distribution of the social income. Pain is regarded as the original price for which goods are purchased from nature, and it seems just that the price should be equal to all. In this view it is evident that any excess over that income which bears the normal or average relation to pain would be unearned. If abstinence is regarded as a " pain," a part of interest is earned, a part unearned, according as capital is saved at normal or less than normal sacrifice. As has been pointed out in the preceding chapter, abstinence connects itself with the appropriation and ownership of land as well as with the formation and holding of capital ; accordingly rent would be partly earned, partly unearned. Just as it is clear that the same thing is true of interest, so it is true of wages. If it is assumed that just wages are such as exactly cover pain-cost, there is almost always a surplus which is not earned. If it is held that shares in the surplus of satisfaction created by society should be proportionate to the pains incurred in production, the large number of workers who produce at low subjective costs and who secure high rewards receive an unearned income. On the basis of pain-cost, then, there is no ground for distinguishing rent as a whole from wages and interest treated as wholes. The unearned portion of the social income includes a part of rent, but it also includes a part of wages and interest.

SEC. 20. At a time when economic thought was dominated by utilitarian ideas, it was natural that emphasis should be laid upon the relation between the pains involved in production and the reward derived from it. Modern economics is subjected to wholly different philosophical influences. The ideal distribution which most nearly meets the requirements of modern thought is that which favors the survival of the individual and of society. Society should so distribute its wealth as to encourage the growth of the classes which are most useful to itself. And these do not consist in those who produce at the greatest pain. The man who can create a great deal of wealth without finding labor disagreeable is of more importance to society than the one who creates little and with great difficulty. Accordingly, if incomes are assigned according to productivity, the survival power of society is increased ; if they are assigned according to subjective cost, society is encumbered with the unfit. Productivity thus comes to be considered the most expedient, and therefore the most just basis of distribution. Incomes that correspond with productivity come naturally to be regarded as earned.

This change in the point of view has been hastened by the fact that a great deal of the labor of modern in. dustry is not only not disagreeable, but affords some of the most substantial of the pleasures of life. The claim has recently been advanced that pleasure is the normal concomitant of all kinds of work.[1] The position is, no doubt, extreme, but it is probably nearer the truth than its opposite, that labor and pain are inevitably as. sociated. Now it would not be denied that pleasurable work is more meritorious than the activities of play. Accordingly, even those who would be inclined to defend the claim that there should be some fixed ratio between pain and recompense would have to admit that as between purely pleasurable kinds of labor, productivity is the most satisfactory test of merit.

By this test great disproportion in incomes, or in the relation of reward to subjective cost, does not indicate the presence of unearned income. In the existing state of society, laborers are, of course, not rewarded exactly in proportion to their productivity, and therefore an unearned element may appear in wages. Yet there is a recognized tendency to eliminate this element. Wages may therefore be regarded as essentially an " earned " income.

The question remains whether interest and rent are earned or not. We may waive for the present the question whether capital and land are productive in the same sense in which labor is productive. Certainly they have a worth to society analogous to that of labor. But that does not make the income which the owner of land or of capital receives an earned income ; nor do the political and social considerations so often employed

[1] Patten, Theory of prosperity, p. 29 *et seq.*

in the defense of private possession of such goods indicate that income from them is ethically based on the same principle as income from labor.

Granting that it is possible to determine exactly how much a man's land or capital contributes, his ethical claim to the enjoyment of that contribution does not necessarily stand on the same footing as does the claim of the laborer to his specific product. It is first necessary to determine how productive goods came into private possession. If they have been acquired in the same method in which wages are earned, we may, perhaps, acquiesce in calling the income from them "earned." From this particular point of view, no one would care to distinguish between the product created by a tool which a laborer makes for his own use and the immediate product of his toil. It would, however, be natural to distinguish between the product of an implement acquired by force or fraud, by inheritance or happy chance, and the product of unaided labor.

The typical capitalist, indeed, does not make, but buys his capital goods. That he turns into capital the wealth which he could have wasted in riotous living is no doubt an advantage to society, but it obviously proves nothing as to whether his income is earned or not. That depends on the method in which the money or wealth which he exchanged for capital was acquired. If that wealth was secured through unfair advantages, the permanent income is also unfair; if it was due to chance, the income from it must be classed with chance incomes, and must be justified as they are.

In exactly the same way the income that the purchaser of land secures is earned or unearned according to the circumstances attending the acquisition of the wealth with which the land was purchased. Land was

originally acquired largely through favoritism; its value
has frequently been enormously increased by unforeseen
movements of population.   Thus it has often served to
turn unfair or chance incomes into the hands of favored
or lucky individuals.   Even at present it is a familiar
fact that there is much irregularity in the valuation of
land, owing to sentimental considerations which influence both buyer and seller, and owing to the fact that
the nature of land deprives it of the benefit of market
laws.   Nevertheless, in this respect land differs from
other producers' goods merely in degree, and the degree is hardly sufficiently marked to justify a distinction
between rent as a whole and interest.

It may be said that by the same test the dividends
from common stock in a monopolistic corporation might
be an earned income.   And that is quite true.   When a
man has purchased in the open market a share of stock,
paying for it out of his wages or other legitimately acquired wealth, it would be absurd to say that the income
he secures from it is unearned, even though the stock
was first put upon the market by a speculator who may
have performed no social service.   Theft does not ad-
here to a coin that has once been stolen.   The terms
"earned" and "unearned" express relations between
incomes or sources of income and the particular individuals who possess them.   They do not designate qualities
that inhere in particular sources of income and that are
therefore transferable.

SEC. 21.   It has long been observed that the income
which the possessor of an economic agent receives may
be distinguished into two parts, one of which is absolutely necessary if the services of the agent are to be
secured, while the other may be withheld without affecting production.   A laborer may receive three dollars a

day, although he would rather work for one dollar than remain idle.   He would not work for less than one under
any consideration.   The one dollar, then, is the wage
which is strictly necessary to make the labor of this particular workman forthcoming.   Interest may likewise
be analyzed into these two elements.   This distinction
has by some writers been identified with the distinction
between earned and unearned income.   One economist
says,

> It is easy to see that in many cases individuals obtain for their capi-
> tal more than is necessary to make it forthcoming or available.   .   .
> Thus we reach the conclusion that in interest, as in economic rent,
> there is an unearned element.[1]

This view is manifestly derived from the notion that
land rent is the type of unearned incomes.   Wages and
interest as private incomes could not wholly disappear
without crippling industry, while the volume and direction of industry would not necessarily be changed if no
private individual received an income from the soil.
The whole of rents, it is said, might theoretically be
taken by taxation without limiting or changing the employment of land, while only a fraction of wages and interest could be thus appropriated to the state without
affecting industry.

It is obvious that it is unjustifiable to designate
as unearned that part of a man's income which he
would sacrifice if the alternative were to lose his employment.   There are a great many laborers who are so
specialized that they can earn their living in only one
occupation.   A fall in their wages, so long as it does not
impair their control over the needs of existence, would
not necessarily, or even probably, cause them to work
less diligently.   The difference between the income that

---

[1] Nicholson, Principles of political economy, III, p. 232.

a specialized laborer actually receives and the minimum which he could be forced to take is necessarily greater than the difference between the actual and the minimum wage of the laborer to whom alternative employments are open.   It would, however, be absurd to say that the latter workman *earns* a greater proportion of his income than the former.   In like manner the capitalist who has invested in fixed forms of property might accept a very low rate of interest, since otherwise he would receive no interest at all, while the one whose capital consists in short-period investments would be able to demand a fairly steady return.   Clearly the one does not earn his income any more than the other does.

SEC. 22.   But though we repudiate the identification of necessary with earned incomes, we may consider the question whether the income of land may as a whole be treated as an income which is not necessary to production, while the incomes of labor and capital are necessary. If labor were perfectly mobile, it is evident that the actual wage that a laborer receives would be the minimum that he would take.   Absolute mobility implies the power to migrate from an industry without loss in productive power; accordingly, if wages were reduced in one branch, laborers would migrate until scarcity of labor restored wages again.   If capital were quite mobile, it is obvious that its entire natural income would at all times be necessary to secure its employment in any industry. If, however, land were quite mobile, no landowner would consent to take a smaller rent than the maximum that could be paid—the whole product of the soil.[1]

---

[1] It may be said that no degree of mobility could make rent a necessary income unless private ownership of land exists.   But private ownership is always assumed when we speak of the mobility of capital, therefore it may fairly be assumed when the mobility of land is under discussion.

If instead of considering the effect of a reduction of rent in a single branch of production, we consider the effect of a reduction of rents in all industries, we see that rent as a private income is not really necessary to production. So long as rent was reduced in a single industry, the landowner could put his land to another employment. Under the present hypothesis, nothing would be gained by so doing. The loss in income would be inevitable. If in like manner we assume a reduction of wages in all industries, production would not necessarily be affected unless the means of subsistence were impaired. Exactly how great a reduction wages would stand it is impossible to say. Yet we may be sure that total wages could be considerably reduced without affecting production. The same is true of interest. The capitalist who has alternative uses for his capital has the power of fixing a minimum far above what he would take if he had no better alternative.[1]

To return to realities, we find that it is the power of the owner of a form of productive agency to withdraw it from one employment and to make use of it in another that actually determines the distinction between the necessary and unnecessary parts of the income derived from it. There are, indeed, forms of land so immobile that their rent could be reduced to practically nothing with-

---

[1] The immediate effect of the fall in income assumed in the text would doubtless be a diminution in production. Laborers would feel aggrieved and would refuse to work, or would work with diminished zeal ; capitalists would be less inclined to keep their stock intact ; landlords would let some of their fields lie fallow. But if the low return continued long enough to establish lower standards, the former volume of production would very probably be restored. At all events, the change would be insignificant as compared with that which takes place in a single industry when the return to mobile agents is abnormally lowered

out lessening the amount of service which they perform ; and this is true, only in less degree, of labor and capital of certain kinds. The real distinction, then, is not between rent as a whole and wages and interest in their entirety, but between the incomes of the immobile and the mobile forms of productive agency, whether land, labor, or capital.

SEC. 23. An unearned income is not necessarily an unjust one. There are many forms of income which can not in any sense be said to be earned by their recipients, which are yet socially expedient and are recognized by the popular consciousness to be perfectly just. Such, for example, are gifts, bequests, and inheritances, as well as ordinary chance increments to normal income in which all who have sufficient enterprise and good fortune may share. Numerous economic writers, while agreeing that rent is unearned, have defended it as they defend these types of abnormal income. There is, however, a large class of writers who regard rent as a subtraction from the incomes either of the laborer and the capitalist or from that of the consumer, and hence as an exploitative income. And with the characteristic looseness of a popular science, it is now the consumer who is thought of as the one who endures the entire wrong, while now the laborer and capitalist are regarded as the only parties aggrieved. As one would expect, Adam Smith advocates both views quite impartially.

As soon as land becomes private property the landlord demands a share of almost all the produce which the laborer can either raise or collect from it. His rent makes the first deduction from the produce of the labor which is employed upon land.[1]

Quite clearly it is here the laborer who is exploited. But elsewhere, while the laborer is indeed thought of as

[1] Wealth of nations, I, chap. viii.

the victim of exploitation, it is in his capacity as a consumer.

The wood of the forest, the grass of the field, and all the natural fruits of the earth, which, when land was in common, cost the laborer only the trouble of gathering them, come, even to him, to have an additional price fixed upon them.[1]

The most familiar presentation of the former conception, as an explicit charge of exploitation, is that of Henry George :

Thus rent or land value does not arise from the productiveness or utility of land.   It in no wise represents any help or advantage given to production, but simply the power of securing a part of the results of production.[2]

One of the most common methods of presenting the law of rent, while not explicitly designed to show that the laborer and the capitalist are exploited, does nevertheless convey that implication.   If labor and capital, it is said, are applied to land in successive " doses, " the later doses are less productive than the earlier.   The employer need not pay more for any dose than he pays for the last one.   In Von Thünen's example[3] the earlier units of labor engaged in gathering potatoes create a large product ; as additional units are employed, and it is necessary to dig and rake the soil more carefully, a much smaller product is created.   The last laborer gets what he gathers only with great difficulty ; the earlier laborers can get no more.   The appearance of an additional workman is thus a signal to the employer to cut the wages of all the rest, and the profit thus secured is soon conveyed to the landlord and becomes a part of the permanent rent.   If we place ourselves in imagination at the time when land was, for all practical purposes, unlimited, and observe the development of landed

[1] Smith, Wealth of nations, I, chap. vi.
[2] Progress and poverty, p. 149.
[3] Der isolirte Staat, 2te Aufl., II, 175.

property and rent, it appears that the entire rent is made up of increments transferred from wages and interest, first to the entrepreneur, and later to the landlord.

It may be said that such a transfer of income is inevitable in a competitive society; that it would be bad business, philanthropy, for the landlord to forego the advantages which the misfortunes of the other factors place in his power. But if rent can be truly described as peculiarly a transferred income, such a defence is merely a reflection upon the ethics of business. If, on the other hand, land becomes more productive upon the appearance of additional labor and capital, it is not necessarily an act of exploitation which gives the landlord a greater rent. If labor and capital become less productive when their quantity increases, they are not robbed because their incomes are reduced; and though the rent of land is increased at the same time that the return to the other factors is diminished, we should regard the changes as merely the effects of causes working simultaneously, not as the transfer of income from one factor to the other. There are certain considerations that make such a view reasonable. Is not land which is at present cultivated intensively of greater social utility, of greater productivity, than it was when merely skimmed by extensive cultivation? And is not capital, when scarce, more productive than it would be if it were approaching a condition of superfluity? These questions can be answered only by an analysis of what is fundamental in our notions of productivity.

Sec. 24. In primitive industrial conditions, it is safe to affirm, productivity was predicated of labor alone. The artisan regarded himself as the sole cause of the goods that issued from his hands. The idea that the tools with which he worked, the materials which he employed, were jointly productive with himself would have seemed utterly absurd to him. He recognized them as conditions essential to production, but as nothing more. If he owned the tools and materials, he regarded the commodities which he created by their aid as the pure product of his exertion. If he had to rent his tools and pay interest on the capital invested in materials, he regarded the payment as a deduction from his wages, a necessary deduction, to be sure, and compensated by the advantages of use, just as a modern day-laborer, mulcted by the " padrone," regards his assessment as a deduction from wages, compensated by sufficient advantages. That this was once a common view is amply attested by the fact that among backward social classes, as, for example, immigrant handicraftsmen and even farmers, a like view prevails to-day.

But even in primitive industry there must have been laborers who were not employed directly upon the commodity, but whose presence was nevertheless necessary for production, as, for example, those engaged in directive and protective labor. Even at a time when its importance was recognized, such labor has been termed " unproductive." The " productive " labor of Adam Smith was obviously that which changed directly the form of materials. With the advent of machinery, however, the laborer ceases to be even in seeming the sole cause of the changes which the material undergoes. It would be illogical to affirm productivity of the smith who forges nails without affirming it of the machine which performs the identical operation. Still less natural would it be to call productive the labor of a man who merely watches a complex machine, while defining as unproductive that labor which is engaged in organizing and directing other labor. An increasingly large proportion of total labor is held aloof from physical contact with the commodities produced; it is nevertheless indispensable to production. The quality of indispensability occupies the economic position once held by the act of imparting utility directly by muscular exertion. If productivity is to be a term of any significance in modern science, it must be used to connote economic importance and nothing else. The labor of the loom-tender is productive, but so also is that of the foreman and the night-watchman. The loom is productive, but so also is the yarn, and so are the bricks of the factory chimney. In this sense the ground on which the factory stands is obviously productive.

Not only can productivity be affirmed of capital and land, but its precise degree is ascertainable. Just as the importance of any unit of consumers' goods can be found by measuring the satisfactions depending upon it, so the importance of any unit of producers' goods can be determined by computing the loss in consumers' goods that would result if it were withdrawn from production. To test the true importance of a unit of producers' goods of any kind, all that it is necessary to do is to withdraw that unit, and after making the best possible rearrangement of complementary agents, to determine the loss in productivity. It is clear that productivity in this, the only natural sense, is a marginal quality. Interchangeable units of productive agency have a like economic importance. " Marginal productivity " is a redundant expression, since there is no intra-marginal productivity which exceeds that of the margin. True, if the capital in the power wheel of a mill were destroyed and could not be replaced the loss would be very much greater than the loss which would result from the destruction of raw material representing an equal amount of capital. That would be true, however, not because a unit of capital of great " total productivity " had been destroyed, but because all the remaining capital of the mill would be sterilized. " Total " or " intra-marginal " productivity results from the imputation to one factor of the products of complementary factors.[1]

Productivity, in the sense of the effective importance of a producers' good, is obviously no absolute quality of that good, but varies according to its economic relations. And the most essential factor in determining productivity is the sufficiency or insufficiency of complementary agents, without which producers' goods are of no importance at all. The productivity of labor changes with every change in the quantity of capital and land upon which it is employed, and this by virtue of no change in the operations performed by labor.[2] Land likewise varies in productivity with every change in its quantitative relations with labor and capital.

When a producers' good is for practical purposes unlimited, its productivity is *nil.* As goods which are to it complementary increase in quantity, it becomes relatively limited, and is endowed with productivity, and with each increase in the quantity of complementary agents its productivity increases. In the nature of the case such a change is at the same time the cause of a decline in the productivity of the complementary agents —not simply a decline in marginal productivity, but a decline in productivity in general. To speak of the productivity of earlier units as unchanged is to mistake certain movements, applications of mechanical force and

---

[1] Wieser, Natural value, 83 *et seq.*

[2] But *cf.* Loria, Analisi, I, 39 *et seq.*

of chemical or vital processes which may or may not have economic importance, for relations that are purely economical. Economically, the productivity of labor and of land change simultaneously. There is no transfer from one to the other.[1]

Few have found difficulty in comprehending the fact that when the quantity of available land is extended, labor becomes more productive. Yet such an extension of the area of economic land normally means a fall in rents, until population again reaches a condition, relatively to land, similar to that which existed before the increase in land. Obviously, if the productivity of land is defined with reference merely to its absolute powers of supporting vegetable life, immediately after each increase land is exploited in favor of the laborer.

The facts of economic history give a semblance of reality to the assumption of unlimited, and therefore unproductive land, while unlimited capital or labor is inconceivable. It is accordingly easier to conceive of the whole of rent as transferred from labor and capital than to conceive of wages and interest as the transferred income of land. But that part of wages which exceeds the subsistence minimum may be so conceived, and must be so conceived in certain analyses of the nature of economic productivity.[2] The conception that any income can be treated as primarily a transferred income is, however, theoretically inexcusable. It is based upon a vague notion of physical productivity which can have no standing in economics. It would be absurd to attempt to distinguish between a part of the total product which is *physically* due to labor alone ; it is likewise absurd to affirm that the pure physical pro-

[1] *Supra*, chap. i, sec. 8.
[2] Clark, Distribution of wealth, *passim*.

duct of labor changes, or that it remains stationary under changing complementary relations. Economic productivity certainly does change with changes in the quantitative relations of productive goods.

In this connection it may be worth while to touch upon the notion that the income from land has a peculiar dependence upon the law of diminishing returns. It has been said that rent is not due to the fertility of the land, but arises because land yields diminishing returns to labor and capital employed upon it.[1] It has been shown that a fixed amount of labor yields diminishing returns to successive units of capital and land combined with it; and that the corresponding fact is true of a fixed amount of capital.[2] Were this not true, neither labor nor capital would be an economic agent. Diminishing or limited returns to increasing quantities of complementary agents are, of course, essential to the productivity of any agent. They play the part that limitation plays in the valuation of a consumers' good.

Sec. 25. The view that rent is an income transferred from the consumer to the landlord was especially common among the older economists, and still survives. It is most clearly stated by Sismondi, Buchanan, and Ricardo.

It is the only part of the product of labor of which the value is purely nominal, devoid of reality. It is, in fact, the result of the augmentation in price which a seller obtains by virtue of his privileges, without which the commodity would really be worth more.[3]

The high price in which the rent or net surplus originates, while it enriches the landlord, who has the produce of agriculture to sell,

[1] Ricardo, Political economy, 63.
[2] Clark, Distribution of wealth, *passim;* also, Hobson, The law of the three rents, *Quarterly Journal of Economics,* V, 270.
[3] Sismondi, De la richesse commerciale (cited by Malthus, Political economy, 138).

diminishes, in the same proportion, the wealth of those who are its purchasers, and on this account it is quite inaccurate to consider the landlord's rent as a clear addition to the national wealth.[1]

It must then be admitted that Mr. Sismondi and Mr. Buchanan, for both their opinions are substantially the same, were correct when they considered rent as a value purely nominal, and as forming no addition to the national wealth, but merely as a transfer of value, advantageous only to the landlords and proportionably injurious to the consumer.[2]

The same view appears sometimes in a slightly different form : "Rent, then, is a creation of value, but not a creation of wealth ; it adds nothing to the resources of a country."[3]

We have here another example of that prejudiced logic which persists in regarding rent from one point of view, wages and interest from another.[4] As a money income, paid by the business undertaker to the landlord, and in the last analysis paid by the consumer, rent is, of course, no net addition to the wealth of a community. The goods that pass into the hands of the landlord existed before in the possession of the buyer of agricultural produce. But wages and interest, as money incomes, represent merely the transfer of wealth that is already in existence, and constitute no net increase in the social wealth. If, however, by wages and interest we mean not the money incomes which are usually designated by those terms, but the specific product in concrete goods that labor and capital produce, regarding

[1] Buchanan, cited by Malthus, 139.

[2] Ricardo, Works, McCulloch's ed., p. 244.

[3] Ricardo, Works, McCulloch's ed., p. 244. Practically the same idea appears even in modern economics. Thus we have the statement of Professor Carver that " the amount of rent, as I understand it, is the excess of the profitableness of the industry over the productiveness of the industry." Publications of the American Economic Association, Papers and proceedings of the fourteenth annual meeting, 198.

[4] Roscher, Political economy, Lalor, ed. p. 32.

the receiving of money wages as a mere exchange of goods for goods, wages and interest are indeed net additions to the wealth of a community. Land, as has been pointed out, is also productive; and the primary form in which rent appears is as the specific product of the land—clearly a net addition to social wealth. In the sense, then, in which rent is not an additition to wealth, wages and interest are not; in the sense in which wages and interest augment the national wealth, rent does also.[1] The flow of goods from which all increase in the wealth of society is derived appears under economic analysis to consist in the products of land and the products of labor and capital; in rent, wages, and interest alike.

[1] Clark, The distribution of wealth, chaps. xxii, xxiii.

SEC. 26. Most of the views that were considered in the preceding chapter conveyed, explicitly or implicitly, the notion that there is an ethical distinction between rent on the one hand and the return to labor and capital on the other. Scientific writers, however, have often tried to avoid introducing ethical ideas into economic discussions, and have attempted to distinguish rent from wages and interest by reference to purely economic characteristics. This they have usually done by describing rent as a differential or as a residual income. Units of labor and of capital, it is claimed, yield equal incomes ; units of land vary in their productivity. Moreover, there is a certain uniformity in the return which labor and capital receive at different periods, while the return to land shows the widest possible range of variation. The rent of land may, therefore, be described as differential, whether we compare the productivity of different units at the same period of time, or the productivity of the same unit at different times.

Since there appears to be this uniformity in the return to labor and capital, while the return to land varies so greatly, it is thought to be most convenient, in the theory of distribution, to establish directly the laws that determine the productivity of labor and capital, leaving rent to be indirectly determined. Whatever is produced above the normal return to labor and capital will be rent or something similar to it in nature. Rent may, therefore, be best treated as a residuum. It is to be noted that the view of rent as a differential is funda-

5

mental, since it attempts to describe the essential nature of the income ; while the description of rent as a residual is merely a matter of convenience in theory.

We may take Walker's statement as fairly representative of this view :

Rent arises from the fact of varying degrees of productivness in the lands actually contributing to the supply of the same market, the least productive land paying no rent, or a rent so small that it may be treated as none.[1]

Stated thus, there is a very old and very obvious objection which will bear repetition. In the classical illustration, it is when lands of the second grade of fertility are brought under cultivation that lands of the first grade begin to yield a rent. With certain reservations we may admit this, and yet deny that it is *because* of the employment of lands of the second grade that rent emerges on the better lands. When the demand for the products of the soil increases, the share of the produce which the landowner can exact becomes greater at once, quite without regard to the extension of cultivation to the poorer grade. This becomes clear if we assume that there is an appreciable difference between the two grades of land. Prices will have to rise considerably before the poorer land can be employed, and since according to the usual assumption the laborer and the capitalist can get no greater returns than before, the landowner must necessarily receive an increase in rent.

If we prefer the other common form of statement of the same "law," namely, that rent is due to the differences in the productiveness of the several powers of a given piece of land, we find that the same objection holds. The first "power" yields a rent, not because the second power is called into use, but quite independently of that

---

[1] Walker, Land and its rent, p. 21. *Cf.* also Macfarlane, Value and distribution, p. 87.

fact. The method of illustration just employed shows
that it is not only possible that rent should emerge on
the better powers before the worse ones are utilized, but
that the utilization of the poorer powers can never
logically be said to cause the better powers to yield a
rent. Emergence of rent on the better grades or
on the better powers of land, and the employment of
the worse land or powers are different effects of the
same cause.

It may be said that in the case assumed the increase
in the income of the landowner is not a true rent, but
a species of monopoly gain, since it is a " marginal "
return, not differential. This is, of course, to assume
the very thing that it is sought to prove, that the income
from land is caused by differences in the fertility of the
soil.

Even if it is assumed that the gradations between the
different kinds of land and the different powers in each
kind are infinitesimal, so that an extension of cultivation is an inevitable concomitant of rise in rent on the
better grades or powers, it would obviously be incorrect
to speak of either phenomenon as the cause of the other.
But under such an assumption it would be quite correct
to speak of rent as being subject to differential measure- ∠
ment. And that is practically all that the classical
position signifies.

The term " differential" has received such wide application in recent economics that the definiteness of its
meaning is in danger of disappearing. When we say
that an income contains a differential element it is by
no means clear what that element really consists in.
It may be merely a quantity of satisfaction, such as that
which is afforded by the earlier units of consumers'
goods ; it may be a part of the price, such as the addi-

tion to normal price due to monopoly control; or again, it may consist in concrete goods. The laborer who works in a community which is well provided with capital and land thus produces an income containing a differential element, measured in goods. If, then, we wish to consider whether rent may be distinguished from wages and interest on the ground that it is a differential return, it is necessary to be on our guard against shifting our point of view. One can readily see that it is execrable logic that will confuse an income which is differential from an objective point of view with the subjective differential that may be attached to any income. Yet it is hardly too much to affirm that this is what modern economic terminology tends to do.

It is accordingly necessary to consider the various points of view from which rent may be regarded as a differential income, and to examine wages and interest from the same points of view. In this way, and in this way only, will it be possible to determine whether we have here a characteristic which sharply distinguishes rent from the two other forms of income.

The subjective differentials which compose the so-called consumers' and producers' rents do not require detailed discussion here. If rent were indeed an income which entailed no subjective cost, while wages and interest served chiefly to cover such cost, we should have one perfectly definite characteristic which would mark off rent from interest and wages. But it is generally admitted that there is a surplus of utility over disutility in the income to labor and capital, and as we have seen, only a part of the rent of land can be considered as such a surplus.[1] Moreover, subjective surpluses, if correctly analyzed, have no effect upon either the production or

[1] *Supra*, chap. ii, sec. 13.

the distribution of wealth. It is a matter of interest to
the social philosopher that the earlier hours of the
working day afford a considerable surplus of pleasure
over pain. But if that surplus were reduced to practically nothing, the laborer would have no reason for
working fewer hours, and hence the volume of production would be unchanged if the surplus ceased to exist.
In like manner the consumers' surplus on the earlier
units of goods acquired does not affect the number of
units which will be demanded, nor does it affect the
utility or the value of the last unit. Objective differentials alone are of importance in economic description.[1]

The most familiar type of objective differential is that
which is illustrated in the Ricardian formula. An economic agent is divided into units which are measured,
not according to their economic qualities, but according
to certain physical characteristics. A unit of land is an
acre, a unit of labor is an individual workman, a unit
of capital is a particular machine. Such units may be
arranged in a series, and their economic importance may
be measured either from the least productive or from the
most productive. If the former method is adopted, as
much of the income of a better unit as exceeds the productivity of the worst unit is a positive differential.
The latter method would create a series of negative differentials.

As it is assumed that the worst unit of land yields no
rent, the product of any other unit is regarded as a positive differential. If it is possible to find capital goods
that pay no interest, there is no reason why the return
to any unit of capital should not be regarded as a differential of the same nature. Professor Clark has pointed
out the fact that there is a point in the life of each

---

[1] *Supra*, chap. i, sec. 6.

perishable capital good when it yields its owner no surplus above the return to the complementary agents that are employed with it.[1]   It may be possible to find laborers so inefficient that they add nothing to the product of industry, in which case the wages of better labor could be described as a differential.   If, however, it is preferred to regard as marginal labor that which receives a wage sufficient for bare subsistence, the greater part, though not all, of the return to efficient labor may be treated as a differential.   The claim has been urged, and with much force, that land requires a minimum return for upkeep ;[2] and the reduction to desert of grazing lands in the West and in Australia proves that even " marginal " lands require a certain care, and so must produce a minimum return similar to the minimum of subsistence for labor.   The differential in rent would then be measured from a minimum return, not from zero.   But whether the differential is measured from zero or from a minimum return is a matter of practically no theoretical significance.   Few economists would now subscribe to Walker's dictum that " the whole theory of rent rests on the assumption that there is a body of no-rent lands." [3]

Although it is possible to conceive of units of labor and of capital that are based upon purely physical characteristics, yet to do so is to violate established usage. A unit of labor in economic theory almost always means an amount of labor of a given efficiency.   If two children are able to do the work of one man, we should naturally say that they represent as many units of labor as a man.   If there are laborers who make no specific addition to production, we should not call them units of no-

[1] Clark, Distribution of wealth, 96.

[2] Hobson, Economics of distribution, 155.

[3] Political economy, 3d ed., 222.

wage labor; we should say that they represent no labor
at all. The capital goods which are at the point of being
discarded and which add nothing to the product of industry are not capital in the economic sense of the word.
" All portions of capital do, in proper economic theory,
bear an equal rate of interest,"[1] and the same thing is
generally held to be true of all units of labor.

Economic usage notwithstanding, there appears to be
no reason in logic why two acres of poor land should
not stand for the same number of units of land as one
acre of good land. To reduce land to units of efficiency
is a process exactly analogous to the reduction of labor
and capital to units of efficiency. No-rent land is no
more an economic agent than is the capital that yields
no interest.

It is not, however, difficult to understand why the
unit of land should have been described in one set of
terms and the units of labor and capital in another. In
the first place, in spite of the variations in the efficiency
of labor, custom has always tended to reduce to a certain
uniformity the work actually performed by ordinary
workmen. A " day's labor " formerly conveyed a far
more definite meaning than " the use of an acre of
ground." It is the tendency of modern improvements
in the technique of agriculture and in transportation to
lessen the differences in the productivity of the soil.[2]
At the same time, modern industry permits of a wider
range of personal differences than did a régime of custom. The term " an average acre of land " thus comes
to possess a more definite significance than formerly,
while the term " an average day's labor " conveys a less

[1] Walker, The source of business profits, *Quarterly Journal of Economics*, vol. ii, p. 287.

[2] Patten, Premises of political economy, p. 27 *et seq.*

definite meaning with the progress of industry. The possibility of reducing land to units of efficiency is at present scarcely less than that of reducing labor to similar units.

SEC. 27. But the chief cause for the difference in the treatment of land on the one hand and labor and capital on the other was the conviction that the differential on the better land bore a relation to price quite different from the relation to price of the analogous portions of wages and interest. One might call the wages of the poorest workers marginal, and the excess over such wages that better labor receives differential. But the relation of the differential and the marginal portions of wages to price was seen to be identical. Whether sugar beets are cultivated by three children, by two Russian women, or by one man, the cost to the entrepreneur and the price to the consumer are the same. To classify portions of the wages of the more efficient workers as differential and non-differential has, therefore, no economic significance whatever. If, however, workers were paid equally, the wages of the least efficient labor might bear a peculiar relation to price, and the distinction would be of economic importance.

The description of rent as a differential of this kind is then of theoretical importance if rent is not a cost, if it does not enter into price. Until it is independently proved that rent is not a cost, the differential analysis which is based upon a comparison of the productivity of unlike units is incapable of distinguishing rent from wages and interest. The discussion of this question must, however, be postponed to the next chapter.

SEC. 28. But even though we describe the units of labor, capital, and land in terms of productivity, so that there are none which do not yield a return, it is nevertheless possible to treat their incomes as differentials. Although such units are by definition equally productive, they must differ in some respects that are of great theoretical importance. They will require very different proportions of complementary agents to endow them with normal productivity.[1] Thus the capital which is embodied in old and inefficient appliances will require a far greater quantity of labor to work it than an equal amount of capital embodied in machinery of the most improved type.

The goods produced by the aid of the former appliances will represent a high labor cost and a low cost in capital.[2] As the machinery deteriorates still more, the cost of the product resolves itself more and more into labor cost until a point is reached where the product is economically created by labor alone. This peculiarity of industrial units is nowhere so obvious as in the case of land. A unit consisting in very poor land will often require a comparatively great expenditure for labor and capital ; and if the land be sufficiently poor, the entire product may be due to the labor and capital.

Under the assumption of perfect competition, the various units of labor will have migrated from point to point until they have become equally productive, whether they are combined with a hundred units of cap-

[1] In his criticism of Professor Clark, Loria objects strenuously to the notion of varying proportions in the combination of industrial agents. The proportions, he says, are fixed by immutable physical laws, (Il capitalismo e la scienza, 19). The fallacy of his position is due to the fact that he conceives of units of capital, labor, and land as physically alike, when in fact they are alike only with respect to some economic quality that we select as relevant to our immediate needs. It would be absolutely impossible to select a unit of capital which would be based both upon static productivity and upon its habits of combining with other units of productive agency. But this is clearly what Loria tries to do.

[2] Clark, Distribution of wealth, p. 96.

ital and land or with one unit, or with practically none at all. If, then, we desire a measure of the efficiency of labor, of its true importance to the economic organism, we have it in the product of the labor which is working virtually unaided.

We may, if we choose, arrange the supply of all commodities with reference to the relation between the value of each unit and its cost in labor alone. Those portions of the supply that are produced by labor which is combined with very little capital and economic land would represent the margin of greatest labor cost ; all other units would have a value greater than their cost, counting only the specific form of cost which we are considering. That surplus value would of course be the income to capital and land described differentially. In the same way it is possible to form a differential series with reference to cost in capital, and another in which the cost in the uses of land receives similar emphasis. The significance of such series of differentials consists in the fact that a field thus appears in which some units of each agent work practically unaided. It will be remembered that one of the chief ends that the classical economists sought to attain was the discovery of a field in which the whole product of industry was divided between labor and capital, where " whatever is not interest is wages." [1] It would be superfluous to point out here the connection between Ricardo's law of rent and his proposition that commodities exchange in proportion to the labor that has been expended upon them. Now it is no more impossible, theoretically, to discover a field where labor works virtually unaided by capital and land than to find one in which labor and capital work without the use of economic land. In

[1] *Cf.* Von Thünen, Der isolite Staat, II, 137 *et seq.*

either case it is necessary to disregard the trifling contribution which is due, even at the margin, to the excluded factor or factors.

The advantage of the method of differential analysis here suggested is that it does not require the existence of no-rent land in order to find a field where the product of labor and capital are practically dissociated from the product of land; nor does it depend upon the margins of labor and capital to distingush pure interest and wages. Where a great deal of labor and capital are e m ployed on a small amount of land, even if that land pays a considerable rent per acre, the value of each unit of commodities produced will more nearly resolve itself into wages and interest alone than where a smaller amount of labor and capital are employed upon a great deal of land that pays a small rent per acre. In a developed economy it is perhaps more likely that the pure product of labor or of capital will appear in connection with the better land than in connection with the poorer.

SEC. 29. Both of the differentials discussed above are phenomena of static society. If industry became quite stationary, it would still be possible to find acres of land, capital goods, and laborers that produce a merely nominal return, or labor combined with such insignificant qualities of intra-marginal capital and land as to be working virtually unaided. But there is another class of differentials illustrated in the so-called intensive law of rent which actually appear as differentials only when dynamic movements of industry take place, and which can be explained only on the assumption of dynamic phenomena.

In any group of producers' goods that are combined for the production of a single commodity, a change in the proportions of land, labor, and capital will mean a change in the productivity of every unit of each factor,[1] provided that the additional units are of the same general character as the original ones, and that no change in the technique of production has altered the normal proportions of combination in that branch of industry. If the amount of labor increases, the productivity of each unit of labor declines, while each unit of capital or of land becomes more productive. We may conceive of the quantity of labor increasing until the productivity of any unit becomes so small as to be quite negligible. We should then have a series of differentials representing the productivity of labor under the widest range of conditions that are of economic importance. Under the worst conditions, from the point of view of labor, the product of a unit is zero ; under the best conditions it is the entire value which labor could create if combined with unlimited capital and land.

If we start with the most favorable possible condition for labor—when the units of labor are few and capital and land are practically unlimited—and gradually increase the number of units of labor, we shall have a decline in the productivity of each unit. The earlier units, it is usually said, are more productive than the later ones ; accordingly, a differential surplus connects itself with them. Accurate analysis shows, however, that at any given time there are no favored units, that in the economic sense of the word the "earlier" and the "later" units are equally productive. The differential series is connected, not with different units at one time and under one set of conditions, but with the same unit, or identical units at different times and under different conditions. At no time, then, does such a differential

---

[1] *Supra*, chap. i, sec. 8.

surplus exist, except in thought.[1] Since, however, a
change in the quantity of labor which reduces the productivity of labor increases at the same time the productivity of the other factors, it is not unnatural, though inaccurate, to identify the increased income of the factors
of which the position has been improved with the diminished productivity of the factor which suffers through
the change.[2]

Such a differential, or pseudo-differential, we may designate as the dynamic differential, to distinguish it from
the kinds of differentials discussed above. It is the one
which appears in the "intensive law of rent." Originally the rent of land alone seemed capable of being described as a differential of this nature. But in recent
years several economists have successfully applied the
same method to the explanation of wages and interest.[3]
Its application to capital and labor are obviously implications of its application to land. Why, then, was this
fact practically overlooked for a whole century, and why
do so many economists of the present day regard it as
merely an over-refinement of theory?

SEC. 30. The conception of a dynamic differential
series rests upon the assumption that one of the factors
of production remains stationary in quantity while the
quantities of the other factors increase. The "earlier"
and "later" increments that figure in the illustration
are units of the factor which varies in quantity. Now
if there were some law that made it inevitable that all
of the factors of production would increase at the same

---

[1] For a slight qualification of this statement *cf. supra*, p. 15, foot-
note.

[2] *Supra*, chap. i, sec. 8.

[3] Clark, Distribution of wealth, p. 319 *et seq.;* Hobson, The law of
the three rents, *Quarterly Journal of Economics,* vol. V, p. 270.

time and in the same degree, such a conception would
be wholly valueless. It would be a description of an
impossible phenomenon. If, on the other hand, one of
the factors increases at a more rapid rate than the
others, it would be quite legitimate to assume that it
alone increases while the other factors remain unchanged. The description would be only approximately
true, but it would gain in clearness what it lacked in
accuracy. If one of the factors is capable of increase,
but is of such a nature that it inevitably lags behind
the others, it would be unnatural to assume that it alone
increases in quantity while the other factors remain unchanged. All of the phenomena of change could be
accounted for by assuming that the factor which is least
subject to dynamic influences remained static, while
assuming that the other factors increased somewhat less
than they do, absolutely considered.

When Ricardo wrote, the quantity of available land
increased slowly, and rents were actually rising;
labor and capital were rapidly increasing in quantity,
and interest seemed to be declining to a minimum,
while wages appeared to manifest a tendency to approximate the barest needs of the laboring population. It
was, therefore, natural to assume that the quantity of
land is fixed for all time, and that labor and capital are
capable of indefinite increase. The assumption that the
quantity of labor remains unchanged while capital or
land increases would have seemed then an utterly fruitless one. It would have been hopelessly abstract even
for Ricardo.

But as we have seen, the land which remains unchanged in quantity is geographic, not economic land;
yet it is the latter which alone has significance in economic theory. And economic land may increase quite

independently of any corresponding increase in capital or labor.[1] Moreover, recent theory has been compelled to abandon the notion that the minimum of subsistence fixes the standard of wages, or that any immutable law fixes a stationary return to capital. Accordingly it is not an absurd assumption that the quantity of land varies while capital and labor remain stationary.

We may conceive of Von Thünen's isolated state annexing, by means of improved transportation, a great area of waste, which thus becomes economic land, not inferior in fertility and effective situation to the lands nearer the metropolis. Assuming the economic fluidity which we always assume when we discuss the effects of increase in capital or labor, we should see each establishment, agricultural or manufacturing, adding new acres or front feet, employing its stationary quantities of capital and labor upon greater areas of land. As the additional units of land are successively taken into these establishments, we should see their productivity gradually decline. No acre could receive for its owner a greater return than the product of the last one of the same degree of productiveness. The greater productivity of the earlier acres would at first appear as a profit in the hands of the entrepreneur; but competition would soon make it over to the stationary factors, capital and labor. Thus we should have a differential series in which the "earlier" units of land appear to be more productive than the "later." This series is precisely analogous to that which is connected with the earlier "doses" of capital and labor, when those factors increase and land does not.

No doubt, under the conditions assumed, the increase in wages and interest would react upon the supply of

[1] *Supra*, p. 38.

labor and capital, and hence would tend to restore the original quantitative relations. But the reaction would not necessarily equal in force the primary dynamic phenomenon, increase in economic land. It must be remembered that high rents, due to relative increase in capital and labor, have a similar influence in increasing the quantity of economic land. In either case there is no reason why the primary dynamic influence would not result in new and higher standards of permanent income.[1]

It is quite conceivable that the birth rate may so decline that population will remain practically stationary during the next century. At the same time capital may increase indefinitely, owing to the greater degree of security and the development of thrift in the general population, and improvements in transportation may greatly increase the amount of effective economic land. Under such circumstances wages would doubtless continue to rise, while the rates of interest and rent would unquestionably fall. In that case it would be natural to regard a great part of wages as a differential on early increments of land and capital. It would be perfectly natural that theorists, in order to give perfect consistency to their systems, should assume a time when labor was for economic purposes unlimited, and explain the whole of wages as a differential on the earlier units of land and capital. Such an assumption would, of course, be historically untrue, but not much more untrue than the classical assumption of unlimited economic land. In every age there have, indeed, been areas of unused land which could be turned to economic account ; but so also have there been classes of workmen unemployed. In either case there was either a temporary misadjustment, or the technique and the control of complementary

[1] *Cf. supra*, chap. i, sec. 8.

factors was not such as would permit of the economic use of the unutilized agents.

SEC. 31. If, then, one of the factors of production is so constituted by nature that it remains relatively stationary in quantity during an indefinite period of dynamic change, it will be quite correct, according to the principles of economic logic, to regard its income as peculiarly subject to the dynamic differential analysis. It would be quite irrelevant that the same analysis could be applied to the other factors by assuming that they in turn remained stationary in quantity while the actually changeless factor increased. Assumptions which are not in some degree generalizations from reality may be employed as a foundation for fictitious logical constructions, but will not assist in the discovery of truth.

Whether the rent of land shall be regarded as a differential income depends, then, upon the question whether or not economic land is capable of increase independently of a corresponding increase in capital. The claim has been advanced in the second chapter of this essay that land is capable of such increase; therefore it is maintained that logic requires the application to capital and labor of the same analysis which is usually applied to land alone. Rent is not characteristically differential from the dynamic any more than from the static point of view.

But while each of the factors of production, treated as a whole, is capable of increase, there are certain forms of labor, capital, and land that remain practically unchanged in quantity. These are usually forms that are specialized to a single use—the monopoly goods of Wieser's analysis. Every increase in the demand for the commodities produced by their aid will tend to

6

change the quantities of mobile productive goods employed in combination with them, and consequently to increase their share in the physical product. Growth in the quantity of the mobile factors will likewise change the proportions of combination with these immobile factors, and will consequently increase the share imputable to them. The return to such "monopoly goods" will therefore be most naturally measured differentially upon the successive units of mobile agency applied to them. Moreover, the productivity of the mobile productive goods is tested in general industry; that of the monopoly goods must be discovered in the isolated combinations in which they occur. And this may be done either by returning the mobile factors to general industry and thus discovering how much value is lost by leaving the monopoly goods unemployed, or by estimating the product of the mobile goods marginally and treating the return to monopoly goods as a residuum. The residual test is, of course, the natural one.

If we consider what concrete forms of productive agency answer to this description, we shall find, indeed, many forms of land, especially land which is peculiarly adapted for certain uses in commerce and industry. But we shall also find numerous forms of capital and labor that for one reason or another do not respond to dynamic influences that affect the general mass of these agents. It is true that such forms of land are likely to retain their monopoly position for a longer period than like forms of capital and labor; but we must remember that at all times there is a complex of capital-goods and of labor which holds a similar position. If, then, we wish to retain the designations "differential" and "residual," we shall probably find it most expedient to apply them to the return to the strictly monopoly factors, whether forms of land, labor, or capital.

The customs and laws of land tenure have a tendency to confuse ordinary land, which is mobile in the economic sense of the term, with the monopoly goods of the foregoing discussion. A great proportion of the entrepreneurs of modern society find it a simple matter to increase the labor and capital under their control, while to rent or purchase additional land involves a considerable amount of friction. To vary the amounts of capital and labor employed with a given quantity of land is a more frequent procedure than to vary the quantities of land with a fixed amount of capital and labor. The conception of land as a fixed quantum and of capital and labor as variables thus gains an established position in the business consciousness. But it is clear that many forms of capital (*e. g.*, a ship or a building, and many forms of labor, such as that of a business manager) share this characteristic with land. It is also clear that the friction which gives rise to such a characteristic is not sufficiently important in modern industry to serve as a basis for a theoretical distinction between sources of income.

CHAPTER V.

THE RELATION OF RENT TO PRICE.

SEC. 32. There is hardly any subject in economic theory that has been more voluminously discussed than the relation of rent to price. The problem, though involved, can hardly be called one of the most intricate with which economics deals ; and it would, therefore, be presumptuous to undertake to add much that is new to the existing controversial material. Yet so long as eminent economists of one school assert that rent obviously bears a relation to price quite different from the relation to price borne by wages and interest, while equally eminent economists of another school assert with equal confidence that in this respect rent does not differ from the other two forms of normal income, it cannot be a wholly superfluous task to examine the premises and the reasoning which lead to the assumption of positions thus diametrically opposed.

A history of the doctrine of rent which we associate with the name of Ricardo would be little more than an enumeration of the names of economists who have subscribed to it. In the form in which it left the hands of Ricardo it appears practically unchanged in all classical economic writings down to the time of Walker, whose statement we may accept as typical.

The normal price of any commodity is fixed by the cost of the production of that part of the supply which is produced under the most disadvantageous conditions. The cost of that part, whatever that cost may be, will determine the price of all other portions, no matter how much more favorable the conditions under which these may be produced. Applying this principle to a single agricultural crop, e. g., wheat, we say that the normal price of wheat will be fixed by the cost of raising it upon the least productive soils which are actually cultivated for the supply of the market. . . . But if the price of the whole crop of wheat is to be fixed by the cost of raising it on the least productive soils actually cultivated, then rent is not a part of the price of agricultural produce, since the least productive soils pay no rent; and therefore rent cannot be part of the price of the wheat raised therefrom, and if not of this wheat, then of no wheat, since, as we have seen, the price of the whole crop is fixed by the cost of that portion which is raised on the no-rent land.[1]

A history of the criticism of the Ricardian doctrine of rent would be somewhat less monotonous than a history of the doctrine itself, since the range of ideas is greater. Yet the points of view of the critics of the doctrine of rent are easily classified. Apart from the attacks of Carey, which spent their force upon a minor detail, the order of cultivation, we find three principal lines of criticism: (1) The poorest land in cultivation may yield a rent, and therefore a part of rent is a constituent element in price. (2) Portions of the supply yield no wages, and other portions pay no interest; therefore the reasoning which is relied upon to prove that rent does not enter into price would prove that neither wages nor interest enter into price. (3) Rent is in the last analysis a portion of the total product of industry, and only secondarily a money income. The existence of rent in its primary form is of the utmost importance in determining price.[2]

[1] Walker, Land and its rent, 27.

[2] A number of objections to the Ricardian doctrine which do not appear in this classification have been presented by Professor Patten in his "Premises of political economy," pp. 21–45. Many of them do not appear to hold when the Ricardian doctrine is broadly interpreted. As a case in point we may cite the sixth count brought against Ricardo (p. 44), namely, that land may remain in cultivation even when the return is not sufficient to pay all costs in labor and capital, including under capital improvements fixed in the soil. This would be a reason for holding that the return to certain kinds of capital may be regarded as a "quasi-rent," to use Professor Marshall's expression, but it does not in itself necessitate any essential modification of the doctrine of rent.

SEC. 33. The first criticism was not entirely overlooked by Mill,[1] it was advanced as an important qualification of the Ricardian theory by Professor Patten in his " Premises of political economy,"[2] and has since become familiar to all students of economics. The poorest land in cultivation is almost certain to yield a rent, since such land has some value for other purposes—pasturage, the chase, the growing of timber. Price must accordingly be sufficient to pay such " marginal rent," as well as wages and interest. More important is the corollary of this proposition, which shows that the rent of land for agricultural purposes must be counted as a part of the cost of the products of a market garden; or, to put it in general terms, rent in any use must be sufficient to keep the land from falling into the best alternative use.[3] If we are permitted to reduce all land to wheat fields, it is necessary to take into account the fact of marginal rent only. But a study of price is a study of relative value. In an investigation of the laws governing the price of wheat little can be gained by ignoring the essential price relations between wheat and other agricultural products. It would be manifestly absurd, in order to determine the laws that govern wages and the price of the product of labor, to assume that all labor produces shoes. If it should be proved, upon such an assumption, that wages do not enter into price, the proof would be valueless, as the premises vitiate the conclusion. It is needless to repeat the argument which shows that the assimilation of all kind of land to wheat land gives equally worthless results.

But the modern defender of classical doctrines, while admitting that it is an essential fact of the problem that

[1] Mill, Principles of political economy, book 3, chap. 5, sec. 2.
[2] p. 22.
[3] Jevons, Theory of political economy, 2d ed., preface.

land enters into various employments, and that in many branches of industry rent is paid for the poorest land used, would still deny that rent enters into the price of the most expensive and price-controlling portion of supply ; and he would point to the well-known intensive law of rent as a sufficient defense of his position. If capital is applied in successive doses, one dose will be found which yields a return only sufficient to cover the cost of the labor and capital employed. Consequently there is a portion of supply which pays no rent.[1]

SEC. 34. The logic of the intensive law of rent has recently been called into question by several economic writers. It is said to overlook the organic nature of industry, and to imply a misadjustment which involves a denial of the theoretically free competition upon which the argument is based. For the first objection we may quote Hobson, who rejects entirely the notion that the productivity of a final unit of any agent is determinable.

It is claimed that the product of the last dose of labor is to be measured by the reduction in the aggregate product of the farm which would have attended the refusal to apply this last dose of labor. Now this is not justifiable. The withdrawal or refusal to apply this last dose of labor would have meant a diminished productivity not only of the other units of labor, but of the units of capital and of land, and part of the result of this diminished productivity of other units is wrongly attributed to the last unit of labor.[2]

Now this would be quite true if the "last dose" is defined loosely enough. If, for example, the dose of capital which is withdrawn from an acre is a bushel of the wheat that would normally be sown, a part of the loss would indeed be due to the sterilization of the uses of land, labor, and other capital employed. But careful economists, in assuming that a "dose" is withdrawn, also

---

[1] *Cf.* Marshall, Principles of economics, 3d ed., p. 475 *et seq.*

[2] Hobson, Economics of distribution, p. 145.

assume that the best possible rearrangement of the remaining productive goods is made, so that only a slight deterioration of all of the forms of the agent in question takes place.[1] It may be that the effect of the addition of a final unit of capital is simply to increase the efficiency of existing goods. Its physical product may be organically related to that of the other elements in production, but this fact does not make its economic productivity less distinctive.

In the same chapter Hobson advances the claim that the premises upon which the intensive law of rent is based involve a previous misadjustment of the factors, thus discarding the principle of free competition without which the whole doctrine is meaningless.

> If a tenant hires a piece of land and puts five doses of capital upon it when he ought to have put six, he pays a rent based on the assumption that he will make a full economic use of the land, *i. e.*, that he will put six doses on it. If, discovering his error, he afterwards adds the sixth dose, he only appears to pay no rent out of its produce, because he has all the time been paying a rent based upon the supposition that he was working the land with six doses.[2]

> The truth is that a certain harmony of combination of factors of production exists for various productive purposes. In a given case a certain proportion of the three factors of production is most productive. If, however, there is a short supply of one of them at the former quality and price, a more than proportionate increase of one or both of the others may be substituted, involving, of course, an increased cost per unit of the increment of supply.[3]

Now it will be admitted that at any given time such a "harmony" exists, and that under the assumption of perfectly free competition no individual will be enabled to vary the productive combination without loss *until some dynamic change in industry takes place.* But if capital increases, the best possible proportions of the factors throughout industry change

[1] Clark, The distribution of wealth, p. 246 *et seq.*
[2] Hobson, Economics of distribution, p. 141.
[3] Hobson, Economics of distribution, p. 137.

also. Free capital is in the market seeking bidders, and under the assumption of free competition it will get just what it adds to industry. It will add less than the former product of like units, because the adjustment existing before the increase in capital implied that in each industrial plant additional units of capital would create a less than proportionate return, and increase in capital would not change this fact. The new capital will, indeed, affect in a very slight degree the productivity of all other units of capital, lowering their return; it will likewise increase the product of all units of labor and land. But these changes cannot take place until it has been ascertained how great a total net increase is due to the new capital. No deduction from that product is made for rent; increase in rent arises from an apparent deduction from the product of other units. There is, therefore, a portion of the supply into the price of which rent does not enter, and that portion actually appears whenever dynamic changes take place.[1]

It is true that if the new units are applied successively, those which are applied first must pay a rent. Moreover, if the final unit is divided into two smaller units, it will appear that a rent is connected with the one which is theoretically first. From this it has been argued that the rentless unit must be infinitesimal, *i. e.*, no unit at all.

No finite unit of product can be shown to be a no-rent unit in the theory of the intensive application of labor and capital with regularly diminishing returns. The concrete units are produced at varying

---

[1] This does not mean that the no-rent portion of supply *exists* only when a dynamic change is taking place. An individual producer can economically make an experiment which will demonstrate the productivity of unaided capital or labor only when new social units of these agents are distributed for employment.

costs for labor and interest on capital, and every one contains an element of rent.[1]

The argument does not, however, seem to be valid from a strictly mathematical point of view. While we cannot conceive of marginal units of labor and capital which are so small that they cannot be divided, and cannot therefore directly conceive no-rent units, a consideration of the relation between the part of the apparent product of a marginal unit of labor and capital due to the labor and capital and the part really due to land will show that as the unit diminishes in magnitude, the ratio of the rent to the labor-capital product constantly grows less. Since this is the case, it is quite legitimate to conceive of the former quantity as becoming infinitesmal while the latter remains finite. To dispute this would be to deny the validity of practically the whole body of theoretical economics, as well as of that part of mathematics into which the Theorem of Limits enters.

There appears, then, to be no reason for denying the validity of the intensive law of rent. There are portions of the supply into which rent does not enter, although such portions appear only when a dynamic change takes place. Even though all units of capital are given equally favorable positions in combination with land, there is yet a unit of product, created by all the units conjointly, which pays no rent.

SEC. 35. To admit this, however, does not compel us to subscribe to the doctrine that rent does not enter into price. For it has been proved conclusively that portions

[1] Fetter, The passing of the old rent concept, *Quarterly Journal of Economics*, vol. xv, p. 439. In a footnote Professor Fetter disclaims any intention of disputing the validity of the method of increments in economic theory, claiming that this is a misapplication of it. The grounds for the difference between this and other applications is not apparent.

of the supply of commodities are produced without the economic aid of labor or of capital; yet it would be absurd to deny that wages and interest form elements in price.[1] There are units of commodities which are virtually produced by labor and capital alone. Some of these units are produced by much labor and little capital; other portions cost a great deal of capital and but little labor. Some units are created at an expense, say, of five units of labor and twenty of capital; others may cost five units of capital and twenty of labor. No economist, however, would affirm that these units are produced at unequal costs, because he would not start with the assumption that the use of either capital or labor is not a cost. If there is a portion of supply which is produced by twenty-five units of labor, unaided by capital, it would not follow that this portion is the most expensive, since increased cost in labor is offset by diminished cost in capital.[2] From this it is clear that those units of supply into which rent does not enter can be considered the most expensive ones only in case it can be shown independently that rent, or more properly the use of land, is not a cost. Accordingly, it is not an injustice to the classical economists to affirm that the argument by which they sought to prove that rent is not an element in cost assumed the conclusion in the premises.

Economic theory deals with three main forms of cost: (1) subjective cost, consisting in the pain and discom-

[1] Clark, Distribution of wealth, p. 360 *et seq.;* Hobson, Economics of distribution, p. 133 *et seq.;* Fetter, The passing of the old rent concept, *Quarterly Journal of Economics,* vol. xv, p. 437 *et seq.*

[2] Those economists who hold that the different agents combine, economically, in fixed proportions in each branch of production will see a gross misadjustment premised in this illustration. For my defense, *cf. supra,* sec. 30.

fort attendant upon production ; (2) entrepreneurs' cost, consisting in payments which the business man must make in order to place a commodity upon the market; and (3) social cost, consisting in the destruction of the commodities, or limited uses of commodities, which are at the disposal of society.

Subjective costs evidently exercise influence upon price through affecting the supply of productive agency. In a dynamic society capital is increasing, and therefore the influence of subjective cost everywhere manifests itself in checking the growth of capital. Economic land is also increasing, and the fact that increase entails subjective cost makes it clear that such costs limit supply and influence values.[1]   In a study of the relations of productive agency to price, limitation is, however, the fundamental factor; and whether or not limitation is due to subjective cost is a matter of secondary importance.   It is quite conceivable that through a process of adjustment, subjective cost to the laborer might become quite negligible,[2] and that capital might normally be saved under condition that no disutility would be involved.   But so long as the quantities of labor and capital remain limited, these agents can still demand and receive, under competitive law, a part of the product of industry; and the relative payments for labor and capital will appear in relative prices.   In the same way,

---

[1] It may be said that when once new land has been brought under cultivation, the fact that a subjective cost was originally connected with its utilization does not act to limit the use of its services.   If society should become static or retrogressive, land would not be limited by reason of such cost once incurred.   We are considering, however, the relation of subjective cost to supply of land, and hence to price, under existing conditions, and under existing conditions it is obvious that the cost of annexing and utilizing new areas is a limiting factor, exerting an influence upon absolute values.

[2] Patten, Theory of prosperity, 8.

even if subjective costs no longer exerted an active influence on the supply of land, land would still be limited,
and its income would appear in price, as will be seen
later.

The relation of rent to entrepreneurs' cost need not be
discussed at length, since it is not disputed by any important modern economist that to the individual entrepreneur rent is an outlay similar to wages and interest.
The farmer who is unable to pay the prevailing rate of
rent for the land he uses is as surely driven out of business as one who cannot pay the ordinary rate of wages
or of interest.   Social customs may, indeed, treat wages
and interest as preferred shares in distribution; but this
is not necessarily true, nor is it normally the case in our
present society.   The rent is fixed before the productive
process begins; if any loss occurs, it falls upon interest,
or even upon capital.

It remains to consider the relation of rent to social
cost—whether the use of land for which rent is paid is
a cost from the point of view of society, in the sense in
which labor and the use of capital are costs.   We must
consider whether, to employ Wieser's expression, the
administrators of a communistic state would be held as
strictly to account for the use they make of land as for
the use of capital or labor force.

Social cost, so far as it is conceived as not merely collective subjective costs, is relative in its nature.   A
workman represents a possible amount of social service;
and when we consider the cost of a commodity to
society, it is necessary to take into account as part of
cost this possible service of laborers engaged in its production.   A commodity which requires the services of
an efficient workman obviously is more costly, from the
point of view of society, than one which requires an

equal number of days' work of a workman who is inefficient, even though the latter may suffer far more subjective cost than the former. Cost in this sense is reckoned ultimately in terms of utility, since every increase in the power of labor to produce utility makes the services of labor count as higher cost.

In a static state costs of this kind would have so close a dependence upon values that the terms "high" or "low" social cost would convey no meaning. Every unit of labor, capital, or land would be placed at the point where its productivity is highest; and the loss occasioned by its withdrawal would have no other measure than the immediate loss in utility. Commodities having an equal utility would have equal social costs. In a dynamic society more units of productive agency may be used in the production of one commodity than in the production of another commodity of equal value. The former may then be said to have a high relative social cost. Now it is obvious that the high cost may be the result of a disproportionate employment of capital, just as well as of a disproportionate use of labor. Exactly the same thing is true of land. Any unit of land represents a quantity of possible social service; and in reckoning the relative cost to society of different commodities, the quantity of land-use withdrawn from general industry must be counted in the same way as the quantity of labor and capital. The commodity produced with a disproportionate use of land has a high social cost, just as the commodity produced with a disproportionate use of labor or capital. One misadjustment is as costly as the other.[1]

It appears, then, that from whatever point of view we choose to consider costs, rent or the use of land does not

---

[1] *Cf.* Wieser, Natural value, p. 207 *et seq.*

differ from wages and interest, or the use of capital or labor force. Under the assumption of free competition and private ownership of land and capital, it is illogical to affirm any difference between the relation of rent to price and the relation to price of wages or interest.

SEC. 36. Yet it would be unreasonable to claim that a doctrine so deeply rooted as is the Ricardian theory of rent can be thus easily disposed of. There remain other factors in the problem which may be best considered in treating the third line of criticism, namely, that the primary form in which rent appears is as a concrete share in the product of industry, as a portion of supply, just as wages and interest are primarily shares in the product.

As money or "real" incomes, wages and interest and rent consist in the wealth given in exchange for such primary shares in industrial product. Thus regarded they have an effect upon price very different from that which is ordinarily considered. As portions of the entire supply, their absence would cause a rise in price. In this sense there is no difference between rent on the one hand and wages and interest on the other.

The real rent of land, as of everything else, consists in goods that the land virtually creates, and these enter into the supply of such goods and help to determine their value. . . . The rent of land, then, as the concrete product imputable to land, is emphatically an element in determining value.[1]

The modern Ricardian would probably admit that from one point of view concrete incomes are products. Yet it is only in a static state that it is possible to identify product with actual shares in the distribution of wealth. Now it is not wages as product, but wages as an actual income, that are supposed to have a controlling

[1] Clark, Distribution of wealth, p. 356.

influence over price. The entrepreneur may withhold a part of the product of labor, in which case we may still call it wages, or better, part of the wages fund, and it will form a part of the supply in the same way in which rent forms a part of the supply, and so will affect price in the way in which it is here claimed that rent affects price. But the wages that are not withheld by the entrepreneur perform a double function. They distribute the wealth that has already been produced, and they serve to show the laborer what he can expect from future production. The disposition of the wages fund of this year may not have much influence upon the supply of wheat of this year, but it will certainly influence the supply of next year. If the workman has been exploited, there will in the future be fewer workmen in the wheat industry. Prices and incomes thus distribute the fruits of present and past production, and distribute productive forces for future production. It is through the distribution of labor that wages influence prices.

If the laboring classes were paid barely enough for subsistence, a lowering of wages would have a further effect on prices, since it would diminish the total supply of labor. But in a society such as our own, it is obvious that a considerable reduction of general wages would not necessarily affect the supply of labor.[1] It is accordingly through the relation between wages and the distribution of labor that wages can properly be said to influence price. It is only by postulating a state in which labor is absolutely free to move from industry to industry

---

[1] A general decline in money wages would no doubt reduce the effective supply of labor even under present conditions. But a decline in real wages, due to a general rise in the price of commodities consumed by the laborer, would hardly diminish the number of workers of the present, or materially check the growth of population.

that we can say that wages in their entirety "enter into" price.

But if instead of postulating a state in which labor is free and mobile—an exceptional and possibly transitional state, if the history of mankind is taken into account—we postulate a condition of society in which a rigid caste system distributes labor independently of income, wages might fall in any industry without reducing the supply of labor. While at first laborers would perhaps refuse to work at all, or would work without much zeal, the need for subsistence would drive the existing body of laborers to work as before in spite of lower wages. So long as the minimum of subsistence were not impaired, a fall in prices could not be prevented by any existing rate of wages. As soon as the price of any product fell so low as to reduce wages below that minimum, the volume of labor in the industry would automatically diminish until prices would rise sufficiently to afford the minimum wage. Under the assumption of wholly immobile labor, then, the minimum wage would alone have the power of fixing prices. Instead of making the comparatively mild assumption of a caste system, we might assume that all labor is of the same quality and produces nothing but shoes. A fall in the price of shoes could not be hindered by labor cost until the subsistence minimum had been impaired for at least an appreciable margin of labor.

In either case it is obvious that the minimum of subsistence would not necessarily be the normal wage, if mobility of capital is assumed, and if capitalists are free to compete with each other for the employment of labor within any particular employment. Neglecting for the present the share assigned to land, we may say that in each branch of industry capital would earn normal interest, and the residue, whether great or small, would go to labor. ' Except in those employments in which that residue actually afforded a mere minimum of subsistence, prices would rise and fall quite without regard to the wages usually paid. Wages would appear to be price-determined, not price-determining. /

SEC. 37. We see, then, that the extent to which wages may be said to enter into price depends upon the degree of mobility that we assume. Where labor is absolutely fluid, it is true, in a modified sense, that the whole of wages enters into price. Where labor is quite immobile, only the subsistence minimum can be said to have any permanent influence in determining price. The same reasoning would obviously apply to capital. If classes of individuals were compelled to invest any capital which they might possess in some particular industry, a fall in price would not necessarily affect supply until it had caused a slackening in the rate of accumulation, or had brought about the consumption of existing capital. When the capitalist is free to invest his capital in any one out of a number of industries, a fall in interest causes an immediate migration of capital. Under the former assumption, the units of capital which bring influence to bear upon price are those which are saved with the greatest difficulty. Under the latter assumption, the units which hold the strategic position are those which find the least difficulty in migrating to other employments. In a competitive economy it is mobility that exercises actual control over prices. /

The only reason why it has seemed worth while to consider the effect upon wages and interest of complete immobility of labor and capital is that in expounding the Ricardian law of rent we are accustomed to make

assumptions of much the same nature. If we assume
that land is absolutely immobile, we must indeed admit
that its actual income has no power to determine price.
Its strategic position is worse than that of labor and
capital, inasmuch as there is no minimum below which
rent cannot fall. If all the land that is capable of growing wheat is capable of growing nothing else, a fall in
the price of wheat will act upon supply only through
the reduction of income to labor and capital, although
a reduction in rent will take place contemporaneously.
If we assume that each kind of land is specialized to a
single use, rents will rise or fall with prices. Land will
have no power to prevent such changes in its income.
Assuming as Ricardo did that all land yields nothing
but corn, the landlord would clearly have no escape
from a fall in rents. He would be reduced to the position of a passive recipient of whatever might be left by
the mobile elements in production.

It appears, then, that the distinction between rent
on the one hand and wages and interest on the other
rests ultimately upon the assumption of immobility
of land and mobility of labor and capital. Labor and
capital are assumed to be subject to competitive law;
land is assumed to be withdrawn from the field of such
law. It would be a shallow argument which would
treat such a discrepancy in assumptions as bad logic. If
the facts of industrial life show that land is far less
mobile than capital and labor, it is quite legitimate to
assume immobility of land while assuming perfect mobility of labor and capital. Such assumptions will not
serve as a basis for absolutely correct conclusions, but
they will make possible generalizations which are
approximate descriptions of reality.

It has already been argued at some length that

land is in reality mobile in the same sense in which labor and capital are mobile; and the burden of proof lies with those who would hold that it is mobile in less degree. In the case of labor and capital, power over price is exercised through marginal mobility. It is not the worst labor nor the poorest capital which holds the position of greatest influence upon price; it is undifferentiated labor and capital in the form of pure purchasing power. If prices fall in a given industry, it is possible that a few of the poorest workmen will starve and that increase in population will be slightly checked. It is also possible that a few marginal savers of capital, accustomed to invest in this particular industry, will consume their capital. But it is obvious that an immeasurably greater influence on price is exercised by the laborers who are free to migrate to other industries and by the capital which is in a position to change its employment.[1] The mobile portions of labor and capital form in reality only a small fraction of the total supply. Now it is here maintained that there is a part of the total supply of land which is so situated that it admits of alternative uses; and that portion is sufficiently considerable to endow land as a productive agent with mobility and to give it the rank of a price-determining factor. There is doubtless land specially adapted to single uses and unrelated through margins to land possessing alternative uses; there is also labor and capital in the like position. These immobile forms of productive agency—the "monopoly" goods of the last chapter—can alone be said to receive price-determined incomes. Under conceivable historical conditions, rent would not "enter into price;" but under the conditions

[1] *Cf.* Patten, Theory of prosperity, 46.

of modern industry there is no satisfactory reason for
treating rent in its entirety as a price-determined income. Ordinary land shifts from employment to employment, seeking the highest possible reward; and in
so doing it affects the supply of different commodities
and exercises a controlling influence upon price.

CHAPTER VI.

RENT, PROFIT, AND MONOPOLY RETURN.

SEC. 38. In the foregoing chapters attention has been devoted exclusively to the relation between rent on the one hand and wages and interest on the other. In the present chapter it is necessary to consider the relation of rent to profit and monopoly return. The task is rendered difficult by the fact that economists are very far from an agreement as to the nature of profit and as to the distinction between profit and the gains from monopoly. Both forms of return, however, represent an excess of income from production above entrepreneurs' cost; and profits may be provisionally distinguished from monopoly return on the ground that the latter income possesses a degree of permanence which the former lacks.

Early economists paid little attention to the concrete form of income which most modern writers now agree in calling monopoly return. Adam Smith, indeed, recognized as monopolistic some of those sources of income which we should now class as legal and customary monopolies, and his earlier followers made certain allowances in their theories for monopoly phenomena. The first thoroughgoing analysis of monopoly, however, appears in Senior's "Political economy," which draws attention to the numerous forms in which monopoly return may exist. Senior agrees with his predecessors in regarding rent and monopoly return as closely related incomes—a point of view which has never lacked defenders.

There are in general three reasons advanced by the

classical economists for classifying rent with monopoly income : (1) land is a monopoly because its value does not correspond to the cost of improvement ; (2) land is a monopoly because it is limited in quantity ; (3) the return from land is a monopoly income because it implies no subjective cost.   Adam Smith may be selected as a representative of the first view, Malthus of the second, and Senior of the third.

The rent of land, considered as the price paid for the use of the land, is a monopoly price.   It is not at all proportioned to what the landlord may have laid out upon the improvement of the land, or what he can afford to take, but to what the farmer can afford to give.[1]

That there are some circumstances connected with rent which have a strong affinity to a natural monopoly, will be readily allowed.   The extent of the earth itself is limited and cannot be enlarged by human demand.   The inequality of the soil occasions, even at an early period of society, a comparative scarcity of the best lands, and this scarcity is undoubtedly one of the causes of rent properly so called.   On this account, perhaps, the term *partial monopoly* may be fairly applicable to it.[2]

The fourth and last class of monopoly exists where production must be assisted by natural agents, limited in number and varying in power, and repaying with less and less relative assistance every increase in the amount of labour and abstinence bestowed on them.[3]

The reason which Senior gives for classifying with monopoly production thus aided is that a greater value is produced than by an equal amount of *labor* and *abstinence* in general industry.[4]   These " natural agents," Senior explains later, consist chiefly in land.   But that part of wages which exceeds the average remuneration of labor is also to be classed with the return to natural agents.[5]

[1] Smith, Wealth of nations, I, chap. xi.

[2] Malthus, Political economy, 140.   For an identical modern view see Macfarlane, Value and distribution, 123.

[3] Senior, Political economy, 105.

[4] Senior, Political economy, 103.

[5] Senior, Political economy, 130.

The above grounds for classifying rent with monopoly income do not, however, appear to be valid, since similar ones would make a monopoly income of wages or of interest, and no one would deny that these incomes when normal differ fundamentally from that which is secured through monopoly.

In the first place we may admit that the value of land does not correspond to the cost of improving the land; but if we were to capitalize the earning power of labor so as to make labor strictly analogous to land, we should find that there is no law that makes the value of the laborer correspond with the outlay in bringing him up. The value of a capital good may tend to equal the entrepreneurs' cost of production, but the value of the pure capital that the goods embody bears no direct relation to entrepreneurs' cost; and it is the relation of pure capital to interest that must be compared to the relation of land to rent. The fallacy of the position is due to the attempt to apply the laws of the normal valuation of finished commodities to one of the permanent agents of production. In the second place it is quite true that rent is due to the fact that land is limited relatively to the demand for its services, but limitation is just as essential if labor or capital are to possess earning power. Partial limitation of the better classes of labor is the cause of the higher productivity of such labor, yet we should feel that it is to use words in a new and strained sense to say that all labor except the very lowest kind receives a monopoly return. Finally, disregarding the question whether the landowner endures subjective costs or not, we may question the usefulness of a classification of income based upon subjective costs, a classification that would make a large part of the income of a laborer who is properly adapted to his calling a monopoly gain, while classing with wages the income of another who performs the identical economic operations, but who is so ill adapted to his calling as to endure extraordinary fatigue and pain. With such a classification one would be forced to adopt Professor Patten's view that when society shall be properly adapted to its environment, all income will be monopoly income.

SEC. 39. In modern economics no definition of monopoly has been agreed upon ;[1] consequently it would be idle to search for an accepted definition of monopoly return. The conception of monopoly profit or net revenue is, however, sufficiently familiar. Manifestly not all of the income of a monopoly, but that portion alone which could not be secured without a control over prices is to be counted as monopoly return.

Monopoly control over prices depends, in almost all cases, upon the power to determine the amount of productive agency which shall assist in supplying a given want in a market of greater or less extent. When any entrepreneur finds himself in a position to treat the price either of finished products or of productive agency as a variable quantity, appreciably influenced by his actions, he has the power to manipulate prices so as to secure a net return. If wages, interest, and rent are practically fixed data, his income results from the raising of prices and the consequent exploitation of the consumer ; if prices are practically fixed, monopoly gain must be subtracted from the earnings of industrial agents.

Although there are numerous circumstances under which the gains of monopoly are virtually extorted from

---

[1] Professor Ely, Monopolies and trusts, p. 14, defines monopoly as "substantial and controlling unity of action." The definition is, perhaps, the most satisfactory we have, but it hardly covers all the phenomena that most would consider monopolistic.

the consumer only, monopoly return is in a strict sense the product of labor, capital, and land, and is diverted ·from the owners of these agents to the profit of the monopolist. The person who holds monopoly control over a commodity may not endeavor to lower the prices paid for productive agency. He may even pay for the use of productive agents a higher rate than that which prevails in the general market. It is, however, obvious that the method by which the monopolist operates is to limit the amount of productive agency in a given branch of industry; and in this way he increases the productivity of each unit. From the enhanced productivity of the several units the monopolist secures his revenue. To illustrate this we may assume that a unit of labor is withdrawn from a monopolistic industrial establishment, and not replaced by labor from outside of it. The net loss, after deducting whatever may be due to the attendant dislocation of industry, will manifestly exceed the net loss which would result from the withdrawal of a similar unit from a competitive branch of industry.[1]

Thus it appears that this particular form of monopoly gain is exploitative,[2] in a sense, since it is a product

---

[1] There are circumstances under which this is apparently untrue. The Standard Oil Company may have men engaged in the manufacture of dyes who are making merely competitive wages. "Every monopoly has some men employed in positions that yield the same net return as do the exposed industries with no monopoly " (Patten, Theory of prosperity, 72.) This merely signifies that an establishment which is monopolistic in some of its enterprises is not monopolistic in others. The manufacture of dyes may be carried on competitively by the Standard Oil Company because it does not interfere with the market for its monopolized produce. To withdraw a workman from such subsidiary enterprises would not result in loss of monopoly gain, but it would not, in reality, be the withdrawal of a workman from the monopoly.

[2] Exploitation, as the term is used in this chapter, conveys no ethical significance. Whenever a productive agent does not receive the product which it creates, it is exploited in this sense of the term.

which is not secured by the agent which creates it. Labor, capital, and land produce the monopolists' net revenue. In any particular establishment they are not necessarily injured by it, since they may still receive a normal or more than normal return.[1] When, on the other hand, prices of finished commodities are not subject to control, but prices of productive agency are, exploitation of the same character takes place, but to the immediate and manifest injury of productive agency.

But there is another form of monopoly income which has been touched upon in the above section, the producers' as contrasted with the entrepreneurs' gain. If laborers, by combination or by control over public opinion or government, are able to exclude men potentially of equal efficiency from their employment, they may maintain a higher degree of productivity than workers in general industry, and may retain the abnormal income for themselves. Under these circumstances it may be that no direct exploitation of any producer takes place. Workers throughout society may gain what they specifically produce. The effect of the producers' monopoly

Ethically, the owner of a productive agent has a clear right to its product only if his claim to the agent is uncontested, and if its productivity is not affected by wrong or favoritism in the distribution of units of agency. The laborers who combine to exclude others from a profitable industry gain an increase in wealth which is counterbalanced by a greater loss on the part of excluded laborers, and it would not be straining the usual meaning of the term to say that the excluded laborers are exploited. But it is. necessary to have terms which will distinguish between the income based upon the productivity of units of agency in one's legal possession and income appropriated by parties in distribution other than the owners of the productive agents that create it. The former income is here classed as productive, the latter as exploitative.

[1] Of course the ultimate effect upon productive agency is unfavorable, since the units arbitrarily excluded from the monopolized branch must seek employment elsewhere, thus abnormally lowering income to labor, capital, and land.

upon the consumer and upon productive agency which is excluded from the favored position does not differ from the effect of the entrepreneurs' monopoly upon the consumer and the outside producer. The distinction between the two forms of monopoly return lies wholly in the distribution of it within the group. If it is secured by the entrepreneur, we may properly term it monopoly profits; if it is shared by labor, capital, and land, these agents may be said to secure monopoly wages, interest, or rent, as the case may be.

Now with what one of these forms of monopoly gain are we to compare rent? It is obvious that an entrepreneur who possesses a monopoly will find it necessary, if he wishes to manipulate prices of finished commodities, to limit the amount of land which he uses, as well as the amount of labor and capital. The withdrawal from his employment of a unit of land will often result in a greater net loss in goods, measured in terms of value, than the withdrawal of a unit of similar land from competitive industry. The land is abnormally productive, and the surplus productivity is appropriated by the monopolist. If, however, the monopolist manipulates the price of productive agency instead of that of finished commodity, the land may be paid at abnormally low rates along with the labor and capital. Again, if a united group of landlords control a given crop and limit the area on which it is grown, the land may be made to yield an exceptionally great value-product for its owners, in which case the land is in a monopoly position, similar to that of the trade-union laborer.\ There may, then, be land which yields a return quite different in its nature from rent, and exactly analogous to the monopoly return secured through labor or capital.

That the withdrawal of a unit of labor from an

industry which yields a monopoly return will result in a greater loss in value-productivity than the withdrawal of a like unit from competitive industry is so self-evident that an apology is due for repeating it here. Does the withdrawal of a unit of labor from an establishment which yields a high competitive ground rent mean a greater loss than the withdrawal of a unit from an establishment yielding a low rent? Does the final unit in extensive culture produce more than the final unit in the forms of intensive cultuie employed in the same country? This is manifestly not true. Unless there is for some reason a greater dislocation of industry and impairment of the productivity of complementary agency, there is no reason for believing that the final unit—*i. e.*, any unit—employed upon good land is more productive than a similar unit actually employed upon poor land. The final unit of labor in a monopolized industry is more productive than similar units placed elsewhere, and this surplus productivity is the monopoly "rent." We may therefore conclude that there is a fundamental difference between the so-called rent of monopolies and the rent of land.

SEC. 40. Assuming that rent is sufficiently defined as a differential surplus above cost, and that profit is a "marginal" or general surplus, Professor Patten has undertaken to prove that monopoly return is simply the same fund as rent, viewed in a different way.[1] On the basis of the "law of substitution," or competition between different kinds of goods in supplying a given genus of wants, he has developed the conception of a series of monopolies, each one producing at a uniform cost for all its units, while the several monopolies differ from each other in the expense of production,

[1] Patten, Theory of prosperity, p. 80 *et seq.*

the one possessing fewest advantages receiving no surplus gain. The income of these monopolies is in this view a profit, although, when the whole class of monopolies is viewed as a group, it is represented by a differential series. \ The income of any monopoly, viewed by itself, is marginal or general; viewed as a part of the income of all monopolies, it is differential. \For this reason Professor Patten concludes that "rent and [monopoly] profit are one fund viewed in different ways." /If we grant for the sake of the argument the existence of a number of monopolies forming a regular series, we still do not lose the distinction between ordinary ground rent and the surplus secured by the more favored monopolies. In those which are most nearly free from competition, land as well as capital and labor will usually be limited artificially. Now there should be no difficulty in distinguishing between that part of the product of the land which depends in no way on monopoly position and which could not be taken away by the freest competition, and that part of the product which exists as a result of artificial limitation, which is secured by one who may not have legal possession of the productive agent to which it is due, and which must disappear with increased freedom of competition.

But there is a more fundamental criticism which may be brought against Professor Patten's position. No profound analysis is required to show that the differentials which figure in this series are quite unlike the differentials which figure in the law of rent. The units of labor, capital, and land in the stronger monopolies are not unlike those in the weaker; they yield a higher return because of their better control of competition. The different "units" of land postulated in the law of

rent are alike only in superficial area—a single one out
of numerous economic characteristics.

No satisfactory reason appears to exist for treating
monopoly return and rent as like forms of income.
Monopoly income is due to artificial limitation which
enhances productivity; rent is due to productivity,
ultimately dependent upon natural limitation. We shall
now consider whether rent bears any close relation to
the other dynamic form of income, profit.

SEC. 41. The concrete forms of income which are at
present termed profit received no adequate treatment
from the classical English economists. In early theory
the fact that returns vary temporarily in the various industries was of course perfectly understood, but the
special income depending upon such variations was not
considered important enough for special treatment. In
his analysis of profit, Samuel Read approaches the problem in a way distinctly in advance of the rest of the
early English economists. He describes the excess of
gain in any industry over and above the ordinary rate of
interest as either wages—" reward for labour or industry, or ingenuity, or skill, in the use and application of
capital,—or otherwise . . . the result of *fortune or
accident*,—that is, of 'secret and unknown causes,'
which sometimes occasion greater or less gain in trade,
or no gain at all, and sometimes a loss,—and falls
properly to be considered as *compensation for risk*."
This latter form of gain, since it is regulated by no
certain causes, Read declares to be " without the pale of
science." [1]

We have here the germ of two of the modern views of
profit. That part which Read treats as " wages " is
manifestly analogous to the reward for superior capacity

[1] Political Economy, London, 1829, p. 263.

in organization which has been regarded by President Walker[1] and Leroy-Beaulieu[2] as the true source of business profits. That part which he regards as compensation for the risks attendant upon business operations is evidently the form of gain which is held to be typical profits by the modern exponents of the " risk theory of profits." This theory was more fully worked out by Von Thünen, who distinguishes between risks which are sufficiently calculable in their nature to be undertaken by insurance agencies, and risks which are wholly incalculable, such as changes in demand, the appearance of new competing products, and similar contingencies, which no insurance could cover and which the entrepreneur must meet himself. It is the latter form of risks for which profit is a compensation. The same economist points out that since the loss which one suffers when deprived of one's fortune far outweighs the gain secured by a doubling of one's means, no one would be an entrepreneur unless the chances of gain outweighed the chances of loss. Business must, therefore, afford to the undertakers as a class a net profit, after deduction has been made for all losses. This net profit Von Thünen calls " Unternehmergewinn."[3]

This theory has been worked out in more detail by other writers,[4] but in its essential features it remains practically unchanged. At present we have in economic literature two theories of profits besides the above. One of these emphasizes the fact that the entrepreneurs as a class enjoy a monopoly position in society. There may

[1] Walker, The source of business profits, *Quarterly Journal of Economics*, vol. i, p. 275 *et seq.*

[2] Académie des sciences morales et politiques, I, 717 *et seq.*

[3] Der isolirte Staat, II, 81.

[4] Especially Mangoldt and Mr. Hawley. *Cf.* Willett, The economic theory of risk and insurance, p. 50 *et seq.*

be numbers of men in humble positions who are potentially able to carry on great enterprises, but who, through lack of business connections, never receive an opportunity to exercise their powers for management. Those who have the good fortune to be placed in charge of business affairs are for this reason enabled to demand for themselves an unduly large share of the product of industry.[1] This point of view is further developed by those economists who investigate the relative monopoly position of individual groups of entrepreneurs instead of that of entrepreneurs as a class.[2] Capable entrepreneurs may be relatively few in any group or sub-group, to employ Professor Clark's terminology; accordingly they have an advantage in purchase of materials, in employment of capital and labor, and in sale of products, and this advantage gives them an opportunity to secure large profits.

Finally we have a theory of profits which takes its point of view from the facts of an intensely competitive, but dynamic society.[3] A new use is discovered for a commodity, and until capital and labor can be diverted to its production, those who are already on the ground reap a rich harvest. A labor-saving machine is invented, and those who are able to apply it at once make great profits before its use becomes general and prices fall in proportion to the fall in cost of production. Frequently the entrepreneur who makes these gains runs no risk whatsoever. The productiveness of a new machine may be accurately calculated. No particularly high degree

---

[1] Macvane, The source of business profits, *Quarterly Journal of Economics*, vol. i, p. 1 *et seq.*

[2] Gross, Die Lehre vom Unternehmergewinn, p. 132 *et seq.*

[3] Clark, Distribution as determined by a law of rent, *Quarterly Journal of Economics*, v.

of managing ability is required in its application. Monopoly position, in the sense of a control over competition, need not be assumed. The fortunate entrepreneur may reap a profit while offering no check to increase of output on the part of others, and while bending every effort to increase his own output. Such gains are of course transient at any one point in the industrial field, but they disappear from one industry to reappear in another. Entrepreneurs as a body always receive a flow of income of this nature.

SEC. 42. It does not fall within the province of this paper to consider what view of profits is on the whole the most satisfactory. All that is necessary for present purposes is to present a sufficiently broad view of the fund which is usually treated as profits, in order to consider the relations of that fund to rent. The income of a fortunate and capable entrepreneur will contain (1) a gain due to chance, offset by a smaller loss[1] (borne, however, by some other entrepreneur); (2) a gain due to his own power of combining labor and capital in ways more effective than those usually employed in the community; (3) a certain share in the first fruits of economic improvements; (4) a part of the gains which entrepreneurs as a class secure through the fact that their services are limited in proportion to the demand for them. It is obvious that the second and third element are dependent in large degree upon the fourth. A system of social selection which would discover the business capacities

---

[1] The mere chance of reward is of course the actual compensation for risk. No compensation is afforded by society for loss. It will be questioned by some whether this form of risk is not really borne by the capitalist. *Cf.* Willett, The economic theory of risk and insurance. If the entrepreneur had no other source of return, it would obviously have to fall on some other factor. As the entrepreneur has other gains, there is no reason why he should not be thought of as bearing part, at least, of these risks.

of members of the working classes would perhaps reduce
many forms of entrepreneurs' activity to the rank of free
goods; it would disseminate much more quickly the results of economic progress. There would still remain
different grades of entrepreneurs, and the better ones
would receive a net gain; there would still be temporary
gains, though smaller and more widely diffused.

The analogies that are alleged to exist between
profit and rent are three in number: (1) that rent and
profit are differential incomes; (2) that they represent a net surplus above cost; and (3) that they are a
price-determined income. We have already considered
at length whether these are the true characteristics of
rent; we may now consider how far they are applicable
to profits, studying separately, for convenience, each of
the elements of the preceding section. It will be necessary, moreover, to examine in detail the economic nature
of each of these elements of profit, in order to obtain a
definite idea of the relations of profit as a whole to rent.

It is obvious that the amount of dynamic risk varies
greatly from industry to industry. If this is correctly
understood by those who undertake the risks of directing
industry, the return above normal wages and interest
will vary in like manner, and thus it is possibe to
arrange industries in a differential series, the industries
with practically no risk representing the no-surplus
units while those in which risks are highest represent the
units of maximum surplus. But since a fall in price
which would diminish any of these alleged surpluses
would at once reduce supply, it appears that the payment for risk forms a part of the necessary costs of production, and therefore has a power to control price.
The analogy between this form of income and rent is

therefore very superficial, even from the Ricardian point of view.

· But there is a more important reason why it is inadmissible to regard this form of income as analogous to rent. If a unit of capital or labor is withdrawn from combination with land where the so-called surplus which constitutes rent is greatest, the loss in product will not normally be greater than when a unit which shows the least rent-surplus is withdrawn. When a unit of labor or of capital migrates from a combination which yields a high risk-surplus, the loss in product is normally greater than when it is taken from a combination in which the risk-surplus is *nil.* The rent surplus is produced by the land, and continues without appreciable loss when any one unit of complementary agency disappears from the establishment. The risk surplus is produced by the units of labor and capital, and is naturally reduced in proportion when these are withdrawn.[1]

We see, then, that the surplus return in an industry in which risks are high is in important respects similar to the income from a monopoly. Economically it is imputable to the units of productive agency, while in the distribution of product it is secured by the entrepreneur, or, in some cases, by the capitalist who assumes responsibility for risk. It differs, however, from monopoly return in other important respects, since it is necessary if production is to continue, and since it presupposes no price manipulation. The contrast with rent may, perhaps, be brought out more clearly by pointing out the fact that when the return to a branch of production is uncertain, the amount of land employed in it will be limited, just as the quantities of labor and capital in that branch are limited;

[1] *Cf.* Willett, The economic theory of risks and insurance, p. 60 *et seq.*

and when production is successful, the land yields a risk surplus which may be distinguished from rent proper.

SEC. 43. We may next consider that element in the profits of the entrepreneur which results from dynamic changes which the entrepreneur is able to foresee and profit by. When a new method of production reduces the cost of a commodity, even though any one is free to adopt the method, some manufacturers will be in a position to increase their output more rapidly than others, thus receiving a profit during the time when prices are falling. It is evident that in such a case the extension of the new method will usually be retarded by the imperfect mobility of labor and capital. Entrepreneurs may be anxious to increase their product; but so long as the requisite kind of labor is scarce, and so long as a sufficient supply of capital in the necessary form does not find its way into the new branch of production, the productivity of each unit of labor and capital will remain above the normal. The imperfections of the market for productive agency prevent wages and interest in the industry affected by the change from rising in proportion to productivity, and therefore a net gain is left in the hands of the entrepreneur.[1]

The analogy of this form of profit with monopoly return is manifest. It is not a necessary form of income; it is an "exploitative"[2] income, *i. e.*, it is not received

---

[1] It is obvious that this element in profit is not wholly independent of the one described in the preceding section. The chance that he will find opportunities for certain gains is one of the lures that induce men to assume the uncertain rôle of the entrepreneur. Reflection, however, will show that the two funds are not coextensive; it is therefore permissible to treat them as separate elements.

[2] It may be superfluous to disavow any intention of conveying an ethical implication by the term exploitative. A new product has ap-

by the owners of the agency to which it is economically imputable. But it is temporary in its nature, while monopoly return has a degree of permanence. Moreover, while it is the acts of the monopolist which prevent a greater quantity of productive agency from entering the industry which yields monopoly return, the activities of the entrepreneurs in seeking to secure a share in profits annihilates the latter form of income.

Analogous to monopoly wages, interest, and rent are the abnormal wages, interest, and rent that may sometimes be paid when the competition of entrepreneurs for a temporarily limited supply of productive agency is active. Like the entrepreneurs' profit, this abnormal productive income is temporary. A given unit of labor may be in a position to produce (1) wages equal to the normal rate; (2) a surplus above this sum, analogous to monopoly wages, but transient in its nature; and (3) a further surplus, likewise transient, appropriated by the entrepreneur. A given unit of land may yield a product which may be analyzed into three similar parts. It is not difficult to see the contrast between the sum of those parts of the surplus product of labor, capital, and land, appropriated by the entrepreneur, representing the element in profits now under discussion, and the normal rent of land.

An effort has been made to minimize the differences between this form of profit and rent by proving that rent is a transient form of income. Emphasis is laid upon the fact that changes in consumption may reduce the rent now of one kind of land, now of another.[1] As well might we maintain that wages are a transient in-

peared which competition will sooner or later give to the agents which create it; but until competition has distributed it among the productive factors, it remains in the hands of the entrepreneur.

[1] Patten, Theory of prosperity, p. 79 *et seq.*

come, analogous to profit, because at one time the hand-loom weavers, at another time the hand compositors find their acquired powers losing their control over income.

SEC. 44. In our analysis of profits two elements remain: the extra product created by the skill of the superior entrepreneurs; and the gain which is due to the fact that the social mechanism is defective in developing potential directive capacity, and therefore in endowing entrepreneurs as a class with abnormal advantages. These elements are not distinct, but are mutually interdependent. The entrepreneur may be paid in proportion to his productivity, but productivity is intimately dependent upon limitation. Skilled laborers may be paid in proportion to their productivity, but their productivity might be indefinitely reduced were all the potential capacities of the unskilled laborers to be developed.

The normal productivity of labor, capital, and land must be understood as the productivity of these agents when combined in the most advantageous proportions that are commonly known. Better combinations are always possible, and an individual employer can by his own energy create them. From such improvements arises the income that Walker understands by profits. It is, in his view, the net product of the employer.[1] If Walker's analysis is correct: this form of income differs widely in nature from those mentioned above. If an entrepreneur has made an improvement that can be applied by no one but himself, there would appear to be good reason for saying that he creates the part of the product that exceeds the normal return to labor, capital, and land.

[1] Walker, The source of business profits, *Quarterly Journal of Economics*, vol. i, p. 275.

If the entrepreneurs who have the capacity necessary for applying the same method are few, relatively to the labor and capital that are capable of being organized by them, it would appear to be quite legitimate to say that labor and capital are no more productive than before, the increased productivity being due to entrepreneurs' activity. When, however, so many entrepreneurs are able to use the new method that all of the labor and capital capable of this form of organization are withdrawn from less productive employment, this particular form of entrepreneurs' activity manifestly becomes a good unlimited relatively to the demand for its services, and the productivity formerly attributable to entrepreneurs' activity shifts to labor, capital, and land. The entrepreneur may still receive a part of that product, but in that case his gains will be a profit of the kind discussed in the preceding section.

Manifestly it would be impossible to draw the line between the gain due to a relatively limited form of managing ability, the exploitative gain into which it may transmute itself, and monopoly profit which appears when the possessors of the new method are able to prevent its extension. But the first form of gain is distinguishable in theory, whether it is properly to be classed with profit or not.[1] And it is the relation to rent of this concrete form of income which we have now to consider.

The capacity to apply a method is in many respects analogous to the three forms of productive agency—labor, capital, and land. It yields an income directly imputable to it. It is subject to a law of diminishing returns ; for

[1] Personally I would be inclined to treat it as a special form of wages. It is manifestly created, not by the method,—methods are capable of indefinite reduplication, and are therefore not economic goods,—but by the limited personal activities which apply it.

however great the capacity of an entrepreneur, it would not be humanly possible for him to organize labor and capital indefinitely. To do so he must depute his method to others, *i. e.*, develop like capacities in his subordinates; and when he does this his special form of activity starts on the road toward becoming a free good. The analogy with those forms of productive agency termed monopoly goods in a former chapter is still closer. The income is price-determined, since the method can not ordinarily be shifted from industry to industry in consequence of changes in price. It is estimated residually, since experimental variation in quantity is unthinkable. But it is extremely volatile, since nothing more easily becomes relatively unlimited than the capacity to apply a combination once invented.

Entrepreneurs' activity, in Walker's sense of the term, is the inventing of new combinations in continual succession—the permanent possession of one or another capacity for combination in its relatively limited stage. This originating capacity is manifestly valued as the elements that compose it; the series of capacities for applying new methods is valued from the productivity of each one while limited. The general capacity, however, may have an influence in determining price, since an entrepreneur possessing it may operate in different employments, increasing supply where prices are relatively high, reducing supply where price is low.

If this element in profits has been correctly analyzed, it is the antithesis of rent, not a "species of the same genus." We have seen that it is inadmissible to confuse rent with either of the other elements in profits. Rent is wholly distinct from monopoly gain; it is no less distinct from each part and therefore from the whole of the composite income which is termed profits.

CHAPTER VII.

CONCLUSION.

SEC. 45. An elaborate conclusion would be wholly superfluous in an essay of such modest proportions as this one. Moreover, a position has already been taken upon each controverted point; and if the argument was not sufficient to sustain the position taken, it would be late to supply the deficiency here. However, a restatement of the writer's view-point and a reiteration of a few of the more important points discussed may not be out of place.

The assumptions upon which the argument is based are two. In the first place it is assumed that the distribution of income is the problem of central importance in economics, and that therefore economic phenomena should be grouped and classified with a view to clearing up the problems of distribution. In the second place it is assumed that competition exists as a powerful factor in economic life, and although it is affected in its working by numerous social forces, it holds the position of the most essential economic principle.

This latter assumption will not pass unchallenged in an age when so many thinkers are impressed by economic developments which seem to be the forerunners of a new monopolistic order of society. It is, however, at least plausible that competition is not less active than it was during the early prime of the factory system, although its form has changed. Competition is less keen among industrial establishments which create one and the same kind of commodity; but it is far keener than formerly between industrial groups which create, not like commodities, but commodities yielding like amounts of satisfaction, from which the consumer selects according to his estimates of utility and cost. It is a noteworthy fact that Professor Patten, who has done more than any other living theoretical writer to convince economists of the wide prevalence of monopoly, stands also as the foremost exponent of the " law of substitution "—competitive law under a new form. The persistence of competition, therefore, is at least a defensible assumption.

Under competitive law there is a tendency for income to identify itself with product. Granting that competition exists among entrepreneurs, it is easy to understand why a unit of productive agency, offering in the market a distinguishable product, should receive that product as its reward. On the further assumption that there is competition among units of industrial agency for the most favored positions in production, it is obvious that the productivity of like units will tend toward equality. The laws of productivity ultimately govern income; and the fundamental classification of incomes, in a competitive society, is the one which is based upon productivity relations.

It is from this point of view that we have classified incomes as productive and exploitative. The former incomes represent wealth which is obtained by the owners of the agents which produce it; the latter incomes represent an element secured by other parties in distribution. The return to a unit of agency is productive if the loss occasioned by its withdrawal is not less than that return; if the loss occasioned by withdrawal is greater, an exploitative income, secured by some other party, is implied.

Exploitative incomes depend upon friction, and fre-

quently exist by virtue of different degrees of resistance
to economic laws in different social media. If, for example, competition among workers is active while entrepreneurs do not compete, the latter are in a position
to take advantage of any abnormal productivity of labor.
If competition of entrepreneurs is checked, and labor is
immobile, it is possible that a portion of normal product
may be secured by the entrepreneur. Incomes of this
kind vary so greatly in permanence and in the laws of
their development that they hardly permit of scientific
classification. The same thing is true of the element
in income due to abnormal productivity which favored
industrial units may secure. According as exploitative
and abnormal incomes are more or less permanent, they
are usually classed as monopoly return or profit. It is
doubtful whether a wholly satisfactory analysis of these
forms of income is possible in the present state of
economic knowledge.

The case is very different with normal productive incomes. A general law of diminishing returns renders
possible a scientific explanation of their nature and a
description of the laws of their development. Certain
dynamic influences affect a wide range of sources of
income; and in order to attain to a view of distribution,
static and dynamic, it is necessary to group together
those incomes which are affected alike by familiar
changes, and to contrast those which undergo effects
unlike in nature or degree. The dynamic movement
which is most fully understood is increase in the productive factors themselves, and it is with this fact in
view that we have grouped incomes as they are affected
by increase in the factors.

SEC. 46. Land, it is here maintained, is productive in
the same sense that labor and capital are productive.

"The only test by which the productivity of the latter agents can be determined, the withdrawal or addition of increments, may equally well be applied to land." The productivity of land, in the economic sense, is dependent upon the fact that land yields diminishing returns to successive units of capital and labor applied to it ; and in the same way capital is productive, economically, because it yields diminishing returns to successive units of labor and land combined with it in production. The two cases are exactly parallel. What is true of capital is also true of labor, and for this reason a sharp distinction has been drawn between rent, wages, and interest on the one hand, and profit and monopoly return on the other.

Land and capital are therefore alike in this respect; are they, however, identical in nature? It has been admitted that land is capable of increase, and the claim has been advanced that the holding of land involves "abstinence" precisely analogous to the "abstinence" involved in holding permanent capital. It has further been claimed that the annexation of new land—by which is meant not only the reclamation of desert and swamp and forest, but also changes in the effective position of land, due to improved transportation, and changes in the productivity of land which are due, not to additional application of labor and capital, but to new methods— involves abstinence akin to that which is undergone by the man who creates new capital. But the motives which lead to the creation of new capital are not necessarily active in the annexation of new land ; the steady frugality which creates a fund of capital is unlike the resolution to join in the search for new homes which is one of the most prominent motives leading to the creation of new economic land. The two sets of

motives are not so closely connected as normally to act
simultaneously; and therefore, while capital may be increased in quantity and diminished in productivity, it
is not unlikely that economic land will remain relatively
stationary in amount and increase in productivity. If
land and capital alike remain stationary while labor increases, the effect of the change would no doubt be
shared by both alike; and in a society, real or assumed,
in which this is the case we should make no distinction
between capital and land.

It is quite possible that a time may come when the
land at the disposal of society will not be capable of increase, using the term "increase" in the broad sense indicated above. The ultimate limit to increase will,
however, be psychical, just as the ultimate limit to increase in capital is psychical, not physical. If that
state were already attained, however, it would not alter
the problem. The fact of different rates of increase is
sufficient in itself to justify difference in classification,
since there are important dynamic phenomena which
cannot be explained without such difference in treatment.

SEC. 47. Whether rent in itself bears any characteristics that will distinguish it from wages and interest is
a question which requires little further discussion. It
is a differential income, but in the same sense wages and
interest are differentials. It may be computed residually;
but this is merely a matter of convenience in theory,
except in the case of land which is not capable of alternative uses, and which is not related through margins to
other land capable of such uses. There is, however,
labor and capital in like position. Residual wages and
interest are no more anomalous than residual rent.
There may be good reason for making a distinction

between the productive incomes of mobile and immobile agents, but that distinction would not mark off wages and interest from rent. Here again there are conceivable historical conditions which would make rent the type of residual income, but it would be difficult to point out a time when they were actually realized.

Relation to price has been selected by a great number of economists as the test according to which incomes are to be classified. "Price-determining" and "price-determined" appear to be characteristics of income which are sharply distinct, and they are characteristics that are certainly of cardinal importance in distribution. Incomes in one aspect are shares in price, and are price-determined; in another aspect they are portions of supply, and are therefore price-determining. In a state of imperfect competition, however, there may be incomes which are price-determining in the sense that if they are not paid the agent which claims them will withdraw from further production. Price must therefore be sufficient to cover them. Other incomes may or may not be paid, the agent having no motive to withdraw.

It is obvious that the prevailing motive leading to the withdrawal of a laborer from one industry is the desire to use his powers in another and better paid industry. If prices fall so that normal wages can not be paid, supply soon decreases through the migration of labor. Similarly if capital does not receive a normal reward, it withdraws from the unsatisfactory employment. "Mobility is the essential feature in price relations." Now it has been pointed out that land is no less mobile than capital and labor, and therefore rent is an income which determines price. It is admitted that many concrete portions of land have no alternative use, and that in a

qualified sense the return to such land is price-determined. But nothing could be more false than that all
units of labor or of capital are mobile. A certain number of units of each agent hold a strategic position, being
able to shift from industry to industry ; and it is through
the action of these that the incomes to the respective
factors control price.

Historical conditions determine whether or not rent
"enters into price." When the land of a country is
almost entirely engaged in producing a single crop, a
fall in price can throw land out of cultivation only by
cutting down the return to labor and capital and forcing
those agents from the land. This, it may be said, is to
yield the essential point at issue, for it appears to be an
admission that rent does not enter into the price of agricultural produce in its entirety. The small amount of
agricultural land which will be turned into building
sites could not materially check a fall in price. It may
be worth while to point out that in like manner wages
and interest would not be elements controlling the price
of manufactured products in their entirety. A fall
in general prices of manufactures could force into agriculture only a small margin of undifferentiated manufacturing labor and capital. The fallacy of the position
lies in the grouping together of phenomena when it is
their interrelations that are to be explained. The real
price of wheat signifies its relation to beef and wool and
corn and vegetables as well as to boots and iron ; and
all of these various relations must be taken into account
if we would explain the laws which govern the rent of
wheat land. Taking into account these relations, we
can but conclude that in its relation to price rent does
not differ from other productive incomes. The laws of
dynamic change, then, alone furnish a basis for giving
to rent the position of an independent form of income.

INDEX OF AUTHORS MENTIONED.